Social Computing Theory and Practice:

Interdisciplinary Approaches

Panagiota Papadopoulou
University of Athens, Greece

Panagiotis Kanellis
University of Athens, Greece

Drakoulis Martakos
University of Athens, Greece

INFORMATION SCIENCE REFERENCE

Hershey · New York

Director of Editorial Content:	Kristin Klinger
Director of Book Publications:	Julia Mosemann
Acquisitions Editor:	Lindsay Johnston
Development Editor:	Joel Gamon
Typesetter:	Michael Brehm
Production Editor:	Jamie Snavely
Cover Design:	Lisa Tosheff

Published in the United States of America by
Information Science Reference (an imprint of IGI Global)
701 E. Chocolate Avenue
Hershey PA 17033
Tel: 717-533-8845
Fax: 717-533-8661
E-mail: cust@igi-global.com
Web site: http://www.igi-global.com

Library of Congress Cataloging-in-Publication Data

Social computing theory and practice : interdisciplinary approaches /
Panagiota Papadopoulou, Panagiotis Kanellis, and Drakoulis Martakos, editors.
     p. cm.
  Includes bibliographical references and index.
  Summary: "This book offers a holistic approach to social computing with
respect to the underlying theory, technology and mechanisms, as well as the
challenges, opportunities and impact of social computing to any application
area"--Provided by publisher.

  ISBN 978-1-61692-904-6 (hardcover) -- ISBN 978-1-61692-905-3 (ebook) 1.
Online social networks. 2. Human-computer interaction. 3. Information
society. I. Papadopoulou, Panagiota, 1975- II. Kanellis, Panagiotis, 1967-
III. Martakos, Drakoulis, 1947-

  HM742.S628 2010
  303.48'33--dc22
                                    2010028955

British Cataloguing in Publication Data
A Cataloguing in Publication record for this book is available from the British Library.

All work contributed to this book is new, previously-unpublished material. The views expressed in this book are those of the authors, but not necessarily of the publisher.

Editorial Advisory Board

Table of Contents

Section 1
Social Computing from a Social Perspective

Chapter 1

From Information Technology to Social Technology: Opportunities and Challenges
Benjamin Yeo, Milken Institute, USA

Chapter 2

Aaron X. L. Shen, City University of Hong Kong, Hong Kong
Matthew K. O. Lee, City University of Hong Kong, Hong Kong
Christy M. K. Cheung, Hong Kong Baptist University, Hong Kong

Chapter 3

Using Theoretical Frameworks from the Social Sciences to Understand and Explain Behaviour
Jacqui Taylor, Bournemouth University, UK

Chapter 4

Thomas Mandl, University of Hildesheim, Germany

Section 2
Social Computing from an Organizational Perspective

Section 3
Social Computing from a Technical Perspective

Detailed Table of Contents

Section 1
Social Computing from a Social Perspective

This section addresses social computing with respect to behavioral, social, cultural aspects.

Chapter 1

    Benjamin Yeo, Milken Institute, USA

This chapter highlights the importance of the social dimension of information technology among regions developing a knowledge economy. Looking at information technology as an integral part of the knowledge economy, the chapter seeks to establish the importance of understanding social technology as opposed to information technology in innovation creation. In order to emphasise the shift in perspective from information technology to social technology, the author uses empirical findings from three case studies conducted in California, Ireland and Singapore.

Chapter 2

    Aaron X. L. Shen, City University of Hong Kong, Hong Kong
    Matthew K. O. Lee, City University of Hong Kong, Hong Kong
    Christy M. K. Cheung, Hong Kong Baptist University, Hong Kong

This chapter deals with the concept of "we-intention"—which reflects an individual's perception of the extent to which all participants in a collectivity will engage in the joint action and act together—as a topic of theoretical and practical interest. The authors discuss the importance of we-intention in social computing research and propose a conceptual framework to understand the impacts of group-based factors, i.e. collective attitude, social influence and collective efficacy, on participation we-intention in social computing communities.

Chapter 3

Jacqui Taylor, Bournemouth University, UK

In this chapter, various theories from social science are discussed to explain psychological processes, at all levels, for users of social computing applications. Social identity and social capital theories are proposed as offering the greatest potential since they consider the social world in a holistic way and therefore they are able to explain human behaviour at all three levels.

Chapter 4

Thomas Mandl, University of Hildesheim, Germany

The author discusses differences between design, functions, use, opinion expression, and the perception of social capital in social software from various countries. Exploring the relationship between culture and information technology, the chapter discusses the influence of culture on social networks for several aspects of social media.

Section 2
Social Computing from an Organizational Perspective

This section deals with the use of social computing within various organizational contexts.

Chapter 5

Gbolahan K. Williams, King's College London, UK
Iman Poernomo, King's College London, UK

The chapter presents a general overview of the use of social computing technologies in various application domains whilst also discussing various considerations, challenges, and a scope for future solutions to those challenges. In this vein, the authors discuss the importance of requirements for social software systems and argue that ethnography could play a particularly useful role in the perception, elicitation and understanding of such system requirements. The authors further illustrate the challenges of social computing technologies by narrowing the discussion to the adoption of such technologies, especially Web 3.0 within organizational enterprise and cultural institutions.

Chapter 6

Chaka Chaka, Walter Sisulu University, South Africa

Employing a thematic synthesis approach, the author argues that social computing in the form of blogs, wikis, social networking sites, and virtual worlds serves as an ideal platform that enterprises can tap into for enterprise social networking purposes. In addition, the chapter explores the way in which social computing can help enterprises leverage the relationship economy inherent in enterprise social networking.

This chapter focuses on aspects related to user practices of social networks and web 2.0 tools that could be used to enhance information systems use in an organizational context. Through the description of two case studies of knowledge and intellectual capital management systems for teaching and learning, the chapter explores the effectiveness of user generated content technology to support knowledge creation and sharing in an academic and business setting.

The authors discuss the implications of social computing on organizations and productivity, showing how social computing applications, particularly social networks, collaborative tagging and multi-user immersive environments, can become platforms for productive activities. The discussion goes into three directions: social networks for project management and coordination, social networks and social bookmarking for supporting academic productivity, and social networks in multi-user immersive environments for learning and training.

Section 3
Social Computing from a Technical Perspective

This section addresses technical issues related to social computing.

In this chapter the authors discuss the relation between social networks and semantics, showing how synergies between these two areas can be used to solve concrete problems. They describe three approaches that demonstrate the potential for interconnecting these technologies. They study semantic profiling of social networks, based on MySpace, they propose a solution for mediating between social tagging systems using Upper Tag Ontology, and, finally, they examine the use of social semantics to qualitatively improve the task of service ranking, based on Delicious.

Chapter 10

This chapter deals with social software development and evaluation and describes how they can be informed by the research and development techniques used within the field of Interaction Design. Particular attention is given towards the challenging area of end-user culture and how different evaluation paradigms and techniques can be applied.

Chapter 11

This chapter addresses human-computer interaction in social computing environments, focusing on multimodal interfaces. An in depth analysis of how multimodal frameworks can be best employed for interaction in social computing is offered, including topics such as multimodal fusion and fission, grammars and languages and data structures representation technologies.

Chapter 12

The chapter deals with mobile social networks and how they can be leveraged for a flawless and optimized media delivery across mobile networks. In their chapter, the authors propose a Content-aware and Network-aware Management System (CNMS) over a converged user-environment of social networking and mobile multimedia services. The system aims to optimize the Quality of Experience in a requested media service, according to the users' preferences, the favorites provided in their social network profile, and prior experiences rated by users themselves.

Section 4
Social Computing from a Marketing Perspective

This section focuses on social computing and marketing.

Chapter 13

This chapter explores the history of marketing and social computing, how the two fields are linked, and how they have come together to revolutionize online marketing today. The chapter examines the current social computing marketing activities in the different major social computing applications and provides a discussion of issues concerning the use of social computing in marketing.

Chapter 14

This chapter examines how major IT companies make use of virtual social worlds, especially Second Life, focusing on the examples of Dell, Hewlett-Packard, International Business Machines (IBM) and Microsoft. Specifically, they investigate whether and how corporate presences within Second Life can be used as platforms to distribute Real Life products and services, so-called virtual commerce (v-Commerce). Based on their results they authors offer valuable insights for the business potential of virtual social worlds.

Chapter 15

This chapter focuses on the role of social networking sites in viral marketing through a case study in a University environment. By using questionnaires and focus groups interviews, the authors ascertain that companies which were active in social networking sites developed a positive effect on attitudes towards them, but little to no effect on the actual customer behavior patterns. The authors conclude that social networking sites suggest an efficient alternative channel for marketing purposes.

Foreword

At a first read, 'social computing', as a term, could refer to the well-known socio-technical nature of information and communication technology and systems. But it seems that the word 'social' had to be explicit and part of a new term, so as to indicate in a sense that it is now possible to exploit this nature for social purposes. And exploiting it we certainly do. Information is produced by users and is made available to users; in other words, information is socially produced and consumed. Social computing applications increasingly proliferate in various areas, with sites achieving exponential growth in their membership numbers. Is social computing here to stay? Will it help to define a new paradigm for defining the value of the next generation applications and of the principles we currently follow for their design? In this new digital context, we at least, need to understand what social computing means in terms of opportunities, implications and challenges, if they are to be faced successfully. This calls for an interdisciplinary approach to the social computing field, from both a research and practical standpoint.

I was very glad to read "Social Computing Theory and Practice: Interdisciplinary Approaches" and see how it comes to respond to this call. It looks at social computing from four key perspectives, social, organizational, technical and marketing which provides a much needed holistic view of the field from diverse disciplines. The book will be a valuable asset for both academics and professionals working and researching in one of the many fields that social computing and social media applications can be encountered. I hope you enjoy reading it as much as I did.

Panagiotis Georgiadis
University of Athens, Greece

Panagiotis Georgiadis *is a Professor at the Department of Informatics and Telecommunications at the National and Kapodistrian University of Athens. He holds a BSc in Physics from the National and Kapodistrian University of Athens, an MSc in Computer Science from Warwick University and a PhD in Computer Science from the National and Kapodistrian University of Athens. He has held several administrative positions, including General Secretary for Information Systems of the Ministry of Economy and Finance, General Secretary for Public Administration and Electronic Government of the Ministry of Interior and President of the Audit Committee of the "Information Society" Operational Programme of the Greek government. He has participated in a number of research projects and has several publications in international journals and conferences. His research interests include distributed systems and applications, electronic government and systems simulation.*

Preface

What is social computing? One could not fail to realize that, in one way or another, computing was always social. Machines were made by humans to serve human needs, wants and aspirations. Information systems were identified as primarily socio-technical systems and have been approached and studied as such: systems that can enable communication, that can help in cutting down costs, that can help an organization achieve a competitive advantage and as such sustain the well-being and safeguard the prosperity of all its members. And then, with the emergence of the World-Wide-Web, their applicability and uses seem to multiply, breaking the threshold barrier that dictated that those were primarily machines we used when at work. A social dimension? Yes. But, they were mostly deemed as things one tends to forget when the office building door is closed behind on the way home after a long day. What happened? What does it really mean when Twitter announces that it's expecting more than 30 million users by the end of the first half of 2010 and Facebook informs us that its membership exceeded 300 million users?

Social computing encompasses many now-familiar terms like *social networking* and *social media*. This broad term has been given to a phenomenon which in so little time has blossomed into a myriad of manifestations, transforming the way we conduct ourselves, build, nurture and sustain relationships, and run business. The social is fusing with the technological, personal lives are being changed in the process, the boundaries of industries as were standing traditionally are becoming fuzzy, and governments are striving to understand how to harness the power of the new or, indeed, control it, so as not to loose the benefits of the prior status quo.

This book aims to paint the landscape. Not exactly to depict in a detailed manner how it stands now or to predict its future form, for the today is already yesterday, and no crystal ball is good enough to be able to predict a future when one is faced with transformative powers of such disruptive power.

We have divided the chapters in this book into four main sections representing the perspectives from which our contributors viewed social computing: from social, organizational, technical and marketing perspectives. Having in mind the prospective audience, these we believe, suffice to organize the material in a manner that can help the reader to choose how to engage with the book; he can begin with the section he is more interested in and continue in this fashion or he can start from the beginning going through the sections and reading the chapters in succession.

The chapters in the first section focus on social aspects by addressing behavioral and cultural issues in tandem. Benjamin Yeo of the Milken Institute holds that social technology differs distinctly to information technology regarding innovation creation. What this assumption entails is that we should perhaps need to re-focus and that what we have learned thus far about information technology may already be outdated or not sufficient in versions 2.0 and 3.0 of the knowledge economy. Yeo builds and backs his argument about a shift in perspective by presenting and analyzing data from three case studies in the

U.S., Ireland and Singapore. Communities are the focus of Shen, Lee and Cheung's chapter on the wisdom of the crowds. What makes us join a community and share its purpose? What is collective attitude and how should we understand influence in the new communities? In addition to these questions, the authors also discuss the concept of *We-Intention*: an individual's perception of the extent to which all participants in a collective will engage in joint-action and act together. In her chapter, Jacqui Taylor from Bournemouth University reviews a number of theories from social science and offers a critical analysis in terms of their effectiveness to help us explain and better understand the psychological processes users of social computing applications undergo. Social identity and social capital theories are, according to the author, the most promising in terms of explanatory power. This section concludes with a chapter by Thomas Mandl, who investigates the hugely influential role culture plays in the design and use of social media. But there is not one culture, and Mandl seeks to pinpoint the main differences in the perception of social media as influenced by the culture of peoples in various countries.

Most organizations today have come to realize the business benefits of applications such as LinkedIn and Twitter, starting to integrate Web 2.0 and social media applications into everyday corporate practices. The second section of the book, which addresses organizational perspectives, begins with Williams and Poernomo from King's College, London, who identify the challenges of the institutionalization process of social computing technologies. Have organizations the choice to opt-out? Maybe not, but in any case the authors correctly point out that as in any business decision one must first elicit the precise social behavioral models in which he is trying to improve or replicate and some measure to gauge those improvements. Chaka Chaka's chapter which follows may indeed be used as a strong argument in favor of a go-for-it decision simply because the benefits of exploring the relationship economy inherent in enterprise social networking can far outweigh any costs. Anyone who ever built an information system in an organizational setting knows that the system's value must be made clear to its users. No perceived value means rapid disillusionment, as users would ignore the system, stick with the old informal way of doing things, and even sabotage it. Why cannot users get what they want? What if you let the user be the designer himself? Through the description of two cases studies on knowledge and intellectual capital management systems for teaching and learning, Jean Eric Pelet's contribution explores the effectiveness of user-generated content technology to support knowledge creation and sharing in an academic and business setting. In doing so he helps us to understand user practices that can be leveraged to enhance the use of information systems in organizations. The final chapter in this section by Sanchez and Valdiviezo discuss the implications of social computing on organizations and productivity in particular showing how applications such as social networks, collaborative tagging and multi-user immersive environments in general can become platforms for enhancing productivity. Is it now, perhaps, the right time to start revisiting the old IT-Productivity Paradox?

The four chapters comprising the third section of the book place the emphasis on the technology itself. Recently, we do encounter all too often the notion of a semantic web as an evolving development towards a stage where machines will be able to process the wealth of information by understanding its meaning and reference. The first chapter by Toma, Caverlee, Ding, Jacob, Yan and Milojevic explores the relation between social networks and semantics, identifying and assessing the synergies between them. Before a truly world-wide semantic web and networks are possible, researcher must confront the ambivalence that language brings into any attempt in defining meaning. To the interested reader, this chapter serves as an appetizer for issues such as these. Everything has (or has not) a value so Christopher Douce from the Open University, UK, seeks to frame the evaluation aspect of software and in particular social software. This is a big field not only for social media but for the more traditional types and forms of information systems and software. The next chapter by Avola, Del Buono and Spongardi address human-computer interaction arguing that the approaches that inform the design of traditional systems do not address adequately the requirements imposed by applications build around social media. Their solution lies on multi-modal frameworks, and they explore the ways in which these can be applied. The contribution by Koumaras, Farnado, Liberal, Sun, Koumaras, Troulos and Kourtis close this section with the identification of the possibilities emanating from the convergence of the multi-modal social networking environment with mobile/fixed networks. They then continue to present an architecture of an environment for the provision of services, adaptable enough to allow for the optimization of Quality of Experience (QoE) level according to user preferences and favorites.

Social media and marketing seems like a marriage made in heaven. The last three chapters in the book deal with a number of issues and particularly how these technologies can be used to drive competition, bring business benefit and even shape whole industries. Jason G. Caudill examines the histories of marketing and social computing and analyzes how the two fields are linked and have come together to revolutionize on-line marketing today. Kaplan and Haenlein, both professors of marketing at ESCP Europe, are targeting the IT industry by examining how the key players in the field such as Dell, IBM and Microsoft utilize virtual social worlds. They conclude, in their own words that "… they have the potential to be of similar importance as the Internet is today." Viral marketing is a term used to refer to techniques used to achieve increases in product sales through self-replicating processes much like the way pathological viruses develop. Social networks lend themselves physically to such techniques and the study by Jayasekera and Papadopoulos ascertains that companies which were active in social networking sites developed a positive effect on attitudes towards them, but little or no effect on the actual customer behavior patterns.

In the foregoing paragraphs we have offered a base outline of the wealth of contributions that make up this book. However, it is the chapters themselves that matter and by going through them the reader will most likely start to acquire a social computing view of reality—perhaps not the most fitting choice of words—to describe what the goal of this book is. It is a worthy, candidate, however, considering the chameleontic nature of social computing itself.

Panagiota Papadopoulou
University of Athens, Greece

Panagiotis Kanellis
University of Athens, Greece

Drakoulis Martakos
University of Athens, Greece

Section 1
Social Computing from a Social Perspective

Chapter 1

From Information Technology to Social Technology:
Opportunities and Challenges in the Knowledge Economy

Benjamin Yeo
Milken Institute, USA

ABSTRACT

Stemming from the information economy, the knowledge economy represents an extension of technology-based production to include the leverage of technologies for value-added products and services. In this chapter, the author defines the knowledge economy and looks at the technology-based economic growth experiences of three places—the San Joaquin Valley in California, Ennis in Ireland, and Singapore—to show the importance of human capital development, social inclusion, and learning contexts in generating the foundation for continuous innovation. These themes highlight the opportunities and challenges involved in their bid to create a knowledge economy. The main argument in the chapter advocates the importance of going beyond the technologies to analyse the social context within which technologies function. Based on the author's larger study of the sustainable knowledge economy, this chapter comprises an empirical analysis of the three cases and a rigorous literature review to emphasise the shift in perspective from the information view of technology to the social perspective of technology.

INTRODUCTION

Amidst the backdrop of the information revolution, regions saw the growth of high technology industries that comprise information technology companies and capital investments in technology firms. High technology centres became key drivers of economic growth in the information economy.

Regions also experienced increasing penetration of information technologies, such as computers, personal electronic devices and electronic services. It is no surprise therefore, that governments, businesses and people began to leverage information technologies to form a networked society. Business activities in particular, became grounded on the flexible, networked society (Castells, 2001).

At the same time, the proliferation of information technologies in a society can facilitate

DOI: 10.4018/978-1-61692-904-6.ch001

increased segmentation among citizens, companies and regions (Rodrigues, 2003). Among other issues, the introduction of information technologies can also bring about unforeseen challenges such as unemployment. According to Menzies, the use of information technologies in labour-intensive regions that do not have a sufficient workforce capable of using and leveraging these technologies can lead to the unemployment of lowly skilled workers (Menzies, 1996).

The knowledge economy represents an extension from the information economy, where value-based inputs become necessary drivers for growth. In the current global economy, the most technologically advanced economies are knowledge-based, where information and knowledge are forces that drive production (World Bank, 1999). The advent of the knowledge economy is characterised by a shift in its economic base from tangible to intangible assets, such as human capital and innovation (DeVol et al., 2004). Knowledge-based inputs, in the form of value-added information, supplement material inputs as key productive forces in the economy.

RESEARCH OBJECTIVES

The goal of this chapter is to highlight the importance of the social dimension of information technology among regions developing a knowledge economy. Concepts such as human capital, social inclusion, learning contexts, continuous innovation as well as high tech initiatives were examined and discussed. The findings were generalised to a theoretical level to emphasise the importance of the social context in the study of technologies and leveraging them in a knowledge economy. For purposes of this paper, the term social technology was used to characterise this social view of technology. Since information technology is an integral part of the knowledge economy, the author refers to social computing

as a social approach to understand innovation in the knowledge economy.

This study comprises a comprehensive literature review on the knowledge economy, information economy, and regional economics, as well as empirical findings from the three case studies. A qualitative method was used, comprising in-depth interviews, observation, and document reviews. These findings are discussed in three layers. The first looks at the challenges extended from the information economy and how they are relevant for the knowledge economy. Based on these challenges, the second focuses on how regions can create opportunities that enable them to grow knowledge-building capacities. The third layer extrapolates these findings to a theoretical level to establish the importance of considering and understanding contextual factors in a successful knowledge economy. Relevant literature was reviewed to support this theoretical generalisation. As regions begin to initiate strategies to enhance their knowledge-building capacities, considerations given to local contextual and cultural characteristics – thus, the term social technology – may be useful to enhance their effectiveness. The chapter concludes with a broad theoretical perspective and possible future research directions.

DEVELOPING A SUSTAINABLE KNOWLEDGE ECONOMY

The knowledge economy is characterised by a rise in knowledge-based activities and increased globalisation. These activities refer to innovation that is the result of research and development (R&D) industries. Yeo (2009) argued that innovation is a key driver of growth in the knowledge economy. Therefore, governments are increasingly executing initiatives to develop knowledge-based industries to reflect a knowledge value chain. Among these initiatives are public policies that are designed to facilitate human capital development and information technology utilisation to increase innovation creation and commercialisation. These involve regional collaboration among different stakeholders in a region to create knowledge value chains. Human capital and information technology utilisation create the foundation for innovation creation and commercialisation.

However, there are challenges involved in harnessing human capital and information technology in the knowledge economy. Pacey (1983) argued that the impact of information technologies must be interpreted within their social contexts. Their leverage for the knowledge economy involves similar contextual challenges as in the information economy.

The research in this chapter makes an argument to advocate a contextual approach to understand the role of information and communication technologies for innovation creation towards the knowledge economy. An inter-disciplinary approach is taken, comprising information science, policy studies, and regional economics, to review the dynamics of the knowledge economy to discuss how the challenges in the information economy are extended to the knowledge economy. Empirical findings from three case studies were used to show the importance of taking a contextual approach to understand how technology can be leveraged in the knowledge economy.

These case studies originated from Yeo's larger study involving the influence of contextual factors in the development of a sustainable knowledge economy (Yeo, 2009). In his study, Yeo developed 12 common themes in three cases – San Joaquin Valley in California, Ennis in Ireland, and Singapore – that posit the importance of contextual factors in the development of a sustainable knowledge economy. A further discussion of Yeo's study is given in a subsequent section entitled "A Qualititative Research Method." Using these findings, the author explains how challenges in the information economy manifest in the knowledge economy and how they translate into opportunities for regions to grow.

DEFINING THE KNOWLEDGE ECONOMY

The knowledge economy is a complex concept. Scholars have had wide variations in the definition, leading to different research operationsations. For purposes of this chapter, the terms "knowledge economy" and "knowledge society" were used inter-changeably. Studies that have utilised either term were deemed to be referring to the same entity.

According to Bell (1973), the knowledge society represents a post-industrial setting. He argued that research and development play an important role in its production processes. Today, scholars have tied the knowledge economy to information technologies and information systems. It is characterised by the availability and effeciveness of information systems, innovation systems, and human resources among others (United Nations Economic Commission for Europe, 2002). It can also be seen as an economic setting that leverages information and communication technologies for education, innovation, knowledge diffusion (Drucker, 2004; Godin, 2003).

Taken together, in a knowledge economy, economic production and services stem from knowledge work (Powell & Snellman, 2004). Economic value is therefore, placed upon knowledge goods (Drucker, 1993). Information technologies (IT) have an important role in the production process whereby based on the leverage of these technologies for knowledge creation. It can be further argued that the knowledge economy is driven by productive and distributive forces based on less tangible inputs as opposed to material ones (Stehr, 2002).

The knowledge economy is based on knowledge creation. According to Yeo (2009), the knowledge economy can be studied as an entity characterised by continuous innovation. This dynamic approach to define the knowledge economy allows researchers to capture the abstract nature of knowledge: The foundation and processes of innovation in a region are at least as important as the output of innovation (such as patents) (Yeo, 2009).

The definition of knowledge work stems from the information hierarchy comprising data, information, knowledge, and wisdom. For purposes of this study, the latter is excluded from the discussion. According to Zeleny (1987), data are neutral. They do not carry with them value-added characteristics. When placed and used in a context, that is, upon processing, they acquire added value that informs users and recipients about them. Here, data become information. Further processing transforms information to knowledge. One who claims to have knowledge is one who knows how to effectively apply the information to solve problems (Zeleny, 1987). This person will be said to be a perform knowledge worker. However, it is important to note that the definition of a knowledge worker is by degree rather than kind. In other words, it is more logical to conceive the extent of knowledge work conducted rather than whether this individual is a knowledge worker. Every worker possesses and performs knowledge work of some sort (Yeo, 2009).

Knowledge is cumulative. Continuous innovation is based on prior innovations. These can occur across different disciplines or fields. Knowledge industries are not restricted to high-tech industries. They cross different disciplines because continuous innovation can occur in all industries (Yeo, 2009). The emergence of knowledge-based fields such as biotechnology, that incorporate biology and information technology, is evidence of inter-disciplinary fields in the knowledge economy.

In summary, the knowledge economy can be seen as one based on information technologies and characterised by innovation. Since knowledge work involves the creation of new entities (Yeo, 2009), it is reasonable to define the knowledge economy as one using continuous innovation in its production process. This chapter will adopt Yeo's (2009) definition of knowledge work as continuous innovation to capture the dynamism of the knowledge economy. This involves human

capital and is influenced by the context within which workers engage in economic production. Therefore, the research in this chapter is focused on information technologies in its context of innovation creation to identify lessons learned for the knowledge economy.

CASE STUDIES

A Qualitative Research Method

This research is based on case studies in three regions: San Joaquin Valley in California, Ennis in West Ireland, and Singapore that are markedly different in terms of their social, political, and economic make-up. As earlier discussed, qualitative method was used to enable the researcher to understand the story behind the statistics. While descriptive statistics can show the extent of regional collaborations, they do not explain the underlying challenges as well as how and why they are important.

The data were collected through a triangulation of in-depth interviews, observation, and document reviews. The study led to the development of twelve themes that were found to be relevant to the development of a sustainable knowledge economy. For purposes of this paper, I focus on the themes on regional economic leadership and general culture, in which I highlight key findings in related to regional collaboration and how they influence of the cultural fabric.

San Joaquin Valley is a region targeted by the state of California's development efforts to position it as a technology-based economy. It is an agriculture-based economy, with other industries such as manufacturing. Ennis is a town in Ireland, a country that developed its economy from an agriculture-based one directly to an information economy (Trauth, 1999). Ennis is attempting to leverage the achievements to build its knowledge economy. It is currently known as an information age town and deemed as an exemplary case of a

Figure 1. Themes in a sustainable knowledge economy

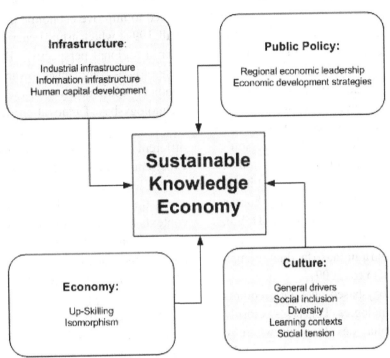

small town having developed its technology base and is attempting to sustain its growth. Singapore is a country in Southeast Asia. It is a modern economy that has well-established industries. Singapore is attempting to sustain its competitiveness amidst intensified global competition. These three regions are in different geographical areas and are at different stages of development with the common goal of developing a sustainable knowledge economy. Furthermore, they are markedly different in their social and cultural make-up.

The following figure shows the 12 themes (categorised into four broad factors) that influence the development of a sustainable knowledge economy (Yeo, 2009). The shaded portions in Figure 1 represent the two factors that are discussed in this study. Within these two factors, this study focuses on the three factors – human capital development, social inclusion, and learning contexts – as underlined below. Through a discussion of these three themes, the author seeks to establish the importance of understanding social technology as opposed to information technology per se in the knowledge economy.

Themes in Focus

Following the preceding discussion, the knowledge economy is an extension of the information economy. It is characterised by the leverage of information technologies for innovation. All three regions in this study have initiated efforts to develop information technological infrastructures and to leverage them.

Within the context of the knowledge economy, human capital, social inclusion and learning contexts are relevant themes that deserve investigation. These three themes constitute the context for building continuous technology-based innovation towards a knowledge economy. They will be discussed individually and subsequently consolidated to identify key lessons learnt.

Nobel Laureate Gary Becker clearly explained the importance of human capital in an economy:

"The continuing growth in per capita incomes of many countries during the nineteenth and twentieth centuries is partly due to the expansion of scientific and technical knowledge that raises the productivity of labor and other inputs in production. The increasing reliance of industry on sophisticated knowledge greatly enhances the value of education, technical schooling, on-the-job training, and other human capital." (Becker, 1992). A region's economic well-being stems from the dynamism and productivity of its technology base. This dynamism can be created from leveraging human capital to promote econmic development (DeVol, 2002). Therefore, regions place importance and invest in education and training to facilitate human capital development (Yeo, 2009).

Creating technology-based innovation requires access to these technologies. This is also closely tied to human capital development whereby highly trained and educated workers must be able to utilise and leverage these technologies. However, social inclusion is a social issue rather than a technological one. Information technology transcends both technological and social boundaries. In information systems research therefore, it is important to understand the social context within which technologies function (Baskerville & Stage, 2000).

According to Sen, social inclusion refers to the availability of egalitarian opportunities, active citizenry, and fundamental well being in a society (Sen, 1999). To this end, information technologies have an enabling potential. Through the provision of access to information technologies, equality, and hence, social inclusion, can be achieved (Philips, 2000). Studies on social inclusion are therefore, highly contextual in their investigation of empowerment and disempowerment through technologies in a society (Cecez-Kecmanovic, 2001; Howcroft & Trauth, 2004). In a similar vein, this theme comprises findings on the social experiences of these regions in creating technology-based continuous innovation.

Education, as a form of learning, has been argued to improve economic productivity (Marshall, 1994), which in turn generates human capital from a regional perspective. Beyond access to technologies, approaches towards learning is yet another important layer in the social fabric of technology-based innovation. Individuals learn in different ways and different regions present different facilitators and inhibitors to learning experiences, thus contributing to the effectiveness of learning.

In this study, findings related to learning contexts include contextual facets that influence the creation of continuous learning to support continuous innovation in a sustainable knowledge economy. These findings include attitudes towards learning in each of the three regions. The following sections describe the social context of these three regions. The subsequent discussion positions these contextual findings within the perspective of creating knowledge work through information technologies. For purposes of this chapter, the social context of each region refers to human capital development, social inclusion, and learning contexts. The knowledge economy refers to continuous technology-based innovation in economic production.

CASE STUDY FINDINGS

San Joaquin Valley Findings

San Joaquin Valley is located in Central California. It comprises nine counties: Fresno, Kern, Kings, Madera, Mariposa, Merced, San Joaquin, Stanislaus, and Tulare. Fresno city, located in Fresno County, lies in the centre of the region. It is deemed as the economic centre of activities within San Joaquin Valley.

The economy in San Joaquin Valley is dependent on labour-intensive agriculture, where farm workers are paid low wages (UC Davis, 2004; Kirch Foundation, 2005). Furthermore, some farm workers prefer these jobs compared to more highly paid non-farm jobs (UC Davis, 2004). Culturally, this finding reflects a resistance towards upward mobility and a comfort with the status quo (Yeo, 2009).

In San Joaquin Valley, approximately 30 percent of high school students graduate. Among them, 15 to 30 percent go on to attend tertiary education (Gradeck & Paytas, 2000). It has been observed that the highly educated leave the region for opportunities elsewhere (Public Policy Institute of California, 2004). Regions that have better advantages in career advancement are better positioned to attract and retain talented professionals (Gradeck & Paytas, 2000). Without these assets, knowledge workers were also found to leave the region for employment elsewhere (Rural Migration News, 2006).

Developing knowledge work involves the growing of human capital, and hence domestic educational institutions to harness the local residents. A strong human capital base facilitates the development of economic opportunities. Locations of major corporations have been at least partially influenced by the access to talents from leading universities. For example, Google has set up operations in Pittsburgh to tap the region's renowned human capital stemming from prominent institutions such as Carnegie Mellon University and the University of Pittsburgh (Wong, Yeo & DeVol, 2006).

In a bid to address the human capital challenges, among others, in the region, the Economic Development Work Group was initiated in 2006 to target the creation of industry clusters and entrepreneurship (Economic Development Work Group, 2006). These two programs in particular, as a part of the Work Group, acknowledge the importance of human capital in the region's economic development (Yeo, 2009).

The first program, industry cluster development, targets specific industries comprising agriculture (including agricultural technology and biotechnology), manufacturing, supply chain management and logistics, healthcare, and renewable energy (Economic Development Work Group, 2006). Knowledge work requires accumulation and interactions (Yeo, 2009). Businesses in a knowledge economy face the need to leverage these networks of establishments (Houghton & Peter, 2004). These networks and their collaboration links among these industries and universities create clusters that are characterised by strong knowledge value chains can be grown. Incubators, as a part of industry clusters, can create a continuous cycle of innovation and commercialisation, thus increasing the value of work in the region.

The second program was aimed at developing entrepreneurship in the region. Resources including the Lyles Center for Innovation and Entrepreneurship at Fresno State University and the Valley Small Business Development Center would be leveraged to support the initiative (Economic Development Work Group, 2006). Entrepreneurship stems from innovation. It involves the creation of a production of the innovation itself, such as a startup company. Entrepreneurship increases competition among more players, with higher expectations, and heightened communication (Hamelink, 1986). On a regional level then, entrepreneurial activities form the link between investments in innovation and economic growth (Hart, 2003).

In June 2005, Governor Schwarzenegger formed the California Partnership for San Joaquin Valley to address economic challenges facing the region (California Economic Leadership Network, 2006). Among the broad strategies, programs related to human capital were created, such as a public outreach effort to create access to education opportunities for the residents, and to create a culture of pursuing tertiary education in the region (California Partnership for the San Joaquin Valley, 2006).

These efforts are aimed at extending opportunities to all residents in the region, that is made up of potentially excluded population segments. Based on education demographics, roughly 30 percent of high school students graduate in the region. Among which, 15 to 30 percent pursue tertiary education (Gradeck & Paytas, 2000). The low education attainment, coupled with a brain drain from the region, could lead to a downward spiral in creating value-added production involving knowledge work.

According to the U.S. Census in 2005, about nine percent of San Joaquin Valley's population is made up of people aged 65 years and above, with 29 percent living in rural regions (Miltiades & Flores, 2008). Incidentally, according to the California Association of Adult Day Care Services in 2002, among all 58 counties in California, Tulare and Fresno (in San Joaquin Valley) are ranked seventh and eighth respectively in terms of the percentage of elders (aged above 65) living below poverty. These two counties have 47 and 45 percent of their population aged above 65 (Miltiades & Flores, 2008). These residents face the possibility of being excluded from economic development initiatives that involve learning and the leverage of ICTs.

Low wage labour also constitutes yet another potential form of social exclusion. Low wage farm workers who rely on manual labour with a per capita income similar to that in Mexico are common in the region (UC Davis, 2004). Many are of them accepted the minimum wage rate due to a lack of job opportunities in their home country of Mexico (Migration Dialogue, 2000). Local farm owners were encouraged by the availability of abundant cheap labour that cost less than machines (Yeo, 2009). As an example, the cost of machine labour in corn farming was 10 percent higher than manual labour in San Joaquin Valley (Campbell-Matthews et al., 2001a). Using green beans as another example, machine labour costs 20 percent more (Campbell-Matthews et al., 2001b).

As an added layer of complications, it is one of the characteristics in the region that residents may not have placed an emphasis on upward mobility. Despite the availability of non-farm jobs that pay better wages, some farm workers choose to remain at their manual jobs (UC Davis, 2004). This constitutes a possible negative learning context, since knowledge work involves continuous learning and innovation.

Taken together, the human capital develop strategies stress the importance of developing value-added work, that is, knowledge work in the region. However, the different segments in the population inhibit the uniform extension of training programs across the region's entire population. Coupled with a complex learning context, San Joaquin Valley's challenges to transform its agriculture base to one premised on knowledge-based production is social rather than technological.

Ennis Findings

Leadership of the Irish government played a key role in the rise of country's information economy in the 1980s and 1990s. The government executed strategies to develop selected high valued-added industries to encourage investment (Yeo, 2009). Studies have shown that among European countries, the Irish are among the most contented. It is not common for them to associate higher income with greater happiness, all else remaining equal (McWilliams, 2006). According to Trauth's (1996, p.255) research findings, the family unit is an important facet of the Irish culture. Taken together, Ennis can be perceived as a laid back traditional town with traditional values (Yeo, 2009).

The Irish government places a heavy emphasis on human capital for technological innovation (Science Foundation Ireland, 2006). The country's focus on tertiary education facilitated the creation of high-tech jobs (Kirchberger, 2002), thus highlighting the recognition of a shift towards knowledge work. Despite this emphasis, the Information Age Town of Ennis "does not have the proximity to or the direct support of a university," (McInerney, 2003, p. 10).

Ennis was an exemplary participant of the 1996 Information Age Town Project that enabled it to grow from a rural town to one that had an increasing presence of information technologies in businesses. This project was aimed at enabling residents and businesses in the town to partake in using information technologies for their purposes. It was deemed as one of the largest community projects in Ireland, and shows the coordinated collaboration among stakeholders (Mc.Quillan, 2000). The organising committee included major development establishments such as Shannon Development, Clare County Council, the Chamber of Commerce, Ennis Task Force Ltd, and eircom (eircom, 2000).

The project was organised into different areas, such as businesses and community, with a staff member in charge of each area. The project focused not only on businesses but also on schools and residential areas. Households were given computers and household members were trained by the task force personnel on using them. Schools were financially supported and encouraged to use information technologies in the classrooms and curricula. Businesses were invited to participate and taught how to use these technologies to support their business objectives (McQuillan, 2000).

As a part of the project, information technologies were integrated into the school curricula. Teachers were encouraged to use computer software to support their teaching in subjects such as mathematics. The use of information technologies in schools has also enabled students to communicate and collaborate with students in other European countries (McQuillan 2000). The initiative has been met with positive reception from school teachers, who perceived themselves as catalytic to the training of students in the use of these technologies (McInerney, 2003). Through the Online Newspapers Program, students were allowed to play key roles in the news reporting and publishing process. Newspaper content included community-related events. This were aimed to create social cohesion among schools and the community (McInerney, 2003). Through regular technology evaluations and collaborations, the program can fuel a value-oriented continuous learning process for the region.

Through the Information Age Town Project, Ennis sought to create a vibrant regional knowledge economy that is characterised by widespread use of information technologies (eircom, 2000). Despite the lofty aspirations of the Information Age Town Project, an evaluation report showed that the local community did not perceive information technologies as critical to their daily activities (McQuillan, 2000). While some business owners expressed their desire to further leverage these technologies, others lamented at their relevance to their operations (Yeo, 2009).

For example, the owner of a business that operates primarily out of local market explained that investing in high-cost information systems does not add value to his current operations. His customer base is essentially local and prefer face-to-face service in their office that is within short distance to inpersonal online experiences. At the same time, another owner expressed his desire to create more user-centred value-added services with an increasing customer base from regions outside Ireland that demands more convenience and value (Yeo, 2009). These two broad segments highlight the social boundary that separates the two groups, thus, inhibiting possible inclusive strategies that encourage the use of informatio technologies.

While these present social challenges, learning attitudes in Ennis make the residents receptive to the deployment of new technologies. This is evident from the Irish culture, that places a heavy emphasis on education (McInerney, 2003, p. 25; Trauth, 1993 p. 209). Interviews with the local residents also showed that education was considered important for the next generation. Parents deemed it as a critical process for their children (Yeo, 2009).

Indeed, an objective of the Information Age Town Project was to create a centre of excellence for lifelong learning in Ennis (eircom, 2000). According to Education Ireland (2007), education participation in Ireland stand among the highest in the world. Eighty-one percent of Irish students complete secondary education while 60 percent pursue post-secondary education. Trauth's (2000) findings on Ireland explain that "education (is) a way of maintaining national and religious identity," (Trauth, 2000, p. 60). This stands in sharp contrast to San Joaquin Valley education landscape.

According to Trauth's (2000) findings on the Irish information economy, young workers were quicker in absorbing new knowledge (Trauth, 2000, p. 56). These were the creative economic actors who facilitated the growth of Ireland's the information economy. The learning context based on the Irish culture sets Ennis in a good position to leverage the infromation infrastructure in place to develop a homegrown knowledge base made up of knowledge workers and continuous learning. However, the existing lack of extra-regional businesses may inhibit the achievement of this goal.

Singapore Findings

Singapore is a small, highly urbanised country in Asia, with established and developed information and knowledge services sectors. Singapore has a collaborative government structure. The government places strong emphases on education and training. The country is known for its rapid economic development, triggered partially by its transparency, efficiency and integrity of its legal system, with highly protected and easily enforceable contractual intellectual property rights (Rechtsanwaltgesellschaft, 2004). It enjoys coordinated policies that were effective in bringing about economic, social, and political changes (Yeo, 2009).

Acknowledging the relevance of the knowledge economy in the late 1980s, the Singapore government introduced TradeNet as the first countrywide electronic trade documentation system that system enhances efficiency and lowered costs for the trading community (United Nations

Social and Economic Commission for Asia and the Pacific, 2006). With this system, a common standard for trading documents was introduced to enhance the exchanges of these documents. This nationwide information system replaced manual labour from workers, thus increasing speeds of transactions (Yeo, 2009).

This new system was introduced before the hype of the information and knowledge economies in Asia in the late 1990s. Therefore, it was a challenge to develop the skills necessary to fully utilise the system and ensure its success. The complexity of information technologies needed new job categories, as well as a re-deployment of existing workers to carry out these news jobs in newly established divisions. Training programs were developed to facilitate the training process and help workers acquire new skills (United Nations Social and Economic Commission for Asia and the Pacific, 2006).

Singapore has a strong and systematic education system. In a bid to develop a platform for continuous upgrading of skills and knowledge, the National Information Technology Literacy Plan was created by the Infocomm Development Authority of Singapire (IDA) and the Ministry of Manpower, and funded with US$30 million over a period of three years (Ministry of Economic Development, 1999). The training costs were kept affordable through the Lifeling Learning Endowment Fund and the Skills Development Fund. Low-income trainees were given financial assistance by the Community Development Council and self-help groups (Ministry of Economic Development, 1999).

Following this in 2003, the BackPack.NET Initiative was developed as a five-year project to enhance students' learning experiences through the use of emerging information technologies, including digital ink and tablet personal computers. The Initiative is also aimed at developing a collaborative platform for the industry and schools to develop software solutions. Lesson resources were available online and teacher-student interactions were supported by the technological infrastructure. Students were also able to communicate in real time with experts on various subjects outside the currricular. Preliminary findings showed that teachers found it easy to use these technologies and the students engaged in more independent learning (International Telecommunication Union, 2005).

However, Singapore has a highly structured meritocracy education system. Annual examinations enable the system to group students into schools and classes based on their academic performances. Although this is an efficient system, this also possibly leads to family pressure on students to perform well. According to Tan, this pressure may facilitate the accumulation of stress among Singaporean students (Tan, 2001). Incidentally, in 2001, a Singaporean student aged 10 years old committed suicide due to the stress she experienced in primary school (Asian Economic News, 2001).

The government's initiatives discussed can be argued to be socially inclusive to prevent the possible repercussions of the efficient education system. It follows therefore, that the benefits of social inclusion is recognised as reflected in the development initiatives. Both the National IT Literacy Plan and the BackPack.NET initiatives were focused at all segments of their respective targeted population.

Singapore's experience shows the strong coordinated fashion of initiatives towards the use of new technologies. Singaporeans also place a strong emphasis on improving themselves (Yeo, 2009). Culturally, there is a race among the population to upgrade their skills. Singaporeans perceive themselves as becoming more competitive and better positioned to reap benefits in the knowledge economy where skills and knowledge are increasingly important.

As a whole, government institutions who introduce and implement new technologies and the population that uses them both recognise the relevance of the knowledge economy. The government uses a heavily coordinated approach to facilitate collaboration among its institutions for common objectives. This controlled approach has proved to be a successful model for Singapore's growth to a vibrant knowledge economy today (Bureau of East Asian and Pacific Affairs, 2006). The population on the other end is conditioned to be receptive because of strong emphases on skills upgrading (Yeo, 2009). Taken together, the supportive learning context coupled with the coordinated and inclusive nature of development initiatives position the country to create knowledge-intensive industries.

ANALYTICAL DISCUSSION AND IMPLICATIONS

The findings portray descriptions of the contextual landscapes pertaining to the leverage of information technologies for economic growth. They suggest how the themes of human capital development, social inclusion and learning contexts influence the development of knowledge-based production, using the definition of the knowledge economy in this chapter. These themes manifested differently in the three cases. However, their relevance to the development of a knowledge economy remains important.

In this section, these findings are generalised to the theoretical level and discussed in three layers related to challenges, opportunities, and contextual factors. These correspond to the three sub-sections that follow: from Technologies to Learning, Opportunities for the Knowledge Economy, and Fitting the Local Context: A Theoretical Discussion. Figure 2 describes the structure of this analytical discussion. In the following sub-sections, the challenges involving the three themes are discussed, followed by the opportunities created through leveraging the social contexts. These include the experiences of each region pertaining to the three themes. Subsequently, the discussion is generalised to make an argument supporting the importance of the social context in the develop-

Figure 2. Structure of analytical discussion

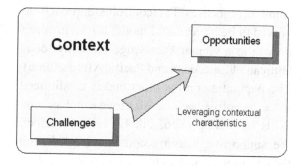

ment of a knowledge economy. This will include a theoretical discussion on the importance of taking into consideration social contexts in policymaking in the knowledge economy.

From Technologies to Learning

In the information economy, access to information and communication technologies (ICTs) was deemed as a factor influencing its egalitarianising characteristic. While ICTs can enable users to a wide variety of services, users must first be able to gain access to these technologies to leverage them. On a regional level therefore, it is common to have policies directed at creating universal access, particularly in developing regions seeking to jump onto the information technology bandwagon. The issue of access is extended to the development of a knowledge. In the three cases, access to training in the use of ICTs was not evenly distributed. Since continuous learning, as a part of human capital development, is a key facet of the knowledge economy, it becomes a challenge for regions to create knowledge work and nurture knowledge workers. The transition involves an emphasis that goes beyond having access to technologies. It involves learning technologies, and leveraging them for innovation.

From the findings in the case of San Joaquin Valley, the extension of opportunities for skill development was inhibited by the different demographic segments of the population. The farm workers were pre-disposed to be excluded from upward mobility in view of the production structure of the region and the learning contexts. On the one hand, the farm workers constituted a source of cheap manual labour that was more lucrative than investments in machines. In a general sense, this can possibly lead to a maintenance of the status quo, that is the reliance on non-machine labour. As a result, deploying universal access to learning and leverage of ICTs becomes inhibited. The large rural population of elderly people and the braindrain augment the presence of the excluded segments of the population. On the other hand, the lack of a desire for upward social mobility constitutes a negative learning context for the region. Without the personal motivation to engage in training, the use of value-added technology-based services becomes limited.

Ennis is relatively uniform in its demographic makeup with seemingly uniform access to learning opportunities. The division in access to learning stems from necessity of information and communication technologies. As shown in the findings, through the Information Age Town Project, the region attempted to create a technology-based information economy with prospects for a knowledge economy. However, different business owners perceived different needs and therefore, had different perceptions on the extent to which ICTs can support their operations. Given that the learning context in Ennis is largely positive, as evidenced in the Irish culture of learning, it may not be difficult to implement new technologies and value-added services in the region. However, the lack of follow-up initiatives after the completion of the Project has led to a divide in the perceived leverage of technologies to create a technology-based knowledge economy.

The case of Singapore is markedly different from San Joaquin Valley and Ennis. Bing multicultural, Singapore has top-down initiatives to ensure universal access to technologies and learning opportunities. Singapore has a strong technological infrastructure base and is well known for its leverage of ICTs to create value-added services. Being a society that values meritocracy and efficiency, the Singapore education system evaluates students regularly to streamline the training process. However, the controlled initiatives ensured that all segments of the population, including the less peforming ones were included in the nationwide development efforts. These orchestrated approaches have been credited for Singapore's strong economy. The positive learning motivation also enables the country to create a vibrant human capital development engine for a technology-based knowledge economy.

Opportunities for the Knowledge Economy

Knowledge is applicable to every industry. This sets the knowledge economy apart from the information economy, that is characterised by information technology industries. Since it transcends industry definitions and boundaries, broad societal characteristics, that is social contexts, become more important in the creation of a knowledge economy. Boston's Route 128 and California's Silicon Valley are renowned high-tech clusters in the U.S. Both regions have proximity to leading universities that have linkages with high-tech anchor companies in the regions. Even though both regions have similar agricultural roots and technology availability, they have different characteristics in their industries. Saxenian (1996) explained that Route 128 is made up of independent and self-sufficient businesses, thus leading to a culture of independence. This characteristic led to its relative decline compared to Silicon Valley. Silicon Valley's cooperative and decentralised industrial system allowed businesses to form social networks in formal and informal ways, thus facilitating conditions for sustained economic growth. Businesses, universities and various institutions leverage this characteristic to build networks where production is organised in

a similar fashion to industry clusters (Saxenian, 1996).

Following the nation's political system, the democratic political freedom in San Joaquin Valley strongly supports both top down government initiatives active grassroots establishments, such as non-profit organisations, to participate in economic development initiatives. This spells heightened representation of different segments of the population. It therefore follows that different segments can seek various forms of representations to be in the spotlight for these efforts. Grassroots organisations are one example of a pivot for representation. While this may be a challenge in itself, it is also an avenue for the potentially excluded segments to reach out. This constitutes a source of opportunities for the region to grow.

Ennis adopts Ireland's parliamentary democracy and enjoys a mix of top down initiatives and bottom up efforts. The town appears to be more dependent on the top down efforts rather than market forces. Business owners were found to be reliant on the Information Age Town Task Force for guidance: when the project ended, some businesses expressed concerns about a lack of follow-up directives. This cultural characteristic suggests that long term structured efforts may be more effective. The presence of the Information Age Town Project was substantially felt among businesses in Ennis. This suggests the effectiveness of the Project in creating awareness and familiarity with ICTs. Subsequent initiatives leveraging this awareness and the culture of learning can be expected to create a process of continuous learning for technology-based production in Ennis.

Singapore relies heavily on top-down initiatives. Economic development is largely initiated through government-led policies. This approach has played a pivotal role in Singapore's economic development (Yeo, 2009). However, this was effective because the public was receptive towards such paternalistic efforts. Singapore's cultural characteristic makes it possible for these top-down initiatives, including planning and execution, to be efficiently and effectively implemented to positive outcomes. Its highly structured system has been proven to effectively generate growth for the country and stands among the highly technology-based economies in the global arena. While not entirely without challenges, the government has leveraged the motivated learning context to extend learning opportunities across its multi-cultural population.

Fitting the Local Context: A Theoretical Discussion

The findings suggest that although human capital, social inclusion, and learning contexts are important themes in technology-based development, they are manifested differently in different regions due to their unique characteristics that may require different development routes. Trauth's (2001) research on Ireland showed that regions' unique competitive strengths can be exploited for growth. Using Ireland's experience, policy-makers adapted work in the information sector to the unique cultural characteristics in Ireland, thus leading to their leapfrog to an information economy (Trauth, 2001).

There may be intended and unintended consequences resulting from policy implementation (Trauth, 1996). Therefore, Trauth (1996) suggested that continuous investigations on regions are important to development. Trauth (1996) explained further that the aim of these assessments is not to strategically adapt policies to local contextual conditions, rather than re-create experiences from another region.

Houghton and Sheehan (2000) argued that effective development policymaking pays attention to the production structure in an economy (Houghton & Sheehan, 2000). It follows that regions must consider their own unique cultures and adapt development initiatives to these settings. According to Mukand and Rodrik, these settings include characteristics such as history, geography, political economy, and institutions (Mukand & Rodrik, 2002).

Feldman argued that localised creation of knowledge creation and deployment can lead to higher productivity (Feldman, 2005). Consideration given to local sensitivities is more effective in economic development because institutions function differently in different regions (Rodrik, 2000). Local adaptation therefore, is important as different regions may present unique challenges to development efforts. These may or may not be applicable to other regions. For instance, San Joaquin Valley's complex social fabric may not be a suitable context for Singapore's top-down approach.

Veugelers explained that structural reforms in societies are complex. They require consideration to many local factors, some of which, some of which are not easily captured by statistical indicators (Veugelers, 2005). However, responding to unique social configurations can produce efficient regional collaborations. Knowledge work, in the form of innovation, is cumulative. Knowledge-based production is based on leveraging prior innovations to produce value-added products and services. A strong collaborative structure can create a vibrant cycle of continuous innovation characterising a knowledge economy.

The cases of Boston's Route 128 and California's Silicon Valley are exemplary examples of how social contexts can influence the economic outcome of knowledge-based industries. The presence of coordinated efforts in all three regions recognise this importance. While their different social contexts have led to different challenges, their opportunities stem from their abilities to take advantage of these contexts. The three cases discussed in this chapter highlight challenges in local contexts in generating technology-based economic growth. However, these unique contexts can also be leveraged to create opprotunities towards the same goal.

CONCLUSION: THE BROADER THEORETICAL PERSPECTIVE

In this chapter, the author argued that in the technology-based development process towards a knowledge economy, it is important to take into account social contexts for initiatives to be successful. However, local conditions may pose challenges at the same time. Scholarly literature posits that policies, and hence economic growth initiatives, must fit local contexts for each region's unique social configuration to be effective in guiding regional development.

This argument advocates a shift in perspective from information technology to social technology, which comprises an acknowledged importance of the unique local contexts. This is increasingly relevant because the knowledge economy is less static than its preceding economic configurations. As Yeo (2009) showed in his review of scholarly literature, knowledge is complex and therefore, difficult to define as opposed to information in the information economy.

Gault argued that established indicators of knowledge creation, such as research and development activities and intellectual property commercialisation, are static indicators that cannot capture the dynamism involved in the knowledge economy (Gault, 2005). Although they capture the concept of innovation, they are restricted to the output of innovation or knowledge work, which is creation based on knowledge. Therefore, these measures may not be suitable in defining knowledge work explicitly for empirical research.

This theoretical perspective forms an impetus for social theories to be used to explain the development of a knowledge economy. It emphasises the need to adopt a broad perspective to include the contextual elements. Future research could therefore, take a focused approach to look at specific cases to identify best practices in which regional collaboration can be introduced and incorporated for technology-based economic growth. Measures on the degree of institutional collaboration can also be developed to study the impact of collaboration on economic growth. As industry bases constantly change in view of innovation flow in the knowledge economy, unique local contexts also become increasingly important to be considered for continued growth and sustainability.

REFERENCES

Baskerville, R., & Stage, J. (2000). Discourse on the interactions of information systems, organizations, and society: Reformation and transformation. In *IFIP WG 8.2 Conference.: The Social and Organizational Perspective on Research and Practice in Information Technology*. Boston, MA: Kluwer Academic Publishers.

Becker, G. (1992). Human capital and the economy. *Proceedings of the American Philosophical Society, 135*(1), 85–92.

Bureau of East Asian and Pacific Affairs. (2006) Background note: Singapore [Web page]. Retrieved from http://www.state.gov/r/pa/ei/bgn/2798.htm

California Economic Leadership Network. (2006). California economic development partnerships [Web page]. Retrieved March 17, 2006, from http://www.labor.ca.gov/cedp/cedpsanjoaquin.htm

California Partnership for the San Joaquin Valley. (2006). *Summary of approved "Scopes of Work" for work groups*. Fresno, CA: California Partnership for the San Joaquin Valley.

Campbell-Matthews, M., Vargas, R., Frate, C., Collar, C., Canevari, M., & Marsh, B. (2001a). *Sample costs to produce corn silage: San Joaquin Valley*. Stockton, CA: University of California Cooperative Extension.

Campbell-Matthews, M., Vargas, R., Frate, C., Collar, C., Canevari, M., & Marsh, B. (2001b). *Sample costs to produce green beans: San Joaquin Valley*. Stockton, CA: University of California Cooperative Extension.

Castells, M. (2001). *The internet galaxy: Reflections on the internet, business, and society*. Oxford: Oxford University Press.

Cecez-Kecmanovic, D. (2001). Doing critical IS research: The question of methodology. In *Qualitative research in IS: Issues and trends* (pp. 141–163). Hershey, PA: Idea Group Publishing.

Davis, U. C. (2004). *Changing face 2004*. Davis, CA: University of California Davis.

DeVol, R. (2002). *State technology and science index: Comparing and contrasting California*. Santa Monica, CA: Milken Institute.

DeVol, R., Klowden, K., Collins, J., Wallace, L., Wong, P., & Bedroussian, A. (2004). *Arkansas' position in the knowledge-based economy: Prospects and policy options*. Santa Monica, CA: Milken Institute.

Drucker, P. (1993). *Post-capitalist society*. New York: Harper Business.

Drucker, P. (2004). The age of social transformation. *Atlantic Monthly, 274*(5), 53–80.

Economic Development Work Group. (2006). *California partnership for the San Joaquin Valley*. California: Economic Development Work Group. eircom. (2000). *Ennis information age town: A connected community*. Dublin, Ireland: eircom.

Feldman, M. (2005, January 10-11). The importance of proximity and location. Paper presented on the panel Knowledge and place: Proximity, mobility, clusters, and institutions at *Advancing knowledge and the knowledge economy*, Washington, DC.

Gault, F. (2005). Measuring knowledge and its economic effects: The role of official statistics. In Kahin, B., & Foray, D. (Eds.), *Advancing knowledge and the knowledge economy* (pp. 27–41). Cambridge, MA: MIT Press.

Godin, B. (2003). The knowledge-based economy: Conceptual framework or buzzword? *Canadian Project on History and Sociology of S&T Statistics,* Working Paper No. 24. Retrieved from http://www.csiic.ca/PDF?/Godin_24.pdf

Gradeck, R., & Paytas, J. (2000). *Migration and regional growth*. Pittsburgh, PA: Carnegie Mellon University Center for Economic Development.

Hart, D. (2003). *The emergence of entrepreneurship policy*. Cambridge, UK: Cambridge University Press. doi:10.1017/CBO9780511610134

Houghton, J., & Sheehan, P. (2000). *A primer on the knowledge economy*. Melbourne City, Australia: Victoria University Center for Strategic Economic Studies.

Howcroft, D., & Trauth, E. (2004). *The choice of critical information systems research. 20th year retrospective: Relevant theory and informed practice? Looking forward from a 20-year perspective on IS research* (pp. 195–211). Boston, MA: Kluwer Academic Publishers.

International Telecommunication Union. (2005). *ITU workshop on ubiquitous network societies*. Geneva, Switzerland: International Telecommunication Union.

Marshall, R. (1994). Job and skill demands in the new economy. In Solmon, L. C., & Levenson, A. R. (Eds.), *Labor markets, employment policy and job creation* (pp. 21–58). Santa Monica, CA: Milken Institute.

McInerney, C. (2003). Wired Ennis: Learning and technology in an informaion age town. *Information Technology. Education et Sociétés, 4*(2), 9–34.

McQuillan, H. (2000). *Ennis information age town: A connected community*. Dublin, Ireland: Eircom.

Menzies, H. (1996). *Whose brave new world? The information highway and the new economy*. Toronto: Between the Lines.

Migration Dialogue. (2000). California: San Joaquin development. *Rural Migration News*, 6(2).

Miltiades, H. B., & Flores, M. (2008). *Aging in the San Joaquin Valley: Present realities and future prospects. Fresno, CA: Calfiornia State University*. Fresno: Central California Institute for Healthy Aging.

Ministry of Economic Development. (1999). *Information technology*. Singapore: Ministry of Economic Development.

Mukand, S., & Rodrik, D. (2002). In search of the Holy Grail: Policy convergence, experimentation, and economic Pperformance. *The American Economic Review*, *95*(1), 374–383. doi:10.1257/0002828053828707

Pacey, A. (1983). *The culture of technology*. Cambridge, MA: MIT Press.

Philips, L. (2000). New communications technologies: A conduit for social inclusion. *Information Communication and Society*, *39*(1), 39–68. doi:10.1080/136911800359419

Powell, W., & Snellman, K. (2004). The knowledge economy. *Annual Review of Sociology*, *30*, 199–220. doi:10.1146/annurev.soc.29.010202.100037

Rechtsanwaltgesellschaft, L. (2004). Legal and court system in Singapore [Web page]. Retrieved September 2005.

Rodrigues, M. J. (2003). *European policies for a knowledge society*. Cheltenham, UK: Edward Eglar Publishing Limited.

Rodrik, D. (2000). *Institutions for high quality growth: What they are and how to acquire them*. Cambridge, MA: National Bureau of Economic Research.

Saxenian, A. (1996). *Regional advantage: Culture and competition in Silicon Valley and Route 128*. Cambridge, MA: Harvard University Press.

Sen, A. (1999). *Development as freedom*. New York: Oxford University Press.

Stehr, N. (2002). *Knowledge and economic conduct: The social foundations of the modern economy*. Toronto, Canada: University of Toronto Press.

Trauth, E. (1996). Impact of an imported IT sector: Lessons from Ireland. In *Technology development and policy: Theoretical perspectives and practical challenges* (pp. 245–261). Aldershot, UK: Avebury Publishing Ltd.

Trauth, E. (2000). *The culture of an information economy: Influences and impact in the Republic of Ireland*. Dordrecht, The Netherlands: Kluwer Academic Publishers.

Trauth, E. (2001). Mapping information-sector work to the workforce: The lessons from Ireland. [Special issue on the Global IT workforce]. *Communications of the ACM*, *44*(7), 74–75. doi:10.1145/379300.379318

Trauth, E. M. (1993). Educating information technology professionals for work in Ireland: An emerging post-industrial country. In *Global information technology education: Issues and trends* (pp. 205–233). Harrisburg, PA: Idea Group Publishing.

United Nations Economic Commission for Europe. (2002). *Concept, outline, benchmarking and indicators*. Geneva: United Nations Publications.

Veugelers, R. (2005). Assessing innovation capacity: Fitting strategy and policy to the right framework. In *Measuring knowledge and its economic effects: Advancing knowledge and the knowledge economy*. Washington, DC: National Academies.

Yeo, B. (2009). *Developing a sustainable knowledge economy: An investigation of contextual factors*. Germany: VDM Verlag.

Zeleny, M. (1987). Management support systems: Towards integrated knowledge management. *Human Systems Management*, 7(1), 59–70.

KEY TERMS AND DEFINITIONS

Knowledge Economy: An economy that is utilises continuous innovation for production.

Knowledge Work: Work characterised by continuous innovation.

Knowledge Worker: A worker who performs knowledge work.

Information Technology: Computer-based systems that use and process data to add value.

Social Context: The environment that involves human interactions at different levels.

Social Technology: A social view of technologies that includes the social settings in which technologies operate.

Economic Development: Increase in output of a region, in terms of goods and services produced.

Case Study: In-depth analysis of a region or event

Chapter 2
Harness the Wisdom of Crowds:
The Importance of We-Intention in Social Computing Research

Aaron X. L. Shen
City University of Hong Kong, Hong Kong

Matthew K. O. Lee
City University of Hong Kong, Hong Kong

Christy M. K. Cheung
Hong Kong Baptist University, Hong Kong

ABSTRACT

Today, the growth and popularity of social computing greatly facilitate online collaboration in creating user-centered networked content. This chapter explores participation behaviors in social computing communities, conceptualizing them as group-referent intentional social actions. The authors identify the concept of "we-intention", which reflects an individual's perception of the extent to which all participants in a collectivity will engage in the joint action and act together, as a topic of theoretical and practical interest. A preliminary conceptual framework was further developed and, in particular, the collectively shared beliefs (i.e., collective attitude and collective efficacy) and the social influence processes (i.e., subjective norms, group norms and social identity) were regarded as the key predictors of participation we-intention in social computing communities. This chapter finally concludes with a discussion on future research directions in the areas of we-intention and social computing.

INTRODUCTION

The usage and diffusion of social computing applications have been growing dramatically in the past few years. According to Alexa's latest ranking (Alexa, 2009), five of the top ten global websites are social computing systems, including Facebook, YouTube, Windows Live, Wikipedia and Blogger.com. The advent and spread of social computing tools greatly change the fundamental way people communicate and share information, and further create opportunities for business world to improve its competitiveness in today's knowledge economy. Nowadays, lots of initiatives have been undertaken in the organizations from diverse industries. For example, in a recent report released

DOI: 10.4018/978-1-61692-904-6.ch002

by The Gilbane Group, the evolution of social computing is believed to enable a new generation of team collaboration in organizations (Bock & Paxhia, 2008). The Gilbane Group has investigated the use of social computing applications across seventeen different industries and it identified five industry trends for collaboration with the use of social media – the growing appetite for innovative technologies, the focus on vertical solutions, the restrained role for IT, the advent of rich media, and the importance of building communities.

It is commonly believed that the success of social computing depends not only on the technology itself but on a strong online community (Parameswaran, 2007). It is thus important and necessary to incorporate community-oriented motivational factors in understanding the adoption and usage of social computing technologies. In addition, prior studies have demonstrated that decision interdependence and collective efforts are essential for the successful implementation of social computing communities (Li et al., 2007). This is because the benefits of social computing applications can be achieved only when the majority of its users accept and voluntarily use the system together. Especially in the new era of social computing, collective action plays an increasingly significant role in creating and maintaining a virtual community, and decision making often involves two or more people who are jointly engaged in the collective action. The participation intention in social computing communities thus can be social in some sense. In this regard, it is recommended that researchers should explore new theories and methodologies from more disciplines to address questions raised by social computing phenomenon, and extend them to the realm of social endeavor (Parameswaran & Whinston, 2007).

The traditional intention-based models primarily focus on individual behavioral intention, but neglect the collective perceptions and efforts involved in the intention formation processes.

Individual behavioral intention is often defined as a "person's motivation in the sense of his or her conscious plan to exert effort to carry out a behavior" by himself or herself (Eagly & Chaiken, 1993, p. 168). In the current investigation context of social computing communities, the traditional individual intention may not be appropriate because the value and power of social computing greatly depend on the simultaneous play of all participants. Some recent studies also have demonstrated that it is necessary to re-specify intention when two or more people are involved and when decision involves mutual, shared and joint processes (Bagozzi, 2007). In this regard, we-intention may be a more appropriate construct, which is rooted in "a person's self-conception as a member of a particular group or social category, and action is conceived as either the group acting as a unit or the person acting as an agent of, or with, the group" (Bagozzi, 2007, p. 248) in social computing research.

Built on the theory of reasoned action (Fishbein & Ajzen, 1975) and the self-efficacy theory (Bandura, 1997), this chapter attempts to develop a preliminary conceptual framework to understand the impacts of group-based factors (i.e., collective attitude, social influence and collective efficacy) on participation we-intention in social computing communities. Specifically, the chapter is organized as follows. First of all, we discuss the definition and the common traits of social computing, as well as the research issues on the motivations for participation in social computing communities. We then explain the importance of we-intention in social computing research and present a detailed overview of we-intention research in related academic disciplines. Third, we propose a conceptual framework and discuss the underlying hypotheses for the purpose of facilitating future research in this area. This chapter concludes with recommendations and suggestions for future research opportunities.

BACKGROUND ON SOCIAL COMPUTING

The concept of social computing begins with the observation that human behavior is profoundly social and it is often described as "any types of computing application in which software serves as an intermediary or a focus for a social relation" (Schuler, 1994, p. 29). This definition can be interpreted in two ways. In the weaker sense, social computing can support any types of social behavior and social interaction through the use of information systems. Examples of social computing technologies in this category include weblogs, wikis, email, instant messaging, discussion forums, social bookmarking, and social networking services. In the stronger sense, social computing supports cooperation and collaboration among groups of people with common interests and concerns. Some typical applications in this category include collaborative filtering, online auction and prediction marketing, etc. Today, most of the social computing applications are capable of supporting group collaboration and communication. In this sense, Forrester Research further defined social computing as "a social structure in which technology puts power in communities" (Charron et al., 2006, p. 1). It also proposed that there are three tenets underpinning social computing: 1) innovation will shift from top-down to bottom-up; 2) value will shift from ownership to experience; 3) power will shift from institutions to communities. In recent years, the scope of social computing has expanded greatly with a shift of emphasis toward new applications and services. The premise of current social computing technologies thus is that it is possible to design systems that support useful functionality by making socially produced information available to their users. In this regard, social computing refers to "systems that support the gathering, representation, processing, use and dissemination of information that is distributed across social collectivities such as teams, communities, organizations, and markets" (Wikipedia, 2009). This information here is often produced by a group of people and can be provided directly or indirectly after being filtered and aggregated.

Social computing applications have some common traits and characteristics that differentiate them from the traditional information technologies (Parameswaran, 2007). First of all, social computing technologies are easy-to-use, lightweight and mostly open-source. Lightweight computing can be seen as a result of the shift from servers to the edge, and represents a shift from intelligent, powerful and complex computers to network-based computing which is closer to end-users. This leads to the empowerment of the edge and further helps to express and communicate human intelligence and creativity more efficiently. Second, information spaces created by most social computing tools are dynamic, socially interactive, portable and location-sensitive. The information space is cultivated and refined by social interactions and resides in the networks with portable identities. It thus has the potential to generate immediately apparent values to end-users and various collectives. Business initiatives also can leverage information from the spaces so as to provide enhanced values to customers. Third, social computing expands the organizational boundary to be much more fluid, enveloping communities of shared interests. There is no obvious direct revenue model, and in this regard altruistic and community-oriented motivational factors are regarded as the dominating factors affecting social behavior in most cases. Fourth, knowledge in social computing communities is often collectively contributed and refined by its users and thus the quality of the collectively user-generated content can be enhanced with the wisdom of crowds. Collective contribution, debate and refinement in social computing communities may tend to produce accurate information, and further lead to better insights than academic research and analyst reports (Parameswaran, 2007). In this sense, the collective participation and the sharing of concerns lie at the heart of social computing. In addition, it is also necessary to recognize that the use of social computing applications may be interdependent and tied in some way to the collective perceptions regarding the technology in question. However, prior studies investigating the motivations for social computing communities have paid little attention on this point.

Previous academic studies have investigated the motivational factors of social action in social computing communities primarily through adopting and extending the social science-based models. Specifically, altruism is often considered as one of the key factors in sustaining cooperation and collective action in online communities (Parameswaran & Whinston, 2007). Altruistic behavior, in this sense, reflects a long-term orientation in contributing and people make the contribution in order to achieve the social benefits. The focus here is also exclusively on the whole community (Wagner & Prasamphanich, 2007). It has been further argued that the uniqueness of human altruism facilitates cooperation in large groups of genetically unrelated individuals and only the psychological altruism is the true altruism because it is not related to psychological striving for advantages (Fehr & Fischbacher, 2003). Wagner and Prasamphanich (2007) also demonstrated that while social computing users have both individualistic and collaborative motives, the collaborative (altruistic) motives dominate the participation and contribution behavior. On the other hand, research on collective action in virtual communities further suggested that the community-oriented motivations are important factors predicting participation and contribution behavior, and individuals may forego the tendency to free ride at provision of public goods due to the concerns for the online community as a whole (Wasko & Faraj, 2000). Prior studies also found that personal benefits from community such as reputation building, reciprocity and organizational rewards are important motivations in social cooperation. People may engage in social computing communities without exact expectation of future returns, but instead for relatively long-term relationships of interests. Social capital is another important area that is believed to provide necessary conditions for users' participation in social computing communities (Parameswaran & Whinston, 2007). It refers to features of social organizations such as norms and networks that facilitate coordination and cooperation for mutual benefits (Putnam, 1995). In this sense, social capital theory provides a basis for understanding and exploring collective action in social computing communities.

WE-INTENTION RESEARCH

The social and interactional nature of computing technologies obviously is a tendency in recent years (Schuler, 1994). Different from the traditional productivity-oriented information technologies, such as word processing, social computing tools heavily rely on the collective intelligence as an important approach for creating and distributing online content. In addition, participation and contribution with the use of social computing technologies are mostly group-referent because it often involves the simultaneous behaviors of participants and people are interdependent in adopting and using the technology together (Bagozzi & Dholakia, 2006). In addition, prior experimental studies on group actions also have found that conditional cooperation may function under voluntary public goods interactions. Individuals contribute more when they expect constructive contribution from other participants. However, cooperation decreases if this expectation is undermined by free riding. In this situation, individuals' contribution decisions to a public good may greatly depend on the simultaneous contributions of other participants (Fischbacher et al., 2001). Therefore, the interdependent decision-making can be regarded as a specific feature of the collective actions in social computing. In this regard, behavioral intention in social computing context may be conceptually different from the traditional individual intention, which is defined as the subjective probability of an individual to perform a specific behavior by himself or herself (Fishbein & Ajzen, 1975). We-intention with reference to shared activity and mutual obligations thus may be more appropriate for the current investigation of social computing.

We-intention represents an individual's self-perception as a member of a particular group or a social category, and the behavior is conceived as the group acting as a unit or the person acting as an agent of the group (Bagozzi, 2007). In this sense, the concept of we-intention is believed to capture the collective perceptions and beliefs involved in the group actions, and is defined as "a commitment of an individual to participate in joint action, and involves an implicit or explicit agreement between the participants to engage in that joint action" (Tuomela, 1995, p. 9). Philosophical work has contributed significantly to the conceptual and logical aspects of we-intention. For example, Gilbert (1989) pointed out that different types of conceptual schemes instead of the more commonly used theme of singular action are required when participation intention is related to plural targets. Similarly, Searle (1990) believed that collective intention among each participant lies at the heart of collective action, and it cannot simply be reducible to individual intention. Bratman (1997) also proposed that two people share an intention to act only when there is common knowledge between them and both parties believe that "I intend that we act." Tuomela (1995) has further identified four presumptions for we-intention to occur: (1) a member of a collectivity intends to perform his or her own part contributory to the group action, (2) each member believes that the joint action opportunities, to some extent, exist and other members will perform their parts, (3) there is a mutual belief among all the participants that the opportunities for joint action will obtain, and finally, (4) the intention to perform one's own part depends on both (2) and (3). In addition, Tuomela (2005) also maintained that the beliefs required for

we-intention are purely subjective and represent one's own perception of the reality. Therefore, if the above conditions are satisfied, a member can even be the only agent with we-intention in a focal group (Bagozzi & Dholakia, 2002). In this sense, we-intention can be considered as an individual's subjective perception of the extent to which all participants in a collectivity will engage in the joint action together (for a detailed discussion on group intention and intentional social action, see Bagozzi, 2000).

Some recent empirical studies have begun to explore how participation we-intention is developed in the online social communities. Specifically, participation and contribution in virtual community have been conceptualized as intentional social action and we-intention to participate are functions of both individual determinants, such as positive anticipated emotions and desires, and community influence, such as social identity (Bagozzi & Dholakia, 2002). For example, a study investigating virtual communities from seven different types of Internet venues has found that group norms, mutual agreement and desires were significant predictors of participation we-intention. In particular, group norms have the largest impact, followed by mutual agreement and desire to act. In the meanwhile, we-intention explained 24% of the variance in actual behavior. Virtual community types (i.e., network-based and small-group-based virtual community) also have moderated the relationships between reasons for participating and social influence factors (Dholakia et al., 2004). Another empirical investigation on open source software user communities revealed several different factors predicting participation we-intention. In particular, cognitive factors, such as attitude and perceived behavioral control, affective factors, such as positive anticipated emotions, and social factors, such as social identity, are the important determinants of participation we-intention. Among these factors, social identity exerted the most pronounced effect on we-intention, which in turn leads to participation in Linux user groups interaction, visiting Linux websites, working with Linux and money spent on Linux (Bagozzi & Dholakia, 2006). A recent study examined why people use online social networks (e.g., Facebook) and further concluded that participation we-intention is strongly determined by social identity and social presence (Cheung et al., 2010). The concept of we-intention also has been investigated in some other social computing contexts such as instant messaging. Building on the belief-desire-intention model and the social influence theory, a recent study found that desire mediates the impacts of group norm and social identity on we-intention to use instant messaging. In addition, usage experience moderates the effects of group norms and social identity on we-intention (Shen et al., 2010a). Gender is another important moderator in we-intention-based models and it is believed to moderate the effects of attitude, anticipated emotions, group norms and social identity on participation we-intention (Shen et al., 2010b). Although some noteworthy initiatives have been starting to investigate we-intention in social computing contexts, the antecedents they identified are primarily based on previous individual intention models. However, as a new and interesting philosophical concept which may be conceptually different from the traditional individual intention, we-intention definitely deserves specific attentions on detailed analysis and structural identification of the major contributing factors.

RESEARCH FRAMEWORK

As we discussed before, prior empirical studies on we-intention suffered from several serious problems. One of the most important drawbacks is that there is a lack of research exploring factors specific to the concept of we-intention. The use of factors contributing to individual intention in we-intention models will fail to capture the possible differences between the two kinds of intention,

and further will be unable to provide new insights into business practice. In addition, the adoption and implementation of social computing require collective participation and team efforts among the group members. In this regard, the participation behavior is driven by the collectively shared perceptions regarding a specific group activity. It is thus important and necessary to take individuals' perceptions of collective consciousness as one of the determinants of participation we-intention in the current investigation context of social computing. As social computing continues to gather momentum, social psychology-based theoretical lenses will become more important to help us understand the new patterns of community user behaviors. Based on the theory of reasoned action (Fishbein & Ajzen, 1975) and the self-efficacy theory (Bandura, 1997), we propose a preliminary conceptual framework, as shown in Figure 1, to investigate the development of we-intention in the realm of social computing.

Collective Attitude

One of the most popular definitions of attitude in social psychology literature is "a learned predisposition to respond in a consistently favorable or unfavorable manner with respect to a given object" (Fishbein & Ajzen, 1975, p. 6). In the theory of reasoned action (TRA), attitude is believed to have a direct impact on behavioral intention, which further affects the actual behavior. It assumes that if an individual has positive feelings about performing a particular behavior, he or she will be more likely to engage in the target behavior. The behavioral attitude in the TRA focuses more on a single person's own view toward the object. However, in the social computing era, the benefits of social computing can be achieved only when a group of people collectively engage in activities that may span over prolonged periods of time. In this regard, Parameswaran and Whinston (2007) indicated that, "requirements that hold for communities are common values and beliefs" (p. 340).

Figure 1. Research framework

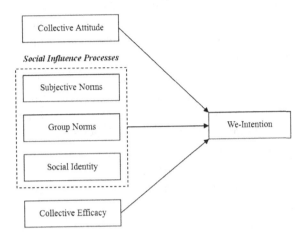

It is thus believed that the collectively-held perception and consciousness among all participants dominate the power of social computing communities. Nowadays, social computing tools greatly facilitate the development and growth of diverse online communities and the success of social computing, to some extent, largely resides in the information distributed across social collectivities. It is thus necessary to focus more on the collective orientation toward participation and involvement in the social computing environment. In this sense, collective attitude jointly-held by plural subjects may be more important than commonly-used individual attitude in investigating social behaviors observed in the social computing world.

Collective attitude may exist in any kinds of social categories and is mutually believed by all participants in the collectivity. Prior philosophical studies have demonstrated that collective attitude obtains if and only if (1) all members in the group share the collective attitude, (2) there is a common belief that everybody in the group share the collective attitude and the initial conditions for the presence of the collective attitude obtain, and (3) there is a common belief that collective attitude is present in the group. The initial conditions for the presence of collective attitude are satisfied when some participants have individual attitudes

of some objects that correspond to a collective attitude of the same objects, and hold the beliefs that other participants also have such individual attitudes. These initial beliefs and attitudes further lead to more complex beliefs and attitude, and after several iterations, there is a common belief among all the participants that everybody in the group has a collective attitude (Balzer & Tuomela, 1997). In this sense, an individual will participate in social behaviors based on his or her own perception towards the collective attitude. In addition, an individual may implicitly expect other participants to perform their roles, however, the expectation is subjective and the collective action may be viewed differently by each participant (Goyal, 2005). Therefore, similar to our conceptualization of we-intention, collective attitude here focuses more on an individual's subjective perception toward the collective beliefs. In the current study, we define collective attitude as an individual's subjective perception that there is a common belief among all the participants about the extent to which the performance of a particular behavior is positively or negatively valued.

Collective attitude is functionally important for social computing research because today's online social behavior pertains to the interdependent relationships of individuals or groups. In this regard, people with positive collective attitude toward participation in social computing community together tend to make a greater effort to engage in community's actual activities. In addition, in accordance with the propositions raised in the theory of reasoned action, attitude contributes significantly to the behavioral intention to perform an action. In our current investigation context of social computing, we believe that an individual may have a we-intention to engage in a joint action if he/she thinks there is a shared belief among all members in social computing communities about the favorableness of the group participation behavior. This leads to our first proposition.

Proposition 1: *Collective attitude is positively related to we-intention to participate in social computing communities.*

Social Influence Processes

Kelman (1958) has identified three distinct aspects of social influence processes, including compliance, internalization, and identification. Compliance occurs when an individual accepts the influence to get support, approval or a favorable reaction from significant others. Internalization represents the process through which people incorporate external things into one's own psychological processes and it occurs when an individual accepts the influence because of the content itself of the targeted behavior. Finally, identification occurs when an individual accepts the influence to establish or maintain a satisfying self-defining relationship with another person or group.

Social influence is believed to affect intentional social action in many different ways. In particular, the theory of reasoned action posits that perceived interpersonal pressure (e.g., subjective norms) to perform an action can be thought as an important form of normative social influence. Subjective norms reflect the influence of directly felt expectations from significant others and are associated with the accompanied "social effects". An individual accepts the influence of subjective norms in order to get support, approval or favorable reactions from the general public whose opinions are important for him/her. It represents the social influence process underlying what Kelman (1958) terms compliance. In the context of social computing, significant others can be either members in online communities or members of other primary reference groups such as family or friends, or both (Bagozzi & Dholakia, 2002). If an individual perceives that most of the people around support his/her participation in the social computing communities, these advocators also may be the users of such communities, and in this case, he/she will develop a we-intention to participate in social computing communities with the significant others. However, prior studies also have demonstrated that subjective norms promote the acceptance of information technology only under conditions of mandatory use and for users with limited experience (Karahanna et al., 1999; Venkatesh et al., 2003). Because of the voluntary choice and inconspicuous participation for most social computing communities (Bagozzi & Dholakia, 2002), we expect that subjective norms, which reflect social influence in a rather general sense, will exert a less positive impact, compared to other particular group influence (e.g., group norms and social identity), on one's participation we-intention in social computing communities.

Proposition 2: *Subjective norms are less positively related to we-intention to participate in social computing communities, compared to group norms and social identity.*

Although subjective norms have received considerable empirical support as an important antecedent of behavioral intention, this concept has often been regarded as one of the least understood aspects in the theory of reasoned action. As demonstrated by Terry and Hogg (1996), the use of subjective norms "may be problematic because it describes norms in terms of the extent to which people perceive that others want them to perform the behavior … for behaviors that do not influence other people or behaviors that are not so directly associated with [impactful] … outcomes, such pressures may be latent and may not be perceived" (p. 778). Eagly and Chaiken (1993) further argued that "features embedded in certain types of role relationships" (p. 683) must be considered in investigating social actions. In this sense, two other modes of social influence – internalization and identification – identified by Kelman (1958) may be more pertinent to the study of group influence and the context of voluntary choice (Venkatesh et al., 2003).

Internalization represents the process through which people incorporate external things into one's own psychological processes and it occurs when an individual accepts the influence because of the congruence of one's values with the values of others (Kelman, 1958). It can be generated from the information communicated between group members and resides in "the personal meaning of that information" (p. 228, Bagozzi & Lee, 2002). In the social computing context, an individual accepts the influence underlying internalization when he/she finds that his/her values match those of other group members. For example, through effective and expressive interpersonal communication, a music fan may find others who are also enthusiastic toward music, and in this case, they have a large overlap of values or goals and may produce socially valuable information together. As a result of this, internalization can be achieved mainly due to the relevance of the themes and issues. In addition, prior studies have found that social influence operates in voluntary contexts primarily through internalization by the process that an individual actively participates in virtual groups with overlapping values (Bagozzi & Dholakia, 2002). In the current research context, internalization process is reflected through the effects of group norms. Group norms are defined as "an understanding of, and a commitment by, the individual member to a set of goals, values, beliefs, and conventions shared with other group members" (Dholakia et al., 2004, p. 245). Group norms thus are facilitated by the similarity of one's values or goals with that of their referent group and it represents a shared agreement among participants about their shared goals and expectations (Turner, 1991). Generally speaking, group norms can be publicized to members through three different ways. First, an individual participates in cooperative group activities and actively seek out the group's goals, values and conventions. Second, a participant may slowly discover the group norms through socialization and repeated communication over a period of time. Third, a

person may come to understand the community's norms beforehand and participate because of the perceived overlap between his/her own values with the group norms (Dholakia et al., 2004). Prior studies have shown that group norms have a strong influence in computer-mediated groups because it can be accessible through resources such as FAQs or be inferred by group members through peer interactions (Postmes et al., 2000). The importance of group norms also lies in the fact that it is not enough for an individual to merely accept the reference group influence to form a we-intention to participate, but all participants must hold one or more common goals. In this regard, the collective participation behavior is becoming intrinsically rewarding in fact. Therefore, if an individual finds collective participation in social computing communities congruent with one's own value systems, he/she will be motivated by the internalized values and be more likely to have a we-intention to participate together with other group members.

Proposition 3: *Group norms are positively related to we-intention to participate in social computing communities.*

In addition to internalization, another type of social influence associated with one's relationships to other specific individuals or groups is identification (Kelman, 1958). Identification refers to one's conception of self in terms of thinking, feeling and acting on the basis of a "group level of self" (as a member of the group) instead of a "personal self" (Turner, 1987). It occurs when an individual accepts the influence to establish or maintain a positive self-defining relationship with another person or group (Bagozzi & Lee, 2002). Identification thus leads to a selective perception of belonging to a collectivity (Workman, 2007). After categorizing himself/herself as a group member, an individual may strive to achieve a positive self-enhancement by discriminating the in-group to which he/she belongs from other out-groups. In the process of seeking distinctiveness, they perceive themselves in terms of "we" rather than "I" (Turner, 1987). For these social computing communities, many-to-many communication can foster a sense of connectedness among participants because users become more aware of one another and their opinions, feelings, likes and dislikes (Chen, 2007). Identification with a virtual community, in this case, is based on social criteria like age, gender, profession or interests, and will induce group-oriented behaviors because group members are often motivated to distinguish their own groups from the out-groups. Specifically, identification is characterized by the social identity in the current study. The most commonly quoted definition proposed by Tajfel (1978) asserts that social identity is "… that part of an individual's self-concept which derives from his knowledge of his membership of a social group (or groups) together with the value and emotional significance attached to that membership" (p. 63). Ellemers et al. (1999) further suggested that social identity involves three related but distinct aspects, including "a cognitive component (a cognitive awareness of one's membership in a social group – self-categorization), an evaluative component (a positive or negative value connotation attached to this group membership – group self-esteem), and an emotional component (a sense of emotional involvement with the group – affective commitment)" (p. 372). Social identity theory recently has been increasingly considered as a remarkably successful theory in explaining human behavior, especially the behaviors of individuals in a variety of virtual communities. More specifically, social identity theory has been proven successful in explaining how virtual community users develop their participation we-intentions in a digital environment (Bagozzi & Dholakia, 2006; Dholakia et al., 2004). If an individual identifies himself/herself with a social group and seeks to reinforce the self-enhancement that perceived as consequences of group memberships, he/she will be more likely to form a we-intention to engage in the group activities. In line with previous research, we obtain the following proposition.

Proposition 4: *Social identity is positively related to we-intention to participate in social computing communities.*

Collective Efficacy

Self-efficacy is the belief in one's effectiveness in performing specific tasks and is often defined as "one's ability to organize and execute given types of performances" (Bandura, 1997, p. 21). Prior studies have demonstrated that self-efficacy beliefs provided the foundation for human motivation and personal performance because unless people believe their behaviors can produce the desired outcomes, they have little incentive to act (Bandura, 1977; 1997). Individuals can use information about the task, past behavior and the environment to evaluate their abilities of performing a behavior in a given context. Prior studies also have demonstrated that individuals' perception of self-efficacy may not be sufficient to explain group performance for highly interactive tasks because the collective outcome cannot be separated from group processes and social interactions (Katz-Navon & Erez, 2005). In this regard, the self-efficacy concept is a social construct and some small-group-based studies have begun to investigate the nature and influence of collective efficacy (Baker, 2001). Collective efficacy can be defined either as individually-held group beliefs (e.g., Riggs & Knight, 1994) or as a group-held belief in the group's capability to attain goals and accomplish desired tasks (e.g., Gibson, 1999). However, by defining collective efficacy as individually held beliefs, researchers can further operationalize and measure it independent of the extent of group development or the existence of group beliefs about performance (Baker, 2001). This is because group members may not share the same expectations in the early stage of group development and in this case collective efficacy ratings may vary significantly within the group. Based on this reasoning, collective efficacy cannot exist if it is defined as a group-held belief. Therefore, it is advisable to keep with the Riggs and Knight's (1994) study to analyze at the individual level and define collective efficacy as an individual's expectation about group's capabilities to organize and execute the courses of action required to produce given levels of attainments on a specific task (Baker, 2001). In this sense, collective efficacy reflects group members' perception of team effectiveness or "what we think of us" (Mischel & Northcraft, 1997). With the development of collaborative group, members develop their perceptions of collective efficacy from past behavior, learn through experience with group tasks, and understand the capabilities of each other. Consequently, group members' beliefs about collective efficacy become increasingly similar and both individual and group levels of the conceptualization of collective efficacy are applicable in this stage. In today's social computing communities, many activities require cooperation, coordination and collaboration among two or more individuals who work together toward the accomplishment of a common goal. The interdependence nature of group tasks provides opportunities for the participants to develop shared understanding and knowledge of the group's abilities. The collective efficacy thus further influences what people choose to do as a group and how much efforts they put into the group action, fosters motivational commitment to group's missions, and improves their resilience to adversity in performance accomplishments (Bandura, 1997). Prior studies also have demonstrated the positive effect of collective efficacy on team performance of a variety of collaborative tasks (Bandura, 2000; Katz-Navon & Erez, 2005). Therefore, in the current investigation context, we propose that if an individual feels that the social computing community is capable of performing certain tasks, he/she will be more willing to act as an agent of the community in doing so.

Proposition 5: *Collective efficacy is positively related to we-intention to participate in social computing communities.*

FUTURE RESEARCH DIRECTIONS

Today, it is believed that social computing leads to a significant degree of innovation being at the community level (Parameswaran & Whinston, 2007). In this chapter, we explore and conceptualize participation behavior in social computing communities as intentional social action, and employ the concept of "we-intention", instead of the traditional individual intention, as the major issue of interest. Participation in social computing communities can be considered as group-referent social behavior since it often involves other members' simultaneous actions and incorporates aspects of influencing and being influenced by them (Bagozzi & Dholakia, 2006). In this situation, the participation intention thus can be formed with reference to the collectivity and obtained by an individual when acting together with other participants. The importance of "we-intention" concept in social computing research also lies in the fact that the individual intention emphasizes an individual's beliefs regarding his/her own performance on actions taken by himself/herself, whereas we-intention implies that a group member believes that his/her own efforts cannot warrant the achievement of a goal, instead it is the group that acts as a whole to achieve the collective goal, which may be more similar to that in social computing research.

Prior studies have called for new theories and methodologies to address questions about incentives and motivations for participation in social computing communities, and suggested extending the scope of current information system usage to social endeavor (Parameswaran, 2007; Parameswaran & Whinston, 2007). In this regard, the concept of "we-intention" should deserve to be given more attention in future social computing research. In particular, future research could empirically test the propositions suggested in this chapter by a large scale survey with different samples. On the other hand, hierarchical linear modeling is appropriate for use with nested data, and a multi-level analysis can be conducted to analyze we-intention at multiple hierarchical levels.

The possible effects of collectively shared beliefs and social influence processes on participation we-intention also may be different for different types of social computing communities. As stated by Dholakia et al. (2004), small-group-based community is constituted by "individuals with a dense web of relationships, interacting together online as a group, in order to accomplish a wider range of jointly conceived and held goals, and to maintain existing relationships" (p. 248), whereas network-based community can be conceived as "a specialized, geographically dispersed community based on a structured, relatively sparse, and dynamic network of relationships among participants sharing a common focus" (p. 248). In this sense, it is reasonable to assume that collectively shared beliefs and social influence processes may have stronger effects on we-intention in small-group-based community because this kind of community represents a strong sense of unity and a kind of fully cooperative group action.

In addition, comparison study examining the differences between individual intention and we-intention in explaining actual participation behavior is certainly required on this point. Particularly, two distinct forms of social intentions should be taken into account in future social computing research (Bagozzi, 2007; Bagozzi & Lee, 2002). The first form of social intention can be regarded as a group-oriented individual intention to do one's part of a group activity so as to contribute to the achievement of group performance, and an individual in this situation is personally committed to the group action. Another form of social intention is what we have termed as we-intention. We-intention is rooted in an individual's perception as a member of a group and the group activity

is viewed holistically instead of in an atomistic sense. In the mode of we-intention, all participants are collectively committed to the group action and it is the group that acts or experiences as a unit in performing an activity. A recent study has demonstrated that both forms of social intentions predicted group-referent contribution behavior in wiki-based virtual communities. However, individual intention is negatively related to the actual group contribution behavior, whereas we-intention is positively related to the behavior (Shen et al., 2009). This seems somewhat contrary to prior empirical findings on the relationship between individual intention and behavior. An explanation given by the authors is that people with individual intention concentrate more on the behavior itself, and thus may be less likely to work with others in group actions. Today, lots of emerging social computing technologies place a greater emphasis on group processes in producing online user-generated content. It is thus necessary and advisable to incorporate the concept of we-intention in future social computing research.

In order to understand the social computing phenomenon in greater detail, much other work needs to be done. As we have mentioned earlier in this chapter, collectively shared perceptions among participants in social computing communities and social influence processes are definitely major areas of concerns. This is because we-intention reflects an individual's perception toward the coordination and implementation of group actions. It is thus can be better understood from the perspectives of shared values, perceptions and beliefs concerning the group activities. Collective attitude and collective efficacy, in this sense, capture an individual's perception of the extent to which the focal group holds a shared belief toward the collective action. Collective attitude thus contributes more in the context of group behavior, and this also may be the reason why prior studies have found that individual attitude significantly predicts individual intention, instead of behavioral we-intention (Bagozzi & Lee, 2002).

The three different routes of social influence also provide important insights into we-intention research (Bagozzi & Lee, 2002; Cheung et al., 2010; Shen et al., 2010a). Since behaviors in social computing communities capture aspects of influencing and being influenced by other participants, it is thus useful to incorporate both social normative compliance and group-referent influence in we-intention models. In fact, the three modes of social influence identified by Kelman (1958) have been proven significant in determining participation we-intention in online social communities (Bagozzi & Dholakia, 2002; 2006; Cheung et al., 2010; Shen et al., 2010a; 2010b).

In addition, prior studies have demonstrated that group action requires three necessary conditions: "(1) mutual responsiveness among participants to the intentions and actions of others, (2) collective commitment to the joint activity, and (3) commitment to support others involved in the activity" (p. 1101, Bagozzi & Dholakia, 2006). Future social computing research thus may focus more on the commitment and mutual responsiveness involved in the development of group-oriented intentions. On the other hand, we-intention can be formulated when participants perceive themselves as "us" or "we" and express their joint readiness to participate in the collective activities (Gilbert, 1989). In this regard, we-intention entails a mutual understanding and cooperation among a group of people who work together toward a shared common goal. These specific mechanisms of we-intention provide a useful baseline for future studies on we-intention in social computing.

Further to the discussion above, it is also necessary to recognize that there is often no explicitly a prior agreement on activities in social computing applications. Therefore, even though the focal action is at the group level, the proper unit of analysis is at the individual level and the emphasis is on an individual's perception of group

action (Shen et al., 2009). The operationalization and conceptualization of individual perception thus is independent of the stages of group development and the existence of actual group beliefs. This is often an issue arousing much confusion in the past, as it was often thought that for group level study the unit of analysis should be at the group level too.

CONCLUSION

In this chapter, we provide a thorough discussion on the importance of we-intention in social computing research and propose a preliminary conceptual framework for future research in this area. Specifically, we believe that the collectively shared beliefs perceived by each participant in social computing communities and social influence processes exerted by group members play significant roles in we-intention formation and should deserve particular attention in future research. Today, with the advent of social computing, the traditional individual intention-based models may not be appropriate because human's behaviors become increasingly interdependent and collaborative. In this regard, the wisdom and intelligence of crowds can serve as a promising approach for the creation and organization of user-driven content, and accordingly, collective action, to some extent, dominates the outcome with the use of social computing technologies. New theories and methodologies thus are strongly required to fully understand the underlying motivations and the intended results. From this point of view, this chapter presents a valuable and timely attempt to identify the research opportunities for those exploring the collective processes in social computing. In addition, social computing is believed to be the trend of future organizational computing (IP & Wagner, 2008). In this regard, research findings regarding we-intention also will benefit managers who rely on collaborative teams in accomplishing various tasks and providing supports to customers. Which methods can be used to harness the collective wisdom of employees and how to develop a positive we-intention among team members should be of great concerns for practitioners. On the other hand, since individual intention and we-intention may be stimulated by different types of factors, managers thus could give priority to corresponding motivational incentives with the types of intended behavior outcomes in mind.

ACKNOWLEDGMENT

The authors acknowledge with gratitude the generous support of the Hong Kong Baptist University for the project (FRG1/09-10/014) without which the timely production of the current report/publication would not have been feasible.

REFERENCES

Alexa. (2009). Top 500 websites. Retrieved September 8, 2009, from http://www.alexa.com/topsites

Bagozzi, R. P. (2000). On the concept of intentional social action in consumer behavior. *The Journal of Consumer Research*, *27*, 388–396. doi:10.1086/317593

Bagozzi, R. P. (2007). The legacy of the technology acceptance model and a proposal for a paradigm shift. *Journal of the Association for Information Systems*, *8*(4), 244–254.

Bagozzi, R. P., & Dholakia, U. M. (2002). Intentional social action in virtual communities. *Journal of Interactive Marketing*, *16*(2), 2–21. doi:10.1002/dir.10006

Bagozzi, R. P., & Dholakia, U. M. (2006). Open source software user communities: A study of participation in Linux user groups. *Management Science*, *52*(7), 1099–1115. doi:10.1287/mnsc.1060.0545

Bagozzi, R. P., & Lee, K. H. (2002). Multiple routes for social influence: The role of compliance, internalization, and social identity. *Social Psychology Quarterly*, *65*(3), 226–247. doi:10.2307/3090121

Baker, D. F. (2001). The development of collective efficacy in small task groups. *Small Group Research*, *32*(4), 451–474. doi:10.1177/104649640103200404

Balzer, W., & Tuomela, R. (1997). A fixed point approach to collective attitudes. In Holmström-Hintikka, G., & Tuomela, R. (Eds.), *Contemporary action theory*. Boston: Kluwer Academic Publishers.

Bandura, A. (1977). Self-efficacy: Toward a unifying theory of behavioral change. *Psychological Review*, *84*(2), 191–215. doi:10.1037/0033-295X.84.2.191

Bandura, A. (1997). *Self-efficacy: The exercise of control*. New York: Freeman.

Bandura, A. (2000). Exercise of human agency through collective efficacy. *Current Directions in Psychological Science*, *9*, 75–78. doi:10.1111/1467-8721.00064

Bock, G., & Paxhia, S. (2008). *Collaboration and social media: Taking stock of today's experiences and tomorrow's opportunities*. Cambridge, MA: Gilbane Group, Inc.

Bratman, M. E. (1997). I intend that we J. In Holmström-Hintikka, G., & Tuomela, R. (Eds.), *Contemporary action theory*. Boston: Kluwer Academic Publishers.

Charron, C., Favier, J., & Li, C. (2006). Social computing: How networks erode institutional power, and what to do about it. Cambridge, MA: Forrester Customer Report.

Chen, I. Y. L. (2007). The factors influencing members' continuance intentions in professional virtual communities: A longitudinal study. *Journal of Information Science, 33*(4), 451–467. doi:10.1177/0165551506075323

Cheung, C. M. K., Chiu, P., & Lee, M. K. O. (2010. (in press). Online social networks: Why do we use Facebook? *Computers in Human Behavior.*

Dholakia, U. M., Bagozzi, R. P., & Pearo, L. K. (2004). A social influence model of consumer participation in network- and small-group-based virtual communities. *International Journal of Research in Marketing, 21*, 241–263. doi:10.1016/j.ijresmar.2003.12.004

Eagly, A. H., & Chaiken, S. (1993). *The psychology of attitudes.* Fort Worth, TX: Harcourt Brace Jovanovich.

Ellemers, N., Kortekaas, P., & Ouwerkerk, J. W. (1999). Self-categorisation, commitment to the group and group self-esteem as related but distinct aspects of social identity. *European Journal of Social Psychology, 29*(2-3), 371–389. doi:10.1002/(SICI)1099-0992(199903/05)29:2/3<371::AID-EJSP932>3.0.CO;2-U

Fehr, E., & Fischbacher, U. (2003). The nature of human altruism. *Nature, 425*(23), 785–791. doi:10.1038/nature02043

Fischbacher, U., Gachter, S., & Fehr, E. (2001). Are people conditionally cooperative? Evidence from a public goods experiment. *Economics Letters, 71*(3), 397–404. doi:10.1016/S0165-1765(01)00394-9

Fishbein, M., & Ajzen, I. (1975). *Belief, attitude, intention, and behavior: An introduction to theory and research.* Reading, MA: Addison-Wesley.

Gibson, C. B. (1999). Do they do what they believe they can? Group efficacy and group effectiveness across tasks and cultures. *Academy of Management Journal, 42*, 138–152. doi:10.2307/257089

Gilbert, M. (1989). *On social facts.* London: Routledge.

Goyal, M. (2005). Attitude based teams in a hostile dynamic world. *Knowledge-Based Systems, 18*, 245–255. doi:10.1016/j.knosys.2004.08.002

Ip, R. K. F., & Wagner, C. (2008). Weblogging: A study of social computing and its impact on organizations. *Decision Support Systems, 45*, 242–250. doi:10.1016/j.dss.2007.02.004

Karahanna, E., Straub, D. W., & Chervany, N. L. (1999). Information technology adoption across time: A cross-sectional comparison of pre-adoption and post-adoption beliefs. *Management Information Systems Quarterly, 23*(2), 183–213. doi:10.2307/249751

Katz-Navon, T. Y., & Erez, M. (2005). When collective- and self-efficacy affect team performance: The role of task interdependence. *Small Group Research, 36*(4), 437–465. doi:10.1177/1046496405275233

Kelman, H. C. (1958). Compliance, identification, and internalization: Three processes of attitude change. *The Journal of Conflict Resolution, 2*(1), 51–60. doi:10.1177/002200275800200106

Li, D., Chau, P. Y. K., & Lou, H. (2005). Understanding individual adoption of instant messaging: An empirical investigation. *Journal of the Association for Information Systems, 6*(4), 102–129.

Mischel, L. J., & Northcraft, G. B. (1997). "I think we can, I think we can...": The role of efficacy beliefs in group and team effectiveness. *Advances in Group Processes, 14*, 177–197.

Parameswaran, M. (2007). Social computing: An overview. *Communications of the Association for Information Systems, 19*, 762–780.

Parameswaran, M., & Whinston, A. B. (2007). Research issues in social computing. *Journal of the Association for Information Systems, 8*(6), 336–350.

Postmes, T., Spears, R., & Lea, M. (2000). The formation of group norms in computer-mediated communication. *Human Communication Research, 26*(3), 341–371. doi:10.1111/j.1468-2958.2000.tb00761.x

Putnam, R. (1995). Tuning in, tuning out: The strange disappearance of social capital in America. *Political Science and Politics, 28*(4), 664–683. doi:10.2307/420517

Riggs, M. L., & Knight, P. A. (1994). The impact of perceived group success-failure on motivational beliefs and attitudes: A causal model. *The Journal of Applied Psychology, 79*, 755–766. doi:10.1037/0021-9010.79.5.755

Schuler, D. (1994). Social computing. *Communications of the ACM, 37*(1), 28–29. doi:10.1145/175222.175223

Searle, J. R. (1990). Collective intentions and actions. In Cohen, P., Morgan, J., & Pollack, M. (Eds.), *Intentions in communication* (pp. 401–415). Cambridge, MA: MIT Press.

Shen, A. X. L., Cheung, C. M. K., Lee, M. K. O., & Chen, H. (2010a. (in press). How social influence affects we-intention to use instant messaging: The moderating effect of usage experience. *Information Systems Frontiers*.

Shen, A. X. L., Lee, M. K. O., Cheung, C. M. K., & Chen, H. (2009). An investigation into contribution I-intention and we-intention in open web-based encyclopedia: Roles of joint commitment and mutual agreement. Paper presented at the Proceedings of the 30th International Conference on Information Systems, Phoenix, Arizona.

Shen, A. X. L., Lee, M. K. O., Cheung, C. M. K., & Chen, H. (2010b. (in press). Gender differences in intentional social action: We-Intention to engage in social network-facilitated team collaboration. *Journal of Information Technology*.

Tajfel, H. (1978). Social categorization, social identity and social comparison. In Tajfel, H. (Ed.), *Differentiation between social groups: Studies in the social psychology of intergroup relations* (pp. 61–76). London: Academic Press.

Terry, D. J., & Hogg, M. A. (1996). Group norms and the attitude-behavior relationship: A role for group identification. *Personality and Social Psychology Bulletin, 22*, 776–793. doi:10.1177/0146167296228002

Tuomela, R. (1995). *The importance of us: A philosophical study of basic social notions*. Stanford, CA: Stanford University Press.

Tuomela, R. (2003). The we-mode and the I-mode. In Schmitt, F. F. (Ed.), *Socializing metaphysics: The nature of social reality* (pp. 93–127). Lanham, MD: Roman & Littlefield.

Tuomela, R. (2005). We-intention revisited. *Philosophical Studies, 125*(3), 327–369. doi:10.1007/s11098-005-7781-1

Turner, J. C. (1987). *Rediscovering the social group: A self-categorization theory*. Oxford: Blackwell.

Turner, J. C. (1991). *Social influence. Milton-Keynes*. UK: Open University Press.

Venkatesh, V., Morris, M. G., Davis, G. B., & Davis, F. D. (2003). User acceptance of information technology: Toward a unified view. *Management Information Systems Quarterly, 27*(3), 425–478.

Wagner, C., & Prasarnphanich, P. (2007). Innovating collaborative content creation: The role of altruism and wiki technology. Paper presented at the Proceedings of the 40th Hawaii International Conference on System Sciences.

Wasko, M., & Faraj, S. (2000). It is what one does: Why people participate and help others in electronic communities of practice. *The Journal of Strategic Information Systems*, *9*(2-3), 155–173. doi:10.1016/S0963-8687(00)00045-7

Wikipedia. (2009). Social computing. Retrieved September 8, 2009, from http://en.wikipedia.org/wiki/Social_computing

Chapter 3

Using Theoretical Frameworks from the Social Sciences to Understand and Explain Behaviour in Social Computing

Jacqui Taylor
Bournemouth University, UK

ABSTRACT

Research over the past 15 years has examined how the Internet is being used to support communication and social interaction across a variety of groups and communities. However, much of this research has been exploratory, rather than explanatory. It is argued here that approaches from the social sciences offer established methods and frameworks within which the psychological and social impacts of computing can be addressed. In discussing various theories, the chapter highlights one problem—that individual theories have tended to be used to explain a single aspect of human behaviour. There is a need to think more holistically and search for a theoretical approach that can explain intrapersonal processes (e.g. cognition and emotion) as well as interpersonal behaviour within social computing. A number of theoretical frameworks from the social sciences (e.g. social identity theory and social capital theory) will be discussed as potentially being able to explain psychological processes at all levels for users of social computing applications. In summary, the objectives of this chapter are to discuss current approaches used to explain the way people interact in social computing contexts, identify shortcomings with these and to highlight approaches that can address these shortcomings.

SOCIAL COMPUTING AND SOCIAL SCIENCE

1.1 Introduction

Social computing covers the area where social behaviour and computer science intersect and

DOI: 10.4018/978-1-61692-904-6.ch003

this chapter will consider the support for all types of social behaviour through computing systems across all facets of society. The focus will be on the potential of social science to explain the psychological impacts of this computing support. For example: an academic online community can support students in the development of critical thinking skills; online support groups can provide empathy and advice for the elderly or ill patients, and online gaming communities can support the social needs of adolescents. The application of theoretical frameworks from the social sciences will be evaluated by drawing on research conducted across a variety of social computing environments (e.g. entertainment, commerce, education and health) and with a variety of users (e.g. adolescents, learners, employees, the elderly, and people with illnesses).

Human beings are social beings who learn, play and work in social contexts; as a result people are extremely sensitive to the behaviour of those around them, and their behaviour is ultimately shaped by their social context. For example, during a learning context a tutor will adapt their teaching style dependent on the students' verbal and non-verbal cues and in an urban context a market seller will adapt prices depending on demand and customer behaviour. People not only adapt their own behaviour but in groups they conform to other's social behaviour, e.g. people will be drawn to a crowd gathering around a street artist or people will look up to a high building if some of those around them are doing so. In the discipline of Psychology this process is known as social influence and it is a two-way process, with an individual able to influence those around them and those around them are able to influence the behaviour of the individual (Baron, Branscombe and Byrne, 2009). In summary, social information provides a basis for making perceptions or attributions about other people and helps us to decide how to think, feel and behave. An understanding of social influence can be used at many levels, for example for crowd control, to direct a learning experience or to influence shopping habits. In the same way that face-to-face interaction is predictable, in many ways online social behaviour is also predictable. In online systems social information can be provided directly; for example, the number of users who have rated a product / service as helpful or products recommended based on people with a similar purchasing

history. Alternatively, social information may be available indirectly, for example the influence of other's opinions through online group discussion. In both direct and indirect ways, social information that is produced by a group changes individuals' perceptions and behaviour and ultimately the functioning of the group. Jarron, Favier and Li (2006) recognise the significance of social influence when they discuss the sources of influence for users of social computing in a commerce context. For example, they discuss the increasing importance that people attach to cues from one another, rather than from institutional sources like corporations, media outlets, religions and political parties. They conclude with advice for companies wanting to thrive using social computing, to weave online communities into their services and products and to use employees and partnerships as significant marketers.

Social computing applications support one-to-one, one-to-many and many-to-many interactions and therefore explanations need to cover individual, group and community processes. It is argued here that social science approaches have a great deal to offer in understanding interactions at each of these levels. At the individual level, social science can explain the impact of personality and individual differences on the use of social computing and the impacts of social computing on self-perception and emotion. At the group level, social science can help to understand group decision making and group cohesion. Increasingly, social computing supports the interactions that are carried out by very large groups of people, or communities (e.g. online auctions and Massive Multiuser Online Role Play Games - MMORPGs). In these contexts, social information processing and social network analysis approaches can be used to track and predict interactions and behaviour (often for commercial use such as market research). Although there are a number of approaches focusing on each level, there is less research exploring how social computing is affecting people at all psychological levels together.

A wide-ranging variety of theories from the disciplines of computing and information systems have been used to explain the impacts of the internet. Many of the early computing approaches were developed to address a specific problem or area of computing use. For example, the 'technology acceptance model' (Chau, 1996) explains the take-up and initial use of systems and the 'task-technology fit theory' (Goodhue, 1998) proposes that if system capabilities match the tasks that users perform, then impacts will be positive and performance enhanced. However, despite the initial usefulness in predicting usability, take-up and performance, many of these approaches were ill-suited to explaining the increasingly interpersonal and intrapersonal nature of online interaction. Therefore, over the last 10 to 15 years, approaches have increasingly drawn on social science concepts which integrate the social and technical. These integrated approaches to understand social computing will now be reviewed in section 1.2, followed by a review of approaches from the social sciences in section 2 which will highlight those theoretical frameworks that can potentially further our understanding of behaviour at all levels (individual, group and community) in social computing.

1.2 Early Approaches to Explain the Impacts of Computing on Behaviour

During the mid-1990s, designers and practitioners began to recognise that social science theories and methods could contribute to the design and evaluation of computer systems. At the same time, social scientists began to focus on the ways that social conventions and social contexts are mediated through the use of software and technology. This resulted in research occurring within three different areas where people interacted with technology. These areas reflect the levels refereed to earlier (individual, group and community) and although some work crosses areas, there was no attempt to explain the impacts of ICT on all levels

of human behaviour. The key research directions within each area will be briefly reviewed before looking in more depth at social science theories and methods and their recent application to social computing.

At the individual level, the computer-user relationship began to be evaluated and the field of HCI (Human Computer Interaction) came into existence. Information processing theory was applied to understand the cognitive demands of computer systems on individuals. However, as highlighted in a review by Wei and Salvendy (2004), although this was useful in predicting individual task performance, it is less able to explain the cognitive demands when using multiple, and often synchronous, communications media within social computing.

At the group level, the relationships between group members when technology such as groupware is used to mediate tasks were evaluated and the discipline of CSCW (Computer Support for Cooperative Working) was born. With the growth of computer-mediated communication (CMC) during the 1980s and 1990s a number of researchers used media theories to explain online group behaviour. The concept of Social Presence (Short, Williams and Rice, 1976) conceptualises CMC as a poor imitation of offline communication. This theory proposes that the low social presence of CMC is conducive to reduced social influence, when compared to other higher social presence media such as face-to-face communication. Media Richness theory (Daft and Lengel, 1984), the Social Information Processing model (Walther, Anderson and Park, 1994) and the Reduced Social Cues (RSC) model (Sproull and Kiesler, 1991) concluded with similar verdicts. A common thread that weaves through these different approaches is that with physical cues gone, the fear of being judged or punished disappears. For instance, using the RSC model, Kiesler et al. (1984) found that when social cues are absent people are more self-orientated and less concerned with the feelings and evaluations of other group members;

in turn their behaviour is more uninhibited. In summary, these 'media' explanations propose that the medium of CMC provides conditions for the likely breakdown and even absence of social norms, however frequently these approaches did not consider the vast research from social psychology investigating social norms.

At a systems level, the impact of new systems on employees and organisations was evaluated and as larger networks of people began to interact, some of the early online communities were investigated using systems theories to help explain and predict online behaviour. While systems approaches, such as General Systems Theory (e.g. Garrity, 2001), consider interactions with wider networks and the changes in organisations and society, they fail to consider changes to individual psychological processes which can be significant. For example, socio-technical systems theory (STS) does not address the impact of the system on changes to a users' sense of identity or self-concept, which is an important factor in much of the social networking research with adolescents (e.g. Joinson, 2003).

THEORIES FROM THE SOCIAL SCIENCES

Since the early work covered above, use of social computing applications has grown exponentially and increasingly these affect our thoughts, emotions and communication. As a result, designers and implementers need to consider concepts and methods from a variety of social science theories to be able to understand and predict the impacts of social computing on behaviour. Theories covered here will include: (i) those that focus on the self (e.g. personality) and experience (e.g. emotion); (ii) those that focus on group level impacts (e.g. social identity theory), and (iii) those that focus on social systems such as organisations (e.g. actor-network theory) and communities (e.g. social capital).

2.1 Individual Level

Experimental psychologists and professional psychologists have contributed much to the development of methods and procedures to investigate and understand the functioning of the human brain. Psychological approaches which can be applied to social computing include those which explore cognitive function and decision making within online auctions to those trying to understand the relationship between clinical disorders and the use of social networking sites.

2.1.1 Self-Efficacy Theory

This theory originated within cognitive psychology and is used to understand the relationship between thoughts and actions. Bandura (2004) defined perceived self-efficacy as people's beliefs about their capabilities to influence events that affect their lives. Self-efficacy beliefs determine how people feel, think, motivate themselves and behave. Social computing allows enhanced control over one's life, mainly relating to the affordances of online interaction, such as asynchronicity and reduced social context cues. Therefore this theoretical approach could be used to help understand and explain online communication behaviour, portrayal of identity, and heightened self-confidence. People's perception of their ability to plan and take action to reach a particular goal has been applied to the computing context by Marakas et al. (1998) who developed a scale which measures 'computer self-efficacy'; which they define as an individuals' judgment of their capabilities to use computers in diverse situations. Later, Eastin and LaRose (2000) developed a scale to measure 'internet self-efficacy', which they define as the belief in one's capabilities to organise and execute courses of Internet actions required to produce given attainments. Both scales have since been used to explore attitudes and behaviour within specific computing-based tasks (e.g. Ko and Myers, 2009), but there is no research which applies the concept to interaction in social computing contexts. The suggestion from Eastin and LaRose that future research could investigate the interplay among internet self-efficacy, stress and on-line support is currently being investigated by Frackiewicz, Taylor and House (2008).

2.1.2 Personality Theory and Abnormal Psychology

Personality theories from Psychology can be used to examine individual differences in the use of social computing applications, for example to investigate the high numbers of people with certain traits in online communities. In particular, the use of social networking sites (SNS) by adolescents have attracted a lot of interest recently and they have been accused of attracting adolescents with communication difficulties (Kim et al., 2009) or social anxiety (Caplan, 2007). Levels of shyness have also been investigated, for example Huang and Leung (2009) related Instant Messaging addiction among teenagers to higher levels of shyness. However, it is unclear whether the individuals in these studies were shy or socially anxious prior to using SNS. In online gaming environments, personality factors (e.g. low self-esteem) have been correlated with high usage (Chou and Tsai, 2007). However, as the research conducted so far has not been longitudinal it is unclear whether extended use of SNS exacerbates psychosocial problems or attracts users who may develop these problems anyway. Also, in contrast to this research on the negative impacts, other researchers have suggested that SNS could improve offline skills by allowing users to experiment and confront social anxieties in a safe environment (e.g. see Kim et al., 2009).

Recently, researchers have proposed that using social computing applications could be leading to mental health problems. Higher incidences of depression have been associated with increasing use of social computing by clinical psychologists. For example, Morrison and More (2010) related

internet dependency with depression using an online survey of 1,319 individuals aged from 16 to 51. They found a small group who were both depressed and internet-addicted; in this group, the average depression score was more than five times higher than that of non-addicted users. To some extent, the impacts of use of computer games and SNS on personality and behaviour have been hyped by the media. There is currently very little empirical research showing significant effects on moral development, aggressive behaviour, communication skills and identity formation. For example, warnings of future psychiatric problems were issued by Tyagi (2008) who proposes that those born since the 1990s "are likely to find the real world boring and will look to more extreme types of behaviour to get a kick out of life". He also warned that current training was not fully preparing psychiatrists to help young people with internet-related problems. However, this was not based on published work. Again it is not clear whether using the internet causes mental health problems, or whether people with mental health problems are drawn to the internet and further research and evidence are needed.

It has been proposed that using social computing applications could also be changing the biological make-up of the brain. This has been shown across the age span but is potentially most worrying in the case of children's brains, which are not fully formed and therefore the impacts could be more significant. However, although evidence from psychologists and others working with children is gathering pace, much of this is anecdotal. For example, Greenfield (2009) one of the top neuroscientists in the UK, warns that adolescent brains are becoming 'infantalised'. She provides examples of adolescents with short attention spans, enhanced need for self-gratification, being attracted by interesting noises and bright lights and being self-centered. Greenfield believes repeated exposure could 'rewire' the brain. Similarly, educational psychologist Healy (1999) believes children should not use computer games until they are at least seven, as most games only trigger the 'flight or fight' region of the brain, rather than the more important areas such as reasoning. Palmer (2006) states in her book 'Toxic Childhood', "we are seeing children's brain development damaged because they don't engage in the activity they have engaged in for millennia...I'm not against technology and computers, but before they start social networking, they need to learn to make real relationships with people". In the area of developmental disorders, it is not clear whether the reported increase in cases of autism is due more to an increased awareness and diagnosis of autism, or whether it can be linked to children spending increasing, and in some cases excessive, time interacting online. At the other end of the age-range, a team of psychiatrists and neuroscientists at UCLA, have examined brain scans of older adults aged between 55 and 78 and compared those who rarely used the internet, with daily users. Small at al. (2009) found that activity in parts of the brain used in memory and decision-making was different. However, perhaps more importantly, after the inexperienced group was asked to use the internet daily it only took a few days for the brains of inexperienced users to change to become similar to those of the experienced users.

2.1.3 Theories of Emotion

Emotion is a fundamental human experience affecting many tasks that we undertake each day, for example, learning, communicating and decision-making. Much of the research has focused on methods for measuring emotion and this is often intimately tied up with the theoretical stance of different groups of emotion researchers. This is mainly because there are many difficulties associated with measuring affect and it is easy to make misunderstandings when interpreting similar emotions. Much of the early work regarding the origin and nature of emotions was developed by James (an American psychologist and philosopher)

and Lange (a Danish physician and psychologist), who worked independently to produce the James-Lange theory. This theory proposed that the autonomic nervous system creates physiological effects (e.g. an increase in heart rate, sweating, muscular tension and a dry mouth) as a response to external experiences. According to this theory, emotions are feelings which arise as a result of the physiological changes, rather than being their cause. Since this work, many psychologists have developed these concepts, but often from different traditions and employing different methods of measurement resulting in different foci. For example, cognitive psychologists have focused on: the mechanisms of appraisal; the relationship of emotion and stress to cognition, and the link between emotion and decision-making. In contrast, social psychologists use different methods to investigate different aspects of emotion relating to interaction, e.g. the development of a social theory of emotion to explain prejudice and the investigation of the use and display of emotions in relation to facial expressions. Advanced methods (e.g. fMRI) are now being used to relate internal changes to overt behaviour to develop a neuroscience approach to emotion.

The research area in which emotion and computing are studied together is known as affective computing. This term was introduced by Picard (1997) and defined as, "computing that relates to, arises from, or deliberately influences emotion or other affective phenomena". Picard's research and the research of those she has stimulated has effectively changed our understanding and approach to the relationship between emotion and technology ever since. Affective computing research is naturally interdisciplinary, combining engineering and computer science with a number of areas in social science, including psychology, cognitive science, neuroscience, sociology and psychophysiology. Since 1997, there has been an explosion of interest in the emotional side of computers and their users, with the aim of much of the research to improve the human affective experience with technology.

This work has developed sensors and systems that are now able to recognise, interpret, model and display human emotions. For example, applications that can detect and interpret emotions such as stress and frustration in users have been integrated into the communication system used by call-centre workers (Millard and Hole, 2008).

Applications in social computing that have drawn on advances in affective computing are often based in the area of online entertainment. For example, game player interaction is supported using systems that detect and interpret the emotional state of a user and this can then be used to adapt avatar behaviour, giving appropriate responses for the emotions detected (Heise, 2004). Such systems rely heavily on the psychological research on emotion, speech, non verbal cues and linguistic analyses. Other research relating positive intra-personal changes to observed behaviour, aims to understand the positive affect relating to video game-playing and online gambling. Users of these social computing applications are frequently observed to lose their sense of time and connection with their real lives; similar to a state known as 'flow' which has been linked to many offline entertainment activities. Csikszentmihalyi (1997) refers to flow as an optimal experience arising from psychological immersion in an activity and results in an energised focus, total involvement, and overall change to positive emotions. Faiola and Smyslova (2009) explored the link between flow and telepresence within the online virtual world Second Life. They found that flow was experienced based on four controlling factors which were related to being present in a virtual world and that there was a significant correlation between flow and telepresence.

2.2 Group Level

Social psychologists and group dynamics researchers have well-developed methods and a systematic approach to theory-building regarding the impact of the group on individuals and the interactions within and between groups. Although much of the work developed from face-to-face groups can successfully be applied to social computing, due to the differences in contextual factors some theorists have argued that new methods and theories are required (e.g. Lyttinen et al., 2004). For example, online groups tend to be larger with sporadic membership and can span large geographical distances and their members may never meet. This section will highlight the key similarities and differences when group processes have been examined and compared in both online and offline contexts.

2.2.1 Group Theories

Strauss (1997) explored group process and group outcomes in both computer-mediated and face-to-face groups and showed that in general traditional theories could be applied to online groups and that the differences were in directions predicted by the theory as a result of the different contexts of online groups. For example, minority / majority influence was found to exist, but the specific context of computer-mediated communication (CMC) determined whether minority opinions were expressed, e.g. they were expressed most under anonymous CMC, then identifiable CMC, then face-to-face. Social loafing was found to be virtually eliminated using online groups, however when contributions became anonymous and non-permanent, once again loafing was evidenced. This finding would be predicted based on social loafing theory where presumably because of the identifiability of comments which reduce face-to-face social loafing. Also, regarding another consistent group effect 'groupthink' again in line with traditional groupthink theory, more alternative points are aired online and therefore there is less possibility of groupthink. Regarding social influence processes research has shown there to be more divergence in electronic groups and group leaders need to exert more effort trying to reconcile contradictory opinions, i.e. online discussion reduces conformity. Group discussions using a risky-shift type task showed that online groups shifted even more towards extreme positions than face-to-face groups, (i.e. group polarisation) due to the broader distribution of views and more extreme attitudes.

Tuckman (1965) was influential in producing his sequential model of group formation and evolution where the following stages were proposed: forming, storming, norming, performing and adjourning. There have been some attempts to apply this model to online groups (e.g. Suler, 1999) and although there are similarities, the model needs adapting to take account of the more dynamic, anonymous and larger size of online groups.

De-individuation theory has been applied to explain both cooperation and conflict in online groups. In face-to-face groups, de-individuation arises under certain conditions such as anonymity or where group salience is high and results in a loss of public self-awareness that leads to a loss of internal standards, less concern about the judgement of others and often results in aggressive behaviour. De-individuation theorists such as Spears, Lea and Lee (1990) have applied this to online behaviour; they suggest that a reduction of accountability cues in online interaction leads to decreased self-regulation and standards and therefore to anti-social behaviour. De-individuation could be used to explain anti-normative behaviour (such as flaming) as well as excessively pro-social behaviour (such as group cohesion and self disclosure) in online groups, depending on which norms were salient at the time.

The problem with many group theories is that they have been developed to explain specific group processes (e.g. cohesion) and frequently do not take account of the wider context in which groups perform (e.g. the community or society norms) and are not holistic in nature. To address this, Social Identity Theory was developed to explain groups at various levels.

2.2.2 Social Identity Theory (SIT)

SIT was developed by the social psychologist Tajfel (1974) to understand the psychological basis of intergroup discrimination and it has been used since then to explain a variety of group processes (such as intra-group cohesion) and processes within society (e.g. inter-racial conflict and prejudice). SIT emphasises the cognitive and motivational processes that underlie group behaviour and rests on the assumption that people are driven by a need to understand themselves and the world around them and do this through processes of social categorisation and social comparison. Tajfel (1974) suggested groups provide us with a sense of social identity and that a person has not one personal self, but several selves which correspond to membership of social categories (e.g. gender and age), and which influence an individual's self-concept.

Taylor and MacDonald (2000) proposed that SIT can be used to explain online behaviour at all levels: intrapersonal perceptions, interpersonal communication, group processes and the development of online community. Regarding group processes, Postmes et al. (2002) explain changes in online decision-making behaviour in terms of an interaction between group immersion and level of identifiability and state that, "there is growing evidence that anonymous CMC leads to increased social influence in line within the group compared to face-to-face interaction" (p.15). In line with SIT, while some behavioural effects were enhanced by anonymity, the outcomes of the interaction depended on the norms that a group subscribes to. Moreover, Lea and Spears (1992) argue that the lack of social rules could actually mean that this might force people to make reference to general norms to regulate their behaviour. Taylor and MacDonald (2002) proposed that social identity theory could explain not only online group processes, but also online intrapersonal experiences such as changes to self-awareness. In their study, they collected measures of self-disclosure and self-awareness in low and high social identity situations within online discussion contexts. This was investigated further by Joinson (2003) who conducted a series of studies to experimentally test: whether self-disclosure was higher in online conditions (compared to face-to-face); whether visual anonymity increased self-disclosure within online interaction; and whether private and public self-awareness interacted to affect self-disclosure during CMC. Joinson concluded that self-disclosure is caused by the contexts of online communication leading to reduced public self-awareness and increased private self-awareness. These findings were predicted by and can be explained by SIT. The findings have implications for online communities, in that high levels of self-disclosure are likely to lead to higher levels of affiliation in online communities and therefore potentially of most use to support groups. The relationship between social identity and social support has recently been investigated in a study exploring computing gaming communities as support networks, Taylor and Taylor (2009) found that enhanced group identity was related to motivation to remain within a gaming community.

Researchers have also used SIT to explore the interaction and influence of the group on individual identities. For example, Pluempavarn and Panteli (2008) set out to examine how the social identity of bloggers influences and are influenced by the blogging community. Their findings showed that bloggers actively selected to participate in those communities that matched their interests, which supports traditional social identity theory (Tajfel, 1974). To explore the impact that blogging has on the identity of the group and the group members, Pluempavarn and Panteli use the three main features of SIT (categorisation, identification and comparison) to analyse the blogs. They note the way that bloggers observe a community before joining and relate this to categorisation of the community into unique characteristics. They concluded that social identities were actually created in blogging communities and that these

have a reciprocal effect on community members as well as on the community in general.

2.3 Social Systems and Networks

Researchers from sociology and biology have significant expertise in theory and methods to explore cultural norms, neurobiological factors and evolutionary issues and can potentially be very influential in helping to understand and model online community behaviour, with respect to behaviour such as motivation and cooperation.

2.3.1 Sociology and Network Theories

A number of approaches developed from the social sciences focus on the complex interaction of social and technical systems. The sociologist Giddens (1984) has written widely on social change and his theory of structuration could usefully be applied to explain the changes that occur to individuals, groups and society through use of social computing applications. Giddens defines structuration as, "the production and reproduction of the social systems through members' use of rules and resources in interaction" (p.25). Based upon Giddens' theory, DeSanctis and Poole (1990) developed their 'Adaptive Structuration Theory' to study the interaction of groups and organisations with information and communications technology (ICT). DeSanctis and Poole emphasise the importance of the social aspects of ICT use, in contrast to other approaches adopting a techno centric view of ICT. Central to their theory is the perceptions formed by groups and organisations about the role and utility of ICT to carry out their activities and how these perceptions influence the way technology is then used and hence mediate its impact on group outcomes. This offers a useful approach to explain the impacts on individuals, groups *and* organisations, but to date there has been little application of this theory to social computing. One exception to this is a review by Merchant (2006) who draws on the work of Giddens to explore the relationship between identity and social network theory. Although he discusses the way that identities are experimented with across both online and offline social networks, as yet he has conducted no empirical research to test this. So far it has been applied almost entirely to e-commerce (Hinds and Bailey, 2003) and teams within organisations (Griffith et al., 2003).

A sociological theory which might offer an understanding of the impact of social computing on society is Actor-network theory. This was developed by a number of theorists (most significantly Latour, 1991) and considers networks as comprising inseparable social and technical parts (i.e. all elements involved in an interaction, including people, their appearance, objects and the organisation) which are referred to collectively as actors. Each actor is equally important to the social network, and as long as an actor-network runs smoothly there will be societal order, but social order breaks down when actors are removed. It has been used to explain the impacts of the telephone and motor car (Walsham, 1997) and could now be used to explore social computing, where the removal of the face-to-face component of communication is having impacts upon society, e.g. in terms of community involvement and breakdown. Other network theories focus on the strength of ties or connectedness between nodes in a network and have also been used to explain the breakdown of community (e.g. Pew, 2001).

2.3.2 Theories of Prosocial Behaviour, Cooperation and Altruism

There is a growing interest in understanding the factors that affect the levels of sharing or cooperative behavior in virtual communities. Theories of prosocial behaviour from social psychology (e.g. Baron, Branscombe and Byrne, 2009) identify three components that need to be considered: the individual who helps, the person who receives help, and the situation in which help occurs. Prosocial theories emphasise reciprocal helping as a

motivating factor and socio-biologists propose that people are social animals and social bonding is necessary to govern our behaviour. Recent approaches view the three-component model as too simplistic though, and increasingly researchers are investigating the interactions between factors; for example, Levine and Crowther (2008) explored social category and group size and found that depending on how they interacted they could encourage or inhibit prosocial behaviour.

Altruism often involves personal cost and is said by some theorists to be key to sustaining cooperation in genetically unrelated groups (Fehr, 2003). Psychological experiments of altruism frequently involve a scenario called the Prisoners Dilemma Game which is a mixed-motive situation where one person must be altruistic for the good of the team. Such experiments have shown players to exhibit altruistic behaviour in set-ups involving unacquainted players interacting anonymously and repeatedly. As such, the theory of altruism may have particular relevance to explore human behaviour in online communities which have similar environments, albeit on a larger scale.

Despite the differences between online and offline communities (e.g. anonymity) many researchers are drawing on theories of prosocial behaviour and altruism. It seems that despite not meeting each other and sometimes not knowing each others' name or identity there are many examples of community life. In MMORPGs teams of players work together to perform adventurous tasks and in many cases success depends on players helping each other, often with a lack of personal gain. Kelly (2006) compared offline and online altruism in game-playing and found that there was significantly more altruistic behaviour within online settings. Also, in a gaming study, Wang and Wang (2008) examined the reasons players help other game players using an online empirical survey. They found that high levels of altruistic traits and reciprocity influence prosocial behaviour simultaneously.

Lin (2007) examined the influence and interaction between three sets of factors: individual factors, organisational factors and technology factors on the extent that people shared knowledge. He found that two individual factors (enjoyment in helping others and knowledge self-efficacy) and one of the organisational factors (support from management) had a significantly influence upon knowledge-sharing. Hsu, Ju, Yen and Chang (2007) proposed a social cognitive theory-based model to explore knowledge-sharing behaviour within the virtual communities of professional societies. This model included knowledge-sharing self-efficacy and outcome expectations for personal influences, and multi-dimensional trusts for environmental influences. The proposed model was then evaluated using structural equation modeling and confirmatory factor analysis which found that the empirical data supported the proposed model.

Further research is needed, especially to investigate theories of altruism based on affect, these theories propose that people are altruistic as it serves to increase positive good feeling or to decrease negative affect, such as guilt. Such research might help to explain motivation for online altruism by relating it to the role of emotion highlighted in section 2.1.

2.3.3 Evolutionary Anthropology

Dunbar (2010) proposes that our brains cannot cope with more than around 150 relationships in offline or online contexts. This relates to his 1990s work studying social groups from various societies, both ancient (e.g. Neolithic villages) and modern (corporate offices). His work led to the notion of "Dunbar's number", which is the size of the "social circle" - identified as a circle of friends in which we know exactly how each friend relates to every other friend. He proposed that the human neo-cortex limits us to 'social circles' of approximately 150 friends. Despite having numerous FaceBook friends, users maintain

a similar size of 'social circle' as that observed in the real world, of around 150. Also, Dunbar identified some interesting gender differences in that females were happy to maintain their social circle by communicating with each other, while males needed physical interaction to maintain their social circle. In a similar way, Sigman (2009) proposed that social networking leads to loneliness which leads to biological harm, and explains this from an evolutionary perspective by highlighting the positive benefits of people being together. Although these approaches are certainly of interest, further empirical study is required and much of the work in this area has attracted criticism for the lack of evidence.

2.3.4 Social Capital

Following on from the concept of support discussed above, a theory ideally suited to understand and explain the social benefits and emotional support within social computing is the theory of Social Capital. Initially developed in the fields of sociology and political science, it was defined by Woolcock (1998) as the "norms and networks facilitating collective actions for mutual benefits" (p.155). The concept of social capital is based on the premise that being part a community brings with it benefits based on reciprocation and trust. Researchers differ in their focus regarding these benefits, with some focusing on the individual benefits and others on the benefits to the wider community. Coleman (1988) believes that social capital exists between individuals and that it can be accumulated and studied at the individual level. White (2002) states that this rests on the premise that, "my connections can help me" (p.260). In contrast, Putnam (1995) focuses on the benefit to the community and defined Social Capital as, "the features of social life – networks, norms and trust – that enable participants to act together more effectively to pursue shared objectives" (p.4). Despite the differences, all researchers consider social capital to be the glue that holds communities and social networks together. Researchers have explored the social, psychological and emotional benefits (Lin, 2001) as well as the economic benefits (Putnam, 1995). This theory has been applied predominantly within the health sector, for example, Halpern (2008) has related social capital to both individual well-being (e.g. the finding that those with lives rich in social capital cope better with traumas and fight illness more effectively) and group well-being (e.g. the link between community involvement in social networks and improvements in community health).

It is clear that a culture of collaboration can help both sustain and strengthen online communities, as well as offline ones. Thousands of online communities exist, all differing in their longevity, composition, goals, and whether they exist solely online or are blended with offline community participation. Online communities have the added benefit of being able to support their members regardless of time zone, distance or cultural differences. They can support a similar range of activities as offline communities (e.g. debate of wider issues, empathy and comfort, shared personal reflection and advice), but can do so more quickly and to a wider or larger membership. To date, there has been little research relating social computing and social capital, despite the clear link of both to networks. Despite discussion of the link by Preece (2002), researchers have been slow to conduct empirical studies. Preece focuses on how ICT can be designed and used most effectively to support communities and to foster the development of social capital. However, the solution is not in software alone, a key factor to a successful community is the community leader who promotes cooperation and trust which helps to foster social capital. The concept of trust is difficult to both define and measure. Much of the literature focuses on the use of historical information that a user will consider to assess whether a person or situation is trustworthy, e.g. good past interactions often lead to an expectation of a trustworthy interactions in the future. Many social computing applications

draw on this concept to produce systems that help to identify who is present and what their past behaviour is to enable a user to make a judgement of trust. For example: a decision to buy a product in a commercial context; to trust another game-player in a MMORPG context, or to disclose a secret in a support group. This capability, which Erickson et al (2002) termed 'social translucence', in social computing systems can help community members to gauge more easily who is present, how long for, what they are doing, what are the roles/status of members and how members value each others' comments. Earlier in this chapter, the concepts of sharing and cooperative behaviour were discussed, whereby various approaches had attempted to explore factors (individual and environmental) which contributed to such behaviour. Social capital theory may offer a more useful approach than just identifying factors as it provides an holistic theoretical framework. This has been investigated by Ju, Chen and Ju (2006) who used social capital to understand information-sharing among internet users and Wasko and Faraj (2005) examined the extent that people contribute and share knowledge in online communities.

Social capital has been used to explain online behaviour in various contexts, with much being conducted in learning and health communities where positive outcomes are at the core of their existence. Within online learning communities, Hiltz and Turoff (2002) draw on nearly 30 years of research to make three recommendations to sustain and build social capital in asynchronous learning networks. These recommendations are that: (i) interaction between tutor and student should be promoted using 'swift trust' (this involves putting aside any feelings of uncertainty and dis-trust and agreeing to cooperate, in order that long-term trust can develop); (ii) use collaborative activities, rather than those perceived as competitive within or between groups, and (iii) generate active participation (e.g. by relating activities to other classroom activities or assessment). Bruckman (2002) also relates social capital to learning in her discussion of the benefits of cross-generational participation in online discussions. She highlights the benefits of online discussion groups made up of students and their peers as well as seniors and other adults as more engaging, productive and providing emotional support as well as fostering creativity. These findings more recently supported by Yuan, Gay and Hembrooke (2006) who also focus on the wider benefits of distributed learning communities. Health-related online communities present one of the most successful in terms of social capital generated, due to their intensely personal nature and positive outcomes. Since the seminal book by Rice and Katz (2001) on the experience and expectations of those involved with communities in the health sector, there have been numerous evaluations of the role of online communication, health websites and social networking in support those with illnesses. However, despite many interesting accounts employing qualitative methods, there is less quantitative data measuring social capital and the impacts on health.

FUTURE RESEARCH DIRECTIONS AND CONCLUSION

In summary, this chapter has highlighted the usefulness of theories form the social sciences to explain the impacts of social computing on human behaviour at each of the three levels. It is proposed that social identity and social capital theories might offer the greatest potential, because they consider the social world in a holistic way and therefore they are able to explain human behaviour at all three levels. For example, social capital theory explains: individual effects (e.g. trust and perception of connectedness), group effects (e.g. group well-being) and community effects (e.g. social cohesion). Similarly, SIT explains: individual effects (e.g. self-awareness), group effects (e.g. group cohesion and conflict) and community ef-

fects (e.g. social norms). However, a number of challenges exist.

One challenge for researchers applying social capital theory is to develop a valid and reliable way to measure social capital; increasingly public services and private companies are required to account for the time and money spent on social computing projects. Despite the many benefits so far highlighted, frequently research programmes have been unable to quantify the improvement, for example in improved quality of life for individuals or a more successful community. Similarly, the costs of developing social computing applications for the purpose of enhancing social capital need to be identified, both in psychological and financial ways. Another challenge is to identify ways to develop trust in online communities, as this is essential for subsequent collaboration and sharing behaviour. One suggestion might be to employ techniques used to develop trust in face-to-face interactions; for example, the techniques employed by tutor-facilitators in learning groups or the methods used by community workers in disseminating public health campaigns. A final challenge is to draw on the experience of social scientists, with their deep understanding of social interaction, to help achieve the positive effects of online social capital. Building online social capital is unlikely to exactly mirror offline community involvement; potential ways forward will need to consider new styles of interaction that are emerging as the boundaries between offline and online communities continue to dissolve, with a future where people interact seamlessly across online and offline worlds. Ideally, enhanced social capital in online communities will cross-over to offline communities and vice versa.

A challenge for SIT researchers is that the very nature of identity is dynamic and therefore difficult to study at one point in time and without reference to contextual factors. There have been many discussions in the literature regarding the impacts of online interaction on identity. For example, one view is that social computing applications help people to create new identities, while another view is that social computing is helping us to see ourselves in new ways. It is becoming clear that for some sectors of the population online interaction is changing social norms and perceptions of identity itself, e.g. it is relatively 'normal' for game players to swap gender in online games (Denegri-Knott and Taylor, 2005). Future research needs to explore new identities that result from the complex interaction between humans via social computing. The world is undergoing change at an unprecedented rate and recently findings from biological and medical research have been useful in predicting attitudes and behaviour resulting from changed identities, in the same way that swarm intelligence is being used to predict responses to viral infections (Salazar-Banuelos, 2008).

In conclusion, the research that is developing around the study of social computing encompasses many theoretical frameworks and without interdisciplinary thinking and debate the answers to many fundamental questions about human behaviour will not be solved. This chapter has reviewed many theoretical approaches from the social sciences and shown how they can be used to explain human thought, emotion and behaviour in social computing contexts. Although many theories can be used to explain specific psychological processes, social identity theory and social capital theory are highlighted as offering the most potential to explain the multiple and dynamic processes in social computing. Research has been reviewed which applies these two theories within various social computing domains (e.g. learning, gaming and health) providing evidence that they can be used robustly across disciplines and contexts. There is no doubt that in order to understand such complex and changing systems further interdisciplinary work is essential.

REFERENCES

Bandura, A. (2004). Health promotion by social cognitive means. *Health Education & Behavior*, *31*(2), 143–164. doi:10.1177/1090198104263660

Baron, R., Branscombe, B., & Byrne, D. (2009). *Social psychology*. London: Allyn & Bacon.

Bruckman, A. (2002). The future of e-learning communities. *Communications of the ACM, 45*(4), 60–63. doi:10.1145/505248.505274

Caplan, S. E. (2007). Relations among loneliness, social anxiety, and problematic internet use. *Cyberpsychology & Behavior*, *10*(2), 234–242. doi:10.1089/cpb.2006.9963

Chau, P. K. Y. (1996). An empirical assessment of a modified technology acceptance model. *Journal of Management Information Systems*, *13*(2), 185–204.

Chou, C., & Tsai, M. J. (2007). Gender differences in Taiwan high school students' computer game playing. *Computers in Human Behavior*, *23*(1), 812–824. doi:10.1016/j.chb.2004.11.011

Coleman, J. S. (1988). Social capital in the creation of human capital. *American Journal of Sociology*, *94*, 95–120. doi:10.1086/228943

Csikszentmihalyi, M. (1997). *Flow: The psychology of optimal experience*. New York: Harper and Row.

Daft, R. L., & Lengel, R. H. (1984). Information richness: A new approach to managerial behaviour and organisation design. *Research in Organizational Behavior*, *6*, 191–233.

Denegri-Knott, J., & Taylor, J. (2005). The labelling game: A conceptual exploration of deviance on the internet. *Social Science Computer Review*, *23*(1), 93–107. doi:10.1177/0894439304271541

Dunbar, R. (2010). Facebook friends are not REAL friends. Retrieved January 21, 2010, from http://technology.timesonline.co.uk/tol/news/tech_and_web/the_web/article6999879.ece

Eastin, M., & LaRose, R. (2000). Internet self-efficacy and the psychology of the digital divide. *Journal of Computer-Mediated Communication* [Online], *6*(1). Retrieved January 21, 2010, from http://jcmc.indiana.edu/vol6/issue1/eastin.html

Erickson, T., Halverson, C., Kellogg, W. A., Laff, M., & Wolf, T. (2002). Social translucence: Designing social infrastructures that make collective activity visible. *Communications of the ACM*, *45*(4), 40–44. doi:10.1145/505248.505270

Faiola, A., & Smyslova, O. (2009). Flow experience in Second Life: The impact of telepresence on human-computer interaction. In Ozok, A. A., & Zaphiris, P. (Eds.), *Online communities and social computing* (pp. 574–583). Berlin: Springer-Verlag. doi:10.1007/978-3-642-02774-1_62

Frackiewicz, U., Taylor, J., & House, B. (2008). An investigation into the role of traditional and computer-based social networking on the psychological identity and well-being of older adults. Unpublished paper presented at the British HCI Conference, Liverpool, Ireland.

Garrity, E. J. (2001). Synthesizing user centered and designer centered IS development approaches using general systems theory. *Information Systems Frontiers*, *3*(1), 107–121. doi:10.1023/A:1011457822609

Giddens, A. (1984). *The Constitution of Society: outline of the theory of structuration*. Berkeley, CA: University of California Press.

Goodhue, D. (1998). Development and measurement validity of a task-technology fit instrument for user evaluations of information systems. *Decision Sciences*, *29*(1), 105–138. doi:10.1111/j.1540-5915.1998.tb01346.x

Greenfield, S. (2009). Social websites harm children's brains. Retrieved January 21, 2010, from http://www.dailymail.co.uk/news/article-1153583/Social-websites-harm-childrens-brains-Chilling-warning-parents-neuroscientist.html

Griffith, T. L., Sawyer, J. E., & Neale, M. A. (2003). Virtualness and knowledge in teams: Managing the love triangle of organizations, individuals, and information technology. *Management Information Systems Quarterly*, *27*(2), 265.

Healy, J. M. (1999). *Failure to connect: How computers affect our children's minds—and what we can do about it*. London: Simon & Schuster.

Heise, D. (2004). Enculturating agents with expressive role behavior. In Payr, S., & Trappl, R. (Eds.), *Agent culture: Human-agent interaction in a multicultural world* (pp. 127–142). London: Lawrence Erlbaum Associates.

Hiltz, S. R., & Turoff, M. (2002). What makes learning networks effective? *Communications of the ACM*, *45*(4), 56–59. doi:10.1145/505248.505273

Hinds, P. J., & Bailey, D. E. (2003). Out of sight, out of sync: Understanding conflict in distributed teams. *Organization Science*, *14*(6), 615. doi:10.1287/orsc.14.6.615.24872

Hsu, M. H., Ju, T. L., Yen, C. H., & Chang, C. M. (2007). Knowledge sharing behavior in virtual communities: The relationship between trust, self-efficacy, and outcome expectations. *International Journal of Human-Computer Studies*, *65*(2), 153–169. doi:10.1016/j.ijhcs.2006.09.003

Huang, H., & Leung, L. (2009). Instant messaging addiction among teenagers in China: Shyness, alienation, and academic performance decrements. *Cyberpsychology & Behavior*, *12*(6), 675–679. doi:10.1089/cpb.2009.0060

Jarron, C., Favier, J., & Li, C. (2006). *Social computing: How networks erode institutional power and what to do about it.* Cambridge, MA: Forrester Research Reports. Retrieved January 21, 2010, from http://www.forrester.com/Research/Document/Excerpt/0,7211,38772,00.html

Joinson, A. (2003). *Understanding the psychology of internet behaviour: Virtual worlds, real lives.* London: Palgrave Macmillan.

Ju, T. L., Chen, H., & Ju, P. H. (2005). Social capital and knowledge sharing in virtual communities. In Khosrow-Pour, M. (Ed.), *Emerging trends and challenges in information technology management* (pp. 409–411). London: Idea Group Publishing.

Kelly, R. (2006). *An investigation of attitudes to altruism amongst achievers, explorers, killers and socialisers: Can massively multiplayer games engineer altruism? Unpublished student project.* UK: Bournemouth University.

Kim, J., LaRose, R., & Peng, W. (2009). Loneliness as the cause and the effect of problematic internet use: The relationship between internet use and psychological well-being. *Cyberpsychology & Behavior, 12*(4), 451–455. doi:10.1089/cpb.2008.0327

Ko, A. J., & Myers, B. A. (2009). Attitudes and self-efficacy in young adults' computing autobiographies. Paper presented at *IEEE Symposium on Visual Languages and Human-Centric Computing,* Corvallis, OR, USA.

Latour, B. (1991). Technology is society made durable: A sociology of monsters. In Law, J. (Ed.), *Essays on Power, Technology and Domination* (pp. 103–131). London: Routledge.

Lea, M., & Spears, R. (1992). Paralanguage and social perception in computer-mediated communication. *Journal of Organizational Computing, 2,* 321–341. doi:10.1080/10919399209540190

Levine, M., & Crowther, S. (2008). The responsive bystander: How social group membership and group size can encourage as well as inhibit bystander intervention. *Journal of Personality and Social Psychology, 96*(6).

Lin, H.-F. (2007). Knowledge sharing and firm innovation capability: An empirical study. *International Journal of Manpower, 28*(3-4), 315–332. doi:10.1108/01437720710755272

Lin, N. (2001). Building a network theory of social capital. In Burt, R. (Ed.), *Social capital: Theory and research* (pp. 3–30). New York: Aldine de Gruyter.

Marakas, G. M., Yi, M. Y., & Johnson, R. D. (1998). The multilevel and multifaceted character of computer self-efficacy: Toward clarification of the construct and an integrative framework for research. *Information Systems Research, 9*(2), 126–163. doi:10.1287/isre.9.2.126

Merchant, G. (2006). Identity, social networks and online communication. *E-learning, 3*(2), 235–244. doi:10.2304/elea.2006.3.2.235

Millard, N., & Hole, L. (2008). In the Moodie: Using 'affective widgets' to help contact centre advisors fight stress. In C. Peter & R. Beale (Eds.), *Affect and emotion in human-computer interaction* (Lecture Notes in Computer Science, Vol. 4868, pp. 186-193). Berlin: Springer-Verlag.

Palmer, S. (2006). *Toxic childhood.* London: Orion Publishing Group.

Pew Internet and American Life Project. (2001). *Online communities: Networks that nurture long-distance relationships and local ties.* Retrieved January 21, 2010, from www.pewinternet.org

Picard, R. W. (1997). *Affective computing.* Cambridge, MA: MIT Press.

Pluempavarn, P., & Panteli, N. (2008). Building social identity through blogging. In N. Panteli & M. Chiasson (Eds), *Exploring virtuality within and beyond organisations: Docial, global and local dimensions*. London: Palgrave Macmillan. Poole, M. S., & DeSanctis, G. (1990). Understanding the use of group decision support systems: The theory of adaptive structuration. In J. Fulk & C. Steinfeld (Eds.), *Organizations and communication technology*. Newbury Park, CA: Sage.

Postmes, T., Spears, R., & Lea, M. (2002). Intergroup differentiation in computer-mediated communication: Effects of depersonalization. *Group Dynamics, 6,* 3–16. doi:10.1037/1089-2699.6.1.3

Preece, J. (2002). Supporting community and building social capital. *Communications of the ACM, 45*(4), 37–39. doi:10.1145/505248.505269

Putnam, R. D. (1995). Bowling alone: America's declining social capital. *Journal of Democracy, 6*(1), 65–78. doi:10.1353/jod.1995.0002

Rice, R. E., & Katz, J. E. (Eds.). (2001). *The internet and health communication: Experiences and expectations*. Thousand Oaks, CA: Sage Publications.

Salazar-Banuelos, A. (2008). Immune responses: A stochastic model. In Bentley, P. J., Lee, D., & Jung, S. (Eds.), *Artificial immune systems* (pp. 24–35). Berlin: Springer-Verlag. doi:10.1007/978-3-540-85072-4_3

Short, J., Williams, E., & Christie, B. (1976). *The social psychology of telecommunication*. London: Wiley.

Sigman, A. (2009). Well connected? The biological implications of social networking. *Biologist (Columbus, Ohio), 56*(1), 14–20.

Small, G. W., Moody, T. D., Siddarth, P., & Bookheimer, S. Y. (2009). Your brain on Google: Patterns of cerebral activation during internet searching. *The American Journal of Geriatric Psychiatry, 17*(2), 116–126. doi:10.1097/JGP.0b013e3181953a02

Sproull, L., & Kiesler, S. (1991). *Connections: New ways of working in the networked organization*. London: MIT Press.

Strauss, S. G. (1997). Technology, group process and group outcomes: Testing the connections in computer-mediated and face-to-face groups. *HCI, 12,* 227–266. doi:10.1207/s15327051hci1203_1

Suler, J. (1999). *The psychology of cyberspace* [Online book]. Retrieved January 21, 2010, from http://www.rider.edu/users/suler/psycyber/psycyber.html

Tajfel, H. (1974). Social identity and intergroup behaviour. *Social Sciences Information. Information Sur les Sciences Sociales, 13,* 65–93. doi:10.1177/053901847401300204

Taylor, J., & MacDonald, J. (2000). Using SIDE to investigate group interaction in a realistic computer-mediated context. In Postmes, T., Spears, R., Lea, M., & Reicher, S. (Eds.), *SIDE issues centre stage: Recent developments in studies of de-individuation in groups* (pp. 17–30). Amsterdam: Elsevier.

Taylor, J., & MacDonald, J. (2002). The effects of asynchronous computer-mediated group interaction on group processes. *Social Science Computer Review, 20*(3), 260–274.

Taylor, J., & Taylor, J. (2009). A content analysis of interviews with players of Massively Multiplayer Online Role-Play Games (MMORPGs). In Ozok, A. A., & Zaphiris, P. (Eds.), *Online communities and social computing* (pp. 613–621). Berlin: Springer-Verlag. doi:10.1007/978-3-642-02774-1_66

Tuckman, B. W. (1965). Developmental sequence in small groups. *Psychological Bulletin*, *63*(6), 384–399. doi:10.1037/h0022100

Walsham, G. (1997). Actor-network theory and IS research: Current status and future prospects. In Lee, A. S., Liebenau, J., & DeGross, J. I. (Eds.), *Information systems and qualitative research* (pp. 466–480). London: Chapman and Hall.

Walther, J. B., Anderson, J. F., & Park, D. W. (1994). Interpersonal effects in computer-mediated interaction: A meta-analysis of social and anti-social communication. *Communication Research*, *21*, 460–487. doi:10.1177/009365094021004002

Wang, C. C., & Wang, C. H. (2008). Helping others in online games: Prosocial behavior in cyberspace. *Cyberpsychology & Behavior*, *11*(3), 344–346. doi:10.1089/cpb.2007.0045

Wasko, M. M., & Faraj, S. (2005). Why should I share? Examining social capital and knowledge contribution in electronic networks of practice. *Management Information Systems Quarterly*, *29*(1), 35–58.

Wei, J., & Salvendy, G. (2004). The cognitive task analysis methods for job and task design: Review and reappraisal. *Behaviour & Information Technology*, *23*(4), 273–299. doi:10.1080/01449290410001673036

Woolcock, M. (1998). Social capital and economic development: Towards a theoretical synthesis and policy framework. *Theory and Society*, *27*, 151–208. doi:10.1023/A:1006884930135

Yuan, Y. C., Gay, G., & Hembrooke, H. (2006). Focused activities and the development of social capital in a distributed learning community. *The Information Society*, *22*(1), 25–39. doi:10.1080/01972240500388347

Chapter 4
Cultural and International Aspects of Social Media

Thomas Mandl
University of Hildesheim, Germany

ABSTRACT

Social software provides powerful tools for people to communicate and interact. Social software networks are popular around the world but there are many differences between tools, functions and their use. The international application of these global tools even bears the risk of misunderstandings between individuals. This article discusses differences between social software from various countries concerning design, functions, use, opinion expression and the perception of social capital. First, a theoretical culture model is presented to provide one potential framework for the analysis. Subsequently, the relation between culture and information technology is explored. In particular, user interfaces need to be adapted to national preferences and cognitive styles. The influence of culture on social networks is then discussed for several aspects of social media.

INTRODUCTION

Recently, social software has received great attention. From 2008 to 2009, the time spent with such systems has increased by 82% (Nielsen, 2010). Many social networks are successfully used by large scale international communities. Even business portals are now using the appeal and the simplicity of social software for knowledge management or they extract relevant business information by text mining (Sohns & Breitner, 2009). Social software tools with their ease for publishing on the web and the creation of virtual networks seem to be of universal appeal and may be used on a global level. Social software appeal to users from many cultures and some might even think that the Internet leads to one unified world culture. However, humans are often unaware of cultural habits and values which have a strong impact on the individual behavior. We see culture as observed human behavior without expressing

DOI: 10.4018/978-1-61692-904-6.ch004

any preference for a particular culture. A definition will be given in the following chapter.

Culture has a great impact on the development and use of IT. Virtual chats are a good example for cultural habits and values in a new environment. In real face-to-face communication, standards and conventions have been established to signal that a partner wants to end the communication. For virtual chats, these signals are not yet established. This lack leads to uncomfortable situations for many users from cultures with an emphasis on politeness. There are also cultural factors which need to be considered when designing social software for economic and community development.

The following naive questions could arise:

- Are there differences between the use of social software in individualistic and collectivist cultures?
- Do individualistic cultures use social software more because it serves as a means of individual expression?
- Do collectivist cultures use social software more because it serves for entering in virtual social interaction?

This article explores the relationship between culture and information technology for social networks. First, the culture model of Hofstede is presented and other culture definitions are shown (Hofstede & Hofstede, 2005). These are applied to information technology in general and to social media in particular. For several examples and based on a few studies we show how the functions of social networks are quite different. One chapter shows how discussion patterns and opinion expression can be influenced by the communication style of a culture.

BACKGROUND: CULTURE MODELS

There are many definitions of culture. The influential Dutch anthropologist Hofstede defined cul-

ture as learned patterns of "thinking, feeling, and potential acting" that form the mental program or the "software of the mind" (Hofstede & Hofstede, 2005) of an individual. As "software" it affects our way of thinking and acting in the world. National or social cultures define how people interact with each other, e.g. in groups and their environment.

Culture is often illustrated by using the metaphor of an onion: the most visible outer layers are easier to access than the hidden inner core, which is difficult to identify (Trompenaars & Hampden-Turner, 1997). Visible aspects of a culture are easily recognizable for anyone. The invisible ways of thinking and dealing with the world are much more difficult to access. This leads to many misunderstandings in intercultural encounters. For example, while the greeting behavior can be easily observed in a different culture, it is much more difficult to find out how a culture deals with unavoidable uncertainties of our existence.

Cultures are often classified in accordance to their relative positions on a number of polar scales which cultural anthropology commonly calls cultural dimensions. The position of a culture on those scales is determined by the dominant value orientations. Such quantified models of culture are difficult to find. Hofstede originally defined four dimensions of culture (Hofstede & Hofstede, 2005):

- Power distance measures the extent to which subordinates (employees, students) respond to power and authority (managers, teachers, parents) and how they expect and accept unequal power distribution. In high power distance cultures, individuals pay more respect to superiors. Guidance from elderly and experienced people is expected and not regarded as patronizing,
- Individualism vs. Collectivism: these value orientations refer to the ties among individuals in a society. In collectivist cultures, individuals define themselves more as members of a social group. They are ex-

Table 1. Examples for Values of Cultural Dimension (http://www.geert-hofstede.com)

Country	Power Distance	Individualism	Masculinity	Uncertainty Avoidance	Long term Orientation
Brazil	69	38	49	76	65
Chile	63	23	28	86	
South Korea	60	18	39	85	75
United States	40	91	62	46	29
Colombia	67	13	64	80	
Germany	35	67	66	65	31
Japan	54	46	95	92	80
France	68	71	43	86	
Germany	35	67	66	65	31
Pakistan	55	14	50	70	0
India	77	48	56	40	61

pected to share their belongings with the group and can rely on the backup within the group. In individualistic countries, the ties to groups are less strong and the individual freedom is highly regarded.

- Uncertainty avoidance: describes the extent to which individuals feel threatened by uncertain or unknown situations. High uncertainty avoidance cultures feel threatened by uncertain or unknown situations. They try to avoid or prepare for risks.
- Masculinity vs. Femininity: these two extreme values of this dimension focus on the differences between the social roles attributed to men and women and the expected behavior of the two sexes. Masculine values are related to competitiveness and assertiveness. Feminine values are related to quality of life.

Later in his research, Hofstede added a fifth dimension which was suggested by researchers from Asia.

Long-term vs. short-term orientation: The attitude toward time differs between cultures. Short-term cultures prefer to gain return on their investment quickly whereas long-term cultures are willing to invest in future returns. Long-term cultures value tradition highly and elders and experience enjoy a high status.

Many other theorists have suggested additional dimensions to describe cultures better. Hofstede argues that these correlate with his dimensions as presented above. This cultural theory discussion cannot be elaborated here. However, some other dimensions can be useful for the analysis of social media which are essentially communication tools. Hall (1966) has suggested the dimension of communication style. Explicit communication style cultures are also called low context cultures. They state important messages explicitly, people say directly what the mean and communication is seen as an exchange of information. On the other hand, high context cultures rely much more on the context of the situation or the social environment. Social status and the private life of people are important in any situation. Direct communication is regarded as impolite and even aggressive. Many messages are conveyed through non-verbal signals or implicitly.

Further dimensions to describe differences between cultures have been introduced by others. We want to mention universalism vs. particularism.

Universalism means that rules are to be followed under all circumstances. Under particularism, the members of a culture follow relax rules according to the circumstances (Trompenaars & Hampden-Turner, 1997).

SOCIAL NETWORKS IN AN INTERNATIONAL PERSPECTIVE

Culture and User Interfaces

Before analyzing the effect of culture on social media, we briefly review the literature on the relation between human-computer interaction and national cultures.

Usability generally defines to which a product or a system is easy to use for customers. Usability encompasses the aspects effective use, efficient use and subjective satisfaction. Good usability can be achieved by designing an interface with the user in mind and by applying testing methods throughout the development process.

The concept of usability is constructed out of several other concepts. The value which is assigned to these differs between cultures. In a survey among Chinese and Danish users, it was shown that perceive different issues of usability as important. Whereas Danish users stressed the relevance of the effectiveness of the interaction, Chinese users found that the software needs to appeal to them (Frandsen-Thorlacius et al., 2009). This shows that the basic understanding on what software and human-computer interfaces should provide differs greatly.

In addition, the basic visual perception of an interface (like a web site) also diverges. Eye tracking studies have revealed that the same web site is perceived differently by test persons from different countries. Users scan other areas and the attention is spread out in other patterns. German test users focused more on the top elements. On the other hand, Japanese participants scanned more areas further down the page (Duda et al., 2008). This

is evidence for a more holistic perception of user interfaces in the Eastern cultures. Even Chinese search engine users tend to click on result pages lower down in the ranked list than American Google users (Enquiro Research, 2009).

Cultural dimensions as presented in the last section have often been a starting point for research because they provide a plausible and quantified culture model. As one of the first researchers, Marcus presented convincing examples of differences for all cultural dimensions (Marcus et al., 2003). He observed, for example, that websites from high power distance countries present more people with a high social status on a web site, whereas cultures with low power distance tend to display persons with a lower status like students or employees. Marcus argues further that cultures with an high uncertainty avoidance have fewer elements on a page, less navigation options and a clear hierarchy. Individualism in web sites is exhibited by emphasizing the options that the user has and by providing further functions. However, these interpretations are based on a small and pre-selected set of web sites (Marcus et al., 2003).

Further studies with larger samples followed. Some hypotheses for the effect of the communication style have also been suggested and researched. In high context Web design, more imagery and less text is used. High context cultures will develop strategies for mimicking human presence online more than low context cultures. Low context are more consistent in layout and use of color (Würtz, 2004). Western websites are characterized by a deep hierarchy and fewer elements on each level. Chinese websites have a flat hierarchy with as many elements on each level as possible (Bucher, 2004). Case studies for specific applications have been carried out, e.g. for e-commerce sites (Aoki, 2000) or university web sites (Callahan, 2005a).

More important than the analysis of interfaces like Web sites are user tests with culturally heterogeneous groups of participants. Such experiments reveal whether users can handle interfaces differently and whether they perform better with sites from their culture.

Dormann and Chisalita try to quantify the differences between the perception of test users from different cultures and the design of web sites from other countries. Their analysis is focused on the dimension femininity vs. masculinity for university web sites in Italy and Scandinavia (Dormann & Chisalita, 2002).

A study with Taiwanese and German test persons revealed several performance and perception differences for search tasks on American university web sites (Schmitz et al., 2008). The results suggest that German users coped better with the information structures of the USA sites which is culturally less distant from them than the Taiwanese users.

The culture also has an impact on the development process of user interfaces. Much literature has focused on the adaptation of usability methods to cultural properties (Clemmensen et al., 2007). Methods need to be carefully adopted to the demands of a culture. Especially the user test is a complex social situation in which the social status of the people involved and administration can lead to problems.

Social Networks in Different Cultures

Social networks have gained popularity over the last few years. Users communicate, exchange information objects such as photographs, organize their existing and find new contacts. Especially among young Internet users, these social software systems are highly popular and markets have been growing.

A specific market situation market emerged in most developed countries. For network systems, it is natural for this market that one competitor emerges and dominates the market. The value of a network with many participants is higher for each participant.

It is striking to observe, that in most countries one or two market leaders have reached a domi-

nant market position (Pingdom, 2008; ComScore, 2007). Exporting a social software system to another country hardly ever leads to a significant market share (Shim, 2008). This seems to be due to the cultural issues involved in social media (UID, 2007). Since these networks are created to support people in their social life and organize their social contacts in the online world, these systems need to be heavily adapted to the way in which social life is organized in a particular culture. It seems that the local market leader can much better adapt to such cultural needs than foreign competitors. On the other hand, many products and services do not need to be adapted too much and foreign companies can enter local markets, since they do not support people in their interaction with each other. An example for such a product is a web search engine.

It is a valuable approach to identify the particularities of the market leaders in order to gain insights into the differences between social software in a variety of cultures. Market leaders are, for example, Xing (www.xing.com) and studiVZ (www.studivz.net) in Germany, Vkontakte.ru and Odnoklassniki.ru in Russia, QQ (www.qq.com) in China, Mixi (mixi.jp) in Japan, CyWorld (www.cyworld.com) in Korea, Orkut (www.orkut.com) in Brazil, Iran and India, Facebook (www.facebook.com) and MySpace (www.myspace.com) in the USA, Friendster and Imeem in the Philippines and Islam Net in the Arab Countries (www.muxlim.com).

Especially in collectivist countries like Korea and China, social networks were founded early and have much success. CyWorld in Korea has been active since 1999 and QQ in China even since 1997. In absolute numbers, there are more users of social networks in the USA than in other countries. Over 140 Million US users compare, for example, to 47 Million Japanese, 30 Million in Brazil, 18 Million in Italy according to a study from 2009 (Nielsen 2010). However, this is due to differences in the technological infrastructure and the wealth of countries. According to a another recent study, 30% of the entire population in South Korea have an account at CyWorld and more than half of the internet users have logged in within the last month, whereas in the USA merely less than 25% have done so (Anderson, 2007). It seems that collectivist countries are more attracted by social networking services. A survey from the media company Universal McCann (2008) revealed that the Philippines, Mexico, India and Pakistan use social networks most and find blogs useful for socializing. All these countries are ranked relatively low on the individualism score determined by Hofstede, with Pakistan being extremely low. Some of the other countries with high collectivism scores are not very technologically developed and, as a consequence, were not included in the survey. More statistical evidence is given in a study from 2006. It shows that already then South Korea was the leader in the use of online networking sites (Ipsos, 2007).

The visual design and appearance of Asian social media applications is different from Western social media sites just like for other web sites as discussed in the previous section. A study on navigation, metaphors, mental models and appearance of social networks for Korea, Japan and the USA has been carried out by Marcus and Krishnamurthi (2009). There are more graphic elements and more functions related to visual information like pictures and videos in the Asian systems than in Western systems. This can be explained by the high context communication style which relies not only on explicit verbal information. Both facilitate the visual display of the current emotion of the user.

Entertainment plays a more important role. QQ includes transmissions of live shows. This supports the findings of different concepts of usability as identified by the survey presented in the previous section (Frandsen-Thorlacius et al., 2009).

The emphasis is on the community and less on the presentation of the individual person. QQ and CyWorld have very successful business models which fit the cultures very well. The companies generate revenue from the sale of digital goods

(e.g. background music, avatars, and small objects for individual homepages or casual games) (Plus Eight Star, 2009). In CyWorld, a large portion of the objects are bought as presents for others. This digital goods culture supports the elaborated present culture in Korea which is typical for a collectivist culture.

The Japanese service Mixi does not allow immediate access to the profiles of other users like many Western systems. It is not meant to find new friends but rather to stay in contact with friends or communities. This can be explained by the long-term orientation and the collectivist nature of the Japanese culture. Safety and trust within the in-group are emphasized. The extension of the social network is mainly based on invitations. Facebook, on the other hand, allows to find new friends more easily like it would be expected from a more individualistic and short-term oriented culture in which new relations are being established more frequently. Facebook lets users use their real names. Combined with the low restrictions on the access to the profiles, it is obvious, that Facebook or MySpace are more oriented toward the self-presentation typical for an individualistic society (Toto, 2008). A recent study on privacy issues and personal openness discusses how the elaboration of privacy settings of social networks in the USA, Brazil, Russia, India and China are directed toward the cultural needs of their audience (Turner, 2008). The same study also shows that within a country two services with substantially different orientation may be successful and attract different personalities within a country.

The Korean CyWorld has an elaborated system with degrees of friendships. These are translations of degrees of blood-relationships in the real world. This shows that in-groups are systematically organized into several layers of friends. Such layers are not common for Western countries and this shows how an extremely collectivist society needs to define more elaborately what a friend and a group are. It is necessary due to the consequences of the membership to a group which requires an high degree of loyalty. CyWorld also allows the creation of a mini-room in pseudo 3D on the homepage of the users (Plus Eight Star, 2009). This feature serves the demand for space in a densely populated country and opens opportunities for the gift culture again typical for a collectivist society like South Korea.

The types of online activities popular also differ among societies. Korean and Chinese seem to be more active and read and write blogs whereas more individualistic societies like France, Germany, the UK and the USA read and write blogs less frequently than the global average (Universal McCann, 2008). For uploading videos, the three big East Asian societies are well above global average and China is well ahead in video consumption (Universal McCann, 2008). Online video consumption is also very popular in Brazil and Mexico. Not for all these phenomena, an explanation based on cultural dimensions can be found easily. They need to be understood as a complex interplay of cultural, personal, economic and political reasons.

Opinion Expression in Social Media

Social software appeals to members of many cultures and some might even think that this indicates the evolvement of an unified international culture. Blogs, for example, are becoming an increasingly important knowledge source not only for individual readers. For this study, blogs were chosen because their content is exploited for opinion analysis even for business portals and because they allow discussions and interaction through so called posts and can consequently be considered as a form of social software.

The expression of opinions is strongly culturally dependent. Some cultures prefer open negative statements whereas other cultures use indirect communication to transfer a negative opinion. This leads to many cultural misunderstanding because both sides may interpret the communication style as negative. Whereas direct communication

Table 2. Comment Types (Mandl 2009)

Reaction	China	Germany
emotional, positive	0.298	0.175
argumentation, positive	0.157	0.226
Mediation	0.256	0.277
argumentation, negative	0.099	0.124
emotional, negative	0.071	0.107
change of topic	0.119	0.090

cultures interpret other cultures as less honest, the cultures preferring indirect communication interpret others as rude. These statements are grossly simplifying the issues for illustration. We do not argue that blogs cannot be understood or typically lead to negative reactions by readers from other cultures. In this study, merely the blogs themselves are analyzed and not their perception by users.

Applications of web mining technologies to extract opinions need to consider these cultural patterns of discussion and opinion expression. Otherwise, they might detect only patterns from the point of view of one particular culture.

A thorough intellectual analysis of 700 blog pages and the comments and reactions attached to them revealed culturally diverse patterns. The study showed that the virtue of "keeping face" is very important for Chinese and has an impact on the discussion and communication patterns. There are less negative reactions in the Chinese set as table 2 shows. A more detailed look at the negative reactions shows that they usually contain more text than negative reactions in the contrastive German set. If Chinese react negatively, they feel the need to elaborate the reasons for that more (Mandl, 2009).

Further differences were found. They can be attributed to high vs. low context communication style and the long-term vs. short-term differences between the German and the Chinese culture (Mandl, 2009).

A quantitative study on the frequency of opinion expressions in news texts shows that there are significant differences of the frequency of expression of subjectivity and their polarity. The subjectivity and polarity differs over a corpus of news extracted form the web in nine languages (Bautin et al., 2008). Consequently, cross-cultural comparisons of sentiments need to include proper normalization methods.

Virtual Social Capital

Social software appeals to users because they allow the creation of networks and because of their social reward systems. Virtual social capital can be built up and users can manage their networks and contacts.

In order to analyze cultural differences for this construction process, we conducted a user test with social software user test with Nigerian and German test users. Twelve test persons of each culture underwent the user test in their own country and in their typical usage context. They interacted with a social sharing site for videos (YouTube). The test revealed many similarities between the groups but also several differences. The interaction with the social software led to a positive emotional reaction in both cultures. The reaction was recorded with a standardized self report questionnaire.

The German test users did not see the integration into a social network as sufficient motivation to interact in the test situation. On the other hand, the Nigerians took advantage of the network and gave real socially motivated feedback.

The social status is the basis for trust and motivation for social interaction in many systems. The size of ones network or the popularity of ones pages are examples of indicators for that kind which are displayed in most social software applications.

It was obvious that both user groups searched for such indicators and that they intended to evaluate the social status of the person they looked at. However, the construction of the virtual social status differed greatly between the cultures. The German test users tried to identify the character of a person based on the content provided. They intensively read the opinions of other members of the network. On the other hand, the Nigerian test users were much more interested in the real world social network of the person. This may be due to their more collectivist nature.

The Germans in the test needed to find and judge more context indicators and took more interest in the comments of others. The Nigerians as a high context communication style culture were less interested in the context and read the comments of other user much less.

Social software is of great interest for members of both cultures. Social values, however, are constructed in very different ways. Situations may occur where community members judge each other or other persons quite different and do not understand the reasons for that. Someone may e.g. wonder why others do not trust him despite of his high social capital in his own culture and the reason for that might be that they cannot even see the issues which are relevant for them to construct social capital.

CONCLUSION

Social software applications bear the risk of misunderstandings in international settings. On the other hand, these systems can also remedy the communication and intercultural problems in ways which are not possible in face-to-face meetings. These methods need to be further explored. We suggest the following list of actions as a basis for discussion.

- Interfaces are culturally adapted and provide information relevant in the culture of the user
- Only a globally safe sub-set of indicators is shown
- Numbers hinting at social status are culturally normalized

- The applications explains potential differences and educates the user context dependent

All these methods have their advantages and disadvantages. There are many further open questions. Some of them refer to the empirical methods to study behavior in social systems. How do test situation influence the use of social software? How can real-world social software use be studied? Ultimately, we need to arrive at a better understanding of social software itself to adapt it to international communication.

The international communication over social media is also made more difficult by language differences. Models and experimental results for the access to multilingual information need to be considered when promoting the exchange over language borders (Berendt & Kralisch, 2009). The complex interplay between competence, assumptions on the language of the content, availability of language tools and information architecture determine the way people access such sites in multiple languages.

For the analysis of social networks in international studies, there remain many questions unanswered. Much could be answered with detailed statistics but other issues require user studies or user observation. For example, it could be analyzed how networks form over time and how many connections people typically have. User studies could explore issues about the perception of networks and how functions are used in particular countries.

Understanding virtual social networks is a hard challenge. Nevertheless, this topic needs to attract more research. A better understanding can ultimately lead to improved international communication.

REFERENCES

Anderson, N. (2007). *Report: South Korea tops in social networking, US fifth.* Retrieved from http://arstechnica.com/

Bautin, M., Vijayarenu, L., & Skiena, S. (2008). International sentiment analysis for news and blogs. In *Proceedings of the Second International Conference on Weblogs and Social Media (IC-WSM-2008)*. Retrieved from http://www.aaai.org/Library/ICWSM/icwsm08contents.php

Berendt, B., & Kralisch, A. (2009). A user-centric approach to identifying best deployment strategies for language tools: The impact of content and access language on Web user behaviour and attitudes. *Information Retrieval, 12*(3), 380–399. doi:10.1007/s10791-008-9086-4

Bucher, H. J. (2004). Is there a Chinese internet? Intercultural investigation on the internet in the People's Republic of China: Theoretical considerations and empirical results. In *Proceedings Fourth International Conference: Cultural Attitudes towards Technology and Communication 2004 (CATAC)*, Murdoch University, Australia (pp. 416-428).

Callahan, E. (2005). Cultural similarities and differences in the design of university websites. *Journal of Computer-Mediated Communication, 11*(1), 12. Retrieved from http://jcmc.indiana.edu/vol11/issue1/callahan.html. doi:10.1111/j.1083-6101.2006.tb00312.x

Callari, R. (2009). *Top ten social networks circumnavigating the globe.* Retrieved from http://inventorspot.com/articles/top_ten_social_networks_circumnavigating_globe_30018

Clemmensen, T., Shi, Q., Kumar, J., Li, H., Sun, X., & Yammiyavar, P. (2007). Cultural usability tests: How usability tests are not the same all over the world. *Usability and Internationalization: HCI and Culture, Second International Conference on Usability and Internationalization, UI-HCII 2007* [HCI International 2007, Beijing, China, July 22-27, Proceedings, Part I] (pp. 281-290).

ComScore. (2007). *Social networking goes global*. Retrieved from http://comscore.com/Press_Events/Press_Releases/2007/07/Social_Networking_Goes_Global

Dormann, C., & Chisalita, C. (2002). Cultural values in Web site design. In *Proceedings of the Eleventh European Conference on Cognitive Ergonomics (ECCE 11)*, Catania, Italy, September 8-11.

Duda, S., Schießl, M., & Nüsperling, S. (2008). See the world with different eyes. *planung & analyse*, pp. 14-18.

Frandsen-Thorlacius, O., Hornbæk, K., Hertzum, M., & Clemmensen, T. (2009). Non-universal usability?: A survey of how usability is understood by Chinese and Danish users. In *Proceedings 27th Intel. Conference on Human Factors in Computing Systems, CHI 2009*, April, Boston, MA (pp. 4-9).

Hall, E. T. (1966). *The hidden dimension*. New York: Anchor Books/Doubleday.

Hofstede, G., & Hofstede, G. J. (2004). *Cultures and organizations: Software of the mind*. New York: McGraw-Hill.

Ipsos. (2007). *Online video and social networking set to drive tomorrow's digital lifestyle*. Retrieved from http://www.ipsos-ideas.com/article.cfm?id=3592

Kamentz, E., & Womser-Hacker, C. (2003). Defining culture-bound user characteristics as a starting point for the design of adaptive learning systems. *Journal of Universal Computer Science, 9*(7).

Krenn, B., Neumayr, B., Gstrein, E., & Grice, M. (2004). Lifelike agents for the internet: A cross-cultural case study. In *Agent Culture: Human-Agent Interaction in a Multicultural World* (pp. 197–229). Mahwah, NJ: Lawrence Erlbaum Associates.

Mandl, T. (2009). Comparing Chinese and German blogs. In *Proceedings 20th ACM Conference on Hypertext and Hypermedia (HT '09)* Torino, Italy, June 29-July 1 (pp. 299-308). New York: ACM Press.

Mandl, T., & Womser-Hacker, C. (2008). Tapping the power of social software for international development. In *HCI for Community and International Development* [Proceedings of Conference on Human Factors in Computing Systems (CHI) 2008, 5th-6th April, Florence, Italy]. Retrieved from http://www.cc.gatech.edu/~mikeb/HCI-4CID/Mandl.pdf

Marcus, A., & Alexander, C. (2007). User validation of cultural dimensions of a Website design. In *Usability and internationalization: Global and local user interfaces* ([). Berlin: Springer.]. *Lecture Notes in Computer Science, 4650*, 160–167. doi:10.1007/978-3-540-73289-1_20

Marcus, A., Baumgartner, V. J., & Chen, E. (2003). *User interface design vs. culture. In Designing for Global Markets 5, IWIPS 2003, Fifth International Workshop on Internationalisation of Products and Systems, (IWIPS) Where East meets West*, Berlin, Germany, 17-19 July (pp. 67-78).

Marcus, A., & Krishnamurthi, N. (2009). Cross-cultural analysis of social network services in Japan, Korea, and the USA. In *Internationalization, Design and Global Development, Third International Conference, IDGD 2009*, San Diego, CA, July 19-24 (pp. 59-68).

Nielsen. (2010, January 22). *Led by Facebook, Twitter, global time spent on social media sites up 82% year over year*. Retrieved from http://blog.nielsen.com/nielsenwire/global

Oard, D. (1997). Serving users in many languages: Cross-language information retrieval for digital libraries. *D-Lib Magazine*. Retrieved from http://www.dlib.org/dlib/december97/oard/12oard.html

O´Murchu. I., Breslin, J., & Decker, S. (2004). Online social and business networking communities In *Proceedings of the ECAI 2004Workshop on Application of Semantic Web Technologies to Web Communities*, Valencia, Spain, August 23-27. Retrieved from http://sunsite.informatik.rwth-aachen.de/Publications/CEUR-WS/Vol-107/paper2.pdf

Pingdom. (2008). *Social network popularity around the world*. Retrieved from http://royal.pingdom.com/

Plus Eight Star. (2009). *Inside CyWorld. Business Report*. Retrieved from http://www.plus8star.com/2009/01/01/publishing/

Schmitz, A., Mandl, T., & Womser-Hacker, C. (2008). Cultural differences between Taiwanese and German Web users: Challenges for intercultural user testing. In *Proceedings of the 10th Intl. Conference on Enterprise Information Systems (ICEIS)*, 12 - 16 June, Barcelona, Spain (pp. 62-69).

Shim, J. P. (2008, October). Social networking sites: A brief comparison of usage in the U.S. and Korea. *Decision Line, 39*(5), 16–18.

Smith, A., Dunckley, L., French, T., Minocha, S., & Chang, Y. (2004). A process model for developing usable cross-cultural websites. *Interacting with Computers, 16*(1), 63–91. doi:10.1016/j.intcom.2003.11.005

Sohns, K., & Breitner, M. (2009). Online content mining & its potential for cruise management. In *Cruise Sector Growth* (p. 171). Wiesbaden, Germany: Gabler Verlag. doi:10.1007/978-3-8349-8346-6_12

Toto, S. (2008). *Taking social networks abroad: Why MySpace and Facebook are failing in Japan*. Retrieved from http://www.techcrunch.com

Trompenaars, F., & Hampden-Turner, C. (1997). *Riding the waves of culture: Understanding cultural diversity in business*. London: Nicholas Brealey.

Turner, B. (2008, November 2). Hypotheses about privacy attitudes. *International values and communications technologies: The blog of the GU-ISD Yahoo! fellow*. Retrieved from https://digitalcommons.georgetown.edu/blogs/isdyahoofellow/hypotheses-about-privacy-attitudes

UID. (2007). *Internationale Web 2.0 Studie über MySpace*. Retrieved from http://www.uid.com/download.php?pdf=uid_referenz_myspace_studie.pdf

Universal McCann. (2008). *When did we start trusting strangers? How the internet turned us all into influencers*. Retrieved from http://www.imaginar.org/docs/when_did_we_start_trusting_strangers.pdf

Würtz, E. (2004). Intercultural communication on websites: An analysis of visual communication of high- and low-context cultures. In F. Sudweeks & C. Ess (Eds.), *Proceedings of the Fourth International Conference on Cultural Attitudes towards Technology and Communication (CATAC)*, Murdoch University, Australia (pp. 109-122).

ADDITIONAL READING

Aoki, K. (2000). Cultural differences in e-commerce: A comparison between the United States and Japan. In *INET 2000 Proceedings* [18-21 July, Yokohama, Japan]. Reston, VA: Internet Society. Retrieved from http://www.isoc.org/inet2000/cdproceedings/7d/7d_1.htm

Aykin, N. (2004). *Usability and Internationalization of Information Technology*. Boca Raton, FL: CRC.

Beneke, J. (1998). Thriving on diversity: Cultural differences in the workplace. *Working Papers in International Business Communcation* (Vol. 4). Bonn, Germany: Dümmler

Callahan, E. (2005). Interface design and culture. [ARIST]. *Annual Review of Information Science & Technology, 39*(1), 255–310. doi:10.1002/aris.1440390114

Enquiro Research. (2009). *Chinese search engine engagement* [White paper]. Retrieved from http://www.enquiroresearch.com/whitepapers

Evers, V., Sturm, C., Rocha, M., Martínez, E., & Mandl, T. (2007). *Designing for global markets 9: Proceedings of the Ninth International Workshop on Internationalization of Products and Systems – Actually Being There (IWIPS 2007),* 28–30 June, Merida, Mexico. Retrieved from http://www.iwips.org

Gudykunst, W. B., & Kim, Y. Y. (1984). *Methods for intercultural communication research.* Thousand Oaks, CA: Sage Publications.

Hodemacher, D., Mandl, T., & Jarman, F. (2005). Ein empirischer Vergleich zwischen Großbritannien und Deutschland. In *Workshop-Proceedings der 5. fachübergreifenden Konferenz Mensch und Computer, September* (pp. 93–101). Linz, Österreich: Kultur und Web-Design.

Jeon, S., Yoon, S. N., & Kim, J. (2008). A cross cultural study of corporate blogs in the USA and Korea. *International Journal of Information Technology and Management, 7*(2), 149–160. doi:10.1504/IJITM.2008.016602

Kralisch, A., & Mandl, T. (2006). Barriers of information access across languages on the internet: Network and language effects. In *Proceedings Hawaii International Conference on System Sciences (HICSS-39)* Track 3. (p. 54b). Retrieved from http://doi.ieeecomputersociety.org/10.1109/HICSS.2006.71

Liebscher, A., Caroli, F., & Mandl, T. (2008). Die Qualitätsbewertung internationaler Websites: Neukonzeption und Evaluierung des Informationsangebots des Außenhandelskammer Singapur. In *Verfügbarkeit von Informationen: Proceedings 30. Online-Tagung der DGI. 60. Jahrestagung der DGI,* Frankfurt, Germany (pp. 217-225).

Märtl, T., Mandl, T., & Womser-Hacker, C. (2009). Mehrsprachige Suche in Social Tagging-Systemen: Eine Untersuchung am Beispiel von Flickr. In *Information: Droge, Ware oder Commons? Proc 11. Internationales Symposium für Informationswissenschaft (ISI 2009),* 1-3 April, Konstanz, Germany (pp. 35-50).

Massey, A., Montoya-Weiss, M., Hung, C., & Ramesh, V. (2001). Global virtual teams: Cultural perceptions of task-technology fit. *Communications of the ACM, 44*(12), 83–84.

Prendinger, H. (2005, October 10-12). Estimating user affect and focus of attention from physiological signals in life-like character based interaction scenarios. Paper presented at *LWATrack . Knowledge Discovery,* Saarbrücken, Germany. Retrieved from http://www.dfki.de/lwa2005/abis/13-Prendinger.pdf

Sturm, C. (2005). Approaches for a successful product localization. In *Workshops–Proceedings der 5. fachübergreifenden Konferenz Mensch und Computer* (pp. 59-68). Retrieved from http://mc.informatik.uni-hamburg.de/konferenzbaende/mc2005/workshops/WS8_B1.pdf

Swigger, K. M., Alpaslan, F., Nur, B., Robert, P., & Monticino, M. (2004). Effects of culture on computer-supported international collaborations. *International Journal of Human-Computer Interaction, 60*(3), 365–380.

Yunker, J. (2002). *Beyond borders: web globalization strategies.* Boston: New Riders.

KEY TERMS AND DEFINITIONS

Collectivism: Describes cultures in which ties between members of social groups are very tight. People define themselves more as members of groups than as individuals. They are loyal to the group and receive security in return.

Cultural Dimension: A cultural dimension is part of a cultural model to analyze the collective behavior of a society. A dimension describes a particular aspect of behavior which is potentially independent to other aspects. Several dimensions can be used in parallel to define an individual culture in comparison to others.

Localization: Software and other products need to be adopted to target markets in international commerce. The adaptation to local technological and cultural customs is called localization.

Long-Term Orientation: This dimension to describe cultures originated in Asia is also referred to a Confucian dimension. It denotes how far ahead members of a society typically plan and whether they expect return for an investment soon or in the long term.

Social Capital: A sociological concept which tries to define the value in social contacts for humans. Social Capital lies in relationships between people and the degree of acquaintance and recognition. People may invest in social capital and receive capital in other forms. Measures can be the size and stability of a social network of a person.

Uncertainty Avoidance: Describes the tendency to avoid uncertainty. Members of a culture with an high uncertainty avoidance try to avoid situations with unclear rules and structures in which they feel threatened. The society defines many rules and rituals to minimize anxiety.

Usability: Denotes the degree to which a product can be used easily and is a key success factor. The aspects of usability are effectiveness, efficiency and satisfaction. They may have different importance for a system. Usability needs to be integrated into the development of a system. User centered design processes guarantee a higher level of usability.

Section 2
Social Computing from an Organizational Perspective

Chapter 5
Social Contexts in an Information Rich Environment

Gbolahan K. Williams
King's College London, UK

Iman Poernomo
King's College London, UK

ABSTRACT

'Information Management' has seen a tremendous transformation over the years from various forms of traditional analogue/digital techniques for managing information to more current digital forms that employ various heterogeneous technologies aimed at enhancing the task of information management to a level that is more robust, reliable and effective. As one would expect, the application of social computing technologies (SCT) to modern information management contexts has played a particularly useful role to facilitate the process of information sharing, document authoring, communication and collaboration between users in various domains. As such, these technologies have seen increased interest from business and industry, cultural institutions, educational institutions and government. This chapter presents a general overview of the use of social computing technologies in various application domains, discusses various considerations and challenges, and presents a scope for future solutions to those challenges. The conclusion is that while it is generally accepted that SCT's have the potential to improve communication and collaboration in various organizational and social settings, one must elicit the precise social behavioral models in which it is trying to improve or replicate and some measure to gauge those improvements. In such an instance, the authors suggest ethnography would be particularly useful.

PREFACE

In this chapter, we will discuss social computing software and web 3.0 technologies with respect to information management systems as used in the context of information rich environments. We narrow our discussion on the topic to the various challenges and issues conferred from the use of the said technologies under various social and digital settings; For example: the use of social computing applications in conjunction with mobile computing and pervasive technologies in the

DOI: 10.4018/978-1-61692-904-6.ch005

enterprise and other organizational settings such as museums and galleries which are representative of cultural institutions.

Both organizational enterprise and cultural institutions are two different examples that we will use to illustrate our points. We argue that the interpretation of the contexts for any environment under study to which must be modeled requires an immersive examination of the natural flow of information and interaction between users from both sociological and technological standpoints.

Thus, the central issues we discuss in this chapter are:

1. We provide a discussion on the aspect of social interaction leaning towards Web 3.0 (the next progressive version of the web), with respect to the next generation of information management systems. We give a general discussion on the topic and subsequently narrow our discussion to the adoption of Web 3.0 and social computing technologies in museums (Museum 3.0) and the enterprise (Enterprise 3.0). Some challenges are outlined, and some directions for possible improvements for some specific challenges.
2. The role of social interaction in information management is also discussed and the issues construed in various domains and application contexts.
3. We also discuss various considerations and requirements for utilizing social software.

1. INTRODUCTION

Information as we know it today typically consists of various forms of structured and/or unstructured data in both analogue and digital formats and can be recognized as a resource independent of its physical properties. Collectively, the management, collection, retrieval, enrichment and maintenance

of such information is commonly referred to as '*Information Management*' (Boaden, 1991).

Information Management (*IM*) is a very broad topic and is a responsibility that has been around for a very long time and has continually evolved over time to meet various demands and challenges presented by modern technological and sociological innovations and the new ways in which people manage, share, create and retrieve information. The primary constituents of Information Management consist of: the actual information content (e.g. information documents, emails, journals etc); the uses of the information (e.g. communication, content publishing, enriching information repositories etc); the processes and rules that govern information management (this encompasses the business rules and constraints that govern how the information is accessed and utilized); and the systems that enforce those processes (this takes into account the various systems that enforce the business rules and constraints specified by the aforementioned IM constituents).

Information Management solutions come in a variety of shapes and forms and range from very simple systems to highly complex systems and encompass systems such as:

1. Content Management Systems (CMS): A CMS is a system that supports the creation, administration and publishing of digital media and/or electronic texts (Bovey, 2005)
2. Wiki Systems (WS): systems that enable collaborative document authoring through participation of various authorized members of the system (Neumann & Erol, 2008).
3. Document Management Systems (DMS): systems used to monitor and track the creation, manipulation and storage of digital documents (Sutton, 1996).
4. Collaboration Software Systems (CSS): systems designed to enable multiple individuals to collectively participate in a common task to achieve a common goal (Grudin, 1994).

Information Management systems are continuously evolving and are continually being updated and developed in order to maximize on *information richness*, which refers to the amount of detail pertaining to a particular piece of information that can be conveyed by a medium and comprises of the main data and some additional parameters that might be specific to the information domain in question.

In literature, information richness has been defined as *"the potential information carrying capacity of data, or simply the capacity of information to provide substantial new consensual understanding"* (Trevino et. al, 1987). The richness of information is indicative of the mediums capacity to carry large volumes of data, and as such, the breadth and depth of information conveyed over a particular medium might be determined by the chosen medium (Daft & Lengel, 1986). This formed the rationalization for the 'information richness theory' (also referred to as the 'media richness theory'), which is a framework that was conceptually proposed to explain media choice (Daft et. al, 1984; Daft et. al, 1987).

In a pervasive computing world, in which computing resources (both hardware and software) and information flow are intended to be transparent, accessible and limitless, information richness transpires thus creating *information rich environments*, environments in which data or other relevant information is provided to a user in a highly accessible way (Addington et. al, 2005). For example, wiki systems in enterprise settings (Neumann & Erol, 2009).

Social computing technologies have recently begun to play an important role in creating and enriching information environments, from the enterprise, to educational institutions, to cultural institutions. Though the topic of social computing has recently seen wide adoption over the last few years, the core ideas of social interaction through software systems have been around for a very long time and can be traced back to Vannevar Bush's *'memex'*, a device conceived to record an individuals data and communications with the aim of making it more accessible to others (Bush, 1945).

Social computing applications, software that derives from a set of tools and technologies that support any form of social interaction or social behavior, include everything from email clients, instant messaging applications to blogging software, wiki systems and social networks (some real life examples of social computing services are presented in Table 1). The strong interest in applications that support social interaction comes from the growing need for software tools that support collaboration and sharing, tools which are also referred to in some domains as groupware (Orlikowski, 1997). It is for this reason that several organizations and businesses employ social computing technologies at the core of their systems and services. Examples of such systems include: CRM applications, blogs, wiki engines and other forms of computer supported cooperative works (CSCW), (Grudin, 1994); while preceding generations of social software included mailing lists, usenet, bulletin board systems etc.

2. SOCIAL COMPUTING VS. SOCIAL THEORY

It is important to make a distinction between the concepts of social computing and social theory because there is often some confusion over the differences between them and often both are used imprecisely or misused interchangeably. Thus, definitions are given here to clarify the usage of terms herein.

Conceptually, social theory relates to the ways in which social life is embodied and often, its life cycle; the way it is organized, managed and evolved (Coleman, 1994). It provides a general framework for the analysis, interpretation and description within a particular social arrangement or configuration. In contrast, social computing and the application of such technologies draw from ideas of social theory and interdisciplinary

Table 1. Real life examples of social computing services

Social Computing Technology	Popular Examples
Instant Messaging Instant messaging is a form of real time communication that utilises technologies that enable multiple participants to communicate over a network (internet or intranet).	MSN, AIM, GoogleTalk, Yahoo! Messenger
Social Networks Allows users to create and manage personal profiles and 'connections' through a virtual *social graph* or *social network*.	Facebook, Bebo, LinkedIn, Friendster, MySpace
Blogs Blog or Web-log, is an online journal that allows users to publish ongoing entries of information in the form of text, audio, video and other media types.	Blogspot, WordPress, BuddyPress, MSN Spaces
Web Search Engines Web search engines are a particular type of information retrieval systems that retrieve information documents from the world wide web commonly based on keyword searches and other types of information queries.	Google, Yahoo, Bing, AltaVista, AskJeeves
Folksonomy, Tagging These are set of social classification technologies	Del.icio.us, magnolia, Google Bookmarks,
Photo Sharing A set of tools that enable a user to share photos online.	Flickr, PhotoBucket, iStockphoto, StockPhoto
RSS A web feed format used for various kinds of media content publishing.	Newsgator, FeedBurner
Wiki and Knowledge Systems Allows the creation of collaborative websites.	Wikipedia, Google Knol, Britannica

research from sociology, philosophy, anthropology and other research communities.

Though it can be seen that the only recognizable advantage of employing social computing technologies and applications is to facilitate the process of various facets of social behavior such as communication and collaboration, it is important to note that these are not standalone goals. Below, we present some of the additional goals of social computing. It is worth noting that some of these goals derive from the experience of issues pertaining to social interaction identified in social theory research.

1. **Widespread distribution of information:** Social computing technologies such as blogs, wiki's and forums provide the tools and capabilities that enable users to create and share content with other users. Users can utilize social media to find insights that matter to them and to maximize information richness.

2. **Improved discovery and aggregation of information:** The use of folksonomy systems which include collaborative tagging and social classification systems have improved the process of classifying and searching for various kinds of information.

3. **Enhanced availability and accessibility of information:** The use of RSS, a web feed format used for content publishing of media content that is updated frequently has enhanced the accessibility of information by content consumers and the ease of broadcasting such information by content publishers. Content providers can simply create information sources and publish content via RSS feeds from those sources,

whilst content consumers can simply subscribe to those feeds using an RSS reader, a software tool for retrieving and managing content from an RSS feed.

4. **Improved Learning:** In educational and organizational contexts, social computing technologies such as forums and blogs have the potential to facilitate learning because of the ease at which information can be broadcasted and communicated to people thus enhancing the way in which information is disseminated and accessed by both content publishers and content consumers.

3. CHALLENGES AND CONSIDERATIONS FOR SOCIAL COMPUTING TECHNOLOGIES

As the topic of social computing is very broad and social computing technologies can be broken up into various categories of tools and applications, the challenges discussed in this section will be limited to two main categories covering the general issues in the problem space. Similarly, as some of the challenges might be specific to particular domains and contexts, we will elaborate on these examples in subsequent sections. In this section, we give a precursor to some of these challenges by discussing some topics which we categorize under 'Behavioral Considerations' and 'System Considerations', categories which might be cast to fall under the 'social' and 'technical' problem spaces respectively. We revisit some of the challenges of social computing technologies in subsequent sections in this chapter.

Behavioural Considerations: Interfaces / Evaluation Techniques

1. **Interface design:** The challenge of developing group centric and collaboration centric user interfaces presents its own challenges. This new paradigm is a complete shift away from single user interface design. Group centered user interfaces inherit all the design challenges of single user interfaces, supplemented by additional challenges arising from the need to support the involvement of group processes (Grudin, 1994). Some of the challenges conceived, directly affect some specific concerns of interface design such as the elicitation of requirements, prototyping, usability testing etc.

2. **Difficulty of Evaluation:** The nature of social computing applications, that are solely group centric and collaborative present several complications for their analysis and evaluation. Grudin (1994) makes an important point about the habits of single users and groups. The preferences of individual users are generally more constant over time. In contrast, users in group-centric applications are difficult to examine. For this reason, most social computing applications and services are evolutionary based and generally evolve over longer periods of time compared to single user interfaces. In such instances, product iterations and enhancements come through some analysis of user behavior and/or through some negotiation of system features between the user and the service provider.

System Considerations: Architectural / Integration / Mashups

1. **Flexibility of Applications:** One of the challenges of social software relates to the flexibility of applications. This relates to specific concerns such as the granularity of features and variability that are required in multiuser environments. A single system can possess multiple types of users, which may all have different and sometimes conflicting requirements of the systems. In a social application, supporting features and services to accommodate such a wide variety

of users may pose several challenges. In a group-centered application, there is hardly a 'one size fits all' solution.

2. **Risk Assessment:** Social computing applications require some sort of evaluation and assessment of the potential risks that may arise following the adoption of the technology. Some specific concerns under the topic of risk assessment include privacy and security of user information. Although privacy and security are challenges affecting all social computing applications, most of the research and discussion around it has focused around privacy and security in social networks (Felt, 2008; Strater et al., 2008; Strater & Richter, 2007).

4. SCOPE FOR PROBLEM RESOLUTION

It is our belief that the issues discussed in the previous section are derived as a result of inadequate or misunderstood software requirements. There is a popular notion that for many reasons, many software systems fail due to poorly understood and/or under-developed requirements. Over the years, there has been increased acceptance pointing towards the adoption of empirical methods for software engineering (Finkelstein, 2000). The recent attention drawn towards social computing technologies used in conjunction with mobile and pervasive computing technologies now presents additional complications to the analysis, design and development of software systems both from social and software engineering perspectives.

4.1 Requirements in Social Software Design

The basic question in requirements engineering is how to identify what users really need and want or how to find out which of their established needs are most important. In the case of social comput-

ing applications, some questions a requirements engineer might face might be: (i) What tools might enable users to collaborate more efficiently? (ii) What measures need to be taken to ensure security and privacy to protect proprietary or confidential information within a social network? etc.

Requirements Analysis (RA) also called Requirements Engineering (RE) involves all the processes and tasks that go into establishing the user needs and expectations of a newly proposed (or previously existing) system/product. Typically, requirements engineering succeeds business planning and comprises several techniques and activities that have been developed in the requirements engineering community (Cheng & Atlee, 2007; Nuseibeh & Easterbook, 2000). Some examples of techniques for requirements analysis include: introspection, interviews, questionnaires etc.

Components of Requirements Analysis

In Nuseibeh and Easterbook, (2000), the core activities of Requirements Engineering are outlined as follows: eliciting requirements; modeling and analyzing requirements; communicating requirements; agreeing requirements; and evolving requirements. However conceptually these tasks represent a finer-grained set of tasks/processes compared to the more generally accepted task definition in RE which consist of:

1. **Eliciting requirements:** This is the process of communicating with users (clients) and gathering requirements about the system in question. It comprises the activities and processes that enable the gathering and understanding of the goals, objectives, and motives for building a proposed software system (Cheng & Atlee, 2007).

2. **Analyzing requirements:** The task involves the verification and validation of the said requirements with the user/client and could require a few iterations of the same. This task (and the task of eliciting requirements)

could also combine the task of modeling requirements as outlined by Nuseibeh & Easterbook (2000). Modeling consists of a set of well-defined properties or an abstract description of the system, which can be used to establish high-level goals and tasks of the system. For example a data model of a large cloud computing system might be used to inform the storage technologies (both hardware and software) used to implement the system.

3. **Recording requirements:** Recording requirements consists of an explicit description of the requirements, aims and goals of the software system in question. This task involves all the processes that involve documenting such requirements descriptions. Several languages (both formal and informal) have been suggested for the purpose documenting software requirements. Some of the various languages are discussed in (Wieringa, 1996).

The process of requirements engineering involves integrating these said activities into the software developmental process, which commonly takes place prior to system design. The anticipation of challenges created by future software systems has drawn some interest in empirical methods that go beyond the standard methods for requirements engineering and guidelines for best practices in requirements engineering. In Cheng & Atlee (2000), some focus is given to the direction of future Requirements Engineering practices. In their work, they identify various challenges in requirements engineering posed by emerging and future software needs. They make a distinction between the challenges faced by both the requirements engineering and software engineering research communities in that requirements engineering problems reside in the problem space while software engineering problems reside in the solution space. That is, requirements are written descriptively in terms of the environment while when software engineering is concerned, the descriptions are written in terms of their effect on the proposed system.

In any case, each of these instances will be affected by the nature of the system in question, in this case – social computing software. The distinction made by Cheng & Atlee (2000) closely fits with the categories of challenges of social computing applications which we described in section 3 – i.e behavioral considerations (social issues) and system considerations (technical issues), thus meaning that the requirements engineer should be concerned with social / behavioral issues whilst the software engineer should be concerned with system / technical issues.

Problems in Requirements Capture / Design

In the requirements engineering community, it is a well-known fact that some of the problems that may occur during the design and development of social software systems may come from the inadequacy of attention paid to social context. Even in standard software requirements analysis, it is also argued that some of the difficulties are because of political and cultural factors (Goguen & Linde, 1993). For example, in the context of museums and cultural spaces how would one understand the information needs of a visitor without practical experience of the tasks performed by a visitor; or through observation of a visitor? Before we expand on such social-centric issues, we briefly outline some of the existing challenges of software requirements analysis. Some of these include:

1. **Insufficient input from the customer/client:** The customer might not participate sufficiently during the requirements gathering stages. This might also be because of poor communication between the requirements engineer(s) and the customer because of several factors such as distance (in the case of an offshore software development model),

frequency of meetings between both parties etc

2. **The customer may not fully understand the requirements:** The customer may not be able to identify with the requirements elicited by the requirements engineer. In an iterative requirements gathering cycle, it is important for the client/customer to confirm and validate the requirements elicited by the requirements engineer. The inability of the client to do this may slow down the software development process. This might lead to very poor understanding of the requirements gathered by the requirements engineer.

3. **The customer may not be able to articulate the requirements of the system:** As the customer may not be adept with specific technical details of the system, certain requirements may be difficult to convey to the requirements engineer, which may end up being omitted entirely.

4. **Conflicting user interests:** Difficulty of balancing priorities of user requirements, which also includes the problem of balancing between what the user requires and what is possible.

5. **Poor interpretation of the requirements by the requirements engineer for various reasons:** This problem may derive from the first two points mentioned, but it is not limited to these points.

6. **Organizational Constraints:** It is often the case that the choice of techniques employed for requirements analysis may be chosen due to strict managerial guidelines. This process might be dependent on resources (e.g. time, cost, availability of equipment etc) available to the requirements team, and the chosen technique may not be appropriate for the task at hand (Nuseibeh & Easterbrook, 2000).

Generally the first two problems mentioned above arise because most often the client is not technically inclined and may not be able to express the important details of the system requirements that the requirements engineer requires. This problem commonly arises during system alteration; in addition to this, the client might not be aware of the full requirements of the system, and may not be able to inform the requirements engineer of other relevant and important details pertaining to the system.

It is intuitive that where these problems are realized, methods for eliciting requirements using ethnographic techniques may prove to be successful. In Goguen & Linde (1993), they discussed various techniques for requirements elicitation. Their argument was that requirements elicitation cannot be solved in a purely technological way because social context matters and is much more vital than in other phases in the software system developmental cycle.

It is apparent that a shift towards a new paradigm, that incorporates new modes of social interactions using digital technologies, would influence new directions of data management including the need for new managed services and organizational models. One would need to address specific technical considerations for the new factors that need to be taken into account for instance, as mentioned in the previous section under behavioral considerations: interface design, evaluation techniques; and under system considerations: application flexibility, risk assessment strategies. Other factors that may exist might include those that emanate from the features or properties of the system – for example: mobility and concurrency of users and devices in isolation (or in clusters) and the management or flow of information between users and devices. These characteristics might make it particularly challenging to uncover important user and system requirements using the standard techniques for requirements capture in software engineering.

4.2 Ethnography in Social Software Requirements Analysis

The elicitation of requirements for software systems that observe social contexts require a more formal and methodological approach to requirements analysis. One of such methods is to perform extensive analyses through observational techniques and other methods derived from ethnography to understand the challenges of the topic under study. In particular, complex areas of social computing software such as communication and collaboration. Our argument is that Ethnography could play a particularly useful role in the perception, elicitation and understanding of such system requirements.

Ethnography refers to the processes associated with developing a description that reflects the concerns, practices, problems and perspectives of those in a setting and the activities under study (Pettinari et al., 1998). A concise definition of ethnography is 'the study of human activities and processes'. There has been a long interest drawn to Ethnography (Hammersley & Atkinson, 1983) because of its empirical and qualitative methodologies (Lethbridge et al., 2004); and, strategies and methodologies that are appropriate for specifying group centric and social software applications. Such processes draw on a particular standpoint and could involve in-depth interviewing, observing, audio/video recording.

Why Ethnography?

It is intuitive that adopting methods and strategies for gaining a clear understanding of a users needs and requirements can potentially alleviate some of the problems that may develop when specifying the system at an early stage in the software developmental life cycle. The appeal of using ethnography for social computing applications draws from the growing acceptance that understanding the social character of 'real world, real time' activities is an important factor in software design and development (Hughes, 1995).

Some of the techniques discussed (as mentioned earlier) include introspection, interviews, questionnaires etc. It is true that some of these techniques can be categorized as ethnographic methods, however in many cases when used individually they possess systematic limitations (Goguen, 1993) and in some cases can or should be supplemented or replaced by additional techniques based on ethnomethodology, ethnography and sociolinguistics, though this is not always where the problem stops.

In the context of requirements analysis for social software, ethnography could prove to be an effective addition to the requirements analysis phase, as it could be used to inform user/system requirements through observation and examination of workflows for instance, and to identify those important underlying requirements that are sometimes overlooked or difficult to identify – where this may not have been originally possible. For example, understanding the flow of information in a distributed and concurrent environment can help identify standard tasks and procedures that could inform a software engineer's design of its workflow.

Ethnography also provides a means of assessing current work practices. For example, it could be used to evaluate current systems in a particular environment, in order to identify critical components of a work process. This relation is expanded upon in Ronkko et al. (2004), where ethnography is discussed with its relation to software engineering.

4.3 Overview of Problem and Illustration

In order to be successful at any kind of information management, one must consider the various complexities and critical factors that may govern various aspects of the process. For example, in the enterprise, are there any security policies that may govern the transfer and/or access of various kinds of information documents in a social application? If so, how should these policies be implemented? In a different light, in the context of museums, what are the roles of users that should be able to create and manage digital documents pertaining to museum exhibits?

A lot of these types of influences and decisions might be based on various business and organizational rules, and must be embedded in the systems in one way or the other. However where specific business rules may not be so apparent, the task of identifying those rules lies in the hands of the requirements engineer. And as mentioned earlier, the current standard traditional techniques might be inadequate for the process of identifying such rules and may need to be supplemented by other techniques. To illustrate this problem, we discuss a problem common to several social computing systems such as social networks and wiki systems: we label this problem as 'The problem of emerging user roles and Groups'.

In social software such as wiki systems, social networks and collaborative software suites, there is the challenge of predicting user behavior on a system, as unexpected types of behavior may begin to emerge due to a variety of factors. For example, originally in the blogging community, the original types of users were the content creators (publishers) and the content readers (consumers). However, over the years new breeds of users began to emerge partly due to the emergence of newer social technologies to complement existing ones, and possibly due to new/changing user requirements that have continuously evolved over time.

As classified by Forrester's Social Technographics (2009), online consumers in these types of systems can be quantified based on their levels of participation. These classes of participation include: *creators*: users that generate content e.g. blog writers, uploaders of music, photos, videos and so on; *critics*: users that generate feedback data e.g. topic reviewers, participants of forums and content moderators; *collectors*: users that

retrieve content from a variety of sources using social technologies such as RSS and other web feed formats; *joiners*: users that simply maintain online profiles on social networks and engage in a variety of activities via their profiles; *spectators*: users that are generally classified as content consumers. Such users include: readers of blogs and wiki's, viewers of online videos etc; *inactives*: users that do not engage in any social media activities and don't fall into the aforementioned categories.

Though the topic of ethnography in software requirements analysis has been incubating for a while, we believe that given the current wave of social computing technologies and the expectations of the next generation of social computing software, it has never been as important as it is now to formally include ethnography in the requirements analysis process. For example, in the example given above, one could argue that a thorough ethnographic evaluation might be successful at uncovering this growing phenomenon of clans and groups emerging within social networks. An analysis of various kinds of users of a particular system might inform the ethnographer of the different kinds requirements to meet the needs for the different kinds of users.

In the next section, we take a look at Web 3.0 in the realm of cultural institutions (museum 3.0) and business organizations (enterprise 3.0), using these topic domains to further illustrate some of the challenges of SCT's.

5. ENTERPRISE 3.0 AND MUSEUM 3.0

So far, we have provided a general orientation to social computing. In this section we continue our discourse on social computing but we narrow this discussion to its adoption within organizational enterprise and cultural institutions. The current research in this space has been very much involved in identifying the ways in which so called 'Web

3.0 technologies' and online social networking environments are changing the ways in which people interact in various domains and settings.

Most recently, there have been increased expectations that new movements will be initiated towards the transformation of current information management systems to the next generation of information management systems. These expectations have generated a lot of buzz and fierce rivalry amongst several technology corporations such as Microsoft, Google, Amazon etc. To this end, there has been an even more renewed interest in social computing applications and the use of new digital contexts in various domains.

Before we expand on Enterprise 3.0 and Museum 3.0, we first look at where these concepts derive from – Web 3.0. Web 3.0 is a blanket term that was coined by John Markoff of the New York Times to represent the next forward-looking step of the Internet towards the semantic web and beyond. As Web 3.0 is inherently an extension of Web 2.0, it expands on previously established Web 2.0 technologies (which encompass virtually all common social computing technologies) such as social networking technologies, tagging & folksonomy technologies, search technologies etc and covers all combinations of technologies that will be used in the next generation of the web. Web 3.0 has been referred to by many as the Semantic Web (or web of meaning) (Bernes-Lee et al., 2001; Lassila & Hendler, 2007), the Service Web (Fensel, 2007) and the web of human communication and cooperation (Raffl et al., 2008). In transition, the business and cultural counterparts of Web 3.0 are Enterprise 3.0 and Museum 3.0 respectively.

In our discussion of social computing technologies with regards to these concepts in subsequent sections, we will pay particular focus on social networks. Unlike other forms of social computing technologies, social networks appear to be the most extensive, as they incorporate other forms of social computing and heterogeneous technologies all in one platform. As such, the examples we provide in this section will be heavily centered on them.

Social Networking (SN): as mentioned previously, is a specific aspect (or technology) of social computing. Social Networks generally incorporate a range of social computing technologies (such as email, instant messaging, tagging, photo sharing, video sharing etc.). SN's are very popular and provide significant benefits when utilized properly as physical networks, connections and affiliations can be orchestrated using the various tools and features embedded in the software.

5.1 Social Software in Enterprise

Enterprise 3.0 has seen a lot of debate in industry because of the different and sometimes conflicting interpretations of the concept. Though the adoption of Enterprise 2.0 (its predecessor) may not have been as wide as one would have expected, the proliferation of new social computing technologies and the popularity of mainstream social media services have called the question of Enterprise 3.0.

What do we mean by Enterprise 3.0 (or its predecessor, Enterprise 2.0)? These concepts simply refer to the use of Web 3.0 technologies in business / organizational contexts. Although the concept of Enterprise 3.0 appears to be new and emerging, social computing have been around since the very beginning of enterprise computing through technologies such as email, web and video conferencing, instant messaging, blogs etc, though these individual technologies have seen numerous future enhancements and iterations over the same period of time. However, although some of these technologies might work well for communication and collaboration, businesses and researchers are beginning to consider social networks in the workplace (Neumann and Erol, 2009).

A recent report by NewsGator Technologies has shown that 7 out of 10 companies are investigating the potential use/adoption of social computing technologies. In the same study, it was revealed that there is no clear understanding of what Enterprise 2.0 actually is which is not surprising as Enterprise 2.0 carries different meanings depending on the person.

Adoption

In the enterprise, social networks are commonly referred to as '*Enterprise Social Networks*'. As one would expect, social computing technologies in the enterprise differ from their mainstream consumer oriented counterparts. These technologies are taken and applied to various domains in different combinations where each domain formalizes the said technologies to meet different challenges and requirements that may conform to a particular set of business goals or organizational constraints. So for example, in a mainstream social network a user would normally be able to upload personal photos and videos of perhaps a holiday trip, however in an enterprise social network such personal digital effects would not be important to the business and as such there may be no facility for photo / video upload or at least not intended for that purpose.

The market for vendors of enterprise social computing technologies and their off-the-shelf solutions has grown significantly over the past few years. Some industry solutions that provide social computing capabilities for communication and collaboration in the work place include: Lotus Notes (from IBM Corporation) and SharePoint (from Microsoft Corporation). SharePoint and Lotus Notes both provide various tools and services that simplify the process of various workplace tasks such as content management, document sharing, document authoring etc. Such tools are coming as a response to the increasing interest and adoption of these technologies in the enterprise because of some of the potential benefits of these technologies. However the challenges of adopting social computing technologies in the enterprise are not trivial. Several factors (for example organizational factors, social factors, technological factors) need to be addressed before these types of systems can be realized. We expand on two of the main problems that hinder or delay the adoption of social computing technologies in the enterprise.

Challenges of Adopting Social Computing Technologies in Enterprise

1. **Business Case for the Technology:** As with any organizational change initiative, one must present a compelling business case to justify the claim that the deployment of new solutions to replace existing solutions or services makes good business sense. In the case of social computing technologies in the enterprise, it may be difficult to present a good business justification that the adoption of these technologies will be beneficial to the organization as the argument "it worked for that company, so it will work for us" might not always be applicable because the deployment of social software in businesses is not as clear-cut as it may seem as companies are naturally structured differently and may require different types of SCT configurations. Also, it is not always the case that a company requires social computing software. Through examination of various organization specific criteria, these companies still need to address whether SCT's are viable for their businesses and their company cultures. This has led to the 'readiness evaluation metric', a metric used to determine whether a company needs social computing technologies and the formats in which they need it in, developed by NewsGator Technologies, a company that assists enterprises in social media adoption.

2. **The sentiment of 'social' networking in the enterprise:** One of the very many misconceptions of Social networking in the enterprise is the way it is presented in its consumer/commercial contexts. In fact many organizations oppose the idea of 'social networking' style participation and communication and argue that it does not have any place in the enterprise because of

the 'social' nature of the tool and various technical and organizational concerns over the use of the technology. Some of these issues and concerns include (i) concerns over security and privacy of documents and proprietary corporate information (ii) concerns over integration of existing systems with new untested systems – following the principles of most I.T managers *"if it is not broken, don't fix it!"*.

5.2 Social Software in Museums

Museum 3.0 is a holistic term that incorporates various processes and methods including multiple forms of analogue and digital technologies both privately and publicly owned which describe the adoption of Web 3.0 (or strategies to incorporate Web 3.0 technologies) in cultural institutions such as museums, galleries and other collecting bodies. One can think of Museum 3.0 as the synthesis of various technologies and practices leaning towards the enrichment of the overall museum experience both from the visitor and curators perspective.

In recent times, there has been a lot of interest in the modernization of museums through the instauration of a combination of various analogue and digital technologies social computing technologies. The aim of museum 3.0 is to improve productivity and collaboration of people (users/ entities) by putting a digital user experience within the bounds of the traditional workflow of a visitors experience at a museum. Technologies such as audio tour guides and personalized PDA based tour guides have almost ubiquitously replaced other forms of tour-guided media such as leaflets, handouts, brochures etc.

Previous work in this area have investigated the use of social software in mobile and PDA based guides (Gallud et. al, 2007; Huang et. al, 2008); personalized access to digital museum collections using semantic-driven recommendations (Aroyo et al., 2008); collaborative models to predict visitor locations in museums (Bohnert et al., 2008); tools that promote social interactions between visitors through cooperative and educational games (Laurillau & Patern, 2004); the design of adaptive museum guides (Goren-Bar et. al, 2005); just to name a few. Evaluative methods of such experiments have been known to be performed using ethnographic techniques. For example, Vom Lehn et al. (2007) reported on an analysis of video-recordings and field observations of visitors' actions and interactions of a gestural interface and a touch screen panel connected to a large projection screen which was deployed at a major exhibition at Tate Britain. The report explored visitors' interactions with and around the systems, how they configured the space around the installation and how they examined and discovered their properties.

In the next section, we expand on two of the main problems that hinder or delay the adoption of social computing technologies in this space.

Challenges of Adopting Social Computing Technologies in Cultural Institutions

1. **Failure of full adoption:** Several of the social computing technologies and other forms of technology solutions in museums have been deployed on a trial basis or in small scale deployments. This might be a reason for slow adoption rate by consumers in this domain even though the research in this space on SCT's is very agile.

2. **Conversion Problems:** Cultural museums are trying to move forward with technology to improve visitors understanding and experience; however there are various challenges with regards to converting various museum collections. Some of which originate because of the types of collection and also because of other factors such as cost of conversion, time scale of conversion, possible disruptions to museum facilities etc.

5.3 Benefits of Social Software

There are several advantages of a shift towards the full adoption of SCT's in cultural institutions and organizational enterprise. In the case of cultural institutions, this includes improved financial capitalization through the realization of new untapped business models, numerous benefits to visitors and a potential positive impact on the tourism industry as a whole.

As highlighted in the introduction, there are several specific instances in which social computing technologies have become invaluable. We expand on each of these instances:

1. **Information Sharing:** Information sharing through blogs and RSS have almost ubiquitously replaced other forms of information publishing mediums. Blogging platforms accompanied with RSS technologies are the most common and prevalent social computing technologies. In a business / enterprise context, social computing technologies can be particularly useful for helping employees to find relevant information resources or skills more quickly and efficiently.

2. **Communication:** social computing technologies can enable the curator of a museum to be more productive with his staff and visitors. SCT's can also give the curator new ways of showing his collection in ways that bring his knowledge to the world in a more tangible and meaningful manner.

Another instance where communication is improved through the use of social computing technologies is outsourcing, which is the transfer of business functions to third party service providers. In any outsourcing model, one must carefully consider all the various governance and knowledge management issues that may ensue given the facts about all the relevant parties involved.

One of the widely known problems of outsourcing is the transfer of knowledge management. In an offshore model, this problem could be particularly difficult because of the numerous problems relevant to the transfer of specification and requirements information. One of such problems could be from the use of tools that are not efficient enough to communicate requirements to the outsourcing service provider. Expanding on the key problem of communication in outsourcing, SCT's can provide the means to possibly alleviate this problem completely, provided the right technologies are used correctly. Various organizations adopt different communication strategies for their outsourced operations. The adoption of SCT's in this context can provide multilayer communicate channels between the relevant parties involved – providing a record of the projects progress and any changes that have occurred over a period of time.

3. **Collaboration:** The adoption of SCT's can create enhanced collaborative communication channels. In the context of the enterprise, this can increase employee engagement. It also has the potential to counteract departmental 'divides' thus maximizing on the potential of the organization to share and better manage organizational skills and resources. However this might not be seen as an advantage in some organizations because of privacy concerns.

6. CONCLUSION

In this chapter, we discussed the aspect of social interaction with respect information management systems. A discussion of the topic of Social Computing and Web 3.0 was also given with specific applications of the said technologies in museums and the enterprise. This overview presented some challenges and benefits of the adoption of social computing technologies in each of these contexts. In this chapter, we claim that specific aspects of social computing make it difficult to uncover requirements for such systems. We propose the formal inclusion of ethnography in the software requirements analysis phase for social software design, as we believe ethnography and other practices from ethnomethodology will be particularly useful for uncovering the requirements of social centric software systems. Potential future work topics include: (i) developing a way of evaluating social computing technologies. (ii) developing a description and a set of guidelines for the inclusion of ethnography in requirements design alongside a formal way of specifying the ethnography.

7. REFERENCES

Addington, D. M., & Schodek, D. L. (2005). *Smart materials and new technologies: For the architecture and design professions*. Boston: Architectural Press.

Aroyo, L., Stash, N., Wang, Y., Gorgels, P., & Rutledge, L. (2008). CHIP demonstrator: Semantics-driven recommendations and museum tour generation. In *Semantic web* ([). Berlin: Springer.]. *Lecture Notes in Computer Science, 4825,* 879–886. doi:10.1007/978-3-540-76298-0_64

Bernes-Lee, T., Hendler, J., & Lassila, O. (2001, May). The semantic web. *Scientific American.*

Boaden, R., & Lockett, G. (1991). Information technology, information systems and information management: Definition and development. *European Journal of Information Systems, 1,* 23–32. doi:10.1057/ejis.1991.4

Bohnert, F., Zukerman, I., Berkovsky, S., Baldwin, T., & Sonenberg, L. (2008). Using collaborative models to adaptively predict visitor locations in museums. In *Proceedings of the 5th international conference on Adaptive Hypermedia and Adaptive Web-Based Systems* (pp. 42–51). Berlin: Springer

Bovey, J. (2005). The content management handbook. *Program: Electronic library and information systems, 39*(4), 387 – 388.

Bush, V. (1945, July). As we may think. *Atlantic Magazine.* Retrieved from http://www.theatlantic.com/doc/194507/bush

Cheng, B. H. C., & Atlee, J. M. (2007). Research directions in requirements engineering. In *Future of Software Engineering* (pp. 285–303). Washington, DC: IEEE Computer Society. doi:10.1109/FOSE.2007.17

Coleman, J. S. (1994). *Foundations of social theory*. Cambridge, MA: Harvard University Press.

Daft, R. L., & Lengel, R. H. (1984). Information richness: A new approach to managerial behavior and organization design. In B. Staw & L. L. Cummings (Eds.), *Research in Organizational Behavior, 6,* 191-233.

Daft, R. L., & Lengel, R. H. (1986). Organizational information requirements, media richness and structural design. *Management Science, 32*(5), 554–571. doi:10.1287/mnsc.32.5.554

Daft, R. L., Lengel, R. H., & Trevino, L. K. (1987). Message equivocality, media selection and manager performance: Implications for information systems. *Management Information Systems Quarterly, 11,* 355–366. doi:10.2307/248682

Felt, A., & Evans, D. (2008, May 22). Privacy protection for social networking APIs. Paper presented at W2SP, Oakland, CA.

Fensel, P. D. (2007). Service web 3.0 [WI'07 and IAT'07 Joint Keynote].

Finkelstein, A., & Kramer, J. (2000). Software engineering: A roadmap. In *Proceedings of the Conference on The Future of Software Engineering* (pp. 3–22). New York: ACM.

Forrester Research, Inc. (2009, August 25). The broad reach of social technologies.

Gallud, J. A., Lozano, M., Tesoriero, R., & Penichet, V. M. R. (2007). Using mobile devices to improve the interactive experience of visitors in art museums. In *Human-Computer Interaction: Interaction Platforms and Techniques* ([]. Berlin: Springer.]. *Lecture Notes in Computer Science, 4551,* 280–287. doi:10.1007/978-3-540-73107-8_31

Goguen, J. (1993, January). Social issues in requirements engineering. In *Proceedings, Requirements Engineering* (pp. 194–195). doi:10.1.1.32.8909

Goguen, J., & Linde, C. (1993). Techniques for requirements elicitation. In *IEEE International Symposium on Requirements Engineering,* San Diego, CA (pp. 152–164). New York: Academic Press.

Goren-Bar, D., Graziola, I., Rocchi, C., Pianesi, F., Stock, O., & Zancanaro, M. (2005). Designing and redesigning an affective interface for an adaptive museum guide. In *Affective Computing and Intelligent Interaction* ([]. Berlin: Springer.]. *Lecture Notes in Computer Science, 3784,* 939–946. doi:10.1007/11573548_120

Grudin, J. (1994). Computer-supported cooperative work: History and focus. *Computer, 27*(5), 19–26. doi:10.1109/2.291294

Grudin, J. (1994). Groupware and social dynamics: Eight challenges for developers. *Communications of the ACM, 37*(1), 92–105. doi:10.1145/175222.175230

Hammersley, M., & Atkinson, P. (1983). *Ethnography: Principles in practice.* London: Tavistock Publications.

Huang, Y. P., Chang, T. W., & Sandnes, F. E. (2008). A ubiquitous interactive museum guide. In *Proceedings of the 5th international conference on Ubiquitous Intelligence and Computing* (pp. 720–731). Berlin: Springer-Verlag.

Hughes, J. (1995, February). Ethnography, plans and software engineering. *IEEE Colloquium on CSCW, 2,* 1–8.

Lassila, O., & Hendler, J. (2007). Embracing "Web 3.0". *IEEE Internet Computing, 11*(3), 90–93. doi:10.1109/MIC.2007.52

Laurillau, Y., & Patern, F. (2004). Supporting museum co-visits using mobile devices. *Mobile Human-Computer Interaction MobileHCI 2004* ([]. Berlin: Springer.]. *Lecture Notes in Computer Science, 3160,* 451–455. doi:10.1007/978-3-540-28637-0_55

Lethbridge, T. C., Sim, S. E., & Singer, J. (2004). Software anthropology: Performing field studies in software companies. *Lingua,* 281–319.

Neumann, G., & Erol, S. (2008). From a social Wiki to a social workflow system. In *Post-proceedings of BPM 2008: 1st Workshop on BPM and Social Software.* Milan: Springer.

Nuseibeh, B., & Easterbrook, S. (2000). Requirements engineering: A roadmap. In *Proceedings of the Conference on the Future of Software Engineering* (pp. 35–46). New York: ACM.

Orlikowski, W. J., & Hofmann, J. D. (1997). An improvisational model of change management: The case of groupware technologies. *MIT Sloan Management Review, 38,* 11–21.

Pettinari, C., Heath, C. C., & Luff, P. (1998). Notes toward an applied ethnography [Technical report]. London: Kings College work interaction technology research group.

Raffl, C., Hofkirchner, W., Fuchs, C., & Schafranek, M. (2008). The web as techno-social system: The emergence of web 3.0. In Trappl, R. (Ed.), *Cybernetics and Systems* (pp. 604–609). Vienna: Austrian Society for Cybernetic Studies.

Ronkko, K., Lindeberg, O., & Dittrich, Y. (2002). 'Bad practice' or 'bad methods': Are software engineering and ethnographic discourses incompatible? In *Proceedings of the 2002 International Symposium on Empirical Software Engineering* (p. 204). Washington DC: IEEE Computer Society.

Strater, K., & Lipford, H. R. (2008). Strategies and struggles with privacy in an online social networking community. In *Proceedings of the 22nd British HCI Group Annual Conference on HCI* (pp. 111-119).

Strater, K., & Richter, H. (2007). Examining privacy and disclosure in a social networking community. In *Proceedings of the 3rd symposium on usable privacy and security* (pp. 157-158). New York: ACM.

Sutton, M. J. D. (1996). *Document management for the enterprise: Principles, techniques and applications*. New York: John Wiley & Sons, Inc.

Trevino, L. K., Lengel, R. H., Bodensteiner, W., & Gerloff, E. (1987). *Managerial media choice: The interactive influences of cognitive style and message equivocality*. Paper presented at the meeting of the Academy of Management, Anaheim, CA.

Vom-Lehn, D., Hindmarsh, J., Luff, P., & Heath, C. (2007). Engaging constable: Revealing art with new technology. In *CHI '07: Proceedings of the SIGCHI conference on human factors in computing systems* (pp. 1485–1494). New York: ACM.

Wieringa, R. J. (1996). *Requirements engineering: Frameworks for understanding*. New York: John Wiley & Sons, Inc.

KEY TERMS & DEFINITIONS

Information: typically consists of various forms of structured and/or unstructured data in both analogue and digital formats and can be recognized as a resource independent of its physical properties.

Information Management (IM): IM is defined as the management, collection, retrieval, enrichment and maintenance of information.

Social Computing Applications (SCA): SCA's include software that derive from a set of tools and technologies that support any form of social interaction or social behavior.

Requirements Engineering (RE): involves all the processes and tasks that go into establishing the user needs and expectations of a newly proposed (or previously existing) system/product.

Ethnography: Ethnography refers to the study of human tasks, activities and processes.

Web 3.0: Web 3.0 is a blanket term that was coined by John Markoff of the New York Times to represent the next forward-looking step of the Internet towards the semantic web and beyond.

Museum 3.0: Museum 3.0 is a holistic term that incorporates various processes and methods which describe the adoption of Web 3.0 in cultural institutions such as museums, galleries and other collecting bodies.

Chapter 6
Social Computing:
Harnessing Enterprise Social Networking and the Relationship Economy

Chaka Chaka
Walter Sisulu University, South Africa

ABSTRACT

This chapter investigates instances of social computing and the affordances it offers enterprise social networking. Employing a thematic synthesis approach, it argues that social computing in the form of blogs, wikis, social networking sites, and virtual worlds serves as an ideal platform that enterprises can tap into for enterprise social networking purposes. In addition, the chapter explores the way in which social computing can help enterprises leverage the relationship economy inherent in enterprise social networking. Against this background, the chapter provides, first, an overview of social computing and enterprise social networking. Second, it characterises, using examples of real world applications obtained through thematic synthesis, how enterprises can exploit instances of social computing cited above to extract business benefits from them. Third, it outlines how enterprises can harness the relationship economy, Value 2.0 and Prosumerism 2.0 to enhance their brand image and boost their online presence. Fourth, it presents caveats regarding how terms such as enterprise social networking, wikinomics, collective intelligence, relationship economy, Prosumerism 2.0 and Value 2.0 may degenerate into mantras. Fifth and last, the chapter delineates future trends likely to characterise enterprise social computing.

INTRODUCTION

Social computing (SC) is making its mark in different spheres of life. For instance, it is an emerging trend in learning, social life, business and organisations. In fact, it is virally diffusing through and colonising almost every aspect of human interaction. Mostly, it facilitates communication, collaboration and socialisation and fosters online networks, friendships, and relationships among individuals and groups or communities, thereby harnessing their relational and social capital. These two forms of capital have to do, in this case, with values embedded

DOI: 10.4018/978-1-61692-904-6.ch006

in and accruing from online relationships and social networks individuals or groups have among themselves while utilising SC applications such as blogs, wikis, social networking sites, and virtual worlds. In relation to enterprises, in particular, SC is increasingly becoming part of the enterprise computing fabric, having outgrown its Cinderella status. So, the affordances and efficiencies SC can provide to enterprises are many and varied. In this regard, affordances are potential benefits - known or unknown - any SC application has that enable users to undertake tasks in their SC environments (see McLoughlin & Lee, 2008), while efficiencies are the value-adds or enhanced performances that SC applications offer users at any given time. These affordances and efficiencies range from the relationship economy, Value 2.0 to Prosumerism 2.0. The last three concepts here refer to the economy deriving from online relationships, business value emanating from SC, and *production* and *consumerism* mediated through SC, respectively.

Moreover, by its very nature, SC offers dynamic, ubiquitous, distributed, real-time, collaborative, many-to-many, value-based and personalised enterprise computing. All this holds the potential for competitive edge for enterprises leveraging SC applications. Instances of the latter are: blogs; wikis; social networking sites; and virtual worlds. Based on this, the chapter explores the manner in which enterprise social networking on the one hand, and the relationship economy, Value 2.0, and Prosumerism 2.0 on the other hand, can be harnessed within the context of SC. Most importantly, thematic analysis was used as a method to select relevant examples of real world applications of SC tools like blogs, wikis, social networking sites, and virtual worlds in the enterprise social networking domain. Thematic analysis is a method for analysing data in primary qualitative research studies with a view to identifying and developing themes. It is similar to meta-synthesis and meta-ethnography. The latter are approaches to synthesising research

whose goal is to produce a new and integrative interpretation of findings. They entail bringing together findings, examining them, discovering the essential features, and synthesising them into a transformed whole (Thomas & Harden, 2008).

However, in this chapter thematic analysis is used in a very narrow sense to refer to identifying and analysing topical and descriptive themes related to online search engine and database search results (see Adesope & Nesbit, 2010) in respect of given key phrases relevant to this chapter. These key phrases were: enterprise social computing; enterprise social computing platforms; enterprise social computing applications; and enterprise social computing – best practices for blogs, wikis, social networking sites, and virtual worlds. That is, a desktop online search (see *Table 1*) of these key phrases was mounted through the following search engines and databases: Google; Google Scholar; Bing; Educational Resources Information Center (ERIC); and Business-Technology Solution (BTS) database. Two selection criteria informed the search: recency/currency and relevance of information. In the first instance, the search was confined to a four-year time span - 2005-2009; in the second instance, relevant information was given priority in the search hits or returns.

Furthermore, a literature search was undertaken by reviewing and selecting online articles providing instances of best practices of enterprise social networking from search returns. Inclusion and exclusion criteria were employed in selecting articles. For example, an article was considered when it focused on any of the four cited SC applications (e.g., blogs, wikis, social networking sites, or virtual worlds) and discussed any of the key phrases identified earlier on. In addition, an article was given preference when it reflected instances of the following networking practices: collective intelligence; crowd wisdom; collective knowledge; network effect/network economy; the long tail economics; collective power of simulation; relational or relationship capital; and social

Table 1. Sources used to search for instances of best practices of enterprise social networking

Search Engine or Database	Description	Usage	Key Phrases	Selection Criteria
Google	Google's search engine	Used for multi-purpose online search needs	Enterprise social computing; enterprise social computing platforms; enterprise social computing applications; and enterprise social computing—best practices for blogs, wikis, social networking sites, or virtual worlds	Recency/Currency (2005-2009), relevance
Google Scholar	Google owned academic search engine	Employed for searching for academic publications	Same as above	Recency/Currency (2005-2009), Relevance
Bing	Microsoft's beta search engine	Utilized for multi-purpose online search needs	Same as above	Recency/Currency (2005-2009), Relevance
ERIC	A US-supported national information system	Provides access to education database (e.g. journal articles, research reports, conference papers, and books	Same as above	Recency/Currency (2005-2009), Relevance
BTS	IGI Global's business and technology database	Provides users with access to a variety of journals, books, and cases on information and technology in the business and management domain	Same as above	Recency/Currency (2005-2009), Relevance

capital. But when an article did not meet these two criteria it was not considered as appropriate.

On the basis of the preceding paragraphs, the following aspects constitute the major sections of this chapter: social computing and enterprise social networking: an overview; tapping into enterprise social networking—affordances and best practices; harnessing the relationship economy; buzzwords or hype?; and future trends.

SOCIAL COMPUTING AND ENTERPRISE SOCIAL NETWORKING: AN OVERVIEW

Social computing (SC) is part of the Social Web, the Editable Web, or the Programmable Web (see Lakshmanan, Pradeep & Harish, 2010). There are three perspectives from which SC is viewed in this chapter. First, it is a collective term referring to a number of new social applications (e.g., wikis, blogs, instant messaging, social networking sites, media sharing sites, and virtual worlds) and services (e.g., Internet protocol television, voice over the Internet protocol, and personal broadcasting) that foster collective action and social interaction online aided by multimedia information and content (see De Ferrari, 2007; Parameswaran & Whinston, 2007a, 2007b). Second, it is a form of computing that enables, encourages and captures especially unstructured interactions between individuals. Such interactions and individuals are the basis for virtual communities such as communities of practice, communities of interest, and communities of trust. In this sense, SC emanates from the confluence of a quest to harness the interactions of communities of individuals that are facilitated by social software platforms (see Sarner, Drakos & Prentice, 2008).

Third, SC is essentially about the manner in which people use the Social Web to serve their personal and social needs and interests in virtual environments. It is about putting technology - in particular the Social Web - in the hands of individuals and communities and allowing them to use it in the way that suits them. This evolving social use of the Web has given rise to a people-centric Web characterised by user-created content, repurposed/remixed content, user-driven artifacts, and user-generated applications. This user-centric development has, in turn, spawned the concept of prosumerism.

Thus, by its very nature, SC moves computing to the edge of the network, thereby empowering individual users to use the Web to harness their creativity, expertise and collective intelligence. SC also taps into lightweight computing tools that facilitate the mashing up of applications and grass-roots innovations by individual users. Additionally, it facilitates a shift from desktop computing to network-centric computing (Parameswaran & Whinston, 2007a; see Charron, Favier & Li, 2006). This move has the potential to radically transform the computing playing field in relation to how individuals interact with the Web. In light of the above, SC encompasses myriad social technologies and tools. These include, on the one hand, blogs, microblogs, instant messaging, wikis, podcasts, social networks, social bookmarks, virtual worlds, and really simple syndication (RSS). On the other hand, they encapsulate search engines (e.g., Google, Firefox, and Bing), open source software, SlideShare, Scribd, Google Docs, and so on (Charron et al., 2006). Given this, there are instances where SC assumes and leverages both cloud and mobile computing and vice versa.

For its part, enterprise social networking refers to the use of social computing networking by enterprises with a view to tapping apparent business value inherent within SC applications. It is an equivalent of Enterprise 2.0 – the use of Web 2.0 applications within the enterprise environment. At the heart of enterprise social networking is the desire to pool diverse external talents and utilise them for enterprise purposes. This can come in the form of crowd sourcing or collective intelligence. There are three main drivers of enterprise social networking: *consumerisation*, *wikinomics* and *networks*. Consumerisation refers to a process in which social technologies traditionally meant for consumers/users are later adopted by enterprises for business use. It is the evolution of social technologies into enterprise technologies. In this way, enterprise social networking facilitates the consumerisation of social technologies and tools and leads to the rise and evolution of social media.

Wikinomics is the online business model advocated by Tapscott and Williams (2006). Based on the Web 2.0 ethos and informed particularly by the wiki idea, this model is underpinned by four new competitive principles: openness, peering, sharing and acting globally. Openness is about enterprises sourcing and harvesting external talent and human capital from outside networks for the purpose of enhancing their performance while peering is related to partnering with peers for co-production purposes. The case in point is co-producing software, media and entertainment brands. This means wikinomics entails a variety of peer production models within an enterprise social networking environment. Sharing, in this case, has to do with smart enterprises sharing some aspects of their business intelligence and their intellectual property with critical business partners on a mutual fund basis. And acting globally means that enterprises need to be global participants in terms of markets, technologies and customers (see Tapscott & Williams, 2006) if they are to have a competitive edge over their competitors. Finally, networks here can comprise enterprises, customers, consumers, individuals, and communities that enterprises tap into through enterprise social networking applications. The bottom line in this case is the value, the competitive edge, the competitive intelligence, and the return on investment (ROI) that enterprises can extract from exploiting such networks. For instance, some of the affordances enterprises can extract from enterprise social networking are the relationship economy (Deragon, 2008a, 2008b), Prosumerism 2.0 (Chaka, 2010a), and Value 2.0 (Porta, House, Buckley & Blitz, 2009).

TAPPING INTO ENTERPRISE SOCIAL NETWORKING: AFFORDANCES AND BEST PRACTICES

Social computing tools such as blogs, wikis, social networking sites, and virtual worlds lend themselves well as enterprise social networking applications that enterprises can exploit for business purposes. When exploiting these applications, enterprises are in a position not only to extract business value and engage in peer production models but to increase their online footprint as well. Thus, this section serves two purposes: it outlines the types of online affordances offered by blogs, wikis, social networking sites, and virtual worlds; and it delineates some of the enterprises utilising these four enterprise social networking applications as instances of best practices.

Blogs and their Enterprise Uses

As instances of enterprise social networking applications, blogs have several enterprise uses. For example, they can be used as:

- Tools for cross-functional communication with employees, managers, clients, partners and investors, thereby delivering critical real-time enterprise intelligence to these stakeholders
- Forums for product/service evaluation, feedback and recommendations
- A means for sourcing company information open to the public
- Instruments for competitive intelligence by sourcing quality research, harvesting

current collective business views and perceptions, and new business solutions
- A platform for promoting company brands to the potential global market
- Tools for knowledge sharing, team knowledge management and team project management
- Virtual environments for networking with a view to tapping into stakeholders' expertise and for co-production of content
- A platform for product/brand development and for leveraging mass user contributions (see Cobb, 2008).

There are several documented instances of best enterprise practices involving blogging. Among these are the following: IBM; Intel; Quark; Sun Microsystems; Microsoft; Google; Macromedia; Wal-Mart; Boeing Commercial Airplanes; McDonald's; and Walt Disney (Disney). There are even CEO (Chief Executive Officer) and employee blogging (Wyld, 2007). The business models of these enterprises that harness blogging for enterprise purposes, logically fit into what can be termed *blogonomics* (blogs and economics) following Tapscott and Williams' (2006) concept of wikinomics.

At IBM, for instance, internal blog usage and participation have spread spirally. At one point, the company's BlogCentral boasted more than 30 000 registered users and 31 000 blogs with more than 74 000 posts and 71 000 comments. Blogging is then shared with social bookmarking within the company (IBM, 2007). In this way the company is able to leverage the collective intelligence (CI) of both its internal and external users. For Sun Microsystems, blogging is seen as an integral part of its organisational culture. The company offers both employee and CEO blogging. Employees, customers and other users are allowed to post comments to the CEO blog concerning the company's products and services (Sun Microsystems, 2006). This practice, undoubtedly, represents one way in which the company tries to tap into users' relationship capital with a view to sourcing both their CI and collective wisdom.

One company that applies *blogonomics* to its business environment and manages to synergise enterprise social networking applications so as to extract maximum business spin-offs is Disney. As a giant conglomerate of multiple divisions spanning, for example, Disney Studios, the ABC cable network, film and music studios, and consumer products, Disney experienced a crunch time in early 2004 as some of its divisions were losing business to their competitors. Then, from mid-2004, it set about implementing composite enterprise social networking tools - blogs, wikis and RSS - into its enterprise architecture. It overhauled its external web presence by leveraging blog technology: it created a customer blog platform to reach out to its customer base; and through its blog interface it was able to launch subtle and targeted advertising. This covered corporate information, product news, and gossip directed at different target groups and demographics (Creese, 2007).

In addition, Disney's ABC site began using RSS feed and content aggregation functionality so as to have a more dynamic web service. Moreover, its movie site allowed user review blogs and offered RSS movie news feeds to users. Most significantly, Disney exploited the RSS technology to broadcast web content to wireless devices, thereby tapping into new markets. Thus, using these enterprise social networking platforms both internally and externally, Disney was able to harness customer feedback, improve its corporate profile and image, open up new business opportunities, and increase its online footprint (see Creese, 2007).

Wikis and their Enterprise Affordances

The enterprise affordances of wikis encompass some of the uses stated above under blogs. In addition, in an enterprise social networking scenario wikis can be employed as:

- A documentation, content and knowledge generating, managing, archiving, sharing, and disseminating system
- An in-house knowledge base
- Communication and collaboration tools
- E-learning 2.0 deployment platform for organisational learning (e.g., training, workshops, meetings, etc., for employees)
- Project and resource management tools
- Repositories for training videos for new recruits and for collective memory
- A medium for virtual communities of practice or for user/customer groups
- Research and development (R&D) tools (e.g., product/brand development and evangelism, service provision, innovation initiatives, etc.)
- Marketing and customer relationship management (CRM) tools (Hasan & Pfaff, 2006; Gandhi, 2008).

On this score, examples of best enterprise wiki practices include the following: Google; Microsoft; Yahoo!; Amazon; Adobe; CommSecure; Lost Boys; Kodak; Sony; Philips; Nokia; Dresdner Kleinwort Wasserstein; Motorola; PDT Design; CoActive Digital; etc. For instance, CommSecure (in Australia) offers e-business solutions on a 24/7 basis. It uses an internal wiki to track the current status of each installation, and to document procedures for handling problems, alerts, changes in contact information, etc. Its wiki is updatable and everyone is encouraged to contribute to it (Wood, 2005). In another instance, PDT Design employs a wiki which replaces employee handbook and human resource documents. An open-source version of the wiki allows any employee to make posts and update or modify any entry. It also enables employees to share code issues on projects and post articles on new design trends, and post, add or change meeting agendas (Baverman, 2008). All this helps facilitate crowd sourcing and build the company's collective organisational memory.

In a different but related scenario, two small groups based at Nokia's Research Centre in Helsinki created their own wikis in 2004 - one to explore an alternative to e-mail, and the other to collaborate on solving specific product design problems. Since, then, a great number of Nokia's 68 000 employees use wikis to trade ideas, edit files, and update schedules and project status. Likewise, Dresdner Kleinwort Wasserstein (a London- and Frankfurt-based investment bank) deployed a Socialtext wiki programme in the same year. The adoption rate was so fast that the company subsequently launched its own corporate wiki for use by its employees (Carlin, 2007). These two cases exemplify both the viral spread of wikis and the triple power of collective intelligence, collective knowledge, and crowd sourcing synergised by enterprise wikis as instances of enterprise social networking applications.

SNSs and their Enterprise Social Networking Applications

SNSs have multiple enterprise applications in the context of enterprise social networking. Leveraged appropriately for enterprise value, SNSs can serve as an ideal competitive differentiator leading, at times, to competitive intelligence in a variety of ways. For example, they can be a platform for:

- Establishing business contacts and links
- Networking (networks of customers or partners, communities of practice, and communities of interest)
- CRM and offering customer-centric service
- Marketing, advertising and promoting products and services
- Increasing brand awareness
- Promoting issues of social concern or related to corporate social responsibility
- Profiling the company/business and enhancing corporate image, reputation and identity
- Sharing knowledge, views, opinions, etc.

- Recruiting and screening/reviewing potential candidates, clients, or partners (Marketing Leadership Council [MLC], 2008).

The following are some of the instances of best enterprise practices harnessing the benefits of enterprise social networking such as CI, the network effect and the long tail economics through SNSs in the Enterprise 2.0 environment: eBay; Amazon; Cisco Systems; Unilever; Xerox; Virgin Mobile; Toyota; JP Morgan; IBM; Burger King; McDonald's; Shell Oil; General Electric; Citigroup; UBS; Oracle; Motorola; FujiFilm Corporation; Casio Computer Co.; and Hitachi Ltd.

In this case, eBay represents a classic case of a company applying wikinomics with a view to synergising and harnessing CI, the network effect, relational and social capital, and the long tail economics. Having started in 1995 as an online auction and shopping website, eBay boasts – at the time of writing - more than 180 million registered global users and 1.7 billion daily page views (Olleros, 2006). It specialises in the selling and buying of a wide range of items: vehicles, electronics, sporting goods, clothing items, garden equipment, furniture, computers, jewellery, aeroplanes, etc. At any given time, it can list more than 25 million items for sale. Its success lies in the viral effect of its user and traffic metrics: its ability to bring together millions of users (people and businesses) to populate its website for buying and selling products and services globally. So, the greater the number of registered users buying and selling products at eBay, the more valuable its network becomes for new users on both sides of its market equation (Olleros, 2006; Tandefelt, 2008). Herein lies its ability to exploit the value of enterprise social networking in the form of the network economy (networks of networks) and the long tail economics.

Another classic instance of a company tapping into the network effect, relational and social capital, and the long tail economics by employing the wikinomics business model is Amazon. Amazon is an online shop selling items such as books, DVDs, software, toys, and furniture whose content is driven primarily by users. It encourages users to review, rate and recommend books, or films that are sold through its enterprise social networking platform. This practice enables potential customers to have a basic idea of the usability, quality and suitability of the products. The site is populated by user content (product previews, reviews, ratings and recommendations) (Tandefelt, 2008). All the company does, is provide an enterprise social networking platform for its users by harnessing their collective groundswell, network effect, and social capital and by applying the long tail approach to selling its products.

Enterprise Affordances of Virtual Worlds

As instances of enterprise social networking applications, virtual worlds (VWs) have enterprise affordances as well. In this context, they serve as ideal platforms for:

- Simultaneous immersive participation from multiple users
- Recruiting potential customers or partners
- Exhibiting and showcasing company brands and services
- Brand and service launches
- Marketing, advertising and branding products and services
- Conducting business or purchasing products
- Virtual monetisation purposes
- In-world meetings, workshops, seminars and conferences
- Enterprise simulations and role plays
- Scenario and project planning
- Corporate training and organisational learning
- Brand and service innovation bed tests

- Research and development (R&D) (Kish, 2007; Sun Microsystems, 2008).

There are many instances of businesses exploiting the affordances and the collective power of simulation offered by VWs. Among them are: American Apparel; Warner Bros.; Adidas; Microsoft; Xerox; Toyota; Nissan; Audi; Cisco Systems; Reuters; Reebok; IBM; and Dell. From this list, American Apparel and IBM warrant a close look as enterprise cases embracing wikinomics within virtual world environments. American Apparel - the Los Angeles-based trendy T-shirt maker - launched its virtual store in Second Life's metaverse on June 17, 2006. This store allows customers to purchase and pay for products in-world (for $1 or less). Customers can outfit their avatars with digital renderings of slim-cut T-shirts and dresses modelled on real-life merchandise. The retailer (American Apparel) often hires virtual sales clerks from among SL (Second Life) residents and test-markets certain new offerings (e.g., jeans) within its SL store a month or two before they hit real life store shelves. Anyone buying items during test-marketing (during the virtual launching of products) is offered a discount coupon on merchandise purchased in physical stores (Jana, 2006). In this context, American Apparel enables customers to exploit the collective power of simulation and the other affordances provided by SL wikinomics.

For its part, IBM owns islands - public and private - on SL. These islands serve as: virtual meeting places for current and former employees and executives; virtual retail areas for IBM customers to meet and discuss products; and information centres for marketing IBM's products and services to customers. For instance, one island has a Circuit City store for showcasing and testing out camcorders and HDTV (high definition television) sets. Additionally, IBM's presence on SL entails regular brainstorming sessions with clients. Moreover, it leverages SL as a platform to host virtual employee meetings and conferences for knowledge sharing purposes. Most importantly, it uses its SL's presence for collaborating with its various global R&D staffers and for experiments related to various aspects of its core business (Brandon, 2007; MLC, 2008). The company even has a Virtual Business Centre dedicated to experimenting with VWs as sales channels. This global virtual centre is anchored in English, German, Portuguese, Spanish, Italian, French, Dutch, and Asian languages. It allows IBM's employees to interface with customers regarding business solutions, content creation, purchasing software or hardware, and talking about the latest business practices. Herein lies IBM's desire to embrace the wikinomics model and its ability to harness the collective power of simulation of SL and the other affordances it provides.

HARNESSING THE RELATIONSHIP ECONOMY

Enterprise social networking applications do offer other affordances. Most importantly, they provide enterprises with value-added benefits. Among these affordances and benefits are the following: the relationship economy, Prosumerism 2.0 and Value 2.0. These three affordances are inter-related, and in particular, the last two feed off the first one.

The Relationship Economy

The relationship economy is intrinsically linked to relational capital which in turn is closely connected to social capital. Capital is that which creates value or adds value to something (see Deragon, 2008a). So, social capital encompasses different forms of connections and networks people establish with families, neighbours, friends, and colleagues. Such social capital is embedded in people's trust, shared identities, common beliefs, norms, and reputation (Cachia, Kluzer, Cabrera, Centeno & Punie, 2007). Given this, relational capital is the

type of capital harnessed in an enterprise social networking environment by users, employees, managers, customers, partners and other relevant stakeholders - through networks of relationships - in a given enterprise.

Thus, in this sense, the relationship economy encapsulates people, resources, and enterprise social networking technologies users are connected to in their virtual networks (see Deragon, 2008a) and everything that adds value to enterprise capital. It is the economy deriving from interconnected relationships and yielding collective relational capital that enterprises leverage through deploying enterprise social networking platforms. Most crucially, it serves as a competitive differentiator and a form of competitive intelligence for enterprise social networking. Understood in this way, the relationship economy is an enterprise model that is more relationship-oriented than simply business-centric. In the main, it is informed more by features falling under the first set than those under the second set in the following relationship- vs. business-centric dichotomy:

- Relationship-driven vs. product-oriented
- Win-win vs. win-lose
- Transparency vs. control
- Reputation vs. brand
- Conversations vs. mass communications
- Networks of relationships vs. pyramids/silos
- All sources of value count vs. only money matters (see Deragon, 2008a)

One way in which enterprises can harness the relationship economy within a competitive differentiation continuum is through tapping into: collective intelligence (CI); collective knowledge systems; the network effect; crowd sourcing; and the collective power of simulation. Enterprise social networking applications that are the main enablers of these five relationship economy based competitive differentiators are - for this chapter - blogs, wikis, SNSs (social networking sites),

Figure 1. Prosumerism 2.0 comprising 8C's and 4P's (Adapted from Chaka, 2010a)

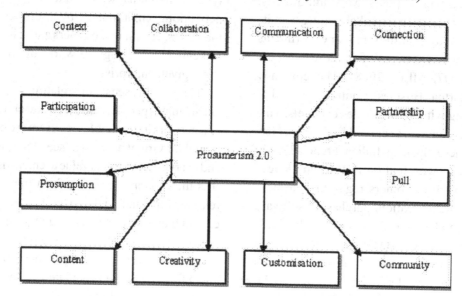

and VWs (virtual worlds), respectively (Chaka, 2010b).

The relationship economy derives from and redounds to wikinomics and the network economy. The latter is the economy spawned incrementally by networks of networks within the enterprise social networking universe. Such networks, in turn, have the potential to cascade spirally within the enterprise social networking environment of which they are a part. Here the bottom line is that as the number of users networking around and participating in the services and products offered by given enterprise social networking applications increases, so does the viral value attached to such services and products. Some of the enterprises exploiting this economy are Amazon, eBay, Facebook, MySpace, YouTube, Flickr, and Google (see Chaka, 2010b; Evans, 2008; Tandefelt, 2008).

Prosumerism 2.0 and Value 2.0

Two other aspects embodied by the relationship economy are Prosumerism 2.0 and Value 2.0. Prosumerism 2.0 is a blend for *production* and *consumerism* - with these two words deriving

from *producer* and *consumer* respectively. Some of its variations are *prosumption, produsage, produserism* and *user-generated brands* (*UGBs*). In this regard, Prosumerism 2.0 refers to an instance in which employees, customers and users add value to enterprise products/brands and services by harnessing composite enterprise social networking applications. They can do so by posting feedback, comments, views, opinions, complaints, recommendations/suggestions, and evaluations in respect of products/brands and services.

Additionally, they can do so through crowd sourcing each other's talent for innovation purposes, and through customer- or user-generated content or applications. In this sense, Prosumerism 2.0 leverages the 8C's (context, collaboration, communication, connection, content, creativity, customisation, and community) and the 4P's (participation, partnership, prosumption, and pull) as depicted in *Figure 1* (see Chaka, 2010a). So, in this way, it is a real embodiment of the participation age. Enterprises exploiting the benefits offered by Prosumerism 2.0 are Google (through its Sandbox), IBM (through its WorldJam), Nokia, Nintendo, Apple and Amazon (see Porta et al., 2009).

Closely allied to Prosumerism 2.0 is Product Development 2.0. At the basic level, Product Development 2.0 is a value chain framework in which employees/employers, partners, customers, and the general users source each other's collective knowledge or wisdom by leveraging enterprise social networking applications. On the one hand, it is about harnessing, collectively, the ideation, innovation, invention and development of enterprise products/brands and services by these stakeholders. On the other hand, it encompasses content, artifact and application creation, and remixing or repurposing data by these stakeholders. By its very nature, Product Development 2.0 encourages a multi-stakeholder participation not only in product/brand and service development, but also in enterprise research and development (R&D).

For its part, Value 2.0 is the virtual business value chain created by tapping into enterprise social networking applications as instances of Web 2.0 technologies. It relates primarily to the value users and customers create and add to enterprises by embracing and participating in the services and products offered by those enterprises exploiting such applications. By its very nature, Value 2.0 harnesses telepresence and the long tail economics - the view that the aggregate niche products at the tail out-value the best-selling products at the head of a demand curve (Porta et al., 2009; Sharp, 2006). Thus, it helps enterprises monetise the long tail of demand. Moreover, it disrupts the Pareto business principle or the *80/20 (eighty-twenty) rule* according to which enterprises concentrate mainly on the critical 20% of the customer/product/service mix that generates 80% of their revenue or profit margins. In line with this rule, enterprises under-value the other 80% they deem non-critical. Value 2.0 challenges this 80/20 approach by leveraging and monetising the non-critical 80% segments. Some of the enterprises and start-ups tapping into this type of Value 2.0 are Amazon, Apple, IBM, Nintendo, Nokia, Craigslist, and Saltworks (Porta et al., 2009).

Moreover, Value 2.0 promotes both the ideas of work swarms and of enterprise as a service (EaaS). Work swarms are instances - within the enterprise social networking framework - in which both professionals and amateurs team up to drive product/brand development and innovation. The notion of EaaS is about enterprises operating as a service in the same way as is the case with SaaS (software as a service). This is a competitive differentiator that allows all the stakeholders to feel that they are part of a given enterprise. Enterprises such as Dell, Proctor & Gamble, and IBM are leveraging work swarms as part of their product development and innovation (Ahlqvist, Bäck, Halonen & Heinonen, 2008). This type of enterprise model has elements of Innovation 2.0 or open innovation and some of its key drivers are mavens and connectors within a given enterprise.

BUZZWORDS OR HYPE?

Concepts such as enterprise social networking, wikinomics, collective intelligence, relationship economy, Prosumerism 2.0 and Value 2.0 do at times serve simply as mantras. This is particularly the case as the term with which they are associated and to which they are indebted, Web 2.0, has itself in most cases, assumed a mantra status (see Madden & Fox, 2006; Skiba, Tamas & Robinson, 2006). For example, wikinomics is built around hyped terms or buzzwords such as mass production, mass creativity and peer production (Van Dijck & Nieborg, 2009). While these terms are intended to capture the emerging business or enterprise models based on Web 2.0 ethos and operating within an SC environment, they nonetheless run the risk of being part of cheap business sloganeering if they are not used with a great deal of circumspection. In addition, wikinomics conjures up images of *the economics of wikis* in the enterprise domain. This is a far cry from what Web 2.0 is fundamentally all about, let alone what its diverse applications in the enterprise world are.

Equally, a term like collective intelligence has blind spots. For instance, while it is a good idea to source the wisdom of multiple collaborators or participants – the wisdom of the crowd – comprising experts and amateurs through diverse enterprise social networking applications, there is no guarantee that crowd-sourced products will always be what enterprises need. This means that for specialist enterprise innovation and product development, crowd sourcing involving communities of experts is one thing, and the one made up of groups of amateurs is quite another. So, collective intelligence is not necessarily a substitute for expertise. In the same vein, terms such as relationship economy, Prosumerism 2.0 and Value 2.0, too, may operate as sheer marketing ploys for enterprise social networking if they are not linked to the enterprise processes they are meant to demonstrate within an SC environment. To avoid this development, each of them must be used to showcase a specific model it represents within a given enterprise social networking instance and within the enterprise social networking applications of which they are a part.

FUTURE TRENDS

Four key future trends are likely to characterise enterprise social computing (SC) in the next 5 years. These are: consumerisation; convergence; virtual value chain; and prosumer capital and economy. Consumerisation refers to SC platforms and applications being embraced by consumers first for social uses and then being adopted accordingly by enterprises for enterprise uses. This trend tallies with the increasing dominance of the Social Web, the Editable Web, or the Programmable Web as a competitive differentiator. Closely linked to consumerisation is the meta-trend of SC as an operating system (OS). This meta-trend will enable a convergence and synergy of the different SC platforms and applications. This convergence and synergy will leverage cloud computing as its critical enabler. Once this happens, it will be possible for users and all other stakeholders to exploit the EaaS (enterprise as a service) model in the same way as is the case with SaaS (software as a service). The EaaS model will foster, inter alia, the practice of *informalising* or *casualising* business.

The other important trend is virtual value chain. This involves creating and building value (e.g., competitive edge, competitive intelligence, corporate image and identity, and online footprint or presence) into the competitive differentiation continuum of enterprises through SC platforms and applications. Finally is prosumer capital and economy. Prosumer capital is the capital enterprises gain from prosumerism which results in prosumer economy. The latter will emerge as one of the critical competitive differentiators for enterprises tapping into SC platforms and applications in the same way as the relationship economy does for many enterprises leveraging SC platforms and applications.

CONCLUSION

Social computing stands to offer enterprises a lot of affordances and benefits. In particular, it provides a lot of value added benefits within the enterprise differentiation spectrum. One of these value added affordances and benefits is that SC serves as a multi-stakeholder medium capable of leveraging users' collective intelligence, aggregate knowledge systems, and collective power of simulation. Other value added affordances and efficiencies in this differentiation equation are social capital, the relationship economy, Prosumerism 2.0 and Value 2.0 that SC enables enterprises and users to exploit. These affordances and efficiencies underscore the pivotal role SC plays as a multi-value medium. It is for this reason that the chapter has set out to investigate the multiple affordances and the multiple values enterprise social networking applications such as blogs, wikis, social networking sites (SNSs), and virtual worlds (VWs) are likely to offer enterprises. In addition, the chapter has provided some of the instances of enterprises harnessing these enterprise social networking applications for their own business benefits. Moreover, it has explored and highlighted the value added benefits accruing from the relationship economy, Prosumerism 2.0 and Value 2.0 all of which serve as part of wikinomics in relation to enterprise social networking. Most significantly, it has argued that these multi-values can provide a competitive edge, a competitive intelligence and a business differentiator if properly leveraged by enterprises. In conclusion, the chapter has concisely outlined the future trends and meta-trends likely to characterise enterprise SC in the next five years.

REFERENCES

Adesope, O. O., & Nesbit, J. C. (2010). A systematic review of research on collaborative learning using concept maps. In Torres, P. L., & Marriott, R. C. V. (Eds.), *Handbook of research on collaborative learning using concept mapping* (pp. 238–255). Hershey, PA: IGI Global. doi:10.4018/978-1-59904-992-2.ch012

Ahlqvist, T., Bäck, A., Halonen, M., & Heinonen, S. (2008). Social media roadmap: Exploring the futures triggered by social media. Retrieved August 18, 2009, from http://www.vtt.fi/inf/pdf/tiedotteet/2008/T2454.pdf

Baverman, L. (2008). Corporate wiki: Sure, it's fun to say, but it's useful, too. Retrieved August 4, 2008, from http://www.bizjournals.com/cincinnati/stories/2008/08/04/focus1.html?b=1217822400%5E1677764

Boutorabi, B. (n.d.). Web 2.0: The next generation of platform. Retrieved May 7, 2008, from http://www.openpublish.com.au/pdf/Bahram_Boutorabi.pdf

Brandon, J. (2007). The top eight corporate sites in Second Life. Retrieved August 18, 2008, from http://www.computerworld.com/action/article.do?command=viewArticleBasic&articleId=9018238

Cachia, R., Kluzer, S., Cabrera, M., Centena, C., & Punie, Y. (2007). ICT, social capital and cultural diversity. Retrieved May 19, 2009, from http://www.kinnisland.nl/binaries/documenten/rapporten/e-inclusion-eur23047en.pdf

Carlin, D. (2007). Corporate wikis go viral. Retrieved August 4, 2008, from http://www.businessweek.com/technology/content/mar2007/tc20070312_476504.htm

Chaka, C. (2010a). Enterprise 2.0: Leveraging prosumerism 2.0 using Web 2.0 and Web 3.0. In Murugesan, S. (Ed.), *Handbook of research on Web 2.0, 3.0, and X.0: Technologies, business, and social applications* (pp. 630–646). Hershey, PA: IGI Global. doi:10.4018/978-1-60566-384-5.ch035

Chaka, C. (2010b). E-learning 2.0: Web 2.0, the semantic Web and the power of collective intelligence. In Yuen, S., & Yang, H. (Eds.), *Handbook of research on practices and outcomes in e-learning: Issues and trends* (pp. 38–60). Hershey, PA: IGI Global. doi:10.4018/978-1-60566-788-1.ch003

Charron, C., Favier, J., & Li, C. (2006). Social computing. Retrieved August 12, 2009, from http://www.cisco.com/web/offer/socialcomputing/SocialComputingBigIdea.pdf

Cobb, J. T. (2008). Learning 2.0 for associations. Retrieved April 29, 2008, from http://blog.missiontolearn.com/files/Learning_20_for_Associations_eBook-v1.pdf

Creese, J. (2007). Web 2.0/business 2.0: New web technologies, organizations and WCM. Retrieved August 7, 2008, from http://eprints.qut.edu.au/archive/00008093/01/8093.pdf

De Ferrari, L. (2007). Wikinomics & co. Retrieved January 18, 2010, from http://www.bioinformatics.ed.ac.uk/TWiki_4.2.4/pub/SysBioClub/ForthcomingTalks/wikinomics_Luna_DeFerrari_20071102.pdf

Deragon, J. T. (2008a). A revolution has begun. In S. Allen, J. T. Deragon, M. G. Orem & C. F. Smith (Eds.), *The emergence of the relationship economy: The new order of things to come* (pp. 13-20). Silicon Valley, CA: Link to Your World. Retrieved May 18, 2009, from http://www.link-tounitedrelations.org/ebook.pdf

Deragon, J. T. (2008b). The relationship factors. In S. Allen, J. T. Deragon, M. G. Orem & C. F. Smith (Eds.), *The emergence of the relationship economy: The new order of things to come* (pp. 39-44). Silicon Valley, CA: Link to Your World. Retrieved May 18, 2009, from http://www.link-tounitedrelations.org/ebook.pd

Evans, M. (2008). The evolution of the Web: From Web 1.0 to Web 4.0. Retrieved May 8, 2008, from http://www.network-research-group.org/presentations/08-11-06-MikeEvans-Web.pdf

Gandhi, A. (2008). The social enterprise: Using social enterprise applications to enable the next wave of knowledge worker productivity. Retrieved May 14, 2009, from http://www.oracle.com/products/middleware/user-interaction/docs/social-enterprise-whitepaper.pdf

Hasan, H., & Pfaff, C. (2006). Emergent conversational technologies that are democratising information systems in organisations: The case of the corporate wiki. Retrieved August 24, 2008, from http://ro.uow.edu.au/cgi/viewcontent.cgi?article=12978&content=commpapers

IBM. (2007). Tapping into collective intelligence: How to leverage the wisdom of the crowd to boost the bottom line. Retrieved May 7, 2008, from http://www-935.ibm.com/services/tw/cio/pdf.empow_wp_collective_intel-gtw01406-usen-00.pdf

Jana, R. (2006). American Apparel's virtual clothes. *Business Week Online*. Retrieved August 20, 2008, from http://www.businessweek.com/innovate/content/jun2006/id20060627_217800.htm

Kish, S. (2007). Second Life: Virtual worlds and the enterprise. Retrieved August 18, 2008, from http://skish.typepad.com/susan_kish/secondlife/Skish_VW-SL_sept07.pdf

Lakshmanan, G., Pradeep, K. M., & Harish, K. (2010). The current and future state of the programmable Web. *Cutter IT Journal, 23*(8), 19–25.

Madden, M., & Fox, S. (2006). Riding the waves of "Web 2.0": More than a buzzword, but still not easily defined. Retrieved February 13, 2008, from http://www.pewinternet.org/~/media//Files/Reports/2006/PIP_Web_2.0.pdf.pdf

McLoughlin, C., & Lee, M. J. W. (2008). The three P's of pedagogy for the networked society: Personalization, participation, and productivity. Retrieved December 17, 2008, from http://www.isetl.org.ijtlhe/pdf/IJTLHE395.pdf

MLC. (2008). Leveraging social networking sites in marketing communications. Retrieved August 11, 2008, from http://www.ittoolbox.com/advertising/pdf/Leveraging-Social-Media-Networking-Sites-in-Marketing-Communications.pdf

Olleros, X. (2006, June). The lean core in digital platforms. Paper presented at the DRUID Summer Conference, Copenhagen. Retrieved August 12, 2008, from http://www2.druid.dk/conferences/viewpaper.php?id=623&cf=8

Parameswaran, M., & Whinston, A. B. (2007a). Research issues in social computing. *Journal of the Association for Information Systems, 8*(6), 336-350. Retrieved May 8, 2009, from http://crec.mccombos.utexas.edu/data/papers/Parameswaran_Social%20Computing_JAIS07.pdf

Parameswaran, M., & Whinston, A. B. (2007b). Social computing: An overview. Retrieved August 8, 2008, from http://crec.mccombs.utexas.edu/works/articles/Parameswaran_Social%20Computing_CAIS07.pdf

Porta, M., House, B., Buckley, L., & Blitz, A. (2008). Value 2.0: Eight new rules for creating and capturing value from innovative technologies. Retrieved May 14, 2009, from http://www-935.ibm.com/services/us/gbs/bus/pdf/gbe03016-usen-02-value2.0.pdf

Sarner, A., Drakos, N., & Prentice, S. (2008). Retrieved May 14, 2009, from http://www.socialtext.net/data/workspaces/m:703/attachments/chris_lane:20081008195322-0-27637/original/the_business_impact_of_social_161342.pdf

Sharp, D. (2006). Digital lifestyle monitor. Retrieved February 15, 2008, from http://www.aimia.com.au/i-cms_file?page=1878/Digital-LifestylesMonitorFullReportPublicVersionReleasedFebFeb2007.pdf

Skiba, B., Tamas, A., & Robinson, K. (2006). Web 2.0: Hype or reality—and how will it play out? A strategic analysis. Retrieved February 13, 2008, from http:www.armapartners.com/files/admin/uploads/W17_F_1873_8699.pdf

Sun Microsystems. (2008). Current reality and future vision: Open virtual worlds. Retrieved August 18, 2008, from http://sun.com/service/applicationserversubscriptions/OpenVirtualWorlds.pdf

Tandefelt, M. (2008). Web 2.0 and network society—PR and communication: The challenge of online social network. Retrieved August 12, 2008, from http://www.diva-portal.org/diva/getDocument?urn_nbn_se_uu_diva-9187-2_fulltext.pdf

Tapscott, D., & Williams, A. (2006). *Wikinomics: How mass communication changes everything.* New York: Penguin Group.

Thomas, J., & Harden, A. (2008). Methods for the thematic synthesis of qualitative research in systematic reviews. Retrieved September 9, 2009, from http://www.biomedcentral.com/content/pdf/1471-2288-8-45.pdf

Van Dijck, J., & Nieborg, D. (2009). Wikinomics and its discontents: A critical analysis of Web 2.0 business manifestos. Retrieved January 18, 2010, from http://www.gamespace.nl/content/Wikinomics_and_its_discontents_2009.pdf

Wood, L. (2005). Blogs & wikis: Technologies for enterprise applications? Retrieved August 4, 2008, from http://gilbane.com/gilbane_report.pl/104/Blogs__Wikis_Technologies_for_Enterprise_Applications.html

Wyld, D. C. (2007). The blogging revolution: Government in the age of web 2.0. Retrieved January 17, 2008, from http://www.businessofgovernment.org/pdfs/WyldReportBlog.pdf

KEY TERMS AND DEFINITIONS

Collective Intelligence (CI): This refers to joint efforts by human collectives to tap into their intellectual capacity so as to exchange ideas and share knowledge online or to create, innovate and invent products online. It can be applied at any level, from small user/employee/customer teams to huge networks. CI is a competitive differentiator in Enterprise 2.0.

Competitive Differentiator: This term is used with the same connotations as competitive edge even though its focus is more on the competitive differentiation brought about by such an edge/advantage in the business market of which a given enterprise is a part.

Connectors: In relation to Product Development 2.0, connectors serve as brand evangelists for enterprises

Mavens: In terms of Product Development 2.0, mavens are product/brand experts who take pride in their knowledge and who can help enterprises establish areas of improvement in their products or services.

Metaverses: These are VWs (such as SL) that are essentially socially inclined as opposed to being game oriented.

Sandbox: This is a new feature that the search engine company, Google, is testing out (at the time of writing) which allows users to provide feedback about their search results.

The Programmable Web: This refers to the Web as a platform facilitating an open programmable environment through user interface, data as resource, infrastructure service, and so on.

The 80/20 (Eighty-Twenty) Rule: Also known as the Pareto principle, the 80/20 rule explores the natural balance between the causes and effects of business activities, and asserts that all business activities display an 80%/20% split. The case in point is when 80% of an enterprise's profits come from 20% of its products/services.

WorldJam: A social networking platform employed by IBM which allows employees to engage in a series of online discussions to promote employee conversations. There are also ValuesJam and InnovationJam that enable employees to create value and engage in innovation respectively.

Work Swarms: Work swarms are online collectives in which both amateurs and professionals coalesce to source each other's knowledge and wisdom for developing, innovating and enhancing enterprise products, brands or services.

Chapter 7
Using Web 2.0 Social Computing Technologies to Enhance the Use of Information Systems in Organizations

Jean Éric Pelet
KMCMS.net, France

ABSTRACT

In the perspective of managing the Intellectual Capital (IC), the user friendliness of User Generated Content (UGC) tools may be preferred over the Information Systems platforms offered in the majority of organizations. Based on a review of literature and actual practices, this chapter focuses on aspects related to user practices of social networks and web tools that could be useful for corporate platforms; its aim is to improve the use of corporate platforms by informing both the research academy and managers about effective practices. Case studies are presented to understand how UGC can be used to implement new ways of sharing information and communicating more efficiently in organizations. Knowledge and IC management systems for teaching and learning are presented, in order to better assess whether or not this technology is effective to support knowledge creation and sharing in an academic and business setting.

"The new technologies have provided us with tremendous potential. Web-based technologies, especially the new Web 2.0 Social Computing technologies, now enable us to search the world and better know what the world is searching for; allow us to self-publish, through blogs and websites, and share knowledge with the world; and enable mass collaboration through wikis, as inspired by pioneers such as Wikipedia. Through the blogosphere, we can now capture our new lessons, insights, ideas and opinions, and much better know and influence what the world is thinking and feeling." Dr. Ron Young, Chief Knowledge Officer, Knowledge Associates International, UK (Young, 2008)

DOI: 10.4018/978-1-61692-904-6.ch007

INTRODUCTION

During discussions with the top leadership of 10 Information Technology (IT) companies on the methodologies for sharing knowledge, suggestions provided by top executives to Gupta (2008) included:

- Soliciting feedback
- Asking questions
- Telling people what you plan to do before doing it
- Asking other people for help; asking someone to work with you in some way – however small
- Telling people what you are doing and more importantly why you are doing it
- Asking people what they think
- Asking them for advice
- Asking people what would they do differently
- Not just sharing information but know-how and know-why

All these suggestions look simple and easy to apply, especially when we think about the tools and advice offered freely on the Internet, to manage knowledge but only a few organizations apply them. The concept of knowledge creation often refers to Nonaka and Takeuchi (1995) and their model of knowledge conversion between tacit and explicit knowledge. The knowledge creation model developed by Nonaka and Takeuchi treat organizations as cognitive and epistemological entities; therefore, their discussion on the topic remains very much at an individual level (Hong, Kianto & Kyläheiko, 2008). Employee reluctance to communicate and share knowledge still exists even if the theory suggests differently. In the last few years, many organizations realized that they own a vast amount of knowledge and this knowledge needs to be managed in order to be useful (Gupta, 2008). Sharing is about being more open at work and in our relationships with other

Figure 1. A drawing representing social networks on the Internet in 2010

people. Organizations must help people to build networks which facilitate relationships because organizations have always used humans to transfer the knowledge across the firm; this in turn, has a positive impact on employee satisfaction (Gupta, 2008). In our everyday private lives, this is exactly what social networks (try to) do: help people share information. The question we ask about the ergonomics and interaction between the users and the social network is: how can companies improve the use of their information systems platforms by applying key success factors of social networks such as Facebook, Twitter or LinkedIn?

Facebook (http://www.facebook.com/) is a social networking website that is operated and privately owned by Facebook, Inc. Users can add friends and send them messages, and update their personal profiles to notify friends about themselves (Wikipedia, 2009a).

Twitter (http://twitter.com/) is a free social networking and micro-blogging service that enables its users to send and read messages known as tweets. Tweets are text-based posts of up to 140 characters displayed on the author's profile page and delivered to the author's subscribers who are known as followers (Wikipedia, 2009b).

LinkedIn (http://www.linkedin.com/) is a business-oriented social networking site mainly used for professional networking (Wikipedia, 2009c).

In the same time, the world is tied together by a network of personal relationships. A and Z come from different parts of the country, yet they have a mutual friend C. Or maybe A knows B, B knows C, and maybe C knows Z. When he discovered these unexpected relationships, Milgram (1967) explained the *small world phenomenon*. A popular hypothesis called *"Six Degrees of Separation"* which explained that given any two people in the world, they can be connected through at most six *"friends of"*. Coming from this interesting theory and thanks to the evolution of technology, social networks boosted the Internet in 2003 with the launch of Friendster and then MySpace.

Friendster (http://www.friendster.com/) is a privately owned social networking website (Wikipedia, 2009d).

MySpace (http://www.myspace.com/) is a social networking website (Wikipedia, 2009e).

UGC, also known as Consumer Generated Media (CGM), refers to content created and shared online by non-media professionals. Nowadays, millions of users in the world make use of these websites in their everyday lives. Several facts demonstrate why it may be fruitful to examine social networks in the perspective of sharing the knowledge from different organizations:

- 3 out of 4 Americans use social technology (Bernoff *et al.*, 2008)
- 2/3 of the global Internet population visit social networks (Nielsen, 2009)
- Visiting social sites is now the 4th most popular online activity—ahead of personal email (Nielsen, 2009)
- Time spent on social networks is growing at three times the overall Internet rate,

accounting for almost 10% of all Internet time (Nielsen, 2009)

Social media is democratizing communications and Murdoch even adds in 2009: *"technology is shifting the power away from the editors, the publishers, the establishment, and the media elite. Now it's the people who are in control"*. A few figures retrieved from June 2009 are good examples of this growth:

- The amount of videos uploaded to YouTube every minute represents 13 hours
- The length of time it would take to view every YouTube video is 412.3 years
- 3,194,018 articles in English are available on Wikipedia (on 02/14/2010)
- 3,600,000,000 photos are archived on Flickr.com

YouTube (http://www.youtube.com/) is a site where users can upload and view videos of almost any kind.

Flickr (http://www.flickr.com/) is a site where users can upload and view photos of almost any kind.

All the figures related to social networks, show how popular the Internet is becoming on an entertainment (YouTube), cultural (Wikipedia), communication (Twitter) or "all in one" (Facebook) basis. Social Networking has therefore been the global consumer phenomenon of 2008. Two-thirds of the world's Internet population visits a social network or blogging site and the sector now accounts for almost 10% of all Internet time. *"Member Communities"* have overtaken personal Email to become the world's fourth most popular online sector after search, portals and PC software applications (Nielsen, 2009).

In this new paradigm of dynamically configured network organizations, a multiplicity of partners requires that the orientation must be broadened to allow dialogue to permeate and to coordinate the network. However, despite the increasing importance of corporate interaction as companies virtualize, few organizations have yet taken into account the potential of social networks to maximize the human-computer interaction, and thus, the strategy of the organization. Indeed, today's most advanced economies are knowledge based: the balance between knowledge and other resources has shifted so far towards the former that knowledge has become maybe the most important factor determining standards of living and market competitiveness (Grant, 1996; OECD, 1996, 1999, 2001).

The aim of this article is to understand and propose solutions to enhance the efficiency of people working on information systems, whatever the purposes of these systems are. In parallel to their everyday life in company or at school, employees, self made men or students contribute to their social network, day after day, hour after hour, minute after minute. Indeed, people incrementally subscribe to social network platforms such as Facebook, where they post information related to their private lives. The time spent on these platforms grows month after month, showing how important a social network can become at least for a population of computer orientated people.

What are the main differences between these information systems? The commitment which is necessary to make a social network function efficiently, by adding new friends, updating *the wall*, uploading pictures, sounds or video, playing the widgets proposed by friends' requests is significant. People interested in maintaining a presence on this type of application must deploy a strategy to save as much time as possible. They have to write and offer the minimum of information to their network, in order to maintain it as long as possible. This strategy is not only interesting for the network and for the account owner; relatives of the owner may appreciate it if he/she does not spend too much time on the social network.

The goal of this chapter is to present a theoretical framework with which to a) assess the transformative potential of UGC and, b) develop design guidelines for making them into more effective social tools, usable in companies and schools. The argument begins with an introduction presenting the ever growing penetration of www technologies in innovative companies. The different tools that are available are then presented. The next section uses this theory to examine how the structure of UGCs can bring greater trust and reliability to online company transactions and e-learning expectations, how specific site design decisions enhance or weaken their trust-conferring ability. The final section examines the transformative possibilities of UGC, in what ways they might change the way employees work or the way professors and students can enhance e-learning, by creating new ways of interaction thanks to these tools. Cases of already used systems are presented as an argumentation. This section leads to the conclusion of the chapter.

SOCIAL NETWORKS: A PRESENTATION

What are the strengths offered on social networks that could be deployed in another context such as the corporate one? Are there any opportunities in terms of usability, ergonomics, ease of use, readability, playability and so on to take into account in order to make the information system used in a company more efficient?

Coming from a marketing and information system point of view, our objective is to explain why the ease of use of a corporate information system can be mirrored by a clever deployment. The analysis of the consumer behavior on social networks and on e-commerce website comes from the marketing approach. It is coupled with an analysis of the ergonomic aspects of social networks and UGCs, coming from the information system ones. Cognitive psychology is also necessary to make this type of system working: it serves as bases of this chapter. Discussions with users of both corporate platforms and users on social networks will be used as raw material, coupled with a presentation of already used tools for the last 6 years, in the e-learning field. We will then try to identify what the strengths and opportunities of the UGCs uses are. These could serve as leverage in using corporate information systems in order to diminish the threats and weaknesses.

Towards (Always More) Innovative Organizations

An organization whose culture is characterized by openness to change and innovation would likely foster human-to-human contact and stress similarities between individuals (Gupta, 2008). In addition, this culture promotes self-actualization, which is likely to increase individual knowledge. For these reasons, Ladd and Ward (2002) hypothesized that organizations with openness to change/ innovation cultures would be positively correlated to high knowledge transfer environments. The benefits of embracing technology in order to gain competitive advantage and capitalize on the opportunity resulting from the globalization of business exist for more than 25 years (Levitt, 1983). The rapid development of the Internet and e-business technology has been one of the most important influences on business. As a result, it is important to develop an understanding of the organization characteristics that lead to higher rates of information systems adoption. The rapid diffusion of a major technology like Internet, in comparison to the uptake of communication technologies such as radio and television, obliterates all records of speed (Simeon, 1999). Rapidly, the commercial side of Internet, the World Wide Web, has evolved from being a novelty, mainly as an entertainment and communication device, into a transforming concept that is now seen as an essential business tool (Simeon, 1999; Poon & Swatman, 1999; Aldridge *et al.*, 1997; Herbig & Hale, 1997; Cotter, 2002). The Internet is a powerful and transforming "disruptive" technology, which initially degrades business performance,

but promises greater long-term potential (Lee, 2001; Foremski, 2005).

Furthermore, levels of Internet and broadband access in 28 OECD countries indicate that more than 90 per cent of businesses have Internet access, and Iceland, Finland, Switzerland, Japan, Denmark and Austria report access rates above 98 per cent (OECD, 1997). Even if most companies in the developed world have an Internet presence (Kraemer *et al.*, 2006), the main reason for engaging in e-business appears to be *"we need to be on the Internet"*, without any clear goals for research to back up the decision (Welling & White, 2006). However, to be successful, an organization or a school must be innovative in the way it learns about and tracks the needs of customers, employees, students and so on. It must also develop new products, functions or services that address those needs. This has to be done in the way it develops and implements internal processes that enhance the understanding of these people needs as well as product and service development. Innovation is viewed as critically important to an organization's strategy in terms of its growth and survival in the marketplace (Damanpour, 1992; Eisenhardt & Brown, 1999; Voola, 2005). A definition of innovation is *"a new technology or combination of technologies that offer worthwhile benefits"* (McDermott & O'Connor, 2002). Technological innovation is widely considered as a key to corporate success (Coviello, Milley & Marcolin, 2001; Rapp, Schwillewaert & Hao, 2008). However, the use of technology and innovative processes has not created a competitive advantage. Organizations have effectively only developed advantages by leveraging these technologies to enhance the intangible aspects of the organization, including human resources, strategic planning, etc. (Powell & Dent-Micallef, 1997).

In parallel, the importance of IC for the success of any organization is nowadays widely acknowledged by both researchers and practitioners. IC-related assets such as brands, corporate image, databases, employee competencies, immaterial property rights, stakeholder relationships are often considered important but quite difficult to manage (Kujansivu & Lönnqvist, 2008). The same exists with regards to a professor's lectures and presentations, knowing that they are often reluctant to share them, whereas schools ask more and more for this particular raw material nowadays. One of the challenges of knowledge management (KM) is that of getting people to share their knowledge. Why should people give up their hard-won knowledge, when it is one of their key sources of personal advantages? In some organizations, sharing is natural. In others the old dictum as following reigns according to Gupta (2008):

- Knowledge is power
- 'Not invented here' syndrome
- Not realising how useful particular knowledge is to others
- Lack of trust
- Lack of time

Trying to get people to do things differently is not so straightforward because people can easily fall back on defensive routines (Argyris, 1990). To get people to change the way that they do things will also require a level of willingness from the individual. People need to feel valued, that they belong in a community and that their involvement is challenging and rewarding (Goffee & Jones, 2001). The path towards KM doesn't appear so easy to take.

FROM INTELLECTUAL CAPITAL TO KNOWLEDGE MANAGEMENT

Knowledge in Organizations

Davenport and Prusak (1998) defined knowledge as a *'fluid mixture of experience, values, contextual information, and expert insight that provides a framework for evaluating and incorporating new experiences and information'*. There is a slightly different definition given by Alavi and Leidner (2001). They see knowledge as a *'justified personal belief that increases an individual's capacity to take action'*. There are two types of knowledge, called explicit and tacit knowledge by Nonaka and Takeuchi (1995). Tacit knowledge has been linked to know-how (Kogut & Zander, 1992) and explicit knowledge to know-that. Tacit knowledge is obtained by internal individual processes and stored in human beings. For Pillania (2007), firms need to put serious effort into identifying the most crucial knowledge and then leveraging that knowledge for sustainable competitive advantage in this era of globalization. It will then be important to share this information. The sharing of this information is commonly called *Knowledge management*.

KM in Organizations

KM is very important in the 21st century because it helps organizations to gain competitive advantage and effective working through sharing and re-using knowledge (Gupta, 2008). For more than a decade, KM has been proposed by many authorities as a viable means to optimise enterprise performance in the face of the rapidly increasing complexity and competitiveness in modern business world (Drucker, 1988; Nonaka & Takeuchi, 1995; Davenport & Prusak, 1998; Von Krogh, 2000; Choo & Bontis, 2002). Managing IC is challenging for a number of reasons. IC subsumes a number of various resources that require different tools and methods. However, managing IC does not necessarily require any specific framework and in many organizations, there are not enough resources available to apply a discrete IC management system. Furthermore, adopting a certain method is not considered reasonable, although IC as such is considered an important managerial issue. According to Lev (2001), organisation's intangible assets are non-physical sources of values (claims to future benefits) generated by innovation (discovery), unique organisational designs or human resource practices. It seems that there is a fairly general consensus that the IC of an organisation consists of three main components:

- Human capital
- Relational capital
- Structural capital (Sveiby, 1997; Seetharaman *et al.*, 2004).

Many specific frameworks, tools and methods, as well as guidelines, have been developed to support the challenging task of IC management, but many companies are still looking for a solution which suits them. A list of principles explaining the basics for a good structure of the information and the building of a good KM has even been established (Leuf & Cunningham, 2001). IC management refers to a managerial activity that focuses on the acquisition, development and utilisation of intangible resources in business (Kujansivu & Lönnqvist, 2008). Zhou and Fink (2003) state that intangible asset management is used at a strategic level to increase an organization's value creating capabilities.

Internet is thus becoming an indispensable tool for organizations that emphasise an employee-service orientation (Levenburg, 2005) and for schools that emphasise a student-service orientation, the whole thing based on IC. It is also interesting to see how it is becoming an interesting tool for companies which bid on KM and communication management tools.

Information systems are effectively massively used in nowadays companies and schools. They mainly take into account Enterprise Resource Planning (ERP), Business Intelligence (BI), Customer Relationship Management (CRM), Application Service Provider (ASP), KM and Supply Chain Management (SCM) platforms for some, e-learning platforms for others. Their objective is to identify, capitalize and value the IC of the company or school by involving the entire staff or professors. They also aim to coordinate all the activities of the company (vertical activities such as the production or the supply, and horizontal activities such as marketing, sales forces, human resources management, etc.) around the same information system; it is almost the same for the educational systems, with administrative tasks on the one hand, and lectures on the other, to simplify.

From UGC platforms to blogs, and from blogs to e-learning platforms, managers, lecturers, businessmen and so on use more and more *Content Management Systems* to improve their way of working and collaborating. This is not without problems, in terms of involvement, use of information technology, comprehension of what is required by the system and sometimes, capacity to express oneself publicly on this type of platform. The perspective where employees can work and obtain greater access to business processes and develop multiple and ephemeral corporate relationships is not so close in organizations. Schools are asking for the same tools to coordinate their entire staff, from students to lecturers and from pedagogical to administrative persons, because a large majority of youth, regardless of their gender, age, or education attained, enters the labor markets through informal social ties.

The Ever Growing Social Networks

Social ties provide many benefits, including companionship, access to information, and emotional and material support (Granovetter, 1983; Wellman, Garton, & Haythornthwaite, 1997; Wellman & Gulia, 1999). Increasing the number of ties increases access to these benefits, although time and cognitive constraints preclude indefinite expansions of one's personal network. Instead of removing lice from each other's hair, people check in with friends and colleagues, ask how they are doing, and exchange a few words about common acquaintances, the news, or the local sports team (Dunbar, 1996, 2004). Communication technologies expand human social reach (Horrigan, Boase, Rainie, & Wellman, 2006). Email makes communication more efficient: sending a message to numerous recipients is as easy as sending it to one, and its asynchrony means that there is little need to coordinate interaction (Donath, 2007). Contact management tools, from paper Rolodexes to complex software systems, increase one's ability to remember large numbers of people (Whittaker, Jones, & Terveen, 2002).

While these technologies provide some of the support an expanded social world needs, they alone are not sufficient. People need to be able to keep track of ever-changing relationships (Dunbar, 1996; Nardi, Whittaker, Isaacs, Creech, Johnson, & Hainsworth, 2002), to see people within the context of their social relationships (Raub & Weesie, 1990), and, most fundamentally, to know whom to trust (Bacharach & Gambetti, 2001; Good, 2000).

Among all the possibilities offered by Internet technologies, UGC encompass social ties as well as tools that are available on the Internet, free, and easy to use since people agree to read and learn how to use them. This facilitation of interactive information sharing constitutes the *"Web 2.0"*. This refers to web development and web design that enhance the use of this type of Information System. The term was coined by O'Reilly Media to describe second-generation Internet-based services (O'Reilly, 2005). Wikipedia underlines that Web 2.0 is about using the web as a "platform" to provide an enhanced user experience via Rich Internet Applications (RIA), and extending the reach of web content through syndication technologies such as Really Simple Syndication (RSS). What make these systems work? As for Information Systems used in companies, taking advantage of e-business strengths in terms of human-computer interaction, for example, there seem to be several advantages coming from UGC in using them in organizations and schools. Consumer recommendations are effectively the most trusted form of advertising around the world. Over 75% of respondents from 47 markets across the world rated recommendations from consumers as a trusted form of advertising. This is to compare to 63%

for newspapers, 56% for TV and magazines, and 34% for search engine ads (Nielsen, 2007). This underscores the notion that people trust people. And it is not only verified with marketing techniques. On a KM platform, students are willing to read what their fellow students post first.

The experience of an MBA student in Information and Technology Management option System Information Organization passed in Canada during two years between 2001 and 2002 shows that students read the content uploaded on the e-learning platform coming from their peer colleagues first, rather than the content uploaded by the lecturer/ professor. Log files can attest to this particularity when they are accessible. They show what content is read first, what page is the most popular and so on, exactly like a teacher does with an e-learning platform. See, for example, logs extracted from the administration of a platform named KMCMS.net (http://www.kmcms.net). The latter is a UGC used for e-learning that is presented in the following chapter. Its name means "Knowledge management and Content Management System" (Table 1).

The same principles as those already used in the e-business industry are followed in the educational one, with rating on one side, and log files on the other, to understand the user behavior more precisely. Another experience of 6 years (between 2003 and 2009) using a 100% *"homemade"* KM platform and content management system, is now presented. It has been built by a professor to help his students to prepare their major projects in different areas such as ergonomics, consumer behavior or marketing adapted to the Internet. The wiki was built in 2003 and today, around 1500 contributions dedicated to very precise topics are available on this platform. The expected work must be published and readable by any logged in student. As time passes, more and more students publish their work (syntheses of academic papers, journalistic ones or reviews of literature on a particular topic) making it available for the overall community of students. The phenomenon is thus becoming autonomous since

Table 1. Log file from kmcms.net

1	2	3	4	Legend:
2009-05-07 15:46:48	[1] ville dangre	/fiche.php?id=1202	s	**1:** date/hour the page has been viewed
2009-05-07 15:46:43	[1] ville dangre	/fiche.php?action=about	5 s	**2:** name of the user (student in this case)
2009-05-07 15:45:01	[1] ville dangre	/fiche.php?action=new	2:18 s	**3:** viewed page
2009-05-07 15:44:15	[1] ville dangre	/fiche.php?id=1202	46 s	**4:** time spent on the page
2009-05-07 15:44:12	[1] ville dangre	/fiche.php?action=about	3 s	
2009-05-07 15:37:30	[1] ville dangre	/fiche.php?action=new	7:18 s	
2009-05-07 15:36:49	[1] ville dangre	/fiche.php?id=1201	41 s	
2009-05-07 15:36:46	[1] ville dangre	/fiche.php?action=about	3 s	
2009-05-07 15:34:55	[1] ville dangre	/fiche.php?action=new	2:9 s	
2009-05-07 15:34:04	[1] ville dangre	/fiche.php?id=1200	51 s	
2009-05-07 15:33:58	[1] ville dangre	/fiche.php?action=about	6 s	
2009-05-07 15:32:55	[1] ville dangre	/fiche.php?action=new	1:3 s	
2009-05-07 15:32:04	[1] ville dangre	/fiche.php?id=1199	51 s	
2009-05-07 15:31:58	[1] ville dangre	/fiche.php?action=about	6 s	
2009-05-07 15:26:44	[1] ville dangre	/fiche.php?action=new	5:14 s	

students get help from the contribution of other students, and also help the others to find easily what they could be interested in by working on it, adding their *"knowledge"*. One of the key success factors of such a tool lies in the search engine mechanism. The latter is embedded into the system in order to accelerate the search and above all, the finding of results. As for any UGC website, the role of the lecturer is to moderate each new contribution by asking the student to modify it if necessary. Here is a presentation of the KMCMS platform (Figure 2).

In order to coach and help students located in other areas than professor's log files show that the first readings are dedicated to what the other students post (Table 2).

The first aim of this platform was to help a PhD student prepare his thesis, by using Information Technology for two reasons: saving time, remembering important ideas thanks to a system that could drill down any piece of information originated from 5 years of readings, in a flash. Thus the platforms first objective was to prepare for the huge task of classifying synthesis of academic papers and book chapters on a database:

this constitutes the raw material needed for the thesis (Figure 3).

Thanks to the assistance of a programmer who thanks to his ability to speak in layman's terms permitted the PhD student to conceive the platform, the task of creating this was achieved in 2 years. Content Management Systems are computer applications used to manage work flow needed to collaboratively create, edit, review, index, search, publish and archive various kinds of digital media and electronic text (Wikipedia, 2009f). They did not exist at this period, in 2003. At least, these systems were not easy to manage and implement without a solid programming experience. This is why this platform has been created, and is still offering lectures and texts related to the PhD topic and other topics, 6 years later. Its objective is to help students in achieving their major project, a dissertation for example, by accessing the works written since its beginning of hundreds of students. Around 2000 students coming from 5 different schools and at least 8 disciplines, subscribed to kmcms.net during the last 6 years. Around 1350 pages have been created on this platform so far, and at least 5 persons

Figure 2. Presentation of the common appearance of kmcms.net

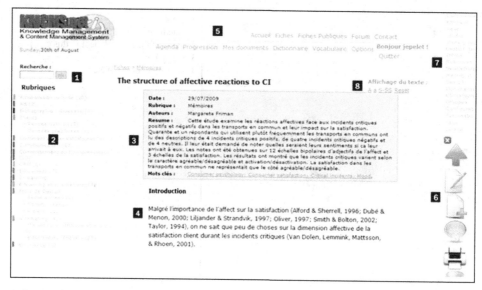

Legend:
1: search engine
2: navigation bar to choose courses
3: title, authors, abstract, keywords of the paper that is synthesized
4: work of the student
5: main navigation bar
6: remote control to assist the student while typing his work
7: navigation administration bar
8: accessibility buttons to increase/decrease the font of the text

Table 2. Tracking of the construction/deletion of pages on kmcms.net

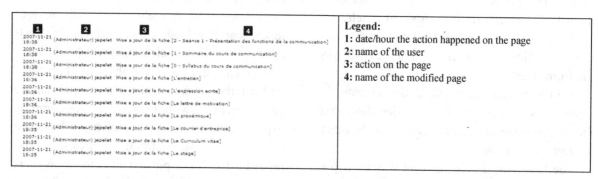

visiting it accidentally try to sign up every month. It is managed by one person only. In an identical manner as the one already described regarding the MBA e-learning experience, log files help to know what content is read first. And once again, the student's writings seem to be preferred as a departure on the KM platform to any other.

On e-commerce websites, alongside professional content are user reviews. Users are asked to rate products on a scale, and are also invited to compose their own reviews, which are compiled

Figure 3. Pages written on the topic of the thesis (212 pages were written at the end of the thesis, with the equivalent of 3 A4 format pages each on average)

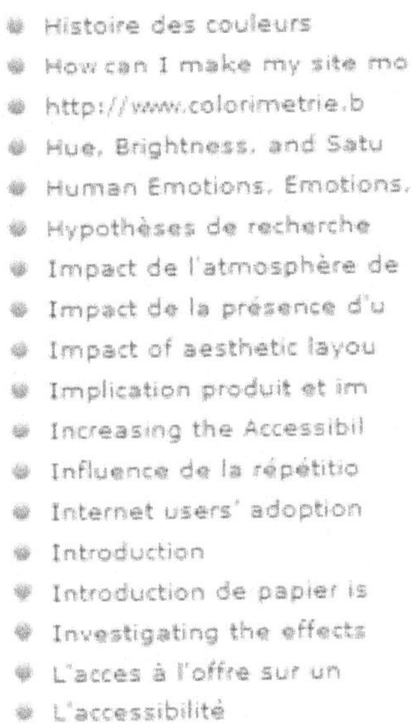

Histoire des couleurs
How can I make my site mo
http://www.colorimetrie.b
Hue, Brightness, and Satu
Human Emotions, Emotions,
Hypothèses de recherche
Impact de l'atmosphère de
Impact de la présence d'u
Impact of aesthetic layou
Implication produit et im
Increasing the Accessibil
Influence de la répétitio
Internet users' adoption
Introduction
Introduction de papier is
Investigating the effects
L'acces à l'offre sur un
L'accessibilité

Figure 4. Marks given by students to another student's work

1. Rating: 3.4/5 (14 votes cast)
2. Rating: 3.2/5 (15 votes cast) Thanks for voting!
3. Rating: 4.3/6 (15 votes cast)
4. Rating: 5.1/8 (12 votes cast)

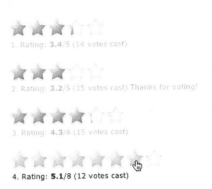

into a separate section. The average user ratings are compiled by the website and displayed on a product's front page. The MBA e-learning platforms already mentioned provided the same system. Each group of students sending a project on the platform was marked by other groups from the same *"virtual class"*, and as a matter of fact, the best mark arises when people have finished reading the work uploaded by the rest of the classroom. The professor knew what content seemed the best (according to the lesson) thanks to the marks student gave to their peer (Figure 4).

Huge numbers of consumers consult peer reviews before making major electronics or technology purchases, and huge numbers of students are consulting mark and peer reviews related to a work made by fellow students on the platform before starting to work on a project, or before reading a solid piece of work already read and synthesized by other students. So, peer reviews, i.e. UGC, must be taken into account when building organizational information systems. They can be useful for managing knowledge, for example.

One of the major contributions of these websites, e-learning or e-commerce platforms comes from the reviewing. Any part of the accessible content is moderated, reviewed within 24 hours, and the offending material is thus immediately removed. Other users are also given the opportunity to easily submit complaints about others' comments that they feel may be out of line. Like any UGC sites, these websites allow users to post comments regarding users' content (Figure 5).

This again fosters a freewheeling exchange of ideas and opinions, sometimes polite, sometimes not. It shows the importance of trust and confidence on these types of UGC tools.

THE ROOT OF CONFIDENCE AND TRUST

In a culture where the knowledge value is recognized, availability of information, sharing of that information, information flows, IT infrastructure, personal networking, system thinking, leadership, communication climate, problem solving, training and many other factors can be supportive factors for successful learning (Warne *et al.*, 2003). For gaining an edge on KM, people-centered skills must be possessed and be used constructively for

Figure 5. Comments left to students at the end of another student's work on kmcms.net

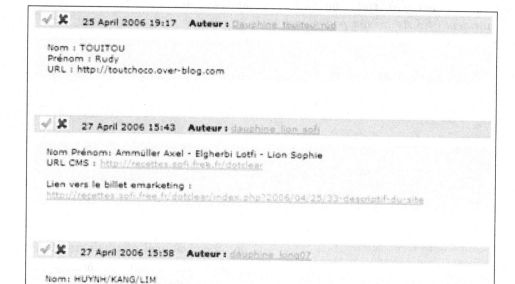

nurturing and motivating people (Bhatt, 2000). Both of the presented sites represent attractive learning, buying or communicating opportunities for obvious reasons: consumers are there because they are in the market for a particular product, or because they are interested in learning more in a precise way. Identically, students and employees look for ways to learn and interact with information or lessons more efficiently. However, the free-flowing opinions provided by members of the general public, of the classroom or desk can be intimidating. This is why it seems important to understand that most review sites do not allow anyone to submit content without agreeing to certain standards or *"user agreements"*. A typical user agreement includes a promise to post no defamation, profanity, threats, or illegal or inappropriate content. Users are told that they are legally

responsible for whatever content they post, and are warned to behave accordingly (IAB, 2008).

It is easy to imagine how employees in companies using platforms could benefit from the use of these types of tools. A growing number of companies ask agencies to design platforms that extract knowledge from individual employees and make it available to the rest of the organization. Each of these companies takes a fundamentally different approach to the problem.

Some applications allow users to drag documents into a special folder, at which point the application parses the documents for key concepts, and goes looking for more information that matches those concepts. The program finds the documents either on the Web or on other users' hard drives. It only looks in user documents that have been marked as sharable. The concept of this type of tool, while creative, require employees or students to think about knowledge in a new way, something corporations or schools might not want to push their employees or students to do.

Another type of tool simply extends the groupware functions that are already used, sharing workspaces between the two clients or students (useful for cross-company or mixed-students teams). Workspaces can for example include:

- all e-mails related to a project
- discussion groups
- shared directories of files
- to-do lists
- calendars
- project management timelines and so on

This type of application provides a new view of a collaborative workspace that users must learn to navigate and use efficiently.

Other types of tools can build profiles of users based on the e-mail they send without storing the e-mails, and then allows other users to find co-workers or students who are knowledgeable in particular fields. But it doesn't force the connection. The system allows the person with expertise to decide if a contact will be made: it just tells them who's asking.

The knowledge-sharing and groupware market is further fragmented because there are many kinds of corporate personalities, and unlike horizontal applications like word processors and browsers, one size doesn't fit all. As additional knowledge-sharing tools come to market, the likely scenario is that none of them will achieve real dominance. Many might find homes in companies that share their communication philosophies, but companies, like people, are too different for a single application to work for all of them.

This limit makes possible the connection to our everyday lives in 2009, where the congruency of all these technologies start to appear on any laptop. The ever growing proliferation of connected laptops or desktops in houses and schools make us understand how knowledge can appear more and more, coming from databases. But the successful implementation of KM platforms should result in the ability of the organization to create a climate in which there is a free flow of knowledge (Gupta, 2008). The process of KM comprises five steps:

- Knowledge generation
- Knowledge sharing
- Knowledge adaptation
- Knowledge application
- Knowledge modification (new knowledge generation)

Knowledge sharing is an important step in the process (Gupta, 2001). Most successful organizations have been following the path of human values oriented practices in their practices. This approach is synthesized in this framework, where the focus is laid on organizational orientation and on the commitment towards the practices which allows the people to apply these skills (Figure 6).

Nevertheless, experiences related to the use of such tools exist in the educational system. Different than e-learning bases, the mixed use of free online tools can be relevant if used in a precise manner. Among these tools, blogs are probably the most famous.

Blogs and Wikis as Starters

"The word blog is irrelevant. What is important is that it is now common, and will soon be expected, that every intelligent person (and quite a few unintelligent ones) will have a media platform where they share what they care about with the world" said Godin (2009), a prolific writer both on books and blogs related to marketing. A blog (a contraction of the term "weblog") is a type of website, usually maintained by an individual with regular entries of commentary, descriptions of events, or other material such as graphics or video (Wikipedia, 2009g). Since the advent of blogs in the mid 1990s, providers of blogging

Figure 6. Framework of knowledge sharing climate (Gupta, 2008)

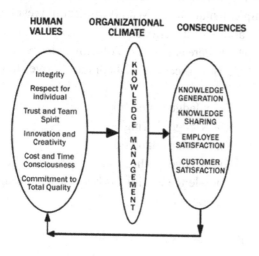

software, facilitate user comments, allowing readers to reply to blog entries allowed for the kind of freewheeling interaction that is today the main concept of blogging and UGC in general. In its purest form, a blog is a personal journal maintained by an individual, updated as often as possible, viewable by anyone on the Internet, and where comments can be left on each written post. The entries (posts) generally appear in reverse chronological order, meaning the most recent is at the top of the page and others can be found by scrolling down, with archived entries available through links at the bottom or sides of the page. Blogs span a wide range of content. Some consist of little more than weekly updates about one's hairdresser, while others serve the nerve centers of political discussions, even influencing debate on a national scale: 5,000,000 active supporters across 15 social networks and blogs helped Obama's campaign by mentioning it on the Internet for example. As of December 2006, 19% of the fastest-growing private companies in the U.S. reported use of blogging as a form of communication (EMarketer, 2007). Users are often invited to leave remarks below each post. They foster, free of restraints, conversations that frequently take on a life of their own. These conversations become a permanent addendum to the original posts, and are often as much of the entertainment as the post itself. This connected community is called the "*blogosphere*".

The Blog's growing rate of 20% every 3 months shows how essential it is for the communications strategies of many brands. Companies actually use it to create a "*buzz*", or simply to communicate and generate traffic on their websites. They can also promote a service or an event, or even measure the impact of the marketing strategy. It helps in tracking and measuring audiences and finally, its success seems mainly due to its independence and credibility.

This type of tool can also be used for other purposes. During the last year, students were studying e-learning with an online professor of e-marketing. Each of them had to create a blog in order to post the expected work on a regularly bases of one post a week minimum. The offer of free blogs is vast on the Internet, but a few were recommended by the professor, because they offer the minimum features which are required in terms of widgets, already prepared links for the syndication and so on: Website Baker (http://start.websitebaker2.org/en/introduction.html), WIM Editor (http://www.wymeditor.org/), Joomla (http://demo.joomla.org/), SPIP (http://www.spip.net/), Dotclear (http://www.dotclear.net/), Wordpress (http://wordpress.com/) count for this purpose and Framasoft (http://www.framasoft.net/rubrique168.html) presents some more.[1]

The task of reading and synthesizing an online text in relation to the content of the course, by adding a post on their blog, permitted the students to know what their peer answers to the lecturer's questions were. The latter could briefly know if the expected work was handed in on each student's blog, at anytime, anywhere. The different tools that are commonly available on a blog once set up, offer the possibility for the students and for the lecturer to stay in touch easily. We refer here to the RSS[2] or Atom[3] links, enabling users to

Figure 7. RSS feeds enable users to receive the last updates of a blog or wiki

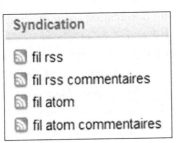

know if something new has been posted on the blog instantly (Figure 7).

Along with this type of technology, wikis are other types of UGC that can easily accompany *"art of blogging"*. Once again, both schools and companies can easily use them to post announcements or present anyone's work.

"Wiki" is the Hawaiian word for 'quick'. In its most basic sense, a wiki is collaborative effort, a Website built through the contributions of many individuals. It is a group collaboration software tool based on Web server technology. It allows the easy creation and editing of any number of interlinked Web pages, using a simplified markup language or a WYSIWYG text editor, within the browser.[4]

Though not all wikis are open to everyone—indeed, many require some kind of membership or qualification to contribute - they appear as the most democratic manifestation of UGC. The principle behind wikis is simple: all the world's expertise, knowledge, and creativity can be harnessed through Internet collaboration. The most instructive and well-known example of a wiki is Wikipedia, the free online, publicly editable encyclopedia. Launched in 2001, it has quickly become one of the most prominent—even trusted—reference sites on the Web. As of December 2007, it boasted more than 2 million articles in 253 languages, making it the largest encyclopedia ever. As already mentioned, 13 million articles are now available in 2009. This shows the potential of

UGC. Nearly every article on Wikipedia is publicly editable, and changes appear immediately, though only registered users can create new articles. For the most part, accuracy and "neutrality" key principles behind Wikipedia, are enforced by the community. There is, however, a hierarchy of volunteer editors, who, at the top levels, have the authority to delete content and lock articles.

Wikis are thus increasingly being accepted as a new breed of collaborative technology. Wiki technology can impact KM, and can support knowledge creation and sharing (Leuf & Cunningham, 2001; Wagner, 2004; Lamb, 2004). Wikis can also support collaborative knowledge creation and sharing in an academic environment. Success in attempts to provide such support may depend on: familiarity with wiki technology, careful planning for implementation and use, appropriate class size, and motivation of students to engage in discovery learning.

One of the interests of these social networks is that they have great potential for a network's demographic, behavioral, or psychographic targeting, providing the quality audience reach that can be attractive to organizations or schools. Once signed up, employees or students are "classified" according to the amount of information they agree to provide when they arrive for the first time on the platform. When users join a social networking site, they are given a page on which they create a profile. They are thus asked to enter personal information such as their sex, age, date-of-birth, hometown, work history, hobbies, favorite songs, interests, etc. They can then upload photos or links to other Web pages that interest or simply please them. This information is displayed on their profile page, and users are given the option of making the page public or viewable only to those within their network. Restricted accesses according to the "owner" exist, permitting him/her to hide certain information. Profile pages serve as launching pads from which users explore these social networking sites. They can search for other individuals, or find people with common interests. Users who identify others they want as part of their networks invite one another to be *"friends"*, and such networks are displayed for others to see and browse. In this way, global networks of people with friends or interests in common get born.

Social networks allow users to place comments, photos, videos and Web links on each others' pages, thereby sharing information and interests with dozens, hundreds, or thousands of people—depending on the size of one's network—with a single click.

This system, when used in organizations where employees have to share their customer's experiences, can be very relevant. A bad experience when selling a product can serve another employee who reads the feedback from his colleague on the company's wiki dedicated to this function. He/she can indeed take into account the weaknesses or threats that occurred with his colleague regarding this bad experience.

The success of wikis depends on the involvement in the participation of each actor of the platform. Wiki technology is an open-source technology and is downloadable at no cost. Easy to learn and understand, once a wiki is installed, anyone can very quickly understand how to use key features within the technology. It permits asynchronous discussion in that it enables students and instructors to engage in continuous discussion, when they have the time. This permits ability to share and update the knowledge base (Bergin, 2002). Once a wiki page is created, it persists and can be updated. Wiki technology can be used as a knowledge repository. It supports many-to-many communication and enables creation of new knowledge based on a given knowledge history (Wagner, 2004). The wiki can support the following goals:

- Sharing of information/knowledge (papers, presentations)
- Demonstrating that there needs to be a benefit for the user otherwise it isn't used

- Showing how information/knowledge needs to be organized to be found easily without duplication (Murali, 2009)

Instructors can use wiki technology as a knowledge base to keep track of student papers, presentations and projects. These can be viewed and updated using simple edit and link functions. The instructor's goal is then to allow the students to explore, test and administer an online collaborative tool and determine whether or not it is a successful KM tool (Murali, 2009). When using wiki technology in e-learning, the system needs to be configured with a tracking mechanism that monitors the contribution level of each participant. Other tools than wikis can reinforce their use, like Social Media, for example.

Social Media Platforms: All in One

The promise of UGC is now becoming hyper-realized thanks to social media. Sites like MySpace, Facebook, and YouTube represent the convergence of user commentary with video, photos, and music sharing, all presented in a user-friendly format, allowing participation on a mass scale. Facebook launched its application platform on May 24, 2007. It is an API that developers can use to create widgets that can easily be distributed on Facebook.[5]

To encourage take-up, Facebook's platform strategy allows developers to keep the revenue they generate through traffic to their applications. Almost a year later, there were nearly 20,000 applications available on Facebook, most created by thousands of 3rd party developers (IAB, 2008). While these applications themselves are forms of UGC, many are also designed to allow individual users to express themselves—their favorites, likes, dislikes, recommendations, etc. The easiness to spread information to particular people taking part of a group of fans on a Facebook account, adds some relevance to the use of it in an academic context. A lecturer can offer text, share pictures, give tasks to achieve in a student context by clicking on a few buttons from his or her Facebook account. This is what actually happens for a professor in marketing. Any information he/she wants to share with his classroom, considered as a "group of fans" in the social media vocabulary, can be sent and delivered easily, without any tool such as a mail server for example. The creation of lists of contacts and the possibility to share any type of content as far as it is online, count as important factors for adopting this type of technology. YouTube, as a platform of video films of any kind, can also provide sources of inspiration when designing social based solutions for information usage within organizations. Companies such as Apple selling Steve Job's show when he promotes the Iphone or Ipad, represent great sources of inspiration for other companies interested in new ways of corporate communication. YouTube is the place to find extracts of this Apple's shows for example. The same type of information exists with Flickr for pictures, thanks to images that can be of interest for photographers who look for new ideas from anybody for example. The strengths of these systems mainly lie in the size of the community of "non experts". It represents a vast amount of ideas that have not been promoted or used yet, in most of the cases. The same interests can be applied in organizations which could be reluctant to afford expensive information systems based on these principles. They even could add some *"tweets"* to their strategy, by using Twitter for example.

Communicating by Tweets

Twitter is a free social networking and micro-blogging service that enables its users to send and read messages known as *tweets* which are text-based posts of up to 140 characters. The latter are displayed on the author's profile page and delivered to the author's subscribers who are known as *followers* (Wikipedia, 2009b). Thanks to this system, people can get news, links and any types of information from people they know (or not) and want to follow. A lecturer may post on his or her

Tweeter account the interesting information he/she reads across the web, and wants to share with his students. The same type of use can apply for an organization where members move and want (or have to) keep in touch with their colleagues. They can update their Tweeter account by using any type of Internet access if they have already signed up on Twitter to create an account. Even if one could find the piece of information quite poor (140 characters is not a lot), it is still useful and so easy-to-use that it represents a real tool for communicating. Tweeter, for example, was used during a project with students in design who had to be present on Second Life for their project. From the professor working with these students to the staff of the school, everybody followed the project thanks to Tweeter and the student's *"tweets activity"*. This system also gives the impression that people are always connected with someone else, minute after minute. This is very important for e-learning, since students call for information from around the world, and expect immediate feedback on their work. They are known as life-long learners as the skills they acquire means that they are continuously challenging and searching for information (Reisman, 2003, p. 240). Another type of social network which can easily benefit an organization or school is named *"social bookmarking"*.

Social Bookmarking: To Keep, Share, and Discover the (Best of the) Web

Social bookmarking allows consumers to share their favorite Web destinations or content with others by submitting links to a public or semi-public web page. The most famous and widely known social bookmarking site is del.icio.us (http://delicious.com/). As publishers and portals add these features to their content and, in turn, those preferences can be tied to a user's profile page, it becomes one more way that users can express their interests to their peers.

An easy way to use this type of tool either in an organization or school is illustrated by an experience with students working on final projects. Year after year, topics vary a little in business or design schools. The aim at the project permits each new generation of students to look at past projects and read what could be interesting for them before starting to work on a new one. A new account has been set up on del.icio.us, dedicated to the group of students of the school. No personal information regarding the websites has been added to this account, only websites related to the project. The instructor then asked the students, by providing them with login and keyword information, to type their title, topic and keywords. Keywords represent a keystone with these social bookmarking technologies (Figure 8).

Also called *"e-tailing folksonomies"*, this collaborative tagging system shows to the community the use of tags and the categorization of tags implications on navigation, content organization and user profiling (Figure 9).

Each student first needs to build a blog, in order to link any of these tags to the social bookmarking website. As explained earlier, the easiness of building a blog permits both students and instructor to read instantly the new contributions of each student thanks to posted data (text, pictures, video, sound etc.) (Figure 10).

Thereby, tag clouds showing keywords enable students to visit an already built blog. This blog has been built by another student from the school in the past. This is especially relevant if they work on a similar topic, for example. The blog acts as a handbook showing progressively each step of the progression of the student's work. One post relates to a book or any other raw material fruitful for the progress of the major project. The

Figure 8. Students projects are incorporated on a special del.icio.us account

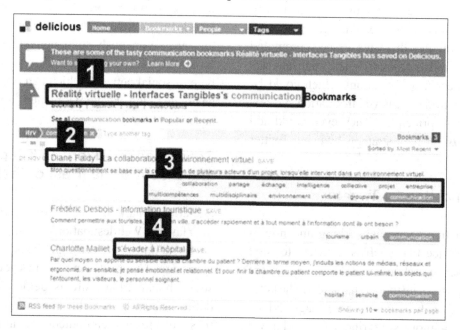

Legend:
1: title of the student's group
2: student's name
3: keywords (tags) of the student's project
4: title of the student's project

ability to click on a word among the variety of words from the tag clouds offers to any student the possibility to read a content that might be close to his own topic.

This is another type of KM possibility merging blogs and social bookmarking systems in order to save time, to avoid the repetition of identical topics, to improve their understanding on topics that they wouldn't have covered if they could not access past student's works so easily.

Why Does it Work? Because it is Free, Easy and Can Be Customized

As for e-commerce websites trying to increase their sales through personalized merchandising mainly based on the *theatralization* of the interface (Pelet & Papadopoulou, 2008), one of the interests of UGC tools is that you can modify many aspects of its interface. However, if online personalization has been extensively studied in information systems research, web users' reactions to such personalization are not known yet (Ho, 2006).

Figure 9. Tag clouds of student projects

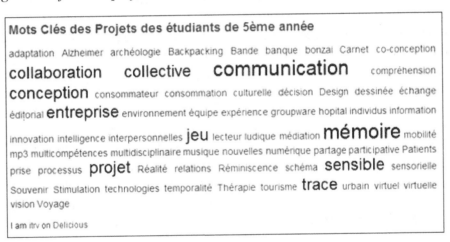

Figure 10. Student's blog

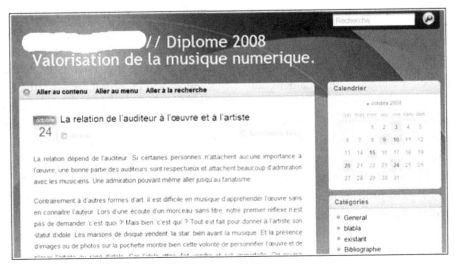

It seems now even more important than ever to admit that KM systems can fail to deliver on their promise (Fahey & Prusak, 1998; Newell *et al.*, 1999; Lindgren & Henfridsson, 2002; Storey & Barnett, 2000). According to Gupta (2008), the true reasons for sub-optimal KM performance are in many cases related to the lack of supportive attitudes and emotions on the part of the organization's employees. By looking at a recent research in the marketing field (Pelet, 2008), positing that e-commerce could be enhanced thanks to a better use of colors as a variable of the design, because its effects on mood and emotion are far from neutral, we can imagine the interest of modifying the appearance of a tool that is used on screens at work.

The personalization of a tool such as a wiki is mainly based on its design and on the capacities it offers to answer users' requests, whatever they are. These requests can be fulfilled thanks to widgets, the most widely used API on the Internet currently.

In this section, we first introduce the capacity to personalize the content of these UGC tools, and then explain how the design of these interfaces constitute an important topic to think about, when using them in organizations or schools.

Widgets: Control Your Content

Widgets are portable applications that allow both users and sites to have a hand in the content (IAB, 2008). They are small programs that users can download onto their desktops, or embed in their blogs or profile pages. A widget imports some form of live content. For example, a windsurfer blogger can embed a widget from Weather.com that always displays weather conditions in his favorite sea spot. The key is helping UGC enthusiasts offer their users some unique content and possibility to offer their content. Most are eager to identify themselves with a brand or service that can make their blogs or profiles more dynamic. They have recently become a popular form of brand or news distribution. In fact, the publisher is able to control the content and the user places

that content on his or her page, be it a blog or social networking profile. Users can also simply pass the widget to friends.

For organizations, widgets can be a way of doing research and development easily. Since a user installs it on his wiki or blog, he/she can then choose to import RSS (or Atom) feeds by using a widget dedicated to this function. RSS feeds can be read using software called *"RSS reader"*, *"feed reader"*, or *"aggregator"*, which can be web-based thanks to the use of a widget for example. Its main benefit is that it syndicates content automatically. An employee working on a precise topic can choose to get information from the web by obtaining it thanks to RSS. After visiting websites around this particular topic, he/she can then subscribe to any RSS feed available. The widget installed on his wiki can then show each feed instantly, avoiding having the employee visit each website. The information comes on its own to him/her. The concept of *"collective intelligence"* here supports the intelligence from experts. This intelligence results from the accumulation of contents and especially from the weaving of more and more dense links between them. This particular use of RSS feeds can be compared with InnoCentive's platform.

InnoCentive (http://www.innocentive.com/) connects companies, academic institutions, public sector and non-profit organizations with a global network of more than 180,000 people (the Seekers). Engineers, scientists, inventors, and business people with expertise in life sciences, engineering, chemistry, math, computer science, and entrepreneurship (the Solvers) thus solve some of the world's toughest challenges. In fact, organizations post their challenges on the InnoCentive website, and offer registered people significant financial awards for the best solutions. Seeker™ and Solver™ identities are kept completely confidential and secure, and InnoCentive manages the entire IP (Internet Protocol) process. Rather than making this process public on a website, one could easily imagine the benefit of installing it on an organization database, and sharing the information from multiple agencies of the company in the world.

In the case of e-learning solution, a professor can manage several students, after asking them to build a blog (or a wiki) where they post their expected project each time they work on it. In a flash, he/she can then access any student's work, after connecting each RSS feed from a student's blog to his own wiki. This wiki owns a widget (installed by the professor), enabling him/her to see what is happening in each student's project without asking them to send an explaining email. As an example of useful wiki to configure in order to receive this type of information, Netvibes (http://www.netvibes.com/) is an option, like Pageflakes (http://www.pageflakes.com/), My Yahoo! (http://fr.my.yahoo.com/), Alot.com (http://www.alot.com/), iGoogle (http://www.google.com/ig), and Microsoft Live (http://home.live.com/). It is a personalized start page or personal web portal organized into tabs, with each tab containing user-defined modules as shown on Figure 10. One tab corresponds to a classroom or group of students in a particular school, for example (Number 1, Figure 11). Beside the tab bar the students' group projects are presented (Number 2, Figure 11).

Built-in Netvibes modules include an RSS/Atom feed reader, local weather forecasts, a calendar, bookmarks, notes, to-do lists, multiple searches, support for email as well as several webmail providers, podcast support with a built in audio player, and several others. A page can be personalized further through the use of existing themes or by creating our own theme. Customized tabs, feeds and modules can be shared with others individually or via the Netvibes Ecosystem. For privacy reasons, only modules with publicly available content can be shared.

By clicking on group names, the professor is able to read each note posted by students of the group in a second, without having to visit each blog, and waste his time trying to understand how the latter has been conceived and where the relevant information is. This is the advantage of the previously mentioned standardized format. Once the professor clicks on a particular student's project, the content originating from his blog appears. A widget could thereby allow a user to share what he/she is revising for an exam or what he/she is studying for exams and get inspiration from others.

As shown on Figure 12, the navigation bar of the student's blog appears on the left of the Netvibes site (Number 1 on Figure 12), whereas the post that the professor wants to read appears on the right hand side of the same screen (Number 2 on Figure 12).

Once again, the interest of using this type of tool mainly lies on its efficiency, speed and easiness of building. Another reason for students,

Figure 11. Netvibes enables professors to follow each student's project

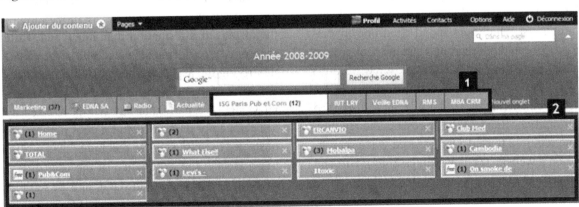

Figure 12. Each student's blog content appears in a standardized format on the Netvibes professor configuration

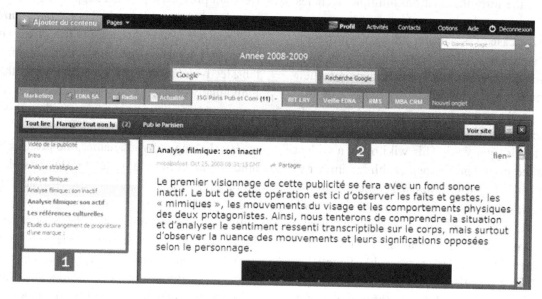

professors, employees and so on to use UGC tools is supported by their easy-to-customize strengths.

Considering the time spent on UGC tools, users may have to take into account aspects related to the content personalization or to ergonomic concerns. The perception of a website's atmosphere lies almost exclusively in its visual aspect since 80% of the information processed by the Internet user's brain comes from sight (Mattelart, 1996). Among the behavioral reactions caused by website atmospherics, the visit duration of a website depends on colors, which are considered as factors of positive influence; on the contrary, a limited use of colors in websites can be considered as a factor of negative influence. These colors reveal the contrast, which correspond to a strong opposition between the foreground and the background colors, as defined by W3C (http://www.w3.org/) (W3C, 2008). The main function of contrast consists of enhancing the readability of the displayed information. Readability represents the reaction time required to find a target word when searching on a website (Hall & Hanna, 2004). Hill and Scharff (1997) have demonstrated the importance of contrast (dynamic color vs. dominant color)

when searching for information within a page. They obtained better readability scores when resorting to chromatic colors (green dynamic color on yellow dominant color). The possibility offered in certain websites to see quality representations of the products or services or information contributes to the user feeling positive about staying on the website. A representation of quality relies on an image being able to be magnified so that the product appears larger. This is why more and more UGC content facilitates the change of color or theme in order to procure to the user more confidence and readability of the content. This seems even more important considering chromatic colors are more likely to enhance the Memorization of the displayed information than black and white (achromatic) colors are (Pelet, 2008). The fact of modifying the aspect of the interface guarantees that each of the millions of users who log onto a UGC site on a particular day will be greeted by a special color or theme. And it does not impose obstacles or extra steps to reaching one's profile page. Hence, the experience of the user differs according to the topic of the UGC and the settings made on the *options* page (Figure 13).

Figure 13. Netvibes offers the possibility to modify its colors and themes

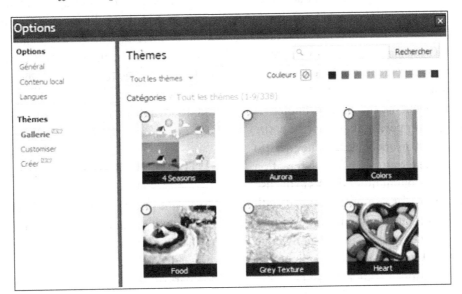

CONCLUSION, DISCUSSIONS, AND LIMITATIONS

As in all case studies, the quality of the research is difficult to verify. For this reason, the following issues should be considered when evaluating this chapter. First, the case studies were described fairly thoroughly in order to make it possible for the reader to assess the validity of the conclusions drawn. Second, the generalizability of the conclusions is problematic, as always in little case studies. Thus, we believe that the main conclusions are not specific to one case, since this is an exploratory study which is also applicable to other companies or schools, in a similar context (Lukka & Kasanen, 1995), i.e. in organizations that are already utilizing business process management and are also interested in applying KM.

This chapter proposes some methodologies that are based on the assessment of practices that have successfully implemented strategies of KM, and their comparison with others. It examines the IC and IC management in the context of the business process of a company such as for the e-learning strategy of a school. This approach can be applied both to large-sized companies, generally interested in the potential of KM and, to schools increasingly interested in the possibility of sharing and communicating between lecturers, students and the entire staff, and to SMEs (Small and Medium Enterprises): any organization in fact can benefit from these tools.

The study contributes to prior research by providing a description of the application of a KM project in practice without applying any specific KM model, since everybody can have his own view on the topic. It also defines and describes conceptually and in practice how the business and school concepts relate to each other and could presumably benefit from embracing a UGC tool or platform in their strategy. Even though this chapter is quite descriptive in nature, it can be considered a valuable contribution due to the very small amount of research published so far on the application of KM in practice, especially when considering UGC tools.

Information technology (IT) has a crucial role in KM because it is the facilitator and the enabler. However, most of the research on the role of information technology in KM has focused on big firms, whereas the IT requirements of SMEs or schools are different from that of big firms,

(Pillania, 2008), this is why the introduction of UGC tools enables us to think about IT differently than for big structures. The examples provided, showing how IC management could be applied within process management, can be viewed as a point of departure.

But as remarkable as the new technologies are, they provide only potential, and not the entire solution to the problems encountered. They need to enable new knowledge processes and the creation of new knowledge communities thanks to the use of social networks, for example, coupled with wikis or blogs and other communicating tools. These new knowledge processes and knowledge communities need to be strategically aligned to the objectives of the organization: this is probably the limit of the proposition of this chapter, since IT projects need to be aligned to the principles of organizational success. It means: the head must accompany the project of implementing this strategy from the beginning until the end.

Wiig (2000) explains that: *"there are emerging realizations that to achieve the level of effective behavior required for competitive excellence, the whole person must be considered. We must integrate cognition, motivation, personal satisfaction, feelings of security, and many other factors"*. This is exactly what e-commerce is facing; this is why this industry is increasingly taking into account ergonomics, cognitive psychology and human computer interaction proposals. One can presume that companies which aim to create and share knowledge should consider with more detail advances in e-commerce before implementing tools such as UGC in their structure. The roles of people in knowledge technologies are integral to their success, like they are the success of e-commerce.

This chapter did not discuss whether other approaches than those used here might have been applicable for linking organizational process management and e-learning to knowledge and IC management. It would be valuable to study what the most useful way to link these approaches might

be, with other UGC tools. It would also be interesting to study how other managerial approaches could be integrated with KM. In addition to just applying KM in practice using different tools such as the UGC ones for organizations and schools, it is important to analyze the effects (i.e. benefits and disadvantages) of such actions.

FUTURE RESEARCH

Most of the literature on KM suggests that it should be adopted considering particular frameworks. At the same time, studies are suggesting that knowledge and IC management can be executed as a part of other management systems such as quality systems or balanced performance measurement systems (see e.g. Lönnqvist *et al.*, 2006). This chapter contributes to the research field by providing examples of adopting UGC tools alongside a conventional management and e-learning approach. It has demonstrated that process and e-learning management provides a suitable way to carry out knowledge and IC management. On the basis of the experience gained from multiple case studies, we conclude that it is possible to identify knowledge and IC management in the organization by analyzing its processes. The following table presents a comparison of which of the technologies that are mentioned in the chapter are more useful in enhancing the use of information systems in organizations. It also presents the combination of the technologies which is more useful, why, and in which situations (Table 3).

Discovery learning requires that people are motivated to learn in this mode. Garrison and Anderson (2003) provide a useful method by classifying different perspectives to understand the role of technology in the context of learning using electronic mediums. From a philosophical stance, they assert that the goal of using technology in education (within the context of e-learning) is to provide students with the ability to manage information effectively. Based on this perspective,

Table 3. Presentation of the facilities offered by each website's assets

		Available websites	Learning, memorizing	Sharing knowledge	Decision making	Sharing information	Specific assets
1	Broadcast, entertainment	**Video** YouTube: http://youtube.com Daily Motion: http://www.dailymotion.com Viadeo: http://www.viadeo.com		✓		✓	Send corporate videos for team building or promote particularly relevant videos on a precise aspect
2		**Picture** Flickr: http://www.flickr.com Picasa: http://www.picasa.com		✓		✓	Facilitate decision on the choices of pictures that are not usually used on a particular field
3		**Sound** Deezer: http://www.deezer.com	✓	✓		✓	Permits to listen to podcasts or soundtracks on different topics
4	Social networks	**Social bookmark** Del.icio.us: http://www.del.icio.us		✓		✓	Bookmarks from everybody become available everywhere, and help to classify topics
5		**Micro blogging** Tweeter: http://www.tweeter.com		✓	✓	✓	Spread a link or information on a particular topic according to the team, students or else from a mobile device or from the Internet
6		**Students** Facebook: http://www.facebook.com		✓	✓	✓	Stay in touch, exchange graphics, images, links, chat with many people at once
7		**Professionals** Viadeo: http://www.viadeo.com LinkedIn: http://www.linkedin.com				✓	Look for profiles of interest and contact them easily without being too involved
8		**Encyclopedia** Wikipedia: http://www.wikipedia.com	✓	✓		✓	Any question, any answer, or build a topic that different people will keep up to date

continued on following page

Table 3. continued

		Available websites	Learning, memorizing	Sharing knowledge	Decision making	Sharing information	Specific assets
9	Content management systems	**Wikis**					
		Elgg: http://www.elgg.com Joomla: http://www.joomla.com	✓	✓	✓	✓	Start to share lectures, data and administrate them person by person or group by group
10		**RSS platform**					
		Netvibes: http://www.nevibes.com iGoogle: http://www.igoogle.com Blogovin: http://www.blogovin.com	✓	✓	✓	✓	Have a look on many CMS at once, share RSS feeds and encourage your team
11		**Blogs**					
		Wordpress: http://www.wordpress.com Dotclear: http://www.dotclear.com Spip: http://www.spip.com	✓	✓	✓	✓	Spread information, images, urls, podcasts, texts
Most useful combinations to use in organizations			All these tools are easy to try/use as far as a minimum of time is invested by the interested person. No particular skill is required, this is their main strength. On top of that, they are free.				

they suggest that the following factors be considered when using technology for academic purposes:

- Create an environment that permits the students/participants not only to learn but also develops the ability to learn to learn;
- Focus on critical thinking;
- The desired outcome of the education process becomes the ability for students to construct coherent knowledge structures to support the learning process;
- Shift towards a constructive view of teaching and learning in general;

The alternative perspective put forth by Garrison and Anderson (2003) is the transactional view. In this context they assert that individual learners should be able to grasp the meaning of knowledge and improve their understanding of a particular subject. This will be hopefully possible once the solutions discussed in this chapter are implemented by organizations and schools.

To conclude, the author has been recently (July 2009) asked to build an intranet in the business school he works in, helping people to elaborate KM as well as communicate. Developers, designers and all the presented tools are already known by him and used in similar contexts. Thus it should not be too difficult to develop it by June 2010. The system will have to serve and help 50 people from the pedagogical and administrative team, 20 researchers and 2000 students, with half of them studying during certain periods in other countries. Another chapter will explain the difficulties encountered, and the new tools that emerged during this period of time in order to reinforce those presented here.

REFERENCES

W3C. (2008). Publication version 1.1 of the AccessiWeb repository. Cambridge, MA: W3C. Retrieved June 9, 2008, from http://www.w3c.org/

Alavi, M., & Leidner, D. E. (2001). Review: Knowledge management and knowledge management systems: Conceptual foundations and research issues. *Management Information Systems Quarterly, 25*(1), 107–136. doi:10.2307/3250961

Aldridge, A., Forcht, K., & Pierson, J. (1997). Get linked or get lost: Marketing strategy for the internet. *Internet Research: Electronic Networking Applications and Policy, 7*(3), 161–169. doi:10.1108/10662249710171805

Argyris, C. (1990). *Overcoming organizational defenses: Facilitating organizational learning.* Boston: Allyn and Bacon.

Bacharach, M., & Gambetti, D. (2001). Trust in signs. In Cook, K. (Ed.), *Trust in society* (pp. 148–184). New York: Russell Sage Foundation.

Bergin, J. (2002). Teaching on the Wiki Web, *ACM. SIGCSE Bulletin, 34*(3), 195. doi:10.1145/637610.544473

Bernoff, J., Pflaum, C. N., & Bowen, E. (2008, October 20). *The growth of social technology adoption: 2/3 of the global Internet population visit social networks.* Cambridge, MA: Forrester Research. Retrieved from http://www.forrester.com/Research/Document/Excerpt/0,7211,44907,00.html

Bhatt, G. (2000). Information dynamics, learning, and knowledge creation in organizations. *The Learning Organization: An International Journal, 7*(2), 89–98. doi:10.1108/09696470010316288

Choo, C. W., & Bontis, N. (Eds.). (2002). *The strategic management of intellectual capital and organizational knowledge.* New York: Oxford University Press.

Cotter, S. (2002). Taking the measure of e-marketing success. *The Journal of Business Strategy, 23*(2), 30–37. doi:10.1108/eb040235

Coviello, N. E., Milley, R., & Marcolin, B. (2001). Understanding IT-enabled interactivity in contemporary marketing. *Journal of Interactive Marketing, 15*(4), 18–33. doi:10.1002/dir.1020

Damanpour, F. (1992). Organizational size and innovation. *Organization Studies, 13*(3), 375–402. doi:10.1177/017084069201300304

Davenport, T. H., & Prusak, L. (1998). *How organizations manage what they know.* Boston: Harvard Business School Press.

Donath, J. (2007). Signals in social supernets. *Journal of Computer-Mediated Communication, 13*(1). Retrieved from http://jcmc.indiana.edu/vol13/issue1/donath.html.

Drucker, P. F. (1988). The coming of the new organization. *Harvard Business Review, 66*(1).

Dunbar, R. I. M. (1996). *Grooming, gossip, and the evolution of language.* Cambridge, MA: Harvard University Press.

Dunbar, R. I. M. (2004). Gossip in evolutionary perspective. *Review of General Psychology, 8*(2), 100–110. doi:10.1037/1089-2680.8.2.100

Eisenhardt, K. M., & Brown, S. L. (1999). Patching: Re-stitching business portfolios in dynamic markets. *Harvard Business Review, 78*(1), 91–101.

EMarketer. (2007, June). *User Generated Content: Will Web 2.0 Pay its Way?* Fahey, L., & Prusak, L. (1998). The eleven deadliest sins of knowledge management. *California Management Review, 40*(3).

Foremski, T. (2005). *If Internet 1.0 was a disruptive technology...where is the train wreck? SiliconValleyWatcher.* Retrieved February 21, 2005, from http://www.siliconvalleywatcher.com/mt/archives/2005/02/if_Internet_10_1.php

Garrison, D., & Anderson, T. (2003). *E-learning in the 21st century: A framework for research and practice.* London: Routledge. doi:10.4324/9780203166093

Godin, S. (2009). *Seth Goodin's blog*. Retrieved from http://www.sethgodin.com/

Goffee, R., & Jones, G. (2001). Followership: It's personal, too. *Harvard Business Review, 79*(11), 148–149.

Good, D. (2000). Individuals, interpersonal relations, and trust. In Gambetta, D. (Ed.), *Trust: Making and breaking cooperative relations* (pp. 31–48). Oxford, UK: University of Oxford Press.

Granovetter, M. S. (1983). The strength of weak ties: A network theory revisited. *Sociological Theory, 1*, 201–233. doi:10.2307/202051

Grant, R. M. (1996). Toward a knowledge-based theory of the firm [in Special issue: Knowledge and the Firm]. *Strategic Management Journal, 17*(2), 109–122.

Gupta, K. S. (2001, July-September). Knowledge management and empowerment: A conceptual relationship. [Bombay: NITIE.]. *Udyog Pragati, 25*(3), 28–35.

Gupta, K. S. (2008). A comparative analysis of knowledge sharing climate. *Knowledge and Process Management, 15*(3), 186–195. doi:10.1002/kpm.309

Hall, R. H., & Hanna, P. (2004). The impact of Web page text: Background color combinations on readability, retention, aesthetics, and behavioral intention. *Behaviour & Information Technology, 23*(3), 183–195. doi:10.1080/01449290410001669932

Herbig, P., & Hale, B. (1997). Internet: The marketing challenge of the twentieth century. *Internet Research: Electronic Networking Application and Policy, 7*(2), 95–100. doi:10.1108/10662249710165226

Hill, A., & Scharff, L. V. (1997). Readability of websites with various foreground/background color combinations, font types and word styles. *Proceedings of 11th National Conference in Undergraduate Research, 2*, 742-746.

Ho S. Y. (2006). The attraction of Internet personalization to web users. *Electronic e-commerce markets, 16*(1) 41-50.

Hong, J., Kianto, A., & Kyläheiko, K. (2008). Moving culture and the creation of new knowledge and dynamic capabilities in emerging markets. *Knowledge and Process Management, 15*(3), 196–202. doi:10.1002/kpm.310

Horrigan, J., Boase, J., Rainie, L., & Wellman, B. (2006). *The strength of Internet ties*. Pew Internet & American Life Project report. Retrieved August 10, 2007, from http://www.pewInternet.org/PPF/r/172/report_display.asp

IAB. (2008). *Platform status report: User Generated Content, Social Media, and Advertising—An Overview*. New York: Interactive Advertising Bureau. Retrieved April 2008, from http://www.iab.net/media/file/2008_ugc_platform.pdf

Kogut, B., & Zander, U. (1992). Knowledge of the firm, combinative capabilities, and the replication of technology. *Organization Science, 3*, 383–397. doi:10.1287/orsc.3.3.383

Kraemer, K. L., Dedrick, J., Melville, N. P., & Zhu, K. (2006). *Global e-commerce, impacts of national environment and policy*. Cambridge, UK: Cambridge University Press. doi:10.1017/CBO9780511488603

Kujansivu, P., & Lönnqvist, A. (2008). Business process management as a tool for Intellectual Capital management. *Knowledge and Process Management, 15*(3), 159–169. doi:10.1002/kpm.307

Ladd, A., & Ward, M. A. (2002). An investigation of environmental factors influencing knowledge transfer. *Journal of Knowledge Management Practice*.

Lamb, B. (2004). The standard wiki overview. *EDUCASEUSE Review, 39*(5), 36–48.

Lee, C. S. (2001). An analytical framework for evaluating e-commerce business models and strategies. *Internet Research, 11*(4), 349–359. doi:10.1108/10662240110402803

Leuf, B., & Cunningham, W. (2001). *The WIKI WAY: Quick Collaboration of the Web*. Reading, MA: Addison-Wesley.

Lev, B. (2001). *Intangibles: Management, measurement and reporting*. Washington, DC: Brookings Institution Press.

Levenburg, N. (2005). Delivering customer value online: An analysis of practices, applications and performance. *Journal of Retailing and Consumer Services, 12*(5), 319–331. doi:10.1016/j.jretconser.2004.11.001

Levitt, T. (1983). The globalization of markets. *Harvard Business Review, 61*(3), 92–102.

Lindgren, R., & Henfridsson, O. (2002). Using competence systems: Adoption barriers and design suggestions. *Journal of Information & Knowledge management, 5*(2).

Lönnqvist, A., Kujansivu, P., & Antola, J. (2006). Are management accountants equipped to deal with intellectual capital? *The Finnish Journal of Business Economics, 3*, 355–368.

Lukka, K., & Kasanen, E. (1995). The problem of generalizability: Anecdotes and evidence in accounting research. *Accounting. Auditing and Accountability, 8*, 71–90. doi:10.1108/09513579510147733

Mattelart, A. (1996). *The invention of communication*. Minneapolis: University Minnesota Press.

McDermott, C., & O'Connor, G. (2002). Managing radical innovation: An overview of emergent strategy issues. *Journal of Product Innovation Management, 19*, 424–438. doi:10.1016/S0737-6782(02)00174-1

Milgram, S. (1967). The small world problem. *Psychology Today, 1*, 61–67.

Murali, R. (2009). Designing knowledge management systems for teaching and learning with Wiki technology. *Journal of Information Systems Education*. Retrieved August 27, 2009 from http://findarticles.com/p/articles/mi_qa4041/is_200510/ai_n15715725/

Murdoch, R. (2009). Global Media Entrepreneur.

Nardi, B. A., Whittaker, S., Isaacs, E., Creech, M., Johnson, J., & Hainsworth, J. (2002). Integrating communication and information through ContactMap. *Communications of the ACM, 45*(4), 89–95. doi:10.1145/505248.505251

Newell, S., Scarbrough, H., Swan, J., & Hislop, D. (1999). *Intranets and knowledge management: Complex processes and ironic outcomes*. Proceedings of the 32nd Hawaii International Conference on Systems Sciences. New York: IEEE.

Nielsen. (2007, October). *Online global consumer study*. Retrieved October 1, 2007, from http://en-us.nielsen.com/main/news/news_releases/2007/october/Word-of-Mouth_the_Most_Powerful_Selling_Tool__Nielsen_Global_Survey

Nielsen. (2009, March). *Global faces and networked places: A Nielsen report on social networking's new global footprint*. Retrieved from http://blog.nielsen.com/nielsenwire/wp-content/uploads/2009/03/nielsen_globalfaces_mar09.pdf

Nonaka, I., & Takeuchi, H. (1995). *The knowledge-creating company. How Japanese companies create the dynamics of innovation*. New York: Oxford University Press.

O'Reilly, T. (2005). What is web 2.0? Retrieved from http://oreilly.com/web2/archive/what-is-web-20.html

OECD. (1996). *The knowledge-based economy*. Paris: OECD.

OECD. (1999). *S&T indicators: Benchmarking the knowledge based economy*. Paris: OECD.

OECD. (2001). *Science, technology and industry scoreboard 2001: Towards a knowledge based economy*. Paris: OECD.

OECD. (2007). *OECD science, technology and industry scoreboard* 2007. Retrieved from http://www.oecd.org/document/21/0,2340, en_2649_33703_16683413_1_1_1_1,00.html

Pelet, J. É. (2008, June). *Effects of the color of e-commerce websites on the memorization and on the intention of purchase of the Net surfer*. Unpublished thesis. Nantes University, France.

Pelet, J. É., & Papadopoulou, P. (2009). Consumer responses to colors of e-commerce websites: An empirical investigation. In K. Kang (Ed.), *E-Commerce*. Vienna, Austria: InTech. Retrieved from http://intechweb.org

Pillania, R. K. (2007). Leveraging which knowledge in the globalization era? Indian facet. [Bingley, UK: Emerald Group Publishing Limited.]. *The Learning Organization, 14*(4), 313–320. doi:10.1108/09696470710749254

Pillania, R. K. (2008). Innovations and knowledge management in emerging markets. [Hoboken, NJ: Wiley Publishers.]. *Knowledge and Process Management, 15*(3), 184–185. doi:10.1002/kpm.308

Poon, S. P. H., & Swatman, P. M. C. (1999). A longitudinal study of small business internet commerce experiences. *International Journal of Electronic Commerce, 3*(3), 21–34.

Powell, T. C., & Dent-Micallef, A. (1997). Information technology as competitive advantage: The role of human, business and technology resources. *Strategic Management Journal, 18*(5), 375–405. doi:10.1002/(SICI)1097-0266(199705)18:5<375::AID-SMJ876>3.0.CO;2-7

Rapp, A., Schwillewaert, N., & Hao, A. W. (2008). The influence of market orientation on e-business innovation and performance: The role of the top management team. *The Journal of Marketing Theory and Practice, 16*(1), 7–25. doi:10.2753/MTP1069-6679160101

Raub, W., & Weesie, J. (1990). Reputation and efficiency in social interactions: An example of network effects. *American Journal of Sociology, 96*(3), 626–654. doi:10.1086/229574

Reisman, S. (2003). *Electronic learning communities*. Charlotte, NC: Information Age Publishing.

Seetharaman, A., Lock, T., Low, K., & Saravanan, A. S. (2004). Comparative justification on intellectual capital. *Journal of Intellectual Capital, 5*(4), 522–539. doi:10.1108/14691930410566997

Simeon, R. (1999). Evaluating domestic and international Web-site strategies. *Internet Research: Electronic Networking Applications and Policy, 9*(4), 297–308. doi:10.1108/10662249910286842

Storey, J., & Barnett, E. (2000). Knowledge management initiatives: Learning from failure. *Journal of Knowledge Management, 4*(2). doi:10.1108/13673270010372279

Sveiby, K. (1997). *The new organizational wealth*. San Francisco, CA: Berrett Koehler.

Von Krogh, G. (2000). *Enabling knowledge creation*. London: Oxford University Press.

Voola, R. (2005). *An Examination of the Effects of Firm Capabilities on E-Business Adoption and Competitive Advantage: A Resource Based Perspective*. Unpublished doctoral thesis. Newcastle University, UK.

Wagner, C. (2004). Wiki: A technology for conversational knowledge management and group collaboration. *Communications of the Association for Information Systems, 13*, 265–289.

Warne, L., Ali, I. M., & Pascoe, C. (2003). Team building as a foundation for knowledge management: Findings from research into social learning in the Australian Defence Organization. *Journal of Information & Knowledge Management, 2*(2), 93–106. doi:10.1142/S0219649203000024

Welling, R., & White, L. (2006). Measuring the value of Internet Web sites. *Journal of Internet Commerce, 5*(3), 127–145. doi:10.1300/J179v05n03_06

Wellman, B., Garton, L., & Haythornthwaite, C. (1997). Studying online social networks. *Journal of Computer Mediated Communication, 3*(1). Retrieved August 10, 2007, from http://jcmc.indiana.edu/vol3/issue1/garton.html

Wellman, B., & Gulia, M. (1999). The network basis of social support: A network is more than the sum of its ties. In *Networks in the Global Village* (pp. 83–118). Boulder, CO: Westview Press.

Whittaker, S., Jones, Q., & Terveen, L. (2002). Contact management: Identifying contacts to support long-term communication. In *Proceedings of the 2002 ACM conference on Computer Supported Cooperative Work* (pp. 216-225). New York: ACM Press.

Wiig, K. M. (2000). Knowledge management: An Emerging discipline rooted in a long history. In *Knowledge Horizons* (pp. 3–26). Boston: Butterworth-Heinemann. doi:10.1016/B978-0-7506-7247-4.50004-5

Wikipedia. (2009a). Facebook. Retrieved from http://en.wikipedia.org/wiki/Facebook

Wikipedia. (2009b). Twitter. Retrieved from http://en.wikipedia.org/wiki/Twitter

Wikipedia. (2009c). Linkedin. Retrieved from http://en.wikipedia.org/wiki/Linkedin

Wikipedia. (2009d). Friendster. Retrieved from http://en.wikipedia.org/wiki/Friendster

Wikipedia. (2009e). Myspace. Retrieved from http://en.wikipedia.org/wiki/Myspace

Wikipedia. (2009f). Content management system. Retrieved from http://en.wikipedia.org/wiki/Content_management_system

Wikipedia. (2009g). Blog. Retrieved from http://en.wikipedia.org/wiki/Blog

Wikipedia. (2009h). Web syndication. Retrieved from http://en.wikipedia.org/wiki/Web_syndication

Wikipedia. (2009i). Atom standard. Retrieved from http://en.wikipedia.org/wiki/Atom_%28standard%29

Wikipedia. (2009j). WYSIWYG. Retrieved from http://en.wikipedia.org/wiki/WYSIWYG

Wikipedia. (2009k). Api. Retrieved from http://en.wikipedia.org/wiki/Api

Young, R. (2008). Back to basics: Strategies for identifying, creating, storing, sharing and using knowledge. In *From Productivity to Innovation: Proceedings from the Second International Conference on Technology and Innovation for Knowledge management*. Tokyo: Asian Productivity Organization. Retrieved August 2009, from http://www.apo-tokyo.org/00e-books/IS-34_FromProdToInnovation/IS-34_FromProdToInnovation.pdf

Zhou, A. Z., & Fink, D. (2003). The intellectual capital web: A systematic linking of intellectual capital and knowledge management. *Journal of Intellectual Capital, 4*(1), 34–48. doi:10.1108/14691930310455379

ENDNOTES

[1]   Web syndication is a form of syndication in which website material is made available to multiple other sites (Wikipedia, 2009h)

2 A RSS (Really Simple Syndication) feed can be used to publish frequently updated works—such as blog entries, news headlines, audio, and video—in a standardized format.

3 The name Atom applies to a pair of related standards. The Atom Syndication Format is an XML language used for web feeds.

4 WYSIWYG: Acronym for What You See Is What You Get, used in computing to describe a system in which content displayed during editing appears very similar to the final output, which might be a printed document, web page, slide presentation or even the lighting for a theatrical event (Wikipedia, 2009j)

5 API: Application programming Interface (API) is an Interface in computer science that defines the ways by which an application program may request services from libraries and/or operating systems (Wikipedia, 2009k).

Chapter 8
Enhancing Productivity through Social Computing

J. Alfredo Sánchez
Universidad de las Américas Puebla, Mexico

Omar Valdiviezo
Universidad de las Américas Puebla, Mexico

ABSTRACT

This chapter posits that social computing applications, when appropriately combined, provide opportunities to facilitate organizational communication and collaboration, and ultimately, to enhance productivity. The authors illustrate this view by discussing ongoing work and initial experiences with the development and deployment of a number of social computing concepts and platforms. They particularly focus on the confluence of social bookmarking and social networks to enhance productivity in academic settings, as well as on the use of social networks for coordinating and managing group projects. They also discuss how social networks in immersive environments can result in opportunities for learning and training that may have a positive impact on productivity. They developed social computing prototypical applications for each of the areas they are exploring. Based upon observation of users and feedback obtained from them, they conclude that it is possible and desirable to take advantage of the collaborative nature of social computing applications so that participants engage in productive activities for the benefit of their organizations.

INTRODUCTION

Millions of people around the world spend time communicating with their contacts that are registered as users of social computing applications, most notably social networks and instant messaging, but also increasingly immersive multi-user

DOI: 10.4018/978-1-61692-904-6.ch008

environments, wikis, blogs and other applications that provide social context for user activities. A few of these applications can naturally be regarded as tools that are oriented to supporting or enhancing productivity. These include collaborative editors, some wikis, and project management environments. Other applications, however, often are seen merely as recreational and are the subject of arguments on whether organizations should discourage their use in productive settings. Social networking, instant messaging and micro-blogging applications are salient examples of this questioned category. A significant number of organizations have banned social networking applications from the workplace over concerns that employees are wasting time on them when they should be working (see e.g. Malkin, 2007). In this chapter, we posit that social computing applications such as social networking and collaborative tagging, when appropriately combined, present opportunities to facilitate organizational communication and collaboration, and ultimately, enhance productivity.

In order for social computing to have a positive impact on the efficacy, effectiveness and satisfaction of participants of group activities, both human and technological issues need to be addressed. On the human side, critical issues include motivation and incentives, training, trust and group dynamics. On the technology side, user interfaces and collaboration environments that are empowering yet secure and privacy-protecting are key. But beyond that, supporting mechanisms are needed that make it possible for users to take advantage of the wealth of knowledge represented by vast collections of documents and the relationships and interactions among their authors and participants of group activities.

We illustrate our views by presenting ongoing work and initial experiences with the development and deployment of a number of social computing concepts and platforms. In particular, we focus on the confluence of social bookmarking and social networks to enhance productivity among knowledge workers, as well as on how social networks may leverage the coordination and management of group projects. We also discuss our explorations of immersive environments and how interactions among multiple users can result in opportunities for learning and training that may have a positive impact on productivity.

The remainder of the chapter is organized as follows: Current related work on productivity and social computing is summarized in the following section to provide an overview of the field. Next, our work that addresses productivity issues is discussed in three sections: (1) project management and coordination based on social networks, (2) social computing for supporting academic productivity, and (3) multi-user immersive environments for learning and training. We discuss the broader implications of social computing on organizations and productivity, and present conclusions that can be derived from our work.

BACKGROUND

In very simple terms, productivity is a measure of output per unit of input. In economic terms, productivity is crucial as the growth of productivity determines the growth of a country's material standard of living (Field, 2008). Concerns over the increasing popularity of social computing and its impact on productivity have prompted discussion and analysis from multiple perspectives and research groups. In this section we sample salient viewpoints and work that examines how various forms of social computing is affecting productivity. These forms include social networks, collaborative tagging, and multi-user virtual environments. We start by reviewing efforts to study the aspects of social computing technologies that may enhance productivity, as well as to provide forums for discussion and analysis. Next we focus on learning as an area of opportunity for social computing applications. Then we consider social bookmarking (or collaborative tagging) and its potential to support knowledge-intensive activities. We then center our attention on immersive virtual environments, which typically have been used for recreational purposes, and refer to work intended to introduce professional and productive applications into these environments. Finally, we review briefly work aimed to help organizations take advantage of social networks in the workplace.

Social Computing and Productivity

A study by Otis (2007) identifies factors of social computing that affect worker productivity. From a thorough review of the literature on the subject published over a decade, Otis suggests criteria for selecting social computing technologies that can contribute to desired levels of worker productivity. Among the aspects that could be addressed by social computing technologies, this study considers usability, pervasiveness, ubiquity, social context and transparency as the most important. Similarly, some of the aspects of worker productivity that require attention include learning, disruptions, accuracy, efficiency, resistance, innovation and motivation. These criteria and their relationships can be helpful not only as a guide to selecting, but also to designing, social computing technologies.

The introduction of social computing into corporations and other organizations has also brought about the formation of special interest groups, such as the one that met at the recent Human Factors in Computing Systems Conference (Blackwell, Sheridan, Instone, Schwartz & Kogan, 2009). The group's motivation includes discussing the business value of social collaboration, design approaches and strategies for integration and adoption. The rise of social networks also has given rise to the need for new methods for observing users and conducting usability studies, as discussed by Hart, Ridley, Taher, Sas, and Dix (2008).

Social Computing and Learning

Researchers also have studied the role and impact of social computing in the realm of education. For example, Liccardi et al. (2007) consider the social dimension of learning and analyze how social networks are formed in educational settings, as well as the influences that institutions may exert on the creation and deployment of social networks for education. They also discuss the advantages and disadvantages of introducing social networks into the learning experience. Advantages have to do with the richness of the digital medium and the availability of a wide variety of supporting applications, as well as the increased sense of community. Disadvantages are more related with issues of trust, privacy and responsiveness of the participants.

One issue that has led some institutions to blocking the use of social networking software in schools is related to student distraction. In contrast, Levy (2007) advocates the use of social networks in schools, which will create durable connections "while developing skills that will help them cope with a world that will always be full of distractions." Cloete, de Villiers and Roodt (2009) consider that students' methods of engagement and the ways students interact nowadays have changed considerably and that it is the instructors who need to keep abreast to take advantage of social computing to support educational activities. They study practices across several universities (in Southern Africa), analyze the student's and lecturer' perspectives, and propose specific individual and group assignments that involve the use of social networks as part of teaching strategies.

Social Bookmarking and Knowledge Workers

Why users engage in collaborative tagging has been researched actively and reported in the literature. Marlow, Naaman, Boyd, and Davis (2006) found five main motivators for tagging: future retrieval, contributing to the visibility of a resource, attracting attention, expressing opinions, competing with other users and leaving persistent marks. Out of these motivations, the first four appear as having particular importance for generating useful tags, which then can be used as the basis for recommendations. The other two (competing with others and leaving marks) are features that could be promoted to increase user motivation and incentives. A taxonomy of incentives, only oriented more specifically to image tagging, has been suggested by Ames and Naaman (2007), whereas the various roles played by users when tagging has been explored by Thom-Santelli, Muller, and Millen (2008).

The taxonomy of tagging styles proposed by Cañada (2006) has had particular relevance for our work. Based upon an analysis of patterns in popular bookmarking software, such as del.icio. us (http://delicious.com) and Flickr (http://flickr. com), he derived four such styles: (1) Selfish tagging, which occurs when users assign tags that are meaningful only to their personal context and most likely not to others; (2) friend-oriented, in which case tags are familiar only to a closed circle of people; (3) altruistic, when the assigned tags are consciously selected as the most descriptive and generally accepted for a wide user community; and (4) populist, which is a pernicious form of tagging in which the assigned tags are attractive but intentionally deceive other users. Evidently, the greatest benefit for the community occurs if users tag altruistically, but it is also true that incentives need to be devised in order for this to happen, as most well-intentioned users tend to tag for themselves or only for a few people. Our approach aims to address precisely this need for incentives, as explained below.

Professional Applications of Multi-User Virtual Environments

Immersive virtual environments represent another group of social computing applications that have raised significant controversy regarding their impact on user activities and their personal relationships. Virtual environments such as There (there. com), Second Life (secondlife.com) and World of Warcraft (worldofwarcraft.com) have attracted the attention of a large user population as well as the media (see, for example, (Dell, 2007) and (Dell, 2008)) and the research community. The potential effects of virtual immersion and interaction on behavior, and even on health, have been researched and documented. For instance, Fox and

Bailenson (2009a) found that virtual self-models or avatars that reflected weight changes had a strong impact on exercising behavior, whereas Fox and Bailenson (2009b) found evidence that indicates that appearance and gaze featured by female characters in virtual environments enhance certain attitudes towards women. It also has been found that racial embodiment in virtual avatars is related to a greater racial bias beyond the digital realm (Groom, Bailenson & Nass, 2009).

Messinger et al. (2009) have examined thoroughly the origin, current situation and future visions of virtual worlds. They propose an initial taxonomy of the area that considers five main classes of virtual worlds: education-focused, theme-based, community-specific, children-focused, and self-determined (or open-objective). They also suggest research directions for virtual worlds in business (e.g., advertising, and e-commerce), education (e.g., distance education and digital libraries), social sciences (e.g., psychological issues, economic models and simulations) and humanities (e.g., digital art and architecture).

Recent work has explored more specifically how multi-user virtual worlds may be used in professional settings. Bessière, Ellis, and Kellogg (2009) identify five challenges in this regard: initial motivation, technical difficulties, interacting competently, becoming socially proficient, and finding compelling activities. They go further to suggest that *constructionism* (Papert, 1990), which promotes learning through the design and production of personally meaningful artifacts, may be a key approach to create opportunities for self-motivated individual or team work in virtual worlds, as it exploits features such as embodiment, 3D shared artifacts and proximity-based social interaction. Our work discussed below explores some of these research issues.

Social Networks in the Workplace

More specifically, Skeels and Grudin (2009) examined patterns of use and attitudes in an organization that uses the popular Facebook and LinkedI social networking software (SNS) n. Their work suggests that people prefer the "pull" technology of SNS, in which the user requests updates when needed or desired, to the "push" nature of email, in which messages arrive in the user's mailbox as a server receives and forwards them. Users of SNS in the workplace feel it provides a form of lightweight awareness, which allows them to monitor events without being interrupted. In addition to reconnecting with old acquaintances and keeping in touch, some study participants reported they considered SNS helped them build stronger relationships and bonding, which emerged from personal information exchange. In the specific organization where the study was conducted, SNS was used and promoted by the upper management levels. However, tensions did appear as a result of crossing hierarchy, status and power boundaries, both within the personal and work spheres.

There are a number of efforts that aim to address productivity related issues in social networks by providing participants with basic functionality to handle tasks and to-do lists (e.g., http://apps. facebook.com/listofthings/). Some applications in this area (such as http://apps.facebook.com/ facebookprojects) go further to provide facilities for sharing related documents. They tend to limit the storage space that can be used for that purpose, and are designed specifically to manage school projects. Most project management applications tend to simplify project representation (e.g., by not considering events other than starting and ending tasks) and make it difficult for project participants to obtain a view of the overall project. Our work aims to address some of these shortcomings.

In what follows, we discuss work we have undertaken which is aimed to devise social computing platforms in which participants take advantage of their networks of contacts to engage in collaborative, productivity-enhancing activities.

SOCIAL NETWORKING AND PROJECT MANAGEMENT

We set out to explore how the distracting features of social network software can be balanced with productivity-oriented functionality. In particular, we are interested in integrating project management functionality that takes advantage of: (1) the network of contacts that users maintain, and (2) the mechanisms that social networks already employ to notify users of events in which they are interested. To that end, our group at the Laboratory of Interactive and Cooperative Technologies (ICT Lab) of the Universidad de las Américas Puebla, developed *wproject*, a software environment that allows users to define projects and related tasks, as well as to assign responsibilities to members of a social network. Tasks can be defined by any members of the team, who may also assign responsibilities to members of their social network. In this way, all contacts that are involved in some related task are eventually included in the project. We developed *wproject* so we can investigate this area and the software can evolve according to our findings.

wproject has been instantiated as a Facebook application, so it is freely accessible to a wide user base. Its main interface displays the projects and tasks in which individual users participate, as well as the activities in which members of their social networks participate. Upon request, the user can be presented with task details, expected dates of completion and participants that are associated with each task. All project participants are selected from the list of members of the users' social network. Task dependencies can be specified so a critical path is automatically constructed. Reminders can be triggered, if the user so requests, for any pending tasks when a deadline is about to be met. Additionally, project participants may upload and share documents they consider relevant.

Figure 1 illustrates how *wproject* is being used to support collaboration and communication in an actual scenario. In this figure, a user is

Figure 1. View of a project's tasks in wproject

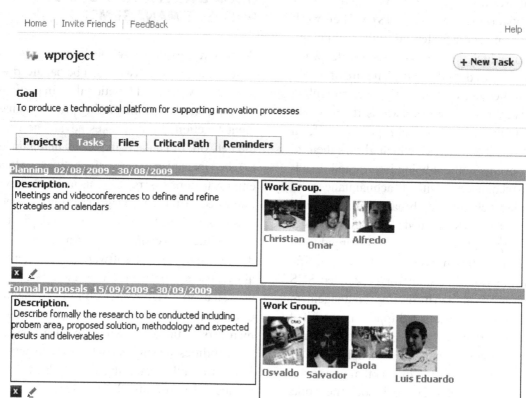

presented with a view of a project's tasks. These are displayed along with a short description and a list of participants and also are represented in a Gantt chart in which the critical path has been highlighted (*Figure 2*). Also, a number of readings have been made available to the project's participants, as displayed in *Figure 3*.

As noted in these figures, everything in *wproject* happens within the context of the social network and even the look and feel of the host environment is maintained. Various reminders have been defined and notifications regarding the project are received along with others related with the regular activities conducted in Facebook.

We currently are using *wproject* experimentally to support various group projects in which participants in México and Germany are users of Facebook. Starting in the Fall Semester of 2009, we also opened *wproject* to the public (via apps.

facebook.com/wproject) and conducted a preliminary survey to receive feedback from users. At the outset, we were particularly interested in participants who were regular Facebook users and were familiar with project management. Thus, we designed projects for our undergraduate students majoring in computer systems engineering and graduate students in computer science and information design, in which *wproject* was used as the project management platform. These students were taking courses in human-computer interaction and computer-supported cooperative work, so they also designed a study in which participants were students from other disciplines, including social sciences and humanities. The projects assigned to a total of 30 participants included activities as diverse as software construction that would span for at least one semester, the production of architectural plans for a building, collaborative

Figure 2. A view of a project's tasks highlighting the critical path

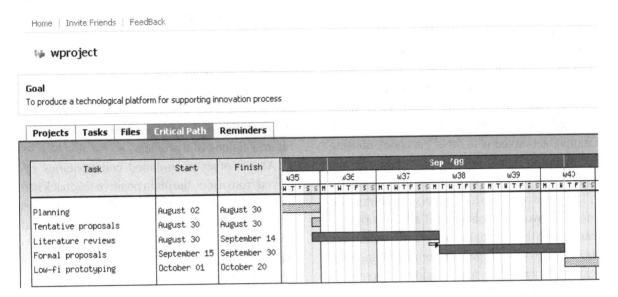

Figure 3. Sharing documents in wproject

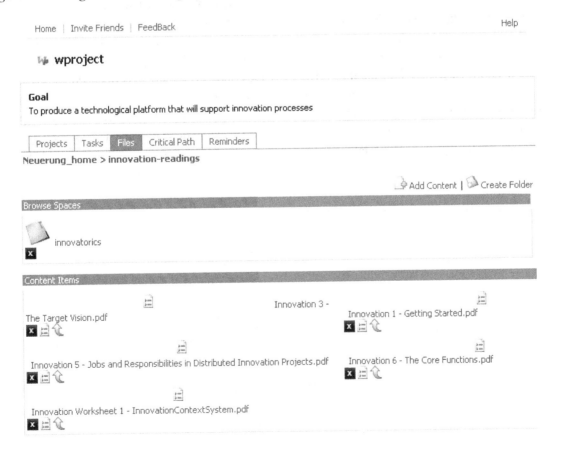

document writing, or a cooking project for a culinary arts group.

In the survey given to participants, they were asked to rate, on a scale from 1 (poor) to 4 (excellent), four main features of *wproject*: Functionality for project management, facilities to define new projects, functionality to have Facebook contacts included into projects, and usefulness of notifications interleaved with other Facebook alerting mechanisms. If all 30 participants assigned the highest rate possible, then a maximum total rate of 120 could be obtained. Conversely, a minimum rate of 30 would be obtained if all users rated a feature with the minimum score. Participants were also asked to provide general comments and suggestions on *wproject*'s functionality and potential.

Figure 4 provides a summary of numerical scores assigned by users to the four main characteristics of *wproject*. As can be seen, participants particularly liked being able to add their Facebook contacts as part of their projects. Most users considered defining a new project (and the tasks it comprises) easy and helpful. Also, receiving notifications about their inclusion as participants of collaborative tasks or upcoming deadlines, interleaved with other Facebook alerts, was considered highly positive (total score of

110). In their comments, participants mentioned that these notifications often made them go back to and keep focused on their projects. Naturally, advanced users missed some of the more sophisticated features available in professional project management software; hence the lower rate assigned to general project management functionality. Advanced features are planned for future versions of *wproject*.

As for other open-ended commentaries received from users, the main positive feedback had to do with the integration of productive activities into their social network, which they typically did not think of as a work environment. Users who were not familiar with project management were pleased with the way *wproject* meshed into their social network's flow of activities and with the notion of getting support for productive work conducted with their friends.

Our initial assessment of the potential of project management in the context of social networks focused mainly on academic projects. It is clear, however, that the concept can be applied in industrial or public sector settings. For example, software development projects, which we explored in our academic realm, also take place both in the private and government sector, and could be sup-

Figure 4. Summary of user feedback for wproject

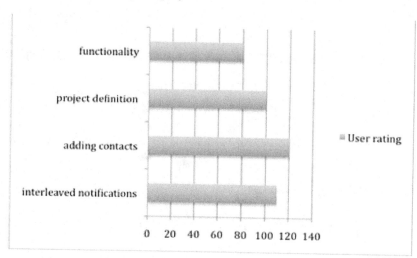

ported by social networking applications such as *wproject*. It is precisely in those settings where, as discussed earlier, the use of social networks software has been questioned or banned. More work is needed to find ways to take advantage of social networks in productive environments, but closing the door to this form of communication and interaction should be pondered by considering personnel's motivation or dissatisfaction.

In the following section we refer to work we have been doing to make sure that users of social networks also benefit from other kinds of social computing applications while remaining in their software environment of choice. We see significant promise in this interaction to enhance productivity in knowledge intensive activities.

SOCIAL NETWORKING AND BOOKMARKING

We also have explored the synergy derived from the interaction of social networks, collaborative tagging (also commonly referred to as social bookmarking) and recommendation mechanisms. In this sense, we consider that, in addition to its well known benefits, such as the generation of so-called *folksonomies* and the potential to improve search over large digital collections, collaborative tagging may have a significant impact on productivity of knowledge workers when strengthened by factors of trust and confidence provided by social networks, and when users are able to direct some of the resources they are tagging to specific users in a community. Our approach relies on the notion of *induced tagging*, which we introduce next.

Induced Tagging

In previous work we introduced the notion of *induced tagging* (Sánchez, Arzamendi-Pétriz & Valdiviezo, 2007), a variation of social bookmarking that addresses issues of motivation while taking advantage of the expertise developed by

information professionals in the context of learning communities. As noted earlier, altruistic tagging, though ideal for generating tags that are useful for a community, poses the need to devise incentives for users to actively participate and think of the other users' interests and information needs. We define induced tagging as a category of social bookmarking with two distinctive characteristics: (1) there is a group of participants who are familiar with the needs and background of a community as well as with the resources they have available; and (2) the task of tagging becomes part of that group's regular responsibilities as a reference team.

Induced tagging takes advantage of the redefinition of the role of information professionals in the digital age. Reference desk personnel have acquired the skills for locating and recommending resources from vast and dynamic digital collections. In this process, staff members often discover resources that are potentially useful for supporting knowledge work conducted by the community, in which case they could bookmark those resources and share their findings. Since they are also familiar with the needs of the community and the vocabulary most commonly used, altruistic tagging should happen naturally (Sánchez, Valdiviezo, Aquino, & Paredes, 2008).

In order for induced tagging to function properly, policies are needed to make collaborative tagging part of the job description for information experts. Whereas users in general are expected and encouraged to tag resources, having a specialized group that tags continuously and consistently as part of their job addresses concerns regarding the need for incentives as well as on the advantages of controlled vocabularies. Given the context in which induced tagging takes place, schemes can also be devised to generate personalized recommendations that are based on tagged resources.

The success of social bookmarking is often discussed in the light of collective intelligence, or what also has been termed *wisdom of the crowds* (Surowiecki, 2004). In this sense, the aggregation of the imperfect judgments of spontaneous crowds may be more effective than the judgments of a few experts. Whereas one may think that this notion is contravened by induced tagging, it is important to note that in our approach the entire community is expected to tag resources, and that the role of experts is to enrich the collaboration by providing consistency and maintaining a stable tag base. Moreover, it is also worth noticing that experiments by Razikin, Goh, Chua, and Lee (2008) suggest that the wisdom-of-crowds theory is not always consistently supported. Based on experimental evidence, they state that tags assigned by experts tend to be better descriptors for resources than tags assigned by the general public, particularly for resource sharing and information retrieval. We consider that induced tagging offers the best of both worlds: It promotes the accelerated growth of a collection of tags and therefore attracts community members to use resources and to participate in tagging. In a stable state, the collection of tags should reflect the wisdom of the community. With appropriate tools, tagging can become part of the regular support offered to users for their information retrieval needs, particularly if it takes advantage of social networks, as illustrated by our work described below.

Recommendations in Social Networks Based on Collaborative Tagging

We have developed "REC", an environment designed to investigate the potential of induced tagging, initially in academic settings. Although the original version of REC functioned as an independent web-based application, user feedback and the popularity of social networks motivated the development of a version of REC that could operate as an application of Facebook. Users are familiar with various social networking systems and also are eager to extend their network of contacts, particularly if that implies some benefit to them. This is the case of information experts, who may continue to provide assistance for scholarly activi-

ties without the users having to leave their social environment of choice. Though we considered several alternatives of social network platforms that could serve as the context for REC, we opted for Facebook on the basis of its popularity and facilities for third-party development.

Users of REC in the context of Facebook can obtain or give recommendations within the same familiar environment. Registration as a user of REC is needed only to enable tagging. *Figure 5* illustrates the interface of REC as a Facebook application. As illustrated in the figure, functionality offered by REC is available via tabs that include options for tagging resources, recommending resources to friends, switching to another language (Spanish or English in the current version), and inviting friends to become users of REC. By clicking on the small icon that appears next to each document in the list, users can generate recommendations for their friends. *Figure 6* is an example of how recommendations of resources can be sent to Facebook friends.

REC has been open to the public for several months, both as an independent web application and as a Facebook application (http://apps.facebook.com/recudla/Principal). We have been observing users and also have been examining systems logs. Six information experts within the Interactive Center of Information and Learning Resources (CIRIA, after is initials in Spanish) of the Universidad de las Américas Puebla (UDLAP) have been tagging resources using REC as part of their regular duties. The number of additional users who tag web resources has varied, depending on publicity of the service and assignments to students of UDLAP that specifically request the use of REC. Currently, there are 596 REC users, out of which 63.4% (382) have tagged resources at some point. As expected, a large proportion of the distinct tags (about 23%) have been assigned by information experts.

The role of personnel expressly designated to do social bookmarking is fundamental for describing the collections managed by CIRIA. Tags

Figure 5. Obtaining recommendations in REC

assigned by CIRIA's information experts have a high descriptive value, as they are expressed in the terms most likely used by the user community. This is of particular importance when requesting recommendations (i.e., the terms employed by the user will very likely be matched by the tags employed to tag resources). Also, given that each information professional has an area of expertise, the available collections and the interests of our community are being covered rapidly, but there is still little overlap among the tags being assigned.

Of particular interest has been a group of 19 users who participated in a formal study of REC,

for whom we designed tasks such as obtaining recommendations on specific topics, tagging resources selected from available digital collections, and finding relationships among documents that had been tagged using REC. This group of users consisted of senior undergraduate students majoring in two areas: information technologies and business and IT. We requested formal feedback from these users through questionnaires. A summary of their responses is illustrated in *Figure 7*. For numerical responses we used a scale from 1 (totally disagree) to 4 (totally agree), so

Figure 6. Recommending resources in REC

Figure 7. Summary of user feedback for REC

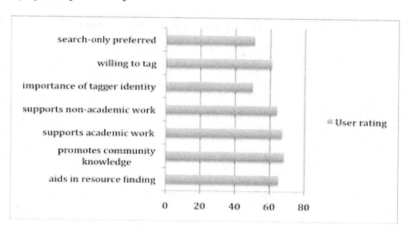

a maximum total score of 76 was possible for each question.

Some interesting issues illustrated by this figure include the following: Users find REC very helpful in finding or recommending resources of their interest and assign a great importance to the generation and use of community knowledge implied by collaborative tagging. From their experience, they consider REC is effective for supporting their current academic activities and expect it will continue to be helpful once they graduate and move to a job. Although most users are willing to participate by tagging digital resources, many also see themselves as relying on REC only for searching and obtaining recommendations. In this process, the identity of users who are tagging may become important in some cases, but not all the time. When asked about this issue, users indicated that they would rely more confidently on recommendations of resources that have been tagged by users they trust. We expect information experts to become the most reliable source of resource recommendations, but still lack evidence to confirm this claim.

As has been the case with project management, discussed in the previous section, users have regarded it positively that REC maintains the look and feel of the social network platform in which it operates and that it facilitates access to their con-

tacts. When responding to questionnaires, users mentioned three positive aspects of REC: (1) the possibility of targeting recommendations directly to friends in their social network; (2) the integration of productive activities into a social network environment that has become a regular element of their daily lives; and (3) the functionality to view their own resources organized according to the bookmarks they have assigned as well as their relationships with other users' tags and resources.

Although more formal observations are still needed, some other effects of introducing REC are worth discussing. Perhaps the most important effect is not an emerging *folksonomy*, in which resources are organized naturally according to the tags assigned by an active user population. Instead, the impact of REC has been on ease of access to very diverse sources and, as a result, on the productivity of a learning community. Our information center subscribes to a wide range of collections, which comprise digital documents provided by vendors such as Ebsco, ProQuest, J-Stor, IEEE and ACM, to name a few, which support academic work in practically all disciplines. These digital collections typically are made available to the user community through highly heterogeneous interfaces. Locating documents on those collections and establishing relationships among them as part of student or faculty research projects often become time-consuming and frustrating tasks. Since information experts and other users are assigning tags to documents, both within commercially available collections and public domain resources, for users who are relying on its collaborative tagging functionality, REC is becoming a uniform interface to a very diverse information space. REC allows users to establish and follow tacit links represented by tags shared by documents that reside in multiple collections, or by sets of tags that overlap and provide access to related documents according to other users' criteria. Thus, REC users discover resources that otherwise would go unnoticed. Tag clouds invite users to explore related resources, which results in an enhanced discovery mechanism. Members of an extended learning community within the university will be able to retrieve documents that have undergone a careful curation process, by just following links recommended by other REC users. It is no longer necessary for our users to visit individual collections or to formulate complex queries.

Based upon our observations and feedback from users, we contend that by combining collaborative induced tagging and social bookmarking we are able to enhance productivity of users by providing support in at least four areas: (1) exploiting the information resources they have available; (2) organizing their information spaces in a personalized manner with the help of their social network; (3) discovering information sources that otherwise would remain hidden, and (4) constructing collaboratively a collection of metadata and annotations that reflects the wisdom of the community, on which they can rely while conducting knowledge-based work.

In the following section we continue to discuss the potential of social computing to impact productivity, only we move to virtual spaces in which users are represented by lifelike characters and are able to interact with three-dimensional objects.

VIRTUAL ENVIRONMENTS AND CONSTRUCTIONIST LEARNING AND TRAINING

At our ICT Lab, we also have undertaken a project aimed at exploring how people may collaborate and learn in the realm of multi-user virtual worlds. This work started as an extension of our previous research with user-defined learning objects (Pérez-Lezama, Sánchez, Paredes, & Valdiviezo, 2008). Considering the potential of three-dimensional representations to convey some concepts, our main goal in this area became to facilitate the construction and manipulation of learning objects that comprise 3D elements, which we refer to as 3DLOs. We have developed instances of 3DLOs and we are developing models and tools for specifying structural and behavioral components of 3DLOs (Paredes, Sánchez, Rojas, Strazzulla, & Martínez-Teutle, 2009). In the process, we have come to realize the enormous potential of the social components of virtual environments to support professional activities, particularly to enhance training based on a constructionist approach.

A learning object (LO) is a digital entity that is designed to promote significant learning. Though the design of LOs may take advantage of the richness of the digital medium, the potential of LOs that comprise 3D representations to foster an exploratory style of interaction and learning has not been fully investigated. In immersive environments much work has focused on generating realistic or believable scenarios. However, users oftentimes continue to be mere spectators and are not encouraged to act upon the 3D objects or to explore cause-effect relationships. This may occur when more traditional instructional approaches are followed or due to technical limitations of immersive scenarios. Our work focuses on providing more interactive features to 3DLOs. We believe that significant learning has to do more with doing, manipulating objects and exploring cause-effect phenomena, than with just visiting and watching 3D scenarios, however dynamic or realistic they may be. In this sense, we are exploring a constructionist approach to learning, as discussed earlier in the chapter. Moreover, we advocate the use of LOs in group settings, as learning is fundamentally a social activity (Meltzoff, Kuhl, Movellan & Sejnowski, 2009). What takes place in a virtual environment when multiple users interact with LOs and socially construct knowledge has been referred to as co-learning (Colazzo, Molinari, & Villa, 2008).

Based on the notions discussed above, we defined a model and created prototypical instances for 3DLOs in the context of the Second Life platform. We refer to our prototype as OA3D (3DLO in Spanish) and we have made it available at http://slurl.com/secondlife/Immintel/36/204/115. Our prototypical 3DLOs illustrate how exploratory learning may take place in areas such as architecture (studying Greek column orders), physics (experimenting with projectile motion) and chemistry (experimenting with ethanol synthesis). We invited three lecturers and four students from two universities (Universidad de las Américas Puebla and Universidad de Guadalajara) to participate in a study in which they were presented with the OA3D prototype and were assigned a number of tasks that involved interacting with the objects and avatars of other users, as well as reaching specific object states (e. g., transforming ethanol into acetaldehyde). Participants filled out questionnaires in which they provided their assessment of various aspects of 3DLOs, as summarized in *Figure 8*. Numerical scores for each aspect ranged from 1 (totally disagree) to 4 (totally agree), so the maximum total score for each aspect was 28.

Clearly, there is consensus on the usefulness of 3DLOs as an aid for learners to grasp abstract concepts, as the digital medium makes it possible to represent and manipulate structures that would require sophisticated equipment to examine, or that cannot be explained easily using a 2D representation. Our subjects were also eager to interact with the avatars of other users, and collaboration occurred naturally, which corresponded to their responses to the question regarding that issue (total score of 24). In general, users felt in control of the objects they manipulated and thought 3DLOs invited them to experiment. The lowest score (16) was assigned to 3DLOs' capabilities to relate virtual and physical objects with each other. This may be due to the richer representations that are possible in the digital medium, which not always match real world objects. Additional feedback we have gathered indicate that learners find handling 3DLOs engaging, and that they consider 3DLOs may help discover concepts or at least reinforce knowledge obtained via more traditional means.

What we find particularly promising is the social dimension of 3DLOs. Not only can the learner experiment with 3D representations, but other users may be present and watch, interact or jointly manipulate objects. *Figure 9* illustrates, for example, a scenario in which two users are manipulating our chemical synthesis model to produce acetaldehyde from ethanol. Collaboration and communication become very rich as users, who physically may be at remote locations, share the 3D model and can manipulate it and immediately observe the results of their actions. Additionally, they may communicate via instant messaging or over a voice channel.

Our initial experiences with 3DLOs and its prototypical OA3D implementation have provided insight into the potential of multi-user virtual environments for other related activities. We envision virtual worlds and constructionist LOs as means to support training in areas that are complex, costly or dangerous. The digital medium makes it possible to model and to manipulate objects and concepts that would require significantly more effort, time and visual aids to explain and comprehend with conventional means (e.g. molecules and chemical synthesis in our illustration). But the social aspect of virtual worlds provides greater opportunities for co-learning and realizing their productive potential.

Figure 8. Summary of user feedback for 3DLOs

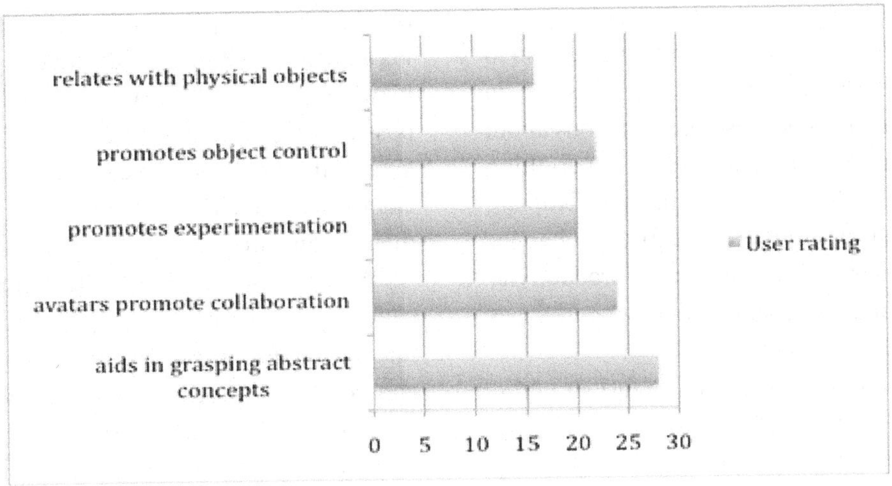

Figure 9. Sharing and manipulating 3D representations in OA3D

FUTURE RESEARCH DIRECTIONS

As discussed throughout this chapter, social computing applications may be used to leverage certain aspects of productivity in very diverse settings. However, much work is needed to investigate how to take advantage of the wealth of explicit and implicit relationships that are continuously being forged by users on the global network. Interdisciplinary work is of particular importance to understand the individual, organizational, cultural and technological implications of introducing social computing into productive processes. Regular users of social computing applications have developed habits that allow them to switch with ease from one context or work sphere to another (González & Mark, 2004). This is related also to what has been called a bi-modal work style, in which a person makes conscious decisions about when to focus on a task and excludes everything else, and when interruptions are allowed (Trapani, 2008). The setting is highly dynamic, as changes in work practices and other aspects of productivity create needs and opportunities for new approaches and new tools.

We plan longitudinal studies to further investigate how social networks, collaborative tagging, project management and virtual environments may effectively be used to enhance productivity. We also are working on mechanisms for automatic discovery of implicit collaboration networks based on vast collections of digital documents. Based on those inference mechanisms, we are planning to provide visualization mechanisms for the users to explore and extend their social networks so they include contacts considering actual work indicators.

We also have started an inter-disciplinary project to develop a technological platform that will support the early stages of innovation processes conducted by geographically distributed teams. This is the project we used in the previous section to illustrate the introduction of project management in the context of social networks. In addition to these technologies, we will be investigating the use multi-touch interactive surfaces, voice input and mobile devices to capture knowledge that is generated during creative group processes. But more importantly, we will be observing users as they follow a specific methodology for innovation and how current tools facilitate or hinder creative work so we can envision the ways in which social computing can make people more productive.

CONCLUSION

Contrary to what has become common belief in some organizations, social computing offers op-

portunities for enhancing productivity in a wide range of activities. Whereas some social computing applications do exhibit distracting features that may hamper productivity if not used wisely, it is possible and oftentimes desirable to take advantage of their collaborative nature so participants engage in productive activities for the benefit of their organizations.

We have discussed how social computing applications, particularly social networks, collaborative tagging and multi-user immersive environments, can become platforms for productive activities. We have described actual software platforms that illustrate how the confluence of social networking, project management, collaborative tagging and virtual worlds can enhance productivity in diverse settings. The results we have been observing are encouraging and indicate that by introducing productivity-oriented functionality into the existing social computing platforms, in many cases users will be motivated to participate in team work and will find it natural to interleave work and personal communication and activities. We are convinced that it is more important to investigate the benefits of social computing and the new habits and skills they are bringing about in workers than blindly fighting against their potential downsides.

Given that social computing applications are becoming deeply ingrained in the daily lives of the new generations, it is important to understand the ways in which people communicate, collaborate and work with their social networks. This necessarily is the work of multi-disciplinary teams.

ACKNOWLEDGMENT

The projects and associated software described in this chapter have been developed with the collaboration of talented members of the Laboratory of Interactive and Cooperative Technologies of the Universidad de las Américas Puebla. We are particularly grateful for the contributions of Emmanuel Aquino, Adriana Arzamendi, Abraham

Ronel Martínez-Teutle, Rosa Paredes, Liliana Rojas, and Israel Zerón. Support for our projects has been provided by our home institution (UD-LAP) as well as by the University Corporation for the Advancement of the Internet (CUDI) through its Program for Advanced Applications.

REFERENCES

Ames, M., & Naaman, M. (2007). Why we tag: Motivations for annotation in mobile and online media. In *Proceedings of the SIGCHI Conference on Human Factors in Computing Systems* (pp. 971-980). New York: ACM Press.

Bessière, K., Ellis, J. B., & Kellogg, W. A. (2009). Acquiring a professional "second life": Problems and prospects for the use of virtual worlds in business. In *Proceedings of the 27th International Conference on Human factors in Computing Systems* (pp. 2883-2898). Boston: ACM Press.

Blackwell, J., Sheridan, J., Instone, K., Schwartz, D. R., & Kogan, S. (2009). Design and adoption of social collaboration software within businesses. In *Proceedings of the 27th international Conference Extended Abstracts on Human Factors in Computing Systems* (pp. 2759-2762). New York: ACM Press.

Cañada, J. (2006). Tipologías y estilos en el etiquetado social [Web log post]. Retrieved August 28, 2008, from http://www.terremoto.net/tipologias-y-estlos-en-el-etiquetado-social

Cloete, C., de Villiers, C., & Roodt, S. (2009). Facebook as an academic tool for ICT lecturers. In *Proceedings of the 2009 Annual Conference of the Southern African Computer Lecturers' Association* (pp. 16-22). New York: ACM Press.

Colazzo, L., Molinari, A., & Villa, N. (2008). From e-learning to "co-learning": The role of virtual communities. In Kendall, M., & Samways, B. (Eds.), *Learning to live in the knowledge society* (pp. 329-338). Boston: Springer. doi:10.1007/978-0-387-09729-9_48

Dell, K. (2007, August 9). Second Life's real world problems. *Time*. Retrieved September 2, 2009, from http://www.time.com/time/magazine/article/0,9171,1651500,00.html

Dell, K. (2008, May 12). How Second Life affects real life. *Time*. Retrieved September 2, 2009, from http://www.time.com/time/health/article/0,8599,1739601,00.html

Field, A. (2008). Productivity. In *The Concise Encyclopedia of Economics* (2nd ed.). Indianapolis, IN: Library of Economics and Liberty. Retrieved August 28, 2009, from http://www.econlib.org/library/Enc/Productivity.html

Fox, J., & Bailenson, J. N. (2009a). Virtual self-modeling: The effects of vicarious reinforcement and identification on exercise behaviors. *Media Psychology*, *12*, 1–25. doi:10.1080/15213260802669474

Fox, J., & Bailenson, J. N. (2009b). Virtual virgins and vamps: The effects of exposure to female characters' sexualized appearance and gaze in an immersive virtual environment. *Sex Roles*, *61*(3-4), 147–157. doi:10.1007/s11199-009-9599-3

González, V. M., & Mark, G. (2004). Constant, constant, multi-tasking craziness: Managing multiple working spheres. In *Proceedings of the SIGCHI Conference on Human Factors in Computing Systems* (pp. 113-120). New York: ACM Press.

Groom, V., Bailenson, J. N., & Nass, C. (2009). The influence of racial embodiment on racial bias in immersive virtual environments. *Social Influence*, *4*(1), 1–18.

Hart, J., Ridley, C., Taher, F., Sas, C., & Dix, A. (2008). Exploring the Facebook experience: A new approach to usability. In *Proceedings of the 5th Nordic Conference on Human-Computer interaction* (pp. 471-474). New York: ACM Press.

Levy, J. (2007). The real reason schools need Facebook. *eLearn, 2007*(12), 1. doi: 10.1145/1361059.1361061

Liccardi, I., Ounnas, A., Pau, R., Massey, E., Kinnunen, P., & Lewthwaite, S. (2007). The role of social networks in students' learning experiences. In Carter, J., & Amillo, J. (Eds.), *Working Group Reports on ITiCSE on innovation and Technology in Computer Science Education* (pp. 224–237). New York: ACM Press. doi:10.1145/1345443.1345442

Malkin, B. (2007, July 27). Facebook banned by City firms. *The Daily Telegraph*. Retrieved August 28, 2009, from http://www.telegraph.co.uk/news/uknews/1558630/Facebook-banned-by-City-firms.html

Marlow, C., Naaman, M., Boyd, D., & Davis, M. (2006). HT06, tagging paper, taxonomy, Flickr, academic article, to read. In *Proceedings of the Seventeenth Conference on Hypertext and Hypermedia* (pp. 31-40). New York: ACM Press.

Meltzoff, A., Kuhl, P., Movellan, J., & Sejnowski, T. (2009). Foundations for a new science of learning. *Science*, *325*(5938), 284–288. doi:10.1126/science.1175626

Messinger, P. R., Stroulia, E., Lyons, K., Bone, M., Niu, R. H., Smirnov, K., & Perelgut, S. (2009). Virtual worlds–past, present, and future: New directions in social computing. *Decision Support Systems*, *47*(3), 204–228. doi:10.1016/j.dss.2009.02.014

Papert, S. A. (1990). Introduction. In Harel, I. (Ed.), *Constructionist learning*. Cambridge, MA: MIT Press.

Paredes, R., Sánchez, J. A., Rojas, L., Strazzulla, D., & Martínez-Teutle, R. (2009). Interacting with 3D learning objects. In *Proceedings of the Fourth Latin American Conference on Human-Computer Interaction* (pp. 165-168). Los Alamitos, CA: IEEE Computer Society Press.

Pérez-Lezama, C., Sánchez, J. A., Paredes, R., & Valdiviezo, O. (2008). A participatory approach for developing learning objects. In *Proceedings of the Third Latin American Conference on Learning Objects* (pp. 15-24). Aguascalientes, Mexico: UAA.

Razikin, K., Goh, D. H., Chua, A. Y., & Lee, C. S. (2008). Can social tags help you find what you want? In *Proceedings of the 12th European conference on Research and Advanced Technology for Digital Libraries* (pp. 50-61). Aarhus, Denmark: Springer-Verlag.

Sánchez, J. A., Arzamendi-Pétriz, A., & Valdiviezo, O. (2007). Induced tagging: Promoting resource discovery and recommendation in digital libraries. In *Proceedings of the Joint Conference on Digital Libraries* (pp. 396-397). New York: ACM Press.

Sánchez, J. A., Valdiviezo, O., Aquino, E., & Paredes, R. (2008). REC: Improving the utilization of digital collections by using induced tagging. *Research in Computing Science*, *39*(1), 83–93.

Skeels, M. M., & Grudin, J. (2009). When social networks cross boundaries: A case study of workplace use of facebook and linkedin. In *Proceedings of the ACM 2009 international Conference on Supporting Group Work* (pp. 95-104). New York: ACM Press.

Surowiecki, J. (2004). *The wisdom of crowds*. New York: Doubleday.

Thom-Santelli, J., Muller, M. J., & Millen, D. R. (2008). Social tagging roles: Publishers, evangelists, leaders. In *Proceeding of the Twenty-Sixth Annual SIGCHI Conference on Human Factors in Computing Systems* (pp. 1041-1044). New York: ACM Press.

Trapani, G. (2008, March 18). Get things done with bi-modal work styles [Web log post]. Retrieved August 28, 2008, from http://lifehacker. com/369128/get-things-done-with-bi+modal-work-styles

ADDITIONAL READING

Ackermann, E. (2001). Piaget's constructivism, Papert's constructionism: What's the difference? Retrieved August 28, 2009, from http://learning. media.mit.edu/content/publications/EA.Piaget %20_%20Papert.pdf

Bailenson, J. N. (2006). Transformed social interaction in collaborative virtual environments. In Messaris, P., & Humphreys, L. (Eds.), *Digital media: Transformations in human communication* (pp. 255–264). New York: Peter Lang.

Bailenson, J. N., Yee, N., Blascovich, J., Beall, A. C., Lundblad, N., & Jin, M. (2008). The use of immersive virtual reality in the learning sciences: Digital transformations of teachers, students, and social context. *Journal of the Learning Sciences, 17*, 102–141. doi:10.1080/10508400701793141

Benkler, Y. (2007). *The wealth of networks: How social production transforms markets and freedom.* New Haven, CT: Yale University Press.

Blascovich, J., Loomis, J., Beall, A. C., Swinth, K. R., Hoyt, C. L., & Bailenson, J. N. (2002). Immersive virtual environment technology as a methodological tool for social psychology. *Psychological Inquiry, 13*, 146–149. doi:10.1207/ S15327965PLI1302_03

Booth, S. (2001). Learning computer science and engineering in context. *Computer Science Education, 11*(3), 169–188. doi:10.1076/ csed.11.3.169.3832

Dalgarno, B. (2002). The potential of 3D virtual learning environments: A constructivist analysis. *Electronic Journal of Instructional Science and Technology, 5*(2). Retrieved September 10, 2009, from http://www.usq.edu.au/electpub/e-jist/docs/ Vol5_No2/Vol5_No2_full_papers.html

Darken, R. P., & Sibert, J. L. (1993). A toolset for navigation in virtual environments. In *Proceedings of the 6th Annual ACM Symposium on User interface Software and Technology* (pp. 157-165). New York: ACM Press.

Dill, S., Eiron, N., Gibson, D., Gruhl, D., Guha, R., & Jhingran, A. (2003). SemTag and seeker: Bootstrapping the semantic web via aut3omated semantic annotation. In *Proceedings of the 12th International Conference on World Wide Web* (pp. 178-186). New York: ACM Press.

DiMicco, J., Millen, D. R., Geyer, W., Dugan, C., Brownholtz, B., & Muller, M. (2008). Motivations for social networking at work. In *Proceedings of the ACM 2008 Conference on Computer Supported Cooperative Work* (pp. 711-720). New York: ACM Press.

Hargittai, E. (2007). Whose space? Differences among users and non-users of social network sites. *Journal of Computer-Mediated Communication, 13*(1), article 14. Retrieved August 28, 2009, from http://jcmc.indiana.edu/vol13/issue1/ hargittai.html

Harris, H., Bailenson, J. N., Nielsen, A., & Yee, N. (2009, December). The evolution of social behavior over time in Second Life. *Presence (Cambridge, Mass.), 18*(6), 434–448. doi:10.1162/ pres.18.6.434

Kafai, Y. B. (2006). Playing and making games for learning: Instructionist and constructionist perspectives for game studies. *Games and Culture*, *1*(1), 36–40. doi:10.1177/1555412005281767

Kim, S. T., Lee, C. K., & Hwang, T. (2008). Investigating the influence of employee blogging on IT workers' organisational citizenship behaviour. *International Journal of Information Technology Management*, *7*(2), 178–189. doi:10.1504/IJITM.2008.016604

Kumar, R., Novak, J., & Tomkins, A. (2006). Structure and evolution of online social networks. In *Proceedings of the 12th ACM SIGKDD International Conference on Knowledge Discovery and Data Mining* (pp. 611-617). New York: ACM Press.

Lin, Y., Sundaram, H., & Kelliher, A. (2008). Summarization of social activity over time: People, actions and concepts in dynamic networks. In *Proceedings of the 17th ACM Conference on Information and Knowledge Management* (pp.1379-1380). New York: ACM Press.

McGrath, J. (1991). Time, interaction, and performance (TIP): A theory of groups. *Small Group Research*, *22*(2), 147–174. doi:10.1177/1046496491222001

Morteo, R., González, V. M., Favela, J., & Mark, G. (2004). Sphere juggler: Fast context retrieval in support of working spheres. In *Proceedings of the Fifth Mexican international Conference in Computer Science* (pp. 361-367). Washington, DC: IEEE Computer Society Press.

Nardi, B. A., Schiano, D. J., Gumbrecht, M., & Swartz, L. (2004). Why we blog. *Communications of the ACM*, *47*(12), 41–46. doi:10.1145/1035134.1035163

Parameswaran, M., & Whinston, A. B. (2007). Research issues in social computing. *Journal of the Association for Information Systems*, *8*(6), 336–350.

Tinto, V. (2000). Learning better together: The impact of learning communities on student success in higher education. *Journal of Institutional Research*, *9*(1), 48–53.

Warburton, S. (2009). Second Life in higher education: Assessing the potential for and the barriers to deploying virtual worlds in learning and teaching. *British Journal of Educational Technology*, *40*(3), 414–426. doi:10.1111/j.1467-8535.2009.00952.x

Wegerif, R. (1998). The social dimension of asynchronous learning networks. *Journal of Asynchronous Learning Networks*, *2*(1), 34–49.

Yee, N., & Bailenson, J. N. (2009). The difference between being and seeing: The relative contribution of self perception and priming to behavioral changes via digital self-representation. *Media Psychology*, *12*(2), 195–209. doi:10.1080/15213260902849943

Zhang, J., & Ackerman, M. S. (2005). Searching for expertise in social networks: a simulation of potential strategies. In *Proceedings of the GROUP Conference* (pp. 71–80). New York: ACM Press.

KEY TERMS AND DEFINITIONS

Collaborative Tagging: A process by which multiple users add metadata in the form of keywords to shared content (also referred to as *social bookmarking*).

Constructionism: A style of learning based on the design and production of personally meaningful artifacts.

Induced Tagging: Social bookmarking with two key characteristics: (1) a well-defined group of participants are knowledgeable on the available resources and the background of a user community; and (2) tagging is required as part of their regular responsibilities as a reference team.

Immersive Multi-User Environments: Software applications, sometimes involving hardware accessories, which generate the impression for the user of being inside a space in which interaction is possible with three dimensional objects and representations of other users (referred to as avatars).

Learning Object: A digital entity that is designed to promote significant learning and involves components such as objectives, requirements, evaluation mechanisms and contents.

Productivity: A measure of a worker's or organization's output per unit of input.

Social Network: A social structure of nodes that represents individuals (or organizations) and the relationships among them within a certain domain.

Three-Dimensional Learning Object (or 3DLO): A learning object that involves three-dimensional components to promote learning, expectedly of a constructionist style.

Section 3
Social Computing from a Technical Perspective

Chapter 9
Social Networks and Semantics

Ioan Toma
University of Innsbruck, Austria

James Caverlee
Texas A&M University, USA

Ying Ding
Indiana University, USA

Elin K. Jacob
Indiana University, USA

Erjia Yan
Indiana University, USA

Staša Milojević
Indiana University, USA

ABSTRACT

This chapter discusses the relation between Social Networks and Semantics – two areas that have recently gained a lot of attention from both academia and industry. The authors show how synergies between these two areas can be used to solve concrete problems, and they describe three approaches that demonstrate the potential for interconnecting these technologies. The first approach focuses on the semantic profiling of social networks. More precisely, they study the characteristics of large online social networks through an extensive analysis of over 1.9 million MySpace profiles in an effort to understand who is using these networks and how they are being used. The MySpace study is based on a comparative analysis of three distinct but related facets: the sociability of users in MySpace; the demographic characteristics of MySpace users; and the text artifacts of MySpace users. The second approach to interconnecting social networks and semantics focuses on a solution for mediating between social tagging systems. The Upper Tag Ontology (UTO) is proposed to integrate social tagging data by mediating between related social metadata schemes. The chapter discusses how UTO data can be linked with other social metadata (e.g., FOAF, DC, SIOC, SKOS), how to crawl and cluster tag data from major social tagging systems, and how to integrate data using UTO. The third approach discusses the use of social semantics to qualitatively improve the task of service ranking. The authors explore the idea of using social annotation technolo-

DOI: 10.4018/978-1-61692-904-6.ch009

gies for ranking web services and show how such an approach can be implemented using information provided by Delicious, one of the largest social networks.

1. INTRODUCTION

Online communities are the fastest growing phenomenon on the Web, enabling millions of users to discover and explore community-based knowledge spaces and to engage in new modes of social interaction. Web 2.0 sites such as Facebook[1], MySpace[2], Delicious[3], YouTube[4], Yahoo! Answers[5], and LinkedIn[6] have grown tremendously in the past few years, garnering increased media and popular attention. The result of this increased awareness is that the Web is socially linked more strongly now than ever before.

Generally speaking, Web 2.0 technologies are transforming the Web environment from a simple repository for documents into the Social Web, a communal platform for connecting people and sharing information. The phrase *Social Web* was introduced in 1998 by Peter Hoschka (1998), who wanted to stress the social functions and capabilities of the Web medium. According to Wikipedia, the Social Web is a global and open distributed data sharing network that links people, organizations and concepts. The Web 2.0 environment is the venue for the Social Web and provides platforms and technologies (e.g., wikis, blogs, tags, RSS feeds, etc.) that facilitate online collaboration and communication. Online social networking is part of the Web2.0 being defined according to Wikipedia as having a core focus on building and reflecting of social networks and social relations among who share interests and/or activities.

Online publishing in the Web 2.0 environment has become so easy that anyone who can write or type can publish on the Web. This revolution has stimulated an ever-growing number of ordinary users, many of them teenagers or seniors, to become involved in Web communication. One of the newest and easiest ways for these users to contribute to the Social Web is through the process of tagging. Tagging is a means for users to add keywords to resources as typed hyperlinks and, cumulatively, reflects community efforts to organize and share information resources. The growing popularity of tagging is furthering the evolution of the Web from a simple repository for hyperlinked documents to a typed hyperlinked Web of data.

As online social networks continue to grow and evolve, an important challenge we face is how to maintain the incredible success of Web 2.0. There is a growing need to understand this new social phenomenon; to understand the processes by which communities come together, attract new members, and develop over time; and to understand what it takes to empower online communities with the ability to gather and retain a core of actively participating members (Backstrom et al., 2006; Coleman, 1990).

Another challenge that we are facing is the increasing heterogeneity and growing amount of data, numbers of resources and users on the Web. Data mediation and data integration have been central concerns of IT for decades (Batini, Lenzerini & Navathe, 1986; Rahm & Bernstein, 2001). With the advent of the Web, interest in these issues has exploded. Currently, there is a focus on providing machine supported meditation on the Web (Antoniou & Harmelen, 2004; Berners-Lee, Hendler & Lassila, 2001) through the medium of machine-processable metadata that has been added to resources. In this context semantics, more particular Semantic Web (Berners-Lee, Hendler & Lassila, 2001), could enable machine supported mediation on a large scale. Using semantics, information becomes machine processable making possible for agents to understand and fulfill users requests.

While Web 2.0 technologies enhance the socially oriented aspects of the Internet, Service Oriented Architectures (SOA) contribute an alternative approach to the current Internet. The service-oriented perspective promotes the notion of service as central to system development, abstracting from implementations and the underlying hardware. While this abstraction provides little more than a common philosophy for the design of distributed applications, the paradigm shift introduces a new set of challenges, including how to organize, search, rank, and select services. Thus, for example, ranking of Web services is a core challenge that any SOA-based system must address. Existing solutions for service ranking are tightly integrated with service discovery and selection solutions and often use service data such as non-functional properties or Quality of Service (QoS) mechanisms to compute rank values for services. In most cases, multiple non-functional properties (e.g., price, availability, etc.) as well as dynamic values are considered (Hwang & Yoon, 1981; Liu, Ngu & Zeng, 2004; Zeng et al., 2004; Zhou, Chia & Lee, 2005); but social information from Web 2.0 is not generally considered in this approach.

In this chapter, we provide a set of solutions to the challenges mentioned above. First, we perform a large-scale study over MySpace, the largest and most active online social network. By studying the characteristics of MySpace, we hope to provide insight into the types of users of these online social networks, how the network itself is organized, and the important text artifacts that may distinguish users. In particular, we study over 1.9 million actual social network profiles with an emphasis on:

- The sociability of users in MySpace, based on relationships, messaging, and group participation;
- The demographic characteristics of MySpace users in terms of age, gender, and location and how these factors correlate with privacy preferences;
- The text artifacts of MySpace users that can be used to construct emergent language models that can distinguish between MySpace users not only by who they say they are but also by the language model they employ.

By studying how MySpace users participate in the social network (sociability), how they describe themselves (demographics), and how they communicate their personal interests and feelings (language models), we hope to encourage the development of new models, algorithms, and approaches for the further enhancement and continued success of online social networks.

The second contribution of this chapter is an analysis of social phenomena on the Social Web in order to identify ways for mediating and linking social data. This analysis is carried out with three major social tagging systems as examples—Delicious, Flickr and YouTube—and focuses on:

- Modeling social tagging data according to the proposed Upper Tag Ontology (UTO);
- Linking data from related social metadata schemes (e.g., FOAF, DC, SIOC, SKOS, etc.) using UTO;
- Crawling data from major social tagging systems and integrating them through UTO; and
- Clustering crawled tagging data.

Last, but not least, this chapter proposes an approach to social ranking for Web service selection and ranking that is based on an analysis of Delicious, one of the largest social networks. We discuss the use of social semantics to qualitatively improve the service ranking task, and we explore the idea of using social annotation technologies for ranking Web services. Annotation data from Delicious is used to discover and rank Web services associated with Delicious bookmarks. Given a set of Web services, the system checks to determine if there are Web pages in the Web services domain that are bookmarked in Delicious; when this is the case, the services are ranked based on the number of users in Delicious who have tagged the associated Web pages. As part of this third approach, an algorithm is proposed that considers interdependencies between services, Web pages, annotations and users to compute the global rank of each service.

The chapter is organized as follows. In Section 2, related work is surveyed and analyzed. In Section 3, we present an extended study of large online social networks that focuses on semantic profiling in social networks. In Section 4, we offer a solution for mediating between social tagging systems and linking social data that is based on an analysis of tagging phenomena on the Social Web. In Section 5, we explore the idea of using social annotation data to improve the quality of the service-ranking task. Section 6 concludes the chapter.

2. RELATED WORK

In this section we survey some of the existing approaches related to our work. We investigate related studies for each of the three approaches proposed in this chapter.

2.1 Social Networks

The study of social networks has a rich history (Milgram, 1967), and the recent rise of online social networks has seen increasing interest in this area. For example, a number of studies have examined the nature and structure of online social networks, including social networks derived from blogspaces (Backstrom et al., 2006; Liben-Nowell et al., 2005), email networks (Adamic & Adar, 2005), online forums (Zhang, Ackerman, & Adamic, 2007), photo sharing sites (Kumar, Novak, & Tomkins, 2006), and many others.

With respect to online social networks such as MySpace and Facebook, there has been some research interest, but most studies have been carried out on a much smaller scale. In one study, researchers analyzed the relationship between a user's profile and friendships over 31,000 Facebook profiles (Lampe, Ellison, & Steinfeld, 2007). Social capital has been studied over several hundred Facebook users by Ellison, Steinfield, and Lampe (2006), and the privacy attitudes of 7,000 Facebook users was studied by Acquisti and Gross (2006). Dwyer, Hiltz, and Passerini (2007) surveyed trust-related issues for over 100 MySpace and Facebook users; and Hinduja and Patchin (2008) studied the revelation of personal information among 10,000 young people on MySpace. Other studies have investigated membership formation for 200,000 Orkut members (Spertus, Sahami, & Buyukkokten, 2005) or looked at the messaging characteristics of four million Facebook users (Golder, Wilkinson, & Huberman, 2007).

2.2 Tagging Ontologies

In 2005, Tom Gruber first proposed the idea of using an ontology to model tagging data. His original idea was further formalized and subsequently published in 2007 (Gruber, 2007). His tag ontology contains the concepts Object, Tag, Tagger, and Source. He then introduced the + or - vote tag to the ontology to be used for collaborative filtering. UTO is based on Gruber's formulation, but it provides enhanced support for ontology alignment and data integration. When compared to Gruber's tag ontology, UTO contains more concepts and relations (e.g., Date, Comment, and has_relatedTaqg) and focuses on mediation between social metadata schemes in order to achieve data integration.

The Social Semantic Cloud of Tags Ontology[7] (SCOT) was developed to represent both the structure and semantics of a collection of tags and social networks of users based on tag sets.

The core concepts of SCOT include Tagcloud and Tag. SCOT uses URIs as a mechanism for identifying a unique tag namespace to link a tag and a resource. The SCOT ontology is based on and linked to SIOC, FOAF and SKOS. It uses SIOC concepts to describe site information and relationships among site-resources, FOAF concepts to represent a human or machine agent, and SKOS to characterize relationships between tags. Although it does not include the concept Tagcloud, UTO is defined in such a way that it can be aligned with many other social metadata schemes in addition to SIOC, FOAF and SKOS (e.g., DC, microformats, etc.)

The Holygoat Tag Ontology[8] models the relationship between an agent, an arbitrary resource, and one or more tags. Using Holygoat, taggers are linked to foaf:agents and taggings reify the n-array relationship among tagger, tag, resource and data. This ontology is also linked to relationships in RSS and DC (e.g., rss:item, rss:category, rss:pubDate, rss:link and dc:subject) through use of rdfs:subClassOf or rdfs:subPropertyOf. Based on these links, it is possible to perform simple subsumption inferences using Holygoat metadata. Thus the Holygoat Tag Ontology provides some support for the emerging Semantic Web by utilizing ontology reasoning and inference. In contrast, because the primary objective of UTO is to support mediation and ease of alignment across metadata schemes, ontology reasoning and inference has not been considered at this stage in its development.

The MOAT Ontology[9] is a lightweight ontology intended to represent how different meanings can be related to a tag. It focuses on providing a unique identifier for each tag that serves to link an associated semantic meaning to the tag. MOAT is based on Holygoat Tag Ontology in its definition of a tag object and assumes that there exists a unique relationship between a tag and a label such that a tag can have a unique MOAT identifier in the Semantic Web. As noted previously, UTO is focused on the structure of the tagging behavior rather than the meanings of individual tags; but the provision of a unique identifier for a tag is always a helpful and an important contribution both to social tagging and to the Web in general.

2.3 Web Service Ranking

We now turn our attention to related investigations of the general ranking problem. Ranking various types of entities has been a challenging research problem over the years, but ranking has gained increasing attention in the context of improving Web search experience of user.

A variety of different approaches has been developed to improve ranking algorithms and ranking results. Classical approaches use statistical information such as term frequency, document length, etc. to compute the similarity degree of a document and a query. An interesting approach that uses social annotations to improve Web search was proposed in Bao et al. (2007). This work was motivated by two basic assumptions: (1) annotations are usually good summaries of the corresponding pages; and (2) the number of annotations indicates the popularity of a Web page. Two algorithms based on these assumptions have been proposed to define how the similarity between queries and annotations can be computed (i.e., the popularity of a Web page based on its relations to annotations and users).

A classification of various types of Web service ranking approaches is proposed in Gekas (2006). The author distinguishes two distinct categorization axes: one measures the localness of the ranking approach depending on whether local or global knowledge is used in computing ranking values; the other measures the absoluteness of the ranking approach depending on whether the measurement is of absolute scope or refers to a particular request.

Two of the more prominent categories of Web service ranking are based either on hubs and authorities, or HITS algorithms, which examine the relations between the number of services that link to a specific service (in-degree) and the number of services to which the service links (out-degree), or on non-functional rankings, which use nonfunctional aspects to compute the rank of services. The first category of methods exploits the given in/out relations between entities, computing rank values using global knowledge. The most prominent representative of this category is PageRank (Page et al., 1998). In the second category, the most prominent approaches have been offered by Hwang & Yoon (1981), Liu, Ngu & Zeng (2004), Zeng et al. (2004), and Zhou, Chia & Lee (2005). For example, in Zeng et al. (2004), a multi-criteria Quality of Service (QoS) model is used to determine the importance or rank of a service. Quality vectors are built for each service and a correspondence matrix is constructed between services and QoS. A simple additive weighting method is then applied to select the optimal Web service(s).

3. SEMANTIC PROFILING OF SOCIAL NETWORKS

3.1 Approach

In our first study of social networks and semantics, we provide the first large-scale demographic study of more than a million actual social network profiles. We analyze these profiles with respect to age, gender, and location, and we study how these factors correlate with privacy preferences. We compare two sampling approaches for extracting social network data, and we provide a unique analysis of text artifacts that can be used to distinguish between types of users.

Data and Setup

To study the characteristics of large online social networks, we selected MySpace as our target social network. MySpace is the largest social networking site, the sixth most visited Web destination according to Compete.com, and a website that has received a tremendous amount of media coverage. In addition to these characteristics, MySpace is one of the few online social networks that provide open access to user profiles. Many other sites require a user account and may restrict access to the entire social network even when a user has a valid account on the site.

On MySpace, as on most online social networks, the most basic element is a profile, a user-controlled Web page that includes descriptive information about the person it represents and that can be connected to other profiles through explicitly declared friend relationships and numerous messaging mechanisms. MySpace allows users to choose between making their profiles publicly viewable (the default option) or private. If a user's profile is designated as private, only the user's friends are allowed to view the profile's detailed personal information (e.g., the user's interests, blog entries, etc.). However, a private profile still provides information such as the user's name, gender, age, location, and last login date.

Because extracting and analyzing all 250 million MySpace profiles would place undue burdens on the resources and network of both MySpace and our local infrastructure, we adopted a sampling-based approach to extract representative profiles from MySpace. We considered two approaches – random-sampling and relationship-based (or snowball) sampling:

- *Random Sampling:* MySpace profiles are sequentially numbered and made publicly Web accessible by constructing a URL containing the profile's unique profile ID. Hence, we can randomly sample from the space of all MySpace profiles by randomly generating profile IDs. By construction, we expect a random sample of MySpace profiles to provide perspectives on the global characteristics of the entire MySpace social network.

- *Relationship-Based Sampling:* Unlike random sampling, the second approach leverages the relationship structure of the social network to select profiles. We begin by generating a set of randomly selected seed profiles. We then extract the IDs of their friends, add these friend IDs to the queue of profiles to sample, and continue in a breadth-first traversal of the social network. When the queue is empty, we generate a new random profile ID and continue the process. In contrast to the random sampling approach, we expect the profiles extracted through the relationship-based sampling approach to provide a more focused perspective on an active portion of the social network.

Data Collection

In practice, we collected two representative datasets from MySpace: the Random dataset was constructed using random sampling and the Connected dataset was constructed using the relationship-based sampling. We wrote two MySpace-specific crawlers (based on Perl's LWP::UserAgent and HTML::Parser modules). Both crawlers disregarded invalid profile IDs (i.e., profiles that were either deleted or undergoing maintenance at the time of the crawl) and entertainment profile IDs (i.e., profiles that were associated with bands, comedians, etc.) so as to focus our collections on active profiles that belong to regular individuals. In June 2006, we deployed ten instances of the random sampling crawler in parallel across ten different servers, collecting profiles for about a week. We repeated this setup in September 2006 with the relationship-based sampling crawler. Summary data for both the Random and Connected datasets are provided in Table 1.

We then wrote a custom MySpace parser to extract the name, age, and other pertinent information from each collected profile. Because some of these features are self-described by the owner of the profile (e.g., age and gender), they may or may not be truthful. Other features (e.g., number

Table 1. Summary data for the two MySpace datasets

	Public Profiles	Private Profiles	Total Profiles	Size
Random	859,347	101,158	960,505	52 GB
Connected	717,337	173,830	891,167	98 GB

of friends) are maintained by MySpace and are therefore expected to be correct. However, MySpace has a limited validation process; thus, we have no assurances that a self-described 20-year old male from Texas is really who he says he is. Having said that, we do believe there is significant value in studying demographics in the aggregate, and, as we will demonstrate in the following section, certain text artifacts specific to certain groups on the social network could be used to detect deceptive profiles.

3.2 Results and Observations

In this section we present the main findings of our study across a series of characterizations: sociability, demographics, language models, and privacy preferences.

Sociability Characterization

We begin our characterization of MySpace by examining the social aspects of users in the network. Since online social networks derive their value from users actively participating in relationships with other users, we are interested to observe to what degree users actually take advantage of these social aspects. To examine sociability over both datasets, we measured the number of friends, the number of comments, and the number of groups a user participates in, values that are only available for public profiles.

In Figure 1, we present the distribution of the number of friends for both the Random and the Connected datasets on a log-log scale. For the

Figure 1. Distribution of friends: The x-axis is the number of friends a user may have; the y-axis is a count of the number of users with a particular number of friends

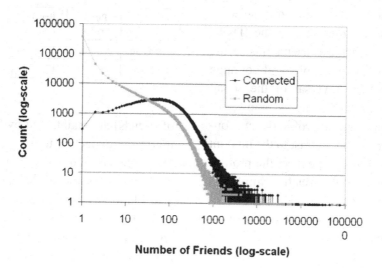

Random dataset, there is a heavy-tailed distribution: That is, most users have very few friends, but a few users have many friends. Such a heavy-tailed distribution has been observed in a number of related domains, and observing it here is no surprise. What was surprising was the number of users with zero or only one friend, which accounted for 426,926 or 50% of the public profiles in the Random dataset. Since MySpace provides each new user with a single default friend, we surmise that more than half of MySpace users had created an account and subsequently abandoned it.

In contrast, we see that, for the Connected dataset, most users had many friends and were actively participating in the MySpace social network. Only 2.5% of the public profiles in the Connected dataset had no or only one friend. Obviously, the relationship-based sampling method used to construct the Connected dataset favored users with many friends.

To further validate the sociability divide, Figure 2 shows the distribution of the number of comments posted to a user's profile for both datasets. The commenting feature of MySpace is one of several avenues for users to communicate with other users. Because comments written to a

particular user are posted on that user's profile, we would anticipate that users with many comments are well known and active in the social network. Again, there is a heavy-tailed distribution for the Random dataset, whereas the Connected dataset shows more skew, since it is, by construction, more connected.

Group participation is another metric of the sociability of a social network. While over 80% of the users in the Random dataset (and, by extrapolation, of the users of MySpace as a whole) participate in no groups, we found that slightly less than half of the users in the Connected dataset belong to at least one group and that nearly 20% of users in the Connected dataset belong to at least eight groups. This evidence further confirms what we observed for the friend and comment measures of sociability: Most MySpace users appear to have effectively abandoned their online profiles, but there remains a large core of active users within MySpace who account for the vast majority of friends, comments, and group activity.

Who, then, are these active users? In an effort to understand if some users are more likely to be active than others, we considered a number of

Figure 2. Distribution of comments: The x-axis is the number of comments posted on a user's profile; the y-axis is a count of the number of users with a particular number of comments posted on their profiles

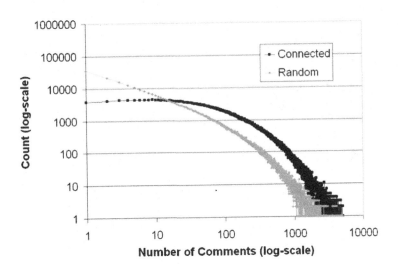

features, including age, location, gender, and the length of time a profile had existed on MySpace. We found that California and other western U.S. states dominated the total number of profiles on MySpace, but that these differences were minor across the Connected and Random datasets, which indicates that location is not a strong indicator of sociability. Likewise, we found little evidence that a profile's self-declared age or gender impacted its relative sociability. In contrast, we did find that the length of time a user has participated in MySpace was a strong indicator of sociability. In order to measure the length of participation on MySpace, we had to augment our original sampling process. Because the profile creation date is provided for each profile on a separate blog page linked off the public profile Web page, retrieving the date of a profile's creation required accessing an additional page for every profile sampled. However, because profile IDs are assigned sequentially in MySpace, we can interpolate the date of creation for each profile sampled. Therefore, in an attempt to avoid overburdening MySpace with a doubling of page requests, we sampled a handful of profiles (e.g.,

profile 10,000, profile 100,000, etc.) to retrieve creation dates and thus construct a time series.

Thus, in Figure 3, each point serves as a bucket that represents all profiles created before that date, extending back in time to the previous point. The y-axis measures the rate of sampling for each bucket. As expected, the random sampling approach provided a nearly uniform sample for each bucket, although we do see a hiccup at the beginning because the bucket is so small and again at the end because the sampling periods are slightly different. In contrast, the relationship-based sampling approach used to construct the Connected dataset indicates that users overwhelmingly joined at an early date. These long-time users are presumably more plugged-in and are thus more active participants in the social network.

Demographic Characterization

In the previous section, we studied the sociability of MySpace users – how active they are and to what degree are they connecting to other users. In this section, we expand our analysis of MySpace to consider the demographics of participants.

Figure 3. Sampling by date: The x-axis shows buckets of profiles organized by their dates of creation; the y-axis shows the fraction of all sampled profiles that were created within a bucket's date range

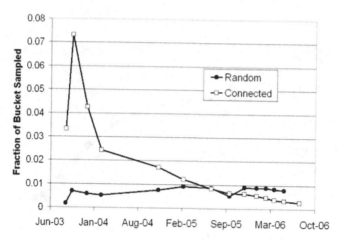

How old are they? Are they predominately male or female? Where are they located? The answers to these questions can provide us with added insight into how a social network grows and what features are attractive to certain participants as well as indicating other interesting avenues. Both the public and the private profiles on MySpace provide basic demographic information; and we found that nearly all MySpace users (> 99.9%) provide some information about age, gender, or location. Only 1,311 profiles in the Random dataset and 1,203 profiles in the Connected dataset declared no age, gender, or location.

Figure 4 shows the distribution of ages in both datasets. As expected, MySpace is dominated by younger users: Nearly 85% of the users on MySpace are 30 or younger. Interestingly, we observed that the Random dataset, which peaks at 17 years of age, skews slightly younger than the Connected dataset, indicating that the most active users on MySpace may, in fact, be in their 20s. We also observed a peak at the age of 69, presumably either a joke age or an age intentionally selected by users interested in sex in order to find one another through the age-based search facility of MySpace (Gradijan, 2007). We also observed

another peak around 100, but we can presume that many of these self-reported ages are also false.

In Table 2, we show the gender breakdown for each dataset. The split between male and female is nearly even: 52% male and 48% female in the Random dataset versus 50% male and 50% female in the Connected dataset. The Other category is a placeholder for profiles that list either no gender information or non-standard gender information. In Figure 5, we consider the gender distribution across both datasets. The results are intriguing: Women are more prevalent at the youngest ages, whereas men are more prevalent at all other ages (barring a few hiccups at the older end, where the data is sparser).

Why are women more active participants at younger ages? It may be either that women intentionally self-report a younger age or that men intentionally self-report an older age; or it may be that there are clear gender differences in how users participate in a social network, with younger women more attracted to certain social aspects than their male counterparts. These are interesting and open questions that deserve further exploration.

Finally, we studied the self-reported location information for each profile. MySpace users hail

Figure 4. Distribution by age: The x-axis is the self-reported age on a user's profile; the y-axis is the fraction of all profiles declaring a particular age

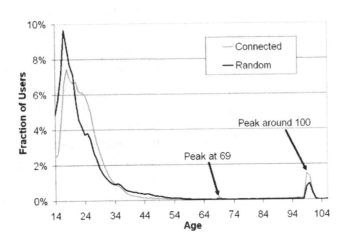

Table 2. Gender breakdown for MySpace datasets

	Random	**Connected**
Male	505,357	440,330
Female	452,240	448,920
Other	2,908	1,917

Figure 5. Gender breakdown by age: The x-axis is the self-reported gender on a user's profile; the y-axis is the fraction of all profiles of a particular age declaring a particular gender

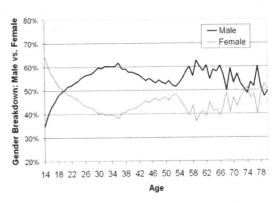

(a) Random Dataset

(b) Connected Dataset

from all fifty U.S. states, and a significant percentage come from other countries. Not all profiles list an intelligible location (e.g. "Somewhere Over the Rainbow"), and some list multiple locations (e.g., "Honolulu and Metro DC"), so we built a best-effort parser. In our initial analysis, we found that the U.S. was the most prevalent location by far, followed by the United Kingdom and Canada. Accordingly, we focused on states in the U.S. for further analysis of location information. For the Random dataset, we found that 77% listed a U.S. state in the location; for the Connected dataset, we found that 87% listed a U.S. state.

In Table 3, we report the top five states that are overrepresented on MySpace, relative to their actual population, as well as the top five under-represented states. We measured the relative presence of a state on MySpace versus its relative share of the U.S. population as:

Table 3. U.S. states most over-represented and most under-represented in MySpace random dataset relative to U.S. census population

Most Over-Represented	Most Under-Represented
Hawaii [+115%]	Mississippi [-58%]
California [+61%]	West Virginia [-53%]
Washington [+41%]	Arkansas [-52%]
Alaska [+40%]	Missouri [-49%]
Nevada [+39%]	South Dakota [-48%]

$$rel_i = 1 - \frac{pop_{i,MySpace}}{\sum_j pop_{j,MySpace}} \bigg/ \frac{pop_{i,US}}{\sum_j pop_{j,US}}$$

where $pop_{i,US}$ is the population of state i based on the latest U.S. Census data and $pop_{i,MySpace}$ is the number of profiles in our dataset that listed state i as their location. For the Random dataset, Table 3 demonstrates that California and other western U.S. states were the most over-represented on MySpace relative to their actual population, while southern and mid-western states tended to lag behind relative to their actual population.

We attribute much of this geographic discrepancy to My-Space's initial launch by a California-based company and its success with Los Angeles area bands (Rosenbush, 2005). Although California accounts for only 12% of the U.S. population, users from California dominated the early adopters of MySpace.

Characterizing Language Models

Thus far in our study, we have characterized how users participate in the MySpace social network (e.g., friendships, comments, etc.) and how users describe themselves. In this section, we examine what users are saying on their profiles through an analysis of the language models of social network users. Our goal is to understand how language use varies across classes of users. For example, do women express themselves differently than men?

Do older MySpace users describe themselves differently than younger MySpace users?

We begin with some definitions. We treated each profile as a sequence of terms drawn from a vocabulary set $V=\{t_1, t_2, ..., t_{|V|}\}$. We considered all terms in a profile that had been generated by the user (e.g., in About Me, Interests, etc.), and we excluded all terms that were most likely generated by other users (e.g., comments). Following the standard information retrieval approach, we can describe the language model of all profiles as a probability distribution over the terms in the profiles according to a unigram language model defined as:

$$\{p(t)\}_{t \in V} \; s.t. \sum_{t \in V} p(t) = 1$$

Terms with high probability are more likely to be observed on a profile than are low probability terms. We can compute $p(t)$ as a function of the count *count(t)* of profiles containing term t relative to the total number of profiles n: $p(t) = count(t)/n$. For example, the top five most probable terms in the Connected dataset are *the, and, straight, friends,* and *with*. Because these common terms provide little insight, we augmented the basic language model by identifying class-specific distinguishing terms for classes based on age, gender, and location. Our goal was to identify terms that were more likely to be generated by a certain class of users (e.g., by women).

To identify these class-specific distinguishing terms, we relied on the information theoretic measure Mutual Information for assessing the importance of a term to a particular class. Mutual Information (MI) between a term and a class is defined as:

$$MI(t,c) = p(t|c)\,p(c) \log \frac{p(t \mid c)}{p(t)}$$

where $p(t|c)$ is the probability that a profile contains term t given that it belongs to class c, $p(c)$ is the probability that a profile belongs to class c, and $p(t)$ is the unigram language model described above for the probability of term t across all profiles. Letting $count(c)$ denote the count of profiles belonging to class c and letting $count(c,t)$ denote the count of profiles containing term t that belong to class c, we have:

$$p\left(t|c\right) = \frac{count(c,t)}{count(c)} \, and \, p\left(c\right) = \frac{count(c)}{n}$$

MI measures how much information a particular term t tells us about class c. Higher MI values indicate stronger associations. In this raw form, however, rare terms that by chance happen to occur only in profiles belonging to a particular class will score highly using MI. Hence, a natural correction is to replace $p(t|c)$ with a "smoothed" version that gives every term a non-zero probability of occurrence across all classes:

$$p^{*}\left(t|c\right) = \alpha p\left(t|c\right) + \left(1 - \alpha\right)p(t)$$

where $0 \leq \alpha \leq 1$. In practice, we selected a smoothing factor of $\alpha = 0.9$. Thus we can interpret

$$\{p^{*}\left(t|c\right)\}_{t \in V} \, s.t. \sum_{t \in V} p^{*}\left(t|c\right) = 1$$

as a class-specific language model.

Class-Specific Distinguishing Terms

Using the MI measure for identifying distinguishing terms, we explored language models of MySpace users according to three characteristics: gender, location, and age. Since we are primarily interested in users who were actively using the social network, we report results from the Connected dataset. Superficially, however, we

Table 4. Distinguishing terms by gender (Ranked by MI)

Male		Female	
dating	sport	love	people
networking	metal	dancing	life
serious	football	shopping	can
relationships	s***	girl	family
single	wars	hearts	being
straight	band	have	notebook
video	f***	are	dance
guitar	gay	favorite	things

saw many similarities with the Random dataset relevant to the presence of distinguishing terms. Furthermore, only public profiles were included in this analysis since the contents of private profiles are hidden.

First, we considered class distinction by gender (i.e., male and female). In Table 4, we report the top 16 class-specific distinguishing terms for profiles declared to be male and for profiles declared to be female. The differences are stark.

Second, we considered class distinction by location for all fifty U.S. states. In Table 5, we report the results from three states that represent distinct geographic regions of the U.S.: the south, the Pacific northwest, and the northeast. We see an interesting mix of geography-specific identifiers (e.g., *protestant* in Alabama versus *catholic* in Connecticut), interests (e.g., *football* in Alabama versus *rafting* and *snowboarding* in Oregon), and word constructions (e.g., *yall, pdx, rad,* and *nas*).

Finally, we consider how the language models of MySpace users vary by age. In Table 6, we report distinguishing terms for ages ranging from 16 to 100. We see how the language model shifts in focus with age and educational level (e.g., high school, college, college graduate, etc.). MySpace users 30 and older used terms like *married, parent,* and *proud,* whereas members under 30 used terms like *lol, single,* and *love.* We can also make a few comments about the older (and perhaps less

Table 5. Distinguishing terms for three representative locations (Ranked by MI): popular location names (e.g., Birmingham, Portland) within each state are excluded.

Alabama	Oregon	Connecticut
christian	camping	catholic
African-descent	pdx	Yankees
tide	hiking	nyc
jesus	northwest	uconn
football	pixies	Hispanic
bama	snowboarding	Bronx
church	coast	boston
chrish	rafting	sox
protestant	floater	nas
gospel	rad	Italian
yall	wine	goodfellas
nascar	vegan	sneakers

truthful) age groups. The 69-year-olds have a clearly expressed interest in sex. The odd language model of 80-year-olds is skewed by the presence of many tribute profiles to Marilyn Monroe, who would have been 80 at the time the datasets were constructed: All of the terms here are relevant to Monroe's movie career and relationships. In contrast, the 100-year-olds display a less coherent

language model, perhaps due to the diversity of users declaring this advanced age.

Identifying Language Model Clusters

In the previous section, we saw how certain classes of MySpace users could be described by distinguishing terms that are relatively strong indicators of class membership. In this section, we continue this analysis by considering clusters of related classes. For example, assuming that most self-declared 100-year-old members of MySpace are not actually 100, what is their true age? MySpace has made some efforts to remove self-declared older members (Gradijan, 2007) through manual inspection. Can the language models we have identified provide a scalable solution?

We begin with the class-specific language models of interest (e.g., by age: $\{p^*(t|c = 16)\}_{t \in V}$, $\{p^*(t|c = 17)\}_{t \in V}$, and so on). Are there clusters of language models by age or by location? In this initial study, we considered a similarity measure for determining the "closeness" of two language models based on the Kullbeck-Leibler divergence (KL-divergence). KL-divergence, or relative entropy, measures the difference between two probability distributions p and q over an event space X:

Table 6. Distinguishing terms by age (Ranked by MI)

16	18	20	25	30	40	60	69	80	100
high	high	college	graduate	networking	parent	parent	networking	scudda	swinger
school	school	someday	college	graduate	proud	proud	swinger	mortenson	our
hearts	someday	student	networking	parent	married	president	sex	gable	kids
junior	love	love	grad	proud	networking	swinger	a**	jeane	capricon
single	best	straight	professional	married	kids	his	f***	showgirl	networking
best	boy	Caucasian	relationship	grad	great	married	rock	asphalt	virgo
hair	ever	white	traveling	professional	our	kids	islander	dimaggio	artists
friend	hair	like	some	art	divorced	united	real	Dougherty	their
lol	lol	girl	reading	cure	daughter	began	our	harlow	please
play	single	know	working	travel	years	retired	night	actress	official

$$KL\ (p,q) \mathrel{\coloneqq} \sum_{x \in X} p\big(x\big).\log(\frac{p\big(x\big)}{q\big(x\big)})$$

Intuitively, the KL-divergence measure indicates the inefficiency (in terms of wasted bits) of using the q distribution to encode the p distribution. In this case, we can measure the divergence of two class-specific language models (i.e. $p = \{p^*\big(t|c = 16\big)\}_{t \in V}$ and $q = \{p^*\big(t|c = 17\big)\}_{t \in V}$). Note that KL-divergence is not symmetric, so we will typically find $KL(p,q) \neq KL(q,p)$.

In Figure 6, we report the KL-divergence for 16-year-olds versus other ages, for 20-year-olds versus other ages, and for 30-year-olds versus other ages. Since there are very few profiles listing an older age, we have omitted these from the graph.

The KL-divergence for 16-year-olds is lowest for profiles closest in age, which indicates that the language model of a 16-year-old is closest to that of a 17-year-old, then an 18-year-old, and so on. A similar pattern holds for the language models of both 20-year-olds and 30-year-olds, pointing to clear clusters based on age.

What do we observe when we consider profiles that are more likely to be deceptive about their true age? Table 7 shows the closest language models

for profiles listing an age of 69 and for profiles listing an age of 100.

For the 69-year olds, the closest matches are other outlier ages: 100, 99, and 101. This provides some evidence that the type of user who lies about his age is bound by some common language model cues. The next two closest matches are with users in their 30s. This is a bit surprising, since we might have expected teenagers to be more likely to engage in such behavior. For the 100-year olds, we see a similar pattern: close matches with other outlier ages (99 and 101) and then close matches with younger profiles that could be presumed more likely to declare true ages. We believe this line of inquiry could be extended in a number of fruitful directions.

Privacy Preferences

Finally, we turned our attention to the important issue of privacy in social networks. A number of researchers have examined some of the aspects impacting privacy on social networks (Barnes, 2006; Boyd, 2007; Nussbaum, 2007) in an effort to comprehend user understanding of privacy and the limits of privacy controls. We examined the privacy choices of MySpace members through the lens of our demographic study. As noted previously, MySpace users can elect to declare their profile as public or private, although younger members of MySpace (i.e., 14- and 15-year-olds)

Figure 6. KL-Divergence by age: Comparison of class-specific language models using KL-divergence (where a lower value is better)

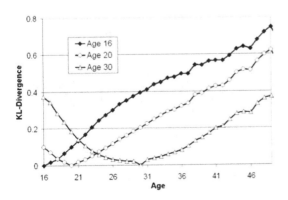

Table 7. Identifying outliers: language model(s) that most closely match the language model of self-described 69-year-olds and self-described 100-year-olds using KL-divergence.

Rank	Age 69	Age 100
1.	100 [0.017]	99 [0.047]
2.	99 [0.021]	101 [0.103]
3.	101 [0.047]	30 [0.105]
4.	33 [0.068]	31 [0.105]
5.	31 [0.072]	29 [0.106]

are required to have a private profile that displays only limited information, such as name, age, gender, and location.

In Table 8, we report on the privacy preferences of the randomly selected MySpace users who comprised the Random dataset, which was constructed to reflect the general MySpace population; and we contrast these preferences with the privacy preferences of the more sociable members of the Connected dataset. Members of the Connected dataset selected private profiles by nearly 2-to-1 over the average MySpace user. These findings are especially surprising since the relationship-based sampling technique used to extract the Connected dataset relied on the friendships declared on public profiles to identify profiles to sample: Private profiles reveal no friendships and so the sampling terminates when it arrives at a private profile. We further examined the private profiles in each dataset and found that nearly all (99.9%) of the private profiles in the Random dataset belonged to 14- and 15-year-olds (see Table 9). In contrast, we found that over 73.7% of the private profiles in the Connected dataset are those of MySpace members who were 16 or older.

Overall, very few users elected private profiles when given the opportunity (0.1%); but, for users who actively participated in the MySpace social network, a larger percentage preferred privacy. These results lend credence to the hypothesis that more sociable members tend to be more likely to choose private profiles.

To further explore the impact of demographics on privacy preferences, Figure 7 presents the percentage of private profiles in the Connected dataset by age and gender. We have truncated the graph over the age of 60 since there are very few profiles for those ages and hence more noise. We find that women favor private profiles 2-to-1 over men and, perhaps counterintuitively, that younger users are more likely to adopt a private profile than older users. Why is this? It may be that older users are less technically savvy and have more difficulty understanding how to configure the privacy setting; or it may be that younger users are more attuned to privacy and security concerns in social networks. We believe this is an area deserving more attention.

Finally, we considered how privacy preferences have changed over time. In Figure 8, each point represents a bucket of all profiles created before that date and extending back to the previous point. The y-axis measures the percentage of profiles created within that bucket that are private (again, relying on MySpace's use of sequential IDs to interpolate profile creation dates). After an initial drop in the privacy rate, we saw a fairly steady growth in the adoption of privacy settings by new members. Overall, the percentage of private profiles increased over time, indicating that new adopters of social networks tended to be more attuned to the privacy risks inherent in the adoption of a public Web presence. We also investigated privacy preferences by location, but found no dramatic swings from state to state.

Table 8. Privacy preferences for MySpace datasets

	Random	**Connected**
Private	101,158 (10.5%)	173, 830 (19.5%)
Public	859, 357 (89.5%)	717,337 (80.5%)
Total	960,505	891,167

Table 9. Private profiles by age for MySpace datasets

	Random	**Connected**
14/15 Years Old	101,017 (99.9%)	45,633 (26.3%)
All Other Ages (16+)	141 (00.1%)	128,197 (73.7%)
Total	101, 158	173,337

Figure 7. Privacy breakdown by age for MySpace connected dataset: The x-axis is the self-reported age on a profile; the y-axis is the percentage of all profiles declaring a particular age that are private

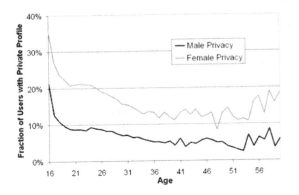

Figure 8. Privacy over time for MySpace connected dataset: The x-axis shows buckets of profiles organized by date of creation; the y-axis shows the percentage of private profiles created within a bucket's range

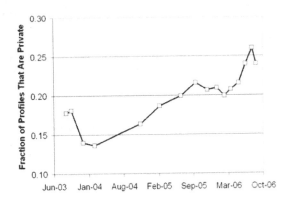

4. MEDIATING AND ANALYZING SOCIAL DATA

4.1 Modeling Social Tagging Data

In our second study of social networks and semantics, we focus on the rise of social tagging and how tagging can be used for mediating and linking social data. A tag is essentially a typed hyperlink: It is a keyword contributed by a user that categorizes or describes an online object. The goal of tagging is to make a body of information increasingly easier to search, discover, share and navigate over time. But tagging by users is not simply the addition of keywords to resources; rather, these tags are social metadata generated through collective intelligence. Thus, social tagging is a bottom-up approach to indexing that reflects the collective agreement of and speaks the same language as the users, making online objects easier to find and leading to the creation of systems of social semantics called folksonomies.

There are many social networks providing tagging services. Users can tag a range of resources, including bookmarks (Delicious), photos (Flickr), videos (YouTube), books (LibraryThing), Music

(Last.fm), citations (CiteULike), and blogs (Technorati). Here we have selected three major social tagging systems—Delicious, Flickr, and YouTube—and analyze their social tagging behavior. Based on this analysis, we propose the Upper Tag Ontology (UTO), which is an adaptation of the Tag Ontology proposed by Tom Gruber (2007). In his tag ontology, Gruber outlined five key concepts: *object*, *tag*, *tagger*, *source* and *vote*. In UTO, we have added an additional three concepts: *comment*, *date* and *tagging*. Most social networks contain information about user-contributed comments, whether they be comments on tags or on objects; and this information can contribute to an understanding of tags or objects. Date is another important concept because it allows us to track the evolution of tags and tagging behaviors. It can also help to reveal hidden social changes occurring within a social network. Although it does not have real meaning, the tagging concept functions to link the core concepts. We have also added the *has_relatedTag* relationship to the tag concept itself. Additional information about modeling social tagging data with UTO is discussed in Ding, Toma, Kang, Fried, and Yan (2008).

Figure 9. Upper tag ontology (UTO)

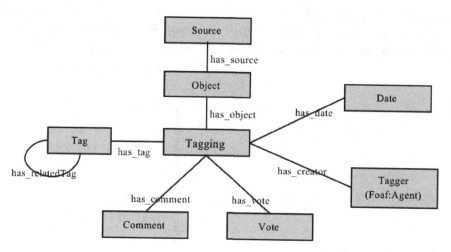

The Upper Tag Ontology (UTO) is defined as follows:

Let O be UTO ontology,

$$O = (C, \Re)$$

Where $C = \{c_i, i \in N\}$ is a finite set of concepts
$\Re = \{(c_i, c_k), i, k \in N\}$ is a finite set of relations established among concepts in C.

In UTO,

$$C = \begin{Bmatrix} Tag, Tagging, Object, Tagger, Source, \\ Date, Comment, Vote \end{Bmatrix},$$

$$\Re = \begin{Bmatrix} has\_relatedTag, has\_tag, has\_object, \\ has\_source, has\_date, has\_creator, \\ has\_comment, has\_vote \end{Bmatrix}$$

Figure 9 represents the concepts and relations in UTO. Obviously, UTO is a small and simple ontology with only eight concepts and eight relationships. The tagging concept acts as a virtual connection for the other concepts of UTO, serving the function of linking core concepts. For example,

it may be difficult to tell whether a date is related to the tag or to the tagging behavior or a comment could be viewed as added to a tag or directly to an object. For this reason, most of the relations in UTO are defined as transitive so that a comment can be connected to an object via tagging or to a tag via tagging.

UTO is very different from a folksonomy, which focuses on the meaning of tags. Following the basic design principle of "making it easy and simple to use", UTO is designed to capture the structure of social tagging behaviours rather than the meanings of the tags themselves. By focusing on the structure of social tagging behaviours rather than the actual tag semantics, UTO aims to model the structure of tagging data in order to integrate tagging data from one social tagging application with tagging data from other applications.

4.2 Linking Social Data

It is becoming increasingly important for data to be interlinked. Linking itself is moving from the traditional hyperlinks of Web 1.0 to the typed hyperlinks of Web 2.0 and, ultimately, to the semantic links of Web 3.0 in the Web 1.0 environment, we began by simply linking documents. Then, we added more metadata to these resources and turned unstructured information into structured information. Now, we are striving to provide semantic links between those structured resources so as to form Web 3.0 or the so-called Semantic Web. Social tagging plays an important role in this process of linking not only by structuring data but also by linking this structured information.

UTO can be aligned with other social metadata schemes such as Friend of A Friend (FOAF), Dublin Core (DC), Semantically-Interlinked Online Communities (SIOC) and Simple Knowledge Organization System (SKOS). With UTO, we try to make alignment between schemes as simple as possible since a more complicated alignment may actually generate more problems or double the complexity of application. In UTO, we have focused primarily on mapping of classes with the consideration of equivalent and sub-class mapping. For instance, the UTO *Tagger* concept is equivalent to foaf:Person and sioc:User and is a subclass of foaf:Agent. The *Tag* concept is equivalent to skos:Concept; the *Object* concept is defined as a superclass of foaf:Document, foaf:Image, sioc:Post, sioc:Item, dc:Text and dc:Image; and the *has_relatedTag* relationship is defined as a superordinate property of skos:narrower, skos:broader and skos:related.

Aligning UTO with other social semantics schemes enables easy data integration, mash-ups, and the interlinking of structured data. Using such integrated data, we can perform tag searches across multiple sites, applications, sources, and hosts and mine relationships (associations) across different platforms and applications. For example, it would be possible to find the friends of Stefan who have used the tag *spicy-Chinese-food* by aligning FOAF with UTO or to identify blogs, wikis or discussion groups where Stefan and his friends have discussed "spicy Chinese food" by aligning FOAF and SOIC through UTO. Associations among tags, taggers and objects can also be mined. For example, we can mine the social network relations of taggers through foaf:knows by aligning FOAF with UTO;

we can mine relations between tags by aligning skos:broader, skos:narrower or skos:related with the UTO relation *has_relatedTag*; and we can use co-occurrence technologies to mine associations among tags, taggers and objects.

4.3 Crawling Social Tagging Data

The Social Tagging crawler (or ST crawler) was developed for crawling major social tagging systems, including Delicious, Flickr, and YouTube (Fried, 2007). It is a multi-crawler based on the "Smart and Simple Webcrawler"[10] and UTO. Figure 10 is a detailed class diagram of the crawler.

The ST crawler is written in Java with Eclipse IDE 3.2 on Windows XP and Ubuntu 6.04, and data is cleaned using linux batch commands. ST crawler can start from either one link or a list of links and has two crawling models:

- **Max Iterations:** Crawling a website through a limited number of links, which needs a small memory footprint and CPU usage.
- **Max Depth:** A simple graph model parser without recording incoming and outgoing links, which uses a filter to limit the links to be crawled.

In the summer of 2007, we used the ST crawler to crawl social tagging data from Delicious, Flickr and YouTube and to model them according to UTO. The data are represented in RDF triples and stored in Jena. After one-week of crawling, the output was contained in a number of RDF files with a total file size of 2.10GB:

- 16 Delicious data files with a total size of 1.64GB
- 3 Flickr data files with a total size of 233MB
- 3 YouTube data files with a total size of 234MB

Figure 10. Class diagram of the ST crawler

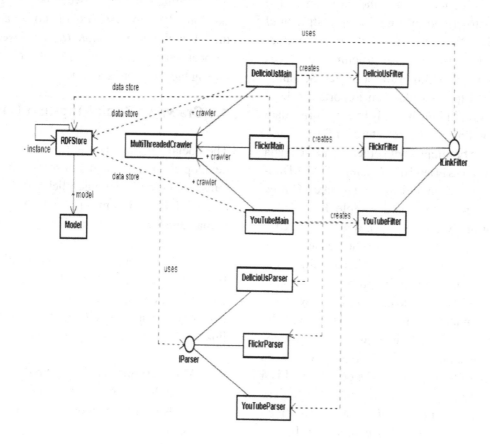

4.4 Social Tagging Data

Table 10 presents an overview of the data collected from the Delicious, Flickr and YouTube social networks. The total dataset contains approximately 1 million bookmarks, 2.8 million taggers and 9.3 million tags from Delicious; 300,000 photographs, 150,000 taggers and 1.4 million tags from Flickr; and 500,000 videos, 200,000 taggers and 1.35 million tags from YouTube. The average number of tags per object ranges from a low of 2.74 in YouTube to a high of 9.31 in Delicious. The average number of tags a single tagger assigns to a resource ranges from a low of 3.33 in Delicious to a high of 8.79 in Flickr. The average number of objects tagged by a single tagger ranges from a low of 0.36 in Delicious to a high of 2.84 in YouTube. The seeming disparity reflected in the low average for objects tagged by a Delicious tagger can be accounted for by the fact that, while users are required to provide a title when uploading bookmarks to Delicious, they are not required to include tags in the tag field: Thus, there may be many bookmarks in Delicious that have titles but no tags. Combined data from the three social networks totals approximately 1.8 million objects, 3.1 million taggers, and 12.1 million tags, of which 648,368 tags are unique.

All tag data are represented in RDF and stored in Jena. We used the tag data as they were retrieved, although we did perform some data cleaning (e.g., stemming and checking with WordNet). By querying the data, we identified the 20 most highly ranked tags and the 20 most highly ranked bookmarks in Delicious for the period 2005-2007, as shown in Table 11.

Table 10. Data from Delicious, Flickr and YouTube for the years 2005-2007

Social Network	Objects	Taggers	Tags	Tag/Object	Tag/Tagger	Objects/Tagger
Delicious	996,748	2,787,860	9,282,058	9.31	3.33	0.36
Flickr	295,837	153,778	1,351,201	4.57	8.79	1.92
YouTube	527,924	185,975	1,443,924	2.74	7.76	2.84
Total	1,820,509	3,127,613	12,077,183	5.54	6.63	1.71

Note: Cells in the column labeled *Tags* represent the total number of tags assigned by taggers (e.g., when TagA is assigned by Tagger X and by Tagger Y, it is counted as two tags).

Table 11. Top 20 tags and bookmarks in Delicious for the period 2005-2007

Rank	Tag	Tag Frequency	Bookmark	Bookmark Frequency
1	blog	141,871	en.wikipedia.org	26,745
2	system	120,673	www.youtube.com	14,990
3	design	109,249	community.livejournal.com	6,594
4	software	87,719	www.google.com	6,376
5	programming	83,665	www.w3.org	6,193
6	tool	83,461	news.bbc.co.uk	5,718
7	reference	74,602	www.flickr.com	5,645
8	web	70,538	java.sun.com	5,538
9	video	65,226	www.nytimes.com	5,222
10	music	61,246	www.microsoft.com	5,219
11	art	57,970	lifehacker.com	5,207
12	linux	47,965	www-128.ibm.com	4,569
13	tutorial	41,844	www.codeproject.com	4,429
14	java	40,780	www.wired.com	4,269
15	news	40,652	video.gooogle.com	4,261
16	game	39,391	www.techcrunch.com	3,818
17	free	39,006	www.bbc.co.uk	3,318
18	development	37,914	www.readwriteweb.com	3159
19	business	35,272	blogs.msdn.com	3,121
20	internet	34,580	msdn2.microsoft.com	2,950

The tag *blog* dominates in Delicious in the period from 2005 to 2007. Because most taggers on Delicious are presumed to be IT gurus, it is not surprising that tags such as *system*, *design*, *software*, *programming*, and *tool* are also included in the top 20 tags. The tags *Web* and *Internet* represent evergreen topics of this commu-

nity. Because people in general like to share music, video, news, and games, these are also popular topics in Delicious. And, because people like things that available without charge, the tag *free* is seventeenth on this list of most highly ranked tags. Highly ranked bookmarks in Delicious include other major social networks (You-

Tube, livejournal, wikipedia, and Flickr), major news (BBC and the New York Times), and major computer giants (Microsoft, Google, IBM, and Sun), which indicates the social impact of these websites.

Power Law Distribution

The tagging data from Delicious, Flickr and You-Tube was merged to form a single, comprehensive dataset. Using this combined dataset, an analysis of tag frequency was conducted. Figure 11 and Table 12 demonstrate that the distribution of tag frequency follows a power law distribution that conforms to Zipf's Law. Table 12 shows the details of this distribution: Only 1,363 of the 648,368 unique tags (or approximately 0.2% of all tags assigned between 2005 and 2007) were assigned more than 1000 times each, while 357,028 (or approximately 55% of all tags) were assigned only once.

In the combined dataset, the most frequently occurring tag is *design*, which accounts for 101,786 or nearly 1% of all tag occurrences. The second most frequently occurring tag is *blog* and accounts for 90,242 or 0.7% of the total tags assigned between 2005 and 2007. The 1,363 most frequently occurring tags account for a total of 6,210,163 tagging instances; these 1,363 tags comprise a core tagging vocabulary that represents

more than 50% of the entire corpus of 12,077,183 tagging instances. (See the Appendix for a list of the 1,363 tags that make up the combined core tagging vocabulary of Delicious, Flickr and You-Tube.) It is hoped that linguistic analysis of this core set of tags will reveal features of the evolv-

Table 12. Tag frequency distribution

Tag Frequency Range	No. Unique Tags	Cumulative %
1	357028	55.07%
2-10	217746	88.65%
11-20	27404	92.88%
21-30	11524	94.65%
31-40	6656	95.68%
41-50	4454	96.37%
51-60	3387	96.89%
61-70	2461	97.27%
71-80	2066	97.59%
81-90	1597	97.83%
91-100	1348	98.04%
101-200	6193	99.00%
201-300	2151	99.33%
301-400	1044	99.49%
401-500	645	99.59%
501-1,000	1301	99.79%
1,001-120,000	1363	100.00%

Note: Cells in the column labeled *No. Unique Tags* represent the total of unique tags (e.g., when TagA is assigned by Tagger X and by Tagger Y, it is counted as one tag).

Figure 11. Distribution of tag frequency

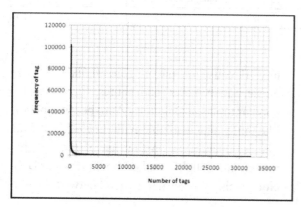 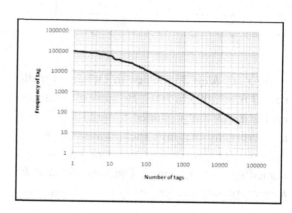

ing vocabulary of tags in each social tagging network.

4.5 Social Tagging Analysis

In order to generate individual portraits of tag use and the composition of tag vocabularies in Delicious, Flickr and YouTube, data from each social network were analyzed independently using three time frames (2005, 2006, 2007).

Delicious

Table 13 shows the 20 most frequently assigned tags in Delicious for the years 2005, 2006, and 2007. These tag sets appear to be relatively stable across the three years. The tags *xml*, *science*, *search*, *games*, *technology*, and *security* appear among the top 20 tags for 2005 but are dropped from the lists of top 20 tags for 2006 and 2007; and the tags *imported*, *research*, and *internet* are dropped from the list of top 20 tags for 2007. The tags *development*, *howto*, *tutorial* and *Web 2.0* appear in the lists for both 2006 and 2007, and the tags *webdesign*, *free* and *opensource* are introduced in 2007, pointing to the emergence of new trends in user interests. Overall, 85% of the top 20 tags are stable across 2006 and 2007, indicating that a shared social vocabulary may be emerging in Delicious.

A profile of Delicious users can be generated through analysis of the lists of popular tags. The dominance of tags such as *blog, web, programming*, and *design* indicate key interests of Delicious users who are tagging bookmarks to store or share. While the tags *music, video, art* and *news* indicate a level of general interest that spans all three years, actual tagging evidence strongly supports the popular assumption that Delicious is a social network for IT gurus and other individuals interested in Web and programming skills. Furthermore, the tags introduced in 2006 and 2007 indicate a growing interest in free or open source resources as well as tutorials and how-to re-

Table 13. Top 20 tags in delicious for the years 2005, 2006 and 2007

Rank	2005	2006	2007
1	blog/blogs	blog/blogs	blog/blogs
2	programming	programming	design
3	software	software	software
4	music	design	programming
5	design	reference	reference
6	web	music	tools
7	reference	web	Web 2.0
8	java	tools	web
9	art	art	video
10	tools	java	music
11	linux	video	art
12	news	Web 2.0	linux
13	xml	linux	webdesign
14	science	news	howto
15	search	tutorial	free
16	games	howto	tutorial
17	research	imported	news
18	technology	development	development
19	security	research	opensource
20	video	internet	java

sources that support learning programming languages or applications and developing new computer skills.

Figure 12 shows the evolution of dominant topical tags used in the Delicious social network for the period 2005-2007. The tag *Web2.0* shows the highest peak in both 2006 and 2007: The raw frequency with which *Web2.0* was used to tag bookmarks increased 16 times in 2006 and 76 times in 2007 when compared with its raw tagging frequency in 2005. The tags showing the most dramatic increase in raw tagging frequency from 2006 to 2007 were *webdesign*, *free* and *Web2.0*, indicating growing interest in these topics on the part of Delicious taggers. The three tags with the least impressive increase in raw tagging frequency from 2006 to 2007 were *java*, *programming*, and

Figure 12. Evolution of the top 20 tags in Delicious for the period 2005-2007

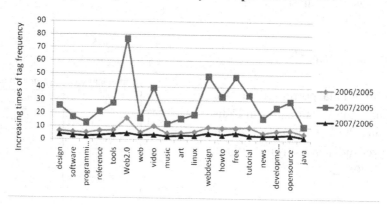

Table 14. Top 20 tags in Delicious for 2007 and frequency of assignment in the years 2005, 2006 and 2007

Top 20 Tags in Delicious for 2007	2005	2006	2007	2006/2005	2007/2005	2007/2006
blog/blogs	6731 (1)	29485 (1)	90474 (1)	4	13	3.1
design	3045 (5)	19273 (4)	78115 (2)	6	26	4.1
software	3558 (3)	19533 (3)	60405 (3)	5	17	3.1
programming	4295 (2)	21789 (2)	55237 (4)	5	13	2.5
reference	2541 (7)	16643 (5)	53971 (5)	7	21	3.2
tools	1943 (10)	13340 (8)	53772 (6)	7	28	4.0
Web 2.0	658 (-)	10620 (12)	50270 (7)	16	76	4.7
web	2743 (6)	14115 (7)	44406 (8)	5	16	3.1
video	1114 (20)	11383 (11)	43847 (9)	10	39	3.9
music	3325 (4)	15523 (6)	39859 (10)	5	12	2.6
art	2344 (9)	12043 (9)	37518 (11)	5	16	3.1
linux	1799 (11)	10434 (13)	34241 (12)	6	19	3.3
webdesign	688 (-)	6542 (-)	33224 (13)	10	48	5.1
howto	962 (-)	8588 (16)	31701 (14)	9	33	3.7
free	643 (-)	5793 (-)	30750 (15)	9	48	5.3
tutorial	895 (-)	8683 (15)	30648 (16)	10	34	3.5
news	1712 (12)	8854 (14)	28086 (17)	5	16	3.2
development	1107 (-)	7588 (18)	27322 (18)	7	25	3.6
opensource	872 (-)	6468 (-)	25735 (19)	7	30	4.0
java	2449 (8)	11606 (10)	25732 (20)	5	11	2.2

Note: Numbers in parentheses in the columns labeled *2005*, *2006* and *2007* reflect the ranking of a term for that particular year. The column labeled *2006/2005* indicates that the value in each cell is the result of dividing the value for 2006 by the value for 2005. The result indicates the increase in raw numbers of frequency of tag assignment from 2005 to 2006. This also applies to the columns labeled *2007/2005* and *2007/2006*.

music. While this might seem to indicate waning interest in these topics, only the ranking for *java*, which dropped from eighth most popular tag in 2005 to twentieth most popular in 2007 (see Table 14), appears to support this conclusion. The tag *programming* drops from second position in 2005 and 2006 to fourth position in 2007; however, this is not a drop in popularity dramatic enough to justify any assumptions about waning interest on the part of Delicious taggers. The tag *music* does demonstrate a more dramatic drop in popularity—from fourth position in 2005, to sixth position in 2006, and to tenth position in 2007—but the fact that Last.fm became one of the more popular social networks for sharing music during this period may help to explain why use of the tag *music* decreased from 2005 through September 2007.

Flickr

Table 15 shows the 20 most frequently used tags in Flickr for the years 2005, 2006, and 2007. In sharp contrast to the more topical tagging culture of Delicious, Flickr taggers like to tag photographs with dates, locations, colors, and seasons. Favorite locations in Flickr include Hong Kong (2005), Germany (2005), USA (2006 and 2007), London (2005-2007), California (2006), and Japan (2007). Favorite color tags are *orange* (2005), *blue* (2006 and 2007), *red* (2006 and 2007), *green* (2006 and 2007), and black-and-white (i.e., *bw* in 2007). Most frequently used tags for seasons are *autumn* and *fall* (2007). In addition, users also favor tagging photographs with time of day or lighting conditions, especially when the photographs are night views. With the exception of tags in the categories year, color and location, topics of the top 20 tag sets differ widely across the three years.

Flickr taggers frequently assign informal tags to photographs (e.g., *me*), indicating that users may be tagging photographs for purposes of storing and retrieving them for their own use rather than with any intent to share them with others.

Table 15. Top 20 tags in Flickr for the years 2005, 2006 and 2007

Rank	2005	2006	2007
1	2005	usa	2007
2	d70	california	canon
3	tsimshatsui	2006	nature
4	hongkong	cameraphone	autumn
5	nightview	celltagged	art
6	germany	zonetag	nikon
7	newkie	sanfrancisco	water
8	ragbrai	blue	bw
9	art	light	red
10	wonder	sky	blue
11	night	urban	sky
12	buttersweet	red	japan
13	15fav	sea	fall
14	central	me	beach
15	light	water	portrait
16	marco	nature	london
17	london	marco	night
18	apargioides	london	green
19	orange	green	usa
20	ads1	music	november

When tagging photographs, users tend to emphasize the eye-catching features of an image such as color, subject (e.g., *sky*, *water*, *beach* and specific locations), and lighting conditions (e.g., *night* and *nightview*). Nonetheless, time (i.e., year, season, or month), locations and colors are the major features of images tagged by users. It could be useful to analyze the tagging culture of Flickr in greater detail given that the annotation of images is an important consideration in image retrieval.[11]

Figure 13 and Table 16 show the temporal history of tag popularity in Flickr for the period 2005-2007. In 2005 and 2006, tagging was not particularly popular in the Flickr community, with the total number of tags at 3,598 for 2005 and 23,066 for 2006. However, as tagging became

Figure 13. Evolution of the top 20 tags in Flickr for the period 2005-2007

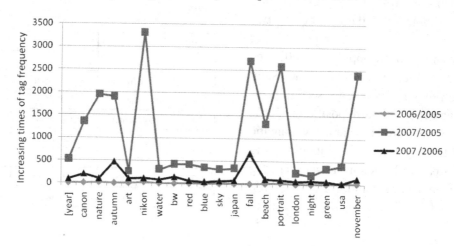

more popular on the Web, tagging behavior in Flickr appears to have changed dramatically: 1,324,537 tags were assigned by Flickr users from January through September of 2007, approximately 50 times more tags than were assigned for all of 2006. Raw tagging frequency for *cannon*, the second most popular tag in 2007, increased 203.5 times over its total use in 2006; but *fall*, the thirteenth most popular tag in 2007, showed the greatest jump, increasing 672.5 times over its raw frequency of assignment in 2006.

Interestingly, an analysis of tagged photographs indicates that there may be two major communities of Flickr taggers. One community appears to consist of non-professional photographers who use Flickr as a platform for sharing photographs with friends and family and thus tag images so that they can be retrieved by others. The second community appears to consist of professional photographers who do not tag regularly but who frequently provide comments on photographs taken by other professionals.

YouTube

Table 17 shows the 20 most popular tags in You-Tube for the years 2005, 2006 and 2007. The topics that are most frequently tagged in this social

network are music, videos, humor, sex and girls, apparently reflecting the broad interests of the general Web community.

Tagging activity in YouTube increased dramatically between 2005 and 2007. The total number of tags assigned in YouTube increased from 4,735 in 2005, to 366,147 in 2006, to 1,073,042 in 2007. Tag use was 78.7 times greater in 2006 and 236.7 times greater in 2007 than it was in 2005. Compared with 2005, the tag [*year*] had the greatest increase in use in 2007, followed by *new* and *sex/sexy*, while *dance* showed the least increase between 2005 and 2007. The tag set in YouTube appears to be more stable than that of Flickr for the same time period, seemingly indicating that areas of user interest have remained fairly steady for the Social Web community as a whole (see Figure 14 and Table 18).

5. UTILIZING WEB 2.0 IN WEB SERVICE RANKING

5.1 System Description

In our third study of social networks and semantics, we propose a social ranking approach for Web service selection and ranking that is based

Table 16. Top 20 tags in Flickr for 2007 and frequency of assignment in the years 2005, 2006 and 2007

Top 20 Tags in Flickr for 2007	2005	2006	2007	2006/2005	2007/2005	2007 /2006
[year]	21 (1)	124 (3)	11112 (1)	6	529	89.6
canon	3 (-)	20 (-)	4070 (2)	7	1357	203.5
nature	2 (-)	39 (16)	3899 (3)	20	1950	100.0
autumn	2 (-)	8 (-)	3804 (4)	4	1902	475.5
art	13 (9)	33 (-)	3416 (5)	3	263	103.5
nikon	1 (-)	30 (-)	3312 (6)	30	3312	110.4
water	10	39 (15)	3126 (7)	4	313	80.2
bw	7 (-)	21 (-)	3028 (8)	3	433	144.2
red	7 (-)	47 (12)	2988 (9)	7	427	63.6
blue	8 (-)	66 (8)	2888 (10)	8	361	43.8
sky	9 (-)	48 (10)	2878 (11)	5	320	60.0
japan	8 (-)	37 (-)	2738 (12)	5	342	74.0
fall	1 (-)	4 (-)	2690 (13)	4	2690	672.5
beach	2 (-)	24 (-)	2636 (14)	12	1318	109.8
portrait	1 (-)	26 (-)	2581 (15)	26	2581	99.3
london	10 (17)	39 (18)	2503 (16)	4	250	64.2
night	13 (11)	35 (-)	2489 (17)	3	191	71.1
green	7 (-)	38 (19)	2417 (18)	5	345	63.6
usa	6 (-)	126 (1)	2406 (19)	21	401	19.1
november	1 (-)	19 (-)	2394 (20)	19	2394	126.0

Note: Numbers in parentheses in the columns labeled *2005*, *2006* and *2007* reflect the ranking of a term for that particular year. The column labeled *2006/2005* indicates that the value in each cell is the result of dividing the value for 2006 by the value for 2005. The result indicates the increase in raw numbers of frequency of tag assignment from 2005 to 2006. This also applies to the columns labeled *2007/2005* and *2007/2006*.

on Delicious, one of the largest social networks. The system is quite simple and straightforward. Given a set of Web services, the system checks to determine if there are Web pages in the Web services domains that have been bookmarked in Delicious. When this is the case, the services are ranked based on the numbers of users in Delicious who have tagged the associated Web pages. For example, a user would like to know which of the shipping services have high social visibility. He identifies relevant keywords and runs his query against the service repository to get a set of .wsdl shipping services. For each Web service, the system then checks to determine if there are Web pages from the same domain already bookmarked in Delicious. These Web pages are retrieved from the Web and stored locally. Finally, the resulting set of Web services is ranked based on how many users have tagged the corresponding bookmarks and then displayed to the user.

5.1.1 Architecture

The system we propose consists of a set of loosely coupled components: an annotations search engine that retrieves relevant Delicious bookmarks given a user query; a Web service finder that crawls the domain of the bookmarks and identifies relevant .wsdl files; and, finally, a Web service ranker that performs the ranking of Web services. The system is implemented in Java and runs as a Web application hosted in the Apache Tomcat container.

Table 17. Top 20 tags in YouTube for the years 2005, 2006 and 2007

Rank	2005	2006	2007
1	music	the	the
2	funny	funny	music
3	video	music	funny
4	the	video	video
5	dance	live	girl
6	crazy	of	of
7	commercial	comedy	sexy
8	dancing	dance	live
9	live	rock	dj
10	AMV	cat	2007
11	fun	Halloween	dance
12	guitar	love	hot
13	hot	girl	comedy
14	girl	movie	rock
15	japan	dj	love
16	anime	in	and
17	Halloween	sexy	sex
18	cat	and	in
19	halo	fight	new
20	of	you	cat

The rest of this section details each component of the system and describes how these components work together.

Access Interface

The access interface component is the visual gateway to the system. It allows the user to formulate a query as a set of keywords and to submit them to the system. Once a request has been processed by the system, the resulting set of ranked services is returned to the access interface, which then displays them to the user. The access interface is implemented using JSP technology.

Annotation Search Engine

The functionality of the annotation search engine can be briefly summarized as follows: Given a user keyword query, the annotation search engine returns a set of Delicious bookmarks relevant to that query. As illustrated in Figure 15, the annotation search engine includes a set of subcomponents: the Delicious Crawler, the Delicious Data Processor, and the Delicious Semantic Repository.

Delicious Crawler: This subcomponent is responsible for crawling social information from the Delicious social network. We chose an internally developed multicrawler designed for crawl-

Figure 14. Evolution of the top 20 tags in YouTube for the period 2005-2007

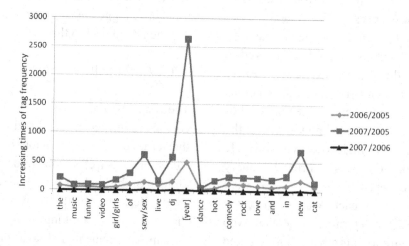

Table 18. Top 20 tags in YouTube for 2007 and frequency of assignment in the years 2005, 2006 and 2007

Top 20 Tags in YouTube for 2007	2005	2006	2007	2006/2005	2007/2005	2007 /2006
the	42 (4)	3240 (1)	9371 (1)	77	223	2.9
music	67 (1)	3080 (3)	6452 (2)	46	96	2.1
funny	58 (2)	3091 (2)	5784 (3)	53	100	1.9
video	53 (3)	2234 (3)	5065 (4)	42	96	2.3
girl/girls	25 (14)	1334 (13)	4647 (5)	53	186	3.5
of	13 (20)	1390 (6)	3955 (6)	107	304	2.8
sexy/sex	9 (-/-)	1338 (17/-)	5601 (7/17)	149	622	4.2
live	17 (9)	1563 (5)	3028 (8)	92	178	1.9
dj	5 (-)	777 (15)	2920 (9)	155	584	3.8
[year]	1 (-)	498 (-)	2641 (10)	498	2641	5.3
dance	56 (5)	1061 (8)	2526 (11)	19	45	2.4
hot	14 (13)	552 (-)	2467 (12)	39	176	4.5
comedy	10 (-)	1245 (7)	2461 (13)	125	246	2.0
rock	10 (-)	1059 (9)	2380 (14)	106	238	2.2
love	10 (-)	817 (12)	2294 (15)	82	229	2.8
and	11 (-)	689 (18)	2190 (16)	63	199	3.2
in	8 (-)	723 (16)	2095 (18)	90	262	2.9
new	3 (-)	544 (-)	2079 (19)	181	693	3.8
cat	13 (18)	977 (10)	1906 (20)	75	147	2.0

Note: Numbers in parentheses in the columns labeled *2005*, *2006* and *2007* reflect the ranking of a term for that particular year. The column labeled *2006/2005* indicates that the value in each cell is the result of dividing the value for 2006 by the value for 2005. The result indicates the increase in raw numbers of frequency of tag assignment from 2005 to 2006. This also applies to the columns labeled *2007/2005* and *2007/2006*.

Figure 15. System Architecture

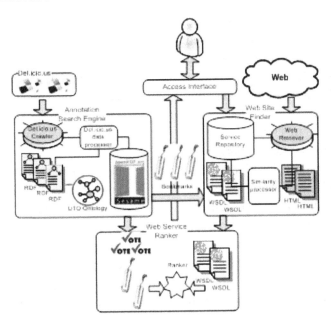

ing major social networks, including Delicious, Flickr and YouTube (Ding, Toma et al., 2008). This crawler is based on the Smart and Simple Webcrawler. Since Flickr and YouTube are platforms for sharing photos and videos and not Web services, they were not considered in our research. Figure 15 shows the detailed class diagram of the crawler. Another option we initially considered to retrieve relevant bookmarks, given a query, was the Delicious API. This might seem a nicer approach, but it faced serious limitations. More precisely, due to authentication issues, a user can only access his own data (i.e., tags, bookmarks, updates and bundles), thus prohibiting access to all bookmarks relevant to a query.

Delicious Data Processor: This subcomponent is responsible for processing .html pages crawled from Delicious, parsing them, and generating structured, light weight semantic annotated data represented in RDF (Manola & Miller, 2004). RDF is a standard language and method for making statements about Web resources in the form of subject-predicate-object. Since RDF is schema independent, we have used the Upper Tag Ontology (Ding, Kang et al., 2008) as a model to structure RDF social data. The Upper Tag Ontology (UTO) is a light ontology that includes concepts such as *Tag, Tagger, Object*, and *Vote* and relations such as *hasTag, hasVote*, and *hasObject*. These ontological elements are used to build RDF representations of the data crawled from Delicious.

Delicious Semantic Repository: This subcomponent stores RDF triples generated by the data processor according to UTO. We chose Sesame (Broekstra, Kampman, & van Harmelen, 2002) as a semantic repository for storing Delicious data because it offers efficient storage for RDF (Manola & Miller, 2004) and RDF schema (Brickley & Guha, 2004), which can be deployed on top of RDBMS repositories. Although an RDBMS repository could have been used, the choice of a semantic repository was motivated by the availability of flexible data structures that can

be stored without the need to extend or change the data model.

Web Site Finder

The website finder is the top-level component responsible for mining correspondences between Web services and possible Web pages in the domain of Web services that have been bookmarked on Delicious. Given a Web service description, this component checks to determine if any Web pages having the same domain have been bookmarked in Delicious. If any such pages exist, they are retrieved from the Web and their similarity with the Web service description is computed. Finally, a correspondence matrix between Web services and the most similar Web pages is built.

As illustrated in Figure 15, the website finder includes a set of subcomponents: the Web Retriever, the Service Repository, and the Similarity Processor.

- **Web Retriever:** This subcomponent is responsible for retrieving .html files from the domain of the Web service. More precisely, the Web retriever component first makes a query to the Delicious semantic repository and receives URLs of Web pages from the same domain as the Web service. It then retrieves the content of these pages from the Web and stores them locally.
- **Service Repository:** This subcomponent stores the .wsdl files identified by the processor subcomponent together with the set of keywords in the query. It is simply a persistent layer implemented using a classic RDBMS. The access interface component interacts with the service repository component, allowing the user to search for services based on the keywords provided as input.
- **Similarity Processor:** This subcomponent determines the similarity between a Web service .wsdl description and each page in its domain that has been bookmarked

in Delicious. To determine the similarity between a Web service and a website, we use two techniques. First, we check for co-occurrence in the set of keywords used to name Web service operations and the keywords in the Web page. Second, we check for co-occurrence in the set of keywords used to name Web service operations and the annotation keywords (or tags) that have been assigned to the Web page in Delicious.

We regard services, Web pages and the set of tags used to annotate a Web page as sets of keywords. To build the vector model for services, we consider only the names of the operations exposed by the services. For Web pages, the initial preprocessing step consists of removing all html tags. For all keyword sets representing services, Web pages, and tags, further preprocessing is performed using stopwords and stemming. We then apply the cosine similarity metric (Manning, Raghavan, & Schutze, 2008) to measure similarity between two sets of keywords representing services, Web pages, or tags.

Web Service Ranker

The Web service ranker component is the core component of the system that is responsible for the actual ranking of Web services. This component first performs a ranking of Delicious bookmarks, which translates into the ranking of associated Web services. The straightforward approach we adopt is to rank each bookmark based on how many people have bookmarked the Web page or how many votes the bookmark has. This information is already available in the Delicious semantic repository, having been crawled from the Delicious website. The ordered list of bookmarks based on the number of votes is then used to generate the ordered list of Web services that is presented to the user.

5.1.2 Algorithm

The current implementation of this Web service ranking system follows a simple and straightforward approach with respect to how the actual ranking of services is determined. Basically, the number of votes received by a relevant bookmark in Delicious becomes the rank value of the service. In the rest of this section, a general algorithm to compute the rank of a Web service is proposed. Our algorithm is based on the Social Page Rank (SPR) algorithm proposed by Bao et al. (2007) and has been extended to address the Web service dimension. The SPR algorithm evaluates the popularity of a Web page based on mutual enhancement among three distinct sets of objects: (a) popular Web pages, (b) Web users, and (c) hot social annotations. We introduce Web services as a fourth dimension or set of objects, and call the new algorithm the Social Web Service Rank (SocWSRank). The algorithm is provided below.

If P is the set of Web pages having N_p elements, U is the set of users having N_U elements, A is the set of annotations having N_A elements, and S is the set of Web service having NS elements, the association matrixes can be defined between annotation and pages (M_{AP}), between pages and

Algorithm 1. Social web service rank (SocWSRank)

```
Require: Set of association matrixes
M_AP, M_PU, M_UA, M_PS Ensure: S* the con-
verged Social Web Service Rank
   1: While S_i not converged do
   2:  P_i = M_ps * S_i
   3:  U_i = M^T_PU * P_i
   4:  A_i = M^T_UA * U_i
   5:  P'_i = M^T_AP * A_i
   6:  A'_i = M_AP * P'_i
   7:  U'_i = M_UA * A'_i
   8:  P_{i+1} = M_PU * A'_i
   9:  S_{i+1} = M_TPS * P_{i+1}
  10: end while
```

users (M_{PU}), between users and annotations (M_{UA}), and, finally, between Web pages and Web services (M_{PS}). The matrix elements are assigned values that capture the associations between each pair of dimensions. For example, the MAP (*pi, uj*) element is assigned the number of annotations (tags) with which a user *uj* annotates a page *pi*. Elements of the matrixes MAP and MUA are computed as described by Bao et al. (2007). Elements of the matrix MPS are assigned the value 1 if there is a correspondence between the Web page and the service or the value 0 if not.

5.2 Experiments and Discussions

We performed a set of experiments using three datasets: a social dataset built using Delicious data and two Web service datasets. The social dataset was created by crawling Delicious data. Once crawled, the data was annotated using the UTO ontology and stored as RDF triples in a Sesame repository. The Delicious dataset totaled 1.64 GB of data.

The other two datasets are .wsdl datasets that were provided by seekda OG, an Austrian company. The first one is an 80 file dataset containing services providing shipping functionality that have valid .wsdl descriptions and are accessible online. The second one is a larger dataset containing 5,000 services from different domains with valid .wsdl files and available online.

For the dataset with 80 shipping services, we found that only three of the domains had pages annotated in Delicious. For each of these domains, we queried Sesame and determined the total number of Web pages annotated to be 14. The distribution of Web pages per Web service domains was between zero and seven Web pages.

For the dataset with 5000 services, 86 of them had Web pages from their domain that were annotated in Delicious. The number of Web pages per domain varied from zero to 131. In total, we found 547 Web pages annotated in Delicious that were connected to the initial dataset.

One can notice that, in both cases, the number of pages annotated in Delicious that actually have a correspondence with the Web services dataset is rather limited. However, for a small number of services we were able to find a considerable number of pages, some of them having a strong correlation/similarity with the Web services. We can conclude that, even though the link between the Web service data and Delicious data is, in general, not very strong, when such a link is visible, it can be used both to determine more information about the services and to rank them.

6. DISCUSSIONS AND CONCLUSION

In this chapter we have investigated the connection between Social Networks and Semantics. We have shown how synergies between these two areas can be used to solve concrete problems and we have described three approaches that show the true potential of interconnecting these technologies. The uniqueness of our three proposed approaches is given by the large-scale social data analysis, the semantic integration of data for social web and the usage of social web data for service ranking. Related studies and approaches suffer from a set of disadvantages that were mentioned in Section 2. These include: (1) a small set of the data considered in the studies, (2) lack of intelligent solutions for data integrating and cross-domain and cross-network search and (3) lack of using the social tagging features for ranking of services. In the following sub-sections we briefly summarize and discuss the contribution of each of our three approaches.

6.1 Semantic Profiling of Social Networks

We have presented the first large-scale study of MySpace in an effort to better understand this new social phenomenon. Our comparative study differs from previous work both in its scale (over 1.9

million profiles) and in its breadth. In particular, we have examined how MySpace users participate in the social network (sociability), how they describe themselves (demographics), and how they communicate their personal interests and feelings (language models). The core findings of the MySpace study are:

- Nearly half of the profiles on MySpace have been abandoned, indicating that perceptions of the overall growth and explosive rate of user interest in social networks may need to be tempered; however, we have also identified a large core of active users within MySpace who account for the vast majority of friends, comments, and group activity.

- Younger users (in their teens and 20s) are most prevalent on MySpace: Women are most prevalent in the younger age groups (14 to 20), whereas men are most prevalent for all other age groups (21 and up).

- There are clear patterns of language use based on user age, location, and gender, which is a useful observation both for text mining and for characterization of applications. We have identified class-specific distinguishing terms and language model clusters that could be used to identify deceptive users attempting to misrepresent their demographics.

- Overall, the fraction of private profiles is increasing with time, indicating that new adopters of social networks may be more attuned to the inherent privacy risks of adopting a public Web presence. We found that women favor private profiles by 2-to-1 over men, and that, perhaps counterintuitively, younger users are more likely to adopt a private profile than older users. We also found that the more connected a user was in the social network, the more likely she was to adopt a private profile.

We have identified a number of surprising and interesting features that motivate our continuing research. In particular, we are interested in augmenting and extending models of social network growth to incorporate the demographic variations we have observed. Along this line, we believe fine-grained language models that move beyond age, gender, and location to capture user interests and expectations of the social network (e.g., for business-development networking, for making friends) could be beneficial.

6.2 Mediating and Analyzing Social Data

Another problem addressed in this chapter was mediation of and alignment between social tagging systems. We have proposed the Upper Tag Ontology (UTO) as a mediating tool and have described how UTO can be used to align metadata represented according to differing tagging ontologies.

To demonstrate the application of UTO and the Social Tagging crawler, we reported on a study of three social networks: Delicious, Flickr and YouTube. When comparing these three social networks, Delicious demonstrates the tightest connection to the use of tags as extended information about resources. In Delicious, every user can tag an object with the tag(s) of his own choice; and any object can be tagged many times and by many different users, thereby indicating that it "belongs" (or is highly relevant) to the Delicious community as a whole. Delicious exemplifies community tagging, where anyone can tag (or bookmark) any online resource (Marlow et al., 2006). Similar social bookmarking networks include CiteULike and Connotea, where tagged resources are bibliographical records, and LibraryThing, where tagged resources are books.

Social networks such as Delicious, CiteULike, and LibraryThing are very different from Flickr, where a resource (i.e., a photograph) is generally tagged only by the individual who has uploaded it.

The major activity of other members of the Flickr community is to "comment on" or "vote for" resources by indicating that a particular photograph is a favourite image. Flickr also provides users with the ability to allow friends to tag photos they have uploaded; but this functionality limits tagging behavior—and thus the development of a sense of community—in that it prohibits open tagging by Flickr users at large. Because tagging a resource in Flickr is not generally open to everyone (one notable exception being the Library of Congress's photostream[12]), Flickr cannot be considered a true community-based tagging system; rather, it is better thought of as a self-tagging system for users and their close friends. YouTube operates in a manner very similar to that of Flickr, allowing an individual to tag the resources (i.e., videos) he has uploaded while limiting the participation of other Flickr users to voting for resources by assigning "stars".

These differences in tagging rights have created differences not only in the roles that tags play in each system but also in the nature of the tags that are assigned (Marlow et al., 2006). Based on an analysis of the top 20 tags in each of the three social networks, it is apparent that tags in Delicious are more content-oriented in that they are generally related to the topics of the resources bookmarked. The tags used in Flickr are more like simplified, one-word descriptions in that they are generally related to the physical features of the photographs themselves, such as colors, lighting and location. While tags in Delicious are likely to reflect the intellectual content of resources and those in Flickr generally represent the physical features of photographs, tags in YouTube tend to focus on the medium or genre of the resources (e.g., *music, video, comedy, movie, tv*) and on the affective judgments of taggers (e.g., *funny, sexy, hot, love, new*).

The role of tags in Delicious is to represent bookmarked resources not only for future retrieval by the tagger but also for sharing them with the larger community. Tags play a major role in Deli-

cious: Without the tags assigned by users of the social network, there would be no means either to share bookmarks or to identify and retrieve resources, which are the main functions of Delicious. In contrast, tagging does not play a major role in Flickr. Because decisions as to whether or not to tag a photograph and who may tag it are left to the individual uploading a photograph, tagging in Flickr is more of a secondary activity or side effect. Furthermore, photographs on Flickr can be searched for and retrieved by their titles and are ranked by comments or votes rather than by the number of tags assigned. This is also the case with YouTube in that videos are most frequently shared based on comments and votes rather than on assigned tags. Indeed, it appears that many YouTube users may not understand the purpose of tagging: Instead of adding specific tags, users often tag their videos by enter a description in the tagging field, which accounts for the occurrence of helping words such as articles, prepositions and conjunctions (e.g., *the, of, in,* and *and*) among the more popular tags in YouTube.

Social tagging behaviors are also related to the community of users that populates each social network. Delicious gathers a community interested in IT-related topics. These individuals are focused on the content of bookmarked resources and tagging provides a way for them to summarize this content. In such a situation, tagging becomes the key function of the system and plays a major role in sharing and retrieving bookmarks. Users of Flickr are more interested in commenting on and sharing their photographs with family and friends. Rather than comprising a single, cohesive community, users in Flickr appear to gravitate toward one of two primary types of community: Communities of professional photographers who upload photographs for comment and feedback from other professionals and communities of non-professional users for whom Flickr provides a place to store personal photographs and share them with family and close friends. Alternatively, the community of YouTube can be viewed as a snapshot of the larger Web community. YouTube is populated by individuals from all over the world who are of different ages and have many different interests. They come to YouTube with many different purposes and expectations, and many of them do not tag their videos because the role of tagging is overshadowed by the roles of rating and/or commenting.

After analyzing social tagging behavior in Delicious, Flickr and YouTube, it is apparent that tagging activities increased tremendously between 2005 and 2007, when evermore individuals were using online social networks to tag resources for purposes of storage, access, and retrieval, both for themselves and for the purpose of sharing those resources with others. Through tag analysis, it is possible to develop a portrait of the social culture of these networks and, in some cases, to identify trends of emerging or waning topical interests among users.

While tag sets in Delicious appeared to have become more stable across the time frame of this study, it was also apparent that collective tagging vocabularies could benefit from both syntactic and semantic normalization of tags. For example, in YouTube in 2007 there were 2,796 uses of the tag *girl* and 1,851 uses of the tag *girls*. Normalization of singular and plural forms as well as acronyms and full names would increase the effectiveness of tags for retrieval purposes, as would standardization of the syntactical formation of tags (e.g., tag phrases with or without a space between individual terms). Perhaps as important is the introduction of user education regarding the potential utility of tags in social networks and the effective choice of tags (Ackerman, James & Getz, 2007).

This study demonstrates that it is possible to profile a social network by analyzing data about the tags and tagging behaviors of that network. For example, analysis confirms the popular assumption that the Delicious community is largely comprised of individuals interested in IT-oriented topics such as design and programming. In contrast, the Flickr community appears to contain two primary groups of users: professional photographers interested in feedback and non-professional photographers interested only in sharing their photographs. In contrast to Delicious and Flickr, the YouTube community is very broad and can be best viewed as a self-selected subset of the general Social Web community. Tagging is a major activity in Delicious but not in Flickr and YouTube. Tagging in Delicious is used primarily for purposes of storing, retrieving and sharing online resources across the community; tagging in Flickr emphasizes indexing objects for retrieval by the tagger and his friends and associates; and tagging in YouTube is undertaken primarily for identifying the genre of a video and for indicating the tagger's affective reaction to it. Thus, taggers are more likely to represent the content of a resource in Delicious, but they tend to focus on the specific features of an image in Flickr and the genre of a video in YouTube.

In Delicious, changing trends in user interest can be identified and tracked by analyzing tag frequencies across time; in both Flickr and YouTube, however, such trends are not obvious, perhaps because the focus of tagging activities is not on the intellectual content of resources but on more superficial features such as color (in Flickr) or affective reactions (in YouTube). Thus, even though YouTube has been characterized as a subset of the general Web population, the results of this research indicate that Delicious is a more representative venue for analyzing social tagging vocabularies and tagging behaviors within a community of users. This conclusion is supported by the finding that the community of users in Delicious is more cohesive than those of Flickr or YouTube; by the dynamic behavior of users that supports tracking of emerging and waning interests within the Delicious community; and by the participatory focus on sharing that characterizes user tagging activity in Delicious. However, these conclusions require better understanding of the concept of "community". How is a community defined? What do we know about how communities form (or are formed) and develop? In that respect, it would be enlightening to compare "online" or "web" communities and their respective vocabularies with communities outside the Web environment (i.e., communities of scientists) and their vocabularies. Such an analysis would be beneficial for enhancing our understanding of both.

6.3 Utilizing Web 2.0 in Web Service Ranking

Another problem investigated in this chapter was the use of Web 2.0 social annotations in Web service ranking. More precisely, we used the annotation data from Delicious, one of the biggest social networks, to discover and rank Web services connected by Delicious bookmarks. Following this straightforward idea, we have proposed a global algorithm to compute the social rank of Web services and designed and implemented a running prototype. In future work, we plan to compare and integrate our system with other approaches for ranking services. We are mainly interested in knowing if and in what situations social-based service rankers perform better than rankers using properties/descriptions of services (e.g., non-functional properties). The focus of this proposed research will not be on the comparison itself but on defining an integrated framework for ranking Web services that is able to select and use, in relevant situations, the most appropriate results of various ranking approaches, including those based on non-functional properties as well as those using socially based ranking.

REFERENCES

Ackerman, G., James, M., & Getz, C. T. (2007). The application of social bookmarking technology to the national intelligence domain. *International Journal of Intelligence and CounterIntelligence, 20*, 678–698. doi:10.1080/08850600701249808

Acquisti, A., & Gross, R. (2006). Imagined communities: Awareness, information sharing, and privacy on the Facebook. In *6th Workshop on Privacy Enhancing Technologies (PET)*. Retrieved August 23, 2009 from http://privacy.cs.cmu.edu/dataprivacy/projects/facebook/facebook2.pdf

Adamic, L. A., & Adar, E. (2005). How to search a social network. *Social Networks, 27*(3), 187–203. doi:10.1016/j.socnet.2005.01.007

Antoniou, G., & van Harmelen, F. (2004). *A semantic Web primer*. Cambridge, MA: MIT Press.

Backstrom, L., Huttenlocher, D., Kleinberg, J., & Lan, X. (2006). Group formation in large social networks. In *Proceedings of the 12th ACM SIGKDD International Conference on Knowledge Discovery and Data Mining,* August 20-23, 2006, Philadelphia, PA (pp. 44-54).

Bao, S., Xue, G., Wu, X., Yu, Y., Fei, B., & Su, Z. (2007). Optimizing web search using social annotations. In *Proceedings of the 16th international conference on World Wide Web* (pp. 501-510). New York: ACM Press.

Barnes, S. B. (2006). A privacy paradox: Social networking in the United States. *First Monday, 11*(9). Retrieved August 23, 2009, from http://firstmonday.org/htbin/cgiwrap/bin/ojs/index.php/fm/article/view/1394/1312

Batini, C., Lenzerini, M., & Navathe, B. (1986). A comparative analysis of methodologies for database schema integration. *ACM Computing Surveys, 18*(4), 323–364. doi:10.1145/27633.27634

Berners-Lee, T., Hendler, J., & Lassila, O. (2001). The semantic Web. *Scientific American, 284*(5), 34–43. doi:10.1038/scientificamerican0501-34

Boyd, D. (2007). Social network sites: Public, private, or what? *The Knowledge Tree: An e-Journal of Learning Innovation*. Retrieved August 22, 2009 from http://www.danah.org/papers/KnowledgeTree.pdf

Brickley, D., & Guha, R. V. (2004, February). Resource description framework (RDF) schema specification 1.0 [Recommendation]. Cambridge, MA: World Wide Web Consortium. Retrieved August, 2009 from http://www.w3.org/TR/2004/RECrdf- schema-20040210

Broekstra, J., Kampman, A., & van Harmelen, F. (2002). Sesame: A generic architecture for storing and querying RDF and RDF schema. In *Proceedings of the 2nd International Semantic Web Conference* (pp. 54-68). Berlin: Springer.

Coleman, J. (1990). *Foundations of social theory.* Boston: Harvard University Press.

Ding, Y., Kang, S. J., Toma, I., Fried, M., Shafiq, O., & Yan, Z. (2008). Adding semantics to social tagging: Upper Tag Ontology (UTO). In *Proceedings of the 70th Annual Meeting of the American Society for Information Science & Technology (ASIS&T)*, Oct 24-29, 2008, Columbus, Ohio, USA.

Ding, Y., Toma, I., Kang, S., Fried, M., & Yan, Z. (2008). Data mediation and interoperation in Social Web: Modeling, crawling and integrating social tagging data. In *Proceedings of the Workshop on Social Web Search and Mining (SWSM2008), 17th International World Wide Web Conference, Beijing, China.* Retrieved August 23, 2009 from http://info.slis.indiana.edu/~dingying/Publication/OTM2008-UTO-CameraReady.pdf

Dwyer, C., Hiltz, S. R., & Passerini, K. (2007). Trust and privacy concern within social networking sites. In *Proceedings of the Thirteenth Americas Conference on Information Systems.* Retrieved August 23, 2009 from http://csis.pace.edu/~dwyer/research/DwyerAMCIS2007.pdf

Ellison, N., Steinfield, C., & Lampe, C. (2006). Spatially bounded online social networks and social capital. In *International Communication Association.* Retrieved August 23, 2009 from http://msu.edu/~nellison/Facebook_ICA_2006.pdf

Fried, M. (2007). Social tagging wrapper. Unpublished bachelors thesis. University of Innsbruck, Austria.

Gekas, J. (2006). Web service ranking in service networks. In *3rd European Semantic Web Conference ESWC '06* (pp. 501-510). Retrieved August 23, 2009 from http://www.eswc2006.org/poster-papers/FP08-Gekas.pdf

Golder, S. A., Wilkinson, D., & Huberman, B. (2007). Rhythms of social interaction: Messaging within a massive online network. In *Third International Conference on Communities and Technologies.* Retrieved August 23, 2009 from http://www.hpl.hp.com/research/idl/papers/facebook/facebook.pdf

Gradijan, D. (2007). MySpace cracks down on 69-year-old members. *CSO.* Retrieved August 29, 2009, from http://www.csoonline.com/article/216376/MySpace_Cracks_Down_on_69_Year_Old_Members?page=1

Gruber, T. (2007). Ontology of folksonomy: A mash-up of apples and oranges. *International Journal on Semantic Web & Information Systems, 3*(2). Retrieved August 23, 2009 from http://tomgruber.org/writing/ontology-of-folksonomy.htm

Hinduja, S., & Patchin, J. W. (2008). Personal information of adolescents on the Internet: A quantitative content analysis of MySpace. *Journal of Adolescence, 31*(1), 125–146. doi:10.1016/j.adolescence.2007.05.004

Hoschka, P. (1998). CSCW research at GMD-FIT: From basic groupware to the Social Web. *ACM SIGGROUP Bulletin, 19*(2), 5–9.

Hwang, C. L., & Yoon, K. (1981). *Multiple attribute decision making: Methods and applications.* Berlin: Springer-Verlag.

Kumar, R., Novak, J., & Tomkins, A. (2006). Structure and evolution of online social networks. In *Proceedings of the 12th ACM SIGKDD international conference on knowledge discovery and data mining* (pp. 611 - 617). New York: ACM Press.

Lampe, C., Ellison, N., & Steinfeld, C. (2007). Profile elements as signals in an online social network. In *Conference on Human Factors in Computing Systems*. Retrieved August 23, 2009 from http://www.msu.edu/~steinfie/CHI_manu-script.pdf

Liben-Nowell, D., Novak, J., Kumar, R., Ragha-van, P., & Tomkins, A. (2005). Geographic routing in social networks. *Proceedings of the National Academy of Sciences of the United States of America, 102*(33), 11623–11628. doi:10.1073/pnas.0503018102

Liu, Y., Ngu, A. H., & Zeng, L. Z. (2004). QoS computation and policing in dynamic web service selection. In *Proceedings of the 13th international World Wide Web conference on Alternate track papers & posters* (pp. 66-73). New York: ACM Press.

Manning, C. D., Raghavan, P., & Schutze, H. (2008). *Introduction to information retrieval*. Cambridge, UK: Cambridge University Press.

Manola, F., & Miller, E. (2004, February). RDF primer [Recommendation]. Cambridge, MA: World Wide Web Consortium. Retrieved August, 2009, from http://www.w3.org/TR/REC-rdf-syntax

Marlow, C., Naaman, M., Boyd, D., & Davis, M. (2006). HT06, tagging paper, taxonomy, Flickr, academic article, to read. In *Proceedings of the Seventeenth Conference on Hypertext and Hyper-media*, August 22-25, 2006, Odense, Denmark (pp. 31-40). New York: ACM.

Milgram, S. (1967). The small-world problem. *Psychology Today, 2*, 60–67.

Nussbaum, E. (2007). Kids, the Internet, and the end of privacy. *New York Magazine*. Retrieved August 23, 2009, from http://nymag.com/news/features/27341/

Page, L., Brin, S., Motwani, R., & Winograd, T. (1998). *The PageRank citation ranking: Bringing order to the web* [Technical report]. Standofrd, CA: Stanford Digital Library Technologies Project.

Pelleg, D., & Moore, A. W. (2000). X-means: Extending K-means with efficient estimation of the number of clusters. In *Proceedings of the 17th International Conference on Machine Learn-ing* (pp. 727-740). San Francisco, CA: Morgan Kaufmann Publishers.

Rahm, E., & Bernstein, P. A. (2001). A survey of approaches to automatic schema matching. *The VLDB Journal, 10*(4), 334–350. doi:10.1007/s007780100057

Rosenbush, S. (2005). News Corp's place in MySpace. *Business Week*. Retrieved August 23, 2009, from http://www.businessweek.com/tech-nology/content/jul2005/tc20050719_5427_tc119.htm

Spertus, E., Sahami, M., & Buyukkokten, O. (2005). Evaluating similarity measures: A large-scale study in the Orkut social network. In *Proceed-ings of the eleventh ACM SIGKDD international conference on Knowledge discovery in data mining* (pp. 678-684). New York: ACM Press.

Zeng, L. Z., Benatallah, B., Ngu, A. H., Dumas, M., Kalagnanam, J., & Chang, H. (2004). QoS: Aware middleware for web services composition. *IEEE Transactions on Software Engineering, 30*(5), 311–327. doi:10.1109/TSE.2004.11

Zhang, J., Ackerman, M., & Adamic, L. (2007). Expertise networks in online communities: Struc-ture and algorithms. In *Proceedings of the 16th international conference on World Wide Web* (pp. 221-230). New York: ACM Press.

Zhou, C., Chia, L. T., & Lee, B. S. (2005). Se-mantics in service discovery and QoS measure-ment. *IT Professional, 7*(2), 29–34. doi:10.1109/MITP.2005.41

ENDNOTES

[1]   http://www.facebook.com/

[2]   http://www.myspace.com/

[3]   http://delicious.com/

[4]   http://www.youtube.com/

[5]   http://answers.yahoo.com/

[6]   http://www.linkedin.com/

[7]   http://scot-project.org/

[8]   http://www.holygoat.co.uk/projects/tags/

[9]   http://moat-project.org/ontology

[10]   https://crawler.dev.java.net/

[11]   An interesting example of ongoing research on social annotation of images and videos is GWAP, the "games with a purpose" project at Carnegie Mellon available at http://www.gwap.com/gwap/

[12]   http://www.flickr.com/photos/library_of_congress/collections/

APPENDIX A: CORE TAG VOCABULARY IN SOCIAL NETWORKS: TOP 1363 TAGS IN DELICIOUS, FLICKR AND YOUTUBE

#s & others   1, 2, 3, 2005, 2006, 2007, -, .net, 3d

A   a, academia, academic, accessibility, accessories, acoustic, action, actionscript, activism, ad, admin, administration, adobe, ads, adsense, adult, advertising, advice, Africa, agency, aggregator, agile, ai, air, airline, airlines, airplane, airport, ajax, algorithm, algorithms, all, alternative, amateur, amazing, amazon, America, American, Amsterdam, analysis, analytics, and, angel, angst, animal, animals, animation, anime, anonymous, anthropology, apache, api, apple, application, applications, apps, architecture, archive, archives, argentina, art, arte, article, articles, artist, artists, arts, as3, asia, asian, asp.net, ass, asterisk, astronomy, at, atheism, atom, au, audio, audiobooks, Australia, authentication, auto, automation, autumn, awards, awesome

B   Baby, backup, bad, ball, band, bands, bandslash, bank, banking, bar, Barcelona, baseball, bass, bbc, beach, beatles, beautiful, beauty, beer, berlin, best, bible, bibliography, bicycle, big, bike, bioinformatics, biology, bird, birds, birthday, bit200f06, bit200w07, bittorrent, black, blackandwhite, blog, blogger, blogging, blogs, blood, blue, Bluetooth, boat, body, boobs, book, bookmarking, bookmarks, books, boston, boy, boys, bpm, brain, branding, brasil, brazil, bridge, Britney, Brooklyn, brown, browser, browsers, Buddhism, building, bus, bush, business, buy, bw, by

C   C, c#, c++, calculator, calendar, California, camera, cameraphone, camping, Canada, canon, car, card, cards, career, cars, cartoon, cartoons, cat, cats, cd, celebrity, cell, cellphone, celltagged, censorship, change, charity, charts, chat, cheap, cheatsheet, chemistry, Chicago, chicken, child, children, chile, china, Chinese, chocolate, chords, chris, Christian, Christianity, Christmas, church, ciencia, cine, cinema, city, class, classic, classification, climate, clip, clothes, clothing, clouds, club, cluster, clustering, cms, cocoa, code, coding, coffee, collaboration, collection, college, color, colors, colour, comedy, comic, comics, commercial, communication, community, company, comparison, competition, compiler, complexity, computer, computers, computing, concert, concurrency, conference, conferences, conspiracy, consumer, content, contest, control, conversion, convert, converter, cooking, cool, copyright, corporate, country, course, courses, cover, crack, craft, crafts, crazy, creative, creativecommons, creativity, credit, crime, crossover, cryptography, cs, css, cultura, culture, curiosidades, custom, cute, cycling

D   Daily, dance, dancing, dark, data, database, datamining, dating, david, day, dc, de, dead, deals, death, debian, del.icio.us, delicious, demo, democracy, design, designer, desktop, deutsch, Deutschland, dev, developer, development, dhtml, dictionary, diet, dig, digital, directory, diseÃ±o, Disney, distributed, distro, diy, dj, django, dns, do, documentary, documentation, dog, dogs, dom, domain, dotnet, download, downloads, drawing, driver, drm, drugs, drunk, drupal, duesouth, dvd

E   Earth, ebay, ebook, ebooks, eclipse, ecology, ecommerce, economia, economics, economy, editing, editor, edtech, educaciÃ³n, educacion, education, effects, el, elearning, e-learning, electronic, electronics, email, embedded, employment, emulation, en, encryption, encyclopedia, energy, engine, engineering, England, English, enterprise, enterprise2.0, entertainment, entrepreneur, entrepreneurship, environment, erlang, esl, espaÃ±a, espaÃ±ol, essay, ethics, eu, europa, Europe, event, events, evolution, examples, excel, exchange, exercise, experimental, extension, extensions, eyes

F   f1, face, facebook, fall, family, fanfic, fanfiction, fantasy, faq, fashion, fat, feed, feeds, female, feminism, festival, fetish, fic, fiction, fight, file, files, filesharing, filesystem, film, films, finance, financial, fire, firefox, firefox:bookmarks, firefox:rss, firefox:toolbar, firewall, fish, fitness, flash, flex, flickr, flight, flights, florida, flower, flowers, fob, folksonomy, font, fonts, food, football, for, forms, forum, forums, foto, fotografia, fotos, framework, france, free, freedom, freelance, freeware, French, friends, from, fuck, fun, functional, funny, furniture, future

G Gadget, gadgets, gallery, game, games, gaming, garden, gardening, gay, gear, geek, gen, gender, genealogy, generator, genetics, geo, geography, George, geotagged, german, germany, ghost, gifts, girl, girls, gis, glass, global, gmail, gnome, gnu, go, god, good, google, googlemaps, government, gps, graffiti, grammar, graph, graphic, graphicdesign, graphics, gratis, great, green, grid, gtd, gui, guide, guitar

H Hack, hacking, hacks, hair, Halloween, halo, happiness, happy, hardware, Haskell, hci, hdr, health, healthcare, heart, Hebrew, help, het, hibernate, high, hip, hiphop, history, holiday, home, hop, horror, hosting, hot, hotel, hotels, house, housing, how, howto, hp, html, http, human, humor, humour

I I, ia, ibm, ical, icon, icons, ict, ide, idea, ideas, identity, ie, illustration, illustrator, im, image, images, imported, in, india, indie, info, informatica, information, innovation, inspiration, install, installation, insurance, intel, intelligence, interaction, interactive, interesting, interface, interior, international, internet, interview, investing, investment, ip, iphone, ipod, iptv, iran, Iraq, irc, Ireland, is, islam, island, Israel, it, italia, Italian, Italy, itunes

J j2ee, jabber, jack, james, japan, Japanese, java, javascript, jazz, jesus, jewelry, job, jobs, john, joomla, journal, journalism, journals, jsf, json, juegos

K Kernel, keyboard, kid, kids, king, kiss, knitting, knowledge, korea, korean

L La, lake, landscape, language, languages, laptop, latex, latin, law, layout, learn, learning, leaves, lectures, legal, lego, lesbian, lessons, libraries, library, library2.0, libros, life, lifehack, lifehacker, lifehacks, lifestyle, light, lighting, lights, linguistics, link, links, linux, lisp, list, lists, literacy, literature, literature, little, live, local, logic, logo, lol, London, long, los, losangeles, love, lyrics

M Mac, macbook, macintosh, macosx, macro, Madrid, magazine, magazines, magic, mail, make, man, management, manga, manual, mÃºsica, map, mapas, mapping, maps, market, marketing, mashup, math, mathematics, maths, mckay/Sheppard, me, media, medical, medicine, memory, men, menu, messaging, metadata, metal, mexico, Michael, microformats, Microsoft, midi, military, mind, mindmap, misc, mit, mix, mobile, model, modeling, models, modern, module, money, monitor, monitoring, motion, motiongraphics, motivation, mountain, movie, movies, Mozilla, mp3, multimedia, museum, music, Musica, musik, my, myspace, mysql

N Naked, naruto, nasa, national, nature, navigation, nc-17, Netherlands, network, networking, networks, new, newmedia, news, newspaper, newspapers, newyork, night, Nikon, Nintendo, nlp, no, nokia, nonprofit, notes, noticias, November, nptech, nude, nutrition, nyc

O Ocean, October, of, office, oil, old, on, one, online, ontology, open, opened, openoffice, opensource, open-source, opera, opinion, optimization, oracle, orange, organic, organization, origami, os, osx, out, outdoors, outlook, owl

P p2p, painting, palm, paper, papers, parenting, paris, park, parody, parser, parsing, party, password, pattern, patterns, paul, pc, pda, pdf, peace, people, performance, perl, personal, personality, pet, pets, philosophy, phone, photo, photographer, photography, photos, photoshop, php, physics, piano, picture, pictures, pink, planning, plants, play, player, plugin, plugins, pocketpc, podcast, podcasting, podcasts, poetry, poker, Poland, police, policy, polish, politics, politik, pop, porn, portable, portal, portfolio, portrait, Portugal, post, power, powerpoint, pr, presentation, presentations, print, printing, privacy, process´, processing, product, production, productivity, products, programming, project, projectmanagement, projects, property, prototype, proxy, psychology, public, publishing, punk, puppy, pussy, puzzle, python

Q   quotes

R   r, race, racing, radio, rails, random, rap, rdf, read, reading, real, realestate, recherché, recipe, recipes, recording, records, recovery, recursos, red, reference, reflection, regex, religion, remix, remote, repair, research, resource, resources, rest, restaurant, restaurants, retro, review, reviews, rights, river, road, robot, robotics, robots, rock, roma, rome, rpg, rps, rss, ruby, rubyonrails, running, Russia, russian

S   Safari, safari_export, sam/dean, san, sanfrancisco, satellite, scary, scheme, school, science, scifi, Scotland, screen, script, scripting, scripts, sculpture, sea, search, searchengine, searchengines, seattle, secondlife, security, seguridad, self, semantic, semanticweb, semweb, seo, series, server, service, services, sewing, sex, sexy, sf, sga, share, sharepoint, sharing, shell, shoes, shop, shopping, short, show, simulation, singing, site, sky, skype, slash, sleep, slideshow, smallville, sms, snow, soa, soap, soccer, social, socialmedia, socialnetworking, socialnetworks, socialsoftware, society, sociology, software, solar, song, songs, sony, sound, source, south, space, spain, spam, Spanish, spears, speech, speed, spirituality, spn, sport, sports, spring, sql, ssh, standards, star, startup, starwars, statistics, stats, stock, stocks, storage, store, stories, story, strategy, streaming, street, streetart, studio, study, stuff, stupid, style, subversion, summer, sun, sunset, super, supernatural, support, sustainability, svn, Sweden, sweet, swing, Switzerland, symbian, sync, sysadmin, system

T   Tabs, tag, tagging, tags, Taiwan, teaching, tech, techno, technology, tecnologia, telephone, television, template, templates, terrorism, test, testing, texas, text, the, theme, themes, theory, thesis, time, tips, to, todo, Tokyo, tom, tool, tools, top, toread, Toronto, torrent, torrents, tour, tourism, toy, toys, trabajo, tracking, trading, traffic, trailer, train, training, translation, transport, transportation, travel, tree, trees, trends, tricks, trip, tuning, tutorial, tutorials, tutorials, tv, twitter, type, typography

U   Ubuntu, ui, uk, uml, uni, university, unix, unread, up, upload, urban, us, usa, usability, usb, useful, usenet, utilities, utility, ux

V   Vacation, validation, Vancouver, vc, vector, vegetarian, viajes, video, videogames, videos, vim, vintage, vinyl, viral, virtual, virtualization, vista, visual, visualization, vmware, voip, vs

W   w3c, wall, wallpaper, wallpapers, war, Washington, water, weather, web, Web 2.0, webapp, webcam, webcomic, webdesign, webdev, webdevelopment, weblog, webmaster, webservice, webservices, website, websites, webstandards, webtools, wedding, weird, white, widget, widgets, wifi, wii, wiki, Wikipedia, wikis, window, windows, wine, winter, wireless, wishlist, with, woman, women, wood, word, wordpress, words, work, workflow, world, wow, writing, wysiwyg

X   X, xbox, xhtml, xml, xp, xslt, xxx

Y   Yahoo, yellow, York, you, young, your, youth, youtube

Z   Zombie, zoo

Chapter 10

Constructing and Evaluating Social Software:
Lessons from Interaction Design

Christopher Douce
Open University, UK

ABSTRACT

The process of developing interactive systems necessitates designers to have a comprehensive understanding of the needs of the user and the context in which a device or system is to be used. Interactive systems are often designed through a series of iterations, guided by a sequence of evaluations. This chapter describes how the research and development techniques used within the field of Interaction Design (ID), a successor to the field of human-computer interaction, can be used to inform the development and evaluation of social software systems. Particular attention is given to the challenging area of end-user culture and how different evaluation paradigms and techniques can be applied. The chapter concludes by presenting pointers towards a number of international standards and highlighting a number of potentially useful research directions.

INTRODUCTION

Social software systems are interactive systems that enable users to share information and collaborate with each other. This chapter presents a very brief overview of a discipline called Interaction Design (ID). Interaction Design is a development of human-computer interaction. It represents a set of tools and techniques that can be used to guide the development of social software and interactive systems. ID draws upon a number of different fields, ranging from computer science and software engineering, through to psychology, sociology, anthropology and design, each contributing useful theories and knowledge that to guide the design and development of interactive devices, systems and environments.

This chapter begins with a description of what ID is and is then followed with a presentation of some of the processes and techniques that can be used to explore product and user requirements, drawing upon the powerful notions of user profiles

DOI: 10.4018/978-1-61692-904-6.ch010

and task scenarios. The 'culture' and 'understanding the user audience' sections provide additional source of useful guidance. The culture section asks designers to consider differences between user groups. The 'understanding the user audience' section calls upon designers to consider the importance of accessibility and inclusion. The design section that follows explores the process of creating a prototype and points to other important design approaches, such as participatory design.

One of the central tenets of effective ID and user-centred design is the notion of evaluation. Evaluating a system, whether it be a low fidelity paper prototype or the first release of an interactive system enables designers to explore whether a system works in the way that we expect it to and ask whether there is anything else that needs to be done to make the system more suitable for its target audience. The evaluation section outlines a number of useful techniques that can be applied by the designers of social software systems. A section that describes a number of technical standards offers useful guidance to facilitate the development of usable and accessible social software systems can be found towards the end of this chapter. This is followed by a very brief example, taken from a current Interaction Design course that illustrates how some of the ideas can be applied. The chapter concludes by outlining a number of current and future research directions before summarising the main themes.

BACKGROUND

Interaction Design can be described as a set of subjects and techniques that can be used to facilitate the design of 'interactive products to support people in their everyday and working lives' (Preece et al., 2002). Interaction Design has emerged from the field of human-computer interaction (HCI). HCI has a long history which encompasses diverse domains such as engineering psychology (Wickens, 1992), human visual and auditory perception, product design and typography. It could also be said to embody a number of different conceptual approaches; an approach that seeks to explain how aspects of interfaces are perceived by users, and another approach that considers the processes that can be used to design effective interfaces.

The emergence of HCI as a subject in its own right has been facilitated by the development of high resolution computer graphics, the creation of new ways to interact with computer systems and increasing levels of computing power. The continual increase in computing power has inspired the creation of new ways in which desktop computer systems can be used. The challenge of HCI was to explore not only how to harness new levels of power but also to create systems that are understandable and comprehensible to different user groups and communities without users having to undergo extended periods of training. User interfaces, in essence, should match the experience and needs of those who need to use them.

As computing and digital communication technologies have evolved, the computer is no longer a tool that is constrained to the desktop. Instead, the notion of an interactive product, or more specifically interactive software system, has expanded considerably due to the emergence of innovations such as mobile phones, personal digital assistants and the ability to embed microcomputer technology into a myriad of different devices. An interactive system can now be thought of as an application found on a desktop computer or an application running on mobile devices. The term can also encompass systems found within public spaces, such as bank teller machines, travel ticket dispensers and so on.

Interaction Design places significant emphasis on the user, drawing upon the notion of user-centered design. The user, it is reasoned, is likely to be the expert of their own needs. Approaching design with the objective of solving a functional problem without understanding the user may yield a product or system that may 'work' in a functional

Figure 1. Interaction design cycle

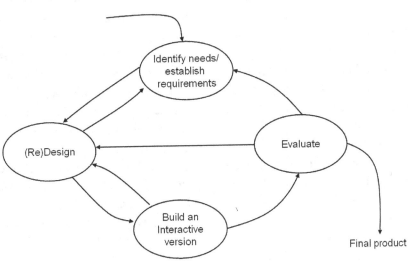

sense but may not be suitable for its intended users. A functional product may provide appropriate information from a set of inputs, but may be unusable in the sense that a user may not have sufficient background knowledge to understand which inputs to provide, or background knowledge to understand the outputs a system may produce. The needs of the user and the challenge of solving a problem through the creation of an interactive system need to be considered simultaneously.

Figure 1, from Preece, Rogers & Sharp (2002, p.186) represents an interaction design process. One of the most powerful principles of the ID process is the important notion of iteration; continual evaluation and re-evaluation has the potential to yield increasingly detailed designs that become increasingly suited to an intended user audience.

The phrase *social software system* is a term that can refer to a wide variety of different tools, ranging from instant messaging products and online discussion tools, through to web based utilities that enable virtual communities to be established. They can be defined as interactive systems that enable people to exchange information, potentially with to the objective of carrying out or supporting the completion of one of more activities or tasks. The precise nature of the information that is shared and the types of activities that are executed depends upon the users and the environment in which the systems are deployed. Different tools can be applied in different situations and social contexts. The requirements for users who wish to organise face to face meetings to support social activities, such as organizing a meal for friends at a local restaurant will be substantially different from users who use social software as a part of a well defined work task, for instance.

Ideally, interactive systems, whether they are social software systems used by many users or solitary applications used by a single user, should be considered 'usable'. The notion of usability differs between users due to variations in personal experience, knowledge, expectations and the physical environment in which interaction takes place. To try to understand or conceptualise usability, there are two sets of goals: usability goals and user experience goals. Usability goals relate to *functional attributes* of a system, such as whether a system is effective, efficient, safe to use, easily learnable and memorable. User experience goals, on the other hand, refer to different *attitudes and experiences* that a user may gather from an interactive system or device. User experience goals aim to consider whether a system is rewarding, fun to use, aesthetically pleasing, entertaining, enjoyable and so on (Preece, Rogers & Sharp, 2002). The challenge that interaction designers face is to find out which of these goals are appropriate given what is known about users and the tasks that they are likely to perform. Designers must then select and apply different tools and techniques to uncover potential designs whilst bearing in mind their chosen goals. When a design is complete, perhaps through the creation of a prototype, designers must then step towards choosing an evaluation method to uncover whether a design supports the chosen goals.

These challenges are addressed as designers move through an interaction design cycle that is similar to the one depicted in Figure 1. The following sections in this chapter expand upon some of the themes that the interaction design cycle encompasses, introducing the designers of social software systems to a number of tools that can be used to learn about the user, their tasks and the environment in which they are situated.

INTERACTION DESIGN THEMES

Gathering Requirements

Interactive products have users. Users differ in terms of their background knowledge and the attitudes that they hold towards a system, a product or problem. Users also differ in terms of the kinds of operations that they wish to perform using a system. Let us consider an example of a vending machine used to dispense train, metro or bus tickets. The vending machine is placed in a public space, perhaps in the concourse of a train station. One user, for example, may wish to purchase a ticket between two locations, whereas another user may wish to obtain some general information about a range of travel options that may exist. Different users may have different reasons to use a system.

Interaction designers can use a variety of tools to uncover assumptions about how a system should work, who it is designed for, and the tasks it should support. The differences between users of a system can be explored through the creation of sets of user profiles, or *persona*. A user persona is a rich description of a potential user. A persona enables the designer to consider the age and gender of a user, the motivations that they may hold, and be used to articulate the knowledge of similar systems that they are expected to possess. Persona descriptions are often named, enabling designers to share references to groups of user attributes quickly and efficiently. They enable hidden assumptions about potential users to be made explicit and invalid or erroneous ideas relating to user identity to be challenged. Designers are encouraged to create groups of personas to enable the boundaries between different users to be considered. One useful approach might be to create 'extreme' users, whose characteristics, values and objectives may be different to the norm (Moggridge, 2006), thus avoiding the possibility of creating systems that only cater for the 'average' user.

User personas can be used in conjunction with task scenarios. A scenario can be considered to be a rich description of an imagined situation, in which a product or system can be used by a particular user or group of users. A scenario, like the persona, allows implicit assumptions to be articulated and issues that need to be considered within the design phase to be highlighted. A scenario can be used to explore the environment in which a product or system is being used, for instance. It can also be used to consider the type of device or interactive mechanism that may be used in a particular product. A named user, for instance, may use a messaging tool to talk with a friend during a lunch break. Alternatively, the same user may use the same application through a mobile device whilst travelling home during the evening to communicate with a work colleague to confirm a meeting time that is to take place the following day. Scenarios enable the various contexts of use to be exposed and considered. Similarly, personas enable requirements and design challenges that relate to the user to be discussed and shared.

Scenarios and profiles are informal descriptions. To further understand the detail of a potential system, it may be useful to convert scenarios into a series of descriptive use cases. A use case can be described as a formal summary of the activities a system may perform, with emphasis placed on the sequence of tasks. There are a number of different types of use cases. Formal modeling languages, such as the Unified Modeling Language (UML) suggest a graphical notation. Other approaches include describing sequences of operations in a textual form, where alternative actions or deviations from the main task flow can be presented as alternative cases. The creation of use cases also permits the formation of higher level 'abstract' use cases, called 'essential use cases' (Preece et al., 2002). These use cases allow designers to consider the pure essence of a series of interactions, devoid of any kind of implementation detail. One advantage of such an approach is that it has the potential to allow designers to consider different forms of interaction mechanisms through different types of devices or technologies.

An important question is this: how do designers find out about the users and the tasks that a system is required to support? A number of different techniques can be applied. These can include interviewing different stakeholders, observing how current systems are used, conducting surveys and questionnaires to identify potential areas for improvement, looking at data that is used and generated by existing systems and examination of associated documentation.

The development of requirements should be considered to be an iterative process, as suggested in Figure 1. Once a set of personas, scenarios and use cases are established, it is the responsibility of the designer to consider whether or not they accurately reflect the required essence of a sys-

tem. To test their assumptions, designers have to design and build simulated or real artifacts that can be used to elicit opinions about the validity of the embodied requirements (as represented by a prototype) from a range of potential users.

Culture

In Interaction Design, the knowledge, experience and levels of motivation of different users is undeniably important when considering the requirements of an interactive system. Another attribute that should be considered is the culture of the user. Culture is a difficult term to define. In some respects, it can be used to refer to national culture, but it can also be considered in terms of other dimensions, such as profession, gender or socio-economic group. Some researchers have posited that culture can influence the design of an interactive system, its interface and the functions it may offer.

The work of Hofstede (1994) is considered to be influential. Hofstede posited a range of *cultural dimensions* that have been drawn from surveys distributed to employees of an international organisation, IBM. Hofstede suggested that, broadly speaking, citizens of different countries differ in their views towards acceptance of power, societal equality and tolerance of change. Power, for instance, is considered in terms of a cultural dimension named Power Distance. In a country with a high power distance score, power is held by a select few, whereas with a country with a low score, power is more equally distributed throughout a society. Similarly, Hofstede proposes a dimension called Uncertainty Avoidance that relates to whether change is likely to be embraced. Marcus and Gould (2000) describe how the cultural dimensions may influence the design of different web sites. Interactive products used in a country with a high power distance rating may present graphical symbols to which power can be attributed. Products used in a culture which has a low uncertainty avoidance rating may encourage users to explore different routes through a system and uncover new ways of working.

Hofstede proposed that different countries differ in terms of his dimensions. It should be stated that his dimensions remain controversial. Firstly, they represent broad generalisations and do not take into account that individuals and subgroups within a country may hold values that are at odds with a cultural norm. Secondly, the research that has been carried out comes from a particular context: a single international organisation and this may influence how the different dimensions have been conceptualized. Whether designers accept the validity of the Hofstede dimensions (or alternative dimensions proposed by other researchers) is perhaps a moot point. Rather than guiding the design and construction of interactive systems, they represent a set of conceptual tools that enables designers to consider the issue of culture and how it, as a concept, can influence the design of a product.

Culture is considered to be an important issue regarding the design of social systems, and one that requires further exploration. It is possible that a single social software system may be available to many different user groups, each of which may have differing values. The way in which the use of these systems can be utilised may be acceptable and desirable for one group but perhaps frustrating and discouraging for another.

Considering User Diversity

The requirements and design phases of ID should also take into consideration the functional diversity of a user population. Not only can users be considered in terms of their culture, background knowledge and experience of interactive systems, can also in terms of how different people can interact with systems. A system that is *accessible* is one that can be used by different people, regardless of whether they have any sensory, physical or cognitive impairments. People who have visual impairments, such as reduced vision or blindness,

can overcome their impairments through the application of assistive technologies, such as screen magnifiers or screen readers.

Whether or not a system will work well with an assistive technology depends upon a number of factors. The first is whether an assistive technology is available on a system or device, whether or not a user is sufficiently skilled or able to make use of the tools that are available, and whether an interactive product has been designed in such a way that enables it to be used with different types of input and output mechanisms. Screen reader software, for instance, converts a visual representation of an application or web page to a linear audio stream, allowing people with visual impairments to listen to what is presented on a screen. Difficulties may arise if an application dynamically downloads and updates on-screen material without informing the user. Users of screen readers may therefore become disoriented or miss essential information. It is therefore essential that developers consider the diversity of not only the user audience, but also the diversity of the interface approaches that users may choose to apply.

Users of screen reader software can most effectively use web pages that use 'semantic markup'. If a web page or interaction screen has a clearly defined semantic structure, in terms of headings, visually impaired users, through the use of assistive technologies, will be more able to effectively navigate through the structure of an application, tool or web page. Designers and developers, therefore, should take effective steps to separate the presentation of content from the mechanisms that are used to present the material. Developers, for instance, should design web pages in such a way that their display can be controlled through cascading style sheets (CSS) rather than embedding presentation and formatting information within the body of a page, for instance. Enforcing this separation enables people who use assistive technologies to more efficiently navigate through interfaces and increase the likelihood that search engines can more effectively index and extract information from pages that are well structured.

The subject of web accessibility, and therefore the accessibility of social software systems, is a subject of continued debate and development. International standards bodies, such as the W3C, (Craig et al., 2009) are considering the most effective approaches to take account of the dynamic nature of Web 2.0 applications whilst ensuring that new innovations in software development and interactive web system design do not create barriers for people who have physical, sensory or cognitive impairments.

The accessibility of interactive systems should *never* be considered as an afterthought. Instead, it should be considered as an integral part of the requirements process. Different users of a system need to be considered from the outset. Excluding certain user groups through poor design is not only undesirable from a moral perspective. The right to accessible applications is now considered as a part of equal opportunity legislation and those organisations that do not take account of user diversity will risk prosecution. Another argument for providing equality of access is an economic one. Excluding users, however accidental, will also exclude opportunities to provide goods and services. Furthermore, research has indicated that systems that are accessible may also achieve higher levels of usability. Increasing accessibility has the potential to benefit all users, regardless of how they interact or consume a social software service (Petrie & Kheir, 2007).

Design

The activity of design broadly refers to the process of constructing or creating an interactive system. In the context of Interaction Design, *design* can also refer to the process of software development. Before any detailed technical development can begin, designers should acquire a firm understanding of the processes users can adopt to request information, and how the information is presented to them. One way to achieve this understanding is to build a number of different prototypes (Lim, Stolderman & Tenenberg, 2008).

Prototypes can be divided into two broad categories: low fidelity and high fidelity. A low fidelity prototype is a 'low tech' presentation of the key elements of a system and can take the form of a 'paper prototype' which can consist of a number of rough pencil sketches. These include a storyboard, a series of task cards, and an interface sketch. A storyboard is used to present a graphical description of how a product is to be used. Users can be represented as simple stick figures and interactive devices can be drawn as crude blocks or squares. Important design influences, such as the weather (which may point towards physical design considerations) or crowds of other people (which may potentially point towards issues of security) can be represented, and can guide the development of a product.

Card sketches allow designers to quickly explore the sequence of actions that are carried out through an interface. A single card can be used to represent the information that is presented through an interface. Cards can be used to explore the question of whether the right information is presented on the screen, and whether a task should be split over a number of displays or pages. An interface sketch represents a development of a card sketch. It allows a designer to create a more elaborate representation of an interface screen, enabling the designer to begin to envisage the look and feel of an emerging design.

To some, the notion of sketching may appear to be somewhat simplistic and unable to convey the true richness of digital interactive systems. Low fidelity prototypes represent the starting point in the development of a system. Sketches have the advantage of being quick and easy to create. Creating higher fidelity prototypes, perhaps by drawing designs in a graphical design tool, requires designers to commit to greater levels of time investment. Since sketches can be drawn quickly, there can be a lower sense of investment in the end result, and a greater inclination to change designs, should they be considered to be unsatisfactory. Furthermore, design sketches can be easily shared between designers, shown in communal spaces, cut out and torn apart and combined with sketches produced by others.

High fidelity prototypes can range from demonstration systems created using screen design tools, where sets of graphical representations of screen mock-ups can be imported into presentation packages, such as Microsoft PowerPoint. Alternatively, high fidelity prototypes or may be operational systems developed tools such as Visual Basic. This type of prototype can differ wildly in terms of how much functionality they implement. A horizontal prototype, for instance, may implement most of the key items of functionality at a relatively superficial level, presenting the salient menu options, for example. A vertical prototype, for instance, may demonstrate, in detail, how a small number of functions operate.

By applying the principle of iteration rigorously it is possible to incrementally develop a prototype into a fully functional product. A low fidelity sketch could be translated into a design that may guide the development of a high fidelity equivalent. The skill of the interaction designer does not only lie with the ability to understand and imagine the user and their tasks, but also their ability to construct useful and effective evaluation activities. An interaction designer must also examine the results of evaluations and listen to potential users and make decisions about what feedback will most effectively guide the design and development of the next version.

Significant questions that need to be asked include: other than following a process of iteration, what occurs within design? Secondly, what can be done to facilitate the generation of new ideas that may find their way into an interactive system or social software system. In his book Designing Interactions, Moggeridge (2006, p.729-732) presents an alternative list of stages (or principles) that may comprise a design process.

Each of these principles outlined in table 1 could be used in sequence, but it is entirely possible that each stage or activity yields new information or insights that takes the designer towards parallel periods of discovery and exploration. Moggeridge writes, 'the fastest progress towards a successful design will be made when these elements are used quickly and repeated frequently, but not usually in the same order!'

Design is an exceptionally creative activity. It relies on the ability of designers to absorb requirements, consider the perspective of others and imagine the circumstances in which products or tools may be used. Designers are also free to use analogies or metaphors to think about and consider designs. Not only do metaphors have the potential to enable potential users to draw upon existing expertise, helping them to understand unfamiliar interactive products, metaphors also have the potential to point designers towards new ways of interacting with a system.

Preece et. al. (2002) introduce the notion of a *conceptual model*. A conceptual model is a 'set of integrated ideas and concepts about what it [a product] should do, behave and look like', p.40. A related concept is the notion of an *interaction mode*. This is the way in which interaction with a system or product may take place. Broadly speaking, an interaction may relate to actions carried to an object (such as a file located within a desktop metaphor), or by carrying out a process or activity. Activity based interactions may include instructing a system to do something (issuing it a command), conversing with it in some way (in the form of an interactive dialogue), manipulating and navigating items within a part of an activity, or exploring and browsing aspects of a system or environment. Metaphors, analogies, conceptual models and interaction modes all represent useful and important concepts that allow designers to consider how to create interactive systems.

Another approach that could be used to facilitate design is to ask users to become directly involved in the design process. Designers may not

Table 1. Design phases

Principle	Description
Constraints	This relates to the starting point of the product or the system. It may emerge in the form of a briefing or specification, either from an individual or a design team.
Synthesis	This is the phase where different ideas collide to produce new ideas after 'all of the relevant issues have been absorbed'. Synthesis comes when a design problem is understood in its entirety, and connections between different themes and issues can be created to form new ones.
Framing	Framing relates to the concept of adding a framework to the activity of thinking about a problem. By framing a problem (or describing it in a particular way) new ideas can be considered.
Ideation	Ideation is the process of creating new ideas. One approach is to hold brainstorming sessions with designers who each have an understanding of the problem. Ideas and related concepts can be sketched or drawn. One approach is to continue to create new ideas and to defer judgement on all ideas until the end of an ideation session.
Envisioning	'Ideas are like dreams until they are visualized into some concrete representation' (Moggeridge, 2006, p.733). The concept of envisioning echoes with the principle of storyboarding, to explore context and consider individual users and their actions through user profile and scenario descriptions.
Uncertainty	Some ideas that are produced may not be clear. After ideation, many ideas may be uncovered but it may be unclear which deserve further attention or consideration. A sense of uncertainty leads to the selection of those which may be worth exploring further.
Selection	This is the phase of culling those ideas that are not considered to be 'good enough' to warrant further exploration.
Visualization	This phase simply consists of taking the idea and drawing sketches. A visualization in this sense can be qualitatively different to the categories of sketches that were described earlier and make up the prototype phase.
Prototyping	'Prototyping is about testing any aspect of the way a design is expected to work. You can create a prototype that represents an idea that has been selected and visualized' p.734. In this phase you can create (low-fidelity) prototypes using index cards, scissors, glue, pencils and pens in a way that is much quicker (and cheaper) than had designs be created using a computer mediated application. Plus, different designers can be directly involved without tools getting in the way.
Evaluation	This may include taking your sketches and presenting them to users or other designers. These sketches may inspire the designer to consider new alternatives. The feedback that is gathered may point the way towards modifications to a prototype, or reapplication of any of the previously described phases.

have all the knowledge, insight and understanding about how to specify a product for a particular user audience. The principle of adopting co-designers, or potential users who are unskilled in the process of design is known as *participatory design*. This approach has the advantage that it is possible to establish a direct dialogue between the user and the designer. Issues such as terminology and functionality can be uncovered and discussed. One important disadvantage is that there may be professional cultural differences between the designer and the co-designer; the cognitive distance between the knowledge of the designer and the user has the potential to cause communication difficulties and yield misunderstandings. Furthermore, it should always be remembered that the co-designers may be tempted to propose designs

that are appropriate for users who are similar to their own, potentially disregarding other equally important user groups. It is important that the interaction designer attempts to maintain a degree of objectivity whilst at the same time trying to effectively harness the insights and knowledge the co-designers may be able to offer.

Evaluation

With iteration being a fundamental principle of ID, the activity of evaluation is one of its foundations. An evaluation aims to determine if a system that is being proposed is going to be useful, understandable or appropriate for a certain group of users. Evaluations can be initiated throughout the ID cycle. User feedback can be solicited from rough sketches or high fidelity prototypes to gather information about the effectiveness of an emerging design. An interaction designer may create several versions of a design and carry out a number of different evaluations.

Since iteration is considered to be both necessary and useful, designers can legitimately ask the question: 'how many alternative designs or prototypes are necessary to build an effective system?' The ultimate answer depends on the product that is being constructed and how much time or budget is available. Different evaluation techniques differ significantly in terms of how much time and resources they require. It is important to remember that the cost of evaluating prototypes and making changes early within a design cycle is likely to be slight in comparison to the cost of making substantial changes to high fidelity prototype or operational system.

Returning to the principle of a 'card prototype', a designer can solicit feedback relating to an early design by 'simulating' the actions of an imagined computer. Mouse clicks or button presses can be simulated by presenting questions to evaluation participants akin to, 'what would you do now?'. When a user has performed an action, the evaluator could then change one interface card for another. Any confusing terms or difficulties with the interaction can then be noted and used as input to a further design iteration.

When faced with a high fidelity prototype or an existing system, perhaps in the form of a web site it is possible to apply a *discount usability* method, such as heuristic evaluation (Nielsen & Molich, 1990). Using a number of well known usability guidelines, a small number of experts can be called upon to assess the operation of a system to determine whether improvements can be made. The advantage to such an approach is that it can provide relatively quick (and low cost) feedback about a proposed design. The disadvantages include the possibility that evaluators may discover faults that are not present, misunderstand

the context in which the system is used, or fail to take account of the attributes of the user.

Another type of evaluation method that could be used is that of laboratory based studies, where users are required to carry out tasks. Using the usability testing methodology, difficulties are noted and analysed with a view to potentially making improvements to the interface of a system. Other human-computer interaction techniques that could be applied include cognitive walkthroughs (Nielsen & Mack, 1994), and predictive evaluations (Card et. al., 1983). These techniques, like heuristic evaluations, have the advantage of not requiring end users. They do, however, suffer from the disadvantage of not being able to fully take into account the complexities that may be present in a real-world setting.

There may be many different users of social software systems, each of whom may have their own patterns of usage formed by their own individual needs and requirements. Techniques such as interviewing and observation (and participant observation) enable evaluators to gain an understanding of how a software system is consumed by different user communities. Ethnographic techniques enable evaluators to uncover whether terminology is appropriate for a given audience, or whether an interactive system ultimately disrupts or facilitates communication between different user groups.

These techniques have the advantage of being able to illustrate problems that other techniques may be unable to show. Whilst the user evaluation and cognitive walkthrough techniques may be able to highlight which elements of a user interface might be confusing or difficult to understand to some users, such approaches will not take into consideration the context in which a device is used. The user, for example, may wish to use a product on a bright sunny day on the side of a noisy street, for instance, and discover that audible alerts do not give appropriate feedback and the screen does not have sufficient contrast. Furthermore, through an observational study, for instance, the information

Table 2. Summary of evaluation approaches

Evaluation method	Attributes
Heuristic evaluation	Usability experts review a system and comment on usability using a set of heuristics (rules) that embody good design practice. More than one expert should be used. Following independent review, the experts then compare their results and arrive at an agreement on their findings. Results are then shared with interaction designer.
Cognitive walkthroughs	Experts simulate users as they step through or use an interactive system with the intention of uncovering whether users will have an understanding of what to do next, given their goals and the information that has been presented to them. No users are required for this approach.
Predictive evaluation	Experts examine an interface to a system and analyse how long a user will take to complete one or more tasks, based upon estimates it takes to carry out certain actions. This approach is used to evaluate performance of one design over another. No users are required, but will not take account of individual differences (such as fatigue) or environment effects (such as environmental noise) on task performance.
User testing	Users are asked to complete a number of tasks (often within a laboratory) to facilitate gathering of evidence in the form of video of user behaviour and device display. Alternatively, with low fidelity prototypes, facilitator can simulate operation of device to gather early feedback. Costly in terms of time. Requires a number of users.
Ethnographic observation	Can be used to gain a rich understanding of how a system 'fits in' with the culture and environment for which it was designed. Requires in-depth observation of user action and gathering of information about usage 'in the field'. Participant observation can be used by an evaluator to immerse him or herself into patterns of use. Most expensive evaluation approach.

storage capacities of a device may be used in ways that were unimagined by the original designer. Such findings may either indicate a shortcoming of a design, or perhaps point the way to new ways in which a system might be used or enhanced. In many respects, there are similarities between the methods that can be used to gather requirements for new systems and the approaches that can be used to evaluate existing systems. Interviews, for instance, can tell us what is required in a new system. They can also be used to tell us how a new system has been used and the opinions users hold about a particular system.

Choosing an effective evaluation strategy depends upon the nature of the product or system that is the focus of an evaluation. The DECIDE framework (Basili et al., 1994, cited in Preece et al., 2002) offers some useful guidance. The 'D' in DECIDE refers to the need to determine the goals of an evaluation, i.e. what issue it is trying to explore. An interaction designer might have an objective to explore whether the steps in a task sequence are understandable to a chosen user group, for instance. 'E' refers to the exploring of questions which are to be asked as a part of an evaluation. Each evaluation goal may yield a number of sub-questions. 'C' refers to the *choice* of the evaluation paradigm or approach, such as one of the approaches that are presented in table 2. The identification of practical issues, such as who is to be involved, where is it to take place and how long it is to take is represented by the 'I'. 'D' represents the need to decide upon how to deal with ethical issues. When conducting user testing, it is necessary to obtain *informed consent* to protect both the evaluator and the participant. When ethnographic studies are performed, the issue of consent is something that may need to be re-negotiated during the period of a study, especially if the number of participants affected by a study widens (Hammersley & Atkinson, 1996). Finally, the 'E' refers to the act of the evaluation itself. The results, of which, should be presented in a form that can guide the on-going development of a product or system.

Standards, Guidelines and Legislation

International standards can provide interaction designers with a rich source of information, particularly regarding definitions of common terms, guidance about design and evaluation processes and information about best practice. ISO 9241-11 is a standard which describes the 'ergonomic requirements for office work with visual display terminals: guidance on usability' defines usability as: 'the extent to which a product can be used by specified users to achieve specified goals with effectiveness, efficiency, and satisfaction in a specified context of use'. This standard presents a usability framework that considers the user, their task, the equipment they use, and the environment in which a product is used. A number of product goals are defined, namely, effectiveness, efficiency and satisfaction. The standard goes on to present some examples that describe how these various goals can be measured or assessed by way of an evaluation.

International standards do not stop at presenting sets of useful definitions that can help to facilitate communication between designers. ISO 13407, for instance, outlines the stages of human-centered design that can be applied for the development of an interactive system. These stages, it should be stated, are similar to those that are depicted in Figure 1. This standard outlines the principles and rationale of human-centred design, presents the importance of iteration and emphasises the importance of evaluation.

ISO represents one of many international organisations that are offering advice about how to best design and implement interactive systems. Other organisations, such as the W3C is an important source of information about emerging internet standards and systems. As suggested earlier, the web content accessibility guidelines (WCAG) is particularly important, offering guidance relating to the construction of systems that can be used by all users, regardless of whether or not they have a disability (Caldwell et al., 2008). In the United Kingdom, the WCAG guidelines feature in the British Standard PAS 78:2006, which is entitled 'Guide to good practice in commissioning accessible websites' (BSI, 2006).

Other domain specific standards and specification communities can also provide useful and practical advice about the construction of social software systems. In the world of e-learning technologies, IMS, for instance, can guide the development of useful and accessible applications and systems (IMS, 2002).

One of the advantages of paying attention to the work produced by standard bodies is that they have often been created by a group of experts who are often from a number of different domains. The published documents can represent distilled expertise and may present examples of good practice. Adhering to standards also exposes the possibility of creating interactive systems that are interoperable with other systems, allowing them to be used in new and imaginative ways. It should be added that the process of creating useful standards is one that is very slow. Useful ideas can emerge many years before they find their way into standards documents. This said, it will be interesting to follow the emergence of new standards and guidelines that facilitate the design of new and exciting social software systems.

A final point is that interaction designers and designers of social software systems need to be aware of the important of international legislation. Designers need to be aware of their obligations in terms of conforming to anti-discrimination legislation. Similarly, designers need to be aware of data protection and privacy legislation in the countries in which they are situated. Since social software provides people with means to communicate and share information, issues of security and data integrity are just as important as developing appropriate interaction mechanisms that are suited to the needs of users.

Applying Interaction Design

Let us consider a hypothetical problem; a collection of products which enable users to share recipes with each other. Firstly, there will be a phase of requirements gathering. This may include a series

Figure 2. A example storyboard

of interviews with potential users and gathering of useful or related documents. Once a set of requirements have been gathered an interaction designer can then begin to consider of a product in terms of user persona and scenarios. The next stage of a design may be to *contextualise* the problem, to allow it to be discussed and further explored by others. As suggested in an earlier section of this chapter, one approach is to create a product storyboard. A storyboard may be a very rough sketch which simply presents a product and the environment in which it may be used and describes the broad interaction paradigm that a particular design is to adopt. A very simple example of a storyboard is presented in Figure 2.

Once the context and interaction paradigm is understood, a designer (or group of designers) may then begin to consider and compose aspects of an interface. Not only must designers consider the actual components of a screen or display, but also how different screens are conceptually connected or linked to each other. One approach to

explore the sequence of screens or interactions is to create what is known as a card based prototype. An example of card sketch is presented in Figure 3.

Using card sketches, designers can quickly evaluate their designs by presenting them to potential future end users. Designers can efficiently simulate the operation of a computer or system with the intention of evaluating the sequence of actions, the language of the items that are presented on the cards, and whether the interpretation of the requirements is correct. When the design of the cards have been agreed upon, the designer then may move onto a further design iteration by creating a more detailed design, such as interface sketch, perhaps similar to the one shown in Figure 4. Note the increase in the fidelity (or detail) as an increase in the number of design decisions have been made

The process of interaction design and user centred design suggests that designers create a number of different prototypes through a number

Figure 3. Example of a card from a card-based prototype

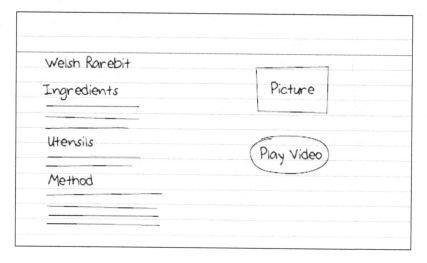

Figure 4. Design of an interface sketch

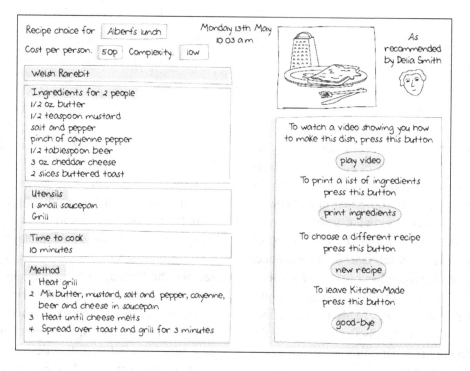

of different iterations with the intention of creating increasingly detailed designs which increasingly match the needs of all those who comprise the target user group. The designer (or designers) must always be mindful to consider the important issues of user culture and accessibility. The issue of product accessibility is especially important, since issues that relate to the interoperability of assistive technology may only become apparent when more detailed prototypes are considered.

FUTURE RESEARCH DIRECTIONS

Historically, interaction design has been predominantly associated with human-machine interaction. With the advent of increasingly mobile computing devices and near pervasive internet access in many developed countries, it is expected that the focus of HCI will move towards how machines or technology can support human-to-human interaction (Harper, Rodden & Rogers, 2008). The move towards human-to-human interfaces raises a number of important issues. Interactive systems will increasingly have the ability to facilitate different kinds of communication between different groups of people. Network technology will increase the levels of connectedness between people, their interests, their organisations and institutions. Due to the differences between groups and the types of interaction tasks that need to take place, the notion of a static 'one size fits all' interface will change. This change may see the emergence of ways of understanding how to present ambient information (information that is always present or available) in a way that is customised to the task that a user is completing. Just as the issues relating to task and information consumption will remain significant, issues relating to individual and group culture will also remain significant.

The Harper et al. (2008) report describe a world that has changed from a situation where a person may have used a single computational device, such as a personal computer, to a situation where we may currently make use of a number of different computational devices; a PC at home, a sophisticated mobile phone, and a PC at work. A vision for the future is that a user may use hundreds of different computer systems located on a network 'cloud'. A challenge for the future is to ensure that the usability and user experience of using many different systems is not compromised. Developments in terms of interoperability and standardization have the potential to help facilitate compatibility between different systems.

The issues of increased levels of connectivity between different systems directly point towards the increasingly important challenge of security and privacy. The emergence of new social software systems may see the development of new higher level concepts or abstractions that can potentially guide the development of new systems. A single user may wish certain types of information to remain private, whereas other information categories may be widely shared. Users will face challenges of how to best control information shared between different groups such as family, friends, work colleagues or a wider group of known associates such as former co-workers, for instance.

The emergence and application of social software may see the increased use of ethnographic methods to gain understanding of whether social software systems can adapt effectively to changing situations and uses. In a situation, where human-to-human communication may change over an extended period of time, longitudinal studies may be the only way to evaluate how successful, powerful and interoperable a particular set of social software utilities are to a chosen group of users. Similarly, just as the development of design principles and heuristics has guided the development of 'discount usability' evaluation for interactive product, the lessons learnt from building and evaluating social software systems may give way to the development of a new generation of social software heuristics.

The notion of usability has given way to the broader concept of user experience. It is prudent to ask whether the processes of ID may eventually take into account wider sets of goals. Whilst the user experience goals that were introduced earlier ask designers to consider whether a system is 'emotionally fulfilling' or whether an interface is 'satisfying', it might be possible to consider user experience in terms of quality of service and the degree to which a social software system permits users to share an emotional experience. The term 'emotional bandwidth' has been used to refer to the extent to which a system permits individuals to either project or detect the emotional expression of others. A challenge for ID theorists and practitioners is to create the tools that enable the expressivity of social software systems to be evaluated.

It is also worth considering the question of whether social software systems themselves might support the design and development of other interactive systems. The process of user-centered design relies on the cycle of producing alternative designs, presenting results to users and making changes based upon the feedback that has been gathered. These processes, given their richness in terms of necessitating communication between different groups of experts is one that has the potential to extensively benefit from the construction of interactive social software.

CONCLUSION

Interaction Design is an interdisciplinary subject that is often situated within the broad boundaries of computer science. There are many themes within interaction design that can be drawn upon to guide the design, development and evaluation of social software systems. Particular attention has been given towards the topics of requirements gathering and evaluation. The techniques used in both situations can be considered to be similar and emphasis has been placed on the potential of ethnographic techniques. These techniques aim to understand the different perspectives of users and the tasks they wish to carry out over periods of time. Standards, guidelines and legislation are considered to be important sources of information for an interaction designer. Standards are considered to be the summary of extended debates about best practice and they have often been created by stakeholders from many different disciplines.

The focus of human-computer interaction has been to understand how people use desktop bound personal computers and how to design effective and usable applications. Computing is now mobile, and through near pervasive web access, users are able to access a myriad of information services quickly and efficiently. Social software systems aim to facilitate human-to-human communication. Interaction design represents a development of HCI which contains sets of techniques and tools that can be used to create useful, exciting and engaging social software systems that can be used by all members of society. It will be interesting to observe how interaction design changes as new ways of interaction and communication emerge.

ACKNOWLEDGMENT

Figures 1, 2, 3 and 4 © Copyright The Open University, Fundamentals of Interaction Design course, M364 (2005).

REFERENCES

Basili, V., Caldiera, G., & Rombach, D. H. (1994). *The goal question metric paradigm: Encyclopedia of software engineering*. New York: John Wiley & Sons.

British Standards Institute. (2006). [—*Guide to good practice in commissioning accessible websites*. London: BSI.]. *PAS, 78*, 2006.

Caldwell, B., Cooper, M., Reid, L. G., & Vanderheiden, G. (2008). *Web content accessibility guidelines (WCAG) 2.0*. Retrieved August 11, 2009, from http://www.w3.org/TR/WCAG20/

Card, S. K., Moran, T. P., & Newell, A. (1983). *The psychology of human-computer interaction*. Hillsdale, NJ: Lawrence Erlbaum Associates.

Carroll, J. M. (Ed.). (1995). *Scenario-based design: Envisioning work and technology in system development*. New York: John Wiley & Sons.

Craig, J., Cooper, M., Pappas, L., Schwerdtfeger, R., & Seeman, L. (2009). *Accessible rich internet applications (WAI-ARIA) 1.0*. Retrieved August 11, 2009, from http://www.w3.org/TR/wai-aria/

Hammersley, M., & Atkinson, P. (1995). *Ethnography: Principles in practice* (2nd ed.). London: Routledge.

Harper, R., Rodden, T., & Rogers, Y. (2008) Being human: Human-computer interaction in the year 2020. Cambridge MA: Microsoft Research Limited. Retrieved August 11, 2009, from http://research.microsoft.com/en-us/um/cambridge/projects/hci2020/

Hofstede, G. (1994). *Cultures and organisations: Intercultural cooperation and its importance for survival*. New York: HarperCollins.

IMS. (2002). IMS guidelines for developing accessible learning applications, version 1.0 [White paper]. Retrieved August 11, 2009, from http://www.imsproject.org

International Standards Organisation. (1998). *9241-11: Definition of usable software*. Geneva, Switzerland: International Organization for Standardization.

International Standards Organisation. (1999). *13407: User-centred design process for interactive systems*. Geneva, Switzerland: International Organization for Standardization.

Kirah, A., Fuson, C., Grudin, J., & Feldman, E. (2005). Ethnography for software development. In Bias, G., & Mayhew, D. J. (Eds.), *Cost-justifying usability: An update for the internet age* (pp. 415–446). San Francisco, CA: Morgan Kaufman. doi:10.1016/B978-012095811-5/50014-6

Lim, Y. K, Stolterman, E., & Tenenberg, J. (2008). The anatomy of prototypes: Prototypes as filters, prototypes as manifestations of design ideas. *ACM Transactions on Human-Computer Interaction, 15*(2).

Marcus, A., & Gould, W. E. (2000). Crosscurrents: Cultural dimensions and global web user-interface design. *Interaction, 7*(4), 32–46. doi:10.1145/345190.345238

Moggridge, B. (2006). *Designing interactions*. Cambridge, MA: MIT Press.

Nielsen, J. (1992, May). *Finding usability problems through heuristic evaluation*. Proceedings of the ACM CHI'92 conference (pp. 373-380).

Nielsen, J., & Mack, R. L. (1994). *Usability inspection methods*. New York: John Wiley & Sons.

Nielsen, J., & Molich, R. (1990, April). *Heuristic evaluation of user interfaces*. Proceedings of the ACM CHI'90 conference (pp. 249-256)

Petrie, H., & Kheir, O. (2007). The relationship between accessibility and usability of websites. In *Proceedings of the SIGCHI conference on human factors in computing systems* (pp. 397-406).

Preece, J., Rogers, R., & Sharp, H. (2002). *Interaction design: beyond human-computer interaction*. New York: John Wiley & Sons.

Wickens, C. D. (1992). *Engineering psychology and human performance* (2nd ed.). New York: HarperCollins.

KEY TERMS AND DEFINITIONS

Accessibility: The subject of designing services and physical objects in such a way that they can be used by people with disabilities, often through the application of assistive technologies. In the context of software systems, an accessible system is one that does not present barriers to end users.

Card-Based Prototype: A series of sketches that can be prepared during to design of a low-fidelity prototype. The operation of a card-based prototype can be demonstrated through the user of a facilitator. Cards are used to explore what should be presented on the surface of an interface and whether the split between different displays are appropriate.

Conceptual Model: A set of integrated ideas about what a product should do and how it should behave. Related to the concept of an interaction mode.

Evaluation: The activity of determining whether a product conforms to a particular set of criteria, for example, whether a product or system is understandable given a particular user audience.

Interaction Design: A multi-disciplinary subject that presents a set of tools and techniques that can be used to design an interactive system.

Interaction Mode: A way of interacting or working with a system. An interaction may be based around an object or based around an activity.

Interaction Paradigm: A way of thinking about how to interact with a system. The most common interaction paradigm is the desktop computer. Alternative paradigms may embody the use of mobile systems and pervasive internet access. Other paradigms include ubiquitous computing, wearable computing and augmented reality, for example.

Persona: A description of a potential user of a system. A persona may include a name, information relating to the users' background knowledge, experience of other similar interactive systems and underlying motivations.

Scenario: A rich textual description of how a particular user (as described within a persona) may use system, device or product. Scenarios can be used as tools to elicit and explore user requirements for interactive products.

Storyboard: A high level sketch that depicts how a product or system is to be used. It contains information that enables designers to understand the environment or the context in which a system is used.

Usability Goal: Design objectives that relate to the functional attributes of a system, such as whether a system effective, efficient, safe to use, offers an appropriate level of functionality, is easily learnable and memorable

Use Case: A textual summary of the interactions between a user and a system, with the focus being upon the normal course of action. Use cases represent one of the ID design tools, and can be created following the production of a scenario description.

User Experience Goal: A wider set of design objectives which relate to how a user may feel about a system.

Chapter 11
Advanced Multimodal Frameworks to Support Human–Computer Interaction on Social Computing Environments

Danilo Avola
University of Rome La Sapienza, Italy

Andrea Del Buono
Computer Science and Knowledge Laboratory, Italy

Angelo Spognardi
University of Rome La Sapienza, Italy

ABSTRACT

In recent years, the growing improvements of the computational capability of the mobile and desktop devices, jointly to the potentialities of the current fast network connections have allowed the wide spread of advanced and complex applications and services belonging to the social computing area. The most current approaches used to interact with this kind of applications and services (hereinafter called social computing environments) do not seem able to provide an effective and exhaustive support to the human-computer interaction process. For this reason, in order to overcome this kind of problems, it is necessary to turn to more suitable interaction methodologies. In this context, human-oriented interfaces can be profitably used to support every kind of social computing environment. More specifically, multimodal interfaces enable users an effortless and powerful communication way to represent concepts and commands on different mobile and desktop devices. This chapter explores the more suitable possibilities to employ multimodal frameworks (and related algorithmic approaches) in order to interact with different kinds of social computing environments.

DOI: 10.4018/978-1-61692-904-6.ch011

INTRODUCTION

The novel hardware technologies used to improve the computational capability of the current mobile (e.g. smartphones, PDAs, palmtops) and desktop (e.g. tablets, workstations, laptops) devices, jointly to the more and more high performances expressed by the current LAN (e.g. ISDN, Cable, DSL, T-Carrier) and wireless (e.g. GSM, GPRS, EDGE, UMTS) network connections have allowed the wide spread of heterogeneous social computing environments that support human activities in everyday life. More specifically, all these novel devices and related connection potentialities have contributed to expand the boundaries of the current digital collaborative and social interaction on almost all main application fields: *professional*, *educational* and *entertainment*.

The most current approaches (e.g. keyboards, keypads, trackballs) used to interact with these innovative devices, and related complex digital environments, do not seem able to provide an effective and exhaustive support to accomplish the increasingly needs required to face the current challenges in the advanced human-computer interaction field. Actually, there are several reasons that lead to an evolution of the current human-computer interfaces used to interact with the mentioned devices and related social computing environments. The first one regards the *pervasive* concept by which the user can interact, anytime and anywhere, with any kind of device and related digital environments. This reason takes on even more significant considering the increasingly main role of the current heterogeneous mobile devices. The second one concerns the *amount of functionalities* related to every single social computing environment. In fact, independently from the kind of the specific digital environment, the current social computing applications and services tend to have an increasing amount of functionalities which often require more suitable ways to be effectively and efficiently used. The third reason regards the growing needs to have *customizable* human-computer interfaces. Indeed, the customization of the access methods to both current and next generation of social computing environments is the actual challenge of the human-computer interaction.

All the mentioned aspects lead to define new types of interfaces able to interact with any kind of both device and related social application or service. In particular, these new interfaces must have three main features: *intuitiveness, human-oriented* and *Web 2.0 designed*. The first feature highlights that the user should perceive the usability criteria of the interface in natural, effortless and simple way. This means that there should be a direct interaction process with the applications or services, regardless of the characteristics of a specific interface (and related device). The second feature focuses on the need to use human-oriented styles during the interaction process. In fact, the final frontier of the human-computer interface research is to allow users to interact with any device, application or service by using the same "tools" employed during human to human interaction, such as: voice (and related tone), expressiveness by handwriting and freehand drawings, gesture, facial expressions, and so on. The last feature regards a technical aspect of the interface design. In particular, this feature expresses the need of a development process compliant with the high standard of the Web 2.0 which is strongly based on two main concepts: *advanced interaction* and *content sharing*. For this reason, the Web 2.0 technologies can be considered the natural support for the social computing interfaces.

Multimodal interfaces provide a powerful tool to solve any kind of mentioned problem tied to the interaction processes: *pervasiveness, amount of functionalities* and *customization*. Besides, they satisfy the features related to the innovative interfaces: *intuitiveness, human-oriented* and *Web 2.0 designed*. In particular, multimodal interfaces, by using human-oriented modalities (e.g. speech, handwriting, freehand drawing, gaze) enable users to express concepts, provide commands and represent ideas in order to interact with any aspect of the social computing environments. Every modality can be exploited, separately or jointly with others, in two ways. In the first one the user provides concepts, commands or ideas in order to convey *inputs* to the digital environments, in the second one the user receives feedbacks in order to obtain *outputs* from them.

This chapter starts introducing some remarkable works about the use of the multimodal interfaces on heterogeneous environments. Afterwards, the chapter explores the more suitable approaches used to develop the multimodal frameworks. In particular, the section analyzes the current algorithms related to every single main modality. The chapter goes on by providing a classification of the main application fields in social computing environments (*professional*, *educational* and *entertainment*) according to the best suitable modalities that can be used to interact with them. Following, the chapter introduces two sections related to the methodologies used to implement multimodal framework functionalities on every kind of social computing application or service. In particular, the first section introduces the general principles regarding the cooperation of the modal inputs (fusion) and the expressiveness of the modal outputs (fission) in multimodal frameworks. More specifically, it shows how different modal inputs can be jointly used in order to provide an advanced human-computer interaction and, at the same time, it highlights how different modalities are used with the aim to provide feedback information to the user in response of its interaction process. The second section shows a novel advanced multimodal architecture suitably conceived to support the implementation of every kind of multimodal framework. In particular, it shows the main problems of the fusion process and the best current solutions (grammars and languages) used to overcome them. A further section regards the current data structures used to support both the working and the interaction of the multimodal frameworks. The chapter

concludes with two brief sections. The first one discusses about the future research directions of the multimodal approaches in social computing environments. The second and last one provides some concluding remarks about the architectures and the approaches described in the chapter.

BACKGROUND

Multimodal interfaces are the future of the human-computer interaction. The growing need to access in pervasive way (i.e. anytime and anywhere) the more and more advanced social computing applications and services has led to a rapid development of human-oriented interfaces able to satisfy user requirements in natural, intuitive and simple way. A single modal interface deals with interpreting the commands, expressed by the users, according to its modality (e.g. a speech-based interface interprets the vocal commands, while a sketch-based interface interprets the drawn commands). Multimodal frameworks support a set of modal interfaces in order to provide a powerful multimodal interface able to drive a specific application or service in consideration of a set of commands expressed by users in heterogeneous ways (e.g. speech, drawings, handwriting). This section shows some of the more remarkable works regarding multimodal frameworks. In particular, it briefly explores the main approaches implemented by other frameworks to support multimodal activity.

Fundamental works about multimodal frameworks (Oviatt, 2003, 2008) and related integration modalities (Koons et al., 1993; Wu et al., 1999) suggest that current advancements, on this field, are tied to the overcoming of problems related to both single modal recognition (i.e. the capacity of the modal interface to correctly interpret user commands) and standardization of the cooperation between several modalities (i.e. the ability of the framework to suitably integrate the different modal commands in order to express a coherent unique interpretation). A remarkable current work that follows these directions is shown in (Gurban et al., 2008). In this work the authors exploit advanced feature extraction processes in order to detect the main characteristics of two basic communication channels: face and speech. The integration and synchronization between the modalities is performed by using spatial and temporal constraints which highlight the logical relationships related to the information content of the modalities. This development approach allows a versatile customization that makes the framework suitable for every kind of context and any kind of application and service, including social computing environments. Another interesting related work is shown in (Alder et al., 2009). The authors describe a proof of concept of a system that supports symmetric multimodal communication for speech and sketching, set initially in the domain of simple mechanical device design. More specifically, the work faces three main aspects of the multimodal frameworks: input processing, dynamic dialogue creation and output generation. The described system is designed to interact with a user who is describing a simple mechanical device using sketching and speech and it has to simulate the behavior of the device using a qualitative physics simulator. Moreover, the system asks the user for additional information whenever it determines that the current physical situation is unclear or ambiguous, or when the user's input has not been understood. A very interesting aspect of the work is the way in which two modalities are both used and combined in order to provide a suitable interpretation of the user interaction. In (Ronzhin et al., 2009) the authors show an advanced example of social computing service. In particular, they describe a multimodal framework, based on speech, movements, poses and gestures interfaces, able to support team meeting in order to determinate the needs of the participants. The framework works by taking into account spatial position of the participants, their current activities, and roles in a current event. In this way, by

associating a semantic meaning to all their actions it is possible to more accurately predict the intentions and needs of the participants. It is important to observe that the mentioned framework can be considered a step forward compared to the current social computing services. In fact, it represents a real intelligent social environment. An advanced framework that can support any kind of social computing environment is shown in (Mendonça, 2009) where the authors propose a multimodal approach designed to perform high-level data integration between two or more modalities. In particular, the framework takes as input and analyzes low level features extracted from different system devices, then it identifies intrinsic meanings in these data by dedicated processes running in parallel. Extracted meanings are compared to identify complementarities and ambiguities to better understand the user intention during the interaction activity.

It is important to observe that our developed multimodal framework architecture, shown in this chapter, follows the main principles expressed by the World Wide Web Consortium (W3C) (Dahl et al., 2008).

MULTIMODAL FRAMEWORKS ANALYSIS

As observed in the previous section, every multimodal framework is able to recognize and to interpret a fixed set of modalities. These modalities are jointly considered from the framework with the aim to interpret the set of commands performed by users during the interaction process with a specific social computing application or service. For this reason, it is important to analyze the main algorithmic aspects involved during the recognition of the three main modalities: *speech*, *sketch* and *handwriting*.

Every mentioned modality (but also the others: gaze, tactile, gesture, and so on) has more than

Figure 1. Multimodal framework architecture

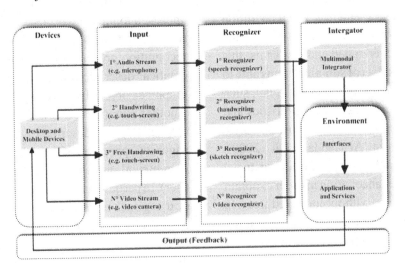

one approach by which it can be recognized, this means that a modal input command (e.g. sketch command) can be interpreted by using different methodologies (i.e. sketch recognition algorithms). The choice of a specific algorithm is tied to several aspects, such as: device, application or service, users needs, indoor or outdoor environments, and so on. Finally, it is important to highlight that the three mentioned modalities can be considered the more suitable approaches by which to interact with social computing environments because they are also the best way to perform the human-to-human communication. In Figure 1 is shown our developed general architecture about multimodal frameworks.

The multimodal commands (e.g. speech, sketch, handwriting) expressed by users on a specific device (desktop or mobile) during the interaction activity, represent the multimodal input of the framework. The main step is the recognition of each modality by a specific recognizer which will provide a suitable interpretation of the related part of input. All these parts will be integrated (by the multimodal integrator) in order to provide a unique interpretation of the multimodal input. This last will be the effective input provided to a suitable interface, related to the social computing applications or services, which

will return to the user (output) a feedback according to the user requirements (i.e. commands performance).

Speech-Based Interfaces

A speech-based interface can be informally defined as a tool able to both identify and perform user vocal activity. In order to accomplish this task, it has to address two main algorithmic aspects. The first one regards the recognition of the users audio stream where every word spoken by users has to detect as a set of specific characters of the related alphabet. This class of algorithms is identified as Speech-To-Text algorithms (STT). The second aspect concerns the semantic meaning linked to the recognized words. This last class of algorithms is tied to the use of the modality according to a specific application or service. In fact, sometimes it could be useful only to associate different practical meanings to different keywords, while in other cases it could be necessary to interpret the real semantic meaning of a whole sentence.

As regards the first class of algorithms, in (Huang et al., 2008) one of the best STT system is presented. As usual, the interface is based on advanced Hidden Markov Model (HMM) (Cappé et al., 2005) by which the voice signal is analyzed in order to provide the set of tokens (i.e. words) that compose a sentence. The recognition algorithm of the mentioned system allows the discrimination of overlapped audio streams; this is due to an advanced set of sub-algorithms able to detect the basic features of a spoken signal, such as: noise, background, signal characteristics and related differences, and so on. Another powerful approach is shown in (Al-Haddad et al., 2009). In this work the authors focus on an advanced algorithm for noise cancellation in order to obtain a suitable robust signal without corrupted areas. In this way the identification of each word is simply performed by analyzing the main features of the signal itself.

The second class of semantic algorithms is not easily explicable. It uses the basic concepts tied to the Natural Language Processing field (NLP) (Manning et al., 1999) with the aim to identify from simple keywords up to complex semantic meaning linked to the whole sentence.

Sketch-Based Interfaces

A sketch-based interface can be informally defined as a tool able to both identify and perform user drawing activity. Also in this case, the task can be accomplished by addressing two main algorithmic aspects. The first one concerns the recognition of the drawn objects performed by users during interaction activity. This class of algorithms is identified as Sketch Recognition algorithms (SR). The second aspect concerns the semantic meaning linked to the recognized graphical objects. This last aspect is easier than other modalities (e.g. speech, handwriting). Indeed, in this case, the modal interface developer assigns a specific meaning and/ or action to a recognized graphical symbol. For example, the developer can decide that the plus sign contained in a circle represents the zoom in action in a map browser application, or that a drawn arrow represents a scroll action of the same application. An interesting and complete sketch-based system is presented in (Fernández-Pacheco

et al., 2009). In this work the authors describe an approach to interpret user sketch, in on-line way, related to advanced graphical environments. The recognition process uses geometrical and mathematical descriptors in order to represent every graphical object by a set of graphical features. Another remarkable work is presented in (Macé et al., 2009). The described system is based on an eager interpretation of the user strokes (i.e. on an incremental process with visual feedback to the user). In particular the authors present the benefits of using such an interactive approach in order to design efficient and robust sketch recognition. However, the whole set of algorithms regarding the sketch recognition systems can be subdivided in three different classes. The first one works by analyzing the mathematical and/or geometrical features of every user stroke. The second one works by identifying the main features belonging to the whole user sketch. The last one uses the statistical models in order to define referenced patterns able to describe different sets of shapes.

Handwriting-Based Interfaces

A handwriting-based interface can be informally defined as a tool able to both identify and perform user handwriting activity. In this case, it is possible to consider a unique algorithmic aspect, that is the recognition of one or more user stroke as a specific character of an alphabet (and a set of characters as a sentence). The whole algorithms class in this application field works taking into account the mathematical and statistical features of the strokes performed by the user during the interaction process. An advanced typical system is shown in (Frinken et al., 2009) where the authors use the combination of both Neural Networks (NNs) and Maximum Margin Hidden Markov Models (MM-HMMs) in order to obtain high level results during the classification activity. Actually, the core process of several systems is quite similar and real differences between them occur during character pre or post processing activity.

MULTIMODAL FRAMEWORKS ON SOCIAL COMPUTING ENVIRONMENTS

Social computing environments can be mainly classified according to the following application fields: *professional*, *educational* and *entertainment*. The specific functionalities of every application or service can drive the modal ways by which the users tend to interact with the related environments. Table 1 summarizes a complete

comprehensive study (Avola et al., 2009) on the classification of the different modal interfaces according to heterogeneous application fields and devices (desktop and mobile). In particular, the preference is highlighted by using three parameters: *high, average,* and *low*. Every parameter identifies the level by which a specific modality is commonly used to interact with related advanced social computing environments.

There are applications or services that can belong to different application fields, this depends

Table 1. Preference in the use of the modalities

Application Fields	Applications & Services	Speech	Freehand Drawing	Hand-Writing	Other Modalities
Professional	Collaborative Computer Aided Design (C-CAD)	High	High	High	Average
	Collaborative Computer Aided Manufacturing (C-CAM)	High	High	High	Average
	Collaborative Computer Support Analysis (C-CSA)	High	High	Average	Low
	Distributed Development Environments	High	High	Low	Low
	Linkages Services	High	Low	Low	Low
	Collaborative Document Management Services	High	Average	High	Average
	Collaborative Control Systems	High	Average	Low	Low
	Distributed Monitoring Systems	High	High	High	High
	Collaborative Simulation Systems	High	High	High	High
	Distributed Trust Systems	High	High	Low	Average
Educational	Collaborative Information Systems	Average	High	High	*Low*
	Distributed Mobile Learning (M-Learning)	High	High	High	*Average*
	Distributed Electronic Learning (E-Learning)	High	High	High	*Average*
	Collaborative Annotation Systems	High	*High*	*Average*	*Low*
	Collaborative Search Systems	Average	*Average*	*Average*	*Low*
	Distributed Scientific Learning	High	High	High	*Average*
	Collaborative Browsing Systems	High	High	*Average*	*Average*
Entertainment	Collaborative Virtual Environments	High	Low	Low	Average
	Collaborative Music Environments	Low	High	Average	Average
	Collaborative Video Environments	Low	High	Average	Low
	Social Networks	High	High	Average	Average
	Collaborative Photo Environments	Low	Average	Average	Low
	Distributed Graphical Resources Management	Low	High	Low	Low
	Games Platforms	High	High	High	High
	Distributed Maps Browsing	High	High	High	Low
	Distributed Communication Environments	High	High	High	Low

on the specific use of the mentioned application or service, but this doesn't influence the preference expressed by the users during the choice of the interaction modality.

MULTIMODAL FUSION AND FISSION

A main aspect of the multimodal frameworks that has to be analyzed regards the interaction process between user and social computing environments. More specifically, the use of multimodal interfaces to interact with an application or service implies the possibility to exploit one or more different modalities to convey a set of suitable commands (e.g. users could use handwriting and speech interfaces with the aim to drive a social e-learning platform functionalities). Within the multimodal frameworks, these different modalities (i.e. different parts of input) will have to be jointly integrated (by the fusion module) with the aim to correctly interpret the user intentions. Similarly, the multimodal frameworks, once obtained the result (i.e. output) of the elaboration process from the specific application or service, have to select the more suitable modalities (by the fission module) in order to provide to the users a representation of the same result (e.g. according to the e-learning platform example, it

could provide a set of information, resulting from an elaboration process, in two different modalities: writing them on the screen and/or speaking them by speakers). The choice and the selection of different modalities by which to both express the input and represent the output related to an application or service is the main matter of the fusion and fission processes. In fact, they depend on four basic aspects: application or service, input and/or output, external environment, and device. In Figure 2 is shown our advanced developed architecture based on recent efforts in fusion e fission processes (Del Valle-Agudo et al., 2009; Ertl, 2009; Kim et al., 2007).

- **Application or Service**: the kind of application or service can influence, on one side, the choice of the modalities used by the user during interaction activity (input) and, on the other hand, the selection of the more suitable modalities detected by the framework with the aim to provide the feedback to the user (output).
- **Input and/or Output**: fusion and fission processes can be influenced by the complexity of the informative content of the same input and/or output.
- **Environment**: the indoor or outdoor external environments have features (e.g. noise,

Figure 2. Multimodal fusion and fission architecture

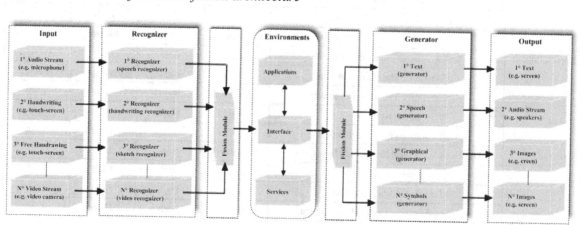

lighting condition) which can influence the way (input) in which users prefer to interact with the applications or services. At the same time, according to specific environments the framework can suggest different modalities in order to represent a same result (output).

- **Device**: the type of device can widely influence the modalities used to both provide input and represent output, to any kind of application or service. This is mainly due to the hardware differences between desktop and mobile devices. In fact, physical features of the devices (e.g. screen dimension, pointing tools, handiness) naturally drive the modalities used during the interaction and representation processes.

MULTIMODAL GRAMMARS AND LANGUAGES

The practical use of multimodal frameworks has its most interesting challenge in the specific approach employed during the fusion process. It is important to highlight this aspect of the multimodal frameworks because it involves two main concrete technical issues. The first one concerns the *effectiveness* and the *efficiency* of the input expressiveness during human-computer interaction. This means that a not suitable fusion process tends to nullify the communication activity by introducing, on the integrated input, both ambiguity problems and misinterpretation phenomena. The second one regards the *coherence* of the input. This means that the whole informative content of each single modal input could not be completely preserved within the integrated input (e.g. if the fusion process introduces noise or loss of information).

The just mentioned issues depend on both technical and methodological choices performed during the development of the fusion process. These choices are tied to different aspects of the contextual domain, such as: kind of application or service, technical requirements, types of modal input, and so on.

There are several different ways to implement fusion process. In recent years, there have been many efforts in order to obtain a process able to both overcome the mentioned issues (*effectiveness*, *efficiency* and *coherence*) and provide a custom tool according to specific applications or services. In particular, this second aspect highlights the need to have a fusion process where the informative content, of the integrated input, can be easily fitted in order to satisfy technical requirements of different devices in pervasive environments. Besides, the customization of the tool has to take into account user needs and/or application and service characteristics.

Multimodal grammars and languages seem to provide the best solution to profitably face each and every aspect related to both mentioned issues and customization matters. More specifically, a modal (or multimodal) human-computer interaction process can be formalized by using a related unimodal (or multimodal) grammar which is used to convey a specific unimodal (or multimodal) language. This language describes the interaction process and, at the same time, it is used to express concepts, provide commands and represent ideas able to interact with any social computing environments. Figure 3 presents our developed multimodal novel framework architecture focused on grammars and languages concepts.

The framework architecture is composed by four main modules: *streaming module, recognizer module, fusion module, output module*. The role of each module will now be detailed, with particular reference to the fusion module. The architecture also shows two further layers (*external device* and *environments*) introduced with the aim to explain the interaction of the framework with the external context (i.e. devices, applications and services). In particular, the external device layer represents the multimodal *input* conveyed

Figure 3. Grammar/language-based multimodal framework architecture

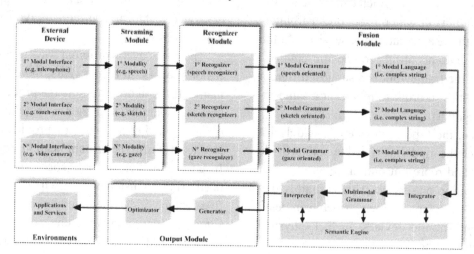

to the framework, while the environments layer represents the target of the multimodal *output*.

External Device

This layer shows two main aspects of the multimodal devices. The first one highlights that every single modality has to have a hardware interface (e.g. microphone) able to catch the human interaction (e.g. user who expresses a vocal command) in order to drive the social computing applications or services. The second one highlights that every modality is expressed separately from the others. This means that the *modal input* provided from every *modal interface* has an informative content tied only to the user expression with relation to the specific modality used during interaction activity. In other words, the content of the user interaction does not depend on contextual aspects, such as: knowledge of other modalities, technical requirements, and so on. It is also important to observe that every *modal input* (and related informative content) is represented by a set of technical information tightly tied to the related modality (e.g. a vocal command can be expressed by an audio stream).

Streaming Module

The aim of the first module belonging to the framework architecture is to take in input every *modal input* coming from the previous layer, and to return as output a "standardized" version of it. The standardization is a complex process that depends on the specific characteristics of the multimodal framework. In general, it can be decomposed in three main tasks that have to be performed on the *modal input* before it is analyzed by the next module (recognizer module). The first one is to carry out the preprocessing activity of the input with the aim to "clean" it from any kind of critical elements, such as: redundancy, noise, defects, and so on. The second one is to analyze every modality in order to "translate" each of them in a suitable standard data structure, according to the technical requirements of every specific framework. This is the first step aimed to express the different modalities in a homogeneous way. The third and final task concerns the *customization* of every *modal input*. In this phase, the framework defines the whole set of parameters related to every modality (e.g. level of detail, complexity of the *modal input*, type of priority among information elements) according to the technical requirements. This kind of activity is tied to the several practical technical aspects of the framework and related social computing environments (e.g. administrator user requirements, specific application or service, indoor/outdoor issues, devices).

Recognizer Module

As mentioned above, the main task of a *recognizer* is to analyze every modality in order to provide an interpretation of its input. For every modality, this second module takes in input the standardized *modal input* and returns as output the related interpretation which can be both complex and heterogeneous. This means that, on one side, the fixed designed choices of each *recognizer* related to a specific modality can provide a recognized element more or less complex and, on the other hand, that the mentioned element can be represented in several different ways. For example, focusing only on the sketch-based interfaces, it is possible to observe that the standard recognition of one or more symbols (e.g. drawn commands to drive a social computing application) is the suitable interpretation of the same symbols themselves. That is, if the user draws a circle, the framework has to recognize the specific geometrical figure. Actually, the geometrical figure can be represented in several different ways, such as: center coordinates and radius of the approximated circle, an advanced vectorial representation including speed of execution and/or drawing direction (clockwise/counterclockwise), the set of drawn pixels, a simple numerical code representing the drawn object, and so on. The just introduced concepts highlight the main issues related to every kind of *recognizer* engine. In particular, they point out both the different degree of complexity related to different recognition processes and the possible heterogeneity of the recognized elements according to different user, application or service needs.

A *Recognizer* has two main further tasks that directly influence the *effectiveness* and the *efficiency* of the whole framework: ambiguity solving and misinterpretation evaluation. The first

task specifies that every modality *recognizer* has to solve its ambiguities. For example, if a user draws a circle in a very confused way, then the related *recognizer* must have "mechanisms" that allow to recognize the shape without any doubt. A common way is to require additional user information about the performed drawing. Another frequent way is to assign a rank, to the recognized element, which will be considered by subsequent modules (in our framework architecture by the *interpretation* process in the *fusion module*). This means that, if other modalities will provide sufficient information to interpret the user interaction, and a specific modality has a low rank, then it will not be considered. A currently used way to overcome any kind of ambiguity problem (in particular for unimodal frameworks) is to consider the *domain knowledge* during the recognition process. More specifically, each modality can be contextualized within a specific application domain. For example, a sketch-based interface could be implemented in order to recognize a fixed set of symbols (i.e. a specific library), if the framework knows the library then this information will support it during the whole recognition process inasmuch it should choose the suitable interpretation according to a limited number of possibilities. The second mentioned task highlights that every modality *recognizer* has to have a tool able to evaluate the possible misinterpretations. This can occur when the user interaction is too confused, or when external events influence the proper work of the modal interface (e.g. outdoor environments, errors, noise). Usually, in order to overcome this kind of problems every *recognizer* checks the recognized element according to the specific state of the framework. This means that, for example, a recognized drawn or vocal command is analyzed taking into account the state of the driven application or service. In fact, a general application or service can accept a defined subset of commands according to its runtime state which defines a specific set of possible user actions.

Fusion Module

The aim of this third module is to take in input the whole set of the *recognized modalities*, and to return as output a unique interpretation. To accomplish this task, the module belonging to our developed architecture performs six main steps: formalization of each recognized modality by a suitable grammar (*modal grammar* process), generation of a related language string (*modal language*), integration of the different language strings (*integrator* engine), possible re-formalization by a further integrated grammar (*multimodal grammar* process), interpretation of the meaning of the whole user interaction process (*interpreter* engine) and possible support to the integration and/or re-formalization and/or interpretation by a semantic engine able to enrich the related informative contents (*semantic engine*).

To detail the mentioned six main steps related to the *fusion module*, it is necessary to introduce some basic definitions about grammars and languages. Initially, the mentioned concepts will be introduced in informal way with the aim to learn their meaning (Parkes, 2002). Afterwards, a more formal way is introduced which will provide the basic terminology used during this section (Crespi-Reghizzi, 2009).

- **Grammar Definition (informal):** A Grammar is a set of rules for generating strings. In this context, a string can be considered as a finite sequence of zero or more symbols taken from a formal alphabet. A typical example of string is any set of symbols belonging to the roman alphabet and/or numerals (e.g. flower, home, acqui30adb110). In the literature, a wide matter related to the formal languages concerns the semantic meaning of the strings (e.g. flower and home have it, while acqui30adb110 does not have it). In our context this problem is overcome taking into account that every string is the representa-

tion of a recognized modality which necessarily has a semantic meaning tied to the related user interaction.

- **Language Definition (informal):** A Language is any subset (with or without semantic meaning) of the whole set of strings generated by a Grammar. A simple example of language can be now introduced. Let the set A = {a, b, c, d} an alphabet composed from a selected letters belonging to the roman alphabet. Then, the following set L = {ab, ad, acd, bcd, abbc, bcdd, bbcdd} can be considered a related language. As mentioned, a language is generated by a grammar. Let G = {rule 1, rule 2,...} the set of rules by which to generate the language L related to the alphabet A. The G set can contain several elements, an example of rule (e.g. rule 1) could be the following: "generate strings where every single letter has a literal ordering greater or equal to its previous and, at the same time, lower or equal to its next (where the literal ordering is the following: a < b < c < d)". Obviously, this is just one of the many rules that should compose the grammar in order to obtain the shown language. A grammar has to generate only the whole set of strings of a specific language. This means that when there is the necessity to create a grammar to generate a language, the main property is that the grammar will not be able to generate any string outside the mentioned language.

Now, with the aim to offer a tool able to provide a high level description of the *recognized modalities*, a more formal definition about Grammars and Languages is given.

- **Grammar Definition (formal):** A Phrase-Structured Grammar (PSG), shortly Grammar, is an ordered quadruple G = {V_N, V_T, P, S} where:

○ V_N: is a set of non-terminal symbols belonging to a suitable alphabet. These symbols are used to support the "working" of the same Grammar, and they do not appear within the strings that represent the language.

○ V_T: is a set of terminal symbols belonging to another suitable alphabet. These symbols are used to compose the strings that represent the language.

○ P : is a set of production rules, shortly productions. They represent a formalization of the rules for specifying strings of the V_T alphabet. A production can be expressed as follows:

■ x→y, where x ∈ $(V_N \cup V_T)^+$, and y ∈ $(V_N \cup V_T)^*$, x and y represent respectively the left-hand and the right-hand of the production. As well known, the symbols " * " and " + " define the composition of strings by using the whole possible combinations of the elements belonging to the related set. The differences between the mentioned symbols is that in the first case also the empty sting is considered. This last consideration highlights that the left-hand of a production cannot be empty. The productions are linked one to each other, this means that it is possible to obtain a path that leads from a production to another (loops are allowed). A finite and ordered set of sequential productions able to generate a string is defined as *derivation*.

○ S: is the non-terminal symbol from which all derivations have to start.

- **Language Definition (formal):** A Formal Language, shortly Language, generated from the Grammar G can be defined as follows:

  ○ L(G) = {w ∈ V_T^*: S →* w }, where:

    ■ w : represents a generic string.

    ■ →* : represents the derivation path in zero or more steps (i.e. the path starting from S that has been obtained to generate the string w can be composed by zero or more productions).

It is important to observe that every modal grammar works according to the just introduced formalisms.

In order to clarify the just introduced formalisms, a simple example of grammar, language and related generation of a specific string is given.

A concrete example of grammar can be expressed as follows: $G_{example}$ = $\{V_N, V_T, P, S\}$, where:

- V_N: {S, B, C}.
- V_T: {a, b, c}.
- P : S → aS | bB ; B → bB | bC |cC ; C → cC | c (the meaning of the symbol " | " is "or", it is used to define a short form of productions (i.e. C → cC | c represents the two productions: C → cC ; C → c).
- S: S.

By the mentioned grammar it is possible to define the related generated language:

- L($G_{example}$) = {$a^i b^j c^k$: i ≥ 0, j ≥ 1, k ≥ 1, if j=1 then k ≥ 2 else k ≥ 1}.

Examples of strings belonging to the specified languages are: bcc, abbcc, aabbccc, aabbbbbccccc, etc.

In order to explain the derivation of the string aabbccc (by using the following sequential set of productions: S → aS, S → aS, S → bB, B → bB, C → cC, C → cC, C → c) the following example is given:

- S → aS ▶ S → aaS ▶ S → aabB ▶ S → aabbB ▶ S → aabbcC ▶ S → aabbccC ▶ S → aabbccc.

The complexity of a derivation depends on the grammar which is tied to a specific modality. A useful way to represent more complex derivations is the *derivation tree*. This new concept is introduced for two main reasons. The first one is that the tree structures are the effective way by which the grammars (and related real data structures) are represented within the current multimodal frameworks. The second one is that this kind of notation allows to specify very complex derivations in intuitive and easy way. In Figure 4 a part of a derivation related to some complex productions of a generic grammar is shown.

As it is possible to observe, the string generation (and related language) is a hard task according to the complexity of the productions. There are several aspects, tied to the productions structure, that has to be considered during the implementation of a grammar. One of the most important, which also covers a primary role in the modal grammar, is the concept of *context*. This new element, belonging to the grammar, highlights the need to have a specific context able to enable

the working of the derivation. For example, the third production of the first level (cBd → RpT) shows that it is necessary to have a particular context (cBd) in order to allow the whole derivation process (RpT).

The theory concerning the formal languages is very wide (see selected references in the additional reading section), many arguments should be discussed (e.g. Chomsky hierarchy, context free and context sensitive grammars, regular languages). But all these concepts are beyond the aim of the section, which has to highlight the main concepts of the formal languages with the aim to explain the real role of the grammars and languages within the multimodal frameworks.

In our context, a grammar used to represent a modality follows the same principles of the just mentioned definitions, but the sets that define it tend to be more complex according to the kind of modality.

For example, a modal grammar used to represent the instances of a sketch-based interface could be implemented as follows: the set of terminal symbols (V_T) should be composed by the primitive graphical elements (e.g. lines and ovals) through which represent every 2D geometrical shape (e.g. circle, square, rectangle). Moreover

Figure 4. Derivation tree

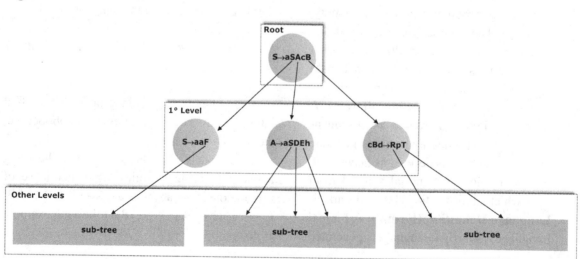

this set should contain other elements representing the spatial and temporal constraints that express the relationships between the mentioned shapes; the set of non-terminal symbols (V_N) should be composed by engines able to support the different steps involved during the recognition process. The main task of the non-terminal symbols is to factorize the recognition process in order to obtain, step by step in the derivation tree, the levels representing well defined states of the mentioned process; the set of productions (P) should contain the whole set of rules used during the recognition process (e.g. the rule to check whether a shape contains another with the aim to introduce a possible constraint of containment); finally the start symbol (S) represent the initial state of the recognition (e.g. the set of pixels drawing by the user during the interaction activity).

In this way, every modal grammar can be seen as the formalization of the recognition process performed by the related *recognizer* within the *recognizer module*.

By the previous introduced definitions it is possible to detail, in a concise way, the six main steps that define the work of the *fusion module*. In particular, the explanation will focus on the main problems that every step has to address in order to support the fusion of the *recognized modalities*.

Modal Grammar

The processes related to this step aim to provide a complete formalization of the whole aspects involved during the recognition process. This means that, independently from how the recognition of a modality happens (*recognizer module*), it is always possible to formalize a process describing it. For example, if the result of a sketch-based recognizer is the shape circle, it is always possible to describe that shape in function of the related geometrical features, regardless of how effectively the circle has been recognized starting from a set of pixels drawn by the user during the interaction activity.

As just mentioned, every modality has a specific pattern of grammar that can be seen as the formalization of a process able to describe the recognition. For this reason, it is not convenient to provide a pattern for every possible modality, but can be useful to introduce an abstraction of a generic modal grammar:

- **Modal Grammar Definition (abstraction):** A Modal Grammar is an ordered six-tuple $G_{Modal} = \{V_N, V_T, P, M, F, S\}$ where:
  - V_N: is a set of non-terminal symbols belonging to a suitable alphabet. Actually, each one of these symbols can be seen as a specific aspect involved during the recognition process of the related modality. Technically, each non-terminal symbol represents an engine that takes in input one or more objects and returns as output an elaboration of it/them. The objects can be considered as raw parts of what will be the final string. In general, the non-terminals symbols depend on the modality, but it has to be taken into account that modalities belonging to a same "context" (e.g. hand-drawing interfaces and free handwriting interfaces) can have symbols that accomplish very similar tasks. The factorization expressed by the non-terminal symbols can be better represented using the derivation tree which, level by level, performs the whole recognition process with the aim to provide the final string. Non-terminal symbols do not appear within the strings, since they are only the "functional" elements of the productions to generate every string.
  - V_T: is a set of terminal symbols belonging to another suitable alphabet. The symbols are tightly tied to the specific modality, moreover they be-

long to one of the following classes: *expression* or *relationship*. The expression class contains all the terminal symbols that are, somehow, a representation of the basic elements of the modality (e.g. for sketch-based interfaces these elements could be: circles, points, lines, squares, and so on). The relationship class contains all terminal symbols that can specify the spatial and/or temporal and/or logical relationships between symbols belonging to the expression class. The symbols belonging to both classes are jointly used to compose the strings that represent the language.

○ P : is a set of production rules, shortly productions. As just observed in the general case of the PSG, they represent the formalization of the rules for specifying strings in the V_T alphabet. More specifically, this kind of productions can be considered as the way in which the sequential steps of the recognition process are related. For example, always taking into account a sketch-based interface, these productions specify how a set of graphical primitives can be tied between them in order to provide a new element belonging to the evolution of the coarse string (or part of it). For this kind of productions, the derivation tree used to represent the generation of the strings is a concrete tool to define the data structures and the interaction processes.

○ M: is a set of meta-information associated to every non-terminal symbol. More specifically, these information represent the semantic description of the work of each non-terminal symbol. They can be informally considered as "labels" linked to every non-

terminal symbol that explain what it does. The meta-information are not tied to a specific modality, but they express a concept that can be the same on different modalities. For example, sketch-based interfaces and free handwriting interfaces both need an engine (i.e. set of non-terminal symbols) able to perform the distance recognition step. Conceptually, the work of the engine is the same in both kinds of interface, insomuch it has always to compute the distance between user drawn objects composed by pixels. So, the meta-information linked to each non-terminal symbol can be seen as the abstract description of the specific aspect involved during the recognition process of the related modality.

○ F : is a function with domain in V_N^*, and co-domain in M^*. This function is designed to link each single or group of non-terminal symbols to the related meta-information (i.e. the labels). This function has a significant role (as shown below) in the process regarding the integrator engine. A representation of the function can be given as follows:

- $F(z \in V_N^+) = k \in M^+$. Notice that z and k cannot be empty elements.

○ S: is the non-terminal symbol from which all derivations have to start. It represents the initial state of the recognition process (e.g. for sketch-based interfaces, it could be represented by an engine that take in input the set of pixels or strokes drawn by the user during the interaction activity and, returns as output a suitable elaboration).

Modal Language

A modal language is represented in a much more complex way than one generated by a common PSG. This is not only due to the fact that the terminal and non-terminal symbols belonging to the modal grammars are very complex compared to those of a common PSG, but this happens because of the difficulties tied to the management of the semantic informative content of the meta-model (supported by M and F elements of the described modal grammar) linked to every string generated by the modal grammar. Similarly to what observed for the grammars, even the languages depend on the specific modality, for this reason can be useful to describe it by introducing a suitable abstraction of a generic modal language:

- **Modal Language Definition (abstraction):** A Modal Language, shortly Language, generated from the Grammar G_{Modal} can be defined as follows:
  - $L(G_{Modal}) = \{w \in V_T^*: S \to^* w\}$ (i.e. in the same way of the PSG, but taking into account the mentioned differences between the sets that define the two kinds of grammar: PSG and modal grammar).

In practical cases, a multimodal framework needs both the generated string of each modality, and the representation of the recognition process used in order to obtain that string. A definition of the just described concept can be provided by the following abstraction:

- $F(z) = k$ (according to the previous definition of F), where:
  - $\delta(w) = z$, the function δ can be considered a projection of the generated string w, to the related set of non-terminal symbols z. More specifically, it takes as argument the string $w \in V_T^*$ generated from the grammar G_{Modal} and returns the set of non-terminal symbols $z \in V_N^+$ that have been used in order to obtain it. This simply means that z represents the set of non-terminal symbols that compose the derivation tree of w.
  - $k \in M^+$: represents a *specular derivation tree* where instead of non-terminal symbols, the related meta-information are given. In other words, the specular derivation tree can be seen as a tree in which every node shows the semantic description of the work of the related non-terminal symbols (that, as just observed, in this context represent specific engines).

Integrator

The aim of this engine is to take in input the different modal languages coming from the heterogeneous modalities, and to provide as output an integrated grammar-based language. This means that the languages related to the different modalities have to be *joined* and *synchronized* in order to express the whole informative content conveyed by each single modality. The join feature specifies that the strings coming from different modalities have to be combined in a unique multimodal string. This new string has to contain both the informative content of the original strings and an added content due to the join of the strings. The synchronization feature highlights that the contents of the strings have to be synchronized during the join process in order to rightly represent the user interaction.

In order to explain as just mentioned it is necessary to introduce the following example. Suppose that a user uses sketch and speech modalities to drive an application related to an annotation social network of scientific documents. The first modality is used to identify (e.g. drawing circles on the screen by mouse or optical pen) which parts of the document have been highlighted from the user. The second modality is used, from the same user, to convey commands to the application. These commands could regard any action allowed from the application, such as: sharing of the mentioned parts, querying about linked annotations, showing of annotations of different users, and so on. Once obtained the strings related to the two different modal languages (w_{Sketch} and w_{Speech}) the integrator engine has to perform two main steps: *verification* and *fusion* (i.e. join and synchronization). The verification step is aimed to identify the rank of the compatibility of the two strings according to their semantic meaning. With the aim to accomplish this task, on each string the linked specular derivation tree is computed ($F(\delta(w_{Sketch})) = k'$ and $F(\delta(w_{Speech})) = k''$). In this case, using a high level of simplification of the specular derivation tree representation, the two semantic informative content can be expressed as follows:

- $k' = \{$"source(WEB document: URL <string>) + command(drawn the object: circle) + action(selection) + circle[center(x, y) + radius(l)] + clockwise + time(15_h:41_m:26_s) + duration(2.21s)"$\}$.
- $k'' = \{$"source(WEB document: URL <string>) + command("share this with the working group") + action(specification) + time(15_h:41_m:32_s) + duration(3.02s)"$\}$.

According to the most advanced Natural Language Processing (NLP) approaches (Béchet, 2009; Parag, 2009; Ravakhah 2009), a rank-based process can be used in order to obtain the "similarity" (i.e. the affinity) of the two concepts. In particular, the rank process performed by the proposed integrator engine works taking into account the whole set of possibilities related to the available elements (in this case: k' and k''). For example, in our context the engine could focus on the following three aspects:

- The concepts "selection" and "specification" have a high level of affinity.
- The derived concepts "selection by circle" and "specification of what share with the working group" have a high level of affinity.
- The starting temporal values of both commands (15_h:41_m:26_s and 15_h:41_m:32) are very close.

According to the mentioned three aspects the engine could decide that the two related strings (w_{Sketch} and w_{Speech}) have to be joined. This leads to the second step, that is the fusion (i.e. join and synchronization) of the described engine. In easy way, the fusion between strings can be expressed as follows:

- $w_{Joined} = w_{Sketch} \cup w_{Speech}$, where:
  ○ w_{Sketch}: represents the string generated from a suitable sketch-based grammar;
  ○ w_{Speech}: represents the string generated from a suitable speech-based grammar,
  ○ w_{Joined}: represents the joined string coming from w_{Sketch} and w_{Speech}.

In this context, it is important to observe that it is not so important to analyze the syntax (i.e. non-terminal symbols and related productions) used to generate the strings, insomuch it can be always represented by the just shown modal grammars and languages formalization. The main matter is to compute the semantic meaning linked to both modal strings and the joined string. Actually, the semantic meaning of the multimodal string w_{Joined} is derived from that expressed by the unimodal strings: w_{Sketch} and w_{Speech}. Obviously this process has to be driven by the syntax of the unimodal language, but semantic and syntax perform a cooperation activity with the aim to provide both w_{Joined} and $F(\delta(w_{Joined}))$. Continuing the given example, the semantic informative contents (k''') of the joined string (w_{Joined}) can be expressed as follows:

- k''' = {"source(WEB document: URL <string>) + command ("share what has been highlighted by the circle with the working group") + action(execute the specification of the selection) + circle[center(x, y) + radius(l)] + clockwise + time(15_h:41_m:26_s) + duration(3:08)"}.

As it is possible to observe, the new string has a semantic informative content that goes beyond the simple union of the contents related to the single strings (k' and k'').

Multimodal Grammar

The aim of this process is to support both the joined strings and the related semantic informative content (i.e. w_{Joined} and k'''). More specifically, the $G_{Multimodal}$ (that contains a suitable fusion of the constructs related to each single modal grammar (G_{Modal})) and the related $L(G_{Multimodal})$ are used to "rewrite" them. The process can be considered an optimization step aimed to solve different issues (e.g. ambiguities).

Interpreter

By using the "rewritten" joined string (w_{Joined}) and the related optimized semantic informative content, the interpreter has to provide a suitable essential interpretation of the joined string ($w_{Interpreted}$).

Semantic Engine

The main purpose of this engine is to support the semantic processes involved in both multimodal engines (i.e. integrator and interpreter) and the multimodal grammar process.

Output Module

The aim of the fourth and last module of our framework is to take in input the *interpretation* of the modalities provided from the fusion module, and to return as output a suitable data structure able to interact with the external social computing environments. The working of this module has two main components: *generator* and *optimizer*.

Generator

This element covers the need to properly prepare the data structures provided by the previous module to obtain a standard representation of them. More specifically, the generator implements the interfaces to interact with the interpretation of the modalities.

Optimizer

The aim of this component is to perform the optimization activity on the just implemented interfaces. This need is tied, on one side, to the software characteristics of the environments that interact with the framework and, on the other hand, to the hardware features of the devices that host these environments. In fact, both aspects drive the set of software technologies that can be used to interact with social computing environments.

Environments

This layer covers the final phase of the whole multimodal frameworks processes, that is the interfacing with the social computing environments. There are two ways to accomplish this task according to specific applications or services. The first one exploits the Application Programming Interfaces (APIs) with the aim to map the functionalities of the environments with a suitable set of multimodal actions. The second one tends to directly introduce a multimodal mapping module, within these applications and services, in order to provide a natural interfacing process.

MULTIMODAL DATA STRUCTURES REPRESENTATION TECHNOLOGIES

The previous section has observed a main aspect of the multimodal interaction: grammars and languages. In this section will be explored, on one side, how effectively these grammars can be represented within the multimodal frameworks (inside of the fusion module) and, on the other hand, in which way the languages can be expressed in order to drive the social computing environments and related devices.

The eXtensible Markup Language (XML) can address both issues (Quin, 2009). It is a simple very flexible text format able to achieve different goals, such as: information exchange, data representation, interfaces formalization, protocols specifications, cooperation between modal inputs (fusion supporting), synchronization between modal outputs (fission supporting), and so on. Actually, in our context the standard XML is used to support two specific activities: interfaces formalization (i.e. the grammars) and data representation (i.e. the languages). The remaining activities are performed by using XML derived languages which have been specifically created to solve a single aspect of multimodal environments. A brief explication about the two different ways to use XML technology is given:

- **Standard XML:** as already mentioned this language is used to define the whole structure of the grammars and the related generated languages. First of all, this means that the productions of a grammar can be easily represented by XML. In fact, XML philosophy allows software developers to define an information (structure or data) without considering particular constraints. For example the production P: S → aS could be easily represented as follows: <Production

Left="P" Right="aS" LeftPr="start" RightPr="terminal, non-terminal"/>

In the same way, it is possible to represent any generated language using simple XML syntax.

- **XML Derived Languages:** unlike the standard XML that support the activities related to the fusion module, these languages deal with to the activities related to the inputs and output aspects, such as: synchronization, data exchanging, compatibility, data presentation, and so on.

Table 2 shows the main features related to selected XML derived languages (Ashimura, 2009). As it is possible to observe every language supports a specific class of multimodal problems.

FUTURE RESEARCH DIRECTIONS

The effectiveness and efficiency of the multimodal frameworks mainly depend on three aspects: recognition quality of every modality, modal and multimodal ambiguity problems, complexity of the fusion according to the set of the selected modalities. The efforts to improve multimodal frameworks interpretation should regard these three aspects. In particular, the resolution of ambiguity problems is the main aspect to address in order to obtain immediate advancements related to the recognition of complex multimodal commands to drive social computing environments.

Another real interesting future research direction regards the representation of the multimodal outputs. More specifically, there are advanced social computing applications and services that need a more representative way to convey a real sense of community or social collaboration. In particular the use of 3D avatars or advanced human agents that show a graphical representation of the outputs could provide a first step within the social computing 3D multimodal environments.

Table 2. XML Derived Languages

XML Derived Languages	Modalities	Purposes	Functions
SMIL (Synchronised Multimedia Integration Language)	Audio, Video, Images, Text, Graphics	Synchronization, Real Time Combining, Managing Temporal and Spatial Constraints, Streaming	Animation, Content Control, Layout, Linking, Media Objects, Meta Information, Transition Effects, Web-Oriented Multimodal Applications and Services
SVG (Scalable Vector Graphics) *(SVG-Tiny: for basic devices SVG-Basic: for advanced devices)*	Graphics	Interactivity, Integration of Multimedia Content, 2D & 3D Graphics	*Document Structuring, Definition of Shapes, Painting, Clipping, Masking, Compositing, Text Manipulation, Styling, Linking, Animation, Alpha Mask, Filter Effects, Zooming,, Object Manipulation and Interaction*
MPML (Multimodal Presentation Markup Language) *(MPML-VR, MPML-FLASH)*	Integration Complex Multimedia, Streaming Management	Description of complex Multimodal Presentations Based on Intelligent Agents, Media Synchronisation	Web, Mobile and Standalone Applications and Services, Multimodal Presentation Contents, Independent Intelligent Agents, Providing a Minimal Set of Tags to Control Presentation, Interactive Presentation Guidance
EMMA (Extensible Multimodal Annotation Markup Language)	Speech, Sketch, Natural Languages	Semantic Interpretations	Prearranged Keystroke Sequence, Speech Recognition Commands, Touch Screen Recognition Commands, Semantic Vocal Streaming Understanding, Semantic Gesture Streaming Understanding, Natural Language Streaming Understanding, Interactive Processes
X-Form (Extendible Form)	Interactive Complex Form	Performing Several Kinds of Data Manipulation	Web Forms, Advanced and Interactive GUI
InkML (Ink Markup Language)	Sketch, Handwriting, Graphics	Digital Ink, Data Representation, Gesture Interpretation, Behaviour Interpretation, Explaining Heterogeneous Semantic Meanings	Providing a Simple Platform to Promote the Interchange of Digital Ink Among Different Kinds of Devices Applications and Services, Data Representation about Interactive Processes Involving: Handwriting, Freehand Drawing, Sketch, Human Expressions, and so on
VoiceXML	Voice	Speech Recognition, Speech Synthesis, Control of Voice, Recognition Capacities	Recognition of Spoken Input and DTMF Input, Recording Spoken Input, Controlling Dialogue Flow, Transferring and Disconnecting Telephone Calls, Synthesising Speech and Audio Files, Identifying and Synchronization Vocal Commands
SSML (Speech Synthesis Markup Language)	Voice	Multimedia Streaming Management	Pronunciation Controlling, Tone, Inflection and Other Characteristics of Spoken Words, Capturing Text Speed, Volume, Prosody
SALT (Speech Application Language Tags)	Voice	Integration of Speech And Video	Integrating Speech and Telephone Interfaces With Web Application and Services, Supporting Speech Input and Output In Visual Interfaces

CONCLUSION

The wide spread of advanced social computing environments due to the growing improvements of both computational capability of the heterogeneous devices and potentialities of the current fast network connections, have led to evolutions in the human-computer interaction. In recent years the main task has been to identify human-oriented interaction ways able to provide natural and intuitive communication processes between users and software environments.

Multimodal interfaces exploit the normal human channels of communication and expression (e.g. speech, freehand drawing, handwriting) with the aim to convey simple or complex commands to drive any kind of social computing environment. Moreover, the different interfaces allow users to perform the interaction processes in pervasive way.

This chapter describes the main matters related to our novel and complete advanced multimodal frameworks, in particular it highlights the different aspects tied to both modal and multimodal interfaces. The described architecture provides a complete point of view about the different steps involved during multimodal interaction processes. Finally, it is important to observe that the architectural and technical solutions expressed in this chapter exploit the best advanced technologies currently used in multimodal environments.

REFERENCES

Al-Haddad, S. A. R., Samad, S. A., Hussain, A., Ishak, K. A., & Noor, A. O. A. (2009). Robust speech recognition using fusion techniques and adaptive filtering. *American Journal of Applied Sciences*, 6(2), 290–295.

Alder, A., & Davis, R. (2009). Symmetric multimodal interaction in a dynamic dialogue. In *Proceedings of Workshop on Sketch Recognition, Intelligent User Interface* (IUI'09), Sanibel Island, FL (pp. 1-10). New York: ACM Press.

Ashimura, K. (2009). Multimodal interaction activity. *Technical dissemination document on multimodal XML-based languages.* Boston: W3C Press. Retrieved from http://www.w3.org/2002/mm1/

Avola, D., & Del Buono, A. (2009). Multimodal interfaces: Classification and usability testing in heterogeneous environments [Technical Research Study, Tech. Report No. 21/09]. Rome, Italy: National Research Centre, Computer Science and Knowledge Laboratory (CSKLab). Retrieved from http://www.csklab.it

Béchet, N., Roche, M., & Chauché, J. (2009). Towards the selection of induced syntactic relations. In M. Boughanem, C. Berrut, J. Mothe & C. Soule-Dupuy (Eds.), *Advances in Information Retrieval* [Proceedings of 31th European Conference on Information Retrieval Research (ECIR'09)], (Lecture Notes in Computer Science, Vol. 5478, pp. 786-790). Berlin: Springer.

Cappé, O., Moulines, E., & Rydén, T. (Eds.). (2005). *Inference in hidden Markov models* [Springer Series in Statistics]. London: Springer.

Crespi-Reghizzi, S. (Ed.). (2009). *Formal languages and compilation*. London: Springer.

Dahl, D., Kliche, I., Tumuluri, R., Yudkowsky, M., Bodell, M., Porter, B., et al. (2008). Multimodal architecture and interfaces. In J. Barnett (Ed.), *Technical dissemination report on multimodal framework.* Boston: W3C Press. Retrieved from http://www.w3.org/TR/mmi-arch/

Del Valle-Agudo, D., Javier Calle-Gómez, J., Cuadra-Fernández, D., & Rivero-Espinosa, J. (2009). Breaking of the interaction cycle: Independent interpretation and generation for advanced dialogue management. In J. A. Jacko (Ed.), *Novel interaction methods and techniques* [Proceedings of Human-Computer Interaction, San Diego, CA] (Lecture Notes in Computer Science, Vol. 5611, pp. 674-683). Berlin: Springer.

Ertl, D. (2009). Semi-automatic multimodal user interface generation. In *Proceedings of the 1st ACM SIGCHI Symposium on engineering interactive computing systems* (EICS'09), Pittsburgh, PA (pp. 321-324). New York: ACM Press.

Fernández-Pacheco, D. G., Aleixos, N., Conesa, J., & Contero, M. (2009). Natural interface for sketch recognition. In *Advances in soft computing* [Proceedings of 7th International Conference on Practical Applications of Agents and Multi-Agent Systems (PAAMS'09)] (Vol. 55, pp. 510-519). Berlin: Springer.

Frinken, V., Peter, T., Fischer, A., Bunke, H., Do, T. M. T., & Artieres, T. (2009). Improved handwriting recognition by combining two forms of hidden Markov models and a recurrent neural network. In *Proceedings of 13th International Conference on Computer Analysis of Images and Patterns* (CAIP'09), Münster, Germany ([]. Berlin: Springer.]. *Lecture Notes in Computer Science, 5702*, 189–196. doi:10.1007/978-3-642-03767-2_23

Gurban, M., Vilaplana, V., Thiran, J. P., & Marques, F. (2008). Face and speech interaction. In Tzovaras, D. (Ed.), *Signals and communication technology: Multimodal user interfaces* (pp. 85–117). Berlin: Springer. doi:10.1007/978-3-540-78345-9_5

Huang, J., Marcheret, E., Visweswariah, K., Libal, V., & Potamianos, G. (2008). The IBM rich transcription 2007 speech-to-text systems for lecture meetings. In R. Stiefelhagen, R. Bowers & J. Fiscus (Eds.), *Multimodal Technologies for Perception of Humans* [Proceedings of International Evaluation Workshops (CLEAR'07 & RT'07), Baltimore, MD] (Lecture Notes in Computer Science, Vol. 4625, pp. 429-441). Berlin: Springer.

Kim, J. H., & Hong, K. S. (2007). An improved fusion and fission architecture between multi-modalities based on wearable computing. In J. Indulska, J. Ma, L. T. Yang, T. Ungerer & J. Cao (Eds.), *Proceedings of the 4th International Conference in Ubiquitous Intelligence and Computing*, Hong Kong, China (Lecture Notes in Computer Science, Vol. 4611, pp. 113-122). Berlin: Springer.

Koons, D., Sparrell, C., & Thorisson, K. (1993). Integrating simultaneous input from speech, gaze, and hand gestures. In Maybury, M. (Ed.), *Intelligent multimedia interfaces* (pp. 257–276). Cambridge, MA: MIT Press.

Macé, S., & Anquetil, E. (2009). Pattern recognition strategies for interactive sketch composition. In *Novel Interaction Methods and Techniques: Proceedings of 13th International Conference on Human-Computer Interaction* (HCI'09), San Diego, CA ([]. Berlin: Springer.]. *Lecture Notes in Computer Science, 5611*, 840–849.

Manning, C. D., & Schuetze, H. (1999). *Foundations of statistical natural language processing*. Boston: MIT Press.

Mendonça, H. (2009). High level data fusion on a multimodal interactive application platform. In *Proceedings of the 1st ACM SIGCHI Symposium on Engineering Interactive Computing Systems* (EICS'09), Pittsburgh, PA (pp. 333-336). New York: ACM Press.

Oviatt, S. L. (2003). Advances in robust multimodal interface design. In [Washington, DC: IEEE Computer Society Press.]. *Proceedings of IEEE Computer Graphics and Applications, 23*(5), 62–68. doi:10.1109/MCG.2003.1231179

Oviatt, S. L. (2008). Multimodal interfaces. In Jacko, J., & Sears, A. (Eds.), *The human-computer interaction handbook: Fundamentals, evolving technologies and emerging applications* (2nd ed., pp. 286–304). Boca Raton, FL: CRC Press.

Parag, M. J., & Liu, S. (2009). Web document text and images extraction using DOM analysis and natural language processing. In *Proceeding of Document Engineering Conference* (DocEng'09), Munich, Germany (pp. 218-221). New York: ACM Press.

Parkes, A. P. (Ed.). (2002). *Introduction to languages, machines and logic: Computable languages, abstract machines and formal logic*. New York: Springer.

Quin, L. (2009). Extensible markup language (XML). *Technical dissemination documents on XML*. Boston: W3C Press.

Ravakhah, M., & Kamyar, M. (2009). Semantic similarity based focused crawling. In *Proceedings of the 1th International Conference on Computational Intelligence, Communication Systems and Networks*, Los Alamitos, CA (pp. 448-453). Washington, DC: IEEE Computer Society.

Ronzhin, A. L., & Budkov, V. Y. (2009). Multimodal interaction with intelligent meeting room facilities from inside and outside. In S. Balandin, D. Moltchanov & Y. Koucheryavy (Eds.), *Smart Spaces and Next Generation Wired/Wireless Networking* [Proceedings of 9th International Conference Next Generation Wired/Wireless Networking and 2th Conference on Smart Spaces (NEW2AN'09 & ruSMART'09), St. Petersburg, Russia] (Lecture Notes in Computer Science, Vol. 5764, pp. 77-88). Berlin: Springer.

Wu, L., Oviatt, S. L., & Cohen, P. (1999). Multimodal integration: A statistical view. *IEEE Transactions on Multimedia*, *1*(4), 334–341. doi:10.1109/6046.807953

ADDITIONAL READING

Abney, S. (Ed.). (2008). *Semisupervised learning for computational linguistics* [CRC Computer Science & Data Analysis series]. Boca Raton, FL: Chapman & Hall/CRC Press.

Bordegoni, M., Faconti, G., Feiner, S., Maybury, M. T., Rist, T., & Ruggieri, S. (1997). A standard reference model for intelligent multimedia presentation systems. *Computer Standards & Interfaces*, *18*(6-7), 477–496. doi:10.1016/S0920-5489(97)00013-5

Daisuke, S., Koichiro, H., Masahiko, I., & Takeo, I. (2009). Sketch and run: A stroke-based interface for home robots. In *Proceedings of the 27th International Conference on Human Factors in Computing* Systems (CHI'09), Boston, MA (pp. 197-200). New York: ACM Press.

Demirdjian, D., Ko, T., & Darrell, T. (2005). Untethered gesture acquisition and recognition for virtual world manipulation. *International Journal on Virtual Reality*, *8*(4), 222–230. doi:10.1007/s10055-005-0155-3

Duarte, C., & Carriço, L. (2009). When you can't read it, listen to it! An audio-visual interface for book reading. In *Proceedings of 5th International Conference on Universal Access in Human-Computer Interaction. Applications and Services* (UAHCI'09) ([]. Berlin: Springer.]. *Lecture Notes in Computer Science*, *5616*, 24–33. doi:10.1007/978-3-642-02713-0_3

Elting, C., Rapp, S., Möhler, G., & Strube, M. (2003). Architecture and implementation of multimodal plug and play. In *Proceedings of the 5th international Conference on Multimodal interfaces* (ICMI'03), Vancouver, Canada (pp. 93-100). New York: ACM Press.

Feldaman, R., & Sanger, J. (Eds.). (2007). *The text mining handbook: Advanced approaches in analyzing unstructured data*. Cambridge: Cambridge University Press.

Forman, I. R., Brunet, T., Luther, P., & Wilson, A. (2009). Using ASR for transcription of teleconferences in IM systems. In *Proceedings of 5th International Conference on Universal Access in Human-Computer Interaction: Applications and Services* (UAHCI'09) ([]. Berlin: Springer.]. *Lecture Notes in Computer Science*, *5616*, 521–529. doi:10.1007/978-3-642-02713-0_55

Forsyth, E. N., & Martell, C. H. (2007). Lexical and discourse analysis of online chat dialog. In *Proceedings of the 1th IEEE International Conference on Semantic Computing* (pp. 19-26). Washington, DC: IEEE Computer Society Publisher.

Horchani, M., Caron, B., Nigay, L., & Panaget, F. (2007). Natural multimodal dialogue systems: A configurable dialogue and presentation strategies component. In *Proceedings of the 9th international Conference on Multimodal interfaces* (ICMI '07), Nagoya, Aichi, Japan (pp. 291-298). New York: ACM Press.

Horchani, M., Nigay, L., & Panaget, F. (2007). A platform for output dialogic strategies in natural multimodal dialogue systems. In *Proceedings of the 12th international Conference on intelligent User interfaces* (IUI '07), Honolulu, Hawaii (pp. 206-215). New York: ACM Press.

House, B., Malkin, J., & Bilmes, J. (2009). The VoiceBot: A voice controlled robot arm. In *Proceedings of the 27th international Conference on Human Factors in Computing Systems* (CHI '09), Boston, MA (pp. 183-192). New York: ACM Press.

Izquierdo, J. L. C., & Molina, J. G. (2009). A domain specific language for extracting models in software modernization. In R. F. Paige, A. Hartman & A. Rensink (Eds.), *Proceedings of Model Driven Architecture: Foundations and Applications* (Lecture Notes in Computer Science, Vol. 5562, pp. 82-97). Berlin: Springer.

Kaindl, H., Falb, J., & Bogdan, C. (2008). Multimodal Communication Involving Movements of a Robot. In *Proceedings of Conference on Human Factors in Computing Systems: Extended Abstracts on Human Factors in Computing Systems* (CHI'08) (pp. 3213-3218), ACM Press.

Leporini, B., Buzzi, M. C., & Mori, G. (2009). Automatically structuring text for audio learning. In *Proceedings of 5th International Conference on Universal Access in Human-Computer Interaction: Applications and Services* (UAHCI'09) ([]. Berlin: Springer.]. *Lecture Notes in Computer Science, 5616*, 73–82. doi:10.1007/978-3-642-02713-0_8

Linz, P. (Ed.). (2006). *An introduction to formal language and automata.* Sudbury, MA: Jones & Bartlett.

Nagy, B. (2009). Permutation languages in formal linguistics. In A. Prieto & J. M. Corchado (Eds.), *Bio-inspired systems: Computational and ambient intelligence* [Proceedings of the 10th International Work-Conference on Artificial Neural Networks (IWANN'09)] (Lecture Notes in Computer Science, Vol. 5517, pp. 504-511). Berlin: Springer.

Nakano, Y., & Yamaoka, Y. (2009). Information state based multimodal dialogue management: Estimating conversational engagement from gaze information. In *Proceedings of 9th Conference on Intelligent Virtual Agents* (IVA'09), Amsterdam, The Netherlands ([]. Berlin: Springer.]. *Lecture Notes in Computer Science, 5773*, 531–532. doi:10.1007/978-3-642-04380-2_77

O'Donnell, T. J., Goodman, N. D., & Tenenbaum, J. B. (2009). *Fragment grammars: Exploring computation and reuse in language* [Technical report MIT-CSAIL-TR-2009-013]. Cambridge, MA: MIT Computer Science and Artificial Intelligence Laboratory.

Oviatt, S. L. (2006). Human-centered design meets cognitive load theory: Designing interfaces that help people think. In *Proceedings of 14th Annual ACM International Conference on Multimedia*, Santa Barbara, CA (pp. 871-880). New York: ACM Press.

Oviatt, S. L., Coulston, R., Tomko, S., Xiao, B., Lunsford, R., Wesson, M., & Carmichael, L. (2003). Toward a theory of organized multimodal integration patterns during human-computer interaction. In *Proceedings of 5th International Conference on Multimodal Interfaces* (ICMI'03), Vancouver, Canada. New York: ACM Press.

Paraiso, E. C., & Barthès, J. A. (2005). An intelligent speech interface for personal assistants applied to knowledge management. *Web Intelligent and Agent Systems, 3*(4), 217-230. Amsterdam: IOS Press.

Ranta, A. (2007). Modular grammar engineering in GF. *International Journal in Research on Language & Computation, 5*(2), 133–158. doi:10.1007/s11168-007-9030-6

Rousseau, C., Bellik, Y., Vernier, F., & Bazalgette, D. (2006). A framework for the intelligent multimodal presentation of information. *Signal Processing, 86*(12), 3696–3713. doi:10.1016/j.sigpro.2006.02.041

Steimle, J. (2009). Designing pen-and-paper user interfaces for interaction with documents. In *Proceedings of the 3rd International Conference on Tangible and Embedded Interaction* (TEI'09), Cambridge, UK (pp. 197-204). New York: ACM Press.

Sun, Y., Shi, Y., Chen, F., & Chung, V. (2007). An efficient unification-based multimodal language processor in multimodal input fusion. In *Entertaining User Interfaces: Proceedings of the 19th Australasian Conference on Computer-Human Interaction* (OZCHI'07) (Vol. 251, pp. 215-218). New York: ACM Press.

Sun, Y., Shi, Y., Chen, F., & Chung, V. (2009). Building a practical multimodal system with a multimodal fusion module. In J. A. Jacko (Ed.), *Novel Interaction Methods and Techniques: Proceedings of Human-Computer Interaction,* San Diego, CA (Lecture Notes in Computer Science, Vol. 5611, pp. 93-102). Berlin: Springer.

KEY TERMS AND DEFINITIONS

Fission: This term points out the possibility to generate an appropriate information using more than one output modalities. Usually, the fission process is used to provide an enriched informative content to the user, it allows the user to have a more suitable output from the devices. In particular, the several redundancy aspects of the output are useful to support the user during output understanding process.

Fusion: This term points out the possibility to integrate information from different input modalities. The fusion process involves several aspects of multimodal interfaces. A common aspect regards the use of multiple modal inputs to improve the semantic meaning of the command and/or concept expressed by the user during communication activities. Another aspect can regard the overcoming of ambiguities during command/concept recognition. However, the fusion process is always aimed to face the critical aspects due to the human computer interaction. The redundancy aspects can be handled to ensure a more valuable interpretation of what has expressed the user.

Interaction: In this context this term points out the communication ways between the human beings and the desktop or mobile systems (that is, the devices). In particular, it highlights the possibility to use "natural ways" (such as: voice, freehand drawing, touch, and so on), both to provide information to the devices (such as: commands, queries, concepts, and so on) and to receive feedback from the devices (such as: information, indications, confirmation, and so on).

Modality: The term is used to describe the distinct methods to interact with a mobile or desktop system. Usually these methods are used to facilitate the human-device communication. There are two types of modality approach: direct and indirect. The direct approach regards those modalities that tend to provide a direct command and/or concept to the system, such as: speech, sketch, handwriting, gesture, and so on. All these modalities make explicit a clear intention of the user to interact with the device. Instead, the indirect approaches are used to catch the intention of the user to interact with a device, such as: gaze, eye-tracking, emotional face recognition, posture recognition, and so on. In is important to observe that, usually, the modalities are used both to provide information to the systems and to receive feedback from the systems.

Multimodality: This term is used to highlight the possibility to interact with a mobile or desktop system using more than one modality. Usually, the term is used to suggest the possibilities for the user both to provide information to the systems and to receive a feedback from the systems using different modalities. There are two main issues for which are used multimodal systems. The first one regards the possibility to provide to the user a set of alternative suitable modalities to interact with the system in order to face every kind of:

environment, situation, location, and so on. The second one regards the possibility use more than one modality to enrich the communication process between the user and the system. Besides, the multimodality is also used to overcome interpretation issues, such as: ambiguity errors, noise errors, misunderstanding errors, and so on.

Pervasively: In this context this term suggests the opportunity, due to the actual mobile devices, by which a user can interact, anywhere and anytime, with every kind of application and/or service. In particular, this term highlights the recent trend of people to use advanced mobile devices to perform any activities of their everyday life.

Chapter 12

A Social Relational Network– Based Architecture for Maintaining the Media Integrity and Optimizing the Quality of Experience:
A Technical and Business Perspective

Harilaos G. Koumaras
University of Bordeaux, France

Jose Oscar Fajardo
University of the Basque Country, Spain

Fidel Liberal
University of the Basque Country, Spain

Lingfen Sun
University of Plymouth, UK

Vaios Koumaras
Business College of Athens, Greece

Costas Troulos
PCN, Greece

Anastasios Kourtis
National Centre for Scientific Research Demokritos, Greece

ABSTRACT

This chapter proposes a Content-aware and Network-aware Management System (CNMS) over a converged user-environment of social networking and mobile multimedia. The proposed CNMS will focus on applying dynamic personalized multi-layer adaptation for the optimization of the Quality of Experience (QoE) level in a requested media service according to the users' preferences, favourites provided in their social network profile, and prior experiences rated by users themselves. By user's preference extraction, a service/content classification will be performed according to an estimation of the user's favourites, which will be used to provide optimized media delivery across the delivery chain. Therefore, the end-

DOI: 10.4018/978-1-61692-904-6.ch012

user will always receive her/his favourite service, like Internet Protocol Television (IPTV), Voice over Internet Protocol (VoIP), interactive application/on-line gaming, web browsing, at requested QoE. The system will ensure optimal allocation of network resources and optimal selection of streaming scheme according to different services/content types and user preferences, and therefore enhance the ratio of price-for-value for the specific subscription and achieve an end-to-end, holistic QoE optimisation. Although QoE is perceived as subjective, it is the only measure that counts for customers of a service. Being able to estimate the user preferences in a controlled manner through the end-user's social networks profiles, helps operators understand what may be wrong with their services and their respective QoE. The proposed multimodal management system is user-centric and applies advanced machine learning techniques in order to extract user preferences from the social network profile of the user and build up a ranking scale of the services/contents. This ranking scale will be translated to adaptation actions per service type at several instances such as before the provision of the service takes place (i.e. Time Zero), during the delivering of the service (i.e. Time T), across all the network layers and delivery-chain nodes, while ensuring throughout the process that the main focus on the QoS-adaptation of the mobile access network is maintained.

INTRODUCTION

One of the visions of mobile communication networks is that necessary capabilities will be developed to support the creation, sharing, locating and delivery of new-media content in a consumer mass market based on the provision of content adapted to the user preferences. There are numerous approaches to this marketing model, but the most important is the Quality of Experience (QoE) concept, because it provides a direct link to user-satisfaction. Today, a typical mobile end-user subscribes to a service in order to have access to, and be able to receive in real-time, media content relevant to his/her preferences. However, the subscription cost usually corresponds to a bouquet of services (e.g., various channels and contents provided through mobile IPTV) without any discrimination or specialization of the available content to the user preferences.

In fact most business models are based on charging once for a bit-pipe content-unaware connection and then for every single content or suite of them. Therefore, a subscriber today pays the same price for content that may not be her/his favourite one, as for content that ranks high in her/his ranking scale. On the other hand, the service/

network provider is not aware of this service un-favouriteness from the user side, and therefore treats any requested media in a similar way both from the engineering and charging aspect, without taking under consideration the user's preference of the requested content.

Thus, current mobile operator's infrastructure does not consider any QoE-aware management mechanism within its service provision and control system. On the contrary, existing management mechanisms (e.g. traffic prioritization and classification etc.) are only network-oriented and perform management without considering user preferences/favouriteness of the requested content. Moreover, from the psychological aspect, an end-user is usually satisfied with a subscribed service when she/he receives the content that she/he likes at good perceptual quality (e.g., her/his favourite TV show), which is also the main reason that she/he has finally subscribed to the specific service.

Consequently, this favouriteness effect is not limited to content but also applies to services themselves. For example, many users would pay for a mobile flat data rate only because they want VoIP services and will make an occasional use of the rest of available services. So, for the remaining contents that may be provided by a service bouquet, and to which the end-user may have access through the specific subscription program, the user will not be dissatisfied even if she/he occasionally does not receive them flawless or even in excellent quality. For example, consider an end-user who is a soccer fan and subscribes to a mobile IPTV service through its mobile operator for watching football games of his/her favourite team when she/he is on the move. Taking the case that during a semi-final game of his/her favourite team, this end-user experiences low perceptual quality and playback problems of the requested live IPTV content (i.e. the semi-final football game). Then this situation will raise a lot of complaints to the mobile operator and the content provider of the specific service, because the specific customer has been subscribed to this service in order to watch football games (good quality is considered as given when you pay for a service). Therefore, it is necessary for a content provider and network operator in order to satisfy its customers, to identify their preferences (through a user-profiling mechanism) and take the appropriate actions that will provide such a QoE level, which will meet the expected standards of the user/customer.

Currently, a place where the users tend to post a lot of information relevant to their preferences, customs, choices, pleasures and tastes is the online social relational networks, which this chapter proposes to exploit as a data repository for user profiling processes.

Nowadays, online social relational networks like Facebook have flourished as a novel component of business Internet strategy of online services, triggering the creation of numerous new social networking sites originating from different countries and offering a variety of languages (Freeman, 2006). A social networking service focuses on building online communities of people who share interests and activities, or who are interested in exploring the interests and activities of others. Most social network services are web based and provide a variety of powerful new ways for users to interact, create, deliver, share, retrieve and fuse multimedia content (e.g., Facebook and its applications). This multimodal environment of social networking in the era of multimedia convergence with mobile/fixed networks is creating new opportunities for high quality and user-responsive service provision management.

Consequently, it is becoming very profound that towards a content-aware network and network-aware applications, the business-affordable and marketing-expected solution may result from the convergence between the mobile operators and the social networking providers. Moreover, this is enhanced by the fact that the mobile operators and the social networking providers are considered the dominant players in the worldwide digital market, under the conceptual umbrella of integrated mobile management systems and infrastructures of the converged mobile media market (e.g., IMS).

The manipulation of Perceived QoS for the optimization of the Quality of Experience during the creation, sharing, delivery and consumption of multimedia services and applications will make the most of both the ever increasing device/edge processing power and network bandwidth, especially for real time and highly demanding immersive collaborative environments. Towards this objective, a key issue for preserving the scalability and commercial viability of any proposed QoE-based approach is the discrimination per user of the content that she/he is interested to receive in optimized scale of perceived quality according to the current network/context conditions. In future, within the expected immersive collaborative environment, users will play a major role either as content producers, consumers or managers. It is therefore becoming more demanding than ever before to develop a new approach to the management of the available contents, and the discrimination and classification of them according to the user preferences.

The chapter will present an architecture of a converged user-environment of social networking and mobile multimedia services, which will be focused on applying dynamic personalized multi-layer adaptation for the optimization of the Quality of Experience (QoE) level in a requested media service according to the user preferences and favorites provided in her/his social network profile and prior experiences rated by users themselves. The chapter will cover both the technological and business perspective of the proposed architecture.

BACKGROUND

The advances and the novel characteristics of the proposed architecture are focused on the following areas: i) User-Profiling ii) Cross layer adaptation techniques iii) Social-Networking iv) Service Management v) Integrated mobile management system and QoE, and vi) Services in an integrated mobile management system. A detailed analysis of each of them follows.

Advances in User-Profile Definition

It is of great importance to provide a personalized system, which can automatically adapt to the interests and interest-levels of users. User profiling is a promising approach towards personalized systems where a user profile, including interests, levels and preference patterns can be assessed when content is requested. Based on the profile setup, personalized content could be generated or proposed to match individual preferences and levels.

User profiling is commonly and currently employed to enhance usability as well as to support personalization, adaptivity and other user-centric features. Application designers model user profiles mainly in an ad-hoc manner, which therefore hinders application interoperability at user profile level, thereby increasing the amount of work to be done, and the possibility of errors or omissions in the profile model (Mislove, 2010). Current techniques for setting and defining a user profile, according to users' interests and preferences are mainly categorized into the following classes:

- *Questionnaires/Ratings*: Most approaches of user profiling are heavily dependent on user feedbacks to construct user profiles. The feedback can be assessed by rating, or implicitly by specific questionnaires that the customer/user is asked to answer or rate specific items/services during service subscription. This procedure is used to define an explicit user profile based on user ratings and/or questionnaires.

- *Stereotypes*: Users with common interests can be grouped, and feedback from a single user can serve as a guideline for information delivery to other members within the same group. The service provider has created user stereotypes that correspond to specific service preferences and each newcomer is classified into one of these, based on such criteria as age, educational background etc.

- *User History*: Observation-based user profiling and profile matching is performed when a service provider classifies users to specific groups with similar preferences, based on their long or short term behaviour. By observing network behaviour instead of necessarily relying on user self-reported data, accurate and objective user profiles can be formed. The user profiles can be with respect to a domain and two or more users can be matched based on their profiles with respect to the same domain.

- *Collaborative Filtering*: Based on item/user based profiling that has been performed per user according to one of the previous methods, it is possible to perform collaborative filtering by correlating preferences of similar user profiles. By this way, the system may recommend or predict specific preferences to a user, for whom a lack of data deprives the direct personalization of the service.

Consequently, user profiling is considered difficult to perform in real time at the time of the content request. At this point, the proposed architecture advances beyond the current state-of-the-art in user profiling systems by proposing real-time user-centric content adaptation based on a hybrid model, which consists of stereotyping, collaborative filtering and user history based on the preferences and data that the user stores in her/his social network profile. The scope of the proposed architecture is to perform personalized multi-layer adaptation of the requested service and an optimization of the delivered QoE-level according to user preferences. Consequently, the proposed architecture creates new circumstances through the proposed sophisticated profiling system, considering that the users/customers/subscribers will be satisfied with the service they are using/paying/subscribed, given that they receive the requested content at the appropriate QoE level (i.e. somewhat relevant to their preferences) without any bandwidth wastage. Hence, the level of user satisfaction with a service can be taken as a rough measure of the personalized multi-layer adaptation that would be performed by this chapter. Thus, the proposed architecture will know who the user is and what their particular preferences and idiosyncrasies are. This will enable a better of a QoE-level to the user that will fully satisfy her/him for the content that she/he is looking for.

Advances in Multi-Layer and Cross-Layer Adaptation

Multi-Layer and Cross-Layer Adaptation (CLA) schemes, especially in the areas of streaming multimedia and wireless/ mobile networks, have attracted significant attention in the last couple of years. A lot of research (Yuana, 2003) aims at offering some kind of CLA. However, all the currently proposed schemes are network-oriented by specializing to specific network technologies and specific transmission conditions, which for the case of PQoS optimization the specific network parameters are mapped according to PQoS impact.

Our approach in this chapter goes beyond all the current approaches, proposing a novel personalized multi-layer adaptation, which takes the following characteristics into consideration:

- The proposed approach does not simply aim at maximizing user satisfaction by optimizing, through adaptation actions, the respective QoS-sensitive network parameters. On the contrary it also aims at applying a personalized/user-centric multi-layer adaptation concept across the network nodes and layers that are involved in the content delivery process in order to provide to the user, the appropriate QoE satisfaction, which is relevant to users' preferences that are stored/contained in her/his social network profile.

- The proposed architecture does not propose just another technique for cross layer adaptation aiming at optimized user experience, but it aims at providing the requested content at the appropriate QoE level based on the end-user preferences. This does not mean that the provision of service will be isotropically maximized for all the users that may experience degraded quality, but it will be specialized at the appropriate QoE level according to user preferences. Thus, the vision of this chapter goes beyond the existing purely engineering and NQoS-specialized adaptation schemes, showing the path and leading the reader towards the future intelligent and personalized user-centric adaptation techniques.

- The proposed approach is not bounded to a specific network technology. On the contrary, it is applied across the network delivery chain of the requested multimedia service, covering heterogeneous network technologies (i.e. DiffServ/MPLS Core and UMTS/HSPA Access network).

- The proposed personalized multi-layer adaptation is content-aware, considering in its adaptation actions the spatial and/or temporal dynamics of the requested media service, moving by this way forward towards a content-aware network.
- It exceeds up to the application layer, integrating in its actions the dynamic adaptation of the encoding/streaming parameters

Advances in Social Networking

Social networking is a phenomenon in the World Wide Web which is simply defined as linking and grouping of individuals into specific groups, like small rural communities. In particular, social networking is perceived as a practice of expanding the number of one's business and/or social contacts by making connections through numerous individuals. While social networking has gone on almost as long as societies themselves have existed, the unparalleled potential of the Internet to promote such connections has been fully recognized and exploited, through Web-based groups established for that purpose, in the last years. This socialization may range from simple actions such as reading the profile pages of other members and possibly even contacting them, up to sharing common interests, such as favourite songs/movies, hobbies, religion, topics, experiences or politics.

The proposed architecture exploits this tendency of online socializing, to propose a Content-aware and Network-aware Management System (CNMS) over a converged user-environment of social networking and mobile multimedia services, which will make use of the data that each user stores/advertises on their social profile as input for performing real time user-profiling when a customer requests to receive a specific media service. Based on this social profile-driven user profiling, the proposed CNMS will adapt the QoE of a requested media service to the appropriate level, which will meet the standards and preferences of the end-user (exactly as these are depicted in her/his social profile).

Therefore, the proposed architecture considers, as a priori, the fact that end-users/customers of future ICT market will also be holders of social network profiles. This requirement does not seem to be in contrast to the current trend of online socializing, considering that according to the HitWise report, Myspace and Bebo were already the leaders in the UK, with 33% market share each back in May 2007 and Facebook coming in third place with a 13% market share. It is clear therefore, that end-users/customers are very eager to perform online socializing and it seems that this trend is going to increase in the next years, based on the facts that i) social networking now accounts for 4% of all UK internet visits, which corresponds to a 79% increase in one year and ii) end-users/consumers spend more time on social networking sites than any others, accounting to an average of 25 minutes. In fact in the speech towards Safer Social Networking given by Viviane Reding on 10 February 2009, new updated data were presented, citing a growth of 35% of European use of social networking between June 2007 and June 2008 resulting in a forecast to rise from today's 41.7 million to 107.4 million in the next four years.

Thus, the proposed architecture taking into account this trend comes to move forward beyond the current state-of-the-art and comes to exploit the information that any user offers freely at his social network profile. More specifically, the vision of this chapter is to create the basis for the next generation social-network profiling, which will move forward from the existing standalone scope for socializing only, and will follow an evolution towards the next generation of social-networking, which will be convergent with the existing mobile operator services. Therefore, the proposed architecture within the convergent environment proposes a personalized multi-layer adaptation with scope the provision of the requested media at the appropriate QoE level, which will cause the respective user satisfaction, subject to preferences and the user-profile ranking that has been created from the data that the user has posted on her/his social network profile.

In addition, the most of the existing social networking sites and standards seem to seriously take into consideration the mere fact of the connection usually existing between users in a social network. In the proposed architecture we will utilize the fact that there is rich semantics of the various connections between users in the social network. People interact with each other directly and indirectly around various objects – such as documents, media items, social events etc. Using this information will enable much better modelling of user's behaviour by not only analyzing user's profile, but also her/his relevant interactions with other users around the social-net graph. By researching the impact of user's behaviour online, the proposed architecture hopes to achieve much better understanding of user's preferences and as such create a superior content adjustment/adaptation system, which will assist QoE requirements of the media users.

The extraction of the preferences and the user-profile-ranking through the proposed architecture will provide an evolutionary social networking, where the clients from typical passive users become active, where the posted data on their profile does not only simply used for networking purposes but define their preferences in many areas and actively affect the QoE/user satisfaction level of received media services at their mobile terminals. Therefore, the proposed architecture does not only provide a novel concept in the area of content-aware network and network-aware applications but it also creates the birth, and causes the advent of a sophisticated and convergent social networking, a service that if exploited appropriately may bring significant wealth to the European market.

Advances in Service Management

Regarding the research in the area of the service management, the proposed architecture leaves back typical network related management systems

and proposes a service management extension to the existing integrated management system of mobile operators, by exploiting the social-network profiles of the customers/users and QoE concept in order to adapt the service provision with twofold objectives:

- Maximization of the end users' satisfaction by taking into account their preferences as they are extracted by the CNMS from their social-network profile.
- Minimization of the impact of possible service degradations by obtaining the greater number of satisfied users.

In accordance to this, the proposed architecture recommends an intelligent machine learning management system, which will scroll the social network profile of the end-user and it will deduce specific decisions concerning the QoE level at which the end-user will be satisfied by the provision of the requested media content. Moreover, the proposed architecture will exploit for the proposed dynamic cross adaptation procedure different mechanisms that are expected to support a better QoE management in the provision of multimedia services. The use and integration of these adapting mechanisms into a common QoE-aware management system is a move beyond the current state of the art, which its novelty is further supported by the integration of the proposed management system within the integrated mobile management system platform.

Some of these service adapting mechanisms that will be integrated in the proposed management system are:

- Content adaptation in the the proposed architecture compliant servers with regard to a set of media parameters such as the codec and bitrate or spatio-temporal characteristics.
- Exploiting more 'classical' network resource management mechanisms (e.g.

DiffServ/MPLS) that guarantee specific NQoS levels associated to the traffic belonging to critical sessions, through intelligent traffic marking and classification of traffic flows to be forwarded to the deployed traffic engineering mechanisms.

- Error resilience adaptation, in order to improve the service robustness at the reception through the use of more efficient FEC schemes at the service generation.

The majority of the current research related to service management have been mainly restricted to technical issues rather than in analyzing their applicability to the management of users' satisfaction. Only limited research has been performed towards the use of QoE evaluations as input for service management mechanisms, but even these cases are in general related to concrete mechanisms or they simply use a limited set of QoE characteristics only for monitoring purposes. The proposed architecture with a pioneering way comes to propose a new concept of service management, which includes QoE-driven service adaptation according to the user-profiling that is performed based on data that have been posted on the user's social-network profile. So, the proposed architecture introduces the new era of the personalized service management, where the social network and the concept of QoE play a major and active role, targeting at user satisfaction according to her/his preferences and tastes.

Advances in Existing Integrated Mobile Management Systems and QoE

Fixed/mobile convergence is a massive trend that requires adequate network and service infrastructures. One of the visions of this trend is that services will be sold in a consumer mass market based on the provision of content at a requested

quality, exploiting the QoE concept. The evaluation of the QoE for multimedia content that have variable bandwidth demands, will provide a user with a range of potential choices covering for example the possibilities of low, medium or high quality levels, indication of service availability and costs. However, the integrated mobile management system infrastructure currently does not consider any QoE management mechanism within its service provision management system, eliminating its traffic policies to the UMTS PCC system (from Release 7), which is a typical traffic differentiation mechanism that classifies the service bearers to different classes with specific QoS constraints.

In this brewing environment, the proposed architecture, going beyond the current state-of-the-art and paving the way to the future interaction between Multimedia Services and integrated mobile management systems, will extend the existing management system capabilities of mobile operators with QoE-aware mechanisms. The proposed introduces the concept of QoE awareness into current converged management systems, towards which the whole traffic engineering is not performed abruptly, but with scope the QoE adaptation at the appropriate level, which will meet the user's standards according to her/his preferences, as they have been extracted and predicted by the posted data on her/his social-network profile.

The concept of this chapter could be applied to a variety of telecommunication platforms that could be used for the needs of the proposed architecture. Among the various candidate platforms, the IMS has been selected for the needs of this chapter because it is believed that according to its specifications and capabilities, it is expected to have the highest market penetration and will finally prevail from the competition and adopted by the big market players.

THE PROPOSED ARCHITECTURE

Conceptual and Technical Description

The manipulation of Perceived QoS for the optimization of the Quality of Experience during the creation, sharing, delivery and consumption of multimedia services and applications will make the most of both the ever increasing device/edge processing power and network bandwidth, especially for real time and highly demanding immersive collaborative environments. As a result, a key issue for preserving the scalability and commercial viability of any proposed QoE-based approach is the discrimination per user of the content that she/he is interested to receive in optimized scale of perceived quality according to the current network/context conditions. In future, within the expected immersive collaborative environment, users will play a major role either as content producers, consumers or managers. It is therefore becoming more demanding than ever before to develop a new approach to the management of the available contents, and the discrimination and classification of them according to the user preferences.

This chapter proposes a Content-aware and Network-aware Management System (CNMS) over a converged user-environment of social networking and mobile multimedia services, which will be focused on applying dynamic personalized multi-layer adaptation policies for the optimization of the QoE level in a requested media service according to the user's preferences and favourites provided in her/his social network profile/graph and prior experiences rated by user her/himself. By user's preference extraction, a service/content classification will be performed according to an estimation of the user's scale of values, which will be used to provide a flawless and optimized media delivery across the delivery chain. The end-user will therefore always receive her/his favourite program without experiencing quality degradation and service unavailability,

facts which will i) minimize end-user's complaints to the network operator/service provider; ii) maximize subscriber's satisfaction; iii) ensure optimal provisioning of network resources (via QoE multiplexing gain); iv) enhance the ratio of price-for-value for the specific subscription. Although QoE is perceived as subjective, it is the only measure that counts for customers/subscribers of a service. Being able to estimate user's preferences in a controlled manner through the end-user's social networks profiles, helps operators understand what may be wrong with their services and their respective QoE level. Thus, this multimodal management system will minimize required network resources and maximize user satisfaction. It will be user-centric (i.e. initiated by any user request performed by a mobile user) and will, firstly apply advanced machine learning techniques in order to extract user preferences/favourites from the social network profile of the user and build up a scale of values (i.e. ranking of services/contents). Afterwards, the CNMS will translate the scale of values of each user in an integrated and coherent way to adaptation actions across all the network layers and delivery-chain nodes by applying intelligent traffic management policies before the provision of the service take place (i.e. time zero T0 of the media lifecycle). The CNMS will check periodically the Access network for possible bottleneck situations, and the whole adapting procedure will be re-performed, reassuring flawless service provision across the media lifecycle, whenever transitory network degradation situation is observed then. The aim of the proposed architecture from the user aspect is to satisfy the customers by providing the appropriate QoE level per content/service according to her/his preferences, while from the network management perspective aims at providing optimized exploitation of the available network resources (at the core/access network) to meet QoE requirement for different types of services and contents.

An overview of the proposed CNMS is depicted in Figure 1. On the left, a social networking relational graph such as Facebook is depicted, where the end-user provides profile information, group memberships, installed applications, friend-relations, and her/his preferences on various categories (e.g. music, cinema, literature, sports etc). The CNMS, upon end-user login, retrieves/ extracts from the social network profile of the end-user, data that is relevant in order to refresh user profile and reconstruct her/his scale of values based on this information and prior user ratings on media content that has already consumed. By extraction of the user-preferences, the CNMS will be able to later classify all requested service/ content to a favouriteness ranking scale according to the user-preferences, using machine-learning techniques, and afterwards accordingly, adapt the network nodes across the media delivery chain in order to apply the policy priorities in the service provision, subject to the user's favouriteness of the specific service/content. CNMS will not only retrieve the end user's profile, but will also analyze the user's interaction with other users. It will then build an augmented social network by taking into consideration the semantics of user's

interactions. For example, if user A read the same document as user B, the document will augment the connection in the graph. It will allow us not only to understand user's preferences by analyzing user's interactions with the content, but also take into consideration both the interactions of the user with other users around the content and also profiles of users related to the user in the context of the content.

The scope of the CNMS is to prioritize the service provision based on end-user preferences, defining the appropriate QoE level and NQoS policies that will i) Assure the suitable QoE level and ii) Guarantee the satisfaction of the end-user. All these requirements will be satisfied according to how much the end-user likes the requested content, based on the extracted user preferences from their social networking profile. Whenever a user requests a service/content her/his entire profile and scale of values is already built up and updated, so that the personalized multi-layer adaptation decision can be easily taken. By applying this kind of asynchronous approach, scalability and responsiveness will be ensured.

Figure 1. Conceptual diagram of the content-aware and network-aware management system (CNMS)

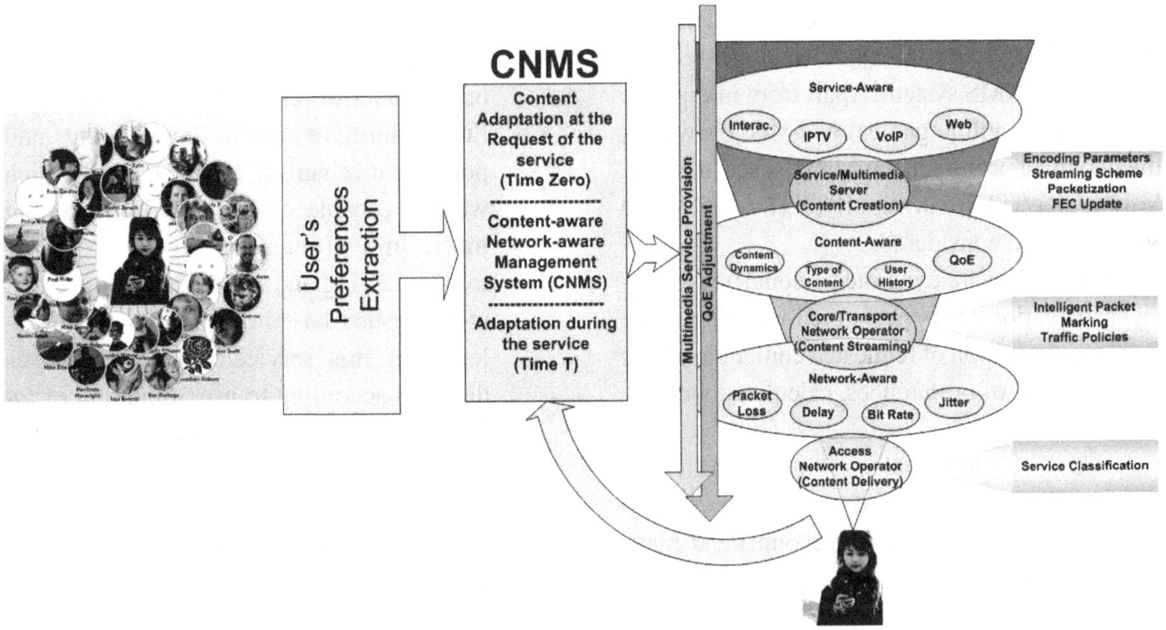

Therefore, as shown in Figure 1, a service-aware, content-aware and network-aware approach is proposed, because upon the service request, CNMS performs a content classification based on the user's preferences that have been extracted from the user's posted data on her/his social profile. Based on this user's preferences-driven ranking of the content, then the CNMS decides at the service layer the encoding/application parameters that must be followed for adjusting the QoE level to the users requirements. Afterwards, the content-aware module of the CNMS decides on the specific network/link QoS parameters, at which the specific service is sensitive (e.g. for interactive services such as online games the lag and latency are the basic QoS-sensitive parameters). Based on this classification, the CNMS decides which QoS policies will be applied during the provision of the requested service. The parameterization of the QoS policies is performed by the network-aware capabilities of the CNMS, which applies the appropriate QoS classification across the media delivery chain of the core network. Therefore, the proposed personalized multilayer adaptation includes service/application layer adaptation (e.g. source codec type, coding parameters and FEC), network layer adaptation (e.g. traffic policies) and link layer adaptation (e.g. service classification), which will all be controlled by an intelligent engine within the CNMS system. Apart from interactive services (i.e. online games) and web browsing, the two most promising multimedia services, i.e. VoIP (voice/video call) and IPTV (live IPTV and VoD) are also considered.

The QoE-aware dynamic personalized multilayer adaptation will be performed according to the forecasted position of requested content in user's ranking scale of preferences, calculated with:

- User's scale of values, built upon her/his profile (previously extracted by her/his social relational network account) and playback history.

- The current network conditions (i.e. to support network-aware content delivery)
- The requested service and content type (i.e. to support service/content-aware network transport)

Consequently, the proposed CNMS module will i) carry out service adaptation actions in those services where coding parameters can be tuned as in VoIP and IPTV cases, and ii) set the rules for intelligent packet marking and prioritizing system, both actions performed at the time To (i.e. In the interval between the service request and the service provision).

- In the first case the CNMS will monitor and adapt the encoding parameters (e.g. codec type, spatial and temporal resolution, encoding scheme structure, frame rate and sender bit rate, if appropriate) and the respective streaming/packetization schemes (i.e. streaming protocol, packet size, hinted encoding for streaming optimization) according to user-preferences on the requested service and content. Moreover, depending on the content dynamics of the requested service in conjunction with the user-*favouriteness* ranking, an optimal FEC value will be applied in order to enhance the error resilience of the service.
- Furthermore, a traffic engineering and policing mechanism is considered, which will be capable of treating the incoming traffic in a differentiated way, according to the marking and classification rules that were applied based on the required QoE-level for this service/content, as it was deduced according to user's ranking of *favouriteness*. The CNMS, depending on the nature of the delivered service (i.e. Video and/or Voice for IPTV or VoIP or interactive services/online gaming or web browsing), its dynamics level (High or Low) and primarily the perceptual importance of the

Figure 5. Voice ARPUs for the European Market

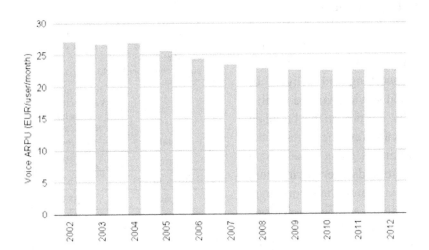

respective traffic packets according to the user-preferences (as these were extracted by her/his social network profile), will perform the appropriate intelligent marking classification before traversing the core network.

Upon the service initiation (i.e. upon To), the CNMS in order to address possible transitory network degradation will monitor continuously the AN by capturing the respective UMTS Traffic Volume Reporting Triggers that are described in the 3GPP TS 25.331 standard. If such a triggering message indicates critical QoS level at the AN, then the whole CNMS adaptation procedure will be re-initiated during the service session for enhancing the delivered QoE level. The proposed architecture considers this continuously monitoring procedure at the AN during the lifecycle of the media provision, because the AN is the conceptual bottleneck (i.e. where the traffic congestion upon the service provision may occur). Finally at the end-user side, typical commercial mobile terminal devices are considered, without any further special equipment and/or firmware modifications.

Business Perspectives of the Proposed Architecture

This section initially describes the current market penetration of the social networks, indicating the existence of a significant user base with increasing adoption trends. The current trend shows that social networking is becoming very popular among the users of various ages and social backgrounds. A short description of current trends in the mobile operator market is presented in the following paragraphs where the conclusion that mobile operators will have to adopt novel business models of data services in order to increase their revenues is formed. It is shown that currently the revenues from data services is lower than the revenues coming from voice services, but considering the increasing penetration rate of the data services and the declining profits from the voice services, the revenues from data services are expected to outperform these of traditional voice services (see Figure 5).

Given this, in the third section we observe the emergence of a new group of users, namely the Mobile Social Networking Users. These are the type of users that maintain one or more public profiles in various social networks and at the same time are using mobile data services. Acknowledging that there exists a significant and constantly increasing volume of such users, it is obvious that the impact of the proposed architecture in the market towards reinforcing positioning of European industry in networking and delivery of multimedia content and services will be significant. More specifically, it is proven that based on the current user trends and revenues rates, if the mobile social networking is going to become a widely adopted application/data service in future mobile communications, providing combined applications with existing traditional voice services, then in the near future the revenues statuses will change. Revenues originating from the mobile social networking service will lead the overall revenues of mobile operators and drive them to a new era of high profitability creating wider market opportunities resulting mainly from innovative business and societal applications (e.g. games, entertainment, or education, culture, and service creations) been based on novel networked media technologies and systems. The proposed architecture impact in the European and international market is underpinned by the mobile operators and social networking market convergence, speeding up the profitability of the mobile operators from the data services, and pushing the mobile operators to high rates and increasing ARPUs (Freeman, 2006).

Social Networking Market Penetration

Social networking is creating new ways to communicate and sharing information among Internet users, regardless of their locale. Social networking websites today are being used regularly by millions of people, and contemporary studies show that social networking phenomenon will be an enduring part of everyday life (Carrington, Scott, & Wasserman, 2005). The mainstream services offered by social networking services are i) directory services and user categorization based on demographic, social and recreational attributes

Table 1. Social networking European market penetration

European Social Networking Reach by Country Total Europe, Age 15+ – Home & Work Locations * December 2008 Source: comScore World Metrix		
Country	Total Unique Visitors (000) to Social Networking Category	% Reach of Country's Total Internet Audience
Europe	210,950	74.6
United Kingdom	29,263	79.8
Spain	13,185	73.7
Portugal	2,705	72.9
Denmark	2,390	69.7
Italy	14,408	69.3
Belgium	3,668	68.2
Germany	24,901	67.3
Ireland	1,131	66.9
Finland	2,061	66.2
Sweden	3,733	65.4
Switzerland	2,804	64.7
France	21,745	63.9
Russia	18,427	63.5
The Netherlands	7,438	63.0
Norway	1,732	58.9
Austria	2,120	49.7

(e.g. former classmates, hobbies, political views, nationality, interests etc), ii) means to connect with friends (usually with self-descriptive profile pages), and iii) recommendation of systems linked to trust (Scott, 2000).

According to the ComScore, Inc., a leading firm in measuring the digital world from a total of 282.7 million European Internet users older than 15 years old, who went online via a home or work computer/access network in December 2008, 211 millions visited a social networking site. This means that social networking attracts approximately three quarters of European Internet users (see Table 1).

Figure 2. Most favorite social network site per country

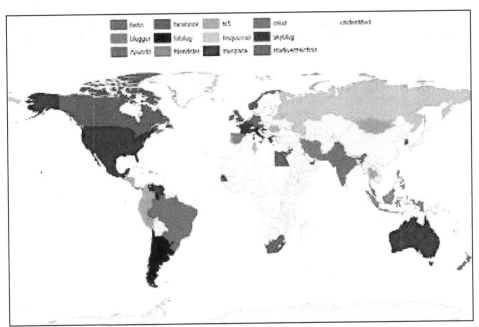

Figure 3. Social networking members worldwide

Apart from European market, social networking seems to becoming a global phenomenon, currently accounting intercontinental members, and high penetration rates in the developed countries. As figure 2 depicts, the total number of the registered users that facilitate a social network profile is distributed from the Caribbean to the Asia-Pacific, creating an international group of users, who are interconnected and exchange information, ideas and preferences. It is also interesting, that as figure 3 shows, the social networking is not limited to a specific service or web site,

rather the opposite. Across the continents various social networking sites seemed to be very popular, making the concept of the social networking a globalized phenomenon and part of the human culture from the very beginning of their appearance over the Internet (Jackson, 2003).

Another interesting parameter of the social network users that figure 4 shows, is that although half of the social networking users come from younger ages (i.e. 15-24 years old), older users (over 45 years old) have their fair share of social networking penetration rates.

Figure 4. Distribution of European social networking by age group

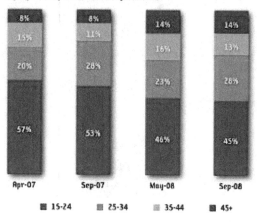

Distribution of European Social Networking
By Age Group (UK, Germany, France)

Apr-07   Sep-07   May-08   Sep-08

■ 15-24   ■ 25-34   ■ 35-44   ■ 45+

Source: JupiterResearch

Table 2. Social network growth in first half of 2008

	June 2008 Total Unique Visitors (000)	December 2007 Total Unique Visitors (000)
Total Internet Users	860.514	815.797
Total Social Network Users	580.510	516.318
Facebook	132.105	97.792
MySpace	117.582	107.167
hi5	56.367	31.428
Friendster	37.080	29.735
Orkut	34.028	25.138
Bedo	24.017	21.282
Other	179.330	203.776

Online social networking has created a critical mass of market, where users from various countries, continents, age and sex are linked online, share, compare and specify their preferences and habits through their profile and/or available applications. Moreover, statistics predict a significant growth in the number of registered users in a social networking service. Table 2 shows the change in active subscribers in the first semester of 2008 (Doreian, 2005).

Current Market Status in Mobile Operators

"Operators must look for innovative strategies aimed at encouraging people to make more – and longer – revenue-generating calls/requests, particularly during off-peak times when little incremental cost is incurred."

Today the mobile industry is on the verge of horisontalization in terms of revenues and market penetration provided by traditional voice services. Mobile voice revenue is set to reach a European plateau, being expected to grow with

a Compound Annual Growth Rate (CAGR) of 0.4% over the next five years. As mobile voice ARPUs are expected to fall in the coming years in Europe (see Figure 5, source: The Western European mobile market: trends and forecasts 2008–2013), the emergence of new data revenue streams is clearly important for mobile operators. The mobile industry in order to identify new products and services that will increase the ARPU rates is gradually moving towards the non-voice based services.

Total mobile voice revenues in the market increased by 31 percent to £126 billion ($188 billion) over the last five-years period, while corresponding data revenues increased by 171 percent to £35 billion ($52 billion). Operators and service providers face challenges to make money from this new demand, as some operators have already resorted to flat-rate tariffs, which encourage adoption of new services, but limit revenue growth once the customer base is established. Operators are, therefore, seeking to promote revenue-enhancing mobile data services, without impairing adoption levels (Cross, 2003). It seems that although the users continue to use as a primary service the voice service, it is obvious from the curves of the total mobile phone subscribers that the customer

Figure 6. Worldwide mobile phone subscribers

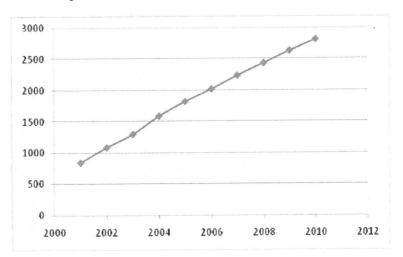

take advantage of the offered flat rate low cost programs that the competitive mobile operators offer and they subscribe to more than one operator in order to exploit and take advantage of the cheap flow rate programs. This has caused an increase in the total number of phone subscribers as figure 6 depicts (based on latest data, GSM/UMTS mobile subscribers passed 3 billions last year and currently is more than 3.7 billion1), but at the same time it has impaired mobile voice revenues due to the spread of the market group (i.e. the customers) across the various mobile operators.

Although mobile voice revenues for the reporting period are still larger than those that are coming from the consumption of mobile data services, the mobile data revenues are growing five times faster than the respective voice-based services. According to figure 7, a detailed distribution of the non-voice ARPUs among Video telephony, M-commerce, Data networking and other data services is presented, showing an increasing penetration rate, which covers almost the 35% of the total ARPUs.

The level of demand for 3G devices, such as the new 3G iPhone, is the clearest indication so far that consumers are interested in mobile data services. Sales of the upgraded iPhone handset reached 1 million in 21 countries in its first week-

end in the market. The demand for 3G-enabled handsets and mobile data services is growing in Western Europe, and 26% of all subscribers now have 3G-enabled phones. Therefore, a great portion of the mobile subscribers are practically prepared to use data services through their mobile device. This consumers-group has the potential to drive mobile operators to higher profitability margins by subscribing to new appealing data services rather than traditional voice services.

Mobile operators are threatened by the emergence of fixed Internet emulation on mobile devices (e.g. 3G-enabled handsets). Operators previously aimed to provide walled gardens for their mobile Internet browsing services, but portals such as Vodafone's live! delivered only limited take-up, until they began to provide their customers with emulated Internet browsing like that available on fixed lines. Mobile operators are seriously threatened and becoming bit-pipe providers, gaining revenue from access, but little from services.

Nowadays as result of open markets and pure competition, mobile operators face continuously increasing competition from service rivals that are also seeking to capitalize on new mobile data services. Whatsoever, mobile operators have a number of advantages that they can leverage on.

Figure 7. Non-Voice ARPUs for the European Market

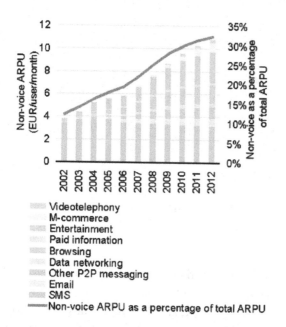

- Videotelephony
- M-commerce
- Entertainment
- Paid information
- Browsing
- Data networking
- Other P2P messaging
- Email
- SMS
- Non-voice ARPU as a percentage of total ARPU

A New Market is Created: Mobile Social-Net Users

In this multimodal environment of continuously increasing numbers of mobile phone subscribers and social network users, a new market is developing that includes the users that choose to install social network applications on their mobile phones. Via these applications the mobile users have continuous access to their social network profiles and applications, creating a continuously updated data environment with their personal data and preferences. Mobile Social Networking, the act of bonding in virtual communities via a cell phone, exploded into the wireless scene in 2007. Broadly defined as the act of generating and sharing media content, ranging from a simple write-up to an elaborate video feed, mobile social networking enables users to keep in touch with friends and establish connections with existing and potential users of a network (Weng, 2007).

According to the European Information Technology Observatory (EITO) in 2012 it is expected that a percentage of 18.8% of the worldwide mobile phone subscribers will be active mobile social network users (i.e. registered users who create, edit and view personal content using their phone), reaching a total number of 803 million users (see Table 3). At this moment, mobile social networking is taking off. More specifically 800,000 mobile subscribers in the UK and 4 million in the US access social networking sites using their phones, spurred on by smart phones, faster network speeds and custom mobile services and applications.

More specifically, mobile operators should take advantage of customer-specific data at their disposal to target subscribers with specific mobile data services; this information also enables them to monitor and optimise the marketing of these services. Customer data also provides a basis for effective mobile advertising, where a premium fee can be added to enable advertiser target specific market groups. Furthermore, mobile operators may be able to make use of their knowledge of service usage patterns to cross-sell other services; for example, a mobile operator with a fixed network offering could provide music services via the fixed line and streamed services via 3G, knowing the customer's musical tastes in more detail than a purely fixed operator.

"Till the year 2012 it is expected that a percentage of 18.8% of the worldwide mobile phone subscribers will be active mobile social network users"

Customers are beginning to use mobile data services, ranging from those that are emulations of fixed broadband, such as Internet browsing, to services that have previously been delivered on other devices. Mobile operators are, therefore, considering how they can best derive revenue from these solutions. It is possible, and some say that it is likely, that service providers will bypass mobile networks entirely in the provision of new

Table 3. Worldwide mobile social network users

	2007	2008	2009	2010	2011	2012
Mobile Phone Subscribers	3078	3417	3697	3894	4150	4275
Mobile Internet Users	406	490	596	757	982	1228
Mobile Social Network Users	82	147	243	369	554	803
Mobile Social Network Users % of mobile phone subscribers	2,70%	4,30%	6,60%	9,50%	13,30%	18,80%

'mobile' services; even if mobile networks are used, the revenue derived may flow straight through them, as in the fixed Internet world.

Operators and content producers are in the best position to use the new opportunities (stemming from the participation of end-users to social networks) and create new revenue sources from innovative services based on existing and new infrastructure and content delivered through mobile networks.

This continuously increasing developing market bodes well for mobile operators, which see a new opportunity to increase data revenue. The success of any pricing strategy depends on the market characteristics, including the traffic patterns and reaction from the competition.

The Impact of the Proposed Architecture

Currently, mobile operators face competition from various service rivals that also seek to exploit the anticipated revenue from new enhanced data services via mobile handsets. Compared to their rivals, mobile operators have a significant competitive advantage that they must leverage on: Information about usage patterns in their networks and potential knowledge of their end-customers preferences.

Figure 8 illustrates concisely the demand functions of data and voice services, and indicates the anticipated impact of the proposed architecture. Voice service market saturation and network upgrades push mobile operators to offer flat rate tariff plans in order to attract/retain customers and fill the capacity potential of their networks. This results in thinner ARPUs in voice services. On the other hand, the novel market of data services exhibits increasing ARPU, indicating that the market has significant growth and profit potentials. Mobile operators are beginning to side out marketing plans for voice services and focusing their marketing and service creation activities in the data market. Predictions show that eventually data services' ARPU will overtake the decreasing ARPU of voice services.

Leveraging the information available on social networking sites and correlating it with the user data residing in their networks, mobile operators can enrich their data offerings with functionality and targeted marketing activities and service creation. Thus, innovative services will be coupled with customer satisfaction stemming not only from the content itself rather from the supplementary attributes of the service (preferences, habits, location-aware content etc

The proposed architecture focuses on showing possible ways to exploitation of this unique opportunity for mobile networks which can further facilitate the expansion of their business scope (extending their reach to content creation, social networking sites etc). Users on both sides (mobile subscribers and social networking sites members) can be provided with the option to describe better their preferences and expectations from mobile services (e.g. QoE level for a specific type of content – sports, TV serials, location preferences, complex ways to handle incoming

Figure 8. Impact on the mobile operators market

	2007	2008	2009	2010	2011	2012
Mobile Phone Subscribers	3078	3417	3697	3894	4150	4275
Mobile Internet Users	406	490	596	757	982	1228
Mobile Social Network Users	82	147	243	369	554	803
Mobile Social Network Users % of mobile phone subscribers	2,70%	4,30%	6,60%	9,50%	13,30%	18,80%

data and – possibly – voice requests – voice mail etc) thus, making their mobile subscription even more valuable.

The convergence of mobile and internet social networks has the potential to completely alter the demand expectation and most importantly the customer value of mobile data services. This will not only increase end-user satisfaction, mobile operators profitability figures, data services adoption rates but can also create an entire ecosystem of services targeting specifically to each user's personal needs and preferences.

From a revenue perspective, the proposed approach can create appealing services (in terms of technical quality and compatibility in preferences) to end customers which in turn will find beneficial to subscribe to. By increasing the number of services a user is subscribed to mobile networks can enjoy higher ARPUs.

From a cost perspective, standardizing the control and transport planes can also lead to operational savings. Standardization leads to savings because network equipment becomes cheaper and off-the-shelf becomes the rule of the day. This means that the value of mobile subscriptions will stem from available applications and not from the connection at hand. Investments can be focused on QoE options and applications. The more forms of QoE, the more users, and the more applications, the higher the ARPUs. In short, one network for all media types is cheaper than multiple overlay networks.

In this framework, from the marketing perspective the proposed approach contributes the following:

- Assists mobile operators to take advantage of customer-specific data at their disposal and target subscribers with specific mobile data services
- Enables mobile operators to monitor and optimise their marketing efforts for the media/data services (via the user-centric and personalized QoE adjustment)
- Facilitates mobile operators to leverage on their knowledge of customer preferences/ patterns to cross-sell available media services.

From the mobile operator's perspective, the proposed approach contributes as follows:

- Creates an ecosystem of new innovative, meaningful services and revenue sources - higher ARPU
- Enables operators to differentiate on service attributes - thus, avoiding price differentiation which reduces ARPU
- Increases customer loyalty - by creating new, engaging experience for mobile users
- Decreases service creation costs – by standardization
- Strengthens the brand name of social-net providers and mobile-operators

From the content provider's perspective, the proposed approach contributes as follows:

- Enables content management and efficient delivery to mobile users
- Could be further exploited to facilitate content billing processes through mobile operators billing systems
- Reduces cost of content production and preparation for QoE-adjustment according to the user preferences

FUTURE RESEARCH DIRECTIONS

The proposed architecture deals with aspects that can completely alter the global market of mobile media services. The knowledge, technical know-how and business operation planning that will be gathered in the proposed architecture can strengthen the place of European mobile industry in the globalized economy.

Furthermore, the business matters and ethical issues been dealt in the proposed architecture require a much larger consensus and thought before put into practice. Both vendors and mobile operators are required to participate in the development process of the business model to secure the long-term sustainability of the model.

Moreover, the human resources and expertise that must be summoned to develop the proposed concept are required to be as diverse, multi-sectoral and inter-disciplinary as possible.

The most serious factors that can affect the proposed concept impact deals primarily with the regulatory implications stemming from the novelty of its business concept. Using user data available in mobile operators data repositories to implement diversified business processes can be confronted by consumer associations. Privacy of data is an important concern that the application of the business model has to consider.

It is further noted that user consent will be required beforehand to secure the success of the business model. However, privacy concerns may affect the success and adoption of the business idea. Although provided the current mentality of Internet users this does not seem to be a big problem (users willingly agree to allow social network sites to use the data stored on their servers for promotional and other purposes), the proposed concept must seriously consider different attitude from the mobile operators user base.

Mobile handsets ownership is much more closely linked to individual privacy than is information available on social networking sites, even though data available on social sites are evidently much more sensitive than those made available upon contracting for mobile service.

CONCLUSION

This chapter has described and proposed a Content-aware and Network-aware Management System (CNMS) over a converged user-environment of social networking and mobile multimedia services, which is focused on applying dynamic personalized multi-layer adaptation for the optimization of the Quality of Experience (QoE) level in a requested media service according to the user preferences and favourites provided in her/his social network profile and prior experiences rated by users themselves. The proposed multimodal management system is user-centric and is expected to have a significant impact on the current business model of social networking.

More specifically, this chapter has provided a marketing analysis aspect on the proposed management systems, towards further boosting the current trend of the mobile social users. The described market perspective, via the personalization and the perceptual awareness of the services according to the user preferences will create the critical mass of customers that will revenues back to the mobile operators, who have experienced limited profit lately.

From a technical aspect, the proposed solution provides a physical gateway between the social networking profiles of the users and the user profiling of the mobile operator, by translating and transforming the stored data into useful user information.

REFERENCES

Carrington, P. J., Scott, J., & Wasserman, S. (2005). *Models and methods in social network analysis.* Cambridge: Cambridge University Press.

Cross, R. L., Parker, A., & Sasson, L. (2003). *Networks in the knowledge economy.* Oxford: Oxford University Press.

Doreian, P., Batagelj, V., & Ferligoj, A. (2005). *Generalized blockmodeling.* Cambridge: Cambridge University Press.

Freeman, L. (2006). *The development of social network analysis.* Vancouver, Canada: Empirical Press.

Freeman, L. C., White, D. R., & Kimball Romney, A. (1992). *Research methods in social network analysis.* New Brunswick, NJ: Transaction Publishers.

Jackson, M. O. (2003). A strategic model of social and economic networks. *Journal of Economic Theory, 71*, 44–74. doi:10.1006/jeth.1996.0108

Mislove, A., Viswanath, B., Gummadi, K. P., & Druschel, P. (2010, February). You are who you know: Inferring user profiles in online social networks. Paper presented at Third ACM International Conference on Web Search and Data Mining (WSDM 2010), New York.

Radcliffe-Brown, A. R. (1940). On social structure. *The Journal of the Royal Anthropological Institute, 70*, 1–12.

Scott, J. (2000). *Social network analysis: A handbook.* Thousand Oaks, CA: SAGE.

Weng, M. (2007). *A multimedia social-networking community for mobile devices.* New York: NYU Tisch School of the Arts, Interactive Telecommunications Program.

Yuana, W., Nahrstedta, K., Advea, S. V., Jonesb, D. L., & Kravetsa, R. H. (2003). Design and evaluation of a cross-layer adaptation framework for mobile multimedia systems. In Proceedings of the SPIE/ACM Multimedia Computing and Networking Conference (MMCN).

KEY TERMS AND DEFINITIONS

3GPP: The 3rd Generation Partnership Project (3GPP) is a collaboration project between telecommunications associations and industrial groups to make a globally applicable 3G system specification within the scope of International Telecommunication Union (ITU)

ARPU: Average Revenue Per User. ARPU is a business/operational compound figure used primarily by consumer communications and networking companies to measure marketing and business efficiency. It is the total revenue divided by the number of subscribers.

CAGR: Compound Annual Growth Rate (CAGR) is an investing term for the smoothed annualized gain of an investment over a certain time period.

DiffServ: Differentiated Services. DiffServ is a computer networking architecture used to classify and manage network traffic and provide QoS on IP networks.

EITO: European Information Technology Observatory. EITO produces reports and studies with up-to-date information on European and global markets for information technology, telecommunications and consumer electronics.

FEC: Forward Error Correction. FEC is a system of error control for data transmission.

GSM: Global System for Mobile Communications. GSM is a mobile telephone systems standard used primarily in Europe.

HSPA: High Speed Packet Access. HSPA extends the performance of existing WCDMA protocols and is comprised of High Speed Downlink Packet Access (HSDPA) and High Speed Uplink Packet Access (HSUPA).

ICT: Information and Communication Technologies

IMS: IP Multimedia Subsystem. IMS is an architectural framework for delivering IP multimedia services.

IPTV: Internet Protocol TeleVision. IPTV is a family of systems (the term mostly refers to commercially available platforms) through which digital television services are delivered via IP-based networks (e.g. Internet, satellite, cable networks etc).

MPLS: Multiprotocol Label Switching. MPLS is a label-based mechanism which directs and carries data from one network node to the next.

QoE: Quality of Experience. QoE is a subjective measure of a customer's experiences with a particular equipment or service. Although it relates to Quality of Service (QoS), it differs in that it focuses on objectively measure the service delivered by a equipment vendor or service provider.

QoS: Quality of Service. QoS refers to resource reservation control mechanisms. Quality of service is the ability to provide different priority to different applications, users, or data flows, or to guarantee a certain level of performance to a data flow.

UMTS: Universal Mobile Telecommunications System. UMTS is a third-generation (3G) mobile telecommunications technology.

VoD: Video on Demand. VoD refers to systems that enable users to watch or listen audiovisual content on demand.

VoIP: Voice over Internet Protocol. VoIP refers to the transmission technologies used for delivery of voice communications over IP networks.

ENDNOTE

[1]   http://www.gsmworld.com/

Section 4
Social Computing from a Marketing Perspective

Chapter 13

Social Computing and the New Market:
How Social Computing is Driving Market Competition

Jason G. Caudill
Carson-Newman College, USA

ABSTRACT

Social computing has revolutionized the way individuals connect with one another and manage their personal lives. The technology has launched billionaire entrepreneurs and influenced presidential elections. For businesses the same technology has meant a revolution in online marketing. Different types of social computing applications offer different opportunities for marketing, but all relate to the opportunity for companies to improve their connections with current and potential customers. This chapter will explore both the history of marketing and social computing and how the two fields have come together to revolutionize online marketing today.

INTRODUCTION

Social computing, the use of technology to connect people personally and professionally, has been one of the central themes of Internet success. Early on, in the days of UNIX connections, bulletin boards became popular for early network users to exchange information and meet other people with similar interests. Later came Yahoo! and their group applications where users could not only post text bulletins, but could also post pictures, schedule events, and even e-mail or use

live chat applications to better connect with their online communities. These early days of social networking, however popular, failed to achieve the kind of market dominance that a true revolution in technology or communication would expect. Just a few years into the 21st century, however, all that changed.

Parameswaran and Whinston (2007) described the change as:

"Through the end of the twentieth century, advances in computing and networking technologies largely manifested themselves in dramatic shifts in business computing. Many of the new

DOI: 10.4018/978-1-61692-904-6.ch013

trends emphasized organizational computing, in diverse domains like enterprise resource systems, customer relationship management, and electronic commerce. However, the 21st Century has seen new trends emerge in social computing, where the scope shifts from corporations to social organizations, and the structure shifts from top-down to bottom-up." pg. 2.

The social networking site MySpace rapidly grew in popularity, but it was almost exclusively in the realm of teenagers and a few college students. The innovation that really got the market moving was Facebook. Originally available only to college students for networking with others in higher education, Facebook grew to be one of the great success stories of the Internet age. Launched in 2004, by the middle of 2009 Facebook counted 250 million users worldwide and boasted a market valuation of $6.5 billion (Oreskovic, 2009).

There are other major players in the social networking universe today, including Twitter, which can interface with Facebook, SecondLife, and sharing sites like YouTube and Flickr. People's basic online habits can be seen changing, with many people now using the messaging features of Facebook and the commenting on Twitter to exchange information instead of more traditional technologies like e-mail. Add to this that, increasingly, these social networks are going mobile through the use of mobile broadband enabled handheld devices and ubiquitous computing in social networking is coming closer and closer to reality.

As with any new media throughout history, the rise of social networking has spurred shifts in marketing and advertising. With such a massive audience, Facebook and similar sites provide opportunities for companies to access target markets and drive those customers to company websites and other promotions. Through the use of profile scanning and actual user feedback on their like or dislike of particular advertisements, advertisers are able to target and capture the attention of

their likely customers among a virtual nation of 250 million. This shift of focus is a generational change from older technologies like banner advertisements or pop-up advertisements that have traditionally been associated with Internet commerce. The enhanced targeting, and the size of the potential customer population, makes the social networking world perhaps the largest potential marketplace in advertising history.

The way that the business community reacts to this shifting market presence, and the ways in which customers interact with their suppliers there, are still emerging trends in 21st century business. How the interactions take place depend on the type of social network that is involved and the goal of both company and customer. Regardless of the details, however, new markets and practices are a part of this new landscape of commerce.

BACKGROUND

The Fundamentals of Marketing

The 4 P's of Marketing

Traditionally the marketing discipline has operated on the principle of the four P's; product, place, price, and promotion (Constantinides, 2006). Three of the four, product, price, and promotion, are still fundamentally the same as they have always been. What a company is producing, how much the product costs, and the manner in which the product is promoted are still central to any marketing strategy. Place is also a core consideration, but for many products and even for an increasing number of services place in the 21st century is a different strategic component than the place of marketing in the 1950's.

Commerce has changed since the 4 P's were first established, particularly with the rise of e-commerce. The core of these principles as marketing guidelines, however, remains in that, "…the basic construction of the 4 P's is still valid and, with some extension and adjustment, is still the core of operative decisions" (Dominici, 2009, p. 20). Dominici (2009), in discussing the traditional 4 P's individually, addresses the idea that the product is still the bundle of benefits obtained by the customer in a purchase. e-commerce does provide opportunities for firms to develop new products based on consumer interaction, but the product is still a bundle of benefits (Dominici, 2009).

The price of a product remains the overall cost to the consumer in terms of financial, time, and effort investment in a product, with the main difference in e-commerce being a more transparent, readily compared set of prices in the marketplace (Dominici, 2009). Promotion in e-commerce continues to build customer relationships, but the media-richness of the technology provides more opportunities to do so and, "Interaction, multimedia, and relationship should be included as elements of the P of promotion" (Dominici, 2009, p. 20).

Place traditionally referred to the physical sales location of the product. The proximity of that place to the product's target market, demographic statistics such as age, median income, education level, and population density of the area all factored into decisions about where to put a storefront or where in a store to place a product. The physical experience of the location itself was also a factor, with atmosphere, entrances and exits, traffic flow, and other human-architecture interface concepts in play. As a basic example, a Rolls-Royce dealership would likely have marble floors, hardwood furniture, and be located in a wealthy metropolitan area, while a Kia dealership would be more likely to have utilitarian building with less expensive furniture in a less affluent area.

With the advent of e-commerce, many of the traditional place considerations have, if not vanished, metamorphosed into different ways of looking at what are very different places. In e-commerce, "The physical place becomes virtual and includes intangible aspects of transaction" (Dominici, 2009, p 20). For products that are eas-

ily shipped or things that do not require shipping at all, e-commerce makes a nation or the planet a single community marketplace. Products that can be affordably shipped directly to residential or office locations can be purchased online and received by the customer wherever they are. Other products or services, such as software, digital music, or technical support, can be delivered electronically and do not require any physical shipping at all. No longer does a store need to be a convenient drive or short walk away from customers to deliver physical products.

The reduced importance of physical place through e-commerce is also being seen in other types of businesses. CarMax, a U.S. national network of used car lots, has their national inventory of used automobiles listed in a customer searchable online database. Automobiles are obviously different from books or DVDs for shipping, but the theory is similar. For a set, pre-arranged price, customers can arrange to have vehicles from any CarMax location in the country shipped to their local CarMax lot for purchase and pick-up. Place matters somewhat here, in that customers still need a physical location at which to complete their transaction, but the e-commerce component gives customers access to a national market instead of limiting them to just what they see at their local store.

Other concepts of place, the ambiance of the store and presentation of the products, translate to e-commerce, but are still unique. Online customers experience an interaction with an e-commerce site, much as a traditional customer experiences an interaction with a brick-and-mortar store. Basic functionality and an intuitive interface are an important component of e-commerce site design, but the feeling of place in an online storefront goes beyond the technical design of the site. Colors, layout, and thematic connections between the online and physical store can all be part of the place experience for an online customer. Mangiaracina, Brugnoli, and Perego (2009) help to define this by applying customer journey maps from traditional retail environments to the e-commerce world. The stages of customer engagement in this e-commerce model are defined as site landing, product discovery, product presentation, cart management, and check out (Mangiaracina, Brugnoli, & Perego, 2009)

E-commerce sites that engage the customer and create a feeling of comfort are more likely to draw repeat business, just as comfortable, engaging brick-and-mortar stores do. In this way, place for e-commerce is just as important as it is for traditional storefronts. While very different, place in e-commerce plays a central role in customer experiences and, by extension, in customer satisfaction.

The core connection between marketing and social computing is another of marketing's 4 P's, promotion. This concept is not different for e-commerce than it is for traditional business models; companies need to provide information to customers that will persuade those customers to purchase the company's products or services. Where traditional promotion included media such as print, radio, and television, social computing has broadened promotional options to the virtual world.

Marketing as Intelligence

The classic 4P model of marketing is an accurate portrayal of how marketing works, but the model does not fully explain the discipline. In practice, marketing is often more listening than speaking. Companies have to communicate the message of their product to customers, but the truly successful companies listen to what their customers are saying so that the company knows what to do. In relation to technology and e-commerce specifically businesses can better learn about and understand their stakeholders, "…primarily through more effective and efficient collection, storage, and analysis of information from the business environment" (Chung, Chen, & Reid, 2009, p. 60).

Traditional marketing techniques for intelligence gathering often took significant effort on the part of the company. Focus groups, customer surveys, test marketing, and even the analysis of sales and service data required the company to deliberately go out and gather information. Even once information was in hand the analysis was not necessarily direct. Competitors would sometimes run promotions of their own products in areas where a test marketing effort was being conducted in order to sabotage results. Sales data, while useful, has to be considered in relation to the levels of competition in the immediate area, current economic conditions, seasonality, and other correlated drivers of consumer behavior.

Social computing has changed the information-gathering role of marketing in the online marketplace. While many online activities are still deliberately designed to gather information, such as questionnaires connected to online ordering forms or the award of coupons in exchange for surveys, there is a new opportunity in social networking. One of the biggest hurdles that companies may face is defining who, exactly, their customers are.

While on the surface this appears to be a simple question it is not. Obviously, a person who has made a purchase can be defined as a customer, and someone who makes repeated purchases of similar products from the same company can even more clearly be defined as a customer. The question for the marketer, however, is how current and potential future customers are defined, what traits combine to make someone a customer.

Demographic statistics are often the foundation of the definition of a customer. Age, gender, income, education level, and cultural background are all recognized drivers of consumer behavior. Much of this data is freely available through census bureaus and other outlets that have already tabulated the data. While helpful, this information is only the beginning of understanding customers. Other information, correlating with demographics, can help marketers more precisely define who a company's customers are and exactly what benefits they may be pursuing in a product.

Related interests are an excellent source of information to the intelligence-gathering component of marketing. If, for example, a company selling MP3 players determines that many of their customers are also Netflix subscribers that connection could help to direct the company's marketing efforts and inform the company of what the customer is actually buying. While their purchase is literally an MP3 player, the benefit to the customer may be mobile media access, entertainment, or a feeling of connectivity. Additional correlations of interest can refine these conclusions. Information such as this is important to marketing efforts and cannot be found in a simple demographic report.

The new marketing territory introduced by social computing is the quick and easy access that many people provide to marketers. Many social computing applications have some method for users to share their interests, their hobbies, even their favorite books or television shows. Using modern marketing technology companies can scan this information and compile data about likely customers, in addition to targeting specific advertisements to potential customers based on their individual preferences. The mechanics of these marketing maneuvers will change in different social computing environments, but the theory underlying those remains the same regardless of URL.

Regardless of the social network forum in question, or the computer code running the application, the primary purpose of marketing in social computing is to achieve an exchange of information. Companies, in gathering marketing information, learn about customers' needs and wants and how those needs and wants interact with other customer choices. Customers, having provided information to companies through the social network, are exposed to company information through various advertising strategies.

Social Computing Networks

Defining the Networks

The march towards ubiquitous computing is changing the way people interact with technology and with each other. The changes occurring today are both extensive and generational. Increasingly traditional e-mail is no longer the primary means of electronic communication for computer-savvy people; new generations are moving to social network messaging and, even more, to text messaging via cell phone. These new interactions among individuals are indicative of their interaction with technology and the influence that new technologies have on how people live each day. Nyland's (2007) research indicated that use of e-mail since the beginning of social media has seen as many users increasing their use as users decreasing their use, but new social computing applications are competing with e-mail.

Boyd and Ellison (2007) defined social network sites as,

"...web-based services that allow individuals to (1) construct a public or semi-public profile within a bounded system, (2) articulate a list of other users with whom they share a connection, and (3) view and traverse their list of connections and those made by others within the system" (pg. 211).

This definition helps to clarify exactly what is meant by the term social network. By this definition simply communicating with technology, such as using e-mail, is not social networking because there is not an accessible profile or network of connections. Many modern services, however, do meet this definition of social networks.

As of this chapter's writing, there are four of what would be considered major social networks; MySpace, Facebook, Twitter, and LinkedIn. Also important to the discussion of social computing is the virtual world of SecondLife, which, while not necessarily classified as a social network, is definitely an application of social computing. Each of these applications has a unique history and a different audience, but the lines between systems are blurring and there are even connections built between many of them. Of these, the largest market players in the United States are MySpace, Facebook, and Twitter, with Facebook being the most popular world-wide (Rooksby et al., 2009).

There is a certain progression of social networks, with many users graduating from one to the other as their lives and needs change. MySpace is primarily a tween and teen site that remains popular through high school. For students going to college, or for adults entering social networking for the first time, Facebook is usually the application of choice. For social networking with a focus on professional development and connectivity LinkedIn is the appropriate choice. This process of natural grouping can benefit marketers by providing some broad guidelines about what kind of customers they are likely to reach through a particular medium.

Twitter is the most recent, and perhaps the fastest growing, of the social networks. There seems to be less segregation among Twitter users than the other social networks, with people of all ages, professions, and interests all taking part. Twitter's microblog format also encourages users to frequently update their activities which may lead to more frequent logins and the connection of Twitter to cell phones for updates.

SecondLife is a unique application that really belongs to a category of its own, separate from the other social networking applications. Instead of being a social network using asynchronous communication through profiles, messaging, and other actions, SecondLife is a live-time synchronous virtual world where users meet and interact in virtual spaces much like they would meet and interact in the physical world. Instead of navigating to a message forum users can walk or fly to a virtual building to interact.

Impact and Size of Social Networks

Facebook has grown to become the king of the social networking sites. Starting in 2004 as just a networking site for college students, Facebook has expanded to include users from all walks of life. The Facebook statistics page lists the following information:

- More than 250 million active users
- More than 120 million users log on to Facebook at least once each day
- More than two-thirds of Facebook users are outside of college
- The fastest growing demographic is those 35 years old and older
- More than 1 billion photos uploaded to the site each month
- More than 10 million videos uploaded each month
- More than 1 billion pieces of content (web links, news stories, blog posts, notes, photos, etc.) shared each week
- More than 2.5 million events created each month
- More than 45 million active user groups exist on the site (facebook.com)

MySpace, historically the first major social networking site in the online social revolution, has less than half the membership of Facebook, with approximately 124 million unique visitors (Smith, 2009). Unlike other social networks, MySpace's user base is actually shrinking as more and more users move from MySpace to rival networks. Even with this changing level of activity, however, a user base of over 100 million is still far beyond the average viewership that can be reached over television or radio airwaves.

Twitter, as the newest social networking entry, is smaller but rapidly growing with an estimated 6 million active users and growth rates that may see the site with as many as 18 million users by the end of 2010 (Ostrow, 2009). Twitter operates as a micro-blog, limiting user posts to just 140 characters. Perhaps more than any other social computing application Twitter has emerged as the closest link between everyday people and celebrities, with many famous actors, athletes, and other well-known individuals maintaining official Twitter pages to send information out to their fans.

LinkedIn is another social network, but instead of the traditional social use of networks LinkedIn is dedicated to professional networking for the purpose of improving or advancing an individual's professional career. LinkedIn reports that they currently have over 43 million users (LinkedIn), and those users are a unique demographic for marketers. Likely due to the professional nature of the network, 28% of users have an average annual income of $104,000 and another 30% have an average annual income of $93,000 (O'Malley, 2008). This self-selected target market may be highly attractive to many marketing efforts as there is a more consistent income level among the LinkedIn population.

SecondLife is distinctly different from the other social networks because of the virtual world component of the program. August 3, 2009 statistics from SecondLife show just over 1.3 million users logged in over the past 60 days (SecondLife, 2009). One of the unique SecondLife aspects is that it actually has its own economy, based on a virtual currency called Linden dollars, which is largely tied to the exchange of real-world currency in outside the program commerce. Thus, in SecondLife, there is not only the opportunity for advertising but also for real profits from virtual commerce activities.

One interesting caveat to this section is that while statistics are a useful reference point, they are of relatively limited use in the examination of social networking. The average production time of an academic text, from the beginning of writing to final publication is at least 18-24 months. Given the speed at which the social computing world is changing the leading application two years from

the time of this writing may be very different from any of today's applications. So, while the statistics listed here may be useful the reader is encouraged to research current conditions on their own when reading this chapter.

The Development of Online Marketing

As already discussed, the interaction of the marketing profession and social computing is unique among all types of media. To better understand this unique interaction, however, the development of online marketing needs to be explored. As Internet access has expanded, so too have efforts to generate profits from it as a medium of communication. The field has grown and changed rapidly over a relatively short period of time, what is really less than 20 years.

When American households first began getting online in large numbers, in the early- to mid-1990's, online marketing was an entirely new concept. While online marketing as a new concept during just the last decade may seem unusual, perhaps unbelievable, the field simply did not exist until there were enough users, a large enough customer base, to justify the time and expense of reaching out to customers through the new medium. In the beginning, this effort relied on the customer taking the first step to reach out to the company.

As Internet access became more common companies began maintaining customer websites. Often these were just simple sites with advertising and opportunities for customers to contact the company via e-mail. Companies on the leading edge of this new technology proudly displayed their URLs on television commercials and printed materials, and early on often had two listings, one for the URL and a second for the AOL keyword.

Early on the marketing relationship between companies and customers online was strictly one-way; customers had to take the initiative to go to the company website and contact the company there. The next evolutionary step was for companies to start compiling mailing lists to contact their customers and actively broadcast information or request customer inputs. Again, this is a tactic that may not seem revolutionary in today's world of SPAM and countless mailing list subscription, but the first companies that made the effort to contact customers caused some excitement because they were first, they were new, and they were, to some extent, revolutionary.

Further developments of the Internet saw growing sites that people frequented. Like print, radio, and television media, website proprietors quickly learned that they could generate revenue by charging companies to post advertisements on their website. Beginning with static banner advertisements and evolving over time to pop-ups, pop-unders, and other animated displays, the use of direct advertising on websites was another step in driving current and potential customers to company websites. With advertising generating traffic, company websites had a greater purpose, and there was better evidence for the entry into e-commerce.

Early banner advertisements may have been targeted, a company advertising a specific product on a related website, or they may have been just general advertisements targeting a wide range of viewers. The rise of search engines gave companies their first chance at more detailed targeting of specific market segments. Search engines gave customers the opportunity to search the Internet for specific products or specific companies. While a properly designed company website would come up near the top of a search page's results, the company could improve their visibility by paying search engines for special placement. These placements might put the company links above or to one side of the search results on a page. In this way companies could ensure that customers who were actively searching for information about their products would find their way to the company website.

Rood and Bruckman (2009) discuss the reasons that companies use online communities.

While these communities may exist outside of social networking environments, communities are certainly a part of social networks. Reasons for company participation in these communities are: provide insight into customer thinking, save money, generate sales, generate ideas for product development, increase customer loyalty and retention, increase customer satisfaction, and acquire new customers (Rood & Bruckman, 2009). This list provides specific goals for online community use by companies. Of particular interest to the discussion of marketing through social computing is that six out of seven reasons companies use online communities, all except save money, are marketing functions.

Over time, the trend in Internet marketing has been to develop closer relationships with customers and, in doing so, give the customer a feeling of connection and loyalty to the company or the product. This background is what has led, one step at a time, to the current connection of Internet marketing and e-commerce to social computing. Wind and Todi (2008) list four reasons that social networks are valuable for advertising strategies; large reach, cost efficiency, targeted advertising, and time spent online. Today, social computing gives companies the best opportunity to personally connect with target markets and develop lasting customer relationships.

MAIN FOCUS OF CHAPTER

Marketing and E-Commerce by Type of Social Computing

Just as there are different kinds of social computing applications, these different applications provide different opportunities for different types of marketing and commerce. The types of individuals involved in the social computing activity, the business model of the firm behind the technology, and the opportunities for interaction within the system all play a part in what e-commerce in social computing looks like. The current social computing marketing activities in the different major social computing applications will be examined.

Marketing on Large-Scale Social Networks

There are multiple large-scale social networks, but Facebook is easily the largest and most pervasive based on numbers of users. Perhaps the broadest range of e-commerce activities in social computing is occurring on Facebook. Facebook's business model depends on advertising revenue; user accounts are free of charge. Perhaps because of this drive for advertising dollars, or perhaps because of its leading position in the realm of social networking, Facebook has many different opportunities for companies to advertise their products and connect with customers.

Some of the advertising on Facebook follows very traditional online methods. Banner advertisements are posted on the sides of pages for different products and services. These advertisements may be for any kind of product or service and may or may not be related to a user's particular interests. While the traffic on Facebook does provide wide exposure to advertisements of this type the tactic does not take advantage of the real potential of social computing for e-commerce.

A step beyond the basic banner advertisement on Facebook is one that takes the concept one step further. Some advertisements are broadcast to the general user population of Facebook but instead of just linking to a product, direct users to some kind of interactive exercise. This not only puts the product or service in front of potential customers, but engages the potential customer and begins the process of building a relationship. Traditional marketing values relationship-based marketing efforts and by bringing a customer into an interactive exercise, even virtually, that relationship can begin to grow.

Neither of these first instances of marketing on Facebook, however, is different from what could be achieved with advertising on search engines, websites, or other online media outlets. The advertising advantage to Facebook is that Facebook is social networking; there is extensive demographic information about potential customers freely shared online. Taking advantage of this information is where social computing takes marketing on a different path from traditional methods.

Facebook user profiles provide information for users to share things like their personal interests, taste in music, favorite television shows, and more. There are also areas for sharing their birth date, education, and work information. Based on these categories a marketer has access to an incredible amount of information. Based on education and work information income can be reasonably extrapolated. Interests, musical tastes, and other aspects of entertainment can provide information about how a user likes to spend their time and, by extension, on what they are likely to spend their money. The combination of all of this information presents companies with the opportunity to participate in highly targeted marketing campaigns.

Based on this demographic information Facebook advertisers can direct their efforts, and more importantly their advertising dollars, at users with an expressed interest in something that relates to the company's advertised product or service. Not only do advertisements find users who are likely to be more interested, but with targeted advertisements users may be less likely to ignore advertisements in the knowledge that the information may be useful to them. This connection between advertisers and potential customers is what the landscape of social computing offers modern marketers; better opportunities to directly connect and build relationships.

Through Facebook these relationships can take on a different identity than just customer loyalty or customer recognition of corporate branding. Customers can actually be "friends", in the virtual sense, with a company or a product. Facebook offers opportunities for companies to create their own profile pages, through which they can invite and accept friends and build a network of people who are interested in the company. Using the profile page the company can also post news and links that they feel will be of interest to customers. Through this process a company can build a network of customers who actively follow company activities and company news. Beyond this, the company will also be visible as a friend of the user to other users, which may serve to expand the company's marketing efforts even further.

Most recently the connection between users and companies or products has taken yet another step with users having the option to become a fan of a particular company or product. This process is similar to adding a company as a friend, but users' fan lists are displayed separately on their profiles, which makes the list more visible to other users, thus creating more exposure for the company. As both friends and fans of a company users also have the opportunity to submit feedback to the company through their online profile. This two-way communication channel makes social computing very different from more traditional forms of media where the company broadcasts information to potential customers and the reply from customers, if any, is delayed and takes place through a different form of media.

The next step in Facebook's marketing services may be coming soon. In 2009 Facebook provided a demonstration of instant polling technology to international business leaders at the World Economic Forum in Davos (Neate & Manson, 2009).

Marketing in Specialized Social Networks

Specialized social networks are smaller and more targeted than the large-scale social networks. As an exemplar this discussion will look at the LinkedIn network. The user population of LinkedIn is a much more limited cross-section of society than that of Facebook. While the total user population of LinkedIn is much smaller than Facebook, the professional networking focus of LinkedIn also leads users to self-select their use. As a professional site the overall environment of LinkedIn is different than that of other social networking sites and the categories of information that users share is also unique.

Instead of listing favorite television shows or taste in music, LinkedIn users share things like detailed histories of their education and work experience. Also unique to LinkedIn is the use of references. Users can request and provide references for other users reflecting an individual's experience and performance in past positions. In many ways, LinkedIn is almost an asynchronous job application, with a resume and references all posted for potential contacts to view and assess.

Because of the unique user population LinkedIn offers unique opportunities to companies' marketing efforts. Services that would not find an appreciative audience in a cross-section of society such as data analysis services, advanced financial management methodologies, or presentation software to network with Microsoft Project are not often seen advertised in traditional or alternative media. LinkedIn, however, provides a market segment that has a need and demand for products and services such as these and others. Educational opportunities are also prevalent in advertisements on LinkedIn, capitalizing on a user base who likely focus on career advancement and, by extension, are interested in continuing education.

The social computing advantage that LinkedIn offers to marketers is not necessarily that of a target market, but of a large target market that encompasses multiple different, but related, target markets. Research or other professional services that are often advertised on LinkedIn can certainly find target market populations in professional journals or related websites in many different fields. The problem lies in the fact that the individual fields all have their own journals, their own websites, and their own locations from which they receive information or view advertising. LinkedIn provides marketers with the opportunity to access many different specialties, all within the realm of highly trained professionals, in a single location for a single advertising fee.

Marketing in Micro-Blogging Environments

As is the case with large-scale social networks there is a leader in micro-blogging environments that will be examined here. Twitter is another unique environment that, more than other social networking sites, is very much still a work in progress. Banner advertisements are not seen on Twitter as they are on many other sites. Twitter, in contrast to other sites, is actually not generating revenue for its own use. The value to marketing in social computing through Twitter, however, is very real and can be seen growing at a phenomenal rate. The reasons users state for their use of Twitter may explain why the service is so popular; users report that they appreciate the technology's brevity, mobility, and pervasive access (Zhao & Rosson, 2009).

The Twitter phenomenon for marketing somewhat mirrors the initial rise of website use by companies. At first the use of Twitter accounts was rare, but then a few forward-thinking media outlets and celebrities started including a "follow us on Twitter" tag as part of their marketing campaign. Very quickly Twitter marketing has grown from an extra, unique idea to a method so important that organizations are actually paying people to, as part of their jobs, keep the organization's or famous individual's Twitter account updated to maintain connections with followers.

Twitter offers what may be the most personally connected relationship between customers and marketers. When a person chooses to follow an account, that account's updates show up on the user's page and, if the feature is activated, they are sent to the user via text message on their cell phone. In this way a follower of a company, news program, or celebrity can receive frequent updates about what is happening or upcoming items of interest.

While Twittering companies are not necessarily following a recognizable traditional format in their advertising, they are very actively pursuing customer relationship building. For customers who are interested enough in a product to keep daily, or even hourly, tabs on the company the ability to feel connected to the company can be an important factor in retaining that customer's business.

On the other side of marketing, customer responsiveness, Twitter is also breaking new ground. While maintaining accounts and sending out updates provides companies with an opportunity to distribute information, Twitter also offers opportunities for companies to receive information. Many major companies keep active searches in progress for their company names in Twitter posts. When an entry is found, an employee reads and analyzes the post. These activities can bring in information to the company, both good and bad, and provide opportunities to impress or retain customers.

There have been many stories of major companies responding much more quickly to Twitter posts than to their own traditional means of service provision. Many people have found that after long periods on the phone with customer service without a resolution, a post to Twitter along the lines of "Company X has run me in circles for 2 hours – can't get any help!" quickly earns an inquiry via e-mail or Twitter from a representative of the firm. Companies, knowing the popularity of Twitter and the network's reach, do not want unhappy customers complaining to the world. This type of proactive response to customer complaints is a new phenomenon, driven in part by the customer's ability to announce to the world what they are thinking at any given moment.

Again, as with some marketing aspects of Facebook, social computing is providing marketers with an opportunity to both provide and receive information from their customer base.

Not only is two-way communication possible, but the communication occurs in an environment of the customer's choosing, where the customer has chosen to connect to the company. Obviously, the ability to best serve customers who are most interested in the company can be a critical component of a company's overall relationship management function.

Marketing in Virtual Worlds

The final social computing application to be investigated here is the virtual world environment. Again, an exemplar will be presented, in this case the virtual world of SecondLife. Unlike social networks that are, more than anything else, user-controlled and customizable websites, SecondLife is an entire virtual world. The interaction in SecondLife takes place among three dimensional, animated figures, avatars, and live chats can occur either through text or audio. It is possible for people to own property in SecondLife and even participate in commerce, which can translate to actual money in the real world, earned as virtual money in the virtual world.

More than any other social computing application SecondLife provides an approximation of real-world marketing efforts. Some things, however, are still unique. One of the major considerations is that place, one of the 4 P's of marketing, is not as critical in the virtual world as it is in the real world. Some areas of SecondLife are more heavily visited than others, and being near as many users as possible is very important, but still not as critical as it is for a brick and mortar location. The SecondLife environment allows users to instantly travel from one point of the virtual world to another using a function called teleporting. Star Trek fans might better recognize it as transporting, although the SecondLife term is teleporting. With this technology it is entirely practical for a customer to move from literally one side of the world to the other to visit a store.

Outside of the place component of the marketing mix SecondLife offers companies most of the other opportunities that the real world does. Companies can build their own buildings, display their own logos and other brand identification, and place staff members in the store to assist customers with questions. By having a full virtual world interaction customers can have substantially the same experience in SecondLife as they achieve in the real world. Granted, the customer has no ability to actually feel the product, but with three dimensional rendering technology they can see the product inside and out from any angle if the company chooses to promote their product in that way.

The SecondLife environment gives users a very different experience from the other aspects of social computing, perhaps most significantly because SecondLife interactions are synchronous while others are asynchronous. The live discussion factor in SecondLife may lend itself to a more realistic experience for users, which is exactly what one would expect from a virtual world environment. The drawback for companies to the advantages of SecondLife is that synchronous communication requires a staff member to be available to customers any time the virtual location is open, which may be 24 hours a day. This factor could mean higher overall costs to support a virtual marketing presence in SecondLife than in other forms of social computing. Table 1 provides a comparison of different marketing activities that are available in different forms of social networking.

Implications for Marketing and Competition

Few people would argue against the idea that technology, and the role technology plays in the lives of individuals, is expanding and changing at an ever-increasing pace. Often, business is working a step behind technology simply because a technology has to exist before a strategy to utilize it can be developed. Because of this, a new

Table 1. Type of marketing activity by technology type

Technology Type	Type of Marketing Activity							
	Banner Ads	Link to Interactive Ad	User Fans and Recommendations	Demographic Targeted Marketing	Direct Connection to Companies	Select User Population	Synchronous Online Interaction	3-D Environment
Large-Scale Social Networks	X	X	X	X	X			
Specialized Social Networks	X	X	X	X	X	X		
Micro-Blogging Environments					X			
Virtual Worlds					X		X	X

technology often needs to be well-established before businesses begin to explore opportunities to expand their customer base, capture market share, or improve revenues with the new technology. Social computing appears to have reached a point at which companies are actively pursuing opportunities through the new media.

Very early in the timeline of home Internet access there were prognosticators who predicted that the Internet would be the great equalizer of society, that through the power of communication and free media there would be profound changes to society around the world. While predictions of world peace springing from a URL were somewhat overly ambitious, the impact of the Internet, and of social media in particular, cannot be ignored. Just one decade into the 21st century many examples have already come forward to prove the power of this new medium.

In the 2004 presidential elections then-candidate Howard Dean may be best remembered for effectively ending his candidacy with a distinctly un-presidential yee-haw yell that exploded on YouTube and other video sharing sites. What is not so well remembered is that prior to his primary candidacy Howard Dean was a virtual unknown in the political arena. Through the power of the Internet and social computing he set the all-time Democratic party record for fundraising by a primary candidate (Anstead and Chadwick, 2008). The market power of the technology can make large, and fast, changes to a reputation.

Another great social computing success story is the rise of DeAndre Way's music career. Better known as Soulja Boy, he gained recognition through promoting his own music and videos through online social networking sites, beginning with the music site SoundClick. What really catapulted his career, however, was the release of a video on YouTube in 2007, which not only launched Way to super stardom but also attracted armies of imitators posting their own video interpretations of Way's original work.

A presidential candidate and a rap star. What do these individuals have to do with one another and what do they have to do with the interaction of marketing and social computing? Dean and Way both relied on the power of social computing to engage in wide-ranging brand marketing. Their brand was their individual reputation and what they had to offer their target markets; leadership from Dean and entertainment from Way. In both cases millions of dollars of revenue were generated, and in Dean's unfortunate case the same media power responsible for putting him into an enviable position was responsible for ending that pursuit.

Companies can learn from these examples and the many more like them that have occurred throughout different industries in the past several years. The focus of customers' attention has shifted, and is continuing to shift from traditional to newer forms of media. While television viewership is still high and people still listen to the radio, online activities, video games, and streaming music choices are all eroding the amount of time that people spend receiving information from the traditional television and radio mediums. With this societal shift away from traditional advertising mediums, marketers must make adjustments and get their messages out, and collect their own information from, the activities to which customers are devoting their time. Failure to do this can, over time, ruin a company.

Historically, companies out of touch with the consumer have failed time and time again. In many ways, the downfall of American manufacturing can be tied directly to a failure to understand and respond to consumer wants and needs. Over time the quality of many American-manufactured products fell while, during the same time, the quality of products manufactured overseas increased. The American consumer came to appreciate quality goods and as a result moved to purchasing more foreign-made goods. Price points were also part of this change, as were labor relations and other issues, but at the root of the problem was a lack of focus on customer desires on the part of the American manufacturing firms.

One particularly stunning example of major failure, followed by what might be the most spectacular turn-around in business history, is Apple Computer. Apple was poised, in the 1980's, to dominate the personal computer market and become the primary operating system and software provider in the United States and perhaps, by extension, the world. The turning point came with the choice of whether or not to license operating systems (OS) to hardware manufacturers and software developers. Microsoft chose to allow anyone to produce hardware and software for their OS and turned into one of the most influential and powerful companies in history. Apple chose to keep their OS proprietary and limited users to only buying Apple hardware and software if they wanted an Apple OS. For years following this decision Apple was relegated to being just the education and artist computer, while Microsoft drove the PC revolution. This occurred because Microsoft followed what the customers wanted; choice.

Years later, however, Apple has once again gained prominence. Following successful launches of new operating systems, the iPod, and the iPhone, many consumers have Apple products on their short list of must-haves for holidays, birthdays, and other events. Apple has recovered by doing exactly what they failed to do in the early fight for the PC market; they focused on what customers wanted.

Social computing is putting exactly this scenario in front of companies and in board rooms around the world. In order to be successful marketing campaigns have to reach the target audience with a message. To be more successful these campaigns have to solicit responses from customers and deliver strategic intelligence to corporate decision-makers.

Issues, Controversies, and Problems

As with any new technology or new application of existing technologies there are issues concerning the use of social computing in marketing. The primary concerns among social computer users and security experts are privacy and security. The more popular social computing becomes, the larger the number of users. As the number of users increase there is increasing value for both marketers and also criminals to take advantage of these users.

Privacy can be a major concern when using social computing technology. While the purpose of the technology is to share information, the scope of that sharing can have unintended and dangerous consequences. Some of these issues are unique to users, but some also involve threats and concerns for companies engaged in marketing efforts.

Implications of Public Information Sharing

Privacy concerns for individual users can range from very personal to distinctly professional. New users, or users who simply possess a certain naiveté about online materials, may post material to social computing applications that they do not want to be seen by the world at large. Unfortunately, many social computing applications are set by default to leave material open to the world. As social computing, and social networking in particular, rose in popularity segments of society quickly came to realize that unprotected, openly shared material could be used to discover details about people's lives.

Merging the personal with the professional, there have been many cases of individuals losing their jobs because of social networking activity. The leading culprit in this type of situation has usually been Facebook. If someone calls in sick to work but then their Facebook status or a new photo album that day show them at a baseball game their boss is unlikely to be impressed. During the 2008 presidential elections a couple of Obama staffers made the national news with a Facebook picture of the two of them acting quite inappropriately with a cardboard cutout of opponent Hilary Clinton. Multiple schoolteachers have been terminated as a result of risqué content they posted to MySpace accounts.

These types of events are not just limited to leading to termination; they may prevent someone from ever being hired. Increasingly, employers have found Facebook and other online profiles to be sources of information about potential employees. Publicly available pictures of job seekers participating in heavy drinking or other activities that present the potential for embarrassment or other trouble for a company may end a company's interest in that individual.

The personal implications of social networking are one issue, but similar problems can be part of marketing efforts. Marketers must understand that while their use of social computing does put their product and reputation in front of the public, they also open themselves to similar problems to those experienced by individual users. Issues of damaging exposure and negative publicity for companies can be a serious concern for social network marketing efforts.

When a company invites the world at large to network with them and be a part of their social network there is the possibility of negative results. The goal of marketing through social networking is to build positive relationships with customers and engender a feeling of connectedness between the customer and the company. For customers who enjoy the company's product or service and have had positive experiences the public availability of social network marketing works.

Unfortunately, no matter how good a company is at what they do there are inevitably negative customer experiences. Marketers are well aware that a dissatisfied customer will talk about their experience to many more people than will a satisfied customer, a problem that makes a company's recovery from customer problems very important. The challenge in using social computing as a part of a company's marketing mix is that dissatisfied customers can very quickly reach a much larger audience much more quickly than customers working with companies that do not use social computing.

As mentioned earlier there are companies who continually search Twitter pages to see if their company's name is mentioned to offer service to dissatisfied customers. This is done, in large part, to try and avoid the negative publicity that can result from a Twitter user posting unflattering things about a company in such a large public forum. In other marketing efforts the effects could be more significant. When set up to be friends with other users or hosting a fan page on sites like Facebook a company may be more open to damaging criticism. A dissatisfied customer would have the opportunity to post to the company's wall or other communication medium through the social network to directly reach other current or interested potential customers of that company specifically. Just as a company can use a social network to directly target their ideal market, so can people who are upset with the company use the same technology to easily reach the company's target market with complaints and other negative facts or assertions that could damage the company's reputation.

In this scenario, the company likely has technical options for removing negative wall posts and other items, but the solution could create another problem. If negative comments are removed by the company customers may view such actions as an attempt to hide from criticism. If complaints are countered by the company they may or may not be believed. Regardless of response, the potential negative implications of opening a company's reputation to comment through social computing technologies is real and must be considered as a part of the overall marketing strategy.

Another potential issue is that of public, online gaffes by a company marketing campaign that can quickly move beyond the company's control. There have been many marketing mistakes in business history, the most famous of them becoming almost famous business school examples. The vacuum company Electrolux coming from Britain to the United States with their wonderful British slogan, which did not quite translate into American English, "Nothing sucks like Electrolux" is one. Some of the Abercrombie and Fitch catalogs protested as pornographic are another. Traditionally marketing efforts through print, radio, and television had a limited shelf life; even the most

disastrous marketing decision could fade away relatively quickly.

Social computing has changed this. A bad choice in a marketing campaign distributed through the Internet can easily be captured, archived, and spread throughout the world through users' own networks. This adds a new pressure to every decision made by marketers. A company's media, much like that of regular users, may no longer be their own once the material is posted in online social forums.

As another privacy concern, even users who keep their information more private may have that privacy compromised by connecting to companies through social computing applications. Many times, even if a user has their privacy settings secured their material is open to their friends. For the user, this means that their information is accessible by the companies they choose to connect to through social computing technology. For companies, this creates a potential burden of liability; what will the company do to safeguard user information?

The potential advantages of social computing use in marketing are substantial, but they are not without risks. Privacy and security are real concerns that need to be addressed in a company's social computing marketing plan and assessed for potential risk and exposure. This is certainly not an argument against using the technology, but a recognition of the potential risks of doing so.

SOLUTIONS AND RECOMMENDATIONS

The best method for a company to pursue marketing through social computing is to approach the project as they would any other marketing initiative. That is, the company should invest sufficient time and study into the market as a whole to determine the optimum course to pursue. Social computing, while a different medium for marketing, follows the traditional model of how the marketing process works.

A company's first step should be to assess how to reach their target market. User statistics, demographic studies, and other information can provide a company with valuable information about what kinds of users participate in what kinds of social computing. This process is similar to what a company will do when investigating television advertising; commercials are aired during shows that attract the company's target customer population.

After determining the best method by which to reach their target market, a company should engage in test marketing through the social computing application they have chosen. A limited release, carefully monitored and periodically assessed will help to define the best way in which to proceed. As with other business strategies, an entry into social computing does not need to be done without considerable study. As results from test marketing are analyzed necessary changes, up to and including terminating the current project if indicated, should be made.

Following appropriate planning and successful test marketing the full-scale rollout of a social computing marketing campaign may proceed. This is not the end of the development cycle. As with any marketing activity social computing activities should be routinely monitored and assessed to determine the continuing viability of the program. Because of the rapid pace of change in social computing, and in technology trends generally, social computing marketing projects may require closer attention and more frequent review than more traditional media. Beyond simply monitoring current activities, companies involved in social computing need to monitor the entire social computing community. While it may be impossible to predict what the next social computing development will be, it is highly likely that new networks and new technologies will continue to emerge and influence the user environment and optimal choices for marketers.

FUTURE RESEARCH OPPORTUNITIES

Due in large part to the relatively recent emergence of marketing in social computing there are ample opportunities for research opportunities in the future. Existing marketing efforts, existing social computing applications, and future developments in both are all rich fields for research. There will also likely be additional directions for research in the future as the field matures.

Security is one area of potential interest. Nov and Wattal (2009) have done some initial work in security preferences and habits of users of social networking applications but recognize substantial potential for much more. Studies of security preferences and practices in multiple social networks, additional research in optimal survey questions, and simply more studies to improve the generalizability of results are all potential avenues in the future (Nov & Wattal, 2009).

Literature addressing the potential of social networking to change human interaction can also be of interest. While interpersonal communications and engagement with a given organization are admittedly different from a pure marketing perspective, human behavior and connections between individuals and organizations are key factors in marketing. Ellison, Lampe, and Steinfield (2009) identify one future research question as, "How can the power of social network sites be leveraged in other contexts, including formal organizations?" (p 9).

There is also a question of how social network-obtained information is integrated with other sources of information available to an individual. Future research could be conducted in examining how users integrate online and offline information and how those different sources influence their decision-making (Brown, Broderick, & Lee, 2007).

Existing marketing efforts could provide good data to marketing researchers. Information collected by companies during their existing social computing marketing efforts could provide a historical perspective of how the field has developed to the current early stage. Access to this data could be difficult as many companies will be hesitant to release information that might be strategically sensitive. If available, a study of one or, ideally, multiple firms could form the beginning of a body of literature on the strategy and execution of social computing marketing.

Studies of existing social computing networks could prove less challenging, but no less relevant to the literature. Both marketing and social computing must be understood to provide a full picture of social computing marketing activities. Study into social computing, and specifically the connections of social computing to business activity, can provide insight into how the industry has developed, how it works, and how companies may capitalize on the industry for their own use. Social computing as a social phenomenon and in relation to eLearning activities has been studied, but there is much less research in the area of social computing and marketing.

The future direction of both fields is not something that can be accurately predicted, but research into existing movements, combined with historical data about related technologies and related business strategies, could form unique theoretical studies. Predicting changes in technology, particularly when those changes are connected to user preferences, is challenging, but there is certainly a place in the literature for hypotheses to be forwarded. As the reach and influence of social computing and the presence of businesses in social computing both continue to grow there will be increased opportunities for the hypothetical study of the future of both fields and their connections to one another.

CONCLUSION

There is little debate that today's world is one of unprecedented technological change, or that the changes are impacting almost every aspect of life. As ordinary people move ever closer to making the theory of ubiquitous computing a reality the potential impact of social computing and companies' interactions with the technology will continue to expand. Today's business leaders, and the leaders of the future, need to be conversant in social networking marketing.

History has shown that new technologies and new media often move from being instruments of competitive advantage and revolutionary firms to being necessary components of an overall marketing mix. Social computing may be the next major media that many companies must focus on in order to remain competitive. Time will tell if social computing or some other new technology will be the next major marketing media to be embraced by industry, but there doubtless will be a technology of some sort that proves to be the next indispensable medium for marketers.

REFERENCES

Anstead, N., & Chadwick, A. (2008). Parties, election campaigning, and the internet: Toward a comparative institutional approach. In Chaswick, A., & Howard, P. (Eds.), *The Routledge handbook of internet politics*. New York: Routledge.

Boyd, D., & Ellison, N. (2007). Social network sites: Definition, history, and scholarship. *Journal of Computer-Mediated Communication, 13*(1), 210–230. doi:10.1111/j.1083-6101.2007.00393.x

Brown, J., Broderick, A., & Lee, N. (2007). Word of mouth communication within online communities: Conceptualizing the online social network. *Journal of Interactive Marketing, 21*(3), 2–20. doi:10.1002/dir.20082

Chung, W., Chen, H., & Reid, E. (2009). Business stakeholder analyzer: An experiment of classifying stakeholders on the Web. *Journal of the American Society for Information Science and Technology, 60*(1), 59–74. doi:10.1002/asi.20948

Constantinides, E. (2006). The marketing mix revisited: Towards the 21st century marketing. *Journal of Marketing Management, 22*, 407–438. doi:10.1362/026725706776861190

Dominici, G. (2009). From marketing mix to e-marketing mix: A literature review and classification. *International Journal of Business and Management, 4*(9), 17–24.

Ellison, N., Lampe, C., & Steinfield, C. (2009, January-February). Social network sites and society: Current trends and future possibilities. *Interactions Magazine, 16*(1), 6–9.

LinkedIn Press. (2009). About us. Retrieved July 24, 2009, from http://press.linkedin.com/about

Mangiaracina, R., Brugnoli, G., & Perego, A. (2009). The eCommerce customer journey: A model to assess and compare the user experience of the eCommerce websites. *Journal of Internet Banking and Commerce, 14*(3), 1–11.

Neate, R., & Mason, R. (2009, February 2). Networking site cashes in on friends. *The Telegraph*.

Nov, O., & Wattal, S. (2009). Social computing privacy concerns: Antecedents and effects. In *Proceedings of the 27th international Conference on Human Factors in Computing Systems* [Boston, MA, April 4 - 9, CHI '09] (pp. 333-336). New York: ACM.

Nyland, R. (2007). The gratification niches of Internet social networking, e-mail, and face-to-face communication. Unpublished master's thesis. Brigham Young University, UT.

O'Malley, G. (2008). Study: LinkedIn users have higher incomes. *Online media daily*. Retrieved July 24, 2009, from http://www.mediapost.com/publications/?fa=Articles.showArticle&art_aid=94128

Oreskovic, A. (2009). Facebook gets $6.5 billion valuation with share sale. *Reuters*. Retrieved July 24, 2009, from http://www.reuters.com/article/internetNews/idUSTRE56C4TH20090714

Ostrow, A. (2009). How many people actually use Twitter? *Mashable: The social media guide*. Retrieved July 24, 2009, from http://mashable.com/2009/04/28/twitter-active-users/

Parameswaran, M., & Whinston, A. (2007). Research issues in social computing. *Journal of the Association for Information Systems, 8*(6), 336–350.

Rood, V., & Bruckman, A. (2009). Member behavior in company online communities. In *Proceedings the ACM 2009 international conference on supporting group work, Sanibel Island, FL* (pp. 209–218). New York: ACM. doi:10.1145/1531674.1531705

Rooksby, J., Baxter, G., Cliff, D., Greenwood, D., Harvey, N., Kahn, A., et al. (2009). *Social networking and the workplace*. Bristol, UK: The UK Large Scale Complex IT Systems Initiative.

Second Life. (2009). SecondLife economic statistics. Retrieved August 3, 2009, from http://secondlife.com/statistics/economy-data.php

Smith, D. (2009). MySpace shrinks as Facebook, Twitter, and Bebo grab its users. *The Observer*. Retrieved July 24, 2009, from http://www.guardian.co.uk/technology/2009/mar/29/myspace-facebook-bebo-twitter

Wind, Y., & Todi, M. (2008). *Advertising on social networking websites*. Wharton Research Scholars Journal.

Zhao, D., & Rosson, M. (2009). How and why people Twitter: The role that micro-blogging plays in informal communication at work. In *Proceedings of the ACM 2009 international Conference on Supporting Group Work*, Sanibel Island, FL, May 10 - 13 [New York: ACM.]. *Group, 09*, 243–252. doi:10.1145/1531674.1531710

KEY TERMS AND DEFINITIONS

E-Commerce: a commercial exchange conducted via electronic means, most often the Internet.

Four P's: the four traditional aspects of the marketing mix, namely product, place, price, and promotion.

Micro-Blog: a social medium where individuals post small updates to express themselves, such as Twitter which limits posts to 140 characters.

Social Computing: the use of Internet-based technology to connect people personally and professionally through a common site and interface.

Ubiquitous Computing: a level of computer and Internet use where individuals are perpetually connected to the technology throughout their daily activities.

Virtual World: an immersive online environment where users operate in a three-dimensional environment and interact with other users synchronously.

Chapter 14

From Real to Virtual and Back Again:
The Use and Potential of Virtual Social Worlds within the IT Industry

Andreas M. Kaplan
ESCP Europe, France

Michael Haenlein
ESCP Europe, France

ABSTRACT

Researchers and practitioners alike have speculated that virtual social worlds and social gaming will likely be major platforms for business operations in the future. This chapter shows how major IT companies make use of virtual social worlds (esp. the online application Second Life), focusing on the examples of Dell, Hewlett-Packard, International Business Machines (IBM) and Microsoft. Specifically, the authors investigate whether and how corporate presences within Second Life can be used as platforms to distribute Real Life products and services, so-called virtual commerce (v-Commerce). They show that although the four firms included in our analysis all have a different perspective on the potential of virtual social worlds, each of them made an active and conscious choice about how to use this medium. With regard to v-Commerce, their results indicate that although the short-term profit potential of this form of distribution is still limited, Second Life residents perceive the idea of buying products through in-world stores as positive and exciting. Based on these results, they derive a set of key insights regarding the business potential of virtual social worlds, consumers' reactions towards corporate presences within Second Life, and advice for firms planning to enter this type of application.

INTRODUCTION

In May 2008, the market research company Gartner, Inc. (Stevens & Pettey, 2008) estimated that

by 2012 around 70 percent of all organizations will have established their own private virtual world. They furthermore forecast that "nine out of ten business forays into virtual worlds fail within 18 months but their impact on organizations could

DOI: 10.4018/978-1-61692-904-6.ch014

be as big as that of the Internet" (Stevens & Pettey, 2008). In a similar spirit Ives and Junglas (2008) predict that virtual worlds will likely be major platforms for business operations within ten years time and Kaplan and Haenlein (2009a) state that virtual worlds are "associated with a set of specific characteristics that offer unique challenges and business opportunities" which make them a "virtually unexplored marketing territory" (Hemp, 2006). These comments show that although press coverage about virtual worlds and social gaming decreased over recent months, many experts still believe in the upside potential of this type of applications. The intention of our manuscript is to continue this line of thought and to show how major IT companies make use of virtual social worlds (esp. the online application Second Life). For this, we focus on the examples of Dell, Hewlett-Packard (HP), International Business Machines (IBM) and Microsoft – all major players in the IT sector – and present the different views these companies have on virtual worlds. Specifically, we are interested in the question whether and how corporate presences within Second Life can be used as platforms to distribute Real Life products and services, so-called virtual commerce (v-Commerce). An analysis of v-Commerce appears particularly important as the growth and evolution of the World Wide Web, as we know it today, has been heavily triggered, shaped and influenced by the corporate use of this medium for the distribution of products and services. Today e-Commerce in its various forms accounts for an important share of all activities on the World Wide Web (for a historical analysis of e-Commerce see: Heng, 2003) and it therefore makes sense to expect v-Commerce to be a similar trigger of virtual world growth and success.

To achieve this objective, our manuscript is structured as follows: In the next two sections, we provide readers with a brief introduction into the virtual social world "Second Life", by highlighting its concept and key functionalities as well as its theoretical foundations, and discuss the ways in which this application differs from other forms of social media, such as blogs, collaborative projects (e.g. Wikipedia), content communities (e.g. YouTube), social networking sites (e.g. Facebook) and virtual game worlds (e.g. World of Warcraft). We then provide an in-depth analysis of how Dell, HP, IBM and Microsoft use Second Life as well as the strategies these companies intend to accomplish by its usage. Subsequently, we focus on the question whether and how virtual worlds can be used as a platform for v-Commerce using the example of Dell Island. We report the results of two customer surveys regarding users' reactions to Dell Island as well as v-Commerce in general and of one interview with Laura P. Thomas (alias *Pyrrha Dell*), the person behind Dell's Second Life strategy. Our article finishes with a discussion of the key insights obtained from our analysis, focusing on three areas: the business potential of virtual social worlds, consumers' attitudes towards corporate presences within Second Life and advice for firms planning to enter virtual worlds.

SECOND LIFE: CONCEPT AND KEY FUNCTIONALITIES

Second Life is a three-dimensional virtual world that has been created by the San Francisco-based company Linden Research, Inc. Users (who are called "residents") can enter it through a downloadable client program and subsequently interact with each other, explore their environment or create new content within the world. Although Second Life had already been launched in 2003, it did not become popular before late 2006, when Linden Research partly abandoned its initial subscription fee-based model and introduced basic (free) accounts next to its fee-based premium services. Since then it has, however, recorded an exponential growth with an estimated 19 million registered residents in 2009. Given that Second Life is a virtual world, residents appear in it in the form of personalized avatars. These avatars are generally of human appearance and can easily be customized depending on the preferences of their user, including modifications in basic body structure (e.g. hairstyle, skin) or appearance (e.g. clothing). This flexibility leads to a high degree of diversity within the Second Life population, which includes male/ female humanoid avatars as well as residents that prefer to appear as robots, mechs (i.e. walking vehicles controlled by pilots) or furries (i.e. anthropomorphic animal characters). Communication between avatars is most often conducted in written format (either chat or instant messaging) although a voice-chat option was introduced in August 2007. To move from one location within Second Life to another, avatars can walk, fly, teleport or ride vehicles such as cars, submarines or hot-air balloons. Residents also have the option to purchase real estate within the virtual social world, ranging from small lots (512 m^2) to whole regions and private islands, on which they can build houses for their avatar to live in which can subsequently be equipped with a wide range of furniture items and appliances. Avatar interaction within Second Life is largely driven by subcultures that either mirror Real Life settings (e.g. shopping malls, nightclubs) or fictional/ historical situations (e.g. ancient Rome).

Some of the products and services within Second Life (e.g. items for avatar customization) are available free of charge (so called "freebies") while the higher quality and branded versions are usually sold for virtual money (Linden Dollars, L$). In order to obtain such money, avatars can either exchange Real Life currencies for Linden Dollars via the Second Life Exchange at a floating exchange rate that is approximately stable at 250 L$ per US$ or derive virtual income by managing businesses, working in stores or providing entertainment services which most prominently include adult entertainment. According to official Second Life economic statistics more than 1,000 Second Life residents have spend more than 1 million Linden Dollars (roughly US$ 4,000) in-world during July 2009. Money that has been introduced into

Second Life can either be kept in one of Second Life's banks (in exchange for interest payments) or re-exchanged into Real Life currency. For some users income earned within Second Life even complements their Real Life salary. The increasing popularity and economic importance of Second Life has also motivated many Real Life companies to start activities within Second Life (Kaplan and Haenlein, 2009b). Consumer corporations, including Telecom Italia, Circuit City and Toyota, maintain Second Life flagship stores to sell virtual (digital) equivalents of their Real Life products (e.g. communication services, consumer electronics, cars) that can be used for avatar enhancement. Others, such as Endemol or Dell, organize virtual reality shows or sponsor events of public interest for Second Life residents. Also, governments and non-profit organizations are increasingly present within Second Life. The Maldives, Sweden and Estonia have opened diplomatic representations, and educational institutions such as Harvard, Stanford and INSEAD are testing Second Life as a tool to enhance interactivity in distance learning programs (Kaplan, 2009b). Recently, public administration officials have even started to discuss the need for official regulation of Second Life, which has previously only been controlled by Linden Research. This resulted in a ban on in-world gambling in July 2007, the closure of virtual banks that did not possess a Real World banking license in January 2008 (Kaplan, 2009a) and rising discussions about the taxation of virtual income derived from activities within Second Life that remains in the virtual social world in the form of Linden Dollars.

From a theoretical perspective, virtual social worlds are founded upon the concepts of postmodernism and hyperreality (e.g. Badot & Cova, 2003; Cova, 1996). According to philosophers such as Jean Baudrillard, Michel Foucault or Umberto Eco, the late 1960s and early 1970s represented a turning point in modern philosophy (e.g. Firat, Sherry, & Venkatesh, 1994). Previously, from the eighteenth century onward, the concerted effort of all scientific domains has been targeted toward the search for universal laws and absolute truths. This period, which is best reflected in the philosophy of the rationalist Bertrand Russell or the management principles of the engineer Frederick Taylor, is often referred to as modernism. In the late 1960s, however, more and more people began to question the foundations of this movement. Evolutions such as nuclear weapons and environmental pollution led to a revolt against authority reflected in the rules of the "establishment" and, ultimately, marked the beginning of postmodernism. Postmodernism is characterized by hostility toward generalizations and a celebration of skepticism. In science it has been reflected in developments such as chaos theory and fractal geometry, in the arts it can be seen in street art and the "happenings" of Christo, and in management it has resulted in the introduction of flexible work practices and matrix organizations. Today, the basic conditions of postmodernism correspond to the new view many managers have of their companies, which puts tangible resources, service delivery and customer–company value co-creation on top of the agenda (e.g. Vargo and Lusch, 2004). Hence, it is not surprising that postmodern ideas have increasingly spread into the business world. One example is the rising use of hyperrealities (e.g. Graillot, 2004), i.e. artificially created settings that appear to be real for the individuals involved in them, as strategic tools to improve the service experience. Hyperrealities are based on "the idea that reality is constructed, and therefore it is possible to construct things that are more real than real" (Venkatesh, Sherry, &Firat, 1993, p. 221). They are a key reflection of the postmodern philosophy as they do not assume that everyone shares the same reality but, instead, simulate alternative realities in which users can perform activities they would be unable or unwilling to do in real life. Places such as Disneyland or Las Vegas were among the first to build seemingly real environments that induce a dream-like state in which consumers tend to spend money more

generously. Virtual worlds, especially virtual social worlds, are just the continuation of this development online.

DIFFERENCES BETWEEN VIRTUAL SOCIAL WORLDS AND RELATED SOCIAL MEDIA

Virtual worlds in general and Second Life in particular are part of a larger group of Internet-based applications often referred to as "social media". This term can be defined as "a group of Internet-based applications that build on the ideological and technological foundations of Web 2.0, and that allow the creation and exchange of User Generated Content" (Kaplan & Haenlein, 2010, p. 61). Social media can take various forms, such as collaborative projects (e.g. Wikipedia), content communities (e.g. YouTube), blogs and microblogs (e.g. Twitter; see also Kaplan & Haenlein, 2011), social networking sites (e.g. Facebook) as well as virtual game worlds (e.g. World of Warcraft). Content communities can be defined as places on the Internet in which consumers connect and which are used as sources of information and social interaction. Compared with virtual social worlds, content communities do not usually allow real-time interaction between users, as content is typically posted within an online forum and replied to later, and are limited to one specific content area (e.g. one product group, media type or area of interest). Additionally, they offer no option to create a customized virtual identity (apart from the use of certain fonts, colors and emoticons), are limited to the exchange of text and/ or media and, hence, two-dimensional, and do not allow users to engage in economic activities such as the buying and selling of virtual products and services. In contrast to content communities, blogs and microblogs provide a much richer base to develop customized virtual self-presentations and to construct digital identities. They allow users to exchange all types of information, independent of content restrictions, except for potential legal boundaries. Virtual worlds share with blogs the ability to create customized virtual self-presentations, although this is done in the form of avatars instead of websites. Social networking sites as well as virtual worlds allow for interaction between users. However, in contrast to virtual worlds, this is usually not done in real time. Additionally, like content communities, exploration of content is limited to two dimensions (graphical websites) and there is no possibility of conducting business-like activities with other users. Within virtual worlds, it is necessary to differentiate between virtual game and social worlds. Virtual game worlds, such as the fantasy-world EverQuest, follow strong rules regarding the type of interactions allowed between users. In the cod-medieval virtual game world "World of Warcraft" users are, for example, obliged to appear in the form of specific character types (e.g. night elf, dwarf, troll). Additionally, trading items or equipment in exchange for real money is usually not permitted and can be punished by exclusion from the game. In contrast, players within virtual social worlds do not need to obey

such strict rules and therefore have the freedom to engage in interactions that closely mirror Real Life settings. Especially the ability to engage in economic activities with other users makes virtual social worlds different from other social media and particularly interesting for corporate use. One way to classify virtual social worlds reflects this ability to conduct economic activities (see Figure 1) and results in four distinct groups, depending on whether there is a real demand possible (i.e. some form of in-world means of payment exists) and whether users/ avatars can offer products and services they generated themselves (vs. generated by the world's owner).

Next to a classification according to economic activities, one also can differentiate between virtual social worlds depending on whether they are specialized on specific user groups (e.g. Webkinz or Teen Second Life, which are targeted toward children and teenagers), geographic regions (e.g. the Chinese HiPiHi) or leisure activities (e.g. Red Light Center for adult entertainment), or if they are open to a broad range of users and preferences. Second Life is part of the latter group

Figure 1. Different types of virtual worlds

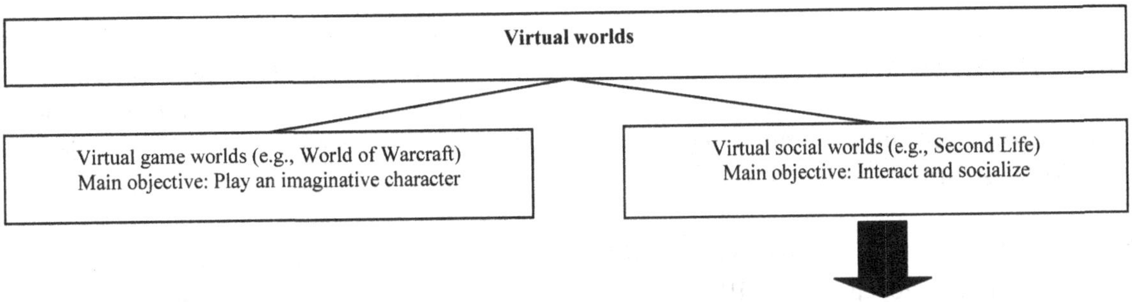

		DEMAND	
		No means of payment exists	**Means of payment exists**
SUPPLY	**Possibility to sell user-generated products and services**	Example: Active Worlds Active Worlds users can build structures and areas from a selection of objects but no in-world currency exists	Example: Second Life Second Life residents can create products and services which can be exchanged using Linden Dollars
	No possibility to sell user-generated products and services	Example: Club Penguin Designed for children between 6 and 14, Club Penguin offers no possibility to create, sell or purchase products and services	Example: Habbo Hotel The owner of Habbo Hotel can create products and services which can be exchanged using credits and pixels

of virtual social worlds, as the only restriction is for users to be of age 18 and above although there is no formal proof of age required to set up a Second Life account. Our manuscript focuses on Second Life as one example of virtual social worlds, as it is one of the most successful and well-known applications in that area. Additionally Second Life has been claimed to offer better functionalities in terms of avatar customization and currency exchange than comparable sites such as ActiveWorlds or There.com.

THE USE OF SECOND LIFE WITHIN THE IT INDUSTRY

In the following section, we will present the views that four major IT companies hold regarding Second Life and the way in which they make use of this virtual world in conducting their business. To select the firms to be included in our sample, we relied on the 2009 Fortune Global 500 ranking and included all companies among the Top 50 firms which maintained activities in either the Computers & Office Equipment, Information Technology Services or Computer Software industry. This resulted in a list of four companies which we focused on in the context of our analysis: Dell, Hewlett-Packard (HP), International Business Machines (IBM) and Microsoft.

Dell: Being Present – Virtual Worlds as End-Customer Channels

Dell entered Second Life in November 2006 and was, therefore, together with IBM one of the first IT companies to be present within this new medium. From the beginning onwards Dell considered Second Life primarily as a potential channel to get in touch with its end-customers and used it as a tool for advertising/ communication and v-Commerce. Dell maintains four connected islands within Second Life that are regularly used to organize events which either complement or mirror Real Life advertising/ communication campaigns. In January 2007 Dell organized a virtual premier party for Universal's "Evan Almighty" movie, which carried Dell's product placement and co-branding in Real Life. Four months later, in April 2007, Dell extended its "Plant a Tree for Me" program into the virtual world and gave residents the opportunity to grow virtual saplings on dedicated Second Life areas. In January 2008, the launch party of the new Crystal monitor line at the Consumer Electronics Show in Las Vegas was mirrored within Second Life in the form of a virtual launch party. Since 2008 Dell also recurrently makes use of SL for its employees by using its virtual conference center to conduct meetings that would ordinarily have conducted by means of a simple conference call. While such activities ensured constant coverage of Dell within virtual and real media, Dell's unique strategy consisted of using Second Life as a tool to distribute Real Life products. At the beginning of its activities Dell distributed free virtual equivalents of its Real Life XPS personal computer line to Second Life residents in the context of an advertising campaign. These PCs were able to perform simple tasks, such as alerting a resident when one of his/ her friends was nearby. Soon afterwards, Dell also offered residents the possibility to fully customize and personalize their PC within the Dell Factory on Dell Island (see Kaplan, 2010 for more detail on virtual mass customization). A virtual equivalent of this PC was then given to the resident free of charge while, at the same time, the user received the option to purchase a Real Life version through the Dell webpage. This makes Dell one of the first companies overall and the only one in our sample that tested Second Life as a potential distribution channel for Real Life products.

HP: Dangerous Endeavors – Virtual Worlds as Risky and Potentially Harmful Environments

Different to Dell, HP always had a more conservative view on Second Life. It is the only company in our analysis that neither maintains an official corporate presence within the virtual world nor appears to be willing to develop one in the near future. In April 2007 HP's Vice President of Global Marketing Strategy, Eric Kintz, wrote on the company's official blog that although Second Life "opens up a window into the future of 3D web", he still needs to be convinced of the potential of this new medium in a broader marketing context. In his essay Kintz listed ten reasons for his skeptical view on Second Life, including the world's complex and non-scalable technology, its misleading subscriber statistics and the danger that the primarily adult-oriented content may pose on a company's image. The critical viewpoint which HP maintains has also been supported by its "Chief Seer" Philip McKinney who highlighted legal difficulties that could arise from the unique structure of this new environment. Especially in the context of cross-border collaboration projects it may not be clear who owns the legal right on a new development and in which country (or even in which reality) legal disputes should be settled. Nevertheless, McKinney also states that virtual worlds are likely to be a growing market segment over the next 20 years, although his firm's own activities within Second Life are limited. In May 2007, HP participated in a virtual job fair, hosted by TMP Worldwide Advertising & Communication on its Second Life island. In February 2009, HP sponsored the in-world Eduverse Talk on "Building Higher Education Campuses in Second Life" hosted by the International Society for Technology in Education (ISTE). Unsurprisingly, the skeptical view which HP holds with respect to virtual worlds in general and Second Life in particular has generated a substantive amount of press coverage for the company. Especially the very divergent views of HP and Dell have been the subject of much debate. For example, 18 days after Eric Kintz's statement Dell provided an official answer on its own corporate blog in which it criticized HP's perspective to solely approach Second Life as a marketing channel instead of seeing it as an opportunity to learn about 3D Internet and get involved with its end-customers (Thomas, 2007).

IBM: Employees First – Virtual Worlds as Tools for Internal Process Management

Although IBM joined Second Life at the same time as its competitor Dell (in November 2006), "Big Blue" used the medium with a different focus and concentrated on its potential in the areas of internal process and human resource (HR) management. It is currently one of the biggest real estate owners within Second Life (the company owns more than 50 islands of 65,536 m2 each) and has set up a \$10 million project to build a three-dimensional internet using the Second Life platform. The company's "Virtual Universe Community" (VUC) consists of 6,100 employees, responsible for identifying new business models within virtual worlds. IBM uses Second Life to conduct meetings, provide training and education (esp. for new employees), organize events and develop new products. By early January 2007, more than 3,000 employees had already created their own Second Life avatar, 10% of them using the medium regularly. According to Linden Lab (2009), IBM saved the impressive amount of \$320,000 by conducting the three-day IBM Academy of Technology's annual world conference in Second Life instead of Real Life. According to the Academy of Technology's president Joanne Martin "the meeting in Second Life was everything that you could do at a traditional conference – and more – at one fifth the cost and without a single case of jet lag" (Linden Lab, 2009). To ensure appropriate conduct in virtual as well as real interactions, IBM even established a set of virtual world guidelines that are supposed to regulate employee's conduct and appearance within Second Life. IBM maintains a recruitment office within Second Life that is linked to the firm's recruiting web pages in each country and provides general information and job offers on information desks and interactive screens. In case a potential candidate is interested, s/he can either get in touch with an HR representative in the form of a Real Life conversation or meet in a virtual private room for a job talk from avatar to avatar. Although IBM's Second Life island was initially reserved for internal use only, the company decided to open part of its space for public use in May 2007. Since then it has been used, among others, to host the official Wimbledon tournament presence within Second Life and to organize IBM's alumni reunion. Although Second Life residents can interact with IBM sales representatives at the firm's virtual business center, Big Blue does not offer the possibility of v-Commerce within the virtual world.

Microsoft: Stepwise Exploration – Virtual Worlds as New Applications for Existing Solutions

Compared to the three aforementioned companies, Microsoft entered Second Life relatively late with its own corporate presence, in June 2007. Before this date, the company's Second Life activities were limited to single, isolated events organized to promote selected products and services. The first activities turned around Microsoft's Visual Studio solution, the company's main integrated development environment. Microsoft invited developers to its Visual Studio Island to solve logic puzzles and rewarded 60 winners with a plot of virtual land. In January 2007, the firm hosted a streaming concert of the rave musician Praga Khan to accompany the launch of Windows Vista. This event resulted in a substantial amount of controversy and mockery as residents running Windows Vista on their PC were unable to con-

nect to Second Life at the time of the event due to an unsupported graphics driver. Besides these end-consumer focused activities, Microsoft also participated in the aforementioned virtual job fair hosted by TMP in May 2007 and, hence, used Second Life internally as a recruiting tool to hire new software engineers. Microsoft decided to get more involved with virtual social worlds and now appears to work on developing its own virtual world application. The company focused on integrating some of its free services (the programming tool Visual C# Express, the relational database management system SQL Server 2005 Express Edition and the identity-management tool Windows Live ID) into the evolving open source package OpenSim. OpenSim (http://opensimulator.org) is an open source server for hosting virtual worlds that relies on libsecondlife, the software library that builds the foundation of Second Life. However, Microsoft's Chief research and strategy officer Craig Mundie stated that "the potential for immersive environments will be likely realized through 3D tools that capture and model the real world" (Lamont 2008) instead of through rather synthetic virtual worlds such as Second Life. One step in this direction could be Microsoft's steady development of Bing Maps for Enterprise (previously Microsoft Virtual Earth), a geospatial mapping platform, comparable to Google Earth. A combination of OpenSim and Virtual Earth would enable Microsoft to create virtual worlds that are fully compatible with Second Life and yet more realistic as they could rely on digital images taken from satellite sensors and aerial cameras.

THE EXAMPLE OF DELL ISLAND: CONSUMERS' ATTITUDES TOWARDS CORPORATE PRESENCES WITHIN SECOND LIFE

In the following section we will focus on consumers' attitudes towards corporate presences within Second Life in general and the possibility of purchasing Real Life products through this medium in particular. For this we will provide an in-depth analysis of Dell's Second Life activities as the company is the only one in our sample that has made first-hand experience with v-Commerce applications and is most advanced in company-consumer interaction on virtual social worlds. We will first give a brief overview of Dell Island before we present the results of two customer surveys as well as of one interview which we conducted with Laura P. Thomas (alias *Pyrrha Dell*), the person behind Dell's Second Life strategy.

A Brief Overview of Dell Island

Dell's corporate presence within Second Life consists of four connected islands: the Orientation Area, Dell City, the Dell Conference Centre and the Dell Factory. The *Orientation Area* has been structured as the first point-of-entrance for any visitor who plans to explore Dell Island. It is designed as a large park with trees, flowers and a parrot in which avatars can inform themselves about the basic structure of Dell Island and its key functionalities (e.g. how to communicate to Dell employees). *Dell City* features a museum displaying Michael Dell's college dorm room at the University of Texas at Austin in which he designed his first computers. Moreover, it includes the Buzz Bean Café, which hosts Dell's Second Life customer service, the Dell Theatre, in which information videos and TV commercials on Dell products are shown, and the Dell Souvenir shop, where avatars can obtain free virtual goods such as a Dell backpack or a stuffed Dell monkey.[1] It also includes a giant walkthrough model of a Dell XPS 710 PC which avatars can enter to explore the interior of a computer and learn about its functionalities and components. The *Dell Conference Centre* offers meeting rooms ranging in size from one-person offices to lecture halls, which can be booked by Dell's employees for internal purposes. It has been used, among others, for educational presentations (e.g. on Windows Vista) and showed

live webcasts of several public speeches made by Michael Dell. The final element, the *Dell Factory* has been designed to mirror the layout of a Real Life Dell manufacturing plant. Within the Dell Factory Second Life residents had the opportunity to customize virtual computers in a way similar to the process implemented on Dell's webpage. In case of technical difficulties, giant "service monkeys" as well as a library were available to help users. While the customized virtual computer was then given to the avatar free of charge, the corresponding user could vote for ordering the corresponding model in Real Life. In this case, customization options were pushed through to the Dell webpage and the order was placed after entering the necessary payment details.

Consumers' Reactions to Dell Island

In order to better understand consumers' reactions to the design and functionalities of Dell Island, we conducted a survey among 142 Second Life residents. We invited participants of a representative panel of Second Life users, managed and maintained by the French marketing company Repères, to visit Dell Island. Subsequently, we asked those participants to list all the thoughts, reactions and ideas that went through their mind while they were visiting Dell Island in the form of an open-ended question, placed in the context of a larger online survey (Haenlein & Kaplan, 2009). Our results indicate that the vast majority of respondents liked the island ("*Beautiful place*"), especially the learning possibilities it offers for visitors ("*The site provides useful information and a usable path to follow and learn about Second Life*"). However, they also frequently highlighted that the island felt empty and lonely ("*There were only very few persons, just two or three*"), difficult to navigate ("*Confusing path inside the island*") and surprisingly un-innovative for a company like Dell ("*Dell is a big company, they should be able to show something different to catch people's attention in Second Life. They could, for example, use Second Life to display Dell's perspective after 1,000 years. I think this would be better than now*"). Recurrently, respondents also pointed out that the island appeared to have been designed with relatively inexperienced Second Life residents in mind ("*I thought the site would be more Dell product and technology oriented. Instead it seemed geared more to new users with instructions on how to do many basic things*"). Overall, the idea of using Second Life as a sales channel for Real Life products received substantial positive feedback ("*I really liked how you could build your own computer in the Dell Factory and then go online to purchase it. Very neat idea!*"), although some users also highlighted that the medium might not (yet) be suitable for such usage ("*I was thinking about buying a new computer, but I mean that it can be more easy and safe to buy it in a normal way in a normal shop or online*").

Consumers' Reactions to V-Commerce in General

While the aforementioned comments provide useful information regarding the potential of v-Commerce within Second Life, they are limited to the specific case of Dell Island. In order to generate a set of broader insights, we therefore also conducted a series of 29 general qualitative in-depth interviews with Second Life residents with an average duration of 50 minutes each (see Kaplan & Haenlein, 2009a). To select our interview partners, we entered Second Life at different moments of the day and teleported to popular locations. Within each location, potential interview partners were approached randomly and asked whether they would be willing to participate in an academic research project. Overall, the feedback received from these respondents also strongly supports the idea of using Second Life stores as an extension of traditional e-Commerce activities to distribute Real Life products. V-Commerce generally seems

to have evoked positive reactions among Second Life users ("*I think this is a good business idea*"; "*This is a great idea! One can already do shopping over the Internet, so why not do the same in Second Life?*"). Especially categories such as music, computers and books were named as prime examples for this form of distribution. In contrast to what one might expect, most users did not consider the resulting connection between Real and Second Life as something negative, as they already see both as being closely linked ("*It is difficult to completely separate the two*") and there is only a small segment that prefers to keep both worlds unrelated ("*If you can buy Real Life stuff in Second Life, where's the magic?*"). The majority of our interview partners did, however, express serious concerns regarding trust/security and user friendliness which would negatively impact their willingness to buy products on Second Life ("*I wouldn't buy any RL products here personally because I don't feel SL is safe enough for such tasks*"). Given these issues, some users said they would only be willing to purchase on Second Life if companies offered them a discount for doing so ("*If Amazon added an extra 10% SL discount, that might make a difference*").

Dell's Own Perspective on the Potential of V-Commerce

Finally, we complemented these customer comments by Dell's internal perspective on the potential of Second Life and v-Commerce. For this, we conducted an interview with Laura P. Thomas (alias *Pyrrha Dell*), the person behind Dell's Second Life strategy. At that time, conducting commerce via virtual worlds was in its beginnings and therefore we decided for a qualitative in-depth interview with an expert in the field. According to Mrs. Thomas, Dell's initial motivation for entering Second Life was the wish to be on the forefront of a new technology and to use the virtual world as a platform to explore the possibilities offered by a three-dimensional version of the World Wide Web. In this context the v-Commerce application on Dell Island was considered as a trial for an alternative form of e-Commerce. The project ran for 12 months after which it was ended due to lack of sufficient profit potential. The integration of the Dell Factory with e-Commerce applications generated substantial cost which were not compensated by associated revenue as the share of Second Life residents actually conducting a purchase was only miniscule. As highlighted by Mrs. Thomas, the current Second Life population still sees the world mainly as a place of fun and diversion and product purchases are not in the mind of most users. Although she sees a promising potential for v-Commerce in the future, current technical difficulties still make it a costly endeavor. Mrs. Thomas highlighted, for example, that there is still a need to conduct all actual transactions outside of the virtual world as the exchange rate of the Linden Dollar remains too volatile to accept this currency in exchange for Real Life products. According to Pyrrha Dell the short-term potential of Second Life lies primarily in the support of internal functions as the highly immersive environment makes virtual meetings in Second Life more efficient than traditional phone- or videoconferencing systems. Only once employees have familiarized themselves through this type of application, will virtual worlds eventually also increasingly be used for external purposes and as end-consumer channels.

KEY INSIGHTS

We will now discuss the key findings that result from our previous analysis. Hereby we focus on three areas: the business potential of virtual worlds, consumers' attitudes towards corporate presences within Second Life and advice for firms planning to enter virtual worlds.

Business Potential of Virtual Worlds

Actively Consider Whether and How Virtual Worlds can be Used in Your Specific Situation

Our comparison of Dell, HP, IBM and Microsoft has shown that all four companies have very different views on Second Life. While HP considers the virtual world as still immature and potentially risky and harmful, firms such as Dell and IBM already leverage the application heavily for end-consumer and employee contacts respectively. Microsoft, on the other hand, appears to consider entering the market with its own solution. While the purpose of our analysis is not to identify which of these strategies may be right or wrong, it is important to recognize that all major players in the IT industry appear to have made an active and conscious decision on how to use virtual worlds. Based on this observation, we strongly encourage firms to actively consider whether virtual worlds can be of benefit in their industry and how they can be used successfully in their specific situation. If not, firms might find themselves in the same situation as the newspaper industry today, which, due to lack of preparation for the upcoming importance of the Internet, has been facing devastating declines in the number of readers and advertising revenue for several years in a row. According to author Philip Meyer, the ubiquitous availability of news on the World Wide Web will lead to the fact that in about 30 years time (around 2040), this industry will disappear from the landscape (Meyer, 2004).

Avoid Overestimating the Short-Term Profit Potential of Virtual Worlds

Virtual worlds are still in their infancy and the potential to earn Real Life money within Second Life today is limited at best. The example of Dell clearly shows that there is not yet a market for v-Commerce applications and that the number of Second Life residents interested in using the medium for something other than diversion is still too low. Also, own employees and other stakeholders still need to learn how to navigate within virtual worlds and often perceive the new medium as difficult to familiarize with and unintuitive. Nevertheless, we think that there are at least two points that speak in favor of companies already entering virtual worlds at this stage: First, setting up a corporate presence within Second Life usually creates some amount of buzz in traditional media - although this effect has substantially decreased since 2007. Back then, if a company wanted to have some good press coverage in popular outlets such as the Wall Street Journal or Financial Times, one very good way was to build an island in Second Life. Second, many experts agree that virtual worlds will be of substantial importance in the near future. Irving Wladawsky-Berger, VP of technical strategy at IBM, compares applications like Second Life with where VCRs were in the early 1980s and where the World Wide Web was in 1993. Setting up a corporate presence in an application such as Second Life is likely to provide learning opportunities that may be invaluable in the near future and represents a (real) option for future expansion in the area.

Consumers' Attitudes Towards Corporate Presences within Second Life

Expect Mainly Positive Initial Reactions to Your Corporate Activities within Second Life…

Most corporate activities within Second Life are likely to lead to initial positive reactions among the residents of the virtual world. The French market research company Repères (2007) interviewed 1,000 Second Life residents in March 2007 to understand their reactions towards Real Life brands entering their world. The results of this survey clearly showed that Second Life residents

consider Real Life brands to increase the realism of the virtual world and to ensure its longevity as they generate wealth and awareness. Also, our own interviews showed that residents like to have the option of using the world for tasks other than diversion and chatting. Purchasing virtual or real products through Second Life is perceived as exciting and new. Although residents may not (yet) want to actually buy a laptop through a virtual flagship store, the concerns raised (e.g. lack of security, unintuitive purchasing process) are very similar to those companies faced at the beginning of the e-Commerce area. For most of its users Second Life is more than a mere computer game (this is why they prefer being referred to as residents, not players) and rather an extension of their Real Life into the virtual space. Hence, they expect to see the same brands and products in both universes at some point.

…But Ensure that Your Design Takes Account of What People are Really Looking for In-World

Yet, this positive first opinion should not be interpreted as an indication that Second Life residents will appreciate all corporate presences in the same way. In one of our research projects we asked Second Life residents for the key motivations that make them enter the virtual world. Besides the obvious desire for diversion, our respondents listed the wish to create personal relationships, the desire to learn and the possibility to earn Real Life money as the main gratifications obtained from their Second Life usage (Kaplan & Haenlein, 2009a). Support for these comments can also be found when looking at the feedback we received with respect to Dell Island. While some residents highlighted the lack of innovative design (diversion) and the limited number of other visitors (social contacts), others considered the learning possibilities offered by the island as particularly noteworthy. In any case, corporate islands need to take account of these factors in order to ensure long-term success. As in traditional e-Commerce applications (see, e.g., Kuk & Yeung, 2002), Second Life islands require a certain level of interactivity in order to be appreciated by residents. One way of doing so may be to organize regular events that drive traffic and attractiveness. The examples of Dell's Crystal monitor promotion, IBM's Wimbledon tournament presence and Microsoft's Visual Studio Island are prime examples in that context. Other firms may decide to provide learning opportunities (as done in Dell City) or to hire Second Life avatars as sales clerks in their virtual stores. Like in traditional marketing campaigns, enduring success requires providing solutions to what your customers are really looking for.

Advice for Firms Planning to Enter Virtual Worlds

Virtual Worlds are More than Simple Replications of Real Life Environments

Virtual worlds are a specific environment and simply replicating activities conducted in Real Life within Second Life is unlikely to be a success for any company. Dell's extension of the "Plant a Tree for Me" program into Second Life has, for example, been heavily criticized as virtual trees, unlike real ones, do not reduce CO_2 emissions but rather increase them since virtual saplings require energy and server capacity to grow. As calculated by the American writer and IT expert Nicholas Carr, the average Second Life resident consumes roughly 1,800 kilowatt hours of energy per year. This is only 25% less than the 2,500 kilowatt hours the average human consumes annually in Real Life and about 1.8 times as much as the 1,000 kilowatt hours consumed by citizens in developing countries (Carr, 2006). Similarly, the Italian fashion label Armani nearly faced a boycott within Second Life because its virtual flagship store, which was essentially a duplicate of a real outlet in Milan, was perceived as lack-

ing interactivity and as not adapted to the virtual world. If your company wants to be successful in virtual worlds, it is necessary to adapt yourself to the specific requirements of this new medium.

Virtual Worlds can also Have Negative Effects on Real Life Companies

Last but not least, firms should not forget that virtual worlds do not only represent a new opportunity for business growth but also a threat to their Real Life operations. Issues like virtual terrorism and organized consumer boycotts are not unheard of and can have similar devastating effects on your company as their corresponding Real Life actions. For example, in September 2007 the Italian IBM staff moved a labor dispute on wage increases into Second Life. For this, they set up information booths inside the virtual world in which residents could equip their avatars with virtual protest shirts with slogans such as "IBM is deaf to its employees' demands". In addition, billboards were created in front of the IBM Island with the slogan "IBM: We deserve our performance bonus agreement" in four languages. Do not forget that customers, employees and competitors may see virtual worlds through the same positive eyes as companies do – and therefore may use them as an efficient means to hurt a firm's Real Life reputation, brand awareness and, ultimately, sales.

CONCLUSION

In 1946 the American writer Murray Leinster published a science fiction short story with the title "A Logic Named Joe", which today is widely considered as one of the first (although fictional) descriptions of the Internet. It took 23 years before this idea was first put into practice in the form of the ARPANET (Advanced Research Projects Agency Network) in 1969 and 43 years until it evolved in 1989 into the World Wide Web. Soon afterwards companies were founded that based their business model entirely on the new functionalities offered by this groundbreaking medium: Amazon in 1994, eBay in 1995 and Google in 1998. Today, the Internet, WWW and e-Commerce have shaped our society to such an extent that life without any of these inventions is barely imaginable.

Interestingly, this historical evolution reflects a lot of the story behind virtual worlds. Roughly 15 years ago, in 1992, the US author Neal Stephenson published a novel titled Snow Crash. In this book Stephenson tells the story of a main character, called Hiroaki Protagonist, who physically lives in Los Angeles during the early 21st century but mentally spends most of his time in a three-dimensional virtual world called the Metaverse. He, as well as other people, access the Metaverse using personal computer terminals that project pictures of a virtual urban environment situated on a virtual artificial planet onto goggles. Within the Metaverse, everyone appears in the form of personalized avatars, i.e. pieces of software that are the audiovisual bodies which people use to communicate with each other in the Metaverse. These avatars, which may have any appearance desired by the user (except for limitations of height "to prevent people from walking around a mile high"), can perform any activities familiar from their Real Life, such as visiting night clubs, making friends or consuming "virtual" drugs, like the pseudo-narcotic Snow Crash. In the 21st century the Metaverse is so popular and attractive that some people even decide to remain continuously connected to it and to spend their Real Life in storage units, surrounded only by the technical equipment necessary to enter the virtual world.

Similar to Leinster's story, the Metaverse was considered as pure fiction at the time of publication and few readers of Snow Crash would have believed that a world like that described in the novel could indeed ever become reality. Nevertheless, the underlying idea of virtual worlds fascinated a lot of people including the US programmer Ron Britvich who used it as an inspiration for the creation of Alpha World in 1995 (later renamed Active

Worlds) – the first widely used virtual world which allows users (or, more precisely, their avatars) to create their own virtual content such as houses, streets and gardens using pre-fabricated objects.

From a theoretical perspective, our analysis provides an indication that virtual social worlds in general and Second Life in particular can indeed serve as distribution channels for Real Life products and services in future. It has recently been discussed that elements such as social interaction (Holzwarth, Janiszewski, & Neumann, 2006) and perceived interactivity (Song & Zinkhan, 2008) are crucial for the success of e-Commerce websites. While traditional online shopping storefronts have difficulties in delivering such value propositions in a convincing manner, they are inherently embedded in the concept of virtual social worlds. Applications such as Second Life therefore have the potential to overcome some of the limitations that have traditionally been associated with e-Commerce, for example the suitability for primarily hedonic goods (e.g. fashion items, cosmetics, food products) vs. primarily utilitarian goods (e.g. information embedded in books or music) – see Dhar and Wertenbroch (2000) for a more detailed discussion of these two product types. Consequently, virtual social worlds represent the potential of taking e-Commerce (in form of v-Commerce) to the next level.

In a broader context the development of virtual social worlds and social media in general likely represent examples of disruptive innovations (Govindarajan & Kopalle, 2006) which firms need to consider actively in their strategy development process. In some cases such active consideration can result in building internal resources based on these technologies to obtain a long-term competitive advantage (Wernerfelt, 1984) – as done for example by Dell or IBM. In other cases it may also represent a conscious and deliberate choice of not using these media – similar to the choice taken by HP. Given that novelty (e.g. by using new transaction structures) and lock-in (e.g. by creating positive network externalities) have been shown to drive e-Business success (Amit & Zott, 2001) the former option might be more appropriate than the latter one. But an active strategic decision will always be necessary to avoid missing out a major trend. Although nobody can say with certainty which role virtual worlds will play in ten, twenty or thirty years, many experts hold the view that they have the potential to be of similar importance as the Internet is today. This argument alone should be sufficient for any company to seriously consider the use of this new form of social media.

REFERENCES

Amit, R., & Zott, C. (2001). Value creation in e-Business. *Strategic Management Journal, 22*(6/7), 493–520. doi:10.1002/smj.187

Badot, O., & Cova, B. (2003). Néo-marketing, 10 après: pour une théorie critique de la consommation et du marketing réenchantés. *Revue française du marketing, 195*, 79-94.

Carr, N. (2006). Avatars consume as much electricity as Brazilians. *Rough Type: Nicholas Carr's blog.* Retrieved December 5, 2006, from http://www.roughtype.com/archives/2006/12/avatars_consume.php

Cova, B. (1996). The postmodern explained to managers: Implications for marketing. *Business Horizons, 39*(6), 15–23. doi:10.1016/S0007-6813(96)90032-4

Dhar, R., & Wertenbroch, K. (2000). Consumer choice between hedonic and utilitarian goods. *JMR, Journal of Marketing Research, 37*(1), 60–71. doi:10.1509/jmkr.37.1.60.18718

Firat, A. F., Sherry, J. F. J., & Venkatesh, A. (1994). Postmodernism, marketing and the consumer. *International Journal of Research in Marketing, 11*(4), 311–316. doi:10.1016/0167-8116(94)90009-4

Govindarajan, V., & Kopalle, P. K. (2006). Disruptive of innovations: Measurement and an assessment of reliability and validity. *Strategic Management Journal, 27*(2), 189–199. doi:10.1002/smj.511

Graillot, L. (2004). Une approche du phénomène d'hyperréalité à partir de l'étude des parcs Disney. *Décisions marketing, 34*, 41-52.

Haenlein, M., & Kaplan, A. M. (2009). Flagship brand stores within virtual worlds: The impact of virtual store exposure on real life attitude toward the brand and purchase intent (Les magasins de marques phares dans les mondes virtuels: L'impact de l'exposition au magasin virtuel sur les comportements et l'intention d'achat de la marque dans la vie réelle). *Recherche et applications en marketing (RAM), 24*(3), 57-80.

Hemp, P. (2006). Avatar-based marketing. *Harvard Business Review, 84*(6), 48–57.

Heng, M. S. (2003). Understanding electronic commerce from a historical perspective. *Communications of the Association for Information Systems, 12*(6), 104–118.

Holzwarth, M., Janiszewski, C., & Neumann, M. N. (2006). The influence of avatars on online consumer shopping behavior. *Journal of Marketing, 70*(4), 19–36. doi:10.1509/jmkg.70.4.19

Ives, B., & Junglas, I. (2008). APC forum: Business implications of virtual worlds and serious gaming. *MIS Quarterly Executive, 7*(3), 151–156.

Kaplan, A. M. (2009a). Second Life: leçons pour le monde reel. *Expansion management review, 133*, 58-60.

Kaplan, A. M. (2009b). Virtual worlds and business schools: The case of INSEAD. In Kingsley, J., & Wankel, C. (Eds.), *Higher education in virtual worlds: Teaching and learning in Second Life* (pp. 83–100). London: Emerald.

Kaplan, A. M. (2010). User participation within virtual worlds. In Dasilveira, G., & Fogliatto, F. (Eds.), *Mass customization: Engineering and managing global operations*. London: Springer.

Kaplan, A. M., & Haenlein, M. (2009a). Consumer use and business potential of virtual worlds: The case of Second Life. *International journal on media management, 11*(3/4), 93-101.

Kaplan, A. M., & Haenlein, M. (2009b). The fairyland of Second Life: From virtual social worlds and how to use them. *Business Horizons, 52*(6), 563–572. doi:10.1016/j.bushor.2009.07.002

Kaplan, A. M., & Haenlein, M. (2010). Users of the world, unite! The challenges and opportunities of social media. *Business Horizons, 53*(1), 59–68. doi:10.1016/j.bushor.2009.09.003

Kaplan, A. M., & Haenlein, M. (2011). The early bird catches the news: Nine things you should know about micro-blogging. *Business Horizons, 54*(1).

Kintz, E. (2007) Top 10 reasons as to why I still need to be convinced about marketing on Second Life. *HP Communities: The digital mindset blog*. Retrieved April 2, 2007, from http://www.communities.hp.com/online/blogs/kintz/archive/2007/04/02/HPPost2964.aspx

Kuk, G., & Yeung, F. T. (2002). Interactivity in e-commerce. *Quarterly journal of electronic commerce, 3*(3), 223-234.

Lamont, I. (2008, September 27). Real life will trump Second Life, Microsoft says. *PC World*.

Linden Lab. (2009). *How meeting in Second Life transformed IBM's technology elite into virtual world believers* [Case study]. San Francisco, CA: Linden Lab.

Meyer, P. (2004). *The vanishing newspaper: Saving journalism in the information age*. Columbia, MO: University of Missouri Press.

Repères. (2007). *Perception of Real Life brand's presence in Second Life: A CB News*. Paris: Repères.

Song, J. H., & Zinkhan, G. M. (2008). Determinants of perceived web site interactivity. *Journal of Marketing, 72*(2), 99–113. doi:10.1509/jmkg.72.2.99

Stevens, H., & Pettey, C. (2008). Gartner says 90 per cent of corporate virtual world projects fail within 18 months [Press release]. Stamford, CT: Gartner. Retrieved November 20, 2009, from http://www.gartner.com/it/page.jsp?id=670507

Thomas, L. P. (2007). Deepening our roots in Second Life. *Direct2Dell: A blog about Dell products, services and customers*. Retrieved April 20, 2007, from http://direct2dell.com/one2one/archive/2007/04/20/12428.aspx

Vargo, S. L., & Lusch, R. F. (2004). Evolving to a new dominant logic for marketing. *Journal of Marketing, 68*(1), 1–17. doi:10.1509/jmkg.68.1.1.24036

Venkatesh, A., Sherry, J. F., & Firat, A. E. (1993). Postmodernism and the marketing imaginary. *International Journal of Research in Marketing, 10*(3), 215–223. doi:10.1016/0167-8116(93)90007-L

Wernerfelt, B. (1984). A resource-based view of the firm. *Strategic Management Journal, 5*(2), 171–180. doi:10.1002/smj.4250050207

ENDNOTE

[1] The monkeys on Dell Island are inspired by a Real Life advertising campaign and TV commercial (the Comcast Monkey), which Dell ran at the time Dell Island was designed.

Chapter 15

Viral Marketing via Social Networking Sites:
Perceptions of Students in a University Environment

Ranadeva Jayasekera
University of Southampton, UK

Thanos Papadopoulos
University of Southampton, UK

ABSTRACT

This chapter focuses on the role of social networking sites in viral marketing through a case study in a university environment. Over the last years, companies are using alternative channels including social networking sites to promote their products. The specific channel provides the opportunity to connect with customers and achieve marketing objectives. The study aims to gather the perspectives of students on social networking sites as a form of marketing and draw on their views to establish implications and practical recommendations for marketers. By using questionnaires and focus groups interviews, the study ascertained that companies which were active in social networking sites developed a positive effect on customer attitudes, particularly brand perception, but had little to no effect on the actual customer behaviour patterns. It is also concluded that social networking sites suggest an efficient alternative channel for marketing purposes.

1. INTRODUCTION

The advancement of the social web over the last years has brought an unprecedented amount of organisations into a dilemma, that is, to utilise the online environment so as to reach their customers more efficiently and effectively, or to remain loyal to the traditional ways of reaching their marketing objectives? Indeed, organisations are using online environments and social networking sites to connect with their customers and promote their offers; this type of informal communication whereby a company uses the communication networks of the customers to promote products and/or services is known as viral marketing (Helm, 2000).

However, to date, there has been very little empirical research on the contribution of social

DOI: 10.4018/978-1-61692-904-6.ch015

networking to viral marketing. Gaining insight into such a phenomenon is important since marketers need to find out the possible ways of using forms of new media such as social networking sites to obtain the maximum anticipated benefits (Weber, 2007). Although the web is a valuable source of information regarding the ways marketers utilize social networking as a means for viral marketing, there are issues arising concerning the form of short blogs, simple how-to guides, or steps to instant marketing success. In particular, they do not provide justified evidence or real results to prove their recommendations. This chapter deals with the aforementioned issues and contributes to both the social networking and marketing literatures since it explores the ability of the social networking to overcome problems associated with the one-way nature (Pitta, 2005) of advertising, providing thereby marketers with suggestions as to how pitfalls of classic marketing channels can be avoided.

Since the focus of marketing has been towards the consumer in e-business (Hagel & Rayport, 1997), it is vital to get the view of customer and see the issues from their perspective. Hence, an empirical study is essential so as to shed light into the correlation of social networking and marketing, as well as the specific characteristics of social networking that make it an efficient channel for promotion of products and services. To gain insights on the way social networking enables viral marketing, a study was conducted at the University of A1. Using questionnaires and focus group interviews, data were gathered regarding the perspectives of students, who are active members of social networking sites, and draw on their views on this form of marketing to form conclusive recommendations for marketers.

The chapter is structured as follows: after a review of the corresponding literature on viral marketing and social networking, the objective of the chapter is presented and the methodology is discussed. It follows the results of the study and a discussion on the implications of social network-

ing for marketers including recommendations. The chapter ends with a presentation of the main research findings, the limitations of the research and future research avenues.

2. AN OVERVIEW OF VIRAL MARKETING AND SOCIAL NETWORKING PHENOMENON

2.1 Viral Marketing

Viral marketing, often used interchangeably with the term word-of-mouth marketing, has been defined as "a form of peer-to-peer communication in which individuals are encouraged to pass on promotional messages within their social networks" (Bampo et al., 2008, p. 273) or a process which "uses electronic communications to trigger brand messages throughout a widespread network of buyers" (Dobele et al., 2005, p. 143). However, there seems to be a continuing debate as to whether the aforementioned term coincides with word-of-mouth marketing, which has been stated in the literature as the most effective, yet least understood marketing strategy (Misner, 1994). Indeed, this is reflected in the literature (e.g. Helm, 2000) where it is stated that viral marketing is the act of managing online word-of-mouth. For the purpose of this chapter, viral marketing is defined as: *online network enhanced communication through which customers promote a supplier, or their products or services.* The process generally involves the supplier contacting only the first few adopters, and from then on the customers act as intermediaries (Helm, 2000).

The history of viral marketing goes back to 1997, introduced by Steve Jurvetson and Tim Draper when free web-based email service, Hotmail, was pioneered (Jurvetson & Draper, 1997). These researchers invented the name because of the evidence related to its speedy adoption through word-of-mouth networks. In the case of Hotmail, each email which users sent out to their friends contained a URL link to join up to Hotmail for free. The friends who then adopted Hotmail would do the same, and thus this snowballing adoption pattern spread out like a virus (Jurvetson & Draper, 1997). However, Modzelewski et al. (2000) discussed the Hotmail example as 'weak' viral marketing since signing up is voluntary and it is easy for the recipient to ignore the message. They suggested that the value of true viral marketing lies in that the value of the message to the original customer should be related to the number of other users it draws in. In other words, the instigator of each branch of the virus should have their own vested interest in recruiting people. Both views however admit the limited costs entailed in the marketing of Hotmail and therefore it is not surprising that after Hotmail's success viral marketing became extremely popular, especially with Internet start-up companies.

The proliferation of viral marketing rendered it soon the buzzword in the marketing world. Many companies were eager to incorporate the viral element into their marketing strategy, a phenomenon expressed through the emergence of marketing sites that promised simple steps to viral marketing success. But, as Shirky (2000) stated, there are two things required for the success of viral marketing, uncommon in the marketing world, that is, honesty and execution. The latter is integral in that the user must be in control and actively endorse the message rather than acting as simply a messenger. The former is important because the recipient of the advertisement must believe it is an honest endorsement by the sender, otherwise it loses its credibility and is likely to be perceived as spam (Shirky, 2000).

Literature has suggested that conversations and information exchange may influence the decisions of customers. This is reflected in the results of Arndt's (1967) study, which discussed the importance of favourable comments in influencing the potential acceptance of a new product, while negative comments hinder this. In this vein, viral marketing uses the Internet as a medium for

greater distribution of such comments, thus aiming to result in increased brand awareness and sales.

Herr et al. (1991) followed the aforementioned idea in their study proving that the face-to-face communication is more persuasive than a printed version; they hence demonstrated that word-of-mouth influences pre-usage attitudes. This study was confirmed by Bone (1992), who also postulated that the creation of original and appealing consumption experiences and the coupling of loyal customers with new customers could inspire word-of-mouth. However, later work discovered the existence of more variables which affect the strength of the influence that word-of-mouth communication has on an individual than previously revealed. She suggested that the influence of word-of-mouth is greater when the information is communicated by an expert in that area (Bone, 1995).

Literature has also discussed the importance of turning customers into marketing force (Phelps et al., 2004). By merely sending "this message to a friend" links, companies believe this strategy will have the same effect as genuine word-of-mouth, but however this is hardly the case. The specific strategy is not to be dismissed, since a friend is more likely to know the taste of individuals than a firm which does not know any given personality (Krishnamurthy, 2001).

Phelps et al (2004) discussed in depth the aforementioned viral marketing strategy, as they undertook a study examining consumer responses and motivations to pass along emails. The increase in the size of inboxes, they suggested, had an impact on the chance of the recipient opening the email; but however, the recipients were more reluctant to delete emails from people they knew. It was also discovered that emails about free goods or containing helpful tips are passed along almost half of the time. These results were corroborated by Dobele et al. (2007) who focused on the reasons why people pass on viral messages. These researchers suggested that the effectiveness of the viral messages does not only depend on the emotion triggered in the recipient, but is more complex. The companies should then achieve fit between the suggested marketing campaigns and the featured emotions, which can vary between genders (ibid). Hence, the study places importance on the clear target of the message and the associated requirements to ensure an increased chance of passing on the message (ibid).

Nevertheless, the study of Leskovec et al. (2007) in analysing the correlation between word-of-moth and person-to-person recommendation networks postulated that on average the recommendations are not as effective at producing purchases as one might have initially thought, and they do not disperse very far. Here though it should be noted that traditional innovation diffusion models assume that people have a consistent probability of 'converting' each time they interact with an infected individual (Goldenberg et al., 2001). This is in contrast to the study of Leskovec and colleagues who found that the probability of "infection" actually decreases with repeated interaction, that is, the more an individual sends out recommendations regarding a product, the less successful the recommendation falls. They did, however, ascertain that in specific communities, products, and pricing categories in which viral marketing seems to be very effective. This is in accordance to Fergusson (2008), who argued that word-of-mouth or viral marketing campaigns are not always successful, but a well-placed provocative campaign can spark an incredible amount of 'buzz' that can sometimes be effective for a number of years, especially in a medium such as the internet.

2.2 Social Networking[2]

The study of social networks has been a popular area in the Sociology field, following Wellman's (1988) phrase that "the world is composed of networks" (p. 37). Networks and the study of ties –that is, connections amongst the network constituents– have been used in the marketing world because of their effect on word-of-mouth behaviour and as a communication channel to promote viral marketing within the communities and social networks of their consumers. Research on social networking as means of marketing goes back to Whyte (1954) who studied the ownership of air conditioners. He concluded that this phenomenon could be explained on the basis of formulating a strong network of neighbours. Later, Katz and Lazarsfeld (1955) found word-of-mouth to be the most important source of influence when purchasing food and household goods, stating that it was seven times more effective than magazines and newspapers. Even during the beginning years of television, word-of-mouth was still proven to be the most influential source (Engel et al., 1969).

The study of Granovetter (1973) on tie strength showed that attention has to be paid to the degree of overlap of two peoples' friendship networks as this varies directly with the strength of their tie to one another. In a later study, Subramani and Rajagopalan (2003) postulated that understanding the formulation of customer social networks and the relationship ties is crucial for marketers to understand the social structures that are essential to knowledge sharing. Factors such as the role of the influencer and the level of network externalities are important in determining the nature of influence in viral marketing (ibid). Moreover, Brown & Reingen's (1987) study used the properties of tie strength to examine word-of-mouth referral behaviour, discovering that strong ties are more influential than weak ties when it comes to referrals.

The random and unmanageable nature of viral marketing renders a need to shed more light into the effects of the social structure of the online networks on viral marketing (Bampo et al. 2008). The specific researchers illustrated that the social structures of digital networks play an essential role in the diffusion of a viral message. In this vein, if marketers decipher the underlying structure to online social networks and estimate the communication behaviour of the target audience, they should then be able to use this knowledge to adapt the campaign strategy as appropriate (ibid).

Nevertheless, up until recently, literature had not fully explored the role of electronic word of mouth processes in influencing the behaviour of customers, especially in an online environment. De Bruyn and Lilien (2008) focused on the role which word-of-mouth plays at each stage of the decision making process of a viral marketing recipient. The study found that characteristics of the social ties influence the behaviour of recipients, but, however, in a different way in each of the stages. This is because the strength of ties is related to awareness and perceptual likeness, which triggers the interest of recipients; on the other hand, demographic similarity influences negatively each stage of the decision-making process (*ibid*).

2.3 Social Networking Sites

Nowadays, the social networking has expanded using various forms of computing, systems and Information Technology. In particular, it is easy to trace hundreds of different types of social networking sites on the web. Some are hugely popular, such as Bebo, MySpace and Facebook, and have attracted millions of users. For the purposes of this chapter, the definition provided here follows Boyd and Ellison (2008) in that social networking sites are web-based services that allow individuals to construct a profile, articulate a list of users with whom they are connected, and view their connections and those made by others within the system.

The history of social networking sites goes back to 1997, when SixDegrees.com was launched. Although the specific site attracted millions of users, it failed to become sustainable business possibly because it was ahead of its time, and closed subsequently in 2000 (ibid). However, the interest into social networking sites was revived again in 2001 with Ryze.com, LinkedIn and Friendster. But Ryze.com never acquired the mass popularity to be successful, and Friendster was an enormous

disappointment (Chafkin, 2007). In 2003, new social networking sites came to the foreground, such as YASNS, which stands for Yet Another Social Networking Site Shirky (2003), and MySpace, which welcomed bands and contacted local musicians to help in promoting the site, a strategy that later proved to be beneficial (Boyd and Ellison, 2008). The introduction of Facebook in 2004 was not really successful; it was not until 2006 that it started to gain the popularity that has now, and its exponential growth. Apart from Facebook, Twitter –a micro-blogging site where people can stay connected through the exchange of quick and frequent messages (Twitter, 2009)– constitutes another successful social networking site which was initiated in 2006 and has been growing in an exceptional rate. In 2009, Nielsen NetRatings predicted that Twitter grew by 1689% from February 2008 to February 2009.

With regards to the promotion of viral marketing, both Twitter and Facebook facilitate viral marketing very well. In particular, companies and politicians have been using Twitter so as to advertise their new products, events, offerings and campaigns. However, researchers suggest that Facebook is more effective since it has a larger audience; companies' profiles come with built in analytics which let the marketer see how well their page is doing, and the viral promotion on Facebook is more effective (Smith, 2009). Twitter enables simple, instant communication based around blogging which is becoming increasingly more credible with customers (Baltazar, 2009).

The aforementioned social networking sites have differences in their underlying technological infrastructure and support a wide range of interests, for instance former social networks or help their members communicate based on their shared political views, interests or activities (Boyd & Ellison, 2008). They also vary in the communication tools they provide; for instance, blogging, photo/video-sharing and mobile connectivity (Boyd & Ellison, 2008).

Figure 1. Timeline of launch dates of many popular social networking sites (Boyd and Ellison, 2008: p. 212)

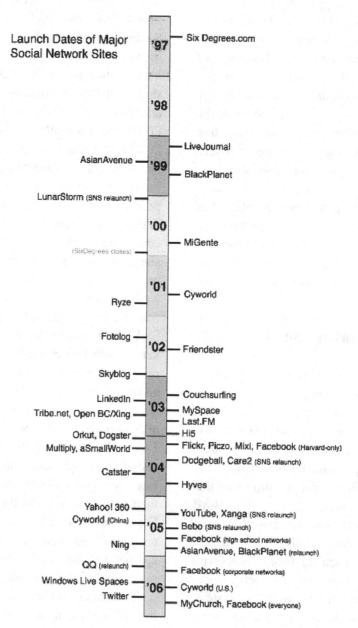

The following figure (Figure 1) depicts the raise in the popularity of social networking sites. Some of these sites have been online for a number of years now, although, as previously mentioned, the popularity of social networking sites did not take off into such an extreme phenomenon until 2004 - 2005.

Research on social networking sites has focused mainly on areas such as 'Frieding' and messaging activities (Golder et al., 2007), the structure of friendship (Kumar et al., 2006), what motivates people to join (Backstrom et al., 2006; Joinson, 2008) and the relationships between different profile elements (Lampe et al., 2007).

For instance, the study of Joinson (2008) looked into the motives of people for using Facebook and found that the primary use included social connection, social investigation, social network surfing and status updating. Boyd and Ellison (2008) studied the role of Facebook in impression management, friendship performance, networks and network structure, and privacy issues.

Since the social networking on the web has increased in popularity over the last years, it is no wonder why marketers have taken on the opportunity to explore another potentially effective platform for reaching viral marketing objectives. According to Mislove et al. (2007), social networking sites, for instance YouTube and Facebook, constitute a powerful means of sharing, organizing, and finding content and contacts over the web. This is because they have a small, well-connected core, and the information via a core node will swiftly spread through the whole network (Mislove et al., 2007), making them an ideal platform for viral marketing. Consequently, from a marketer's point of view, social networking sites provide an opportunity to disseminate marketing information rapidly and efficiently. This is because they are the gateways for connection between millions of users around the globe; these connections would not otherwise be made (Boyd & Ellison, 2008). Literature, however, has found that the effectiveness and efficiency of viral messages' communication is dependent on active communication between the members, since it deepens the relationships between customers and brands (Merisavo & Raulas, 2004). This was later confirmed by the study of Gay et al. (2007) who postulated that customer involvement strengthens the relationships between the customers and the company.

Li and Bernoff (2008) have studied the impacts of customer reviews using social networking tools and sites (e.g. blogs, and YouTube) on the products and/or services provided by companies. However, many businesses may be afraid that by enabling customers to post their own evaluations of products and services they are eliminating their control over product information (Chen and Xie, 2008). But while companies see this as a threat, it should really be seen as an opportunity. The facilitation of this communication through online platforms such as social networking sites enables customers to share their views and impacts positively the growth of loyalty to specific products or services. This is because social networking sites attract large numbers of users keen to engage with their favourite companies or brands (Li, 2007b). The sole use, hence, of traditional marketing methods such as banner and of-site advertisements to drive messages into networks results in leaving out the full potential to connect with customers in a more personal relationship. This means that the realization of the full value of marketing lies on connecting with users on social networking sites and provide them with information and brand elements that can be passed on to their friends and acquaintances.

For social networking to act as a viral marketing channel, two factors are needed, namely trust and engagement (Merisavo & Raulas, 2004). This is because they provide the opportunity to the companies to achieve greater levels of trust and deeper personal relationships with a large number of customers and potential customers. Appearing on social networking sites also increases the frequency that consumers will see a company's brand name or logo, and this type of repeated exposure can enhance brand attitudes (Merisavo & Raulas, 2004). However, this is not to say that the aim is to secure sale straight away; rather, marketing through social networking sites has to do mainly with creating an attractive social environment and community online where people feel comfortable spending time, which will eventually lead to sales (Weber, 2007), since the customer is often led to the product by a fellow user. This constitutes informal communication of products because the consumer has asked for it (Helm, 2000).

The work by Li (2007b) is one of the few pieces of research which looks into marketing via social networking sites. Li mentions that SNS campaigns do not follow traditional marketing rules and marketers should consider the establishment and growth of personal relationships through these sites and especially their members and visitors at the core of their marketing campaigns. Her results reveal that social networking site users are young, they want to engage with their favourite brands, and they are viral leaders (Li, 2007b). Additionally, a study conducted by Ballard at WorkPlace Media (2009) seeks for answers regarding a brand's presence on social networking sites and its influence to visitors. The results of this study suggest that out of a sample of 753 American workers who have access to the Internet only 11% have connections with big brands on social networking sites. A large majority of respondents say their opinion of a brand does not change if that brand is on a social networking site (Ballard, 2009).

However, out of the sample, only 11% are actually connected with companies. This seems to make the results less valid. This is because, when asking respondents about their perceptions of companies on social networking sites, it is better if a significant proportion of the sample is actually connected with companies in order to state their perceptions of the effects of such connections more accurately. Additionally, since the study of Li (2007b) many more companies have joined social networking sites in an attempt to achieve more personal relationships with customers, just as she recommended. Hence, it is believed that in order to find out the role of social networking impact on viral marketing, a study needs to look into other factors, and analyse a wider range of variables, now that the number of companies on social networking sites has greatly increased.

From the review of the aforementioned literature it is made apparent that a gap exists in exploring the role of social networking sites on viral marketing. This chapter aims to fill that gap and provide empirical evidence in the hope of answering some of the outstanding questions on viral marketing via social networking sites. Why

users of social networking sites engage with certain brands and not others and the extent to which marketing via social networking sites has an effect on users' attitudes and behaviours towards those brands need to be explored in order to discover the role of social networking sites in marketing.

3. RESEARCH STRATEGY

The main objective of the study was to gather students' opinions on companies who become members of social networking sites in order to achieve their marketing objectives.

The research involved two separate data collection methods including a questionnaire and then a focus group interview. Using a multi-method approach also has the advantage that it enables triangulation (Saunders et al., 1997) which led to greater confidence in the conclusions drawn. The study was conducted in a way that only those respondents who are connected with companies answered questions relating to how this impacts on their perceptions and behaviours towards such companies. This ensured the data gathered was not affected by those who have no interest in ever connecting with a company over a social networking site. For those students who are not connected with companies, different variables were tested, in order to establish why they are not connected and if they may in the future. This was intended to overcome the drawback of Ballard's (2009) research where it appeared all respondents were tested on whether their perceptions of brands change because of companies' presence on social networking sites, when very few were connected with companies.

Questionnaire

Since Li (2007b) has suggested that young adults are the largest user group on social networking sites, it was sensible to have a sampling frame for this study consisting of mostly young adults as there is likely to be a larger proportion who are members of social networking sites. Because of this, the sampling frame for the questionnaire was decided on as 400 students currently enrolled in the School of Management at the University of A. The students were contacted by email; while email is usually not a reliable form of contact due to its characteristic to perceive that everyone has access to the internet which is not always the case, since every member of the university has a university email address which they normally check regularly, and access to the internet at numerous locations on campus.

The conjectures tested during the study were:

- Being connected with companies on social networking sites has a positive effect on students' attitudes and behaviours towards these companies.
- Students think it is a good idea for companies to use social networking sites for marketing purposes.

The questionnaire (appendix 1) was structured in a sequential manner. A thorough process was undertaken when initially deciding on which questions to ask to test the appropriate variables and answer the research question. Having in mind that the outcome of the research is exploratory, the researchers subdivided the research question into more specific investigative questions. Variables to be tested through each specific question were identified and the questions were composed. The researchers aimed to express the questions in simple words so that there is no ambiguity regarding the meaning of the questions and they do not deter interest or bore the respondent. Where the answer involved selecting options of ordinal ranking, these rankings were consistent throughout questions where this was appropriate to make it easier for the respondent to answer. The questions investigated issues regarding attitude, belief, and behaviour to thoroughly test the appropriate variables.

To ensure the reliability and validity of the questionnaire, the following additional aspects were employed:

- A cover letter was included to explain the purpose of the questionnaire. This can often positively impact on the response rate.
- Questions of all types were included, for instance list questions, scale questions, category questions and open ended questions.
- The researchers asked for feedback from experts to ensure the questions were understandable and clear. Additionally it was pilot tested so as to amend questions which caused confusion.

The results from the questionnaire were analysed using measures of central tendency where appropriate. More specifically, as a large number of the questions were ordinal, the mode has been used to express the trends in the data. Graphs have also been presented to illustrate the data.

Focus Group

The focus group participants were selected by convenience sampling and consisted of five students at the University of A. This method was used because random sampling is not appropriate in focus group research, as the sampling needs to be purposeful and the participants must been chosen based on the objective of the study. The rationale behind focus groups was to get the views of an homogenous group of people (students) with something in common that is relevant to the study (Saunders et al., 1997) (that is, they are all members of social networking sites, and they are all confident individuals).

The focus group (appendix 2) results were to be compared with those from the questionnaire. The questions were based around key themes and issues concerning the research question; but, as the discussion went on, new themes and additional issues emerged. The participants were made to feel

Figure 2. Respondents and participation in SNS

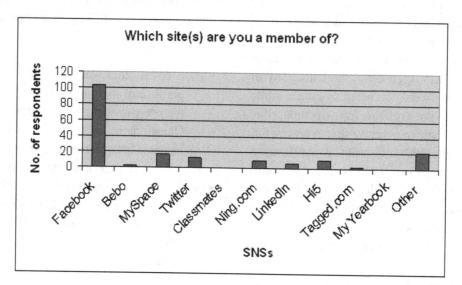

comfortable, and this made them more willing to share their views and experiences of companies on social networking sites. Each student had the opportunity to answer each question. The interviewer summarised the responses after all participants had answered each question. This made sure the responses were being interpreted correctly, that no important information or opinion was being left out, and it also gave the participants the opportunity to make any corrections to the interpretation. Although the question topics and structure was determined before, the discussion emerged by the answers of the informants.

The analysis of the focus group data was conducted by analysing the tape recording of the meeting while taking notes. The data was then categorised into meaningful and related categories which allowed it to be rearranged and analysed more meticulously (Miles and Huberman, 2002). This process revealed key themes in the data set and relationships between the themes (Saunders et al., 1997). The categorisation of the results made it easy to be compared with the theoretical framework of the study, and also with the results from the questionnaire.

4. RESULTS AND DISCUSSION

4.1 Questionnaire Results

Through the questionnaire the researchers obtained 157 responses, which were refined to a set of 124 once the data was cleansed. Of this 124, 18 were found to not be members of Social Networking Sites (SNS) and therefore they did not need to complete the rest of the questionnaire, leaving a final sample size of 106.

User Behaviour

In the first section of the questionnaire, the aim was to establish aspects of user behaviour on SNS. 103 out of the 106 respondents are members of Facebook, which is one of the leading web SNS. The respondents were requested to select all of the social networking sites that they are active members of, with 49 respondents being members of more than one site (Figure 2).

While it was found that participants access SNS more than once a day, the study also found that their majority spends less than or equal to

Figure 3. Length of time spent on SNS in one sitting

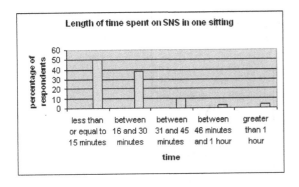

Figure 4. The connection of respondents with SNS-companies

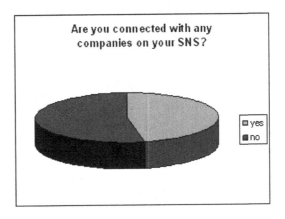

fifteen minutes on the site in one sitting (Figure 3).

Despite the fact that SNS can facilitate viral marketing, the respondents did not see this as a prominent reason as to why they are members of them. When they were presented with 6 potential reasons as to why they are members of the sites and asked to rate each reason from 1-6, with 1 being the most prominent reason and 6 being the least, the reason "to be informed about companies or brands" received the most 6's (63 out of 94) and therefore came out as the least prominent reason overall. "To stay in touch with people easily" was rated the number one reason by most respondents.

Connections with Companies

The questionnaire helped in gathering data regarding the percentage of respondents who have connections with companies, brands or products over their SNSs. The results revealed that 47% of respondents have a connection with at least one company, brand or product over their SNS (Figure 4).

Since the researchers wanted to get the reasons behind the unwillingness of SNS members to have any connections with companies, brands or products over their SNSs, the questionnaire presented them with a list of potential reasons and asked the respondents to select, on a scale, how much

they agree, disagree, or neither with each reason. The following results were obtained:

- 'I have not yet come across a company which appeals to me enough for me to connect with them.' The majority (63%) of respondents who are not connected with companies agree with this statement.
- 'I was not aware you could become friends with companies or brands on social networking sites.' The majority (63%) of respondents who are not connected with companies disagree with this statement, verifying that they are aware that they can form connections with companies or brands.
- 'I have no desire to ever be connected with a company over a social networking site.' Just over half (54%) of the respondents who are not connected with companies agree with this statement.
- The majority of respondents who are not connected with companies neither agree nor disagree with the phrase "I have no interest in companies who use social networking sites for marketing purposes".

On the other hand, the respondents who stated that they are connected with companies, brands

Figure 5. Increase in information through connection with a company

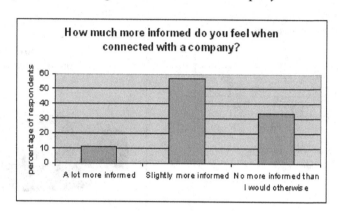

or products on their SNSs were asked a series of questions relating to the effect which this connection has on their attitudes and behaviour towards these companies, brands or products. This was to establish whether or not the following conjecture is supported.

Conjecture (a): Being connected with companies on social networking sites has a positive effect on students' attitudes and behaviours towards those companies.

Each of the questions provided a result which either supported, or did not support, the conjecture. This inconsistency represents the fact that companies on SNSs have a positive effect on certain attitudes or behaviours and have no effect on others. To address this conjecture, the participants were asked how much more informed they feel about a company's products, services or offerings when connected with them over a social networking site. 68% of respondents answered that they feel either slightly more informed, or a lot more informed, about these companies' products, services or offerings because of this connection, thus supporting conjecture (a) (Figure 5).

The participants' brand perception was the next variable to be evaluated. The questionnaire aimed to establish whether respondents' perceptions of brands increased because they were con-

nected with them over their social networking site. 53% of students said that their perception of a brand increased when they were connected with them over the social networking site. This also supports conjecture (a), however quite a large proportion of 46% of respondents stated that this connection neither increases, nor decreases, their perception of the brand.

The questionnaire then went on to determine whether respondents' purchase intentions are increased, decreased, or neither, towards companies, brands or products that they are connected with over a social networking site.

The graph above (Figure 7) shows that a large number of respondents (67%) believe being connected with a company, brand, or product has no effect on their intentions to purchase from that company. The results of this question do not support conjecture (a), in that the connections with companies do not affect students' behaviour when it comes to purchasing. Additionally, Figure 8 shows the results from the question "what sort of companies, brands or products are you connected with, or more likely to be connected with, over a social networking site? Please select from the list."

In determining which types of companies, brands or products students would be least likely to form a connection with over a social networking site, respondents were able to select more than one option, and the graph below represents the

Figure 6. Effect of connection to brand perception

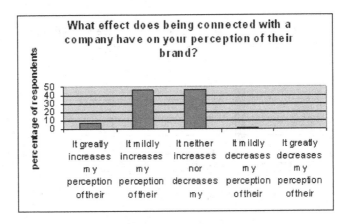

Figure 7. Intentions to purchase and connection to companies

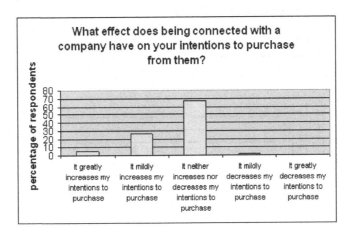

Figure 8. Types of companies and likelihood of connection

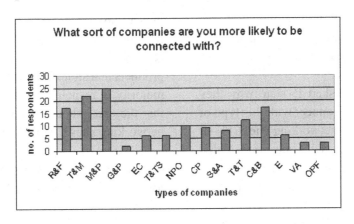

Figure 9. Types of companies and least likelihood of connection

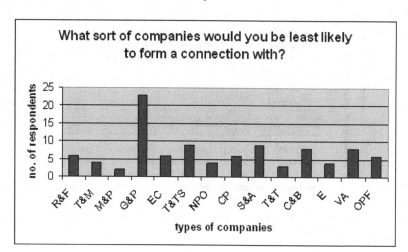

Figure 10. Types of companies and members of SNS

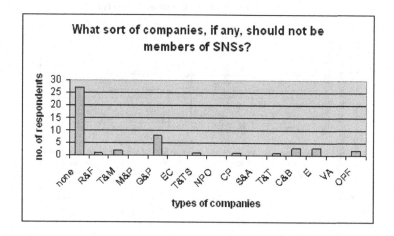

results. 'Government, Politicians and Political Views' was selected as the type of company most respondents would be least likely to connect with (Figure 9).

Respondents were asked to state why they would be less likely to connect with this type of company over a social networking site. 61% of respondents who answered this question said that they would not connect with certain companies simply because it's not in their personal interest. A percentage of the respondents will readily connect with certain types of companies, brands or products over social networking sites; however, they do have strong opinions as to why they would not connect with others. Interestingly, when asked regarding any sorts of companies, brands or products that should not be members of SNS, the majority of respondents said that there are none that they feel should not be members of social networking sites (Figure 10).

Conjecture (b): Students think it is a good idea for companies to use social networking sites for marketing purposes.

Figure 11. Companies as members of SNSs for marketing purposes

Figure 12. Social networking and effectiveness of offer communication

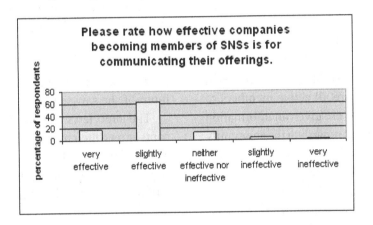

A vast majority (78%) believed it is a good idea for companies, brands and products to become members of social networking sites in order to advertise their products, services, and offerings thus strongly supporting conjecture (b) (Figure 11).

This was confirmed when respondents were asked whether or not they believe there is a place for companies, brands or products on SNS; the vast majority (76%) again answered yes to this question, further supporting conjecture (b). When asking the respondents to rate how effective is for companies to become members of SNS to communicate their products, services, offerings, news and events, conjecture (b) was supported again; 81% of respondents believe joining social networking sites is either slightly or very effective for communicating their offerings (Figure 12).

Finally, when asked if they have ever found themselves wishing a particular company, product or brand was on their social networking site, the respondents (88%) answered "no" (Figure 13).

The overall analysis of the data shows that conjecture (a) is partially supported, in that being connected with companies on SNS has a positive effect on respondents' attitudes towards these companies. However, the connection was found to have little or no effect on respondents' behaviours towards these companies. This would need to be re-confirmed through further research which tested user behaviours as a result of connections with companies on SNS. Conjecture (b) is fully supported, as the results strongly suggest that respondents think it is a good idea for companies

Figure 13. Companies as potential members of the respondents' SNS

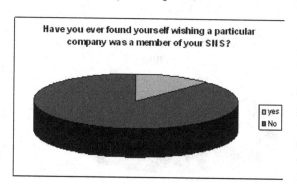

to use social networking sites for marketing purposes.

4.2 Focus Group Results

The focus group consisted of five students from the University A who are all active members of SNS. The participants were given an information sheet and were informed regarding the anonymity of their answers. The interview agenda shed light into some other areas of students' perceptions of viral marketing via SNS which were not unveiled through the questionnaire, such as their perceptions on how companies can attract users to connect with them and sustain the connection. This method was conducted to gain a more complete understanding of the topic and to compare the results with those from the questionnaire, however, the concept from this study may be transferable to another similar environment.

Three of the participants said they are connected with companies. However, two out of three made the initial connection in the 'spur of the moment' and have not gone back since then to look at the profiles of these companies. The third participant who is connected with companies stated that he was only connected with charities such as Oxfam and Amnesty and that these companies update their profiles regularly, communicating with those with whom they are connected. The fourth participant clearly stated

that she was not connected with any companies, brands or products and had no intention to do so in the future. She believes it is a "weird way of finding out information", whereas the fifth participant of the group said that she is not connected with any companies but might consider doing so in the future if she saw something that appealed to her.

The interviews revealed that all of the participants agreed their main reason for being a member of a social networking site is to talk to friends, stay in touch, and connect with people easily. Additionally, they felt that if companies are to attract the attention of users more effectively, they will need to provide actual benefits or discounts which users can only obtain through being connected with them. The need for more updates from the actual company was brought up often throughout the interview. The participants believe they feel more in contact with those companies who update their profile regularly.

The participants believe that companies being members of SNS does not decrease their perception of those brands, and it might increase it if they were interested in a particular brand; it can be annoying if you are connected but you no longer wish to receive information or communication from the company. Moreover, being connected with companies does not necessarily increase purchase intentions, because the purpose of connecting is not about purchasing. They can be connected to something as it may be intriguing or appealing, not because they necessarily want to purchase it. Finally, the awareness and familiarisation generated by companies on SNSs does not necessarily mean that SNS can be used for finding out information about products or services. There is, however, a place for companies on social networking sites since their presence is not irritating. However, the participants also mentioned that companies have to do it properly, by updating their profiles regularly and communicate with their 'friends' or 'fans'.

4.3 Comparison of Results from Questionnaire and Focus Group

A number of interesting comparisons come to the foreground, stemming from the results of the questionnaire and the focus group discussion. To begin with, the questionnaire results revealed that their perception of a brand increased when they were connected with them over a SNS, whereas the focus group response suggested that their perception of the brand would only increase if they were very interested in that particular brand or product. This indicates that the more interested they are in that product, brand or company the more likely the connection is to increase their perception of the brand further. Therefore, an increase in brand perception can depend on the company, product or brand as well as depending on the individual's level of interest.

Regarding purchase intentions, the questionnaire ascertained that the majority of students believe that being connected with companies neither increases nor decreases their intentions to purchase. The focus group discussion revealed that the participants have no intentions to purchase to begin with when they connect with a company; connecting with companies is not about purchasing at all. The connection, hence, has no impact on intentions to purchase. Finally, there was an agreement in terms of the responses from questionnaire and focus group discussion regarding the use of SNS as viral marketing channel. Both stated that they think it is a good idea for companies to be

on SNSs for marketing purposes, and that it is an effective way of communicating their offerings. The members of the focus group agreed, but did not feel quite so strongly about this.

5. IMPLICATIONS FROM RESEARCH FINDINGS

As discussed in the literature review, social networking is so important it is everywhere, and marketers need to embrace this (Li, 2007a). In this study, the fact that the majority of students spend only 15 minutes or less on the social networking site in one sitting does not give marketers sufficient time to grab their attention and encourage them to form a connection. This challenge is heightened by consumers' short attention spans due to an abundance of choices these days (Godin, 2007). Getting users to connect with companies is one of the most important challengers marketers face on social networking sites, since joining new customers with loyal customers can inspire word-of-mouth even further (Bone, 1992). This task is also difficult because, like most word-of-mouth promotional tactics, once the message is out there it is out of the marketer's control (Gay et al., 2007). Therefore, marketers need to look for alternative ways to get users to connect, for instance enable simple one-click registration with the company over their SNS –for example the 'Facebook Connect' (Catone, 2009). This can be justified by the 47% of students who completed the questionnaire; they are connected with companies. While this is a substantial amount, there remains a large number who are not connected with companies. By providing links on their websites, it widens the marketer's possibility of connecting with a greater audience.

Our results indicated that for the majority of students 'to be informed about companies or brands' was their least prominent reason for being a member of a SNS. This means that users are not actively seeking information about companies when they are on the SNS. Thus, marketers need to be aware of this, since it influences the importance of building a relationship with users, rather than bombarding them with obvious and tacky promotion. The basic characteristic of SNS is to connect people, and this fact needs to be made explicit and a priority for companies as well. However, the fact that students do not seek to join SNS to be informed about specific products and services highlights how important it is to attract users through alternative mediums as well. The reason 'to stay in touch with people easily' was found to be the majority of respondents' most prominent reason for being a member of a social networking site. This supports the results from Joinson's (2008) study which found that social connection is a common motive for using Facebook.

In terms of influencing user attitudes, the majority of the questionnaire respondents stated that being connected with companies increases their awareness of the brand, but still there was a large number that indicated that the connection neither increases nor decreases their brand perception. Hence, the results partly reinforce the study of Merisavo and Raulas (2004), who found that repeated exposure does lead to enhanced brand attitudes. Their findings are strengthened by our result which implies that it is possible to increase users' perceptions of a companies' brand over SNSs, however marketers need to focus more attention on this in order to increase it further. The more often companies update their profiles, the more they appear in users' newsfeeds thus exposing them to the brand. According to Merisavo and Raulas (2004) this should lead to an increase in brand perception.

However, the results suggested that the connections created by SNSs do not necessarily lead on intentions to purchase. The respondents connect to a SNS because they find a company interesting or appealing but it is never about purchasing. This means that marketers need to lessen the focus on making sales, and focus more on building relationships with users. In accordance to Weber

(2007), the aim of marketing through the social web should not be to secure sales right away. Marketers need to be subtle with their advertising and focus on informal communication and relationship building.

The results indicated that the majority of the students are more likely to connect with businesses in the retail and entertainment industries, although these results are reflective of the students' lifestyles and interests. To address this issue, a survey of a wider audience with a variety of lifestyles and demographics would uncover different results. Marketers need to be aware who their target market is and where they are spending their time on the web. Despite the fact that SNSs constitute a useful channel for companies for marketing purposes and connecting with customers and potential customers, this place needs to be effectively coordinated into the organisation's overall marketing strategy (Godin, 2007). Companies need to grasp the structure and communication behaviour of the online social networks they wish to target, and adapt the campaign to suit their needs (Bampo et al., 2008). In this vain, by ensuring they suit the communication behaviours of the customers, they will avoid being ignored.

However, it is not only the establishment of the connection that is important; it is also important for the marketer to sustain the relationship with those users, and this can be achieved by regular communication. According to the literature (Gay et al., 2007; Merisavo and Raulas, 2004) active communication with customers deepens consumer-brand relationships. Having said that, marketers should think of their profile on social networking sites as a place where people can spend time, share information, and casually communicate with the company, and other fans, on a personal level. This should ensure the connection is more than just a latent tie between them and their customers (Haythornthwaite, 2002); without communication, there is no relationship.

In accordance to our focus group result that companies should offer benefits through the connection on a social networking site to keep customers and potential customers connected, Phelps et al. (2004) discovered that jokes, sad stories, inspirational messages, free goods or helpful tips are more likely to be passed on when it comes to viral promotional messages. This suggests a useful strategy for marketers, who can offer benefits in the form of entertainment and information for example fun facts, jokes, interesting video clips or images, information about promotions or competitions.

The importance of regularly updating profiles has been mentioned briefly, and is highlighted here as another very important task a company should undertake in order to solidify their relationship with users. Updating entails various tasks, such as communicating with the users regularly, encouraging feedback and responding to users, as well as regular updates and general page maintenance. This is in accordance to Bone (1995), who found that information which is communicated by an expert in the area has a greater influence, in other words, communication from the company itself can generate highly influential word-of-mouth. Hence, marketers have to know their audience well, fill out the entire profile thoroughly, post information about news and events regularly and provide links to other relevant web pages or blogs (Shawbel, 2009); but more importantly, they should update the status of the company regularly, so as to increase the frequency that their brand or product name is being shown on the homepages of users.

6. CONCLUSION

Over the past few years, the social web has developed and had a dramatic effect on the marketing world. A vast range of brands are seeing the benefits obtained from viral activities such as launching videos on websites like YouTube, posting product information on social networking sites, and encouraging word-of-mouth through customer

review forums and blogs (Ferguson, 2008). The objective of this research project was to discover the perceptions of students who are members of social networking sites on viral marketing via those sites, and the effects which this has on their attitudes and behaviours.

By using a questionnaire and focus group interview, the study found that being connected with companies on SNSs has a positive effect on attitudes towards those companies, but little to no effect on their behaviours. Moreover, the results ascertained that it is a good idea for companies to use SNSs for marketing purposes. Other key themes which emerged include the importance of updating the company's profile on social networking sites, communicating and encouraging feedback with visitors, and offering some form of benefits to the visitors through the connection.

There were no major barriers which occurred throughout the research process, but there were some limitations to the study. The response rate for the questionnaire was relatively low, but this is often the case with e-mail based surveys. Additionally, because of the time constraint on the study, there was not enough time for a further round of questionnaires to be sent out and analysed thoroughly to increase the response rate. Nevertheless, the use of the focus group helped to overcome this by providing an additional set of results to be compared with those from the questionnaire. One further limitation was the fact that all the participants in the focus group were members of the same social networking site, that is, Facebook. Had several of them been members of different sites further insights may have been discovered.

It is also important to note that while the results of this study can not be generalised, the concept may inform current theory on SNS and marketing. As Li (2007a) mentioned, social networking is so important now, it is like air. Companies should embrace social networking and use it to their advantage, since people are spending time on SNSs. Many companies are not effectively utilising the gateway to communicating with consumers that SNSs provide; but, however, joining social networking sites is not an 'easy way out' for marketers to communicate with consumers. Marketers need to be aware of what will attract visitors, and most importantly what will keep them.

This study may be one of very few on viral marketing via SNS, but there are several ways in which this topic can be explored more thoroughly with results which can be generalised to a wider population. For instance, a future study looking at an audience with a broader range of demographics and psychographics would provide more accurate perceptions of users, as apposed to just a small group of students. Additionally, the effect marketing via social networking sites has on user behaviours would also provide more insights, as this study looked at purchase intentions. If purchase perceptions are understood as attitudes, further research on actual purchase behaviour may also be needed.

This study does shed some interesting insight on the debate of weather marketing through social networking sites actually constitutes to be an effective form of viral (on line) marketing. If viral marketing is the on line analogy of word of moth marketing which is universally accepted to be the most effective method, then marketing through SNS (if one accepts this to be a form of viral marketing) should possess similar kind of attributes in terms of its effectiveness. However, the conjectures tested out on the sample, although admittedly the sample may not be representative and the methodology may not confirm to a rigorous statistical testing approach, do not reinforce this. In essence the study finds that although there is a positive attitude towards companies that maintains a presence in social networking sites, this does not necessarily influence the customer purchase patterns. Thus, the results appear to favour the fact that marketing through SNS does not constitute to be an "on line" word of mouth form of marketing.

Following previous research examining the characteristics of social ties influence recipients'

behaviours (e.g. De Bruyn & Lilien, 2008), it would be fruitful to look into tie strength between 'friends' on SNSs and the underlying social networks and the way they can spread their viral promotion more effectively. Research could also be undertaken in the form of a case study which analyses the strategy of a company which has employed successful viral marketing via SNSs to uncover winning techniques and critical success factors that can be followed by other companies that wish to use SNSs for viral marketing.

SNSs are the places to be on the internet today, but the social web is constantly advancing. There have been various predictions by marketing experts about the future of the social web. Weber (2007) believes SNSs will have smaller, more focused networks which are related to specific interests whereas Owyang (2009) believes the future of the web will involve a transformation from separate social sites to one shared social experience. Whatever occurs, viral marketing on the social web will continue to be vital in the future because all companies need to get their name into the social networks and e-communities where their target audiences spend their time (Weber, 2007).

ACKNOWLEDGMENT

The authors acknowledge the contribution of Ms. Rebecca Lewis in the research that produced the chapter.

REFERENCES

Arndt, J. (1967). The role of product-related conversations in the diffusion of a new product. *JMR, Journal of Marketing Research*, *4*, 291–295. doi:10.2307/3149462

Backstrom, L., Huttenlocher, D., Kleinberg, J., & Lan, X. (2006). Group formation in large social networks: Membership, growth, and evolution. Paper presented at *KDD '06*, Philadelphia, PA.

Ballard, M. (2009). Can big brands crash the social network party? *WorkPlace Media*. Retrieved August 11, 2009, from http://www.scribd.com/doc/17155840/Can-Big-Brands-Crash-the-Social-Networking-Party

Baltazar, A. (2009). World wide networking. *NacsOnline.com*. Retrieved August 10, 2009, from http://www.visibletechnologies.com/PR/NACS_May09_22-28.pdf

Bampo, M., Ewing, M., Mather, D., Stewart, D., & Wallace, M. (2008). The effects of the social structure of digital networks on viral marketing. *Information Systems Research, 19*(3), 273–290. doi:10.1287/isre.1070.0152

Bone, P. (1992). Determinants of word-of-mouth communications during consumption. *Advances in Consumer Research. Association for Consumer Research (U. S.), 19*, 579–583.

Bone, P. (1995). Word of mouth effects on short-term and long-term product judgements. *Journal of Business Research, 32*, 213–223. doi:10.1016/0148-2963(94)00047-I

Boyd, D., & Ellison, N. (2008). Social network sites: Definition, history and scholarship. *Journal of Computer-Mediated Communication, 13*, 210–230. doi:10.1111/j.1083-6101.2007.00393.x

Boyd, D., & Ellison, N. (2008). Social network sites: Definition, history and scholarship. *Journal of Computer-Mediated Communication, 13*, 210–230. doi:10.1111/j.1083-6101.2007.00393.x

Brown, J. J., & Reingen, P. (1987). Social ties and word-of-mouth referral behavior. *The Journal of Consumer Research, 14*(3), 350–362. doi:10.1086/209118

Catone, J. (2009). 10 impressive new implementations of Facebook Connect. *Mashable: The Social Media Guide*. Retrieved August 11, 2009, from http://mashable.com/2009/07/21/facebook-connect-new/

Chafkin, M. (2007). How to kill a great idea! *Inc. Magazine*. Retrieved August 10, 2009, from http://www.inc.com/magazine/20070601/features-how-to-kill-a-great-idea.html

Chen, Y., & Xie, J. (2008). Online consumer review: Word-of-mouth as a new element of marketing communication mix. *Management Science, 54*(3), 477–491. doi:10.1287/mnsc.1070.0810

De Bruyn, A. D., & Lilien, G. L. (2008). A multistage model of word-of-mouth influence through viral marketing. *International Journal of Research in Marketing, 25*, 151–163. doi:10.1016/j.ijresmar.2008.03.004

Dobele, A., Lindgreen, A., Beverland, M., Vanhamme, J., & Wijk, R. (2007). Why pass on viral messages? Because they connect emotionally. *Business Horizons, 50*, 291–304. doi:10.1016/j.bushor.2007.01.004

Dobele, A., Toleman, D., & Beverland, M. (2005). Controlled infection! Spreading the brand message through viral marketing. *Business Horizons, 48*, 143–149. doi:10.1016/j.bushor.2004.10.011

Easterby-Smith, M., Thorpe, R., & Lowe, A. (1991). *Management research: An introduction*. London: Sage.

Engel, J. E., Blackwell, R. D., & Kegerreis, R. J. (1969). How information is used to adopt an innovation. *Journal of Advertising Research, 9*, 3–8.

Facebook. (2009). Statistics. *Press Room* [facebook blog]. Retrieved August, 20, 2009, from http://www.facebook.com/press/info.php?statistics

Ferguson, R. (2008). Word of mouth and viral marketing: Taking the temperature of the hottest trends in marketing. *Journal of Consumer Marketing, 25*(3), 179–182. doi:10.1108/07363760810870671

Gay, R., Charlesworth, A., & Esen, R. (2007). *Online marketing: A customer-led approach*. New York: Oxford University Press.

Godin, S. (2007). *Meatball sundae: Is your marketing out of sync*. London: Portfolio, Penguin Group Inc.

Goldenberg, J., Libai, B., & Muller, E. (2001). Talk of the network: A complex systems look at the underlying process of word-of-mouth. *Marketing Letters*, *3*(12), 211–223. doi:10.1023/A:1011122126881

Golder, S., Wilkinson, D., & Huberman, B. (2007). Rhythms of social interaction: Messaging within a massive online network. Paper presented at the *Third International Conference on Communities and Technologies*. Retrieved August 10, 2009, from http://www.hpl.hp.com/research/idl/papers/facebook/facebook.pdf

Granovetter, M. (1973). The strength of weak ties. *American Journal of Sociology*, *78*(6), 1360–1380. doi:10.1086/225469

Hagel, J., & Rayport, J. F. (1997). The coming battle for customer information. *Harvard Business Review*, *75*, 53–65.

Haythornthwaite, C. (2002). Strong, weak and latent ties and the impact of new media. *Information Communication and Society*, *18*(5), 385–401. doi:10.1080/01972240290108195

Helm, S. (2000). Viral marketing: Establishing customer relationships by 'Word-of-Mouse'. *Electronic Commerce and Marketing*, *13*(3), 158–161.

Herr, P., Kardes, F., & Kim, J. (1991). Effects of word-of-mouth and product-attribute information on persuasion: An accessibility-diagnosticity perspective. *The Journal of Consumer Research*, *17*, 454–462. doi:10.1086/208570

Joinson, A. (2008). 'Looking at', 'looking up' or 'keeping up with' people? Motives and uses of facebook. Paper presented at the *Conference on Human Factors in Computer Systems*. Retrieved August 12, 2009, from http://people.bath.ac.uk/aj266/pubs_pdf/1149-joinson.pdf

Jurvetson, S., & Draper, T. (1997). Viral marketing phenomenon explained. *Draper Fisher Jurvetson*. Retrieved July 15, 2009, from http://www.dfj.com/news/article_26.shtml

Katz, E., & Lazarsfeld, P. F. (1955). *Personal influence*. Glencoe, IL: Free Press.

Krishnamurthy, S. (2001). Understanding online message dissemination: An analysis of 'send-this-message-to-your-friend' data. *First Monday*, *6*(5).

Kumar, R., Novak, J., & Tomkins, A. (2006). Structure and evolution of online social networks. Paper presented at the *International Conference on Knowledge Discovery in Data Mining*. Retrieved August 10, 2009, from http://wiki.cs.columbia.edu/download/attachments/1979/Structure+and+Evolution+of+Online+Social+Networks-kumar.pdf

Lampe, C., Ellison, N., & Steinfeld, C. (2007). A familiar Face(book): Profile elements as signals in an online social network. Paper presented at CHI 2007, San Jose, CA.

Leskovec, J., Adamic, L. A., & Huberman, B. (2007). The dynamics of viral marketing. *ACM Transactions on the Web*, *1*(1), 1–39. doi:10.1145/1232722.1232727

Li, C. (2007a). Social networking is like air says marketing guru Charlene Li. *Marketing voices*. Retrieved July 16, 2009, from http://www.podtech.net/home/2719/social-networking-is-like-air-says-market-guru-charlene-li

Li, C. (2007b). Marketing on social networking sites. *Forrester.com*. Retrieved July 16, 2009, from http://www.retailing.org/new_site/eweb/forrester/Marketing%20on%20Social%20Networking%20Sites.pdf

Li, C., & Bernoff, J. (2008). *Groundswell* [Excerpt]. Boston: Harvard Business Press. Retrieved July 16, 2009, from http://a964.g.akamaitech.net/7/964/714/397c4414501aa8/www.forrester.com/groundswell/assets/groundswell_excerpt.pdf

Merisavo, M., & Raulas, M. (2004). The impact of email marketing on brand loyalty. *Journal of Product and Brand Management, 13*(7), 498–505. doi:10.1108/10610420410568435

Mislove, A., Marcon, M., Gummadi, K. P., Druschel, P., & Bhattacharjee, B. (2007). *Measurement and analysis of online social networks*. Retrieved July 10, 2009, from http://www.imconf.net/imc-2007/papers/imc170.pdf

Misner, I. R. (1994). *The world's best known marketing secret*. Austin, TX: Bard & Stephen.

Nielsen NetRatings. (2009). Twitter's tweet smell of success. *Nielsen Wire*. Retrieved August 7, 2009, from http://blog.nielsen.com/nielsenwire/online_mobile/twitters-tweet-smell-of-success/

Owyang, J. (2009). The future of the social Web: In five eras. *Web-Strategist.Com*. Retrieved July 16, 2009, from http://www.web-strategist.com/blog/2009/04/27/future-of-the-social-web/

Phelps, J. E., Lewis, R., Mobilio, L., Perry, D., & Niranjan, R. (2004). Viral marketing or electronic word-of-mouth advertising: Examining consumer responses and motivations to pass along email. *Journal of Advertising Research, 44*(4), 333–348.

Pitta, D., & Fowler, D. (2005). Internet community forums: An untapped resource for consumer marketers. *Journal of Consumer Marketing, 22*(5), 265–274. doi:10.1108/07363760510611699

Saunders, M., Lewis, P., & Thornhill, A. (1997). *Research methods for business students*. London: Pearson Professional Limited.

Shawbel, D. (2009). How to: Build your personal brand on facebook. *Mashable: The Social Media Guide*. Retrieved July 11, 2009, from http://mashable.com/2009/04/02/facebook-personal-brand/

Shirky, C. (2000). The toughest virus of all. *Clay Shirky's Writings About the Internet*. Retrieved July 15, 2009, from http://www.shirky.com/writings/toughest_virus.html

Shirky, C. (2003). People on page: YASNS. *Corante's Many-to-Many*. Retrieved August 10, 2009, from http://many.corante.com/archives/2003/05/12/people_on_page_yasns.php

Smith, W. (2009). 5 reasons facebook is better than Twitter for your business. *Social Media School*. Retrieved August 10, 2009, from http://socialmediatoday.com/school/112208

Subramani, M. R., & Rajagopalan, B. (2003). Knowledge-sharing & influence in online social networks via viral marketing. *Communications of the ACM, 45*(12), 300–307. doi:10.1145/953460.953514

Twitter. (2009). *Twitter support*. Retrieved August 10, 2009, from http://help.twitter.com/forums/10711/entries/13920

Weber, L. (2007). *Marketing to the social Web*. Hoboken, NJ: John Wiley & Sons, Inc.

Wellman, B. (1988). Structural analysis: From method and metaphor to theory and substance. Retrieved August 10, 2009, from http://homepage.ntu.edu.tw/~khsu/network/reading/wellman2.pdf

Whyte, W. H. (1954, November). The Web of word of mouth. *Fortune, 50*, 140–143.

ENDNOTES

[1] For confidentiality reasons the actual name of the University is not disclosed.

[2] We refer to social networking instead of "social networks" to depict that we are not dealing with structural properties of networks, but with the act of organising.

Compilation of References

Ackerman, G., James, M., & Getz, C. T. (2007). The application of social bookmarking technology to the national intelligence domain. *International Journal of Intelligence and CounterIntelligence, 20,* 678–698. doi:10.1080/08850600701249808

Acquisti, A., & Gross, R. (2006). Imagined communities: Awareness, information sharing, and privacy on the Facebook. In *6th Workshop on Privacy Enhancing Technologies (PET).* Retrieved August 23, 2009 from http://privacy.cs.cmu.edu/dataprivacy/projects/facebook/facebook2.pdf

Adamic, L. A., & Adar, E. (2005). How to search a social network. *Social Networks, 27*(3), 187–203. doi:10.1016/j.socnet.2005.01.007

Adesope, O. O., & Nesbit, J. C. (2010). A systematic review of research on collaborative learning using concept maps. In Torres, P. L., & Marriott, R. C. V. (Eds.), *Handbook of research on collaborative learning using concept mapping* (pp. 238–255). Hershey, PA: IGI Global. doi:10.4018/978-1-59904-992-2.ch012

Ahlqvist, T., Bäck, A., Halonen, M., & Heinonen, S. (2008). Social media roadmap: Exploring the futures triggered by social media. Retrieved August 18, 2009, from http://www.vtt.fi/inf/pdf/tiedotteet/2008/T2454.pdf

Alavi, M., & Leidner, D. E. (2001). Review: Knowledge management and knowledge management systems: Conceptual foundations and research issues. *Management Information Systems Quarterly, 25*(1), 107–136. doi:10.2307/3250961

Alder, A., & Davis, R. (2009). Symmetric multimodal interaction in a dynamic dialogue. In *Proceedings of Workshop on Sketch Recognition, Intelligent User Interface* (IUI'09), Sanibel Island, FL (pp. 1-10). New York: ACM Press.

Aldridge, A., Forcht, K., & Pierson, J. (1997). Get linked or get lost: Marketing strategy for the internet. *Internet Research: Electronic Networking Applications and Policy, 7*(3), 161–169. doi:10.1108/10662249710171805

Alexa. (2009). Top 500 websites. Retrieved September 8, 2009, from http://www.alexa.com/topsites

Al-Haddad, S. A. R., Samad, S. A., Hussain, A., Ishak, K. A., & Noor, A. O. A. (2009). Robust speech recognition using fusion techniques and adaptive filtering. *American Journal of Applied Sciences, 6*(2), 290–295.

Ames, M., & Naaman, M. (2007). Why we tag: Motivations for annotation in mobile and online media. In *Proceedings of the SIGCHI Conference on Human Factors in Computing Systems* (pp. 971-980). New York: ACM Press.

Amit, R., & Zott, C. (2001). Value creation in e-Business. *Strategic Management Journal, 22*(6/7), 493–520. doi:10.1002/smj.187

Anderson, N. (2007). *Report: South Korea tops in social networking, US fifth.* Retrieved from http://arstechnica.com/

Anstead, N., & Chadwick, A. (2008). Parties, election campaigning, and the internet: Toward a comparative institutional approach. In Chaswick, A., & Howard, P. (Eds.), *The Routledge handbook of internet politics.* New York: Routledge.

Antoniou, G., & van Harmelen, F. (2004). *A semantic Web primer*. Cambridge, MA: MIT Press.

Argyris, C. (1990). *Overcoming organizational defenses: Facilitating organizational learning*. Boston: Allyn and Bacon.

Arndt, J. (1967). The role of product-related conversations in the diffusion of a new product. *JMR, Journal of Marketing Research, 4*, 291–295. doi:10.2307/3149462

Ashimura, K. (2009). Multimodal interaction activity. *Technical dissemination document on multimodal XML-based languages.* Boston: W3C Press. Retrieved from http://www.w3.org/2002/mm1/

Avola, D., & Del Buono, A. (2009). Multimodal interfaces: Classification and usability testing in heterogeneous environments [Technical Research Study, Tech. Report No. 21/09]. Rome, Italy: National Research Centre, Computer Science and Knowledge Laboratory (CSKLab). Retrieved from http://www.csklab.it

Bacharach, M., & Gambetti, D. (2001). Trust in signs. In Cook, K. (Ed.), *Trust in society* (pp. 148–184). New York: Russell Sage Foundation.

Backstrom, L., Huttenlocher, D., Kleinberg, J., & Lan, X. (2006). Group formation in large social networks. In *Proceedings of the 12th ACM SIGKDD International Conference on Knowledge Discovery and Data Mining,* August 20-23, 2006, Philadelphia, PA (pp. 44-54).

Badot, O., & Cova, B. (2003). Néo-marketing, 10 après: pour une théorie critique de la consommation et du marketing réenchantés. *Revue française du marketing, 195*, 79-94.

Bagozzi, R. P. (2000). On the concept of intentional social action in consumer behavior. *The Journal of Consumer Research, 27*, 388–396. doi:10.1086/317593

Bagozzi, R. P. (2007). The legacy of the technology acceptance model and a proposal for a paradigm shift. *Journal of the Association for Information Systems, 8*(4), 244–254.

Bagozzi, R. P., & Dholakia, U. M. (2002). Intentional social action in virtual communities. *Journal of Interactive Marketing, 16*(2), 2–21. doi:10.1002/dir.10006

Bagozzi, R. P., & Dholakia, U. M. (2006). Open source software user communities: A study of participation in Linux user groups. *Management Science, 52*(7), 1099–1115. doi:10.1287/mnsc.1060.0545

Bagozzi, R. P., & Lee, K. H. (2002). Multiple routes for social influence: The role of compliance, internalization, and social identity. *Social Psychology Quarterly, 65*(3), 226–247. doi:10.2307/3090121

Baker, D. F. (2001). The development of collective efficacy in small task groups. *Small Group Research, 32*(4), 451–474. doi:10.1177/104649640103200404

Ballard, M. (2009). Can big brands crash the social network party? *WorkPlace Media*. Retrieved August 11, 2009, from http://www.scribd.com/doc/17155840/Can-Big-Brands-Crash-the-Social-Networking-Party

Baltazar, A. (2009). World wide networking. *NacsOnline.com.* Retrieved August 10, 2009, from http://www.visibletechnologies.com/PR/NACS_May09_22-28.pdf

Balzer, W., & Tuomela, R. (1997). A fixed point approach to collective attitudes. In Holmström-Hintikka, G., & Tuomela, R. (Eds.), *Contemporary action theory*. Boston: Kluwer Academic Publishers.

Bampo, M., Ewing, M., Mather, D., Stewart, D., & Wallace, M. (2008). The effects of the social structure of digital networks on viral marketing. *Information Systems Research, 19*(3), 273–290. doi:10.1287/isre.1070.0152

Bandura, A. (1977). Self-efficacy: Toward a unifying theory of behavioral change. *Psychological Review, 84*(2), 191–215. doi:10.1037/0033-295X.84.2.191

Bandura, A. (1997). *Self-efficacy: The exercise of control*. New York: Freeman.

Bandura, A. (2000). Exercise of human agency through collective efficacy. *Current Directions in Psychological Science, 9*, 75–78. doi:10.1111/1467-8721.00064

Bandura, A. (2004). Health promotion by social cognitive means. *Health Education & Behavior, 31*(2), 143–164. doi:10.1177/1090198104263660

Bao, S., Xue, G., Wu, X., Yu, Y., Fei, B., & Su, Z. (2007). Optimizing web search using social annotations. In *Proceedings of the 16th international conference on World Wide Web* (pp. 501-510). New York: ACM Press.

Barnes, S. B. (2006). A privacy paradox: Social networking in the United States. *First Monday, 11*(9). Retrieved August 23, 2009, from http://firstmonday.org/htbin/cgiwrap/bin/ojs/index.php/fm/article/view/1394/1312

Baron, R., Branscombe, B., & Byrne, D. (2009). *Social psychology*. London: Allyn & Bacon.

Basili, V., Caldiera, G., & Rombach, D. H. (1994). *The goal question metric paradigm: Encyclopedia of software engineering*. New York: John Wiley & Sons.

Baskerville, R., & Stage, J. (2000). Discourse on the interactions of information systems, organizations, and society: Reformation and transformation. In *IFIP WG 8.2 Conference.: The Social and Organizational Perspective on Research and Practice in Information Technology.* Boston, MA: Kluwer Academic Publishers.

Batini, C., Lenzerini, M., & Navathe, B. (1986). A comparative analysis of methodologies for database schema integration. *ACM Computing Surveys, 18*(4), 323–364. doi:10.1145/27633.27634

Bautin, M., Vijayarenu, L., & Skiena, S. (2008). International sentiment analysis for news and blogs. In *Proceedings of the Second International Conference on Weblogs and Social Media (ICWSM-2008)*. Retrieved from http://www.aaai.org/Library/ICWSM/icwsm08contents.php

Baverman, L. (2008). Corporate wiki: Sure, it's fun to say, but it's useful, too. Retrieved August 4, 2008, from http://www.bizjournals.com/cincinnati/stories/2008/08/04/focus1.html?b=1217822400%5E1677764

Béchet, N., Roche, M., & Chauché, J. (2009). Towards the selection of induced syntactic relations. In M. Boughanem, C. Berrut, J. Mothe & C. Soule-Dupuy (Eds.), *Advances in Information Retrieval* [Proceedings of 31th European Conference on Information Retrieval Research (ECIR'09)], (Lecture Notes in Computer Science, Vol. 5478, pp. 786-790). Berlin: Springer.

Becker, G. (1992). Human capital and the economy. *Proceedings of the American Philosophical Society, 135*(1), 85–92.

Berendt, B., & Kralisch, A. (2009). A user-centric approach to identifying best deployment strategies for language tools: The impact of content and access language on Web user behaviour and attitudes. *Information Retrieval, 12*(3), 380–399. doi:10.1007/s10791-008-9086-4

Bergin, J. (2002). Teaching on the Wiki Web, *ACM. SIGCSE Bulletin, 34*(3), 195. doi:10.1145/637610.544473

Berners-Lee, T., Hendler, J., & Lassila, O. (2001). The semantic Web. *Scientific American, 284*(5), 34–43. doi:10.1038/scientificamerican0501-34

Bernoff, J., Pflaum, C. N., & Bowen, E. (2008, October 20). *The growth of social technology adoption: 2/3 of the global Internet population visit social networks*. Cambridge, MA: Forrester Research. Retrieved from http://www.forrester.com/Research/Document/Excerpt/0,7211,44907,00.html

Bessière, K., Ellis, J. B., & Kellogg, W. A. (2009). Acquiring a professional "second life": Problems and prospects for the use of virtual worlds in business. In *Proceedings of the 27th International Conference on Human factors in Computing Systems* (pp. 2883-2898). Boston: ACM Press.

Bhatt, G. (2000). Information dynamics, learning, and knowledge creation in organizations. *The Learning Organization: An International Journal, 7*(2), 89–98. doi:10.1108/09696470010316288

Blackwell, J., Sheridan, J., Instone, K., Schwartz, D. R., & Kogan, S. (2009). Design and adoption of social collaboration software within businesses. In *Proceedings of the 27th international Conference Extended Abstracts on Human Factors in Computing Systems* (pp. 2759-2762). New York: ACM Press.

Bock, G., & Paxhia, S. (2008). *Collaboration and social media: Taking stock of today's experiences and tomorrow's opportunities.* Cambridge, MA: Gilbane Group, Inc.

Bone, P. (1992). Determinants of word-of-mouth communications during consumption. *Advances in Consumer Research. Association for Consumer Research (U. S.), 19,* 579–583.

Bone, P. (1995). Word of mouth effects on short-term and long-term product judgements. *Journal of Business Research, 32,* 213–223. doi:10.1016/0148-2963(94)00047-I

Boutorabi, B. (n.d.). Web 2.0: The next generation of platform. Retrieved May 7, 2008, from http://www.openpublish.com.au/pdf/Bahram_Boutorabi.pdf

Boyd, D., & Ellison, N. (2007). Social network sites: Definition, history, and scholarship. *Journal of Computer-Mediated Communication, 13*(1), 210–230. doi:10.1111/j.1083-6101.2007.00393.x

Boyd, D. (2007). Social network sites: Public, private, or what? *The Knowledge Tree: An e-Journal of Learning Innovation.* Retrieved August 22, 2009 from http://www.danah.org/papers/KnowledgeTree.pdf

Brandon, J. (2007). The top eight corporate sites in Second Life. Retrieved August 18, 2008, from http://www.computerworld.com/action/article.do?command=viewArticleBasic&articleId=9018238

Bratman, M. E. (1997). I intend that we J. In Holmström-Hintikka, G., & Tuomela, R. (Eds.), *Contemporary action theory.* Boston: Kluwer Academic Publishers.

Brickley, D., & Guha, R. V. (2004, February). Resource description framework (RDF) schema specification 1.0 [Recommendation]. Cambridge, MA: World Wide Web Consortium. Retrieved August, 2009 from http://www.w3.org/TR/2004/RECrdf- schema-20040210

British Standards Institute. (2006). [—*Guide to good practice in commissioning accessible websites.* London: BSI.]. *PAS, 78,* 2006.

Broekstra, J., Kampman, A., & van Harmelen, F. (2002). Sesame: A generic architecture for storing and querying RDF and RDF schema. In *Proceedings of the 2nd International Semantic Web Conference* (pp. 54-68). Berlin: Springer.

Brown, J., Broderick, A., & Lee, N. (2007). Word of mouth communication within online communities: Conceptualizing the online social network. *Journal of Interactive Marketing, 21*(3), 2–20. doi:10.1002/dir.20082

Brown, J. J., & Reingen, P. (1987). Social ties and word-of-mouth referral behavior. *The Journal of Consumer Research, 14*(3), 350–362. doi:10.1086/209118

Bruckman, A. (2002). The future of e-learning communities. *Communications of the ACM, 45*(4), 60–63. doi:10.1145/505248.505274

Bucher, H. J. (2004). Is there a Chinese internet? Intercultural investigation on the internet in the People's Republic of China: Theoretical considerations and empirical results. In *Proceedings Fourth International Conference: Cultural Attitudes towards Technology and Communication 2004 (CATAC),* Murdoch University, Australia (pp. 416-428).

Bureau of East Asian and Pacific Affairs. (2006) Background note: Singapore [Web page]. Retrieved from http://www.state.gov/r/pa/ei/bgn/2798.htm

Cachia, R., Kluzer, S., Cabrera, M., Centena, C., & Punie, Y. (2007). ICT, social capital and cultural diversity. Retrieved May 19, 2009, from http://www.kinnisland.nl/binaries/documenten/rapporten/e-inclusion-eur23047en.pdf

Caldwell, B., Cooper, M., Reid, L. G., & Vanderheiden, G. (2008). *Web content accessibility guidelines (WCAG) 2.0.* Retrieved August 11, 2009, from http://www.w3.org/TR/WCAG20/

California Economic Leadership Network. (2006). California economic development partnerships [Web page]. Retrieved March 17, 2006, from http://www.labor.ca.gov/cedp/cedpsanjoaquin.htm

California Partnership for the San Joaquin Valley. (2006). *Summary of approved "Scopes of Work" for work groups.* Fresno, CA: California Partnership for the San Joaquin Valley.

Callahan, E. (2005). Cultural similarities and differences in the design of university websites. *Journal of Computer-Mediated Communication, 11*(1), 12. Retrieved from http://jcmc.indiana.edu/vol11/issue1/callahan.html. doi:10.1111/j.1083-6101.2006.tb00312.x

Callari, R. (2009). *Top ten social networks circumnavigating the globe.* Retrieved from http://inventorspot.com/articles/top_ten_social_networks_circumnavigating_globe_30018

Cañada, J. (2006). Tipologías y estilos en el etiquetado social [Web log post]. Retrieved August 28, 2008, from http://www.terremoto.net/tipologias-y-estlos-en-el-etiquetado-social

Caplan, S. E. (2007). Relations among loneliness, social anxiety, and problematic internet use. *Cyberpsychology & Behavior, 10*(2), 234–242. doi:10.1089/cpb.2006.9963

Cappé, O., Moulines, E., & Rydén, T. (Eds.). (2005). *Inference in hidden Markov models* [Springer Series in Statistics]. London: Springer.

Card, S. K., Moran, T. P., & Newell, A. (1983). *The psychology of human-computer interaction.* Hillsdale, NJ: Lawrence Erlbaum Associates.

Carlin, D. (2007). Corporate wikis go viral. Retrieved August 4, 2008, from http://www.businessweek.com/technology/content/mar2007/tc20070312_476504.htm

Carr, N. (2006). Avatars consume as much electricity as Brazilians. *Rough Type: Nicholas Carr's blog.* Retrieved December 5, 2006, from http://www.roughtype.com/archives/2006/12/avatars_consume.php

Carrington, P. J., Scott, J., & Wasserman, S. (2005). *Models and methods in social network analysis.* Cambridge: Cambridge University Press.

Carroll, J. M. (Ed.). (1995). *Scenario-based design: Envisioning work and technology in system development.* New York: John Wiley & Sons.

Castells, M. (2001). *The internet galaxy: Reflections on the internet, business, and society.* Oxford: Oxford University Press.

Catone, J. (2009). 10 impressive new implementations of Facebook Connect. *Mashable: The Social Media Guide.* Retrieved August 11, 2009, from http://mashable.com/2009/07/21/facebook-connect-new/

Cecez-Kecmanovic, D. (2001). Doing critical IS research: The question of methodology. In *Qualitative research in IS: Issues and trends* (pp. 141–163). Hershey, PA: Idea Group Publishing.

Chafkin, M. (2007). How to kill a great idea! *Inc. Magazine.* Retrieved August 10, 2009, from http://www.inc.com/magazine/20070601/features-how-to-kill-a-great-idea.html

Charron, C., Favier, J., & Li, C. (2006). Social computing. Retrieved August 12, 2009, from http://www.cisco.com/web/offer/socialcomputing/SocialComputingBigIdea.pdf

Chau, P. K. Y. (1996). An empirical assessment of a modified technology acceptance model. *Journal of Management Information Systems, 13*(2), 185–204.

Chen, I. Y. L. (2007). The factors influencing members' continuance intentions in professional virtual communities: A longitudinal study. *Journal of Information Science, 33*(4), 451–467. doi:10.1177/0165551506075323

Chen, Y., & Xie, J. (2008). Online consumer review: Word-of-mouth as a new element of marketing communication mix. *Management Science, 54*(3), 477–491. doi:10.1287/mnsc.1070.0810

Cheung, C. M. K., Chiu, P., & Lee, M. K. O. (2010. (in press). Online social networks: Why do we use Facebook? *Computers in Human Behavior.*

Choo, C. W., & Bontis, N. (Eds.). (2002). *The strategic management of intellectual capital and organizational knowledge.* New York: Oxford University Press.

Chou, C., & Tsai, M. J. (2007). Gender differences in Taiwan high school students' computer game playing. *Computers in Human Behavior, 23*(1), 812–824. doi:10.1016/j.chb.2004.11.011

Chung, W., Chen, H., & Reid, E. (2009). Business stakeholder analyzer: An experiment of classifying stakeholders on the Web. *Journal of the American Society for Information Science and Technology, 60*(1), 59–74. doi:10.1002/asi.20948

Clemmensen, T., Shi, Q., Kumar, J., Li, H., Sun, X., & Yammiyavar, P. (2007). Cultural usability tests: How usability tests are not the same all over the world. *Usability and Internationalization: HCI and Culture, Second International Conference on Usability and Internationalization, UI-HCII 2007* [HCI International 2007, Beijing, China, July 22-27, Proceedings, Part I] (pp. 281-290).

Cloete, C., de Villiers, C., & Roodt, S. (2009). Facebook as an academic tool for ICT lecturers. In *Proceedings of the 2009 Annual Conference of the Southern African Computer Lecturers' Association* (pp. 16-22). New York: ACM Press.

Cobb, J. T. (2008). Learning 2.0 for associations. Retrieved April 29, 2008, from http://blog.missiontolearn.com/files/Learning_20_for_Associations_eBook-v1.pdf

Colazzo, L., Molinari, A., & Villa, N. (2008). From e-learning to "co-learning": The role of virtual communities. In Kendall, M., & Samways, B. (Eds.), *Learning to live in the knowledge society* (pp. 329–338). Boston: Springer. doi:10.1007/978-0-387-09729-9_48

Coleman, J. S. (1988). Social capital in the creation of human capital. *American Journal of Sociology, 94*, 95–120. doi:10.1086/228943

Coleman, J. (1990). *Foundations of social theory*. Boston: Harvard University Press.

ComScore. (2007). *Social networking goes global.* Retrieved from http://comscore.com/Press_Events/Press_Releases/2007/07/Social_Networking_Goes_Global

Constantinides, E. (2006). The marketing mix revisited: Towards the 21st century marketing. *Journal of Marketing Management, 22*, 407–438. doi:10.1362/026725706776861190

Cotter, S. (2002). Taking the measure of e-marketing success. *The Journal of Business Strategy, 23*(2), 30–37. doi:10.1108/eb040235

Cova, B. (1996). The postmodern explained to managers: Implications for marketing. *Business Horizons, 39*(6), 15–23. doi:10.1016/S0007-6813(96)90032-4

Coviello, N. E., Milley, R., & Marcolin, B. (2001). Understanding IT-enabled interactivity in contemporary marketing. *Journal of Interactive Marketing, 15*(4), 18–33. doi:10.1002/dir.1020

Craig, J., Cooper, M., Pappas, L., Schwerdtfeger, R., & Seeman, L. (2009). *Accessible rich internet applications (WAI-ARIA) 1.0*. Retrieved August 11, 2009, from http://www.w3.org/TR/wai-aria/

Creese, J. (2007). Web 2.0/business 2.0: New web technologies, organizations and WCM. Retrieved August 7, 2008, from http://eprints.qut.edu.au/archive/00008093/01/8093.pdf

Crespi-Reghizzi, S. (Ed.). (2009). *Formal languages and compilation*. London: Springer.

Cross, R. L., Parker, A., & Sasson, L. (2003). *Networks in the knowledge economy*. Oxford: Oxford University Press.

Csikszentmihalyi, M. (1997). *Flow: The psychology of optimal experience*. New York: Harper and Row.

Daft, R. L., & Lengel, R. H. (1984). Information richness: A new approach to managerial behaviour and organisation design. *Research in Organizational Behavior, 6*, 191–233.

Dahl, D., Kliche, I., Tumuluri, R., Yudkowsky, M., Bodell, M., Porter, B., et al. (2008). Multimodal architecture and interfaces. In J. Barnett (Ed.), *Technical dissemination report on multimodal framework*. Boston: W3C Press. Retrieved from http://www.w3.org/TR/mmi-arch/

Damanpour, F. (1992). Organizational size and innovation. *Organization Studies*, *13*(3), 375–402. doi:10.1177/017084069201300304

Davenport, T. H., & Prusak, L. (1998). *How organizations manage what they know*. Boston: Harvard Business School Press.

Davis, U. C. (2004). *Changing face 2004*. Davis, CA: University of California Davis.

De Bruyn, A. D., & Lilien, G. L. (2008). A multi-stage model of word-of-mouth influence through viral marketing. *International Journal of Research in Marketing*, *25*, 151–163. doi:10.1016/j.ijresmar.2008.03.004

De Ferrari, L. (2007). Wikinomics & co. Retrieved January 18, 2010, from http://www.bioinformatics.ed.ac.uk/TWiki_4.2.4/pub/SysBioClub/ForthcomingTalks/wikinomics_Luna_DeFerrari_20071102.pdf

Del Valle-Agudo, D., Javier Calle-Gómez, J., Cuadra-Fernández, D., & Rivero-Espinosa, J. (2009). Breaking of the interaction cycle: Independent interpretation and generation for advanced dialogue management. In J. A. Jacko (Ed.), *Novel interaction methods and techniques* [Proceedings of Human-Computer Interaction, San Diego, CA] (Lecture Notes in Computer Science, Vol. 5611, pp. 674-683). Berlin: Springer.

Dell, K. (2007, August 9). Second Life's real world problems. *Time*. Retrieved September 2, 2009, from http://www.time.com/time/magazine/article/0,9171,1651500,00.html

Dell, K. (2008, May 12). How Second Life affects real life. *Time*. Retrieved September 2, 2009, from http://www.time.com/time/health/article/0,8599,1739601,00.html

Denegri-Knott, J., & Taylor, J. (2005). The labelling game: A conceptual exploration of deviance on the internet. *Social Science Computer Review*, *23*(1), 93–107. doi:10.1177/0894439304271541

DeVol, R. (2002). *State technology and science index: Comparing and contrasting California*. Santa Monica, CA: Milken Institute.

DeVol, R., Klowden, K., Collins, J., Wallace, L., Wong, P., & Bedroussian, A. (2004). *Arkansas' position in the knowledge-based economy: Prospects and policy options*. Santa Monica, CA: Milken Institute.

Dhar, R., & Wertenbroch, K. (2000). Consumer choice between hedonic and utilitarian goods. *JMR, Journal of Marketing Research*, *37*(1), 60–71. doi:10.1509/jmkr.37.1.60.18718

Dholakia, U. M., Bagozzi, R. P., & Pearo, L. K. (2004). A social influence model of consumer participation in network- and small-group-based virtual communities. *International Journal of Research in Marketing*, *21*, 241–263. doi:10.1016/j.ijresmar.2003.12.004

Ding, Y., Kang, S. J., Toma, I., Fried, M., Shafiq, O., & Yan, Z. (2008). Adding semantics to social tagging: Upper Tag Ontology (UTO). In *Proceedings of the 70th Annual Meeting of the American Society for Information Science & Technology (ASIS&T)*, Oct 24-29, 2008, Columbus, Ohio, USA.

Ding, Y., Toma, I., Kang, S., Fried, M., & Yan, Z. (2008). Data mediation and interoperation in Social Web: Modeling, crawling and integrating social tagging data. In *Proceedings of the Workshop on Social Web Search and Mining (SWSM2008), 17th International World Wide Web Conference, Beijing, China*. Retrieved August 23, 2009 from http://info.slis.indiana.edu/~dingying/Publication/OTM2008-UTO-CameraReady.pdf

Dobele, A., Lindgreen, A., Beverland, M., Vanhamme, J., & Wijk, R. (2007). Why pass on viral messages? Because they connect emotionally. *Business Horizons*, *50*, 291–304. doi:10.1016/j.bushor.2007.01.004

Dobele, A., Toleman, D., & Beverland, M. (2005). Controlled infection! Spreading the brand message through viral marketing. *Business Horizons*, *48*, 143–149. doi:10.1016/j.bushor.2004.10.011

Dominici, G. (2009). From marketing mix to e-marketing mix: A literature review and classification. *International Journal of Business and Management*, *4*(9), 17–24.

Donath, J. (2007). Signals in social supernets. *Journal of Computer-Mediated Communication, 13*(1). Retrieved from http://jcmc.indiana.edu/vol13/issue1/donath.html.

Doreian, P., Batagelj, V., & Ferligoj, A. (2005). *Generalized blockmodeling*. Cambridge: Cambridge University Press.

Dormann, C., & Chisalita, C. (2002). Cultural values in Web site design. In *Proceedings of the Eleventh European Conference on Cognitive Ergonomics (ECCE 11)*, Catania, Italy, September 8-11.

Drucker, P. (1993). *Post-capitalist society*. New York: Harper Business.

Drucker, P. (2004). The age of social transformation. *Atlantic Monthly, 274*(5), 53–80.

Drucker, P. F. (1988). The coming of the new organization. *Harvard Business Review, 66*(1).

Duda, S., Schießl, M., & Nüsperling, S. (2008). See the world with different eyes. *planung & analyse*, pp. 14-18.

Dunbar, R. I. M. (1996). *Grooming, gossip, and the evolution of language*. Cambridge, MA: Harvard University Press.

Dunbar, R. I. M. (2004). Gossip in evolutionary perspective. *Review of General Psychology, 8*(2), 100–110. doi:10.1037/1089-2680.8.2.100

Dunbar, R. (2010). Facebook friends are not REAL friends. Retrieved January 21, 2010, from http://technology.timesonline.co.uk/tol/news/tech_and_web/the_web/article6999879.ece

Dwyer, C., Hiltz, S. R., & Passerini, K. (2007). Trust and privacy concern within social networking sites. In *Proceedings of the Thirteenth Americas Conference on Information Systems*. Retrieved August 23, 2009 from http://csis.pace.edu/~dwyer/research/DwyerAMCIS2007.pdf

Eagly, A. H., & Chaiken, S. (1993). *The psychology of attitudes*. Fort Worth, TX: Harcourt Brace Jovanovich.

Easterby-Smith, M., Thorpe, R., & Lowe, A. (1991). *Management research: An introduction*. London: Sage.

Eastin, M., & LaRose, R. (2000). Internet self-efficacy and the psychology of the digital divide. *Journal of Computer-Mediated Communication* [Online], *6*(1). Retrieved January 21, 2010, from http://jcmc.indiana.edu/vol6/issue1/eastin.html

Economic Development Work Group. (2006). *California partnership for the San Joaquin Valley*. California: Economic Development Work Group. eircom. (2000). *Ennis information age town: A connected community*. Dublin, Ireland: eircom.

Eisenhardt, K. M., & Brown, S. L. (1999). Patching: Re-stitching business portfolios in dynamic markets. *Harvard Business Review, 78*(1), 91–101.

Ellemers, N., Kortekaas, P., & Ouwerkerk, J. W. (1999). Self-categorisation, commitment to the group and group self-esteem as related but distinct aspects of social identity. *European Journal of Social Psychology, 29*(2-3), 371–389. doi:10.1002/(SICI)1099-0992(199903/05)29:2/3<371::AID-EJSP932>3.0.CO;2-U

Ellison, N., Lampe, C., & Steinfield, C. (2009, January-February). Social network sites and society: Current trends and future possibilities. *Interactions Magazine, 16*(1), 6–9.

Ellison, N., Steinfield, C., & Lampe, C. (2006). Spatially bounded online social networks and social capital. In *International Communication Association*. Retrieved August 23, 2009 from http://msu.edu/~nellison/Facebook_ICA_2006.pdf

EMarketer. (2007, June). *User Generated Content: Will Web 2.0 Pay its Way?* Fahey, L., & Prusak, L. (1998). The eleven deadliest sins of knowledge management. *California Management Review, 40*(3).

Engel, J. E., Blackwell, R. D., & Kegerreis, R. J. (1969). How information is used to adopt an innovation. *Journal of Advertising Research, 9*, 3–8.

Erickson, T., Halverson, C., Kellogg, W. A., Laff, M., & Wolf, T. (2002). Social translucence: Designing social infrastructures that make collective activity visible. *Communications of the ACM, 45*(4), 40–44. doi:10.1145/505248.505270

Ertl, D. (2009). Semi-automatic multimodal user interface generation. In *Proceedings of the 1ˢᵗ ACM SIGCHI Symposium on engineering interactive computing systems* (EICS'09), Pittsburgh, PA (pp. 321-324). New York: ACM Press.

Evans, M. (2008). The evolution of the Web: From Web 1.0 to Web 4.0. Retrieved May 8, 2008, from http://www.network-research-group.org/presentations/08-11-06-MikeEvans-Web.pdf

Facebook. (2009). Statistics. *Press Room* [facebook blog]. Retrieved August, 20, 2009, from http://www.facebook.com/press/info.php?statistics

Faiola, A., & Smyslova, O. (2009). Flow experience in Second Life: The impact of telepresence on human-computer interaction. In Ozok, A. A., & Zaphiris, P. (Eds.), *Online communities and social computing* (pp. 574–583). Berlin: Springer-Verlag. doi:10.1007/978-3-642-02774-1_62

Fehr, E., & Fischbacher, U. (2003). The nature of human altruism. *Nature*, *425*(23), 785–791. doi:10.1038/nature02043

Feldman, M. (2005, January 10-11). The importance of proximity and location. Paper presented on the panel Knowledge and place: Proximity, mobility, clusters, and institutions at *Advancing knowledge and the knowledge economy*, Washington, DC.

Ferguson, R. (2008). Word of mouth and viral marketing: Taking the temperature of the hottest trends in marketing. *Journal of Consumer Marketing*, *25*(3), 179–182. doi:10.1108/07363760810870671

Fernández-Pacheco, D. G., Aleixos, N., Conesa, J., & Contero, M. (2009). Natural interface for sketch recognition. In *Advances in soft computing* [Proceedings of 7ᵗʰ International Conference on Practical Applications of Agents and Multi-Agent Systems (PAAMS'09)] (Vol. 55, pp. 510-519). Berlin: Springer.

Field, A. (2008). Productivity. In *The Concise Encyclopedia of Economics* (2nd ed.). Indianapolis, IN: Library of Economics and Liberty. Retrieved August 28, 2009, from http://www.econlib.org/library/Enc/Productivity.html

Firat, A. F., Sherry, J. F. J., & Venkatesh, A. (1994). Postmodernism, marketing and the consumer. *International Journal of Research in Marketing*, *11*(4), 311–316. doi:10.1016/0167-8116(94)90009-4

Fischbacher, U., Gachter, S., & Fehr, E. (2001). Are people conditionally cooperative? Evidence from a public goods experiment. *Economics Letters*, *71*(3), 397–404. doi:10.1016/S0165-1765(01)00394-9

Fishbein, M., & Ajzen, I. (1975). *Belief, attitude, intention, and behavior: An introduction to theory and research*. Reading, MA: Addison-Wesley.

Foremski, T. (2005). *If Internet 1.0 was a disruptive technology…where is the train wreck? SiliconValleyWatcher*. Retrieved February 21, 2005, from http://www.siliconvalleywatcher.com/mt/archives/2005/02/if_Internet_10_1.php

Frackiewicz, U., Taylor, J., & House, B. (2008). An investigation into the role of traditional and computer-based social networking on the psychological identity and well-being of older adults. Unpublished paper presented at the British HCI Conference, Liverpool, Ireland.

Frandsen-Thorlacius, O., Hornbæk, K., Hertzum, M., & Clemmensen, T. (2009). Non-universal usability?: A survey of how usability is understood by Chinese and Danish users. In *Proceedings 27ᵗʰ Intel. Conference on Human Factors in Computing Systems, CHI 2009*, April, Boston, MA (pp. 4-9).

Freeman, L. (2006). *The development of social network analysis*. Vancouver, Canada: Empirical Press.

Freeman, L. C., White, D. R., & Kimball Romney, A. (1992). *Research methods in social network analysis*. New Brunswick, NJ: Transaction Publishers.

Fried, M. (2007). Social tagging wrapper. Unpublished bachelors thesis. University of Innsbruck, Austria.

Frinken, V., Peter, T., Fischer, A., Bunke, H., Do, T. M. T., & Artieres, T. (2009). Improved handwriting recognition by combining two forms of hidden Markov models and a recurrent neural network. In *Proceedings of 13th International Conference on Computer Analysis of Images and Patterns* (CAIP'09), Münster, Germany ([). Berlin: Springer.]. *Lecture Notes in Computer Science, 5702,* 189–196. doi:10.1007/978-3-642-03767-2_23

Gandhi, A. (2008). The social enterprise: Using social enterprise applications to enable the next wave of knowledge worker productivity. Retrieved May 14, 2009, from http://www.oracle.com/products/middleware/user-interaction/docs/social-enterprise-whitepaper.pdf

Garrison, D., & Anderson, T. (2003). *E-learning in the 21st century: A framework for research and practice.* London: Routledge. doi:10.4324/9780203166093

Garrity, E. J. (2001). Synthesizing user centered and designer centered IS development approaches using general systems theory. *Information Systems Frontiers, 3*(1), 107–121. doi:10.1023/A:1011457822609

Gault, F. (2005). Measuring knowledge and its economic effects: The role of official statistics. In Kahin, B., & Foray, D. (Eds.), *Advancing knowledge and the knowledge economy* (pp. 27–41). Cambridge, MA: MIT Press.

Gay, R., Charlesworth, A., & Esen, R. (2007). *Online marketing: A customer-led approach.* New York: Oxford University Press.

Gekas, J. (2006). Web service ranking in service networks. In *3rd European Semantic Web Conference ESWC '06* (pp. 501-510). Retrieved August 23, 2009 from http://www.eswc2006.org/poster-papers/FP08-Gekas.pdf

Gibson, C. B. (1999). Do they do what they believe they can? Group efficacy and group effectiveness across tasks and cultures. *Academy of Management Journal, 42,* 138–152. doi:10.2307/257089

Giddens, A. (1984). *The Constitution of Society: outline of the theory of structuration.* Berkeley, CA: University of California Press.

Gilbert, M. (1989). *On social facts.* London: Routledge.

Godin, S. (2007). *Meatball sundae: Is your marketing out of sync.* London: Portfolio, Penguin Group Inc.

Godin, B. (2003). The knowledge-based economy: Conceptual framework or buzzword? *Canadian Project on History and Sociology of S&T Statistics,* Working Paper No. 24. Retrieved from http://www.csiic.ca/PDF?/Godin_24.pdf

Godin, S. (2009). *Seth Goodin's blog.* Retrieved from http://www.sethgodin.com/

Goffee, R., & Jones, G. (2001). Followership: It's personal, too. *Harvard Business Review, 79*(11), 148–149.

Goldenberg, J., Libai, B., & Muller, E. (2001). Talk of the network: A complex systems look at the underlying process of word-of-mouth. *Marketing Letters, 3*(12), 211–223. doi:10.1023/A:1011122126881

Golder, S., Wilkinson, D., & Huberman, B. (2007). Rhythms of social interaction: Messaging within a massive online network. Paper presented at the *Third International Conference on Communities and Technologies.* Retrieved August 10, 2009, from http://www.hpl.hp.com/research/idl/papers/facebook/facebook.pdf

González, V. M., & Mark, G. (2004). Constant, constant, multi-tasking craziness: Managing multiple working spheres. In *Proceedings of the SIGCHI Conference on Human Factors in Computing Systems* (pp. 113-120). New York: ACM Press.

Good, D. (2000). Individuals, interpersonal relations, and trust. In Gambetta, D. (Ed.), *Trust: Making and breaking cooperative relations* (pp. 31–48). Oxford, UK: University of Oxford Press.

Goodhue, D. (1998). Development and measurement validity of a task-technology fit instrument for user evaluations of information systems. *Decision Sciences, 29*(1), 105–138. doi:10.1111/j.1540-5915.1998.tb01346.x

Govindarajan, V., & Kopalle, P. K. (2006). Disruptive of innovations: Measurement and an assessment of reliability and validity. *Strategic Management Journal, 27*(2), 189–199. doi:10.1002/smj.511

Goyal, M. (2005). Attitude based teams in a hostile dynamic world. *Knowledge-Based Systems*, 18, 245–255. doi:10.1016/j.knosys.2004.08.002

Gradeck, R., & Paytas, J. (2000). *Migration and regional growth*. Pittsburgh, PA: Carnegie Mellon University Center for Economic Development.

Gradijan, D. (2007). MySpace cracks down on 69-year-old members. *CSO*. Retrieved August 29, 2009, from http://www.csoonline.com/article/216376/MySpace_Cracks_Down_on_69_Year_Old_Members?page=1

Graillot, L. (2004). Une approche du phénomène d'hyperréalité à partir de l'étude des parcs Disney. *Décisions marketing, 34*, 41-52.

Granovetter, M. S. (1983). The strength of weak ties: A network theory revisited. *Sociological Theory*, 1, 201–233. doi:10.2307/202051

Granovetter, M. (1973). The strength of weak ties. *American Journal of Sociology*, 78(6), 1360–1380. doi:10.1086/225469

Grant, R. M. (1996). Toward a knowledge-based theory of the firm [in Special issue: Knowledge and the Firm]. *Strategic Management Journal, 17*(2), 109–122.

Greenfield, S. (2009). Social websites harm children's brains. Retrieved January 21, 2010, from http://www.dailymail.co.uk/news/article-1153583/Social-websites-harm-childrens-brains-Chilling-warning-parents-neuroscientist.html

Griffith, T. L., Sawyer, J. E., & Neale, M. A. (2003). Virtualness and knowledge in teams: Managing the love triangle of organizations, individuals, and information technology. *Management Information Systems Quarterly*, 27(2), 265.

Groom, V., Bailenson, J. N., & Nass, C. (2009). The influence of racial embodiment on racial bias in immersive virtual environments. *Social Influence, 4*(1), 1–18.

Gruber, T. (2007). Ontology of folksonomy: A mash-up of apples and oranges. *International Journal on Semantic Web & Information Systems, 3*(2). Retrieved August 23, 2009 from http://tomgruber.org/writing/ontology-of-folksonomy.htm

Gupta, K. S. (2001, July-September). Knowledge management and empowerment: A conceptual relationship. [Bombay: NITIE.]. *Udyog Pragati, 25*(3), 28–35.

Gupta, K. S. (2008). A comparative analysis of knowledge sharing climate. *Knowledge and Process Management, 15*(3), 186–195. doi:10.1002/kpm.309

Gurban, M., Vilaplana, V., Thiran, J. P., & Marques, F. (2008). Face and speech interaction. In Tzovaras, D. (Ed.), *Signals and communication technology: Multimodal user interfaces* (pp. 85–117). Berlin: Springer. doi:10.1007/978-3-540-78345-9_5

Haenlein, M., & Kaplan, A. M. (2009). Flagship brand stores within virtual worlds: The impact of virtual store exposure on real life attitude toward the brand and purchase intent (Les magasins de marques phares dans les mondes virtuels: L'impact de l'exposition au magasin virtuel sur les comportements et l'intention d'achat de la marque dans la vie réelle). *Recherche et applications en marketing (RAM), 24*(3), 57-80.

Hagel, J., & Rayport, J. F. (1997). The coming battle for customer information. *Harvard Business Review, 75*, 53–65.

Hall, E. T. (1966). *The hidden dimension*. New York: Anchor Books/Doubleday.

Hall, R. H., & Hanna, P. (2004). The impact of Web page text: Background color combinations on readability, retention, aesthetics, and behavioral intention. *Behaviour & Information Technology, 23*(3), 183–195. doi:10.1080/01449290410001669932

Hammersley, M., & Atkinson, P. (1995). *Ethnography: Principles in practice* (2nd ed.). London: Routledge.

Harper, R., Rodden, T., & Rogers, Y. (2008) Being human: Human-computer interaction in the year 2020. Cambridge MA: Microsoft Research Limited. Retrieved August 11, 2009, from http://research.microsoft.com/en-us/um/cambridge/projects/hci2020/

Hart, D. (2003). *The emergence of entrepreneurship policy.* Cambridge, UK: Cambridge University Press. doi:10.1017/CBO9780511610134

Hart, J., Ridley, C., Taher, F., Sas, C., & Dix, A. (2008). Exploring the Facebook experience: A new approach to usability. In *Proceedings of the 5th Nordic Conference on Human-Computer interaction* (pp. 471-474). New York: ACM Press.

Hasan, H., & Pfaff, C. (2006). Emergent conversational technologies that are democratising information systems in organisations: The case of the corporate wiki. Retrieved August 24, 2008, from http://ro.uow.edu.au/cgi/viewcontent.cgi?article= 12978&content=commpapers

Haythornthwaite, C. (2002). Strong, weak and latent ties and the impact of new media. *Information Communication and Society, 18*(5), 385–401. doi:10.1080/01972240290108195

Healy, J. M. (1999). *Failure to connect: How computers affect our children's minds—and what we can do about it.* London: Simon & Schuster.

Heise, D. (2004). Enculturating agents with expressive role behavior. In Payr, S., & Trappl, R. (Eds.), *Agent culture: Human-agent interaction in a multicultural world* (pp. 127–142). London: Lawrence Erlbaum Associates.

Helm, S. (2000). Viral marketing: Establishing customer relationships by 'Word-of-Mouse'. *Electronic Commerce and Marketing, 13*(3), 158–161.

Hemp, P. (2006). Avatar-based marketing. *Harvard Business Review, 84*(6), 48–57.

Heng, M. S. (2003). Understanding electronic commerce from a historical perspective. *Communications of the Association for Information Systems, 12*(6), 104–118.

Herbig, P., & Hale, B. (1997). Internet: The marketing challenge of the twentieth century. *Internet Research: Electronic Networking Application and Policy, 7*(2), 95–100. doi:10.1108/10662249710165226

Herr, P., Kardes, F., & Kim, J. (1991). Effects of word-of-mouth and product-attribute information on persuasion: An accessibility-diagnosticity perspective. *The Journal of Consumer Research, 17,* 454–462. doi:10.1086/208570

Hill, A., & Scharff, L. V. (1997). Readability of websites with various foreground/background color combinations, font types and word styles. *Proceedings of 11th National Conference in Undergraduate Research, 2,* 742-746.

Hiltz, S. R., & Turoff, M. (2002). What makes learning networks effective? *Communications of the ACM, 45*(4), 56–59. doi:10.1145/505248.505273

Hinds, P. J., & Bailey, D. E. (2003). Out of sight, out of sync: Understanding conflict in distributed teams. *Organization Science, 14*(6), 615. doi:10.1287/orsc.14.6.615.24872

Hinduja, S., & Patchin, J. W. (2008). Personal information of adolescents on the Internet: A quantitative content analysis of MySpace. *Journal of Adolescence, 31*(1), 125–146. doi:10.1016/j.adolescence.2007.05.004

Ho S. Y. (2006). The attraction of Internet personalization to web users. *Electronic e-commerce markets, 16*(1) 41-50.

Hofstede, G. (1994). *Cultures and organisations: Intercultural cooperation and its importance for survival.* New York: HarperCollins.

Holzwarth, M., Janiszewski, C., & Neumann, M. N. (2006). The influence of avatars on online consumer shopping behavior. *Journal of Marketing, 70*(4), 19–36. doi:10.1509/jmkg.70.4.19

Hong, J., Kianto, A., & Kyläheiko, K. (2008). Moving culture and the creation of new knowledge and dynamic capabilities in emerging markets. *Knowledge and Process Management, 15*(3), 196–202. doi:10.1002/kpm.310

Horrigan, J., Boase, J., Rainie, L., & Wellman, B. (2006). *The strength of Internet ties*. Pew Internet & American Life Project report. Retrieved August 10, 2007, from http://www.pewInternet.org/PPF/r/172/report_display.asp

Hoschka, P. (1998). CSCW research at GMD-FIT: From basic groupware to the Social Web. *ACM SIGGROUP Bulletin, 19*(2), 5–9.

Houghton, J., & Sheehan, P. (2000). *A primer on the knowledge economy*. Melbourne City, Australia: Victoria University Center for Strategic Economic Studies.

Howcroft, D., & Trauth, E. (2004). *The choice of critical information systems research. 20th year retrospective: Relevant theory and informed practice? Looking forward from a 20-year perspective on IS research* (pp. 195–211). Boston, MA: Kluwer Academic Publishers.

Hsu, M. H., Ju, T. L., Yen, C. H., & Chang, C. M. (2007). Knowledge sharing behavior in virtual communities: The relationship between trust, self-efficacy, and outcome expectations. *International Journal of Human-Computer Studies, 65*(2), 153–169. doi:10.1016/j.ijhcs.2006.09.003

Huang, H., & Leung, L. (2009). Instant messaging addiction among teenagers in China: Shyness, alienation, and academic performance decrements. *Cyberpsychology & Behavior, 12*(6), 675–679. doi:10.1089/cpb.2009.0060

Huang, J., Marcheret, E., Visweswariah, K., Libal, V., & Potamianos, G. (2008). The IBM rich transcription 2007 speech-to-text systems for lecture meetings. In R. Stiefelhagen, R. Bowers & J. Fiscus (Eds.), *Multimodal Technologies for Perception of Humans* [Proceedings of International Evaluation Workshops (CLEAR'07 & RT'07), Baltimore, MD] (Lecture Notes in Computer Science, Vol. 4625, pp. 429-441). Berlin: Springer.

Hwang, C. L., & Yoon, K. (1981). *Multiple attribute decision making: Methods and applications*. Berlin: Springer-Verlag.

IAB. (2008). *Platform status report: User Generated Content, Social Media, and Advertising — An Overview*. New York: Interactive Advertising Bureau. Retrieved April 2008, from http://www.iab.net/media/file/2008_ugc_platform.pdf

IBM. (2007). Tapping into collective intelligence: How to leverage the wisdom of the crowd to boost the bottom line. Retrieved May 7, 2008, from http://www-935.ibm.com/services/tw/cio/pdf.empow_wp_collective_intel-gtw01406-usen-00.pdf

IMS. (2002). IMS guidelines for developing accessible learning applications, version 1.0 [White paper]. Retrieved August 11, 2009, from http://www.imsproject.org

International Standards Organisation. (1998). *9241-11: Definition of usable software*. Geneva, Switzerland: International Organization for Standardization.

International Standards Organisation. (1999). *13407: User-centred design process for interactive systems*. Geneva, Switzerland: International Organization for Standardization.

International Telecommunication Union. (2005). *ITU workshop on ubiquitous network societies*. Geneva, Switzerland: International Telecommunication Union.

Ip, R. K. F., & Wagner, C. (2008). Weblogging: A study of social computing and its impact on organizations. *Decision Support Systems, 45*, 242–250. doi:10.1016/j.dss.2007.02.004

Ipsos. (2007). *Online video and social networking set to drive tomorrow's digital lifestyle*. Retrieved from http://www.ipsos-ideas.com/article.cfm?id=3592

Ives, B., & Junglas, I. (2008). APC forum: Business implications of virtual worlds and serious gaming. *MIS Quarterly Executive, 7*(3), 151–156.

Jackson, M. O. (2003). A strategic model of social and economic networks. *Journal of Economic Theory, 71*, 44–74. doi:10.1006/jeth.1996.0108

Jana, R. (2006). American Apparel's virtual clothes. *Business Week Online*. Retrieved August 20, 2008, from http://www.businessweek.com/innovate/content/ jun2006/id20060627_217800.htm

Jarron, C., Favier, J., & Li, C. (2006). *Social computing: How networks erode institutional power and what to do about it.* Cambridge, MA: Forrester Research Reports. Retrieved January 21, 2010, from http://www.forrester.com/Research/Document/Excerpt/0,7211,38772,00.html

Joinson, A. (2003). *Understanding the psychology of internet behaviour: Virtual worlds, real lives.* London: Palgrave Macmillan.

Joinson, A. (2008). 'Looking at', 'looking up' or 'keeping up with' people? Motives and uses of facebook. Paper presented at the *Conference on Human Factors in Computer Systems.* Retrieved August 12, 2009, from http://people.bath.ac.uk/aj266/pubs_pdf/1149-joinson.pdf

Ju, T. L., Chen, H., & Ju, P. H. (2005). Social capital and knowledge sharing in virtual communities. In Khosrow-Pour, M. (Ed.), *Emerging trends and challenges in information technology management* (pp. 409–411). London: Idea Group Publishing.

Jurvetson, S., & Draper, T. (1997). Viral marketing phenomenon explained. *Draper Fisher Jurvetson.* Retrieved July 15, 2009, from http://www.dfj.com/news/article_26.shtml

Kamentz, E., & Womser-Hacker, C. (2003). Defining culture-bound user characteristics as a starting point for the design of adaptive learning systems. *Journal of Universal Computer Science, 9*(7).

Kaplan, A. M., & Haenlein, M. (2010). Users of the world, unite! The challenges and opportunities of social media. *Business Horizons, 53*(1), 59–68. doi:10.1016/j.bushor.2009.09.003

Kaplan, A. M., & Haenlein, M. (2011). The early bird catches the news: Nine things you should know about micro-blogging. *Business Horizons, 54*(1).

Kaplan, A. M. (2010). User participation within virtual worlds. In Dasilveira, G., & Fogliatto, F. (Eds.), *Mass customization: Engineering and managing global operations.* London: Springer.

Karahanna, E., Straub, D. W., & Chervany, N. L. (1999). Information technology adoption across time: A cross-sectional comparison of pre-adoption and post-adoption beliefs. *Management Information Systems Quarterly, 23*(2), 183–213. doi:10.2307/249751

Katz, E., & Lazarsfeld, P. F. (1955). *Personal influence.* Glencoe, IL: Free Press.

Katz-Navon, T. Y., & Erez, M. (2005). When collective- and self-efficacy affect team performance: The role of task interdependence. *Small Group Research, 36*(4), 437–465. doi:10.1177/1046496405275233

Kelly, R. (2006). *An investigation of attitudes to altruism amongst achievers, explorers, killers and socialisers: Can massively multiplayer games engineer altruism? Unpublished student project.* UK: Bournemouth University.

Kelman, H. C. (1958). Compliance, identification, and internalization: Three processes of attitude change. *The Journal of Conflict Resolution, 2*(1), 51–60. doi:10.1177/002200275800200106

Kim, J., LaRose, R., & Peng, W. (2009). Loneliness as the cause and the effect of problematic internet use: The relationship between internet use and psychological well-being. *Cyberpsychology & Behavior, 12*(4), 451–455. doi:10.1089/cpb.2008.0327

Kim, J. H., & Hong, K. S. (2007). An improved fusion and fission architecture between multi-modalities based on wearable computing. In J. Indulska, J. Ma, L. T. Yang, T. Ungerer & J. Cao (Eds.), *Proceedings of the 4th International Conference in Ubiquitous Intelligence and Computing*, Hong Kong, China (Lecture Notes in Computer Science, Vol. 4611, pp. 113-122). Berlin: Springer.

Kintz, E. (2007) Top 10 reasons as to why I still need to be convinced about marketing on Second Life. *HP Communities: The digital mindset blog.* Retrieved April 2, 2007, from http://www.communities.hp.com/online/blogs/kintz/archive/2007/04/02/HPPost2964.aspx

Kirah, A., Fuson, C., Grudin, J., & Feldman, E. (2005). Ethnography for software development. In Bias, G., & Mayhew, D. J. (Eds.), *Cost-justifying usability: An update for the internet age* (pp. 415–446). San Francisco, CA: Morgan Kaufman. doi:10.1016/B978-012095811-5/50014-6

Kish, S. (2007). Second Life: Virtual worlds and the enterprise. Retrieved August 18, 2008, from http://skish.typepad.com/susan_kish/secondlife/Skish_VW-SL_sept07.pdf

Ko, A. J., & Myers, B. A. (2009). Attitudes and self-efficacy in young adults' computing autobiographies. Paper presented at *IEEE Symposium on Visual Languages and Human-Centric Computing,* Corvallis, OR, USA.

Kogut, B., & Zander, U. (1992). Knowledge of the firm, combinative capabilities, and the replication of technology. *Organization Science, 3,* 383–397. doi:10.1287/orsc.3.3.383

Koons, D., Sparrell, C., & Thorisson, K. (1993). Integrating simultaneous input from speech, gaze, and hand gestures. In Maybury, M. (Ed.), *Intelligent multimedia interfaces* (pp. 257–276). Cambridge, MA: MIT Press.

Kraemer, K. L., Dedrick, J., Melville, N. P., & Zhu, K. (2006). *Global e-commerce, impacts of national environment and policy.* Cambridge, UK: Cambridge University Press. doi:10.1017/CBO9780511488603

Krenn, B., Neumayr, B., Gstrein, E., & Grice, M. (2004). Lifelike agents for the internet: A cross-cultural case study. In *Agent Culture: Human-Agent Interaction in a Multicultural World* (pp. 197–229). Mahwah, NJ: Lawrence Erlbaum Associates.

Krishnamurthy, S. (2001). Understanding online message dissemination: An analysis of 'send-this-message-to-your-friend' data. *First Monday, 6*(5).

Kujansivu, P., & Lönnqvist, A. (2008). Business process management as a tool for Intellectual Capital management. *Knowledge and Process Management, 15*(3), 159–169. doi:10.1002/kpm.307

Kuk, G., & Yeung, F. T. (2002). Interactivity in e-commerce. *Quarterly journal of electronic commerce, 3*(3), 223-234.

Kumar, R., Novak, J., & Tomkins, A. (2006). Structure and evolution of online social networks. In *Proceedings of the 12th ACM SIGKDD international conference on knowledge discovery and data mining* (pp. 611 - 617). New York: ACM Press.

Ladd, A., & Ward, M. A. (2002). An investigation of environmental factors influencing knowledge transfer. *Journal of Knowledge Management Practice.*

Lakshmanan, G., Pradeep, K. M., & Harish, K. (2010). The current and future state of the programmable Web. *Cutter IT Journal, 23*(8), 19–25.

Lamb, B. (2004). The standard wiki overview. *EDUCASEUSE Review, 39*(5), 36–48.

Lamont, I. (2008, September 27). Real life will trump Second Life, Microsoft says. *PC World.*

Lampe, C., Ellison, N., & Steinfeld, C. (2007). Profile elements as signals in an online social network. In *Conference on Human Factors in Computing Systems.* Retrieved August 23, 2009 from http://www.msu.edu/~steinfie/CHI_manuscript.pdf

Lampe, C., Ellison, N., & Steinfeld, C. (2007). A familiar Face(book): Profile elements as signals in an online social network. Paper presented at CHI 2007, San Jose, CA.

Latour, B. (1991). Technology is society made durable: A sociology of monsters. In Law, J. (Ed.), *Essays on Power, Technology and Domination* (pp. 103–131). London: Routledge.

Lea, M., & Spears, R. (1992). Paralanguage and social perception in computer-mediated communication. *Journal of Organizational Computing, 2,* 321–341. doi:10.1080/10919399209540190

Lee, C. S. (2001). An analytical framework for evaluating e-commerce business models and strategies. *Internet Research, 11*(4), 349–359. doi:10.1108/10662240110402803

Leskovec, J., Adamic, L. A., & Huberman, B. (2007). The dynamics of viral marketing. *ACM Transactions on the Web, 1*(1), 1–39. doi:10.1145/1232722.1232727

Leuf, B., & Cunningham, W. (2001). *The WIKI WAY: Quick Collaboration of the Web.* Reading, MA: Addison-Wesley.

Lev, B. (2001). *Intangibles: Management, measurement and reporting.* Washington, DC: Brookings Institution Press.

Levenburg, N. (2005). Delivering customer value online: An analysis of practices, applications and performance. *Journal of Retailing and Consumer Services, 12*(5), 319–331. doi:10.1016/j.jretconser.2004.11.001

Levine, M., & Crowther, S. (2008). The responsive bystander: How social group membership and group size can encourage as well as inhibit bystander intervention. *Journal of Personality and Social Psychology, 96*(6).

Levitt, T. (1983). The globalization of markets. *Harvard Business Review, 61*(3), 92–102.

Levy, J. (2007). The real reason schools need Facebook. *eLearn, 2007*(12), 1. doi: 10.1145/1361059.1361061

Li, D., Chau, P. Y. K., & Lou, H. (2005). Understanding individual adoption of instant messaging: An empirical investigation. *Journal of the Association for Information Systems, 6*(4), 102–129.

Li, C., & Bernoff, J. (2008). *Groundswell* [Excerpt]. Boston: Harvard Business Press. Retrieved July 16, 2009, from http://a964.g.akamaitech.net/7/964/714/397c4414501aa8/www.forrester.com/groundswell/assets/groundswell_excerpt.pdf

Liben-Nowell, D., Novak, J., Kumar, R., Raghavan, P., & Tomkins, A. (2005). Geographic routing in social networks. *Proceedings of the National Academy of Sciences of the United States of America, 102*(33), 11623–11628. doi:10.1073/pnas.0503018102

Liccardi, I., Ounnas, A., Pau, R., Massey, E., Kinnunen, P., & Lewthwaite, S. (2007). The role of social networks in students' learning experiences. In Carter, J., & Amillo, J. (Eds.), *Working Group Reports on ITiCSE on innovation and Technology in Computer Science Education* (pp. 224–237). New York: ACM Press. doi:10.1145/1345443.1345442

Lim, Y. K, Stolterman, E., & Tenenberg, J. (2008). The anatomy of prototypes: Prototypes as filters, prototypes as manifestations of design ideas. *ACM Transactions on Human-Computer Interaction, 15*(2).

Lin, H.-F. (2007). Knowledge sharing and firm innovation capability: An empirical study. *International Journal of Manpower, 28*(3-4), 315–332. doi:10.1108/01437720710755272

Lin, N. (2001). Building a network theory of social capital. In Burt, R. (Ed.), *Social capital: Theory and research* (pp. 3–30). New York: Aldine de Gruyter.

Linden Lab. (2009). *How meeting in Second Life transformed IBM's technology elite into virtual world believers* [Case study]. San Francisco, CA: Linden Lab.

Lindgren, R., & Henfridsson, O. (2002). Using competence systems: Adoption barriers and design suggestions. *Journal of Information & Knowledge management, 5*(2).

LinkedIn Press. (2009). About us. Retrieved July 24, 2009, from http://press.linkedin.com/about

Liu, Y., Ngu, A. H., & Zeng, L. Z. (2004). QoS computation and policing in dynamic web service selection. In *Proceedings of the 13th international World Wide Web conference on Alternate track papers & posters* (pp. 66-73). New York: ACM Press.

Lönnqvist, A., Kujansivu, P., & Antola, J. (2006). Are management accountants equipped to deal with intellectual capital? *The Finnish Journal of Business Economics, 3*, 355–368.

Lukka, K., & Kasanen, E. (1995). The problem of generalizability: Anecdotes and evidence in accounting research. *Accounting. Auditing and Accountability, 8,* 71–90. doi:10.1108/09513579510147733

Macé, S., & Anquetil, E. (2009). Pattern recognition strategies for interactive sketch composition. In *Novel Interaction Methods and Techniques: Proceedings of 13th International Conference on Human-Computer Interaction* (HCI'09), San Diego, CA ([]. Berlin: Springer.]. *Lecture Notes in Computer Science, 5611,* 840–849.

Madden, M., & Fox, S. (2006). Riding the waves of "Web 2.0": More than a buzzword, but still not easily defined. Retrieved February 13, 2008, from http://www.pewinternet. org/~/media//Files/Reports/2006/PIP_Web_2.0.pdf.pdf

Malkin, B. (2007, July 27). Facebook banned by City firms. *The Daily Telegraph.* Retrieved August 28, 2009, from http://www.telegraph.co.uk/news/uknews/1558630/ Facebook-banned-by-City-firms.html

Mandl, T. (2009). Comparing Chinese and German blogs. In *Proceedings 20th ACM Conference on Hypertext and Hypermedia (HT '09)* Torino, Italy, June 29-July 1 (pp. 299-308). New York: ACM Press.

Mandl, T., & Womser-Hacker, C. (2008). Tapping the power of social software for international development. In *HCI for Community and International Development* [Proceedings of Conference on Human Factors in Computing Systems (CHI) 2008, 5th-6th April, Florence, Italy]. Retrieved from http://www.cc.gatech.edu/~mikeb/ HCI4CID/Mandl.pdf

Mangiaracina, R., Brugnoli, G., & Perego, A. (2009). The eCommerce customer journey: A model to assess and compare the user experience of the eCommerce websites. *Journal of Internet Banking and Commerce, 14*(3), 1–11.

Manning, C. D., Raghavan, P., & Schutze, H. (2008). *Introduction to information retrieval.* Cambridge, UK: Cambridge University Press.

Manning, C. D., & Schuetze, H. (1999). *Foundations of statistical natural language processing.* Boston: MIT Press.

Manola, F., & Miller, E. (2004, February). RDF primer [Recommendation]. Cambridge, MA: World Wide Web Consortium. Retrieved August, 2009, from http://www. w3.org/TR/REC-rdf-syntax

Marakas, G. M., Yi, M. Y., & Johnson, R. D. (1998). The multilevel·and multifaceted character of computer self-efficacy: Toward clarification of the construct and an integrative framework for research. *Information Systems Research, 9*(2), 126–163. doi:10.1287/isre.9.2.126

Marcus, A., & Alexander, C. (2007). User validation of cultural dimensions of a Website design. In *Usability and internationalization: Global and local user interfaces* ([]. Berlin: Springer.]. *Lecture Notes in Computer Science, 4650,* 160–167. doi:10.1007/978-3-540-73289-1_20

Marcus, A., & Gould, W. E. (2000). Crosscurrents: Cultural dimensions and global web user-interface design. *Interaction, 7*(4), 32–46. doi:10.1145/345190.345238

Marcus, A., & Krishnamurthi, N. (2009). Cross-cultural analysis of social network services in Japan, Korea, and the USA. In *Internationalization, Design and Global Development, Third International Conference, IDGD 2009,* San Diego, CA, July 19-24 (pp. 59-68).

Marcus, A., Baumgartner, V. J., & Chen, E. (2003). *User interface design vs. culture. In Designing for Global Markets 5, IWIPS 2003, Fifth International Workshop on Internationalisation of Products and Systems, (IWIPS) Where East meets West,* Berlin, Germany, 17-19 July (pp. 67-78).

Marlow, C., Naaman, M., Boyd, D., & Davis, M. (2006). HT06, tagging paper, taxonomy, Flickr, academic article, to read. In *Proceedings of the Seventeenth Conference on Hypertext and Hypermedia* (pp. 31-40). New York: ACM Press.

Marshall, R. (1994). Job and skill demands in the new economy. In Solmon, L. C., & Levenson, A. R. (Eds.), *Labor markets, employment policy and job creation* (pp. 21–58). Santa Monica, CA: Milken Institute.

Mattelart, A. (1996). *The invention of communication.* Minneapolis: University Minnesota Press.

McDermott, C., & O'Connor, G. (2002). Managing radical innovation: An overview of emergent strategy issues. *Journal of Product Innovation Management, 19*, 424–438. doi:10.1016/S0737-6782(02)00174-1

McInerney, C. (2003). Wired Ennis: Learning and technology in an informaion age town. *Information Technology. Education et Sociétés, 4*(2), 9–34.

McLoughlin, C., & Lee, M. J. W. (2008). The three P's of pedagogy for the networked society: Personalization, participation, and productivity. Retrieved December 17, 2008, from http://www.isetl.org.ijtlhe/pdf/IJTLHE395.pdf

McQuillan, H. (2000). *Ennis information age town: A connected community*. Dublin, Ireland: Eircom.

Meltzoff, A., Kuhl, P., Movellan, J., & Sejnowski, T. (2009). Foundations for a new science of learning. *Science, 325*(5938), 284–288. doi:10.1126/science.1175626

Mendonça, H. (2009). High level data fusion on a multimodal interactive application platform. In *Proceedings of the 1st ACM SIGCHI Symposium on Engineering Interactive Computing Systems* (EICS'09), Pittsburgh, PA (pp. 333-336). New York: ACM Press.

Menzies, H. (1996). *Whose brave new world? The information highway and the new economy*. Toronto: Between the Lines.

Merchant, G. (2006). Identity, social networks and online communication. *E-learning, 3*(2), 235–244. doi:10.2304/elea.2006.3.2.235

Merisavo, M., & Raulas, M. (2004). The impact of email marketing on brand loyalty. *Journal of Product and Brand Management, 13*(7), 498–505. doi:10.1108/10610420410568435

Messinger, P. R., Stroulia, E., Lyons, K., Bone, M., Niu, R. H., Smirnov, K., & Perelgut, S. (2009). Virtual worlds–past, present, and future: New directions in social computing. *Decision Support Systems, 47*(3), 204–228. doi:10.1016/j.dss.2009.02.014

Meyer, P. (2004). *The vanishing newspaper: Saving journalism in the information age*. Columbia, MO: University of Missouri Press.

Migration Dialogue. (2000). California: San Joaquin development. *Rural Migration News, 6*(2).

Milgram, S. (1967). The small world problem. *Psychology Today, 1*, 61–67.

Milgram, S. (1967). The small-world problem. *Psychology Today, 2*, 60–67.

Millard, N., & Hole, L. (2008). In the Moodie: Using 'affective widgets' to help contact centre advisors fight stress. In C. Peter & R. Beale (Eds.), *Affect and emotion in human-computer interaction* (Lecture Notes in Computer Science, Vol. 4868, pp. 186-193). Berlin: Springer-Verlag.

Miltiades, H. B., & Flores, M. (2008). *Aging in the San Joaquin Valley: Present realities and future prospects. Fresno, CA: Calfiornia State University*. Fresno: Central California Institute for Healthy Aging.

Ministry of Economic Development. (1999). *Information technology*. Singapore: Ministry of Economic Development.

Mischel, L. J., & Northcraft, G. B. (1997). "I think we can, I think we can...": The role of efficacy beliefs in group and team effectiveness. *Advances in Group Processes, 14*, 177–197.

Mislove, A., Marcon, M., Gummadi, K. P., Druschel, P., & Bhattacharjee, B. (2007). *Measurement and analysis of online social networks*. Retrieved July 10, 2009, from http://www.imconf.net/imc-2007/papers/imc170.pdf

Mislove, A., Viswanath, B., Gummadi, K. P., & Druschel, P. (2010, February). You are who you know: Inferring user profiles in online social networks. Paper presented at Third ACM International Conference on Web Search and Data Mining (WSDM 2010), New York.

Misner, I. R. (1994). *The world's best known marketing secret*. Austin, TX: Bard & Stephen.

MLC. (2008). Leveraging social networking sites in marketing communications. Retrieved August 11, 2008, from http://www.ittoolbox.com/advertising/pdf/Leveraging-Social-Media-Networking-Sites-in-Marketing-Communications.pdf

Moggridge, B. (2006). *Designing interactions.* Cambridge, MA: MIT Press.

Mukand, S., & Rodrik, D. (2002). In search of the Holy Grail: Policy convergence, experimentation, and economic Pperformance. *The American Economic Review, 95*(1), 374–383. doi:10.1257/0002828053828707

Murali, R. (2009). Designing knowledge management systems for teaching and learning with Wiki technology. *Journal of Information Systems Education.* Retrieved August 27, 2009 from http://findarticles.com/p/articles/mi_qa4041/is_200510/ai_n15715725/

Murdoch, R. (2009). Global Media Entrepreneur.

Nardi, B. A., Whittaker, S., Isaacs, E., Creech, M., Johnson, J., & Hainsworth, J. (2002). Integrating communication and information through ContactMap. *Communications of the ACM, 45*(4), 89–95. doi:10.1145/505248.505251

Neate, R., & Mason, R. (2009, February 2). Networking site cashes in on friends. *The Telegraph.*

Newell, S., Scarbrough, H., Swan, J., & Hislop, D. (1999). *Intranets and knowledge management: Complex processes and ironic outcomes.* Proceedings of the 32nd Hawaii International Conference on Systems Sciences. New York: IEEE.

Nielsen, J., & Mack, R. L. (1994). *Usability inspection methods.* New York: John Wiley & Sons.

Nielsen NetRatings. (2009). Twitter's tweet smell of success. *Nielsen Wire.* Retrieved August 7, 2009, from http://blog.nielsen.com/nielsenwire/online_mobile/twitters-tweet-smell-of-success/

Nielsen, J. (1992, May). *Finding usability problems through heuristic evaluation.* Proceedings of the ACM CHI'92 conference (pp. 373-380).

Nielsen, J., & Molich, R. (1990, April). *Heuristic evaluation of user interfaces.* Proceedings of the ACM CHI'90 conference (pp. 249-256)

Nielsen. (2007, October). *Online global consumer study.* Retrieved October 1, 2007, from http://en-us.nielsen.com/main/news/news_releases/2007/october/Word-of-Mouth_the_Most_Powerful_Selling_Tool__Nielsen_Global_Survey

Nielsen. (2009, March). *Global faces and networked places: A Nielsen report on social networking's new global footprint.* Retrieved from http://blog.nielsen.com/nielsenwire/wp-content/uploads/2009/03/nielsen_global-faces_mar09.pdf

Nielsen. (2010, January 22). *Led by Facebook, Twitter, global time spent on social media sites up 82% year over year.* Retrieved from http://blog.nielsen.com/nielsenwire/global

Nonaka, I., & Takeuchi, H. (1995). *The knowledge-creating company. How Japanese companies create the dynamics of innovation.* New York: Oxford University Press.

Nov, O., & Wattal, S. (2009). Social computing privacy concerns: Antecedents and effects. In *Proceedings of the 27th international Conference on Human Factors in Computing Systems* [Boston, MA, April 4 - 9, CHI '09] (pp. 333-336). New York: ACM.

Nussbaum, E. (2007). Kids, the Internet, and the end of privacy. *New York Magazine.* Retrieved August 23, 2009, from http://nymag.com/news/features/27341/

Nyland, R. (2007). The gratification niches of Internet social networking, e-mail, and face-to-face communication. Unpublished master's thesis. Brigham Young University, UT.

O'Murchu. I., Breslin, J., & Decker, S. (2004). Online social and business networking communities In *Proceedings of the ECAI 2004Workshop on Application of Semantic Web Technologies to Web Communities,* Valencia, Spain, August 23-27. Retrieved from http://sunsite.informatik.rwth-aachen.de/Publications/CEUR-WS/Vol-107/paper2.pdf

O'Malley, G. (2008). Study: LinkedIn users have higher incomes. *Online media daily*. Retrieved July 24, 2009, from http://www.mediapost.com/publications/?fa=Articles. showArticle&art_aid=94128

O'Reilly, T. (2005). What is web 2.0? Retrieved from http://oreilly.com/web2/archive/what-is-web-20.html

Oard, D. (1997). Serving users in many languages: Cross-language information retrieval for digital libraries. *D-Lib Magazine*. Retrieved from http://www.dlib.org/dlib/december97/oard/12oard.html

OECD. (1996). *The knowledge-based economy*. Paris: OECD.

OECD. (1999). *S&T indicators: Benchmarking the knowledge based economy*. Paris: OECD.

OECD. (2001). *Science, technology and industry scoreboard 2001: Towards a knowledge based economy*. Paris: OECD.

OECD. (2007). *OECD science, technology and industry scoreboard* 2007. Retrieved from http://www.oecd.org/document/21/0,2340, en_2649_33703_16683413_1_1_1_1,00.html

Olleros, X. (2006, June). The lean core in digital platforms. Paper presented at the DRUID Summer Conference, Copenhagen. Retrieved August 12, 2008, from http://www2.druid.dk/conferences/viewpaper.php?id=623&cf=8

Oreskovic, A. (2009). Facebook gets $6.5 billion valuation with share sale. *Reuters*. Retrieved July 24, 2009, from http://www.reuters.com/article/internetNews/idUSTRE56C4TH20090714

Ostrow, A. (2009). How many people actually use Twitter? *Mashable: The social media guide*. Retrieved July 24, 2009, from http://mashable.com/2009/04/28/twitter-active-users/

Oviatt, S. L. (2003). Advances in robust multimodal interface design. In [Washington, DC: IEEE Computer Society Press.]. *Proceedings of IEEE Computer Graphics and Applications, 23*(5), 62–68. doi:10.1109/MCG.2003.1231179

Oviatt, S. L. (2008). Multimodal interfaces. In Jacko, J., & Sears, A. (Eds.), *The human-computer interaction handbook: Fundamentals, evolving technologies and emerging applications* (2nd ed., pp. 286–304). Boca Raton, FL: CRC Press.

Owyang, J. (2009). The future of the social Web: In five eras. *Web-Strategist.Com*. Retrieved July 16, 2009, from http://www.web-strategist.com/blog/2009/04/27/future-of-the-social-web/

Pacey, A. (1983). *The culture of technology*. Cambridge, MA: MIT Press.

Page, L., Brin, S., Motwani, R., & Winograd, T. (1998). *The PageRank citation ranking: Bringing order to the web* [Technical report]. Standofrd, CA: Stanford Digital Library Technologies Project.

Palmer, S. (2006). *Toxic childhood*. London: Orion Publishing Group.

Papert, S. A. (1990). Introduction. In Harel, I. (Ed.), *Constructionist learning*. Cambridge, MA: MIT Press.

Parag, M. J., & Liu, S. (2009). Web document text and images extraction using DOM analysis and natural language processing. In *Proceeding of Document Engineering Conference* (DocEng'09), Munich, Germany (pp. 218-221). New York: ACM Press.

Parameswaran, M. (2007). Social computing: An overview. *Communications of the Association for Information Systems, 19*, 762–780.

Parameswaran, M., & Whinston, A. B. (2007). Research issues in social computing. *Journal of the Association for Information Systems, 8*(6), 336–350.

Parameswaran, M., & Whinston, A. (2007). Research issues in social computing. *Journal of the Association for Information Systems, 8*(6), 336–350.

Parameswaran, M., & Whinston, A. B. (2007a). Research issues in social computing. *Journal of the Association for Information Systems, 8*(6), 336-350. Retrieved May 8, 2009, from http://crec.mccombs.utexas.edu/data/papers/Parameswaran_Social%20Computing_JAIS07.pdf

Parameswaran, M., & Whinston, A. B. (2007b). Social computing: An overview. Retrieved August 8, 2008, from http://crec.mccombs.utexas.edu/works/articles/Parameswaran_Social%20Computing_CAIS07.pdf

Paredes, R., Sánchez, J. A., Rojas, L., Strazzulla, D., & Martínez-Teutle, R. (2009). Interacting with 3D learning objects. In *Proceedings of the Fourth Latin American Conference on Human-Computer Interaction* (pp. 165-168). Los Alamitos, CA: IEEE Computer Society Press.

Parkes, A. P. (Ed.). (2002). *Introduction to languages, machines and logic: Computable languages, abstract machines and formal logic*. New York: Springer.

Pelet, J. É. (2008, June). *Effects of the color of e-commerce websites on the memorization and on the intention of purchase of the Net surfer*. Unpublished thesis. Nantes University, France.

Pelet, J. É., & Papadopoulou, P. (2009). Consumer responses to colors of e-commerce websites: An empirical investigation. In K. Kang (Ed.), *E-Commerce*. Vienna, Austria: InTech. Retrieved from http://intechweb.org

Pelleg, D., & Moore, A. W. (2000). X-means: Extending K-means with efficient estimation of the number of clusters. In *Proceedings of the 17th International Conference on Machine Learning* (pp. 727-740). San Francisco, CA: Morgan Kaufmann Publishers.

Pérez-Lezama, C., Sánchez, J. A., Paredes, R., & Valdiviezo, O. (2008). A participatory approach for developing learning objects. In *Proceedings of the Third Latin American Conference on Learning Objects* (pp. 15-24). Aguascalientes, Mexico: UAA.

Petrie, H., & Kheir, O. (2007). The relationship between accessibility and usability of websites. In *Proceedings of the SIGCHI conference on human factors in computing systems* (pp. 397-406).

Pew Internet and American Life Project. (2001). *Online communities: Networks that nurture long-distance relationships and local ties*. Retrieved January 21, 2010, from www.pewinternet.org

Phelps, J. E., Lewis, R., Mobilio, L., Perry, D., & Niranjan, R. (2004). Viral marketing or electronic word-of-mouth advertising: Examining consumer responses and motivations to pass along email. *Journal of Advertising Research, 44*(4), 333–348.

Philips, L. (2000). New communications technologies: A conduit for social inclusion. *Information Communication and Society, 39*(1), 39–68. doi:10.1080/136911800359419

Picard, R. W. (1997). *Affective computing*. Cambridge, MA: MIT Press.

Pillania, R. K. (2007). Leveraging which knowledge in the globalization era? Indian facet. [Bingley, UK: Emerald Group Publishing Limited.]. *The Learning Organization, 14*(4), 313–320. doi:10.1108/09696470710749254

Pillania, R. K. (2008). Innovations and knowledge management in emerging markets. [Hoboken, NJ: Wiley Publishers.]. *Knowledge and Process Management, 15*(3), 184–185. doi:10.1002/kpm.308

Pingdom. (2008). *Social network popularity around the world*. Retrieved from http://royal.pingdom.com/

Pitta, D., & Fowler, D. (2005). Internet community forums: An untapped resource for consumer marketers. *Journal of Consumer Marketing, 22*(5), 265–274. doi:10.1108/07363760510611699

Pluempavarn, P., & Panteli, N. (2008). Building social identity through blogging. In N. Panteli & M. Chiasson (Eds), *Exploring virtuality within and beyond organisations: Docial, global and local dimensions*. London: Palgrave Macmillan. Poole, M. S., & DeSanctis, G. (1990). Understanding the use of group decision support systems: The theory of adaptive structuration. In J. Fulk & C. Steinfeld (Eds.), *Organizations and communication technology*. Newbury Park, CA: Sage.

Plus Eight Star. (2009). *Inside CyWorld. Business Report*. Retrieved from http://www.plus8star.com/2009/01/01/publishing/

Poon, S. P. H., & Swatman, P. M. C. (1999). A longitudinal study of small business internet commerce experiences. *International Journal of Electronic Commerce, 3*(3), 21–34.

Porta, M., House, B., Buckley, L., & Blitz, A. (2008). Value 2.0: Eight new rules for creating and capturing value from innovative technologies. Retrieved May 14, 2009, from http://www-935.ibm.com/services/us/gbs/bus/pdf/gbe03016-usen-02-value2.0.pdf

Postmes, T., Spears, R., & Lea, M. (2000). The formation of group norms in computer-mediated communication. *Human Communication Research, 26*(3), 341–371. doi:10.1111/j.1468-2958.2000.tb00761.x

Postmes, T., Spears, R., & Lea, M. (2002). Intergroup differentiation in computer-mediated communication: Effects of depersonalization. *Group Dynamics, 6*, 3–16. doi:10.1037/1089-2699.6.1.3

Powell, W., & Snellman, K. (2004). The knowledge economy. *Annual Review of Sociology, 30*, 199–220. doi:10.1146/annurev.soc.29.010202.100037

Powell, T. C., & Dent-Micallef, A. (1997). Information technology as competitive advantage: The role of human, business and technology resources. *Strategic Management Journal, 18*(5), 375–405. doi:10.1002/(SICI)1097-0266(199705)18:5<375::AID-SMJ876>3.0.CO;2-7

Preece, J. (2002). Supporting community and building social capital. *Communications of the ACM, 45*(4), 37–39. doi:10.1145/505248.505269

Preece, J., Rogers, R., & Sharp, H. (2002). *Interaction design: beyond human-computer interaction.* New York: John Wiley & Sons.

Putnam, R. (1995). Tuning in, tuning out: The strange disappearance of social capital in America. *Political Science and Politics, 28*(4), 664–683. doi:10.2307/420517

Putnam, R. D. (1995). Bowling alone: America's declining social capital. *Journal of Democracy, 6*(1), 65–78. doi:10.1353/jod.1995.0002

Quin, L. (2009). Extensible markup language (XML). *Technical dissemination documents on XML.* Boston: W3C Press.

Radcliffe-Brown, A. R. (1940). On social structure. *The Journal of the Royal Anthropological Institute, 70*, 1–12.

Rahm, E., & Bernstein, P. A. (2001). A survey of approaches to automatic schema matching. *The VLDB Journal, 10*(4), 334–350. doi:10.1007/s007780100057

Rapp, A., Schwillewaert, N., & Hao, A. W. (2008). The influence of market orientation on e-business innovation and performance: The role of the top management team. *The Journal of Marketing Theory and Practice, 16*(1), 7–25. doi:10.2753/MTP1069-6679160101

Raub, W., & Weesie, J. (1990). Reputation and efficiency in social interactions: An example of network effects. *American Journal of Sociology, 96*(3), 626–654. doi:10.1086/229574

Ravakhah, M., & Kamyar, M. (2009). Semantic similarity based focused crawling. In *Proceedings of the 1ᵗʰ International Conference on Computational Intelligence, Communication Systems and Networks,* Los Alamitos, CA (pp. 448-453). Washington, DC: IEEE Computer Society.

Razikin, K., Goh, D. H., Chua, A. Y., & Lee, C. S. (2008). Can social tags help you find what you want? In *Proceedings of the 12th European conference on Research and Advanced Technology for Digital Libraries* (pp. 50-61). Aarhus, Denmark: Springer-Verlag.

Rechtsanwaltgesellschaft, L. (2004). Legal and court system in Singapore [Web page]. Retrieved September 2005.

Reisman, S. (2003). *Electronic learning communities.* Charlotte, NC: Information Age Publishing.

Repères. (2007). *Perception of Real Life brand's presence in Second Life: A CB News.* Paris: Repères.

Rice, R. E., & Katz, J. E. (Eds.). (2001). *The internet and health communication: Experiences and expectations.* Thousand Oaks, CA: Sage Publications.

Riggs, M. L., & Knight, P. A. (1994). The impact of perceived group success-failure on motivational beliefs and attitudes: A causal model. *The Journal of Applied Psychology, 79*, 755–766. doi:10.1037/0021-9010.79.5.755

Rodrigues, M. J. (2003). *European policies for a knowledge society.* Cheltenham, UK: Edward Eglar Publishing Limited.

Rodrik, D. (2000). *Institutions for high quality growth: What they are and how to acquire them.* Cambridge, MA: National Bureau of Economic Research.

Ronzhin, A. L., & Budkov, V. Y. (2009). Multimodal interaction with intelligent meeting room facilities from inside and outside. In S. Balandin, D. Moltchanov & Y. Koucheryavy (Eds.), *Smart Spaces and Next Generation Wired/Wireless Networking* [Proceedings of 9th International Conference Next Generation Wired/Wireless Networking and 2th Conference on Smart Spaces (NEW2AN'09 & ruSMART'09), St. Petersburg, Russia] (Lecture Notes in Computer Science, Vol. 5764, pp. 77-88). Berlin: Springer.

Rood, V., & Bruckman, A. (2009). Member behavior in company online communities. In *Proceedings the ACM 2009 international conference on supporting group work, Sanibel Island, FL* (pp. 209–218). New York: ACM. doi:10.1145/1531674.1531705

Rooksby, J., Baxter, G., Cliff, D., Greenwood, D., Harvey, N., Kahn, A., et al. (2009). *Social networking and the workplace.* Bristol, UK: The UK Large Scale Complex IT Systems Initiative.

Rosenbush, S. (2005). News Corp's place in MySpace. *Business Week.* Retrieved August 23, 2009, from http://www.businessweek.com/technology/content/jul2005/tc20050719_5427_tc119.htm

Salazar-Banuelos, A. (2008). Immune responses: A stochastic model. In Bentley, P. J., Lee, D., & Jung, S. (Eds.), *Artificial immune systems* (pp. 24–35). Berlin: Springer-Verlag. doi:10.1007/978-3-540-85072-4_3

Sánchez, J. A., Valdiviezo, O., Aquino, E., & Paredes, R. (2008). REC: Improving the utilization of digital collections by using induced tagging. *Research in Computing Science, 39*(1), 83–93.

Sánchez, J. A., Arzamendi-Pétriz, A., & Valdiviezo, O. (2007). Induced tagging: Promoting resource discovery and recommendation in digital libraries. In *Proceedings of the Joint Conference on Digital Libraries* (pp. 396-397). New York: ACM Press.

Sarner, A., Drakos, N., & Prentice, S. (2008). Retrieved May 14, 2009, from http://www.socialtext.net/data/workspaces/m:703/attachments/chris_lane:20081008195322-0-27637/original/the_business_impact_of_social_161342.pdf

Saunders, M., Lewis, P., & Thornhill, A. (1997). *Research methods for business students.* London: Pearson Professional Limited.

Saxenian, A. (1996). *Regional advantage: Culture and competition in Silicon Valley and Route 128.* Cambridge, MA: Harvard University Press.

Schmitz, A., Mandl, T., & Womser-Hacker, C. (2008). Cultural differences between Taiwanese and German Web users: Challenges for intercultural user testing. In *Proceedings of the 10th Intl. Conference on Enterprise Information Systems (ICEIS),* 12 - 16 June, Barcelona, Spain (pp. 62-69).

Schuler, D. (1994). Social computing. *Communications of the ACM, 37*(1), 28–29. doi:10.1145/175222.175223

Scott, J. (2000). *Social network analysis: A handbook.* Thousand Oaks, CA: SAGE.

Searle, J. R. (1990). Collective intentions and actions. In Cohen, P., Morgan, J., & Pollack, M. (Eds.), *Intentions in communication* (pp. 401–415). Cambridge, MA: MIT Press.

Second Life. (2009). SecondLife economic statistics. Retrieved August 3, 2009, from http://secondlife.com/statistics/economy-data.php

Seetharaman, A., Lock, T., Low, K., & Saravanan, A. S. (2004). Comparative justification on intellectual capital. *Journal of Intellectual Capital, 5*(4), 522–539. doi:10.1108/14691930410566997

Sen, A. (1999). *Development as freedom.* New York: Oxford University Press.

Sharp, D. (2006). Digital lifestyle monitor. Retrieved February 15, 2008, from http://www.aimia.com.au/i-cms_file?page=1878/DigitalLifestylesMonitorFullReportPublicVersionReleasedFebFeb2007.pdf

Shawbel, D. (2009). How to: Build your personal brand on facebook. *Mashable: The Social Media Guide.* Retrieved July 11, 2009, from http://mashable.com/2009/04/02/facebook-personal-brand/

Shen, A. X. L., Lee, M. K. O., Cheung, C. M. K., & Chen, H. (2009). An investigation into contribution I-intention and we-intention in open web-based encyclopedia: Roles of joint commitment and mutual agreement. Paper presented at the Proceedings of the 30th International Conference on Information Systems, Phoenix, Arizona.

Shim, J. P. (2008, October). Social networking sites: A brief comparison of usage in the U.S. and Korea. *Decision Line, 39*(5), 16–18.

Shirky, C. (2000). The toughest virus of all. *Clay Shirky's Writings About the Internet.* Retrieved July 15, 2009, from http://www.shirky.com/writings/toughest_virus.html

Shirky, C. (2003). People on page: YASNS. *Corante's Many-to-Many.* Retrieved August 10, 2009, from http://many.corante.com/archives/2003/05/12/people_on_page_yasns.php

Short, J., Williams, E., & Christie, B. (1976). *The social psychology of telecommunication.* London: Wiley.

Sigman, A. (2009). Well connected? The biological implications of social networking. *Biologist (Columbus, Ohio), 56*(1), 14–20.

Simeon, R. (1999). Evaluating domestic and international Web-site strategies. *Internet Research: Electronic Networking Applications and Policy, 9*(4), 297–308. doi:10.1108/10662249910286842

Skeels, M. M., & Grudin, J. (2009). When social networks cross boundaries: A case study of workplace use of facebook and linkedin. In *Proceedings of the ACM 2009 international Conference on Supporting Group Work* (pp. 95-104). New York: ACM Press.

Skiba, B., Tamas, A., & Robinson, K. (2006). Web 2.0: Hype or reality—and how will it play out? A strategic analysis. Retrieved February 13, 2008, from http:www.armapartners.com/files/admin/uploads/W17_F_1873_8699.pdf

Small, G. W., Moody, T. D., Siddarth, P., & Bookheimer, S. Y. (2009). Your brain on Google: Patterns of cerebral activation during internet searching. *The American Journal of Geriatric Psychiatry, 17*(2), 116–126. doi:10.1097/JGP.0b013e3181953a02

Smith, A., Dunckley, L., French, T., Minocha, S., & Chang, Y. (2004). A process model for developing usable cross-cultural websites. *Interacting with Computers, 16*(1), 63–91. doi:10.1016/j.intcom.2003.11.005

Smith, D. (2009). MySpace shrinks as Facebook, Twitter, and Bebo grab its users. *The Observer.* Retrieved July 24, 2009, from http://www.guardian.co.uk/technology/2009/mar/29/myspace-facebook-bebo-twitter

Smith, W. (2009). 5 reasons facebook is better than Twitter for your business. *Social Media School.* Retrieved August 10, 2009, from http://socialmediatoday.com/school/112208

Sohns, K., & Breitner, M. (2009). Online content mining & its potential for cruise management. In *Cruise Sector Growth* (p. 171). Wiesbaden, Germany: Gabler Verlag. doi:10.1007/978-3-8349-8346-6_12

Song, J. H., & Zinkhan, G. M. (2008). Determinants of perceived web site interactivity. *Journal of Marketing, 72*(2), 99–113. doi:10.1509/jmkg.72.2.99

Spertus, E., Sahami, M., & Buyukkokten, O. (2005). Evaluating similarity measures: A large-scale study in the Orkut social network. In *Proceedings of the eleventh ACM SIGKDD international conference on Knowledge discovery in data mining* (pp. 678-684). New York: ACM Press.

Sproull, L., & Kiesler, S. (1991). *Connections: New ways of working in the networked organization.* London: MIT Press.

Stehr, N. (2002). *Knowledge and economic conduct: The social foundations of the modern economy.* Toronto, Canada: University of Toronto Press.

Stevens, H., & Pettey, C. (2008). Gartner says 90 per cent of corporate virtual world projects fail within 18 months [Press release]. Stamford, CT: Gartner. Retrieved November 20, 2009, from http://www.gartner.com/it/page.jsp?id=670507

Storey, J., & Barnett, E. (2000). Knowledge management initiatives: Learning from failure. *Journal of Knowledge Management, 4*(2). doi:10.1108/13673270010372279

Strauss, S. G. (1997). Technology, group process and group outcomes: Testing the connections in computer-mediated and face-to-face groups. *HCI, 12,* 227–266. doi:10.1207/s15327051hci1203_1

Subramani, M. R., & Rajagopalan, B. (2003). Knowledge-sharing & influence in online social networks via viral marketing. *Communications of the ACM, 45*(12), 300–307. doi:10.1145/953460.953514

Suler, J. (1999). *The psychology of cyberspace* [Online book]. Retrieved January 21, 2010, from http://www.rider.edu/users/suler/psycyber/psycyber.html

Sun Microsystems. (2008). Current reality and future vision: Open virtual worlds. Retrieved August 18, 2008, from http://sun.com/service/applicationserversubscriptions/OpenVirtualWorlds.pdf

Surowiecki, J. (2004). *The wisdom of crowds.* New York: Doubleday.

Sveiby, K. (1997). *The new organizational wealth.* San Francisco, CA: Berrett Koehler.

Tajfel, H. (1974). Social identity and intergroup behaviour. *Social Sciences Information. Information Sur les Sciences Sociales, 13,* 65–93. doi:10.1177/053901847401300204

Tajfel, H. (1978). Social categorization, social identity and social comparison. In Tajfel, H. (Ed.), *Differentiation between social groups: Studies in the social psychology of intergroup relations* (pp. 61–76). London: Academic Press.

Tandefelt, M. (2008). Web 2.0 and network society—PR and communication: The challenge of online social network. Retrieved August 12, 2008, from http://www.diva-portal.org/diva/getDocument?urn_nbn_se_uu_diva-9187-2_fulltext.pdf

Tapscott, D., & Williams, A. (2006). *Wikinomics: How mass communication changes everything.* New York: Penguin Group.

Taylor, J., & MacDonald, J. (2002). The effects of asynchronous computer-mediated group interaction on group processes. *Social Science Computer Review, 20*(3), 260–274.

Taylor, J., & Taylor, J. (2009). A content analysis of interviews with players of Massively Multiplayer Online Role-Play Games (MMORPGs). In Ozok, A. A., & Zaphiris, P. (Eds.), *Online communities and social computing* (pp. 613–621). Berlin: Springer-Verlag. doi:10.1007/978-3-642-02774-1_66

Taylor, J., & MacDonald, J. (2000). Using SIDE to investigate group interaction in a realistic computer-mediated context. In Postmes, T., Spears, R., Lea, M., & Reicher, S. (Eds.), *SIDE issues centre stage: Recent developments in studies of de-individuation in groups* (pp. 17–30). Amsterdam: Elsevier.

Terry, D. J., & Hogg, M. A. (1996). Group norms and the attitude-behavior relationship: A role for group identification. *Personality and Social Psychology Bulletin, 22,* 776–793. doi:10.1177/0146167296228002

Thomas, J., & Harden, A. (2008). Methods for the thematic synthesis of qualitative research in systematic reviews. Retrieved September 9, 2009, from http://www.biomedcentral.com/content/pdf/1471-2288-8-45.pdf

Thomas, L. P. (2007). Deepening our roots in Second Life. *Direct2Dell: A blog about Dell products, services and customers.* Retrieved April 20, 2007, from http://direct2dell.com/one2one/archive/2007/04/20/12428.aspx

Thom-Santelli, J., Muller, M. J., & Millen, D. R. (2008). Social tagging roles: Publishers, evangelists, leaders. In *Proceeding of the Twenty-Sixth Annual SIGCHI Conference on Human Factors in Computing Systems* (pp. 1041-1044). New York: ACM Press.

Toto, S. (2008). *Taking social networks abroad: Why MySpace and Facebook are failing in Japan.* Retrieved from http://www.techcrunch.com

Trapani, G. (2008, March 18). Get things done with bi-modal work styles [Web log post]. Retrieved August 28, 2008, from http://lifehacker.com/369128/get-things-done-with-bi+modal-work-styles

Trauth, E. (1996). Impact of an imported IT sector: Lessons from Ireland. In *Technology development and policy: Theoretical perspectives and practical challenges* (pp. 245–261). Aldershot, UK: Avebury Publishing Ltd.

Trauth, E. (2000). *The culture of an information economy: Influences and impact in the Republic of Ireland.* Dordrecht, The Netherlands: Kluwer Academic Publishers.

Trauth, E. (2001). Mapping information-sector work to the workforce: The lessons from Ireland. [Special issue on the Global IT workforce]. *Communications of the ACM, 44*(7), 74–75. doi:10.1145/379300.379318

Trauth, E. M. (1993). Educating information technology professionals for work in Ireland: An emerging post-industrial country. In *Global information technology education: Issues and trends* (pp. 205–233). Harrisburg, PA: Idea Group Publishing.

Trompenaars, F., & Hampden-Turner, C. (1997). *Riding the waves of culture: Understanding cultural diversity in business.* London: Nicholas Brealey.

Tuckman, B. W. (1965). Developmental sequence in small groups. *Psychological Bulletin, 63*(6), 384–399. doi:10.1037/h0022100

Tuomela, R. (1995). *The importance of us: A philosophical study of basic social notions.* Stanford, CA: Stanford University Press.

Tuomela, R. (2005). We-intention revisited. *Philosophical Studies, 125*(3), 327–369. doi:10.1007/s11098-005-7781-1

Tuomela, R. (2003). The we-mode and the I-mode. In Schmitt, F. F. (Ed.), *Socializing metaphysics: The nature of social reality* (pp. 93–127). Lanham, MD: Roman & Littlefield.

Turner, J. C. (1987). *Rediscovering the social group: A self-categorization theory.* Oxford: Blackwell.

Turner, J. C. (1991). *Social influence. Milton-Keynes.* UK: Open University Press.

Turner, B. (2008, November 2). Hypotheses about privacy attitudes. *International values and communications technologies: The blog of the GU-ISD Yahoo! fellow.* Retrieved from https://digitalcommons.georgetown.edu/blogs/isdyahoofellow/hypotheses-about-privacy-attitudes

Twitter. (2009). *Twitter support.* Retrieved August 10, 2009, from http://help.twitter.com/forums/10711/entries/13920

UID. (2007). *Internationale Web 2.0 Studie über MySpace.* Retrieved from http://www.uid.com/download.php?pdf=uid_referenz_myspace_studie.pdf

United Nations Economic Commission for Europe. (2002). *Concept, outline, benchmarking and indicators.* Geneva: United Nations Publications.

Universal McCann. (2008). *When did we start trusting strangers? How the internet turned us all into influencers.* Retrieved from http://www.imaginar.org/docs/when_did_we_start_trusting_strangers.pdf

Van Dijck, J., & Nieborg, D. (2009). Wikinomics and its discontents: A critical analysis of Web 2.0 business manifestos. Retrieved January 18, 2010, from http://www.gamespace.nl/content/Wikinomics_and_its_discontents_2009.pdf

Vargo, S. L., & Lusch, R. F. (2004). Evolving to a new dominant logic for marketing. *Journal of Marketing, 68*(1), 1–17. doi:10.1509/jmkg.68.1.1.24036

Venkatesh, V., Morris, M. G., Davis, G. B., & Davis, F. D. (2003). User acceptance of information technology: Toward a unified view. *Management Information Systems Quarterly, 27*(3), 425–478.

Venkatesh, A., Sherry, J. F., & Firat, A. E. (1993). Postmodernism and the marketing imaginary. *International Journal of Research in Marketing, 10*(3), 215–223. doi:10.1016/0167-8116(93)90007-L

Veugelers, R. (2005). Assessing innovation capacity: Fitting strategy and policy to the right framework. In *Measuring knowledge and its economic effects: Advancing knowledge and the knowledge economy*. Washington, DC: National Academies.

Von Krogh, G. (2000). *Enabling knowledge creation*. London: Oxford University Press.

Voola, R. (2005). *An Examination of the Effects of Firm Capabilities on E-Business Adoption and Competitive Advantage: A Resource Based Perspective*. Unpublished doctoral thesis. Newcastle University, UK.

W3C. (2008). Publication version 1.1 of the AccessiWeb repository. Cambridge, MA: W3C. Retrieved June 9, 2008, from http://www.w3c.org/

Wagner, C. (2004). Wiki: A technology for conversational knowledge management and group collaboration. *Communications of the Association for Information Systems, 13*, 265–289.

Wagner, C., & Prasarnphanich, P. (2007). Innovating collaborative content creation: The role of altruism and wiki technology. Paper presented at the Proceedings of the 40th Hawaii International Conference on System Sciences.

Walsham, G. (1997). Actor-network theory and IS research: Current status and future prospects. In Lee, A. S., Liebenau, J., & DeGross, J. I. (Eds.), *Information systems and qualitative research* (pp. 466–480). London: Chapman and Hall.

Walther, J. B., Anderson, J. F., & Park, D. W. (1994). Interpersonal effects in computer-mediated interaction: A meta-analysis of social and antisocial communication. *Communication Research, 21*, 460–487. doi:10.1177/009365094021004002

Wang, C. C., & Wang, C. H. (2008). Helping others in online games: Prosocial behavior in cyberspace. *Cyberpsychology & Behavior, 11*(3), 344–346. doi:10.1089/cpb.2007.0045

Warne, L., Ali, I. M., & Pascoe, C. (2003). Team building as a foundation for knowledge management: Findings from research into social learning in the Australian Defence Organization. *Journal of Information & Knowledge Management, 2*(2), 93–106. doi:10.1142/S0219649203000024

Wasko, M., & Faraj, S. (2000). It is what one does: Why people participate and help others in electronic communities of practice. *The Journal of Strategic Information Systems, 9*(2-3), 155–173. doi:10.1016/S0963-8687(00)00045-7

Wasko, M. M., & Faraj, S. (2005). Why should I share? Examining social capital and knowledge contribution in electronic networks of practice. *Management Information Systems Quarterly, 29*(1), 35–58.

Weber, L. (2007). *Marketing to the social Web*. Hoboken, NJ: John Wiley & Sons, Inc.

Wei, J., & Salvendy, G. (2004). The cognitive task analysis methods for job and task design: Review and reappraisal. *Behaviour & Information Technology, 23*(4), 273–299. doi:10.1080/01449290410001673036

Welling, R., & White, L. (2006). Measuring the value of Internet Web sites. *Journal of Internet Commerce, 5*(3), 127–145. doi:10.1300/J179v05n03_06

Wellman, B., & Gulia, M. (1999). The network basis of social support: A network is more than the sum of its ties. In *Networks in the Global Village* (pp. 83–118). Boulder, CO: Westview Press.

Wellman, B. (1988). Structural analysis: From method and metaphor to theory and substance. Retrieved August 10, 2009, from http://homepage.ntu.edu.tw/~khsu/network/reading/wellman2.pdf

Wellman, B., Garton, L., & Haythornthwaite, C. (1997). Studying online social networks. *Journal of Computer Mediated Communication, 3*(1). Retrieved August 10, 2007, from http://jcmc.indiana.edu/vol3/issue1/garton.html

Weng, M. (2007). *A multimedia social-networking community for mobile devices*. New York: NYU Tisch School of the Arts, Interactive Telecommunications Program.

Wernerfelt, B. (1984). A resource-based view of the firm. *Strategic Management Journal*, 5(2), 171–180. doi:10.1002/smj.4250050207

Whittaker, S., Jones, Q., & Terveen, L. (2002). Contact management: Identifying contacts to support long-term communication. In *Proceedings of the 2002 ACM conference on Computer Supported Cooperative Work* (pp. 216-225). New York: ACM Press.

Whyte, W. H. (1954, November). The Web of word of mouth. *Fortune*, 50, 140–143.

Wickens, C. D. (1992). *Engineering psychology and human performance* (2nd ed.). New York: HarperCollins.

Wiig, K. M. (2000). Knowledge management: An Emerging discipline rooted in a long history. In *Knowledge Horizons* (pp. 3–26). Boston: Butterworth-Heinemann. doi:10.1016/B978-0-7506-7247-4.50004-5

Wikipedia. (2009). Social computing. Retrieved September 8, 2009, from http://en.wikipedia.org/wiki/Social_computing

Wind, Y., & Todi, M. (2008). *Advertising on social networking websites*. Wharton Research Scholars Journal.

Wood, L. (2005). Blogs & wikis: Technologies for enterprise applications? Retrieved August 4, 2008, from http://gilbane.com/gilbane_report.pl/104/Blogs__Wikis_Technologies_for_Enterprise_Applications.html

Woolcock, M. (1998). Social capital and economic development: Towards a theoretical synthesis and policy framework. *Theory and Society*, 27, 151–208. doi:10.1023/A:1006884930135

Wu, L., Oviatt, S. L., & Cohen, P. (1999). Multimodal integration: A statistical view. *IEEE Transactions on Multimedia*, 1(4), 334–341. doi:10.1109/6046.807953

Würtz, E. (2004). Intercultural communication on websites: An analysis of visual communication of high- and low-context cultures. In F. Sudweeks & C. Ess (Eds.), *Proceedings of the Fourth International Conference on Cultural Attitudes towards Technology and Communication (CATAC)*, Murdoch University, Australia (pp. 109-122).

Wyld, D. C. (2007). The blogging revolution: Government in the age of web 2.0. Retrieved January 17, 2008, from http://www.businessofgovernment.org/pdfs/WyldReportBlog.pdf

Yeo, B. (2009). *Developing a sustainable knowledge economy: An investigation of contextual factors*. Germany: VDM Verlag.

Young, R. (2008). Back to basics: Strategies for identifying, creating, storing, sharing and using knowledge. In *From Productivity to Innovation: Proceedings from the Second International Conference on Technology and Innovation for Knowledge management*. Tokyo: Asian Productivity Organization. Retrieved August 2009, from http://www.apo-tokyo.org/00e-books/IS-34_FromProdToInnovation/IS-34_FromProdToInnovation.pdf

Yuan, Y. C., Gay, G., & Hembrooke, H. (2006). Focused activities and the development of social capital in a distributed learning community. *The Information Society*, 22(1), 25–39. doi:10.1080/01972240500388347

Yuana, W., Nahrstedta, K., Advea, S. V., Jonesb, D. L., & Kravetsa, R. H. (2003). Design and evaluation of a cross-layer adaptation framework for mobile multimedia systems. In Proceedings of the SPIE/ACM Multimedia Computing and Networking Conference (MMCN).

Zeleny, M. (1987). Management support systems: Towards integrated knowledge management. *Human Systems Management*, 7(1), 59–70.

Zeng, L. Z., Benatallah, B., Ngu, A. H., Dumas, M., Kalagnanam, J., & Chang, H. (2004). QoS: Aware middleware for web services composition. *IEEE Transactions on Software Engineering*, 30(5), 311–327. doi:10.1109/TSE.2004.11

Zhang, J., Ackerman, M., & Adamic, L. (2007). Expertise networks in online communities: Structure and algorithms. In *Proceedings of the 16th international conference on World Wide Web* (pp. 221-230). New York: ACM Press.

Zhao, D., & Rosson, M. (2009). How and why people Twitter: The role that micro-blogging plays in informal communication at work. In *Proceedings of the ACM 2009 international Conference on Supporting Group Work,* Sanibel Island, FL, May 10 - 13 [New York: ACM.]. *Group, 09,* 243–252. doi:10.1145/1531674.1531710

Zhou, A. Z., & Fink, D. (2003). The intellectual capital web: A systematic linking of intellectual capital and knowledge management. *Journal of Intellectual Capital, 4*(1), 34–48. doi:10.1108/14691930310455379

Zhou, C., Chia, L. T., & Lee, B. S. (2005). Semantics in service discovery and QoS measurement. *IT Professional, 7*(2), 29–34. doi:10.1109/MITP.2005.41

About the Contributors

Panagiota Papdopoulou holds a BSc (Hons) in Informatics from the National and Kapodistrian University of Athens, an MSc (Distinction) in Distributed and Multimedia Information Systems from Heriot-Watt University, and a PhD in Information Systems from the National and Kapodistrian University of Athens. She is a research fellow in the Department of Informatics and Telecommunications at the National and Kapodistrian University of Athens. She has extensive, university-level teaching experience, as an adjunct faculty member at the University of Athens, the University of Pireaus, the University of Peloponnese, the University of Central Greece and other educational institutions in Greece. Papadopoulou has also actively participated in a number of European Community and National research projects. She has published more than 30 papers in international journals and conferences, with her current research interests focusing on social computing, e-commerce, web-based information systems, interface design and online trust.

Panagiotis Kanellis is currently an Executive Director with Ernst & Young in Athens, Greece. Before that he worked for the Greek Government as a program manager and held senior consulting positions with Arthur Andersen and Ernst & Young. He was educated at Western International University in Business Administration (BSc), at the University of Ulster in Computing and Information Systems (Post-Graduate Diploma), and at Brunel University in Data Communication Systems (MSc) and Information Systems (PhD). He is a research associate in the Department of Informatics and Telecommunications at the National and Kapodistrian University of Athens and was an adjunct faculty member at the Athens University of Economics and Business having edited books and published more than 60 papers in international journals and conferences. He is a Fellow of the British Computer Society and a Chartered Information Technology Professional (FBCS CITP), a Chartered Engineer (CEng) and Scientist (CSci) and a Certified Information Systems Auditor (CISA).

Drakoulis Martakos is an Associate Professor at the Department of Informatics and Telecommunications at the National and Kapodistrian University of Athens. He holds a BSc in Physics, an MSc in Electronics and Radio Communications and a PhD in Real-Time Computing from the National and Kapodistrian University of Athens. Professor Martakos is a consultant to public and private organizations and a project leader in numerous national and international projects. He is the author or co-author of more than 70 scientific publications and a number of technical reports and studies. His research interests focus on information systems, internet and web technologies and e-services.

* * *

Danilo Avola obtained his degree in Computer Science from the "Sapienza" University of Rome. He has spent few years in different research and development departments belonging to several national and international ICT companies. Afterwards, he has started several collaborations with both National Research Councils and National and International Universities. Currently, he also a senior researcher at the National Research Center: Computer Science and Knowledge Laboratory (CSK Lab). His main research interests include Human-Computer Interactions (HCIs), Human Centered Systems (HCSs), MultiModal Interactions (MMIs), Visual Languages (VLs), Visual Interfaces (VIs), Image Processing (IP), Video Processing (VP), Computer Aided Diagnosis Systems (CAD Systems), Pattern Recognition (PR), Natural Language Processing (NLP), Semantic WEB, and Ontology Management (OM).

Andrea Del Buono obtained his degree (cum laude) in Computer Science from the "Sapienza" University of Rome. He has spent few years in different research and development departments belonging to several national and international ICT companies. Afterwards, he has started several collaborations with both National Research Councils and National and International Universities. Currently, he also a senior researcher at the National Research Center: Computer Science and Knowledge Laboratory (CSK Lab). His main research interests include Human-Computer Interactions (HCIs), Human Centered Systems (HCSs), MultiModal Interactions (MMIs), Visual Languages (VLs), Visual Interfaces (VIs), Geographic Information Systems (GISs & WebGISs), Satellite Image Interpretation Systems (SII Systems), Artificial Intelligence (AI), Soft Computing (SC), and Advanced Software Engineering Systems (ASE Systems).

Jason Caudill holds a bachelor's degree in Business, an MBA, and a PhD in Instructional Technology from the University of Tennessee and currently serves as an Assistant Professor of Business Administration at Carson-Newman College where he teaches Information Systems and Management. Caudill's research interests include online education and technology integration into organizations. Outside of work, Caudill enjoys the outdoors, working with his hands, and watching college sports including American football and basketball. He is very involved in service activities, primarily as a national staff officer with the United States Coast Guard Auxiliary.

James Caverlee is an Assistant Professor in the department of Computer Science and Engineering at Texas A&M University. He received his PhD from Georgia Tech in 2007 (advisor: Ling Liu; co-advisor: William B. Rouse). Caverlee graduated magna cum laude from Duke University in 1996 with a BA in Economics. He received an MS in Engineering-Economic Systems & Operations Research in 2000, and an MS in Computer Science in 2001, both from Stanford University. His research interests span web-scale information management, distributed data-intensive systems, and social computing. Caverlee directs the TAMU infolab focused on enabling efficient and trustworthy information sharing and knowledge discovery over dynamic, heterogenous, and massive-scale networked information systems, including the World Wide Web, distributed databases, and emerging social+mobile information systems.

Chaka Chaka is a senior lecturer in the Department of English at Walter Sisulu University (Eastern Cape, South Africa). His research interests include collaborative learning (CL); concept mapping; computer-mediated communication (CMC); electronic learning (e-learning); computer assisted language learning (CALL); mobile learning (m-learning); mobile assisted language learning (MALL); Web 2.0 learning/Mobile Web 2.0 learning; Enterprise 2.0; Web 3.0/Mobile Web 3.0 learning; Semantic Web/ Mobile Semantic Web; online genre and discourse analysis; online/virtual and digital identities; knowledge management (KM); and learning organisation (LO).

Christy M. K. Cheung is an assistant professor at Hong Kong Baptist University. She received her PhD from City University of Hong Kong. Her research interests include virtual community, knowledge management, social computing technology, and IT adoption and usage. Her research articles have been published in *MIS Quarterly, Information & Management, Journal of the American Society for Information Science and Technology, e-Service Journal*, and *Information Systems Frontiers*. She received the Best Paper Award at the 2003 International Conference on Information Systems and was the PhD fellow of 2004 ICIS Doctoral Consortium.

Ying Ding is an Assistant Professor in School of Library and Information Science, Indianan University. Before she worked as a senior researcher at the University of Innsbruck, Austria and as a researcher at the Division of Mathematics and Computer Science at the Free University of Amsterdam, the Netherlands. She completed her PhD in School of Applied Science, Nanyang Technological University, Singapore. She has been involved in various European-Union funded projects: research-oriented EU projects (EASAIER, OntoKnowledge, IBROW, SWWS, COG, Htechsight, Esperonto, SEKT, DIP, Triple Space Computing), thematic network (Ontoweb, knowledgeweb), and Accompanied Measurements (Multiple). She has published more than 70 papers in journals,conferences and workshops. She has served on the Programme Committee for more than 80 international conferences and workshops. Her current interest areas include Webometrics, Semantic Web, citation analysis, information retrieval, knowledge management, and application of Web Technology.

Christopher Douce is a Senior Research Fellow within the Open University Institute of Educational technology where he is currently performing research to learn how to improve the accessibility of virtual learning environment systems. Chris is a tutor for two different courses: a postgraduate course entitled Accessible e-Learning, and an undergraduate computing course called Fundamentals of Interaction Design. Chris holds a PhD in Computation from the University of Manchester, UK. Before joining the Open University he worked in industry for a number of years where he helped to design a range of educational technology products that could be used to help teach scientific and engineering principles.

Jose Oscar Fajardo works as research fellow in the Department of Electronics and Telecommunications of the University of the Basque Country at the Faculty of Engineering in Bilbao, where he received his diploma in Telecommunications Engineering in 2003. Since then, he has been involved in several R&D projects in the area of QoS and service performance monitoring, PQoS assessment and QoS-aware networking. He is currently a PhD applicant.

Michael Haenlein is Professor of Marketing at ESCP Europe. He holds a PhD and a MSc from the WHU, Otto Beisheim Graduate School of Management. Michael's research lays in the areas of customer relationship management (CRM) and database analysis, as well as stochastic marketing models and structural equation modeling. Within these domains, Haenlein is particularly interested in the management of unprofitable customer relationships and the inclusion of social network effects and Word-of-Mouth behavior into customer lifetime value (CLV) calculations. He is author of various research publications in leading English-speaking journals, including the *Journal of Marketing*, the *Journal of Product Innovation Management and the European Management Journal*. He is part of the Editorial Review Board of the *Journal of Marketing*. As a consultant, he has collaborated with major companies in the telecommunications and financial services industry to develop and refine their CRM strategy.

Elin K. Jacob is an Associate Professor in School of Library and Information Science, Indiana University. She received her PhD from University of North Carolina – Chapel Hill in 1994. Her research interest lies on representation of knowledge, including theories of classification and categorization; indexing systems as cognitive scaffolding; design, implementation and evaluation of ontologies and metadata schemes; and information architecture; and philosophy of information.

Ranadeva Jayasekera is a Lecturer in Accouting and Finance at the School of Management of the University of Southampton, UK. He holds a bachelors degree with a first class in mathematics and physics from the University of Colombo, and an MBA from the same University, where he graduated with honours and was awarded the Ceylon Chemical Industries Gold Medal Award for Strategic Management & Business Policy. He also holds a PhD in Accounting and Finance from Judge Business School, University of Cambridge, UK. He has served as a manager in various managing positions in the UK financial sector and developed financial models to re-organise the then existing accounting structure and reporting systems to highlight and provide more value added information for decision making for Gonville and Caius College of the University of Cambridge. He joined the quantitative finance team of Deloitte in London at a senior capacity in 2007 and has been involved in the Valuation, structuring and modelling of complex financial instruments of major investment banks.

Andreas M. Kaplan is Professor of Marketing at the ESCP Europe Business School (Paris campus). After starting his career as marketing professor at the ESSEC Business School and Sciences Po Paris, he migrated to ESCP Europe. Professor Kaplan did his Habilitation (HDR) at the University of Paris 1 Pantheon-Sorbonne and his PhD at the University of Cologne in cooperation with HEC School of Management Paris. He holds a Master of Public Administration (MPA) from the École Nationale d'Administration (ENA; French National School of Public Administration), an MSc from ESCP Europe, and a BSc from the University of Munich. Additionally, Andreas was visiting PhD at INSEAD. His research deals with analyzing and decrypting social media in general and virtual worlds in particular. Additionally, Andreas has carried out research in the areas of customer lifetime valuation, mass customization and public sector marketing.

Harilaos Koumaras was born in Athens, Greece in 1980. He received his BSc degree in Physics in 2002 from the University of Athens, Physics Department, his MSc in Electronic Automation and Information Systems in 2004, being scholar of the non-profit organization Alexander S Onassis, from the University of Athens, Computer Science Department and his PhD in 2007 at Computer Science from the University of Athens, Computer Science Department, having granted the four-year scholarship of National Centre of Scientific Research "Demokritos". He has received twice the Greek State Foundations (IKY) scholarship during the academic years 2000-01 and 2003-04. He joined the Digital Communications Lab at the National Centre of Scientific Research "Demokritos" in 2003 and since then he has participated in numerous EC-funded projects, namely SOQUET-IST/FP5, ATHENA-IST/FP6, ENTHRONE-II-IST/FP6 and ADAMANTIUM-ICT/FP7, in which he is the assistant project manager. Since 2004, he is a principal lecturer at the Business College of Athens (BCA) teaching modules related to Information Technology and Mathematics, and at the City University of Seattle teaching Data Networks and Local Area Networks. His research interests include objective/subjective evaluation of the perceived quality of multimedia services, video quality and picture quality evaluation, video traffic modelling, digital terrestrial television and video compression techniques. Currently, he is the author or co-author of more than 30 scientific papers in international journals, technical books and book chapters, numbering 47 non-self citations. He is a member of the editorial board of Telecommunications Systems Journal and a reviewer of EURASIP Journal of Applied Signal Processing and IEEE Transactions on Broadcasting. Dr. Koumaras is a member of IEEE, SPIE and National Geographic Society.

Vaios Koumaras received his BSc degree in Business Administration with major in Computer Information Systems from the American College of Greece and his MBA in Project Management from the City University. Since 1997, he has worked in several positions as computer analyst and software developer, participating in major IT projects. For the last 5 years, he holds the position of R&D software engineer, with participation and collaboration in R&D IT projects of numerous shipping companies worldwide. In parallel, he has a ten-year teaching experience of Business and IT courses in various grades. For the last 3 years he is an associate lecturer at the Business College of Athens (BCA), at the Departments of Business and Computer Science, teaching modules related to Information Technology, Business and Mathematics. Currently, he has participated in EC-funded projects as associate R&D Business consultant for business planning and marketing strategy development. Additionally, he is part of the research team of the Business College of Athens (BCA) scientific centre.

Anastasios Kourtis received his BS degree in Physics in 1978 and his PhD degree in Telecommunications in 1984, from the University of Athens. From 1986 he is a member of the research stuff in the Institute of Informatics and Telecommunications of the Greek National Centre for Scientific Research "Demorkitos". Currently he is a Researcher Director. His technical and research activities have been in the area of digital modulation techniques, spread spectrum systems, multimedia applications, Quality of Services (Perceived and Network), broadband wireless networks, interactive digital terrestrial TV (DVB-T/T2), satellite communications (DVB-S/S2-RCS) and networks convergence. He has participated in a number of EU-funded research and development projects : ESPRIT (FCPN, OFSES), ACTS (CRABS, WATT), IST/FP5 (WIN, MAMBO, SOQUET, REPOSIT), IST/FP6 (ATHENA, IMOSAN, ENTHRONE-I, ENTHRONE-II, UNITE) and ICT/FP7 (ADAMANTIUM, HURRICANE). He has been Project Manager of ATHENA and IMOSAN and Technical Manager of REPOSIT projects. Currently he is the PM of ICT-214751 ADAMANTIUM project. Kourtis has also co-ordinated a number of National funded projects. He is the author of several papers on telecommunications, broadband wireless networks and digital interactive TV.

Thomas Mandl studied information and computer science at the University of Regensburg and at the University of Illinois at Champaign/Urbana. He worked as a research assistant at the Social Science Information Centre in Bonn, Germany and as Associate Professor at the University of Hildesheim in Germany where he is teaching in the programme International Information Management. He received a doctorate degree and a post doctoral degree from the University of Hildesheim. His research interests include information retrieval, human-computer interaction and internationalization of information technology.

Staša Milojević is an Assistant Professor in School of Library and Information Science, Indianan University. She received her PhD from University of California, Los Angeles in 2009. Her research interests include science studies, scholarly communication, scientometrics, bibliometrics, social network analysis, representation of knowledge and scientific classification.

Matthew K. O. Lee is Associate Dean and Chair Professor of Information Systems & E-Commerce at the College of Business, City University of Hong Kong. His research interests extend across innovation adoption and diffusion, knowledge management, e-commerce, and social media. He is an Assessor of the Innovation and Technology Commission in Hong Kong and a member of the Hong Kong Research Grant Council (RGC) Business Studies Panel. He has published well over 100 research articles in international journals, conference proceedings, and research textbooks. His work has appeared in leading research journals (e.g. *Journal of MIS, Communications of the ACM, MIS Quarterly, Journal of the American Society for Information Science and Technology, Decision Support Systems, Information & Management,* and *Journal of International Business Studies*). He serves on the editorial board of a number of journals and is a special Associate Editor of *MISQ*. He holds a PhD from the University of Manchester, England.

Fidel Liberal works as lecturer at the Department of Electronics and Telecommunications of the University of the Basque Country at the Faculty of Engineering in Bilbao. He graduated in Telecommunications Engineering in 2001 and received his PhD in 2005 from the University of the Basque Country in the area of management in quality of telecommunications services. He is currently cooperating in different R&D projects regarding QoS and Security in computer networks.

Thanos Papadopoulos is a Lecturer in Knowledge and Information Systems Management in the Centre for Operational Research, Management Science, and Information Systems (CORMSIS), School of Management, University of Southampton, UK. He obtained his PhD from Warwick Business School, University of Warwick, UK. He also obtained a Diploma (Dipl-Eng- Equivalent to MEng) in Computer Engineering and Informatics from the School of Engineering of Patras University, Greece and an MSc in Information Systems from the Department of Informatics of the Athens University of Economics and Business, Greece. His research interests include innovation and change in public services, business transformation and networks and information systems' assessment strategies.

Jean-Eric Pelet has a doctorate in marketing with distinction and a MBA in information systems with distinction. He works as an assistant professor at SupAgro Montpellier on problems related to interfaces and to the consumer behaviour towards websites and other information systems (e-learning, knowledge management, e-commerce platforms). His main interest lies in the variables helps people navigate efficiently. He works as a visiting professor in several places in France, including the Knowledge Management and Content Management System platform in Design School (Nantes), Business Schools (Paris, Reims), and Universities (Paris Dauphine – Nantes), lecturing on e-marketing, ergonomic, usability, and consumer behaviour. Pelet has also actively participated in a number of European Community and National research projects. His current research interests focus on web-based information systems, interface design and usability.

Iman Poernomo heads the Predictable Assembly Laboratory (Palab) at King's College London. His research involves the intersection of formal methods and model-based techniques to improve the quality of the software development process. He holds a PhD in Computer Science, a BA in Philosophy and a BSc with Honours in Pure Mathematics from Monash University. Prior to joining King's he worked as a Senior Research Scientist and Team Leader at the DSTC, working on metamodelling and trust. His work with the Palab proceeds involves utilising model-driven architecture and formal techniques to improve both functional correctness and non-functional reliability and performance of enterprise systems. He is the author of one book and over 50 research papers.

Alfredo Sánchez is professor of computer science and directs the Laboratory of Interactive and Cooperative Technologies (ICT) at Universidad de las Américas Puebla (UDLAP). He holds MSc and PhD degrees in Computer Science from Texas A&M University, and a BEng degree in Computer Systems from UDLAP. Since 1996, he has conducted R&D projects in areas such as digital libraries, human-computer interaction and computer-supported cooperative work. Results from these projects have been reported in more than 90 refereed and invited publications. Sánchez has been a visiting professor at the University of Waikato, New Zealand, and a visiting scientist at the Center for Botanical Informatics of the Missouri Botanical Garden. Sánchez serves at the editorial board of the International Journal of Digital Libraries and coordinates the Digital Libraries Community of the Mexican Internet 2 Consortium. He also has served as president of the Mexican Computer Science Society and has been a member of the National Researchers System in Mexico.

Angelo Spognardi obtained his degree (cum laude) and in his PhD in Computer Science from the "Sapienza" University of Rome. He has spent few years as post-doc position at INRIA Rhône-Alpes, working on the European UbiSec&Sens project. Currently is a post-doc at "Sapienza" University of Rome. His main research interests include: Security and Privacy for RFID, Wireless and Wireless Sensor Network Security, Security and Multimediality Integration, Intrusion Detection, Security and Privacy, Cryptography.

Aaron X. L. Shen is currently a Senior Research Assistant in the Department of Information Systems at the City University of Hong Kong. He received his PhD from City University of Hong Kong and University of Science and Technology of China. His research interests include IT-based innovation adoption and diffusion, virtual community, electronic commerce and knowledge management. Shen has published in *Journal of Information Technology, Information Systems Frontier,* and the *International Conference on Information Systems.* He was also the PhD research fellow of 2008 PACIS Doctoral Consortium.

Lingfen Sun received her PhD in Computing and Communications from University of Plymouth in 2004. She holds a MSc in Communication and Electronics System (1988) and BEng in Telecommunications Engineering (1985). She is currently a lecturer in the School of Computing, Communications and Electronics. She leads a work package (PQoS models and adaptation mechanisms) within the EU FP7 ADAMANTIUM project. She was a co-leader for a subproject on eDelivery within the EU FP6 BIOPATTERN Project and has led an industry funded project on voice/video quality measurement for 3G networks. She has published over 50 papers in peer-refereed journals and conference proceedings. Her publications on VoIP have received more than 150 non-self citations by peer researchers. She is a reviewer for journals including *IEEE Transactions on Multimedia* and *IEEE Transactions on Speech and Audio Processing.* She has served on the TPCs of a number of international conferences, including IEEE Globecom. Her main research interests include VoIP, QoS, voice/video quality assessment (objective and subjective), QoS prediction and control for multimedia over packet, mobile and wireless networks, network performance measurement and characterisation, and multimedia quality management. She is a member of IEEE and a Voting Member of IEEE Multimedia Communication Technical Committee.

Jacqui Taylor has a BSc(Hons) degree in Psychology and a Masters degree in Information Systems. For her doctorate, she researched the Psychology of Internet Behaviour, which applied Social Identity Theory to explain online communication. Since then, she has been conducting research and supervising and examining research projects in this area, ranging from personality and video gaming to online identity deception. She currently supervises two PhD students investigating the use of online social support networks by the elderly and for those with chronic illness. She helped to develop an innovative BSc(Hons) Psychology & Computing degree at Bournemouth University and currently leads a final year unit on this degree called Social Psychology of Mediated Communication. She is an external examiner for the MSc CyberPsychology at NTU and is planning a Second Conference on the Internet and Psychology for 2011.

Ioan Toma works as a Researcher at STI Innsbruck, University of Innsbruck, Austria. His current research areas include Semantic Web Services, more precisely modeling QoS aspects of service and ranking of services based on QoS descriptions. Before joining STI Innsbruck, he obtained his graduated engineer of computer science (Dipl. Eng.) and MS titles from Technical University of Cluj-Napoca. Toma was a member of several conference and workshop program committees including SMR2-□2007, in conjunction with ISWC2007, ICIW06 (the "Web Service-based Systems and Applications" track), MoSO2006, WSCOMPS05 and the "Web Service Choreography and Orchestration for Business Process Management" workshop in conjunction with BPM2005.

Costas Troulos was an Electrical and Computer Engineering graduate from the National Technical University of Athens in 1997 and holds an MBA from Louisville University, USA (2005). He is also pursuing a PhD degree on public involvement in broadband development from NTUA. He is working with PCN Greece on telecom infrastructure, technology & research projects. Next to PCN Greece, he is a researcher at the Institute of Communication and Computer Systems (ICCS) of the National Technical University of Athens (NTUA) since 2005. Prior joining ICCS, from 2003 to 2005, he was the Technical Director of Vivodi Telecommunications. He has a total of 15 years of business and academic experience in the Telecom and IT industry where he served in various positions. His area of expertise involves fiber investments, social media, next generation access networks and broadband business models. His research interests include telecommunications regulation and policy, techno-economic and engineering models, public policy, universal service and access and social impact of broadband.

Omar Valdiviezo holds a Bachelor of Engineering degree in Computer Systems from Universidad Autónoma de Aguascalientes (UAA) and currently is working on a master's degree in Information Design at Universidad de las Américas Puebla (UDLAP) where he is also working as coordinator of digital services for the Interactive Center of Information and Learning Resources (CIRIA). At UDLAP, he is in charge of designing, developing and implementing projects related with innovative digital tools for information and knowledge management for the university community. Some of these projects have been funded by the National Council of Science and Technology (Conacyt) and the Mexican Internet 2 Consortium (CUDI). His professional experience includes the development of interactive learning resources for distance education courses at UAA, and the multimedia collaborative rooms at UDLAP. He is interested in topics related with human-computer interaction, computer-mediated collaborative learning and interaction and information design.

Gbolahan Williams is a doctoral candidate in Computer Science in the Predictable Assembly Laboratory (Palab) at King's College London. He received his MSc in Computer Science (by Research) from the University of Warwick, UK and his BSc in Computer Science from King's College London. His research interests include social computing, requirements engineering and service orientation.

Erjia Yan is a doctoral student in School of Library and Information Science, Indianan University. His research interest involves social network analysis, scientometrics, and informetrics, with a focus on new indicators for scientific evaluation, heterogeneous scientific networks, and measures of prestige and popularity.

Benjamin Yeo is a Senior Research Analyst in Regional Economics at the Milken Institute and serves as an adjunct faculty at the Fashion Institute of Design and Merchandising and Loyola Marymount University. His research interests include knowledge- and technology-based economic development, social informatics, and ICT policies. He is the author of a 2009 book entitled, *Developing a Sustainable Knowledge Economy: The Influence of Contextual Factors*. His other recent publications include an article in the *International Journal of Contemporary Management Research* entitled "Driving the Knowledge Economy: The Impact of Regional Innovation Capacity," and a Milken Institute report on The Greater Philadelphia Life Sciences Cluster. He received his PhD from the College of Information Sciences and Technology at the Pennsylvania State University, and holds bachelor's and master's degrees from the School of Communication and Information at Nanyang Technological University in Singapore.

Index

A

academic online community 36
anti-normative behaviour 43
avatars 286, 287, 289, 293, 297, 298, 299

B

Bebo 305
Becker, Gary 5, 6, 15
Bing 86, 87, 88
Blogger.com 19
blogs 133
bookmarking 157, 158, 171, 174, 175, 177, 181, 182, 184, 185, 188, 190, 194
Bush, Vannevar 70
business portals 54, 60
Business-Technology Solution (BTS) database 86, 87

C

CarMax network 267
cascading style sheets (CSS) 202
cognitive psychology 104
collaboration software systems (CSS) 69
collaborative filtering 245, 246
collaborative tagging 134, 135, 141, 144, 145, 148
collective attitude 19, 20, 25
collective efficacy 19, 20, 28, 29, 30, 32
collective intelligence 85, 86, 88, 89, 91, 93, 95, 96, 97, 98
collective knowledge 86, 91, 93, 95
computer-mediated communication (CMC) 38, 39, 42, 43, 44

computer supported cooperative works (CSCW) 38, 70, 83
consumer generated media (CGM) 103
consumerisation 88, 96
content-aware and network-aware management system (CNMS) 242, 247, 248, 250, 251, 252, 253, 261, 262
content management systems (CMS) 69
continuous innovation 1, 2, 3, 4, 6, 14, 18
cross-layer adaptation (CLA) 246
crowd wisdom 86
culture 54, 55, 57, 58, 59, 60, 61, 63, 64, 65, 66, 197, 198, 201, 202, 210, 211

D

de-individuation 43
Delicious 156, 157, 158, 171, 173, 174, 175, 176, 177, 178, 179, 181, 182, 184, 185, 186, 187, 188, 189, 190, 194
Dell 285, 286, 287, 290, 291, 292, 293, 294, 295, 296, 297, 298, 300
document management systems (DMS) 69

E

e-business 302
e-commerce 266, 267, 268, 272, 273, 286, 294, 295, 296, 297, 298
Editable Web 87, 96
educational applications 216, 217, 221
Educational Resources Information Center (ERIC) 86, 87
Ennis, Ireland 1, 3, 4, 8, 9, 10, 12, 13, 16, 17
Enterprise 2.0 88, 91, 97, 99
entertainment applications 216, 217, 221
ethnography 76, 83, 84

V

Value 2.0 85, 86, 89, 93, 94, 95, 96, 97, 99
viral marketing 301, 302, 303, 304, 305, 307, 308, 311, 316, 317, 319, 320, 321, 322, 323
viral messages 303, 307, 321
virtual chats 55
virtual commerce (v-commerce) 285, 286, 290, 292, 293, 294, 295, 298
virtual networks 54
virtual worlds 285, 286, 287, 288, 289, 290, 291, 292, 293, 294, 295, 296, 297, 298, 299, 300
voice-over Internet protocol (VoIP) services 243, 252, 263

W

Web 2.0 88, 95, 97, 98, 99, 156, 157, 172, 177, 178, 180, 190, 196, 203, 216, 288
web 3.0 technologies 68, 69, 77, 78, 80, 81, 82, 83, 84

Web service 157, 159, 160, 180, 181, 184, 185, 186, 190, 191
wikinomics 85, 88, 89, 91, 92, 93, 94, 95, 97, 98, 99
Wikipedia 19, 21, 35
wikis 133
wiki systems (WS) 69
Windows Live 19
word-of-mouth 302, 303, 304, 305, 317, 319, 321, 322, 323
World of Warcraft 136
wproject software environment 137, 138, 139, 140, 141

Y

Yahoo! Answers 156
YouTube 19, 103, 116, 117, 125, 156, 157, 171, 173, 174, 175, 176, 177, 180, 182, 183, 184, 187, 188, 189, 194, 266, 277